Advancing Socio-Economics

Advancing Socio-Economics

An Institutionalist Perspective

EDITED BY
J. ROGERS HOLLINGSWORTH,
KARL H. MÜLLER,
AND
ELLEN JANE HOLLINGSWORTH

ROWMAN & LITTLEFIELD PUBLISHERS, INC.
Lanham • Boulder • New York • Oxford

ROWMAN & LITTLEFIELD PUBLISHERS, INC.

Published in the United States of America
by Rowman & Littlefield Publishers, Inc.
A Member of the Rowman & Littlefield Publishing Group
4720 Boston Way, Lanham, Maryland 20706
www.rowmanlittlefield.com

PO Box 317
Oxford
OX2 9RU, UK

British Library Cataloguing in Publication Information Available

Library of Congress Cataloging-in-Publication Data

Advancing socio-economics : an institutionalist perspective / edited by
J. Rogers Hollingsworth, Karl H. Müller, and Ellen Jane Hollingsworth.
         p. cm.
Includes bibliographical references and index.
     ISBN 0-7425-1176-6 (alk. paper)
     1. Economics—Sociological aspects. I. Hollingsworth, J. Rogers
(Joseph Rogers), 1932– II. Müller, Karl H. III. Hollingsworth, Ellen
Jane.
     HM548 .A38 2002
     306.3—dc21
                                                         2002011418

Printed in the United States of America

♻™ The paper used in this publication meets the minimum requirements of American
National Standard for Information Sciences—Permanence of Paper for Printed Library
Materials, ANSI/NISO Z39.48-1992.

For
Robert Boyer, Amitai Etzioni, and
Wolfgang Streeck

Contents

Advancing Socio-Economics: An Institutionalist Perspective

Preface

J. Rogers Hollingsworth, Karl H. Müller, Ellen Jane Hollingsworth

While the field of socio-economics has undergone a remarkable renaissance during the past decade, its roots extend back more than two centuries. In short, the broad framework for engaging in a social and economic approach to the world has long been rather pervasive. For example, although Adam Smith, in the latter part of the eighteenth century, is often portrayed as one of the fathers of modern economics, in fact he was a Professor of Moral Philosophy at the University of Edinburgh and was vitally concerned with many of the same issues which today concern those of us who have a strong identity as socio-economists.

During the past century, however, the study of the social, the political, the economic, the philosophical—in short, most of the areas constituting the area of socio-economics—became increasingly differentiated into separate fields of knowledge, and in turn each has become further differentiated into subspecialties. The modern university, especially in the second half of the twentieth century, has become a "Babel" type of institution in which many of its inhabitants constitute separate "tribes" which can hardly communicate with each other. Contrary to the fragmentation of fields and sub-fields within the social sciences, very broadly conceived, the nature of societal problems and the patterns of societal changes have clearly advanced towards greater complexity and towards greater scope and inter-linkages. Thus, in the course of creating more and more disciplinary diversity, the relevance and the impact of social science expertise and problem solutions with respect to critical societal problems has decreased. In reaction against this fragmentation, there has been in recent years a concerted effort to build bridges across various social science disciplines, to promote greater integration of the social sciences. Numerous new academic journals have emerged as part of this activity, the following being a few examples: *The Journal of Evolutionary Economics, The Journal of Socio-Economics, The Review of International Political Economy, Industrial and Corporate Change, Politics and Society.* And it is in this context, that the field of socio-economics has become energized.

Socio-economics has always emphasized its inter-disciplinary nature and its hybrid status between and beyond different disciplines within the social sciences, broadly conceived. Therefore, it is no wonder that there is now considerable cognitive diversity in what one can identify as the broad parameters of socio-economics. But we are now at a critical junction in the field of socio-economics. We can simply stand back and let the diversity evolve in a very amorphous way, with most of the participants very weakly linked and with no cognitive transfers between the various "tribes" and fields. Or, in an effort to advance the theoretical core, the methods, and the modeling techniques for a richer and more interactive field of socio-economics, we can attempt to order and systematize this diversity. To be more precise, organizing the existing diversity means, above all, to generate a "nested structure," that is, to embed the various socio-economic disciplines and sub-disciplines within a rich and common socio-economic core or, alternatively, within a common socio-economic paradigm. Such a socio-economic paradigm serves as the common platform for cross-disciplinary communications and is responsible, above all, for directed and inter-linked disciplinary changes. This volume represents a first step in attempting to impose some order and nested structures to the field of socio-economics.

The key concern is to focus on the basic ingredients for studying the dynamics of contemporary societies with a socio-economic perspective. In chapter 1, J. Rogers Hollingsworth begins this task with a stage-setting essay in which he focuses on a core agenda of socio-economics which consists of a combination of institutions, innovations, and inequalities—"the Triple I." Obviously, these three themes do not exhaust the totality of a theoretical agenda for socio-economics, but they are an important starting point for the defining of a core agenda. It would be particularly useful for the socio-economic community to understand how processes of institutions, innovations, and inequalities feed back and interact with each other and how these constrain and shape societal change.

The next task in structuring the field of socio-economics is to define several broad methodological parameters in which socio-economics operates. In part 1, Hollingsworth suggests that socio-economists engage in a multi-level analysis if they are to understand the world in which we live: the global, the transnational regional, the nation-state, the sub-national regional, and the local community.

As citizens of the world, we are nested in each of these levels. Unfortunately, our relationship generally focuses on only one level—the nation-state, the subnational region, or the global—but our understanding of the linkages of multiple levels remains poorly developed. That chapter is followed by chapter 3 in which Amitai Etzioni, the founder of the Society for the Advancement of Socio-Economics, presents an essay in which he puts forth essential elements for a socio-economic paradigm. Next Robin Stryker perceptively discusses the future of the field of socio-economics and its relationship with the Society for the Advancement of Socio-Economics. That chapter is one of particular relevance, for it is essential that the leaders of a research area have some vision of where the field should and can go and to suggest how it might move in that direction.

Karl H. Müller (chapter 5) spells out the relationship between socio-economics and the neoclassical analysis of the social world. Whereas neoclassical scholars have been relatively successful in establishing their dominance within the world of social science, Müller defines a radically new relationship between these two research programs. He demonstrates his considerable respect for the strength of the neoclassical program, but proposes a Copernican inversion, arguing that the neoclassical perspective should be viewed as a special case and special-purpose program within the far more diversified and far more general socio-economic paradigm. Like any true Copernican inversion, the hitherto established center of analysis—the neoclassical paradigm—becomes de-centered or marginalized and the previously special and marginal domains of socio-economics acquire core and central status. In the spirit of a Copernican revolution, Müller's chapter 5 on socio-economic embeddedness provides a great deal of cognitive support for "de-centering" the neoclassical program and for treating it as a significant, though highly special, case within the more encompassing socio-economic paradigm.

A key assumption of this volume is that socio-economics begins either with institutional analysis or at least with sensitivity to institutional analysis. Today, virtually all the social sciences have institutional analysis relatively high on their research agenda, with the exception of psychology, but even there the analysis of institutions is gaining greater currency. Unfortunately, across the social sciences there is no consensus as to what is meant by institutions, and hence there is no agreement as to how scholars should go about doing institutional analysis. The chapters in part 2 by J. Rogers Hollingsworth, Tom R. Burns and Marcus Carson, Geoffrey M. Hodgson, Frans van Waarden, and Claus Offe are efforts to define institutional analysis, to identify a few of the major problems in undertaking institutional analysis of contemporary societies, and to propose strategies for doing institutional analysis. Underlying themes implicit in the chapters of part 2 are the issues of institutional complementarity and complexity—the suggestion that particular institutions and specific coordinating mechanisms function as they do because of the way they interact with other institutions and coordinating mechanisms.

Part 3 is an effort to connect a socio-economic agenda, its methods, and models to specific applications. The chapter by J. Rogers Hollingsworth on social systems of production offers an example of an application of socio-economics for macro-societal analysis. Similarly, the chapters by Peter A. Hall, Steven Casper, Sigurt Vitols, Raymond Russell and Robert Hanneman, and Marie-Laure Djelic also provide applications of socio-economic strategies for macro-societal analysis. The concluding chapter by Jerald Hage and J. Rogers Hollingsworth, "Institutional Pathways, Networks, and the Differentiation of National Economies" is a paradigmatic example of innovational analysis at the national level, reflecting the richness of the theoretical core of socio-economics and the strength of comparative analysis.

This volume offers a number of innovative suggestions as the first steps in developing a socio-economics research agenda with institutional analysis as the central focus. Moreover, the volume provides a number of examples of how institutional analysis can be operationalized not only in multi-level analysis but also in comparative societal analysis. In related activities, we emphasize various socio-economic core methods for conducting comparative research for both contemporary and past societies.

Financial support for this and related projects was provided by the National Science Foundation under grant SBR 9618526; the Graduate Research Committee of the University of Wisconsin; the Andrew W. Mellon Foundation; the Alfred Sloan Foundation; the Netherlands Institute for Advanced Study; the Swedish Collegium for Advanced Study in the Social Sciences; the Rockefeller Foundation Study and Conference Center in Bellagio, Italy; the Neurosciences Institute in La Jolla, California; and the Wissenschaftszentrum Berlin. Furthermore, we want to thank the Austrian Ministry for Education, Science, and Culture for its financial support to bring this volume into its current layout and graphical design.

We wish to express our thanks and gratitude to a number of individuals. Our special thanks go to David Gear and his extremely careful efforts in bringing this volume to completion, to Greg Greenberg who was enormously helpful in bringing together the materials in the early stages of the project, and to Stanley Walens, whose exceptional editorial work and technical skills have been very important for the completion of this project. We also thank Michael Eigner of Vienna who was responsible for the graphic designs, Gertrud Stadler at the Institute for Advanced Studies (IHS) in Vienna who transformed the tables of the volume into their current design, and a number of referees and commentators on the papers in the volume. We are also very grateful to our editor, Mary Carpenter of Rowman & Littlefield, whose patience and advice were extremely helpful in bringing this project to completion. We also wish to thank Jerald Hage, Christel Lane, Egon Matzner, Yoshitaka Okada, David Soskice, Richard Whitley, and numerous other colleagues for their stimulating discussions over the years about socio-economics. We are especially grateful to Amitai Etzioni who provided much of the intellectual inspiration for the contemporary revitalization of socio-economics. His continuing support for this field has been vital. For these reasons, we dedicate this volume to him. We also dedicate it to Robert Boyer and Wolfgang Streeck, for their role in teaching us about the institutional environment in which actors are embedded.

May 2002

J. Rogers Hollingsworth
University of Wisconsin, Madison

Karl H. Müller
WISDOM, Vienna

Ellen Jane Hollingsworth
University of Wisconsin, Madison

1

Advancing Socio-Economics

J. Rogers Hollingsworth

Socio-economics in the early twenty-first century seeks to be cross-disciplinary and to draw on a variety of academic disciplines. Unlike neoclassical economics it does not operate from a relatively closed set of assumptions and propositions. This has been both a strength and a weakness. The strength is perhaps obvious, in that socio-economics has been able to draw upon several sizable and strong disciplines during a period of great expansion in the scholarly enterprise. On the other hand, there has been a problem in terms of how knowledge in the social sciences has evolved during the past century.

During this period, new knowledge has become increasingly specialized, narrow, and fragmented. Whole new social science disciplines have emerged in the twentieth century. What was called political economy or moral philosophy in the late eighteenth and early nineteenth centuries has been split into separate disciplines of politics, economics, and philosophy.

In its short history, socio-economics has emerged as a vibrant "hybrid field" at the intersection of economics, sociology and other disciplines such as law, political science, anthropology, and social psychology, to name only a few. In this chapter, I set myself three basic goals.

First, I will briefly review the past decade of socio-economics and some of its spectacular achievements. Second, I will suggest a research profile for socio-economics as an interdisciplinary research program, focusing on essential parts of its core-agenda, on the research design of socio-economics and on its range of possible applications. Third, I will distinguish six main areas of discourse which, on the one hand, stand at the core of this volume and which, on the other, differentiate the dominant neoclassical approach from the socio-economic approach.

SOCIO-ECONOMIC ADVANCES IN THE PAST

To what extent have scholars in socio-economics been successful in creating a socio-economics research agenda? In some respects, the performance appears impressive. After all, it was only a little more than a decade ago (1988) that Amitai Etzioni's book, *The Moral Dimension: Toward a New Economics,* was published and that the first of what would become an annual meeting of the Society for the Advancement of Socio-Economics (SASE) occurred at the Harvard Business School. Since then, a number of widely noted books in the area of socio-economics have appeared. There have been major collections of papers in socio-economics edited by Amitai Etzioni and Paul Lawrence (1991), Richard Coughlin (1991), Richard Swedberg (1990), Rogers Hollingsworth and Robert Boyer (1997), Sven-Erik Sjöstrand (1993), and John Campbell, Rogers Hollingsworth, and Leon Lindberg (1991), among others. Neil Smelser and Richard Swedberg edited the very valuable *Handbook of Economic Sociology* (1994) in which several dozen scholars have essays which focus on topics in socio-economics.

During the past decade, Francis Fukayama (1995), Charles Sabel (1992), Wolfgang Streeck (1992), and others have considerably advanced our understanding of trust, a major concept in the socio-economics research agenda. In related scholarship, there has been substantial advance on the study of the community (Putnam, 1993; Selznick 1992), economics and morality (Etzioni, 1988), and issues pertaining to the governance of a modern economy (Hollingsworth, Schmitter, and Streeck, 1994; Hollingsworth and Boyer, 1997), all falling under the umbrella of socio-economics.

Moreover, entire subfields of socio-economics are flourishing—e.g., scholarship on the welfare state, on law and economics (Scharpf and Schmidt, 2000; Leibfried and Pierson, 1995); the impact of globalization on nation-states and national economies (Berger and Dore, 1996; Ash and Thrift, 1995; Hirst and Thompson, 1996; Smith, Solinger, and Kopik, 1999; Boyer and Drache, 1996; Gilpin, 2000); on knowledge, economy, and society (Weingart and Stehr, 2000; Nelson, 1993; Lundvall, 1992; Badaracco, 1991; Gibbons, et al., 1994; Hage and Hollingsworth, 2000).

In the Society for the Advancement of Socio-Economics, there has been a vigorous effort to launch research networks designed to advance research on a number of sub-fields within socio-economics. These networks include, but are not limited to knowledge and society, the institutional determinants of innovations, the welfare state and societal well-being, organizations, communitarianism, and law and socio-economics. While the Society for the Advancement of Socio-Economics is a scholarly organization, a complementary organization, more action oriented has emerged: The Communitarian Network, with its own journal and a flourishing agenda on both sides of the Atlantic (Etzioni, 1998).

At the same time that these things have been occurring, there have been dramatic changes taking place in social science methodology. For example, in the past decade we have witnessed many advances in qualitative methodology. For many years economists have relied heavily for research tools on mathematical models and econometrics (McCloskey, 1985). Using regression approaches, most economists have long controlled for a group of variables while measuring the impact of a single variable on some outcome. But with recent qualitative methods, particularly qualitative comparative analysis (QCA), scholars can now see what group of variables configure together in order to shape a particular outcome. With this kind of strategy, analysts can determine what variables or processes are both sufficient and necessary in order to achieve a particular outcome (Abell, 1989; Ragin, 1987, 1994a, 1994b; Ragin and Bradshaw, 1991; Hollingsworth, Hanneman, Hage, and Ragin, 1996; King, Keohane, and Verba, 1994).

Moreover, a number of social scientists are advancing socio-economics by doing sophisticated case studies over time. In these studies, they are able to determine the causal processes involving multiple variables (Yin, 1993, 1994). Not surprising, these various qualitative methods have enormous potential for stimulating theoretical advance in socio-economics (Caporaso, 1995; Collier, 1995; Tarrow, 1995).

A reminder is hardly necessary that the field of socio-economics is far from theoretically poverty stricken. Socio-economics has a long and distinguished theoretical tradition "to locate the study of economic phenomena within the context of society, politics, history, and philosophy" (Coughlin, 1991:4). Socio-economics follows from a tradition built on the work of Adam Smith, Durkheim, Weber, Marx, Schumpeter, and others.

In brief, theoretically, socio-economics does not represent a new paradigm (Coughlin, ibid.). Rather, it should be seen as a comprehensive platform for a variety of theoretical traditions stressing the complexity of relations or the "entangled nature" of interactions among individuals, institutions, organizations, knowledge, and societies.

THE RESEARCH AGENDA OF SOCIO-ECONOMICS

Despite the remarkable success over the last decade, the research agenda of socio-economics is seriously hampered by the organizational and institutional environment of today's science system. In the contemporary world, the university has become the major site for the production of knowledge. Universities are of course fragmented into many different disciplines. And in large research universities, many disciplines are further divided into sub-specialties. Much of this fragmentation poses serious problems for communication both within and across disciplines (Hollingsworth and Hollingsworth, 2000; Messer-Davidow, et al., 1993; Bechtel, 1986; Klein, 1996).

Hence, one of the most serious obstacles impeding the advancement of socio-economics as a field of inquiry is the structure of the modern research university, especially as it exists in the United States. Socio-economics is committed to having rich and intense communication among scholars in all the social sciences as well as in a number of professional schools (e.g., law and business). But this kind of discourse across academic disciplines is difficult, if not impossible in today's internally differentiated university. Paradoxically, the vast scale of higher education, the setting which has done so much to advance the field of socio-economics, also greatly constrains socio-economics as it attempts to move toward a more theoretical, coherent approach. The size of the academy, with its richness and variety, which has helped to create socio-economics, also hinders theoretical development of the field. In view of the fragmented nature of the contemporary university, socio-economics is devoted to a large number of crucial societal problems at the intersection of many social science fields such as the following:

- the role of social institutions in structuring socio-economic development, performance standards, and markets
- the relations between markets and democracy
- the difficult transitions of state socialist societies
- the growing inequalities of income, wealth, and economic opportunities, and their connections to gender, ethnicity, and age cohorts
- the relationships among knowledge, society, and economy

This list reflects some of the key issues of the "Madison Declaration" which was proposed at the annual SASE meeting in Madison, Wisconsin, in 1999. This list suggests three research areas of particular relevance for the future advancement of socio-economics: the study of institutions, innovations, and inequality, and the next three sections of this volume will highlight essential features of a socio-economic research agenda, present and future.

Institutions and Institutional Analysis in Socio-Economics

One of the major tasks presently confronting socio-economics is to comprehend the linkages—and tensions—among a society's institutions and institutional arrangements, the structure of its industrial and societal sectors, firms and organizations, and their technological capabilities and processes of individual decision making. In the final analysis, individuals and firms have a high degree of autonomy.

But because their learning is influenced by the institutional environment in which they are embedded, there are always institutional constraints on their decision-making processes. Hence, actors are always confronted with the tension between being constrained by the inertial forces of the past and attempting to move beyond the past into the future. And it is this tension which must be comprehended if we are to understand how institutions, governance arrangements, societal sectors, organizations, individual actors, and innovativeness are intertwined.

In order to understand the process by which this occurs we obviously need a rich body of socio-economic theory of how the various components of institutional change are linked with innovations. At the present time, however, our theories of both institutional change and innovativeness are poorly developed. Indeed, much of our recent literature on technological innovation has emerged from a focus on the firm.

For example, Alfred Chandler's great corpus of work (1962, 1977, 1990) has tended to emphasize how the success of a firm's technological innovativeness—both across countries and over time—has been influenced primarily by whether it has used the right strategy and structure. For Chandler, firms which have the right strategy and structure end up having the organizational capabilities which permit them to have economies of scale and scope to develop cost advantages over their competitors. Chandler's work has had a profound effect in influencing the management literature of the past couple of decades. Hence, in the Chandlerian tradition, much of that literature suggests that the key to understanding the competitive advantage of firms results from their having the right strategies and organizational structure (see the discussion in Teece, 1993).

Over time, however, there has slowly emerged a literature which emphasizes the importance of the institutional environment of firms for understanding why firms in some countries excel in some industries but not in others, and why the firms in a specific country may excel in a particular country at one moment in time but may eventually lose that advantage (Landes, 1969, 1998; North, 1981, 1990).

More recently, Richard Nelson and his co-workers have been advancing this literature by integrating contemporary theories of institutions, firm strategies, technological innovation and evolution (Nelson, 1994, 1995a, 1995b, 1996; Mowery and Nelson, 1999; Murmann, 1998; Arora, Landau, and Rosenberg,

1998). The Nelson school has collectively been developing descriptive studies of how institutions, firms, capabilities, and technologies co-evolve so that particular societies and firms at specific moments in time excel in particular kinds of innovations. The goal of this work is to develop, by working inductively, a better understanding of the processes of how technologies, firms, and institutions co-evolve across a number of industries and countries.

One of the most exciting statements of this strategy is the recent cross-national and cross-temporal study by Murmann (1998) of the synthetic dye industry in Britain, Germany and the United States. Murmann (1998: chapter 7) demonstrates that it is the variety of endowments in the institutional environment which provide economic actors/firms with initial advantages or disadvantages to engage in a particular type of technological activity.

But over time everything is dynamic, and the larger global environment, the institutional environment, the capabilities of firms, and the performance of firms all co-evolve and feed back onto one another. However the institutional environments differ widely from on society to another, and the successful firms and organizations are those which can best adapt their activities to the institutional environment within which they are embedded. Once a number of firms in a particular industry are successful, however, they may or may not be able to engage in collective action to modify their institutional environment in order to enhance their innovativeness and their technological competitiveness.

The studies by Nelson, Murmann, and others have been particularly important in advancing the argument that the interaction among actors and their institutional environment is a multi-faceted process and that successful actors over time must not simply respond to their institutional environment within which they are embedded, but they must be able to modify their environment in order to maintain competitive advantages. Nevertheless, socio-economics does not presently have an adequate theory of how institutions, firms, and technologies co-evolve, and for that reason we are not yet at a stage whereby we can test a set of formal hypotheses which flow from some well-defined model involving institutional analysis (see figure 1.1).

Indeed, in the social sciences, there is at present no consensus as to what is meant by institutions or by institutional analysis. For this reason, I propose in part 2 of this book a set of different approaches to institutional analysis which are inter-connected by increasing degrees of generality and which suggest the descriptive material and the necessary typologies which provide the basis for doing institutional analysis from a socio-economic point of view. My framework provides five types of institutional analysis, the study of (1) institutions, (2) institutional arrangements, (3) institutional sectors, (4) organizations, and (5) outputs and performances. A key assumption of this book is that of institutional complementarity—the idea that particular institutions and coordinating mechanisms function all the better because of the way they interact with other institutions and coordinating mechanisms (Amable, 2000; Hall and Soskice, 2001).

Figure 1.1 A Perspective on the Interactions among Institutions, Firms, and Economic Performance

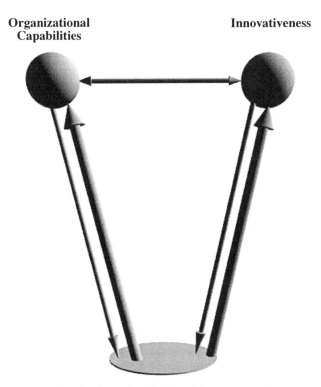

Institutions, Institutional Arrangements
and Institutional Sectors

Studying the Socio-Economics of Innovations

A domain of vital concern for socio-economic research lies in understanding the cultural and structural conditions under which major breakthroughs in hybrid fields of knowledge occur in research organizations, especially in research universities. If we are to make substantial advance in hybrid fields of knowledge such as socio-economics, we need to understand the kinds of processes which facilitate major breakthroughs in such areas of knowledge. Because our understanding of such social processes is limited, I wish to share some of the findings of a large research project in which I am engaged. While the empirical analysis of this project focuses on the problem of why research organizations in Britain, France, Germany, and the United States have varied in their capacity to make major discoveries in bio-medical science (Hollingsworth, 1986; Hollingsworth and Hollingsworth, 2000; Hollingsworth, Hollingsworth, and Hage, 2002 forthcoming), the theoretical findings are very relevant to other fields of a hybrid nature, such as socio-economics. Thus, it would be useful if socio-economists were aware of the conditions which have led to new breakthroughs in bio-medical science. Time after time in the history of science, one field has been able to create substantial new knowledge by borrowing strategies from other disciplines (Mitman, 1992; Fischer and Lipson, 1988; Kohler, 1982, 1994).

Several prerequisites are necessary if major advances are to occur in hybrid fields. First, the organization in which scholars attempt to advance knowledge must be sufficiently flexible so that it can quickly adapt to changes taking place in the larger world of learning. Second, organizations must have structures and cultures that facilitate rich horizontal interaction across academic disciplines. Good science may take place within academic disciplines or sub-specialties, but major breakthroughs or the creation of fundamental new knowledge in hybrid fields tend to occur as a result of frequent and intense interaction across academic disciplines. And for intense and frequent interaction to occur, it must take place in a particular site. It is less likely to occur by e-mail or at an occasional conference.

Science, both natural science and social science, has been very dynamic and has grown in unpredictable ways in the twentieth century. Yet, research organizations experience considerable institutional inertia, which hampers the development of new knowledge. They are quite socially conservative and change rather slowly. As a result, they have difficulty adapting to the fast pace of scientific and technological change. Time and time again, a research organization has been a world-class leader in science, but because of organizational inertia and failure to adapt to new trends, it has lost its leading edge. In fact, most research organizations, which perform extremely well over a period of approximately thirty years, do not continue to perform well during the next period (Hollingsworth and Hollingsworth, 2000; Hollingsworth, Hollingsworth, and Hage, 2002 forthcoming).

Over time, knowledge in hybrid fields has become increasingly more complex (e.g., involving both more fields of knowledge and greater depth in terms of scientific skills), and if scholars are to create radically new knowledge, and/or new discoveries, it is necessary for them to incorporate scientific diversity and depth by interacting with intensity and frequency across diverse fields of knowledge. As research organizations add greater scientific diversity and depth, it is important that the parts of the organization remain well integrated and not highly differentiated from one another, lest there not be horizontal communication with frequent and intense interaction across diverse fields, prerequisites if major advances in new knowledge are to occur.

The diversity and depth of knowledge within a well-integrated research organization have the potential to change the way people view problems and to minimize their tendency to make mistakes and to work on trivial problems. The greater a research group's diversity and depth, the less likely it is that scholars will stray into unproductive areas. Frequent and intense interaction among people of like minds (i.e., with low levels of diversity) tends not to lead to major breakthroughs. When people work with clones of one another, they may be more productive (e.g., produce more papers). But if scholars work in environments with considerable diversity and depth, and have frequent and intense interaction with those having complementary interests, they increase the probability that the quality of their work will improve. It is the diversity of disciplines and paradigms to which individuals are exposed with frequent and intense interaction that increases the tendency for creativity, and for breakthroughs to occur.

As research organizations increase in diversity, depth, and size, there is a tendency for them to experience more differentiation and less integration. These changes in turn tend to lead to increases in hierarchical coordination, with negative consequences for making major breakthroughs in knowledge. When research organizations respond to growth by differentiating into new departments and by imposing hierarchical controls, these processes lead to a decline in organizational communication and integration and reduce the possibility of making major advances in hybrid fields of knowledge.

Although the research reported here is on bio-medical research, the structural and cultural conditions as well as the social processes associated with major discoveries have obvious relevance for other fields of hybrid knowledge, such as the world of socio-economics. The university and departmental processes making for, and inhibiting, creativity are much the same. That is, as research organizations incorporate greater scientific diversity and depth, they create more differentiation and bureaucracy, which inhibit the kind of integration and interaction necessary for major achievements. It should be noted that the kind of visionary leadership needed for nurturing creative scholars is also threatened, as the demands of paper processing overcome agendas of nurturing and identifying top notch talent, and the setting of meaningful research agenda.

Among the most successful research organizations world wide in making major discoveries in bio-medical science during the twentieth century have been two relatively small American organizations: the Rockefeller Institute, later Rockefeller University, and the California Institute of Technology. Significantly, each of these organizations historically has been highly successful, primarily because each has been small, neither has had a clear departmental structure, scientists at both have had a high degree of communication across different parts of the organization, both have had a low level of bureaucratization, and each has had leaders with strategic vision who have helped to facilitate the organization's adaptation not only to new knowledge, but to pioneering new knowledge (see figure 1.2).

Figure 1.2   Socio-Economic Key Factors for Radical Scientific Breakthroughs

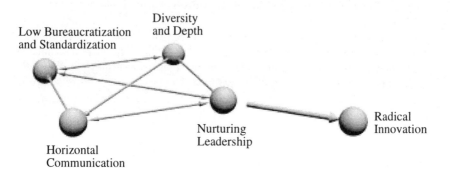

Within universities, disciplinary-based departments tend to be socially conservative, with a tendency for professors to reproduce their own thinking as they recruit others. This conservatism and tendency toward reproduction prevents most academic institutions from adapting rapidly to new knowledge.

At Rockefeller, the institution has been structured around labs, and historically when the head of a lab left, the lab was closed, so that the organization could easily move in different directions. And at Cal Tech, historically there has been a divisional structure. Because there was a single biology division without rigid walls between different fields of biology, it was much easier for scientists to communicate horizontally than in organizations with large numbers of differentiated biological disciplines (e.g., botany, plant pathology, zoology, biochemistry, genetics).

The problem is how an organization can incorporate the expansion of knowledge and growth in size. When research organizations respond to growth by differentiating into new departments and by imposing hierarchical controls, these processes lead to a decline in communication across different fields of knowledge and diminish the possibility of making major discoveries.

Significantly, neither Rockefeller Institute/University nor Cal Tech was differentiated into numerous academic departments or disciplines. Furthermore, at each, a great deal of attention was devoted to the problem of social and scientific integration. As at Rockefeller, Cal Tech's faculty ate at small lunch tables (with high-quality food) where serious science was discussed. While it would be inaccurate to argue that the field of biophysics developed at Cal Tech, its emergence as a field of research was certainly accelerated as biologists and physicists interacted not only socially and in seminars but also as scientific collaborators.

Moreover, graduate training for biologists at both institutions required broad training programs, with students expected to have extensive training in chemistry and physics as well as in biology. A famous part of Cal Tech's biology program over the years was the fact that the faculty, post-docs, and graduate students spent leisure time together, which had positive consequences for intellectual cooperation (Fischer and Lipson, 1989; Kay, 1993; Kohler, 1994).

The enormous success of these two organizations, making major advances in the biomedical sciences throughout much of the twentieth century, is widely recognized. The organizational conditions at Rockefeller and at Cal Tech were such that whole new fields of science were either created or substantially advanced, and their faculties had enormous impact on creating and moving forward scientific agenda that set the tone of subsequent decades.

Moreover, a recent analysis of innovation studies (Hage, 2000) reveals that the main organizational factors which have been identified as facilitating innovativeness in scientific institutes can also be found in business firms. Crucial factors like a complex division of labor or flexible, organic forms of organization or a commitment to "leadership" and strategic visions play a vital positive role in the shaping of new economic products, services or processes.

The Socio-Economics of Inequality

Another core-part on the socio-economic agenda where academic research has failed remarkably in the last two decades of the twentieth century, lies in the understanding of inequality both nationally, internationally, and above all, globally. Both the "Capitalist World System" and national economies have become considerably more unequal, a process which has found vivid expression in the new catchphrase of "social exclusion" (Wallerstein, 1980).

Processes of inequalities in contemporary societies must be studied in a far more comprehensive way, utilizing the full theoretical, methodological, and empirical potential of the socio-economic approach. In my view, five essential domains of inquiry should stand high on the socio-economic inequality agenda.

First, the traditional concepts of "social classes" as well as the contemporary versions of "classes" (Bourdieu, 1982, 1985, 1999) suffer from a too narrow focus on the capitalist production process alone, leaving out a variety of essential dimensions like gender, ethnicity, or regional disparities. Thus, a new and more comprehensive framework is needed in socio-economic analysis, one which is able to generate a multi-dimensional understanding of social inequalities at the local, societal, and global levels of analysis. The new picture must be based on a rich variety of dimensions, including not only the position within the labor process, but also one which includes such resources as the cognitive and emotional capacities of persons, their civil embeddedness, and the like.

Second, a new socio-economic framework for social inequality must be able to account for another recent phenomenon which has been labeled as "individualization" (Beck, 1986). Here, Beck draws the attention to the fact that bio-graphical life courses within the "world risk society" (Beck, 2000) have become more and more diversified and heterogeneous. Thus, a new socio-economic approach to social inequality must be able to account for the increasing variation in "life styles" as well.

Third, the socio-economic approach needs better theoretical and methodological perspectives on how income levels within and across countries depend on the institutional settings and, above all, on the organizing capacities and mobilization of workers (Hollingsworth and Hanneman, 1982; Streeck, 1992). In view of the current trends towards globalization, the negotiating power between global players and national trade unions has shifted considerably in favor of the management side (Scharpf and Schmidt, 2000). It should become one of the key inequality issues within socio-economics to be able to describe and to explain the growing asymmetries both globally and nationally.

Fourth, the rise of the Internet economy has made it imperative that the problem of social inequality also be extended to the accessibility and restrictions inherent in virtual domains. Thus, the issues of great "digital divides" both globally and nationally and their overall consequences for various groups such as the elderly, persons with poor literacy skills, as well as for the distribution of overall life chances have to be studied by socio-economics in an in-depth manner.

Fifth, socio-economics must place on the policy agenda the problem of what remedies and counter-measures should be used against the rising tide of ine-quality both globally and nationally. There is presently a general consensus that the traditional Keynesian path of redistribution by higher taxes or redistributive efforts through prolonged periods of "deficit spending" can no longer be followed. Hence, new socio-economic models must be developed on how new recombinations between the enormously expanding financial markets on the one hand and the composition of workers' wages on the other hand can be achieved in a more re-distributive manner.

With these perspectives on future socio-economic research strategies about the domain of socio-economic inequalities, the first steps have been completed for advances and breakthroughs in the hybrid field of socio-economics.

SOCIO-ECONOMIC RESEARCH-DESIGNS

The core topics described above can be summarized as a "Triple I-Agenda" for socio-economics—the analysis of institutions, innovations, and inequalities. While the "Triple I-Agenda" does not focus on all core issues on the socio-economic agenda, it does represent the central issues for the sustainability of contemporary societies, both nationally and globally. Ideally, socio-economics should pursue its agenda by organizing interdisciplinary work teams which choose one of the target domains within or outside the "Triple I-Agenda" as its research objective. In order to achieve the desired results, the "Triple I-Agenda" should not be restricted to research co-operation between sociologists and economists alone.

Rather, much broader interdisciplinary work groups on socio-economics should be composed. Depending on the domain and scope of investigation, socio-economic analysis may require expertise from the environmental sciences, from the bio-medical sciences, from the cognitive sciences, and/or from computer and information science. Critical issues like the detrimental effects of growing inequalities on less obvious domains like health, sicknesses, mental disorders, and life styles may require combinations of experts from sociology and economics with individuals from fields involving the bio-medical and the cognitive sciences in order to achieve major socio-economic breakthroughs.

Figure 1.3   The Dominant Design for Socio-Economic Research

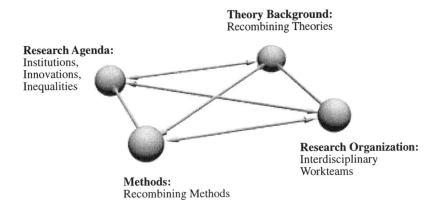

Theory Background:
Recombining Theories

Research Agenda:
Institutions,
Innovations,
Inequalities

Research Organization:
Interdisciplinary
Workteams

Methods:
Recombining Methods

Aside from the hybrid composition of teams and the non-permanence of the organizational settings, the most important cognitive characteristic for socio-economic research lies in a proper recombination of basic research within the context of applications. However, it is important to emphasize the inter-linkages between applied and basic research within a socio-economic context. Taking the issue of scientific innovations and breakthroughs as a reference case, a socio-economic research strategy should not be restricted only to understanding historical case studies of societal and organizational factors associated with innovations, but these studies should also be designed to produce appropriate "organizational designs" and corresponding "institutional blueprints" for highly innovative research institutes. Thus, innovation research socio-economic style should assume a far more active role in the proliferation of tools, instruments, institutional blueprints, or organizational prototypes. Likewise, socio-economic research on inequality is and should be linked with the proliferation of new and manageable programs of a redistributive nature which may serve as a substitute to the programs of the old welfare state regimes (see figure 1.3).

In sum, socio-economics research settings should be very responsive to new forms of societal responsibilities and accountabilities. While this point will be emphasized in greater detail in the final part of this chapter, two general remarks are appropriate. On the one hand, socio-economics must play a far more active role within the public arena, especially within the world of mass communication and mass media. In a period of rapid globalization of news and news assessments, the socio-economic perspective on maintaining security, solidarity, equality, and redistribution in an increasingly complex and diversified global village must find its way much more rapidly and forcefully into the realm of public discourse. On the other hand, the current wave of brave new worlds constructed in virtual space makes it imperative that socio-economics move forward in the digital domain as well and act as a source of rich or "thick" information on the "Triple I-Agenda" and of instruments, research-designs, or tools, necessary to generate genuinely socio-economic research operations.

Aside from a proposed transcending research design for socio-economic analyses, it is also useful to make several methodological comments in order to distinguish once again between the neoclassical agenda and the socio-economic program. Thus in the next few paragraphs, I present a short list of preferences which constitute the methodological corollary to the "Triple I-Agenda."

First, socio-economics is strongly committed to the traditional criteria of measurement, observation, and empirical adequacy of theoretical approaches. This point is particularly opposed to the "possible world approaches" of neoclassical economics where problems of empirical testing, empirical data generation, and the like play a marginal role at best. In particular, the requirements of socio-economics oppose all forms of "neoclassical double-binds" where the "freedom to choose" the relevant modeling structures and model assumptions is often misused as a justification for the empirical.

Second, in terms of spatial dimensions and levels, socio-economic analyses can and should be performed consistently across the whole range of available spatial levels. In terms of conventional micro-macro distinctions, socio-economics must be considered as a hybrid field, concentrating its efforts on all major spatial levels and their inter-linkages. Socio-economics is not to be misjudged as a "micro-perspective" or a "macro-approach," but as an integrated effort, distributed equally across major spatial levels. Additionally, the topic of "multi-level analysis," its major promises and its methodological and theoretical challenges is at the core of my subsequent introduction to part 1.

Third, socio-economics is not committed a priori to either side of the "Great Divide" between qualitative and quantitative research. On the contrary, the socio-economics research agenda supports ways and means for a "triangulization" (Giddens, 1989) i.e., for a simultaneous utilization of both quantitative and qualitative methods. Thus, socio-economics research designs should integrate the comparative strengths of quantitative and qualitative methods of inquiry. It must be emphasized that the chapters included in this book reflect this integrative spirit, since they rely on elements from both methodological "clusters."

Fourth, a large number of highly interesting socio-economic studies have been comparative in nature. Thus, comparative research, while not a methodological requirement in the strict sense, should be seen as the preferred mode for socio-economic analyses. Especially in view of characteristic features of social and economic systems like "path dependencies," "lock-ins," high variations of institutional or organizational arrangements and the like, comparative research becomes a very helpful instrument in differentiating more general patterns across regions or nations from its more special local or national variants.

In this manner, I have presented a short list of methodological requirements and preferences which constitute the methodological corollary to the "Triple I-Agenda."

ON THE POLITICS OF SOCIO-ECONOMICS

While the new "socio-economic synthesis . . . makes economics and the other social sciences more practically and theoretically relevant" (Madison Declaration), it is equally important to stress the need for using the results of socio-economic analyses as an essential input for reforming contemporary social, political, or economic systems around the globe into more "decent societies" (Margalit, 1996) and into overall configurations of more equally distributed life chances and opportunities.

To put it in a different way, the utilization of the socio-economic agenda in particular and of socio-economic research in general should not remain at the level of pure research and an activity for the leisure classes within academic ivory towers. Rather, the socio-economic agenda should be "accountable" and be held "responsible." Thus, the "Triple I-Agenda" on "institutions, innovations, inequalities" should be seen as a genuine scientific contribution to address the most pressing societal problems in today's societal fabric. Thus, the results of socio-economic analyses should serve as a platform and as a "catalyst" for ongoing local, regional, national, or global discussions about the future development of contemporary societies.

During the second half of the twentieth century, economics, the social science discipline with the greatest parsimony (i.e., the fewest variables) but a low degree of predictive accuracy (i.e., the number of confirmed predictions), has become the most dominant social science in the United States (Hirschman, 1984). But note the words of the Nobel Laureate in economics, Herbert Simon, in a discussion about neoclassical economics: its "bad theory survives; it does not predict very much, and when it does, it predicts incorrectly" (quoted in Etzioni, 1988:19). Even so, the rational choice approach ingrained in neoclassical economics has penetrated other fields of social science partly because of its parsimony and mathematical elegance.

Many social scientists have become increasingly frustrated by the neoclassical economists' disdain for all the huge amounts of information that are simply ignored in the course of neoclassical modeling, and as a result there has been a strong backlash. The very existence of a scholarly organization such as the Society for the Advancement of Socio-Economics is symbolic of this backlash. Nevertheless, socio-economics as a field of inquiry finds itself confronting a variety of barriers that hinder its advancement of new knowledge. The tasks of elaborating new multi-disciplinary theoretical frameworks, and demonstrating their utility for understanding society are complex and, so far as socio-economics is concerned, in the early stages.

Part I

On Socio-Economic Concepts and Methods

J. Rogers Hollingsworth, Karl H. Müller

The following chapters take several steps toward advancing some of the methods and concepts which are essential for the ordering of the field of socio-economics. In chapter 2, "On Multi-Level Analysis," J. Rogers Hollingsworth emphasizes the importance of recognizing that we are nested in a multi-spatial world made of the following levels: the global, the transnational region, the nation-state, the sub-national region, and the local. Each level constantly interacts with every other level, and if we are to understand the processes which take place in the world, it is imperative that we comprehend this level of complexity. It is true that in recent years, many analysts who write about the national and regional economies have recognized that these economies are nested in a multi-layered world (Hollingsworth and Boyer, 1997), but even so, most scholarship still proceeds as though each level is independent of the other. The failure to recognize that as individuals we are nested in a multi-level world is equally a serious problem as we reflect about the world of politics. Decisions about the quality of our own lives are constantly made at multiple levels, but our theories of democracy—and of governance generally—do not recognize this kind of nestedness. Indeed, our age requires a new theory of democracy which will take into consideration how citizens can have effective participation and representation at multiple levels of reality almost simultaneously. We believe socio-economics has a vital role to play in placing a multi-level analysis high on the research agenda of the social sciences.

In his very stimulating chapter 3, Amitai Etzioni lays out a paradigmatic framework for socio-economics. It is this core statement which shapes the relevance of all subsequent papers in this volume for the socio-economic agenda. While Etzioni defined the broad parameters of a socio-economic agenda in his book *The Moral Dimension: Toward a New Economics* (1988), this chapter is the clearest statement today of a paradigm of socio-economics. He points out that there are presently two paradigms in the social sciences, one centered around the "individual" with very clear normative and political consequences, and that is the neoclassical perspective. The other is the socio-economic one and is more centered around the "social." These two perspectives make quite different assumptions about our ability to reshape the world in which we live and how we might go about such a task. By sharpening the differences between these two, Etzioni helps to clear the path for building a richer socio-economics.

The Society for the Advancement of Socio-Economics (SASE) is a very eclectic scholarly organization, and one its main functions is to advance the scholarship on socio-economics. Robin Stryker in chapter 4 plots the future of both the field of socio-economics and the SASE. Her chapter resonates very much with most of the other chapters in this volume by emphasizing "institutionalism" as a key building block for socio-economics. Her chapter recognizes that the future of socio-economics is dependent on the capacity of individuals who have been trained in separate disciplines to find common terrain in which they can build on their common interests. And if we attempt to work and learn together across disciplines, we are more likely to build a better world than if we simply work within the confines of a single discipline or a narrow sub-specialty of a particular discipline. In the concluding chapter, Karl H. Müller discusses one of the most important concepts which has emerged within the field of socio-economics: embeddedness. Once we recognize that we are nested (i.e., embedded) in the kind of multi-level society which Hollingsworth discusses in chapter 2, we immediately recognize that individuals, organizations, communities, regions, nation-states, etc. are embedded in a larger social order, and hence we must attempt to understand and de-construct the meaning of the concept embeddedness. Müller undertakes the most extensive analysis of this concept which we have to date, and as a result of this kind of deconstruction of the concept embeddedness, it should now acquire greater precision in the literature. And with the advance which he has made in defining the concept, we should be able to use it more effectively to understand complex interactions at multiple levels of society.

2

On Multi-Level Analysis

J. Rogers Hollingsworth

This introduction to part 1 addresses an important issue for socio-economic analysis which goes well beyond the reach of socio-economic methodology. Here, considerable attention is devoted to the fact that the coordination of economic, political, or social institutions is occurring simultaneously at various spatial levels (e.g., local, sub-national region, nation-state, transnational region, global). The institutional arrangements which at one time were congruent at the national levels are now more dispersed at multiple spatial levels. Impressive economic performance now requires that economic actors be well coordinated at all spatial areas simultaneously. In short, actors are increasingly nested in institutional arrangements which are linked at all levels. The parts of each system have become far more interdependent than was the case only two decades ago, and the increasingly complex distribution of power and resources across geographical levels is further evidence of how economic, political, or social institutions have become nested in multiple worlds. This perspective about the diffusion of power suggests that there is slowly evolving a set of institutions for the governance of societies at multiple levels, but this process is poorly understood and its long-term consequences are rarely discussed.

THE EMERGENCE OF MULTI-LEVEL ANALYSIS

In the decades following World War II, the basic institutional arrangements for most societies were embedded primarily at the level of the nation-state. The major exceptions were federal systems. During the fifties and the sixties, an international regulatory regime provided predictability and permitted ambitious national strategies, at least in most OECD member countries. High growth dividends brought about an increase in welfare and tended to consolidate national compromises between labor and capital. True, regional economies experienced uneven growth, but due to redistributive mechanisms, undesirable consequences of such imbalances were minimized. With the passage of time, however, the embeddedness of economic institutions at the level of the nation-state has been progressively eroded. Because the search for increasing returns to scale has made the domestic market too small, firms in many sectors must compete in the international economy if they are to survive, but the international economy has become an arena of fierce competition. Moreover, financial innovations have permeated and vigorously asserted themselves at the global level. Economic interactions among nations have increased, with rising interdependence among nation-states. The American economy is no longer shielded from other major economic competitors. National economies are now nested into a set of interdependent flows involving trade, finance, and technology, and this has created new problems for nation-states.

It is useful to contrast the post–World War II period of *embeddedness* of national institutions with the present *nestedness* of major institutions which is a complex intertwining of institutions at all levels of the world, from the global arena to the regional level, also including nation-states and such continental entities as NAFTA and the European Union. The concept of nestedness implies several distinct but currently interacting features:

First, the institutional arrangements from the Fordist era which tended to operate mainly at the national level, but with few constraints from the super-national or sub-national levels, are now dependent on a variety of international trends as well as on the capability of sub-regional entities. This is the first and basic meaning for nestedness. Simultaneously, market-type activities tend to escape domestic boundaries, and they increasingly exercise more and more influence on regions and nations all over the world.

Second, nestedness implies that multi-faceted causality runs in virtually all directions among the various levels of society: nations, sectors, free-trade zones, international regimes, super-national regions, large cities, and even small but well-specialized localities interact according to unprecedented configurations. This is a novelty with respect to most, if not all, past economic regimes. It is neither a bottom-up approach, from purely local competitiveness toward an anonymous world market, as pure economic theory might imply, nor is it a top-down mechanism. In figure 2.1 we can observe how the various levels are interacting as an entire system.

The third feature of nestedness is that no single authority, let it be supernational, continental, national, or local, has the power to monitor and to regulate such a complex system. If, for example, a national government wishes to curb the negative influences of highly speculative financial markets operating at the world level, its strategy might end with consequences worse than taking no action—possibly substantial currency depreciation, higher interest rates, and/or foreign capital flight. Such a system is very different from the consequences which would have followed from similar regulations in the sixties. Today, the emerging international forces are generally not able to complete a re-definition of national institutions. International trade agreements, for example, are concerned with the nature of products and public subsidies, but hardly at all with the type of organizations, policies, and resources necessary for the delivery of social welfare services within a particular country. Hence competitive wars tend to take place among countries, based on arguments of social dumping, and with very serious consequences. There is one more reason why coherence in economic coordination is becoming increasingly difficult. Not all the institutional arrangements for implementing the various functions of society occur at the same level. For example, finance and money tend to be highly internationalized, whereas welfare remains strictly limited to the national boundaries. Hence, possible conflicts between contradictory forces operate at different levels: business may prefer market freedom and may operate at the sub-national, nation-state, and global level, while the overall population may look to the nation-state to protect them at the sub-national level from the adverse effects of market logic.

Nestedness makes economic policy and institutional change more difficult than ever, since no super-national central authority is effectively able to monitor a series of innovations. Some developments appear initially to be highly innovative but then turn counter-productive when inserted into the whole system. For example, financial deregulation in the late seventies was initially assumed to promote more efficiency in capital allocation across countries and sectors. Fifteen years later, however, the "short termism" of financial markets increasingly permeated most areas of economic, social, and political life, thus introducing major and new sources of instability in economic expectations. Thus, the global effectiveness of financial deregulation may be mitigated. Some experts argue that the effects of financial deregulations have been negative, and they propose to tax "short run" capital movements. But no single country has an interest in doing so alone. Thus, no country takes action to confront the problems. This is a prisoner-dilemma-type configuration which is an indirect consequence of the nestedness of national and international institutions.

This perspective about the diffusion of power leads to the speculation that the evolution of capitalist institutions will produce a series of governance modes at various levels of society. This is exhibited by scenario four in figure 2.4

(alternative scenarios will be discussed below). Competition might be coordinated partially at a multi- or supra-national by free trade agreements, under the supervision of general rules of the game established worldwide. This, however, would not exclude some specific sectoral arrangements between two countries concerning the auto and textile industries, movies, and agriculture. But individual societies at the level of the nation-state may regulate the way health care and welfare benefits are distributed according to long-run national legacies. But again, the most localized interactions are plugged into the world international system, as demonstrated by the problem of pollution, ozone layer, biological diversity, and many other issues dealt with by the Rio world summit in the early nineties. Acute conflicts of interest among industrialized and industrializing as well as poor and rich countries have made compromise especially difficult to achieve.

Given the structural character of such a shift from national embeddedness of economic institutions to their nestedness within a multi-level system, the national sources of competitiveness have been altered and have become much more complex. The quality of national systems of innovations, the nature of industrial relations systems, the level of skills, and the ability of economic actors to respond quickly to economic fluctuations and uncertainties mean that the nature of interactions among firms, between employees and employers, and between private business and public authorities has become crucial for the performance of national economies. But increasingly, the complexity and dynamism of these economies must be expressed at the sub-national, regional, or local level. Nevertheless, the nature of the linkages between national and regional institutions plays an important role in shaping the ability of societies to evolve into different social systems of production. And some of the previous chapters provide examples of how economic dynamism is influenced by the linkages between local and national institutions. For example, the high quality of differentiated production in Germany results, in large part, from the combination of a de-centralized system organized at the level of the "Länder" which is intricately linked with a national system of co-determination (Herrigel, 1990). But in Britain, these tight linkages between regional and national institutions are not so well established. As a result, there are weakly developed industrial districts and a weakly performing national economy (Zeitlin, 1994). Like Germany, Japan is a good example of complementarity between dense localized networks (Nagoya City as a company town) and strong national institutions (major banks, spring offensives, development agencies, etc.). In the contemporary world, regional, national, and international institutions must be nested together. The British case suggests how weakly developed regional structures may erode the vitality of previously quite successful institutional arrangements at the level of the nation-state (Zeitlin, 1994).

In more analytical terms, the institutional arrangements which at one time were congruent at the national levels are now more dispersed at multiple spatial levels (see figure 2.1).

Figure 2.1 Contemporary Institutional Arrangements

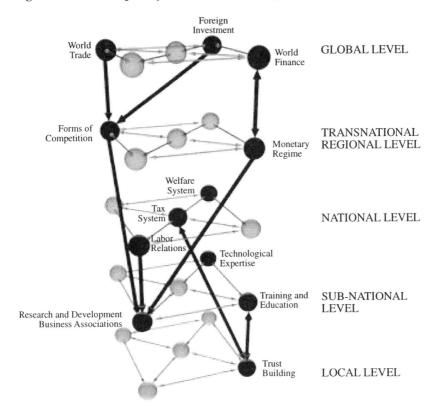

Impressive economic performance now requires that economic actors be well coordinated at all spatial areas simultaneously. In short, actors must be nested in institutional arrangements which will be linked at all levels of reality. At the international level, for example, a trade regime is regulated by international agreements and tends to be much more multi-lateral than bi-lateral in nature: rules are increasingly more of a constraint than a choice made by an individual nation-state. Increasingly, manufacturing and service firms are engaged in international competition. Moreover, the monetary systems are becoming more transnational in nature. For example, currency adjustments are no longer a safety valve to be manipulated in response to extra competitiveness or inferior performance at the level of the nation-state. Indeed, nation-states have lost much of their capacity to control interest and exchange rates. And this declining autonomy over these issues diminishes the capacity of states to regulate social policy and many other policy areas.

Conversely, the constitutional order which allocates power and resources differently between central and local authorities increasingly plays a role in shaping the ability of firms in a particular country to compete in the international arena. Thus, the parts of each system have become far more interdependent than during the sixties, and the increasingly complex distribution of power and resources across geographical levels is further evidence of how economic institutions have become nested in the multiple world of reality.

CORE CONCEPTS FOR MULTIPLE-LEVEL ANALYSIS

As a next step, the concept of levels will be introduced in a rigorous way. Level analysis operates at times with different types of actors like local enterprises, regional agencies, the state, transnational regional agencies like the European Union, transnational enterprises or global non-government organizations (NGOs) and with different spatial domains like regions, nations, transnational regional areas or the global arena.

Starting with the notion of spatial levels, the essential demarcation criterion between various levels lies in the mere scope of a physical space and its distances and scope. Thus, a household, a street, a neighborhood, a city, a region, a nation, a multi-national compound or the entire world occupy different spatial arenas. These spatial arenas can be measured in spatial units like square meters or square miles and have in most instances well-defined boundaries. For operational convenience, these different levels can be introduced in the following way. A simple notion is the "national level," since it is equivalent to the physical territory which is occupied by a single nation. From here, the regional level can be introduced as any spatial sub-component of the national level which fulfills one of the following criteria. The choice of regions should be in accordance with (a) administrative boundaries (a nation is divided into federal states or provinces) or (b) with economic, social, cultural, ethnic, or other boundaries. The only requirement for regional differentiation lies in the application of the regional version of "Occam's razor": regions should not be multiplied without necessity and their number should not exceed the range of 50 to 100 subnational units—"regiones non sunt multiplicandae propter necessitatem." Thus, the local level can be introduced as a proper partitioning of regional levels. Here, local levels comprise a rich variety of different domains like highly localized areas (a street, a collection of private homes, etc.) or wider domains (communities, villages, city districts, cities, etc.) The smallest possible local domains consist in the physical area of a private household, the physical space of a small-scale shop, of a small bar or restaurant and the like.

Proceeding from the national level upwards, the multi-national level can be introduced as any collection of two and more national areas. Thus, the multinational level comprises different spatial ensembles like the supra-national territory of the European Union, a collection of several nations or an entire continent like North America, Latin America, Africa, Asia, or Europe since all these continents are composed of several independent nations. Finally, the global level represents the entire "world" and can be conceptualized as the total sum of national or multi-national levels. Moreover, spatial levels are ordered in a strictly hierarchical manner. The national level is higher than the regional levels, the transnational regional level higher than the national levels, and the global level is the highest possible level. Finally, the level-relation is asymmetrical and transitive. If level L_1 is higher than Level L_2 and Level L_2 is higher then Level L_3, then L_1 is higher than L_3. In this manner, the notion of spatial levels can be given a precise and well-defined meaning.

The concept of "actors" can be introduced in a similar fashion. Here, the notion of "actors" is not to be restricted to individuals but also to groups of individuals which are organized as firms, as associations, as networks, as hierarchies, and the like. Actors can be separated according to the boundaries in which they can physically operate simultaneously.

The paradigmatic example for a local actor is the individual as a private person, living in a single home or apartment. Other typical examples for local actors are small shops, small enterprises without any other branches in other areas, a local school, a local theater and the like. While a small-scale firm may be accessible globally via the Internet and while it may export even 100 percent of its output abroad, the physical operations of the company can be only within a local setting. Likewise communities are practically in all instances in local character since they operate within a single local domain. In the same manner, one finds local associations which do not transcend the boundaries of their local environment and a large number of actors which act strictly in a local sense.

In contrast, regional actors operate predominantly in a regional scope. Thus, a bureaucracy of a federal state can be qualified as regional actor, regional associations with regional memberships fall under this category, small and medium-scale enterprises, operating with different branches across a region can be classified as regional actors as well. Likewise, political movements with a regional agenda and membership are regional in nature. Thus, all ensembles with a strictly regional operation are included in the class of regional actors.

Similarly, the national context is the criterion for identifying national actors. Thus, the federal bureaucracy, large-scale political parties, the government, or the legislative bodies of a nation-state are typical examples of national actors. Similarly, national associations such as trade unions or employers associations fall under the category of "national actors." Likewise, large-scale enterprises which are operating in different parts of a country or which are, due to their sheer employment size, of vital importance to the national economic system, are to be considered important "national players." National associations of universities and national artistic or cultural groups enter as "national actors" into the national arena as well. Thus, all ensembles with a national operation potential are to be qualified as national actors.

Multi-national actors are to be understood, then, as all operating units with a clearly recognizable multi-national scope. The paradigmatic example for a multi-national actor is the European Union with its collection of multi-national actors like the European Commission, the European Parliament or the European Council. Other examples of multi-national actors are multi-national trade unions, multi-national corporations, multi-national cultural or scientific associations like the European Science Foundation (ESF), and the like. The most im-

Table 2.1 The Correspondence between Alternative Institutional Arrangements and Level of Coordination: Paradigmatic Examples

| | *Institutional Arrangements* | | | |
	Markets	*Networks*	*Associations*	*Hierarchies*
Level of Coordination				
Local		Third Italy Silicon Valley	Guilds, Craft Unions, Business Associations	R&D, Education and Training
Sub-National		South Germany	Business Associations	R&D, Education and Training
National	Fordist Regime U.S. (1950–70)	Promotional Networks in	Labor Unions, Business Associations	Defense Taxes
Transnational-Regional	Financial Services Interest and Exchange Rates	Joint Ventures, Licensing Agreements, Sales and Distributional Ties	Very Weak	Safety and Environmental Standards
Global	Financial Services Interest and Exchange Rates	Joint Ventures, Licensing Agreements, Sales and Distributional Ties	Very Weak When Existing	Trade Regulations

portant demarcation criterion for "multinational actors" lies in the fact that these actors normally do not transcend different "continental zones" (Hollingsworth and Boyer, 1997). Thus, they are actors in multi-national arenas, not in the global one.

Global actors, finally, are characterized, above all, by the global scope of their operations. Thus, transnational enterprises (TNE) are distributed over the entire globe with simultaneous operations in at least two different continental zones. Global non-government organizations (NGOs) are representing members from a multiplicity of different countries around the world. Political organizations like the United Nations are operating simultaneously in various economic, social, cultural, or health areas around the world. Thus, the simultaneity of operations around the world must be considered as the most important criterion of demarcation for global actors.

It should be added that the same spatial distinctions which have been introduced for levels and actors can be made with respect to the institutional side, too. Institutions, understood as norms, regulations, rules, conventions, laws, and the like, can be separated according to various spatial dimensions, too. Thus, institutional arrangements like trade regulations can be undertaken on a global or multi-national level, regulations can be of local, regional, national, multi-national, or global scope, etc.

Thus, the differentiation into five distinctive spatial units—local, regional, national, transnational regional, global—belongs to the core domain of socio-economic analysis. As a next step, some important characteristics of multi-level analysis can be introduced at greater length. While some of these features are fairly obvious, other heuristic rules and devices require a more careful discussion.

The first important feature for multi-level analysis lies in the fact that different levels have become particularly well suited for different modes of co-ordination. Each of these various institutional arrangements has its own logic—its own rules, its own procedures for enforcing compliance, its own norms and ideologies which help to reduce the costs of enforcement. These are summarized in table 2.1, which provides further elaboration about the various coordinating mechanisms one finds in almost every capitalist society. Table 2.1 lists the organizational structures, the rules of exchange, and means of enforcing compliance associated with each type of coordinating mechanism. While each type of institutional arrangement has various positive features—or else it would be strongly opposed by various economic actors—nevertheless each institutional arrangement does have particular failures, and these are featured in figure 2.2 as well as in table 2.1.

Another obvious feature, already directly visible in figure 2.1, lies in the massive parallelism and in vertical arrows of causality from above as well as from below. Multi-level analysis is situated beyond the conventional single level designs, mostly centered around the nation-state or beyond the "bottom-up ap-

Figure 2.2   Spatial Levels and Modes of Co-ordination: Degrees of Coordination Effectiveness

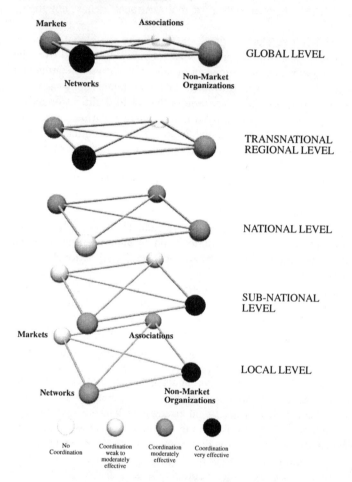

proaches, associated with the micro-aggregations of neoclassical economics or rational choice. For an explanation or explanation sketch to be successful, a pattern or a process at a specific level requires components from higher levels as well as from lower levels. Thus, regional or local factors as well as global arrangements may be of decisive importance for transnational regional or global processes.

A third striking element of the multi-level architecture lies in the absence of an overt or even a hidden coordination center. The interplay between these levels happens in a mode of "self-organization" which produces over time new "mixtures" and "recombinations" for governance and for level specialization.

FOUR TYPES OF MULTIPLE-LEVEL ANALYSIS

Given the basic features of multiple-level analysis, the next step will differentiate between four different "types" or "clusters" of multiple-level investigations. The first two clusters correspond to well-established social science approaches; the third and the fourth clusters will move into more complex areas of investigations which, so far, have been rarely explored and mastered.

The first type is the most traditional one, focusing on changes within a single level using one type of actor only. Thus, the interaction patterns in a local community, using exclusively local actors, or the pattern formation at the national level, utilizing only macro-economic or macro-social variables, may be considered as a paradigmatic case of the first cluster. Here, processes or patterns at one level are accounted for or explained in terms of components or actors from the same level.

For the second type of multiple-level analyses, simultaneous development patterns across at least two levels are to be considered, using one type of actors only. A typical example for the second cluster is the neoclassical and/or rational choice approach which uses the strategic interactions between individuals, households or firms and arrives, by way of aggregations, at the corresponding changes on the national level. Figure 2.3b provides a paradigmatic example for such an aggregation, using all relevant information within a lower level in order to arrive at the development patterns at the national level.

Leading into more "troubled waters" of analysis, type III focuses on the evolution of a particular domain within a single level, using multiple actors across the entire spatial range. Taking an important "hot field" like bio-technology as reference case, a typical investigation for the third cluster would consist of the national development patterns in various sectors of bio-technology (food, medicine, pharmaceuticals, instruments), using actors from the European Union (Commission, Parliament, Council), from global NGOs, from transnational pharmaceutical companies, national legislative bodies, from regional parliaments, from local enterprises, etc. Figure 2.3c exemplifies a typical pattern for type III analysis, demonstrating that changes at the national levels come about as an interplay between actors from all five different levels.

Finally, sticking to the bio-technology arena, a paradigmatic example for the fourth and most comprehensive as well as the most challenging type of investigation would be to analyze the simultaneous changes in actor formations, public support, and institutional regulations within bio-technology for the European Union and for EU member states.

Thus, the fourth cluster of analyses seeks to comprehend the simultaneous changes within two or more levels. Here, one is confronted with a very crowded and heterogeneous set of multiple actors which include, inter alia, the European Commission, transnational and multi-national bio-technology enterprises, the European parliament, universities, multi-national research institutes, national media, national scientific associations, national legislative bodies, local and regional economic actors (farmers, food processing companies, small pharmaceutical firms, hospitals, etc.), global, multi-national, national or regional NGOs and many other actors which "have their exits and their entrances" in the multiple-level, multiple-actor arena of bio-technology. Thus, the crucial requirement for the fourth type of analysis is the search for simultaneous changes in at least two spatial arenas, using multiple actors. Figure 2.3d shows the complexities involved in the fourth cluster of investigations which so far have not been sufficiently mastered and accounted for even within socio-economic analyses.

In sum, figure 2.3 recaptures the increasing degrees of complexities separating the single-level/single-actor type (figure 2.3a) from the multiple-actor/multiple-level type (figure 2.3d). It goes without saying that both the traditional methodologies within the neoclassical domain are of little use and value when it comes to the considerably complex research designs of figure 2.3c and 2.3d.

FOUR SCENARIOS FOR LEVEL-DIFFERENTIATION

Coordination of economic actors at the level of the nation-state has not completely disappeared and will probably not vanish, since it remains the level at which some social solidarity is still embedded and channeled into labor laws, a national tax system, and many welfare services. However, the future of many national institutional arrangements is extremely uncertain. So many contradictory forces are operating that it is difficult to imagine that the complete institutional environment into which firms were embedded in the sixties will survive another generation. Irreversible forces have developed forms of social systems of production which are transnational, have shifted the division of labor among regions, and have transformed the relations between the state and the economy. As a result of these changes, one can imagine four different scenarios (see figure 2.4).

Scenario One—The Return to the National Level

If the contradictions inherent in the internationalization of the economy become too acute (massive and persisting unemployment, rising inequality, major regional imbalances, xenophobist movements, etc.), some governments may attempt to return to a so-called "Golden Age" by becoming increasingly nationalistic and by erecting barriers to finance, trade, and migration of persons. Given the extreme division of labor and interdependencies which now operate at the international level, such nationalistic policies for any particular country would lead to a substantial reduction in productivity and standards of living. Should this occur, any state implementing such policies would be acting contrary to its society's general economic welfare. Indeed, such a state would suffer such a major loss in legitimacy that such policies could not long be sustained.

Scenario Two—The Dominance of Multi-National Levels

Considering the emergence of the European Union, the North American Free Trade Agreement, and the further development of an Asian trading bloc, one can easily imagine that increased international economic uncertainty will foster the development of monetary and economic zones designed to minimize the discrepancies in interest and exchange rates originating from the two other zones of the triad. In varying degrees, this scenario has been operating for more than a decade, and further developments along these lines are expected. Nevertheless, conflicting national interests within particular trading blocs might collide and provoke states to flirt with the first scenario, i.e., the effort to seek more autonomy at the level of individual nation-states. One could clearly observe this type of tension operating among Britain, southern Europe, and the European Community during the period between 1990 and 1993.

Scenario Three—"Blind Variation"

This assumes that the juxtaposition of numerous conflicting sectoral and/or global regulatory regimes will nevertheless be sufficient to bring compatibility among conflicting interests, unequal competitiveness and diverging trajectories among nations. For example, a GATT agreement on agricultural trade; the replacement of GATT by the WTO in order to remove bilateral self-restraint accords in the car, electronic, textile, and other industries; international regulation of banking and finance; a minimal social charter under the aegis of ILO; the development and implementation of an ecological tax for industrialized and industrializing countries; a codification of patents and intellectual rights; and a powerful group of seven to ten nation-states attempting to regulate interest and exchange rates—all of these things could eventually become a relatively coherent system of coordination, without any explicit design to do so. This would be a self-building of institutions at the international level, in accordance with an Austrian vision "à la Hayek." However, the likelihood of such a plural-

Figure 2.3 Four Types of Actor-Level-Analysis

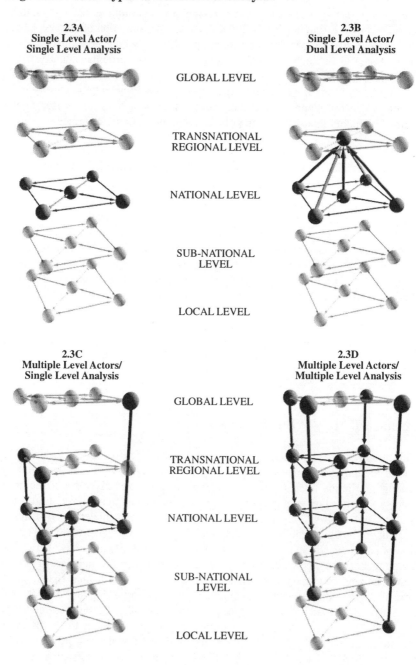

2.3A
Single Level Actor/
Single Level Analysis

2.3B
Single Level Actor/
Dual Level Analysis

GLOBAL LEVEL

TRANSNATIONAL
REGIONAL LEVEL

NATIONAL LEVEL

SUB-NATIONAL
LEVEL

LOCAL LEVEL

2.3C
Multiple Level Actors/
Single Level Analysis

2.3D
Multiple Level Actors/
Multiple Level Analysis

GLOBAL LEVEL

TRANSNATIONAL
REGIONAL LEVEL

NATIONAL LEVEL

SUB-NATIONAL
LEVEL

LOCAL LEVEL

Figure 2.4 Four Scenarios of Multiple-Level Development

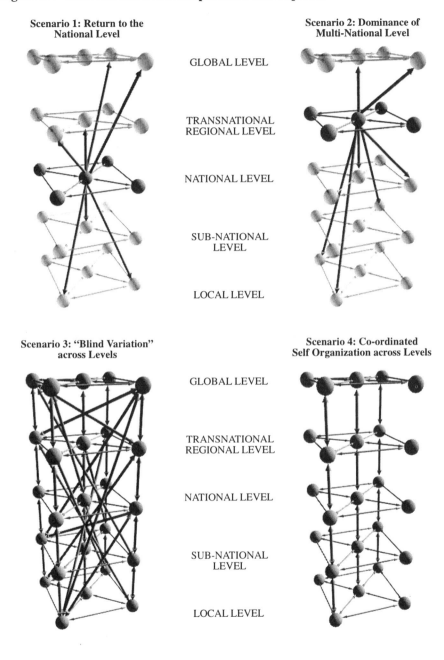

Scenario 1: Return to the National Level

Scenario 2: Dominance of Multi-National Level

Scenario 3: "Blind Variation" across Levels

Scenario 4: Co-ordinated Self Organization across Levels

GLOBAL LEVEL

TRANSNATIONAL REGIONAL LEVEL

NATIONAL LEVEL

SUB-NATIONAL LEVEL

LOCAL LEVEL

istic system of coordination without a powerful state or a single hegemon to orchestrate such behavior and to act as an enforcer appears to be problematic.

Scenario Four—Coordinated Self-Organization

The nestedness of a complex system of regional, national, continental, and world institutional arrangements into a legacy of national intervention, complemented by sectoral agreements, has been emerging for at least a decade. Nestedness means that sub-national regimes, sectoral, national, and international logics are intertwined—with none being dominant—in a two sided type of causality. For example, decisions in Brussels about economic regulations for the European Union have an increasing impact on the competitiveness of single nation-states, sub-national regional dynamics, and the capacity of nation-states to shape their own economic and social policies. At the same time the cohesiveness of national and sub-national regional interests of member states plays a role in shaping the regulations designed in Brussels. Another example of nestedness refers to the links among product, credit, and labor markets at multiple spatial levels. In the sixties, wage formation was embedded in a variety of national compromises between capital and labor, and monetary and exchange rate policies were designed to reflect the specificity of national political and economic institutions. In the nineties, however, the intense international competition of product markets and the strong flows of money across countries have undermined the strength of national systems of industrial relations and labor contracts. In some advanced industrial societies, low wages are threatening to become a basic ingredient in shaping national competitiveness and the capacity of a society to attract foreign capital. All of this is intertwined at the sub-national regional, national, continental, and global levels and feeds back and influences the degree of stability and instability of the economy of any nation-state.

Thus in the sixties, the way that institutions were embedded at the level of the nation-state influenced not only behavior and economic performance at the level of sub-national regions but also the coordination of the international economy. But in the nineties, the world trade regime and continental trade zones influenced national policies and the structure and behavior of sub-national regional groups. The flexibility and nature of national labor markets are subject to a double squeeze—from the outside by the international financial regime and from the inside by the ability of sub-national regional groups to manufacture cooperation and trust among themselves.

Scenario Four is more ordered and less chaotic than the third scenario. How all of the fourth scenario will play out is uncertain, even though this scenario presently has considerable dynamism to it. Where is the theory which allows us to understand and guide such a process? Will public opinion accept such a complex set of institutional arrangements, especially in weaker countries which are more adversely affected by the ongoing transnationalization? What is the capacity of public authorities to build barriers to the process of transnationalization in order to preserve distinctive national institutions, macro-economic performance, and high employment? Will the "satanic mills" created by the market that Karl Polanyi had discussed during the forties re-emerge and undermine the potential for social solidarity? Will nation-states have the capacity to respond to economic, social, and political innovations sufficiently quickly in order to prevent economic crises—even the repetition of a great depression?

The future is very much open, but a perspective on long-term historical trends suggests that taming the market has always been more rewarding over the longer term than myopically following it. Moreover, modern economic theory is slowly converging toward such a vision: only short-run and marginal choices can be left to the market, whereas imaginative collective forms of coordination are addressing many of more important social and political issues of our time. The most competitive firms, regions, or nations are not mimicking the market but on the contrary, they are struggling to manufacture consensus, trust, collective forms of governance, and long-term vision. The core message of this essay brings unconventional conclusions about economic policies for the future. As a neo-Polanyian, I must move away from the rhetoric of what free marketers promise and attempt to convince our societies to build more livable communities and to construct new forms of a mixed economy. But as our institutions are increasingly nested in a world of sub-national regions, nation-states, continental and global regimes, do we have the capacity to govern ourselves democratically? Clearly one of the major challenges of our time is to create a new theory of democracy for governing institutions nested in a world of unprecedented complexity, one in which sub-national regions, nation-states, and continental and global regimes are all intricately linked.

NOTE

I am very indebted to Robert Boyer for helping me to work out many of the ideas in this chapter. Without his assistance this chapter would not exist. For complementary ideas, see Hollingsworth and Boyer (1997).

3

Towards a Socio-Economic Paradigm

Amitai Etzioni

This chapter contains three parts. The first outlines the reasons I believe the time has come to develop a shared disciplinary core for socio-economics. The second then turns to the principles that ought to guide us in developing such a core, and finally, the third suggests several specific elements for such a discipline. While my discussion benefits from a document formulated when SASE,[1] a society founded to advance socio-economics, was first founded, all that follows reflects my current views as to what is to be done and feed into a dialogue on this subject. Clearly, the only way such a core can be developed is through an extended and extensive dialogue among those of us who are concerned about the future of socio-economics as an academic discipline, as a basis for public policy, and as a source for our fellow persons to better understand and guide the social and economic world in which we all live.

NEXT: A DISCIPLINARY CORE

Socio-economics has come a long way over the last decade. Energetic and dedicated leadership and fine executive directors have put the International

Society for the Advancement of Socio-Economics on sound footing. Attendance at annual meetings is solid. Colleagues attend because they find the meetings stimulating; the meetings hardly provide a job market, a reason many feel they ought to attend the meetings of many other disciplinary associations. The executive council is much stronger than it used to be. Several new books have been published that cover socio-economic topics.

With this in mind, three next steps seem to suggest themselves: (a) Socio-economics ought to become institutionalized, in the sense that we need to find or form some graduate departments or schools that are willing to train students in socio-economics and accord degrees in this field. There is a steady demand for socio-economists, especially by CEOs and heads of NGOs, but no supply. (b) We need a journal in which to publish solid socio-economic works rather than a grab bag of papers that happen to come in over the transom, many of which should not have been published in any place, and most of which have not a socio-economic bone in them.

(c) Both developments are conditioned on the third one, that socio-economics develop a limited core of shared principles. Neoclassical economics, for instance, is built around the perfect competition model and all that it entails. Law and economics, which now commands the loyalty of maybe as many as a third of the legal scholars in the United States, in turn is based on the neoclassical model. Biology long took one form or another of Darwinism as its core. As a result, members of these disciplines can take certain core assumptions for granted. These serve to establish what is part of the discipline and what belongs elsewhere; to allow members of the discipline to build on rather than continually examine elementary terms and the basic approach; and—most important—to provide a base for the accumulation of knowledge generated by different scholars. This is what socio-economics seems to be ready for and indeed requires, if it is to grow significantly as a discipline beyond its current level.

A PARADIGM SHIFT

My argument is that to develop the said shared socio-economic core, we require a paradigm shift—a basic change in perspective. There are now two fundamentally different paradigms of social science, which in turn have deep connections to distinct bodies of social philosophies, ethics, social values, and even political ideologies.

One paradigm is centered around the individual, who is assumed to be the agent, the choice maker, the foundation of liberty. (Among those who speak in this way are classical liberals, contemporary classical liberals, laissez-faire conservatives, and libertarians).

When economics is formulated in the terms of this paradigm, as neoclassical economics is, we find as a core concept that of consumer sovereignty, the examination of which will stand for many others. This is the notion that the direction of the economy in toto arises out of an aggregation of individual choices and transactions. This is the cardinal assumption that guides much of the work in the neoclassical approach. Thus, if a neoclassical economist is studying how to make people save more, she will "naturally" think about increasing the incentives for people to save (e.g., increase the amount one may contribute to an IRA) or the disincentives for not saving (e.g., introduce a tax on consumption). She is much less likely to start the analysis by considering increasing the budgetary surplus and/or paying off more of the national debt, much more effective ways to boost saving than trying to affect the choices of millions of individuals. Of course, there are macro-economists who study national budgets, but they cannot find in their paradigm the principles and concepts that nourish analysis that are not based on aggregating individual choices.

One should also note that the neoclassical approach has clear normative and political roots and consequences. Granted, it would be wrong to imply that all or even most neoclassical economists—those who build on the individualist paradigm—are laissez-faire conservatives or libertarians, Thatcherites or Reaganites. It would be, though, accurate to observe that there are certain basic assumptions shared by neoclassical economics and by these ideologies. They nourish each other.

Socio-economics, as I see it, best draws on a different paradigm, one that builds on different core assumptions and implicit normative content. So far it has been much less well articulated than the individual-centered one, but nevertheless, it has been and is very influential. One may refer to it as a societal-historical, institutional, or cultural approach.[2] Because it focuses on factors that affect the preferences and choices of millions of individuals—such as the epoch in which people live and the culture that surrounds them—I will refer to it for short as a macro-approach. And just as the individualistic paradigm does not reject macro factors (although it has a hard time accommodating them), so socio-economics has room for the study of aggregations of individual choices, although this is not at its core. Note that an overwhelming majority of the topics listed in the Madison Declaration on the Need for Socio-economic Research and Theory concern macro-elements.[3] (Robin Stryker correctly points out that further sophistication requires a multi-layered approach that goes beyond that macro-micro dichotomy, a point not further discussed here.)[4]

If one accepts, for the sake of discussion, that socio-economics requires a different paradigm than neoclassical economics, two insights follow. First, it is counter-productive to try to convince neoclassicists that they are making wrong assumptions, or to chastise them for not incorporating societal, cultural, and historical factors in their paradigm. It is futile because once a discipline has acquired a definite core, its members' "job" is to defend it, to try to work within it, and to try to incorporate into it pesky challenges rather than abandon the paradigm. (See, for instance, the way social norms have recently been treated by neoclassical scholars.)[5]

Moreover, if one examines how paradigms have historically shifted, one finds that new paradigms have not emerged because followers of the old, obsolescent paradigm were won over to new ways of approaching the world. Rather, a group breaks away from the old tradition or a new group is formed, giving rise to a legitimate conflict between the old and new paradigms. Then the "market" decides which paradigm has more evidence and is more compelling, although often both the old and the new coexist for long periods of time. The main contest is over new followers rather than converting the old-timers.

Ergo, if there is going to be a socio-economic disciplinary core it will rise out of the work of socio-economists, not neoclassical ones, and most of them—at least the hard core—will not be won over. New generations and those who have not previously committed themselves to any particular paradigm are going to be the carriers of the new one. It also follows that socio-economics, by definition, is an interstitial discipline; it is a bridging discipline. In that sense, it is similar to biochemistry and social psychology, rather than biology or chemistry, sociology, or psychology. Its variables are derived from two or more social science disciplines rather than from any one. (The term "socio" in socio-economics does not stand for sociology; it includes major segments of psychology and anthropology, history, and political science—the whole complex of disciplines that are examined the relationships between society and the economy.)

Moreover, the paradigm at the foundation of socio-economics points to the "location" of causality (or independent variables). Socio-economics requires, on the face of it, that one deal with one or more social variables and one or more economic variables. If one deals only with economic variables—for instance, if one studies whether low levels of unemployment and high rates of inflation are correlated—one is not in socio-economics. It is a fully legitimate subject for study, but an intra-economic one. And if one explores the question of the effects of fundamentalism on science, this study, too, is not part of socio-economics, because all the variables are social and none are economic. Socio-economics arises when analysis starts with the independent variables in the social realm, and then moves to economic dependent variables. For instance, do people who are more conservative in their political ideology save more than those who are not? Do people who are alienated make for less productive workers? Does lobbying affect prices and to what extent? What social and political conditions make for higher economic growth? And so on and so on.

Next, and on the same point, it is a grave error to treat the economy as self-sustaining system, to view the market as separate from society (and its polity). The starting point of socio-economic analysis is that the economy is a sub-system of the societal system. Much of what is occurring within the economy is best explained by attributes and processes that occur outside of it. To cite just one very well-known and compelling example: Max Weber's study of the social (and religious) conditions under which capitalism arises and thrives.

To make the difference between neoclassical and socio-economics less abstract, here is an example. George Stigler wanted to provide an example of the governing assumption of neoclassical economics, that the market (an aggregation of the choices of all participants) ultimately set the context in which individual choices must be made. Thus, if a manager reads the market correctly in terms of what will sell at what price, then that manager's corporation will stay in business; if the manager misreads the market's signals and persists in not responding to its dictates, the firm will be soon bankrupt. To illustrate this point, Stigler focuses on wheat farmers. Each farmer cannot decide what he or she will charge for a bushel of wheat; they can charge only what the market will bear. The market decides. The core assumption is that the market works like an anonymous box into which suppliers throw in their bids and buyers throw theirs, and out of this invisible hat the "correct" price prints out.

A socio-economist, not bound by the aggregate individualist paradigm, will note that in the United States, farmers are not merely "in the market" but also in the polity; they are members of one of two political lobbies. These lobbies influence Congress to enact various legislation that greatly affects the price of wheat. While this is now changing, for the last forty years, the price of wheat was not determined by an autonomous machine: it couldn't fall below a certain level because the government protected the price. (The details were a bit more complicated. To protect their egos, the farmers did not want to take money directly from the government; handouts were for despised welfare recipients. Farmers, therefore, gave their wheat as collateral to the government, which in turn gave them loans. If the market price moved up, they took the wheat out and sold it; if it fell, they left the wheat in the silos, the government fortified and kept it, and it rotted. When all was said and done, the government ensured that the price the farmers got did not fall below a certain level, as determined by politics and not the market.) The price reflected the fact that the farmers lived in both the polity and the economy, and they used their lobbying citizen's hat to influence the economy. Farming is hardly the only sector in which this occurs. If you look at textiles, you will find that we have something called a multi-fiber agreement, through which the government controls how much textile is imported from what country and at what prices. For many years, we had a trigger price for steel; reflecting pressure from Congress, we had a so-called voluntary quota limiting the importation of cars from Japan to 1.25 million. The same can be found in many other areas. About the only sectors in the United States that truly approximate the neoclassical model are Chinese restaurants and laundromats and even they are regulated by the city that tell them they cannot open one too close to another.

A CORE THEOREM: SELF-INTEREST AND VALUES

To reiterate, socio-economics, by definition, is an interstitial science. To apply this essential observation—just illustrated on a macro, societal level—to the micro, individual level, the following core theorem might be considered as a cardinal building block of socio-economics: Individuals' decisions and behaviors, far from following one unified principle, or seeking to maximize pleasure and minimize pain, or marching to one overarching utility, reflect empirically the conflict between two—at least two—irreducible utilities. The first is our desire for pleasure; the other, our moral obligations.

To start with an extremely simple example: When one says, "I would like to go to a movie, but I ought to visit my friend in the hospital," the statement contains what is pleasurable and what is morally called for. Indeed, most of our values are dedicated to pulling us against the pleasure principle. Whether religious or secular, they call on people to fast, to give to the church, to not engage in sex, and so on and on. In other words, there are certain things one is supposed to do which are of virtue for a variety of reasons, but the common variable they share is that they pull us in directions that are counter to where the pleasure principle pushes us.

Our nature is to be conflicted between these two "utilities." Much of what we do reflects this inevitable tension between things we would like to do and things we ought to do. Many empirical observations support this generalization. Let's start with the question of why people vote. Economists find it surprising that people vote; such behavior doesn't fit the standard economic model. Individuals are expected to do things for a return, for profit, or for some other form of benefit. When one votes, one cannot reasonably expect that the vote will make a difference. So the question economists ask is, Why do people expend the time standing in line and lose leisure or work time, when there will be no specific outcome for the person?

For a socio-economist, this behavior is not puzzling. The number one variable that explains the difference between people who vote and those who don't is the sense of civic duty. Those people who do, feel they have an obligation to vote. To them, it is the right thing to do. Those who have this sense are much more likely to vote than those who don't have such a sense.[6] This is not to suggest that the length of lines, the weather, etc., don't make a difference; they do affect the "costs" of voting and do affect behavior. But the number one factor explaining the variance is the relative strength of the person's sense of civic duty.

Another illustration. If people were to act only to maximize their pleasure, those who smoke would vote against taxes on cigarettes, and those who do not would favor these taxes. The fact, though, is that there are a large number of smokers who vote *for* taxes on cigarettes, because they feel they are damaging the public and ought to do something to compensate for that. And there are a fair number of non-smokers who vote *against* these taxes because they are libertarians, or they feel the government should not interfere. A study found that individuals told that conserving energy during peak demand periods would be good for the community were likely to lower their electricity use during such periods, if they felt that households as a group could make a difference.[7] People's moral concepts, their social philosophies, are not the only factors used to make decisions, but they are important ones for understanding their social political economic behavior.

One last example: neoclassical economists try to explain why people—most people—with spouses who have Alzheimer's stay with them. These economists treat marriage as an economic contract, in which an exchange of services takes place for income and services. But with Alzheimer's, there is no payback because there's no reasonable hope that the person who is afflicted will recover and take care of the other person. One may say that the treating spouse does so because of the kudos he or she will receive from members of their extended family and neighbors and friends. However, tending to an Alzheimer's patient day-in and day-out is so taxing that all the kudos in the world could not make up for it. And finally, economists use the notion of psychic income. But again, that explanation fails because the afflicted person does not respond with a warm appreciation for the service; indeed, they become ever more abusive as time goes on. So why do most spouses not walk out on their afflicted husband or wife? When one interviews these people, one repeatedly hears the statement that "this is the right thing to do;" the same sentiment is found in Roberta Simmons's studies of kidney donations. People have a strong moral commitment, a powerful factor which outweighs the pain they have to endure.

My thesis is not that values drive behavior but that there is a continual conflict and tension between self-interest and the pleasure principle on one hand, and powerful moral commitments on the other. It follows that socio-economists would benefit if they took as their starting hypothesis that people are conflicted, and then tried to understand their inconsistencies and tendencies to zigzag as resulting from their being subject to these two competing super-utilities.

THE SOCIO-ECONOMIC MIND

No theory of human behavior can be developed without a core assumption about the intellectual capabilities of the person. I suggest that our deliberations use as their starting point the key observation that people are poor processors of information—just the opposite of what used to be the neoclassical economists' assumption that information flows instantaneously and is absorbed instantaneously, all without any costs. The economists wisely retreated from these assumptions, and they now recognize that information is not immediately absorbed and the process has costs. In this and several other contexts they refer to "imperfect" systems. This is a tricky concept that is inadvertently misleading. The term implies that there is a speck of dust on the perfect scale. Actually, people's limits on information processing are much larger. Indeed, strong evidence shows that people start with little knowledge and that they are slow and poor learners.

A simple case in point: every day millions of people all over the world call their brokers and either ask their advice on which stock to purchase or order them to buy one, on the assumption that these individual investors could beat the market averages. (Otherwise they would buy index funds and save costs.) However, there is strong, consistent, robust data to show this is an irrational act; one cannot consistently out-perform the market. Moreover, brokers have a conflict of interest with the callers; brokers benefit from high turnovers in the accounts, while investors benefit from low turnover and low transaction costs. Moreover, despite the fact that studies supporting the use of index funds rather than brokers have been repeatedly publicized in the popular press, in class-rooms, and on television, millions persist in such untutored behavior.

NEXT STEPS: FIRST APPROXIMATION, SCIENTIFIC DISCOURSE AND CORE BUILDING

Where might we go from here as a discipline? We should draft a small number of core assumptions and hypotheses of the kind I have illustrated in the previous pages and in *The Moral Dimension* (summarized in the lists below). In doing so we ought not seek definitive statements but first approximations. One reason socio-economics has been slower to develop than it might have otherwise been is that we have been seeking a higher level of precision or closure than is possible or necessary at this stage.

One example: a socio-economist may well consider the observation that be-havior (including choices) is more group than individually determined as either too obvious to be included in our set of core assumptions or too general to deserve to be noted. A solid socio-economist may well wish to first ask: Is there not more than one group that influences the same individual? How much of the variance does each group determine? Under what conditions does this determi-nation increase versus subside? All these are valid, but second-order, specifica-tions. We should not belittle the importance of simple first approximations because they clearly differentiate socio-economics from neoclassical economics and, above all, because they provide a theoretical home for thousands of much more specific observations (e.g., the way people vote, what they consume, which media they are exposed to, and much else, is largely determined not by their individual choices but by the social groups to which they belong).

Moreover, as preliminary and elementary as these observations are, they point to numerous policy recommendations as to how to reach people when we seek to change their behavior. One example: if one seeks to curb alcoholism the principle that the group is pivotal and that people chose largely within and with their group leads one to see that policies that are group-centered work much better (as Alcoholics Anonymous does) than those that try to directly reach the individual through ads, one-on-one rehab, and so on. I am not suggesting that we should forego specifying such core observations along the suggested and other lines, but we would do well to start now by formulating a set of first approximation core assumptions to make up our shared disciplinary core.

To make it shared, we should—once such a core is drafted—submit its assumptions to intensive and extensive scientific discourse among our members. In the process we may find that these core assumptions need to be revised, that some of our colleagues need to be persuaded of their merit, and that they elicit still other ones. Assuming that a core of such assumptions could survive such scrutiny, we would have the beginning of a shared core for socio-economics, which would then be a shared discipline and not merely as association of colleagues interested basically in the same part of the universe. This core would then nurture our teaching, meetings, and future work.

The following much revised list is culled from *The Moral Dimension*. It does not provide the core of principles we need, but is presented to stimulate further discussion leading to such a core.

"Divided Selves"

People have divided selves, part pleasure driven and part morally committed.

- Actors pursue two or more goals (utilities): seek pleasure (and hence self-interest), and seek to abide by their moral commitments. They are internally conflicted and hence tend to pursue a nonlinear course.
- The more individuals act under the influence of moral commitments, the more they are expected to persevere (when circumstances change). Conversely, the more individuals heed their pleasures or self-interest, the less likely they are to persevere.
- Moral commitments stretch out the learning curve.
- Moral commitments lower the transaction costs.
- When people violate their moral commitments to enhance their pleasures, such violations activate various defensive mechanisms before, during, and after the violation, and these have specific behavioral consequences.
- Violations of moral commitments cause guilt that leads, among other consequences, to compensatory pro-social behavior.
- Conflicts between pleasure motives and moral commitments are a major source of dissonance, leading to inaction and/or denial.

- Conflicts between pleasure valuations and moral valuations result in inter-psychic stress, leading to the diminished capacity of the actor to render rational decisions.
- Choices that are relatively heavily loaded with moral considerations, including many economic choices, are expected to be unusually difficult to reverse (are asymmetrical), to be very "lumpy" (or highly discontinuous), and to reveal a high "notch" effect.
- When moral commitments are prominent they generate non-markets in some areas ("blocked exchanges"), e.g., in constitutional rights, and poor markets in others, e.g., in adoption.

Limited Information

People have limited intellectual capabilities. They are poor processors of information and are defective decision makers. Actors' choices of means are largely based on values and emotions. To the extent that they draw on logic and evidence, their limited intellectual capabilities lead the actors to typically render sub-rational decisions.

- Most choices are made without the processing of information, drawing of inferences, or deliberations. That is, they are not decisions.
- Most choices (whether deliberative or not) are made to a significant extent on the bases of values/emotions. (Not just the selection of goals but also of means.)
- Values/emotions either fully form many choices, or set a context that limits the range of those options that are considered.
- Values/emotions affect deliberations of those options that are considered by "loading" options with non-empirical, non-logical weights.
- Values/emotions interrupt deliberations, preventing completion of reasoned decision-making sequences.
- Values/emotions legitimate some sub-areas as those in which logical/empirical choices are mandated. That is, the extent to which decision making strives to be rational is deeply affected by values/ emotions.
- Choices made on the basis of values/emotions are not necessarily inefficient.
- Knowledge plays a limited role in most decisions.
- Even when knowledge is extensively used, such decisions are inefficient as compared to the results objective observers find could be reached.

The Social System

- Individual (I) and collectivity (We) are both essential elements and have the same basic conceptual and moral standing.
- The I and We is in a perpetual, but in part creative, conflict.
- While individuals shape the social entities of which they are members, and these groups and communities shape individuals, each individual on his or her own is more socially determined than determining.
- Many kinds of decisions are, on average, made more efficiently by organizational units of collectivities (such as executive boards of firms) than by individuals.
- The scope and level of innovation is in part collectively determined: the lower the culture ranks economic goals, productivity, efficiency, technology, science and the higher it ranks social cohesion, stability, and religion, the lower the scope and level of innovation.

Market as Sub-System; Society as System

- The scope of the transactions organized by the market is largely determined by the social capsule.
- Competition is not *self*-sustaining. Its very existence, and the scope of transactions organized by it, depend to a significant extent on the attributes of the societal capsule within which it takes place; i.e., it is to a significant extent externally determined.
- The divergent interests and pursuits of actors in the market do not automatically mesh to form a harmonious whole; i.e., specific mechanisms are needed to keep competition (as contained conflict) from escalating into all-out conflict. Unregulated competition will self-destruct.
- The strength of the capsule is determined by the strength of the moral legitimacy it commands; by the intensity of the social bonds that competitors share; and by the relative power of the government compared to those in the market.
- Three mechanisms substitute for one another. Up to a point, each has its own role; at the same time, they affect one another and not just the capsule.
- The relationship between social bonds and competition is curvilinear; weak bonds are one factor that allows for all-out conflict; tight bonds will restrain, if not suppress, competition. Bonds of intermediate strength are most compatible with competition.
- Governments sustain competition to the extent they are the ultimate defender of rules and prevent violence; they undermine competition when they seek to determine the outcomes of competitions.

Social Structure

- There are no transactions among equals. Power is the source of structure.
- The price of an item reflects its costs, and the relative economic and political power of producers (providers, sellers, etc.) as compared to users (buyers etc.) and other parties (government regulators, consumer unions, farm lobbies, etc.). In short, cost + power = price.
- The capsule is maintained to the extent that economic power is dispersed or prevented from concentrating, or economic power is being prevented from conversion into political power. The more economic power is segregated from political power, whatever its level of concentration, the higher the probability that the capsule will survive and be effective.
- Structures able to limit the *political* power of economic competitors are as important to sustaining competition as is preventing a large concentration of economic power.
- Manipulation of the government by powerful economic actors generates pseudo-concentration effect (comparable to that caused by the concentration of economic power, without there being any such concentration or collusion among economic actors).

Methodological Positions (Interdisciplinary)

- Two kinds of forces affect the social realm as they affect one another. Deontological conceptions set the context within which utilitarian orientations—pleasure, self-interest, and rationality—are operative.
- Changes in behavior (such as amount saved, level of effort at work, extent to which taxes due are paid) reflect in part changes in preferences and in part changes in constraints. Value changes affect *both* preferences and constraints, but especially preferences. Changes in market forces affect both preferences and constraints, but especially constraints.
- Socio-economics is to rely more on induction, less on deduction than neoclassical economics.
- Parsimony is to be sacrificed to a limited extent in order to expand the scope of the variables covered (especially social, psychic, and political) and to explain more of the variance of the behavior under study.
- Tautologies must be avoided.

NOTES

1 See the "Madison-Declaration" by the Society for the Advancement of Socio-Economics, issued in summer of 1998.

2 For a fine recent discussion of institutionalism in this context see Robin Stryker's article on "The Future of Socio-Economics and of the Society for the Advancement of Socio-Economics," chapter 4 in the present volume.

3 See, once again, the "Madison Declaration" by the Society for the Advancement of Socio-Economics.

4 See the work of Robin Stryker (chapter 4) in the present volume.

5 On this point, see a more detailed analysis in the chapter on "Social Norms" in my book *The Monochrome Society* (2001).

6 On voting behavior, see especially Brian Barry (1978).

7 On this point, see J. S. Black (1978).

4

The Future of Socio-Economics and of the Society for the Advancement of Socio-Economics

Robin Stryker

The idea of combining economics, the social sciences and some of the humanities to get a better handle on production, distribution, and consumption processes and their effects is a worthy goal. If we do it, we ought to make progress toward another worthy goal—using the resulting expertise to help make a better social world. Some people might dispute these goals, but they probably are not SASE members. Those of us in the Society for the Advancement of Socio-Economics (SASE) probably can agree this far. But agreeing beyond this gets trickier. We have to ask exactly what and how we are combining to get socio-economics. What is our image of the result after the combining? Our answers have consequences, both intellectual and practical. There are consequences for us, for others, and—we hope—for society. Since the consequences play out in terms of interests, values, and identities, when we confront the future of SASE, we really are confronting a large, complex set of issues.

Any person or organization confronting a task does so under diverse social constraints and opportunities. In considering the future of SASE, our constraints and opportunities stem basically from three inter-related sources. First is the current intellectual and institutional situation within our organization. Second is the current intellectual and institutional situation in SASE's organizational environment. And third are the intellectual and institutional situations prevailing for each of us as conjoint members of SASE and of various other networks and communities, professional and otherwise. I would like now to explore briefly what I think are some key intellectual and institutional constraints and opportunities confronting us as we consider the future of SASE. I will be optimistic and talk first, and at more length, about the opportunities. Then I will return to mention some key constraints. I will end with a few words about what, given this array of constraints and opportunities, we might expect the process of getting there from here to look like. And what is the likely content of the "there" toward which we are moving?

OPPORTUNITIES

Timing may not be everything, but it counts for a lot. Happily, now is a reasonably auspicious time to be contemplating the future of socio-economics and of SASE. It is so for numerous reasons.

First, we are confronting social change of such magnitude and with such huge consequences for people that we are challenged to think broadly and deeply, as were an earlier era's intellectuals confronting the Industrial and French revolutions. Globalization, democratization, and marketization and their emergent governance issues may or may not promote the level of intellectual creativity and synthesis that we find in, for example, a Marx or a Weber. But the intellectual and practical demands for such creativity and synthesis clearly are there. There are urgent problems to be solved around the world, and policy makers, academics, economic elites and subordinate groups, and citizens personally experience many of these. They personally experience the embedding of economic phenomena in complex cultural and institutional environments. They personally experience the shaping effect that economic transactions and institutions have on other arenas of social life. All this ought to intensify the demand for socio-economics.

Second, there is a complementary supply factor. Due in large part to increasingly poor job markets for many academics in the late seventies and early eighties, increasing numbers of people who previously might have been trained in only one discipline got serious training in two or more academic fields. As a result, we have many skilled persons with multiple doctorates or with doctorates coupled with such other professional degrees as medical degrees, law degrees, and business degrees. Knowing more than one discipline and the actors in it in-depth and from the inside makes a person a more credible spokesperson across fields. It provides us with a group of people who have facility in translating the language of one field to that of another. It also provides people who bring to core problems in one of their fields the insights and skills that they have gained through training in another of their fields. It provides more people who currently are constructing elements of inter- or multi-disciplinary syntheses.

Third, in part as a result of the supply and demand factors that I have mentioned, interdisciplinarity in the sciences, social sciences, and humanities is actually fashionable these days. It is the good kind of interdisciplinarity—the kind rooted in multiple, strong disciplinary understandings. As a critical adjunct, there is an increasing amount of research money—though of course never enough—earmarked to interdisciplinary efforts. We are reasonably rapidly creating and legitimating new fields like cognitive science, which combine the knowledge bases of multiple more established fields (see, e.g., Dennett, 1995).

Fourth, many of the fields that currently are contributing to socio-economics are also contributing to and benefiting from an intellectual movement dubbed new or neo-institutionalism. Today, varieties of institutionalism float around current economics, sociology, history, law, and political science (see, e.g., Cuff, 1973; Williamson, 1975, 1985; North, 1990; Powell and DiMaggio, 1991; Selznick, 1996; Thelan, Steinmo, and Longstreth, 1992; Streeck, 1995; Scharpf, 1997; Powell, 2000; Regini, 2000). Institutionalism provides a substantial intellectual resource for building socio-economics.

On the one hand, institutionalism provides a sensitizing framework congenial to cross-disciplinary conversation and research. On the other, institutionalism is quite encompassing and non-dogmatic in its ability to ground multiple specific theories of socio-economic phenomena. With institutionalist thought gaining popularity across the social sciences, we have at least some common orientation and language to help our research programs cross-fertilize and cumulate. And this can happen without pre-empting our intellectual diversity or pluralism. It also can happen without operating as a colonizing device, making one discipline—such as economics—paramount over all others.

Fifth, at least in some quarters we have managed to get beyond unproductive debates about quantitative versus qualitative. Within the quantitative world, scholars are increasingly building mathematical models, simulations, and statistical estimation procedures that can capture more of the complexity of empirical phenomena than we could even twenty years ago (see, e.g., Casti, 1994). Artificial neutral networks and related statistical models may hold particular promise, allowing researchers to model complex dynamic systems, such as those with continuous interactions between markets and other institutions (see, e.g., Carley, 1996; Cheng and Titterington, 1994).

Modelers purposely reduce the world's complexity to get to the guts of some social process. But now they can accommodate more realistic assumptions about how social processes work. And they can incorporate the knowledge generated by their qualitative counterparts that suggests all kinds of multi-level and dynamic complexity. To the small extent that barriers to moving beyond neo-classical economics or to integrating elements of neo-classicism with other theoretical strands were methodological, advances in modeling surely will help Meanwhile, electronic means for collecting and analyzing textual data help qualitative, interpretive scholars convince quantitative scholars that they can and do produce valid, reliable, and replicable knowledge (see, e.g., Stryker, 1996; Stryker, Scarpellino and Holtzman, 1999).

Sixth, we are starting to get beyond the micro-macro dichotomy to work toward explicitly multi-level theories to explain socio-economic phenomena. One research program that I find fascinating is that of my former colleague Edward Lawler, now at Cornell. Lawler and his collaborators are systematically theorizing and empirically examining how and what kinds of individual level exchanges create what kinds of solidarities and attachments at what level of organizational structure (e.g., Lawler, 1992; Lawler and Yoon, 1993). We then can consider the consequences of these emergent solidarities for how complex organizations work and how much social justice they are likely to provide.

Seventh, though again only in some quarters, we are starting to get beyond sterile confrontations about the merits of deductive versus inductive logics for explaining socio-economic phenomena to realize that there are various ways that the two logics productively combine in constructing theories and explanations (e.g., Stryker, 1996). All these represent real opportunities for the growth of inter- and multi-disciplinary dialogue.

Eighth, SASE itself is at an auspicious moment. We have benefited from the immense creativity and mobilizing capacities of our founder, Amitai Etzioni (Etzioni, 1988, 1996, 1998). We also have benefited from the years of hard work and commitment by many people and groups who have been active in SASE since its beginning. Those of us like me—who came later, but are no less committed—know that without those active at the beginning, there would be no SASE. At the same time, we now have recruited to SASE people who are especially good institutionalizers, and who are working hard to ensure that we have procedures that are coherent, efficient, and effective enough that SASE will endure. As we have known at least since Weber's (1978) writings, intellectual movements, like ours for socio-economics, must be institutionalized and socially and organizationally rooted to endure.

CONSTRAINTS

In short, we now have abundant opportunities for building socio-economics. Butwe also face clear constraints. Here, I shall mention only a few of these. Part of the point of training in any given discipline is that one becomes professionally socialized to a particular cognitive view of the world and how to gain knowledge about it. Normative and instrumental commitments to one's cognitive worldview, whatever it is, usually follow. They do so for many reasons that I, among others, have written about in a more scholarly fashion and that, indeed, most academics will recognize from their own professional lives (e.g., Chesler, Sanders, and Kalmuss, 1988; Eisner, 1991; S. Stryker 1980). We can deduce some corollaries from this. As well, many of us probably could induce some of the key corollaries from our experiences. Whether we arrive at these corollaries deductively or inductively, they include the following.

First, we all operate in atmospheres of partial knowledge punctuated with some black holes of ignorance. For example, I wrote a scholarly article in the 1980s about the politics of economics at the U.S. National Labor Relations Board (Stryker, 1989). At some point during the review process, I discovered that my editor did not realize that any kind of economics other than the neo-classical had been considered legitimate economics in the United States. My editor was an eminent sociologist, one who had worked in industrial relations and the sociology of work, and who had had some training in labor economics.

Second, cross-disciplinary dialogues can get bogged down in commitments to multiple, sometimes overlapping, but sometimes seemingly incommensurable foundational ideas. For example, Deirdre McCloskey, a noted economic historian (McCloskey, 1973, 1990, 1998) and I, a sociologist, are friends and colleagues. We both are trained in multiple disciplines. We share a commitment to understanding economic phenomena in their cultural and institutional contexts. Yet, even our discussions have floundered at times because we were talking a different language and right past each other. On one such occasion a few years ago, I was talking about the constraints or coerciveness engendered by markets. This is not atypical language for a sociologist. But Deirdre's response was that markets cannot possibly represent any kind of external constraint or coercion at all because markets are all about individual choice.

In short, it is difficult for people socialized and networked into different cognitive and normative communities to continue to remain open to each other, and to learning about and from each other, let alone to work together in sus-tained fashion to build something cumulative and synthetic. The factors that I have already mentioned get exacerbated by time constraints and by the strategic considerations of career building and legitimacy within fields. Fields that are organized with one hegemonic or clearly dominant paradigm—like neo-classicism in economics—are especially problematic because these fields create large, though clearly not insurmountable disincentives for people trying to move beyond the hegemonic paradigm.

TOWARD THE FUTURE

Still speaking institutionally, but moving to consider SASE itself, once we get inside such a composite, interdisciplinary organization, we are likely to find only a tenuous equilibrium. SASE is old enough as an organization to have developed its own lines of internal conflict and controversy. These internal conflicts overlap in part but not completely with disciplinary affiliations. Our internal conflicts are about cognitive understanding, but they also are about normative commitments and the instrumental exploitation of extant skills. Equally, they are about power and prestige. How our current internal conflicts are resolved is critical to the future of SASE as an organization and to the intellectual contours of socio-economics. Even this cursory rendition of opportunities and constraints suggests a number of conclusions for the future of socio-economics as an intellectual and pragmatic enterprise and for the future of SASE as a professional organization devoted to building socio-economics. In short, it suggests conclusions both intellectual and institutional.

First, we should expect socio-economics as an intellectual endeavor, and SASE as an organization to experience growing pains while institutionalizing. Interests, identities, values and commitments are at stake. We cannot expect to negotiate all this without a lot of ongoing discussion and some conflict.

Second, it matters what and how we institutionalize. What we say and do today provides a rough script for the future. Adopting the Madison Declaration or a similar broad foundational statement, as we have done, is very important.[1] But beyond a broad foundational statement, we should look for socio-economics to emerge from our practices and not from some a priori statement we make about what it is. Based on where we are now intellectually and institutionally, it seems to me that institutionalism currently provides the best cross-disciplinary framework for building socio-economics. Institutionalism is an emerging common language among a broad array of social scientists. My hunch is that it can provide a framework in which we can maintain what is helpful and useful from neoclassicism, while also viewing neoclassicism as an institutionally embedded normative discourse. Think, for example, of all the useful institutionalist work on the development of hierarchy and of internal labor markets (see, e.g., Osterman, 1984; Doeringer and Piore, 1971; Locke, Kochan, and Piore, 1995). At the same time, institutionalism should provide us with a major building block for the provision of a counter-discourse and explanatory framework to neoclassicism. Of course, not everyone will agree on all of this.

It follows that we should assume that for the foreseeable future, socio-economics will be a multi-paradigm and pluralistic field with somewhat shifting boundaries. We ought to try to organize its current form and practices so that they provide the maximal opportunity for our different theoretical, normative, and empirical strands to grow, to repeatedly confront each other, and to fashion opportunities where synthetic combinations are more, rather than less, likely. We ought to arrange discussions and subgroups that maximize us talking to and with each other. This in turn ought to give us lots of little steps that provide us with elements toward synthesis.

These considerations suggest that SASE as an organization is on the right track by organizing research networks around topics and problems, and not around disciplinary pockets or theoretical perspectives. But these considerations also suggest that we continue and put more effort into recruiting into SASE and maintaining the ongoing involvement of diverse types of economists. I do not think that we will be able to fold in, get beyond, and develop a counter-discourse to neo-classical economics in a way that is maximally useful unless we have the involvement of some key people who know the hegemonic discourse very well from the inside. Pragmatically, I do not think that it is possible in the current environment, at least in the United States, to have a maximally legitimated field called socio-economics without some highly respected economists. These should be persons who themselves have chosen to go beyond neo-classicism and who are interested in developing and testing economic ideas and models against real-world processes. We also should organize more of our panels so that we have panelists with multiple disciplinary backgrounds, orientations, and expertises addressing the same topic at the same time in the same place.

In short, it probably will not come as a shock that I view the future of socio-economics and of SASE through the very same conceptual lens that I developed in my scholarly work on the politics of alternative institutional logics for law enforcement and the politics of alternative institutional logics for government regulation (Stryker, 1994, 1996, 2000). I do not see the development of socio-economics in terms of a neat, linear progression toward an endpoint that we can set a priori today or any other day. I do see socio-economics being defined, and socio-economic knowledge cumulating more dialectically through diverse kinds of conflicts and controversies. We can expect a process of intellectual and organizational change in which socio-economics emerges as some kind of combination of what currently are multiple, sometimes overlapping, and sometimes competing logics for theoretical and empirical inquiry. I do not know exactly where we will get to, and I doubt that anyone can. This will probably be one of those path dependent processes in which, even if we faithfully captured all the relevant initial conditions, these alone would not determine the outcome. There will be contingencies en route that we cannot now predict but that socio-economics as a developing field and SASE as a developing organization devoted to building that field surely will confront. Still, I am confident that if SASE can recruit and retain enough smart, thoughtful, and committed persons from economics and from other social sciences and humanities—including sociology, political science, psychology, law, history, and anthropology, and if we can keep these persons together in an organization in which they talk to and with each other, we will get somewhere useful in the building of socio-economics.

NOTE

1 The Madison Declaration is available on the SASE website, www.sase.org.

5

On Socio-Economic Embeddedness

Karl H. Müller

This chapter[1] will provide a general conceptual and theoretical outline of the core-concept in socio-economics, namely of the notion of "embeddedness."[2] Fortunately, there exists a short, classical summary of the nature of embeddedness which will act as a guiding principle. In his article on "Economic Action and Social Structure: The Problem of Embeddedness," Mark Granovetter gives a highly illuminating picture of the embeddedness of economic actions within a wider social environment.

> the behavior and institutions to be analyzed are so constrained by ongoing social relations that to construe them as independent is a grievous misunderstanding. (Granovetter, 1985: 481)

Although this idea of embeddedness strikes everyone as intuitively sound, the concept needs to be carefully unpacked and desegregated. In particular, this chapter argues that important distinctions exist among different forms of embeddedness. Nevertheless, the short sentence from Mark Granovetter will become the "leitmotif" for the entire article.

BEHAVIORAL SCHEMES AND BUILDING BLOCKS

The starting point lies in the introduction of the notion of a "behavioral scheme" which covers the entire range of scientific ways of constructing behaviors, economic and otherwise. Following Mario Bunge, Fred Dretske, John H. Holland, Stuart Kauffman, Nicholas Rescher, Roger C. Schank, and others,[3] behavioral schemes can be viewed as any scientific arrangement which accounts for a given behavior by an actor or a system of actors.[4] Behavioral schemes comprise, in essence, four different groups, namely descriptions, explanations, models, and mechanisms which are able to generate a specific behavior. An economic action like the purchase of a commodity can be scientifically constructed by way of a narrative of the event under consideration, with the help of a nomic explanation for consumer choices, by using a model for consumer behavior or by specifying a mechanism for purchasing behaviors.

Moreover, behavioral schemes are assumed to consist of building blocks or components. Very generally speaking, any behavioral scheme can be separated into various components, sub-components, sub-sub-components, etc., which are here called building blocks. Thus, behavioral schemes and their constitutive building blocks are both linguistic entities, ordered by subset relations. Take as a paradigmatic example for a behavioral scheme a multivariate regression model for consumption of the general form

$$y = f(\beta X) + \varepsilon$$

Its basic building blocks consist of a dependent variable y, of a group of independent variables X where each of the independent variables x_1, x_2, . . . x_n, in turn, can be categorized as building block as well, of a set of parameters β, of a disturbance term ε, of an empirical data set, of basic statistical assumptions on the independent variables and on the disturbance term and of an estimation procedure like ordinary least squares, maximum likelihood, etc.[5]

Quite obviously, the notion of an economic building block in a behavioral scheme needs some further elaboration. Taking Gary Becker's *The Economic Approach to Human Action* (1990) as a reference point for an economic model of economic behavior, the four main economic building blocks of the neoclassical paradigm consist, in essence, of

- decision sets as primary concepts
- the assumption of stable preferences by actors
- a maximization rule, stating that actors, while subject to various constraints, are maximizing their utility[6]
- equilibrium as the outcome of the maximizing decision-behavior of actors

In the words of Gary Becker these four basic building blocks constitute the neoclassical behavioral scheme in its essence, though not in its entirety.[7]

The combined assumptions of maximizing behavior, market equilibrium, and stable preferences, used relentlessly and unflinchingly, form the heart of the economic approach as I see it. (Becker, 1990: 5)

Thus, features like maximizing behavior, equilibrium, or stable preferences can be classified, following Becker, as paradigmatic instances for economic building blocks, used in neoclassical models or mechanisms for economic action. In this chapter, economic building blocks will become directly associated with the structure and composition of the neoclassical paradigm itself. In other words, the neoclassical approach will be used as the crucial gatekeeper for economic building blocks and all non-statistical and non-formal components necessary for the neoclassical paradigm will be classified as economic building blocks.

Becker's arguments in his book on the economic approach to human action[8] suggest very strongly that these economic building blocks are both necessary and sufficient for constructing behavioral schemes of economic action. Not only that, behavioral schemes with economic building blocks alone are able, following Becker, to shed new light on many non-economic processes like marriage, fertility, and the family (ibid., 169ff.), or on social interactions (ibid., 251ff.).

Within the socio-economic tradition, the self-sufficiency of the neoclassical approach has been seriously questioned from its very beginnings.[9] The most important argument against this self-proclaimed monopoly has been under the heading of embeddedness. Following the Granovetter quotation above, socio-economics has emphasized again and again that "the behavior and institutions to be analyzed are so constrained by ongoing social relations that to construe them without them" constitutes a fatal shortcoming. In other words, economic behavior has to be studied and constructed with the help of behavioral schemes which are built up as an intertwined compound or as a complex mixture of economic and social elements or building blocks.[10] Since the notion of social relations in Granovetter's embeddedness principle covers a wide variety of different domains like social relations proper, emotions, spatial contexts of action, or institutions (rules, norms, laws, etc.), to name just a few, the term social relations will be replaced by the more general notion of non-economic building blocks. Socio-economics is the search for complex behavior schemes, integrating and combining economic as well as non-economic building blocks. Embeddedness refers to the fact that economic building blocks are subsets of a larger class of components within behavioral schemes and are, thus, embedded within this larger set. With the notions of behavioral schemes and building blocks it will become possible to define different forms of embeddedness in a more transparent manner. These two concepts will help to separate Mark Granovetter's guiding principle into three distinct types of embeddedness.[11]

These three forms of embeddedness will establish the basic structure of socio-economic behavioral schemes for economic action.[12]

But this chapter will establish an even stronger and more powerful conclusion on the status of economic building blocks of the neoclassical variety by showing that they are neither necessary nor sufficient[13] for the construction of socio-economic behavioral schemes of economic action. Rather, the economic approach to economic action should be considered as a useful, but highly special case within a much broader range both of special cases and complex socio-economic behavioral constructions.

"Quod erat demonstrandum."

HORIZONTAL EMBEDDEDNESS

Starting with a truism, actors or systems of actors across different levels exhibit an internal organization and are situated, in turn, within a larger environment in which they act. This truism has, however, important consequences for socio-economic behavior schemes since it will lead to two different groups of non-economic building blocks and, thus, to two forms of embeddedness as well. The first group refers to building blocks which reflect the internal side of actors or systems of actors whereas the second group of building blocks captures the contextual aspects of economic action.[14]

Internal Embeddedness

Following the different spatial actor types introduced in Hollingsworth's essay on multi-level analysis (chapter 2 herein), it is obvious that the internal constitution of actors means a variety of different arrangements, depending on the particular type of actor, whether a single individual, a regional firm, a national enterprise, a multinational agency, or a global NGO. Thus, the internal constitution of an individual comprises, inter alia, her or his cognitive and emotional organization and neuro-physiological architecture. The internal organization of a small local firm is dependent, among other things, on the number of employees and their division of labor, and the internal composition of a transnational enterprise refers to globally operating and highly diversified intra-organizational networks. Focusing on a local actor like a single individual, a socio-economic design for the internal actor side is given by Etzioni's notion of "divided selves"[15] where each actor is assumed to be "part pleasure driven and part morally committed." In turn, behavioral schemes of the Etzioni-variety must be constructed as a compound of economic building blocks like utility maximization and of non-economic building blocks like moral obligations.[16]

Aside from the role of moral obligations which figure so strongly in Etzioni's chapter, four other broad domains for potential non-economic building blocks, also mentioned in Etzioni's work, can be added which constrain, interfere, or interact with utility maximizing behavioral rules or other internal elements of the neoclassical approach.

- Social building blocks like the amount of personal trust[17] or many other forms of bonding relations beyond social obligations and norms
- Knowledge ("information") building blocks which include the actor-specific spectrum of everyday knowledge, cognitive routines for problem solutions, for learning, remembering, for knowledge retrieval, etc.
- Emotions, addictions, and visceral factors as building blocks, reflecting the neurobiological architecture of an individual in general—emotions like admiration, anger, depression, fear, joy, pride, sadness; addictions like alcohol, drugs, gambling, overeating, overspending; or visceral factors like hunger, thirst, sexual desire, pain, fatigue, vertigo, nausea, etc.
- "Past-dependency" as building blocks, i.e., past routines, experiences, learning processes, emotions, successes, failures, etc., of an actor and their impact on present practices.[18]

These four domains offer a rich source for identifying internal building blocks outside the economic arena of preferences or maximizing rules. In turn, the inclusion of non-economic building blocks leads, by necessity, to enriched behavioral schemes which are capable of embedding economic building blocks. To provide a concrete example, an enriched socio-economic behavioral model for a seemingly simple economic action like buying or selling something could include, aside from economic building blocks, varying degrees of subjective fears and anxieties, of perceived risks, of experiences with past product choices, of trust or of moral obligations to others, etc. In fact, in a number of instances non-economic building blocks may be the only ones that are needed.

Table 5.1 exhibits a variety of potentially embedding elements for various types of actors, going from local actors up to global players. Accordingly, actors across different spatial levels have a rich internal composition which should be reflected in the construction of behavioral schemes, socio-economic style. Thus, the internal side of actors requires the construction of socio-economic behavioral schemes which contain, in essence, two groups of building blocks, one from the economic side and a second one from a multiplicity of non-economic domains (social, knowledge, culture, history, etc.).

Table 5.1 reproduces the spirit as well as the substance of Etzioni's methodological *tour d'horizon* in chapter 3 of this volume and of Robin Stryker's view on recombinant socio-economic perspectives. Focusing on a single local actor, economic behavior can and should be constructed as a compound of economic maximization motives, social obligations and bonds, cognitive routines, emotional dispositions as well as past experiences. In essence, the four embedding modules of knowledge, emotions/culture, sociality, and the past in table 5.1 should exemplify Etzioni's complex, nonlinear interplay of behavior-relevant constraints, rules, goals, or learning strategies from economic as well as non-economic domains.

Table 5.1   Internal Forms of Embeddedness

Actor-Level	Economic Building Blocks	Embedding Building Blocks
Global (e.g., trans-national enterprise)	Profit Maximizing Goals, Preferences, et al.	Social Goals, Organizational Culture, Knowledge, Past, et al.
Multinational (e.g., multi-national firm)	Profit Maximizing Goals, Preferences, et al.	Social Goals, Organizational Culture, Knowledge, Past, et al.
National (e.g., national enterprise)	Profit Maximizing Goals, Preferences, et al.	Social Goals, Organizational Culture, Knowledge, Past, et al.
Regional (e.g., regional firm)	Profit Maximizing Goals, Preferences, et al.	Social Goals, Organizational Culture, Knowledge, Past, et al.
Local (e.g., individual)	Utility Maximizing Goals, Preferences, et al.	Social Bonds, Emotions, Knowledge, Past, et al.

External Embeddedness

So far, the analysis has concentrated on internal building blocks for behavioral schemes for different types of actors across various spatial levels. However, much of economic action involves special contexts or environments in which typical economic routines like selling, buying, exchanging, investing, saving, consuming, etc., take place Thus, the external side refers to specific characteristics of settings and to their essential roles in determining economic behavior. Using, the Becker-approach to human action as a reference point, one can see that this research program is essentially context-free since economic actions like household productions or consumption do not involve additional contextual building blocks. In general, the only contextual building block from neoclassical theory for economic action comes from the economic relations among actors, i.e., from inter-personal economic relations, from economic inter-firm relations, etc.

In sharp contrast, the socio-economic perspective emphasizes the point of situated action[19] and assumes that contextual characteristics become of essential relevance for the shaping of economic behavior. Focusing on a single individual as local actor[20] and taking a typically economic action like buying or shopping, then one can see a high diversity of socio-economic settings in which this type of economic action can be performed. Buying in supermarkets, in the street, in a small shop, from children, online, from a friend, within a household or from neighbors implies a rich variety of different contexts. More systematically, at least four contextual building blocks can be identified which, according to the general literature, exert a nontrivial role for economic actions and action-sequences.

- First, an important group of potentially relevant building blocks comes from the characteristics of concrete settings. Here, the emphasis turns to the architectural and to the interior design of settings or to specific conditions like noise, crowdedness, etc. Continuing the example with buying something in a supermarket, specific attributes of the supermarket setting like the arrangement of products, the sheer reachability and visibility of products, the placement of price tags, the ways of announcing special offers, etc., could become an important element in determining the choice of a specific product.
- Second, social relations within a concrete setting could enter as an important ingredient for determining a product choice, too. For example, an angry shopkeeper or friendly and responsive personnel within a setting may have a serious effect on the decision to buy something or on the available exit or voice strategies.
- Third, the socio-technical infrastructure, i.e., the constraints or enhancements set by the socio-technical environment, exerts a potentially significant influence on the course of economic actions and interactions as well. Calculations with pencil and paper, without them, with a desk-calculator or with a cash registrar and an optical scanner may lead to a diverse set of voice and exit-options up to the point of canceling an intended purchase. More generally, a consumer-friendly socio-technical environment may induce individuals to buy more or may be an essential reason to choose specific shops.
- Fourth, the wider socio-economic or natural environment is to be included in the list of essential socio-economic building blocks. Shops within an area perceived as unsafe or risky can be excluded from the list of avail-

able options or weather conditions may play an essential role in the course of the economic decision to buy a certain product.

In short, external building blocks can be specified for different types of actors.[21] Shifting to the composition of behavioral schemes, the construction of contextual building blocks will come, due to the largely context-free character of the neoclassical perspective, mainly from the spatial, social, civil, technological or other characteristics of action-settings. These four context domains offer a rich source for identifying external building blocks outside the neoclassical arena. In turn, the inclusion of external non-economic building blocks leads, by necessity, to enriched behavioral schemes which are capable of embedding the available external economic building blocks.

To sum up, the horizontal embeddedness for a single actor, in both its internal and its external version, suggests a construction of behavioral schemes (descriptions, explanations, models, mechanisms) where economic building blocks from the neoclassical approach are embedded in a wider and far more diversified set of internal as well as external building blocks of non-economic origins. Towards the end of this article, table 5.3 will offer some hints on current paradigms or behavioral schemes which reflect the requisite variety of internal as well as external building blocks and exemplify the horizontal embeddedness both of the economic mind and of the economic context.

VERTICAL EMBEDDEDNESS

Vertical embeddedness has always stood at the center of socio-economic analysis since it comprises the institutional domains and their impact on the behavior of economic actors or on the outputs and performances of economic systems. Due to the marginalization of institutions within the neoclassical approach,[22] vertical embeddedness implies that economic building blocks from the neoclassical paradigm become embedded in a wider set which is composed of institutional building blocks, i.e., of rules, norms, regulations, conventions, etc. Here, the notion of institutions follows very closely along the lines which have been specified by Hollingsworth in his first chapter on "Advancing Socio-economics" and in more detail in chapter 6 herein. Chapter 1 by Hollingsworth provides a rich survey of the relevant literature on neo-institutionalism socio-economic style. Chapter 6 introduces five different designs of institutional analysis within socio-economics, varying in their degree of stabilities and temporal horizons. Thus the following discussion on vertical embeddedness here will complement the institutional designs in chapter 6.

Figure 5.1 conveys the basic structure of vertical embeddedness in which behavioral schemes for actors or economic systems include an institutional environment which, following the analyses of Hollingsworth, are to be considered as very powerful constraints or facilitators for economic action or for the performance of economic systems. Figure 5.1 includes several additional features of vertical embeddedness.

Figure 5.1 The Vertical Embeddedness of Actors and of Systems of Actors

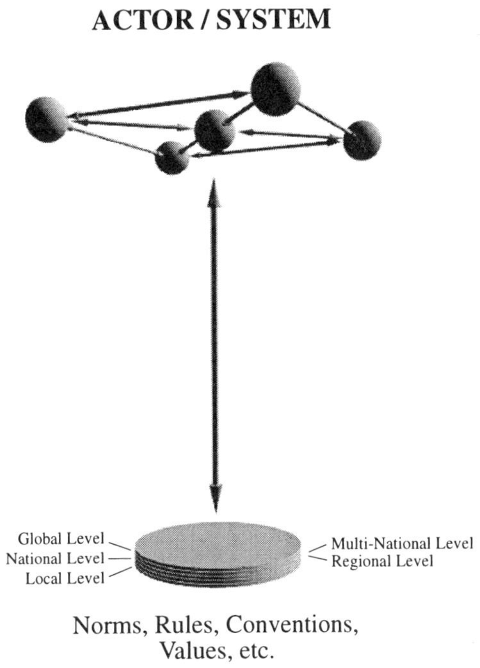

ACTOR / SYSTEM

Global Level
National Level
Local Level

Multi-National Level
Regional Level

Norms, Rules, Conventions,
Values, etc.

To start with, the institutional bases have been separated into different spatial levels. This point is worth mentioning since it reminds one of the fact that rules, norms, or conventions can be distributed across different spatial levels, starting from strictly local rules within local contexts (like the rules within a single school, the rules within a local organization, for a local building, etc.) and going all the way to global rules and regulations like the Declaration of Human Rights and trade regulations within the WTO. Moreover, these rules, norms, laws, regulations, etc., may be of economic nature, specifically designed for economic interactions (like the institutional requirements for setting up new firms, for labor contracts, for business loans, etc.), of a specific non-economic domain like science and technology (e.g., the rules and requirements for creating a new research institute, for starting a postgraduate teaching program, safety regulations in high-tech laboratories, etc.) or of a more general and societal character (like constitutional laws, criminal laws, etc.).

With respect to the basic relations between the institutional bases and the actor/systems side, it must be emphasized that direct relations like "one rule ⇒ one behavior" or "one behavior ⇒ one rule" are very special cases. In most instances, no clearly recognizable 1:1 relations between the institutional bases and the behavior levels can be observed. Rather, institutions play an important co-determining role and do not replace horizontal building blocks but complement them.

Another general point worth mentioning lies in the circular feedback structure between institutional bases and the behavior of actors or systems of actors. Thus, the arrows in figure 5.1, pointing simultaneously upwards and downwards, symbolize the circularity of this relationships. A circular feedback organization exhibits several characteristics.

- First, both domains, i.e., the institutional bases and actors or systems of actors are undergoing mutual adaptations and changes. Institutional changes may effect the behavior of actors and lead to the emergence of new types of behaviors which, in turn, induce institutional changes, which, then, generate new behavioral responses, and so on and so on. Circularly connected domains are, following Douglas E. Hofstadter (1982, 1985) or Heinz von Foerster (1982, 1985), entangled and intertwined in a mode of mutual self-generation.

- Second, a complex circular feedback organization like the one between institutional bases and actors or systems of actors does not lead towards a global optimum (Holland, 1995, 1998). In other words, configurations of this type are permanently under way without reaching a final destination or an ultimate goal domain.

- Third, due to the circular feedback pattern, causal relationships of the classical single-cause variety become difficult to establish since the institutional domains are the result of permanent adaptations from the actor or systems of actor side and vice versa.

As a final general comment, the strength of the arrow in figure 5.1, connecting the institutional domains with the actors/systems side, remains a matter of empirical research. All that can be said at this point is that in the circular feedback processes between institutions and actor/systems behavior the entire range of different patterns can be observed.

- Starting with the bottom up-arrow (institutional base ⇒ actor/system) the spectrum goes from total institutional ineffectiveness (zero strength) to total effectiveness (hundred percent strength). Norms, rules, conventions, regulations, or laws, though formally, may exert zero strength. On the other hand, institutional arrangements may be accompanied with a specific behavior, indicating a maximum degree of strength. In the first case of total irrelevance, no institutional building blocks are to be included in the construction of socio-economic behavioral schemes; in the second instance of a total institutional impact, no other institutional building blocks are required to account for a specific economic action. In between these two extremes, all other instances of institutional effectiveness are situated, ranging from marginal to almost total effectiveness.

- Similarly, the top-down arrow can exhibit the entire range of possible degrees of strength. The most obvious instance for a zero degree top-down strength lies in all those instances where an economic action or a systemic behavior has no tangible consequences or effects on the institutional bases. In fact, most actions, economic or otherwise, fall under this category since they do not bring about any changes in the institutional realm of codified norms, rules, conventions and the like. Similarly, the most important process of high or exclusive top-down strength lies in the codification of new norms, conventions, regulations, etc. Writing down the rules for a new game for example comes as close to the other extreme as possible since this process is almost exclusively dependent on the actor side only, and it has clearly recognizable effects and consequences for the enlargement of the institutional basis.

In essence, the circular relations between the institutional bases and the side of actors/systems cover all possible forms of mutual relations as well as mutual strength. A priori, the linkages between both domains remain under a veil of indeterminacy. The slow and gradual lifting of this veil of indeterminacy belongs to one of the most challenging tasks for research socio-economic style.

Thus, the general format for socio-economic behavioral schemes, incorporating aspects of vertical embeddedness, lies, in a proper integration and combination of economic building blocks with additional components from the institutional domains.[23] Any explanation, model, or mechanism for economic behavior, composed of economic and institutional building blocks, leads, by necessity, to a vertical embeddedness since economic building blocks are subsets of a wider class of building blocks.

COMPLEX EMBEDDEDNESS

Both forms of embeddedness open up the way for the third and final group of embeddedness which consists in behavioral schemes with a proper recombination or integration of institutional, internal and external non-economic building blocks with economic components. The reference case for behavioral schemes socio-economic style should be the one where economic building blocks are embedded into a rich and diversified set which includes both institutional building blocks and internal as well as external components of non-economic nature. Table 5.2 and figure 5.2 exhibit this complex interplay of socio-economic embeddedness formations where economic building blocks become horizontally embedded (embeddedness of economic building blocks in a wider class of non-economic components) as well as vertically embedded (embeddedness of economic building blocks in a multi-level institutional base). Table 5.2 and figure 5.2 summarize the essential requirements for the construction of complex behavioral schemes socio-economic style where, aside from neoclassical components, three groups of additional building blocks are needed, namely internal, external as well as institutional building from essentially non-economic domains. From a socio-economic point of view, the inclusion of non-economic building blocks from these three arenas—the internal side of actors, the contexts of action, and the institutional bases—becomes the reference case in order to account for economic behavior. Thus, economic building blocks are, by necessity, not sufficient for the construction of socio-economic behavior schemes. Rather, they are to be embedded both horizontally and vertically in a richer and more diversified set of non-economic elements. At this stage, the first part of the central thesis in this chapter—the insufficiency of economic building blocks—has been firmly established.

The final part of this essay will be devoted to several important theoretical consequences which are based on the general composition and structure of socio-economic behavioral schemes, as expressed in figure 5.2 and in table 5.2. Moreover, in the course of the subsequent discussion, the second part of the central thesis—the unnecessary status of economic building blocks—will be justified as well.

MAIN CHARACTERISTICS OF SOCIO-ECONOMIC BEHAVIORAL SCHEMES

The extended explorations into socio-economic embeddedness so far can be compressed into six theoretical principles which will conclude this chapter. These six principles should help to boost and to empower the cognitive status of socio-economic behavioral schemes against the dominant neoclassical approach.

First, the general structure of socio-economic behavioral scheme, expressed in table 5.2 and in figure 5.2, has not been designed as an exercise in wishful thinking. Rather, one finds a large set of current best practices in the construction of complex socio-economic schemes which reflect the multiplicity of necessary domains and building blocks. The following group of paradigmatic examples helps to clarify this important point. Moreover, in all these paradigmatic examples, economic building blocks are either embedded in a much more complex class of building blocks or they are entirely absent and have been successfully substituted.

- For behavioral descriptions socio-economic style, a paradigmatic perspective is seen in Jane Lave's study (1988) on the role of elementary arithmetic calculations while shopping in supermarkets. Based on a rich theoretical background in cognitive theory, anthropology, and ethnography, Lave stresses in her descriptive accounts of shopping behavior, the external embeddedness of this type of economic action. Even in the case of the economic core routine of buying and the seemingly trivial and instrumental use of elementary arithmetic calculations, the observed practices exhibit basically an "in situ logic" which emerges as a combination between characteristics of supermarket settings like the placement and advertisement of products and of highly special cognitive routines by buyers like simplifying the available options, a satisficing rank-ordering of products, etc. Moreover, the role of arithmetic calculations appears to be more of an ex post interpreter or justifier of specific product selections and not as an efficient ex ante instrument for decision making itself.
- With respect to traditional explanations, a characteristic framework within the socio-economic variety comes from so-called situation theory which is mainly focused on individuals and which is to be characterized as a predominantly qualitative approach to economic behavior with a small number of nomic statements.[24] Within this program, economic practices become conceptualized as a structured interplay between building blocks from all three embeddedness domains. Thus, observable behavior is linked within the situation theory framework to building blocks from the knowledge bases, to the contexts or situations, and, finally, to mental states and internal representations by situated actors. While situation theory offers only a few law-like generalizations, it has, due to its firm roots in linguistics or computer science, a high potential for reaching such generalizations in the near future.

Another typical socio-economic approach, this time a program mainly for organizations and not for individuals as actors, lies in the DiMaggio and Powell framework[25] for imitative and innovative organizational behavior, including the investment and innovation behavior of firms. Towards the end of their article on "The Iron Cage Revisited," they formulate six assumptions on organizational changes, stressing factors like organizational dependence, degree of centralization, uncertainty, ambiguity of goals, reliance on academic credentials or the managerial participation in trade and professional associations, and their strong impact on producing similarities between organizations. These six non-economic building blocks, arranged in a series of correlative assumptions, offer a highly interesting socio-economic explanation-set traditional style, applicable to the world of economic action and nevertheless far from the equilibrium/utility/preference elements of neoclassical theory.

Table 5.2 Horizontal/Vertical Actor/Systems-Embeddedness and Complex Socio-Economic Behavioral Schemes[26]

		Complex Behavioral Schemes
Economic Behavior of Actors		Economic Building Blocks (Internal), Non-Economic Building Blocks (Internal)
	Horizontal	
		Economic Building Blocks (External), Non-Economic Building Blocks (External)
	Vertical	Institutional Building Blocks (Economic, Non-Economic)

Figure 5.2 Complex Socio-Economic Behavioral Schemes

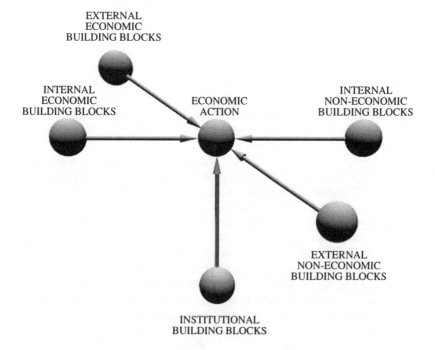

- For quantitative and formal modeling within the socio-economic variety one may invoke approaches like ecological psychology,[27] prospect-theory, or from the groups of complex modeling-frameworks, master-equations.[28] In the case of prospect theory in its current structure for example, the set of alternative building blocks like nonlinear decision weights, reference-dependence, and loss aversion (Kahnemann and Tversky, 2000: xiii), framing effects and mental accounting or an emphasis of experienced utility (Kahnemann and Tversky, 2000: 673) is utilized in addition to the traditional economic components of decision sets, preferences, or maximization rules. Here, the first two components are to be qualified as variations to the neoclassical core whereas the third element of framing effects and mental accounting as well as the fourth factor of experienced utility clearly fall outside the neoclassical realm and belong to the fields of cognitive organization (framing effects, mental accounting) and past-dependencies (experienced utility) respectively.

- Finally, genetic algorithms are a highly illuminating instance for behavioral simulations, too. In genetic algorithms, one can study in a stepwise fashion the gradual specialization of an initially unspecialized set of general rules.[29] Moreover, the basic architecture of genetic algorithms with a special emphasis on attributes like a high context-sensitivity, gracefulness, local maxima, past strength, randomness, recombinations via a crossover mechanism, and the like runs counter to the basic structures of neoclassical theory. In fact, utility maximization and stable preferences, especially if "used relentlessly and unflinchingly" (Becker), are totally inconsistent with constantly changing rules (via crossing-over) and random selections from a group of viable action-sequences. Although no genetic algorithms have been specified, so far, for economic actions like buying or shopping, it can be safely assumed that the evolution of such an actor-specific rule system from few unspecialized general rules to a multiplicity of specific rules will cover both the internal, the external and the vertical aspects of embeddedness in an elegant fashion.[30]

Table 5.3 summarizes different behavioral schemes socio-economic style which, taken together, constitute the current best practice platform for constructing the economic behavior of actors or actor systems. Thus, complex socio-economic behavioral schemes are not a research agenda for the future but have already been developed within the social sciences, very broadly conceived, the cognitive sciences or within hybrid arenas like cognitive anthropology, cognitive psychology, evolutionary theorizing on learning and adaptations, etc.[31] The set of best practices in socio-economic behavioral construction, summarized in table 5.3, reproduces different aspects of the horizontal and vertical embeddedness formations as they have been introduced in the present article. Moreover, the common platform of table 5.3 should become the center stage for actors, systems, roles, and plays after the successful decentralization and deconstruction of the once dominant neoclassical paradigm.

Second, the list of paradigmatic examples as well as table 5.3 make it clear that the entire argument on the multiple forms of embeddedness does not adhere to an explicit or tacit principle of "linking everything with everything" and is not a variant of a "the more, the merrier approach" to economic action. Complex behavioral schemes socio-economic style require the selection of sufficiently diversified building blocks, reflecting both the horizontal as well as the vertical embeddedness of building blocks from the neoclassical paradigm. The notion of a socio-economic mix or a heterogeneous socio-economic compound may be of special relevance here since it reminds one of the necessity to integrate a diverse and even inconsistent group of building blocks into a single and coherent approach. Additionally, socio-economic behavioral schemes should provide the requisite variety and diversity which are necessary for the handling and integration of different groups of building blocks. Due to this heterogeneity, socio-economic behavioral schemes, in order to be successful, will have to exhibit a high degree of complexity.

Third, the multiplicity of complex behavioral schemes within the socio-economic framework should open up the way for a more subtle understanding of general behavioral mechanisms or of laws of behavior both for actors and for systems of actors. These general patterns and laws of behavior should come about in a second-order analysis or in a mode of meta-analysis. Second order or, alternatively, meta-analysis means, on the one hand, the availability of a large number of first-level approaches and applications, and on the other hand, an in-depth second-order or a meta-level investigation of first-level studies. In a typical second-order investigation, general patterns which are to be found in a large number of first-level studies and investigations are identified. Despite the small number of paradigmatic examples given throughout this chapter, a typical second-order pattern could result in a catchphrase like "the power of contexts" or, alternatively, "the power of the local" since many of the examples as well as most of the approaches in table 5.3 point to the overriding importance of contextual factors and their essential role in determining the course of economic actions and interactions. Moreover, the search for second-order patterns follows closely and directly some recent suggestions on the proliferation of socially robust knowledge. (On this point, see especially Nowotny, Scott, and Gibbons, 2001.)

Fourth, the introduction of diversified and rich behavioral schemes socio-economic style is not to be confused with an attempt to bring control and prediction back to behavioral analysis. On the contrary, the complex nature of socio-economic behavioral schemes as well as the search for second-order patterns may well lead to fundamental insights on insurmountable and necessary barriers with respect to the accessible human potential for predictions and controls. In the end, second-order analysis may have the paradoxical effect that we gradually learn to see that we cannot see.

Table 5.3 Paradigmatic Examples for Socio-Economic Behavioral Schemes with Embedding Horizontal and Vertical Building Blocks

Type of Scheme	Essential Requirement	Paradigmatic Examples
Descriptions	In-Depth Descriptions of Socio-Economic Settings	Ethnomethodology, Social Anthropology, et al.[32]
Explanations	Nomic Hypotheses on the Socio-Economic Mix	"Bounded Rationality," Post-Weberian Action Types (Normative, Emotional, Addictive, etc.),[33] "Situation Theory," Capital Spaces and Habitus Formation,[34] "Structuration Theory,"[35] et al.[36]
Models	Socio-Economic Behavior Functions (preferably non-linear)	Master-Equations, Cognitive Modeling, "Prospect Theory," et al.[37]
Mechanisms	Socio-Economic Design of Mechanisms	Multiple Agent-Systems, Cognitive Simulations, Artificial Life, Genetic Algorithms, Classifier Systems, et al.[38]

Fifth, socio-economic behavioral schemes aim at a complete inversion with respect to general and special cases in behavioral accounts. Too often, socio-economics has appeared under the heading of special constraints, of deviations, of exceptions, or of limitations with respect to the more general case of rational action. In other words, the building blocks for constructing "homo oeconomicus" were assumed to define the general or the reference case whereas the embedding social part was confined to the role of exceptions or distortions from the general case only. In view of the dual horizontal as well as vertical embeddedness formations for actors or actor systems across various levels, a complete "Copernican inversion" can and must be undertaken. Complex socio-economic behavioral schemes should be viewed as the general or as the reference case in which economic building blocks become embedded both horizontally and vertically in a rich socio-economic factor set. Following this logic of inversion, the neoclassical approach should be seen as a highly special and ideal case, neglecting almost all other relevant embeddedness domains in table 5.2 or in figure 5.2 and setting them practically at zero values. In other words, the neoclassical approach has to be qualified as a special case since it uses its homespun building blocks relentlessly and unflinchingly and excludes the internal, external, as well as the institutional domains. As a special-case investigation, such an approach is legitimate and methodologically sound. But it has to be clearly recognized and classified as a special case within a far more general and considerably more complex socio-economic framework.

An analogy may be drawn from the history of science where fundamental paradigm changes have been brought about by exchanging or inverting special and general cases. In the instance of the replacement of Aristotelian physics with the new physics of Kepler, Galileo, and above all, Isaac Newton, the central terms of rest and motion underwent such an inversion. Motion was assumed as a special case within Aristotelian physics but became the reference state within Newtonian physics. Likewise, the revolution of non-linear dynamics in the last decades of the twentieth century has seen such an inversion with respect to static and dynamic configurations. Similarly, the distortions, exceptions, and deviations from the neoclassical path are to be inverted to become the general or normal reference state. Following this line of inversion, the economic approach to economic behavior should be viewed as a special case with specific utilization contexts and niches.[39]

Sixth, table 5.2 and figure 5.2 allow one to distinguish between several special or ideal cases which come into play whenever the emphasis is shifted to a particularly relevant aspect within the overall socio-economic behavioral reference scheme. Following the general logic of special cases, they can be constructed by safely neglecting several components of the socio-economic behavioral schemes and by focusing on a clearly defined subset only. For individuals as actors, special cases include, inter alia, a primary focus on emotions only, on obligations, norms, or rules exclusively, on past habits and routines alone, etc. Here, the effects and consequences can be studied by assuming social universes, composed of emotional or past-dependent actors only. By ways of special cases, the well-known hierarchical scheme of action types, as put forward by Max Weber,[40] can be reestablished as variants of different special cases within the reference frame of complex and diversified socio-economic behavioral schemes. More concretely, the ordering of different groups of reasons for different action types has been constructed by Weber along different stages of rationality, starting with traditional action and emotional or affective action with no rational calculation and blind habits or wild desires at the bottom line and going up to the middle stage of value-based action, Weber's "wertrationale Handlung," where a special value, target, or goal is to be followed under all circumstances and independent of contexts or costs and, finally, to the top stage of rationality where rational action and in-depth means-end calculations prevail.[41] Interestingly, the hierarchical ordering of action types as well as the Weberian strict independence of these groups of reasons can be transformed into a non-hierarchical sequence of special cases with the following characteristic features.

- Special case of traditional action, i.e., the sole concentration on relevant building blocks from the history of actors and their past- and path-dependencies, neglecting all other components of the socio-economic behavioral reference frame, especially the economic building blocks
- Special case of emotional action, putting emotional building blocks into the center of behavioral schemes and marginalizing all other potentially relevant elements
- Special case of value-based action, i.e., the obligation to specific norms, rules, and targets irrespective of contextual constraints and variations
- Special case of rational action, i.e., an exclusive focus on economic building blocks alone and setting the entire range of other embedding components to zero

Following this logic of special cases, the neoclassical approach becomes a variant of the special case of rational action. At the same time, the inclusion of the neoclassical paradigm as one among several special instances, helps to refute the second part of the initial thesis on the necessity of economic building blocks within socio-economic behavioral schemes. Due to the special case-configuration, economic building blocks are, by necessity, not necessary for the construction of socio-economic behavioral schemes since many special cases can be constructed which, following the requirements of special-case analysis, do not need the inclusion of economic components. Special cases of socio-economic behavioral schemes for economic action can be constructed which are entirely focused and concentrated, for example, on emotional building blocks and, thus, on a society of emotional actors, on past-dependent components and, consequently, on a society of path- and past-dependent actors, on normative elements and, thus, on a society of normative actors and the like. In all these different special instances, economic building blocks are to be excluded in order to comply with the rules and requirements of special-case analyses. And this leads, once again, to the immediate conclusion that economic building blocks are not necessary for the construction of economic behavior either.

To sum up, due to the complex forms of embeddedness, economic building blocks cannot become sufficient for the construction of socio-economic behavioral schemes. And due to the potential for creating a large number of special cases within socio-economic behavioral schemes beyond the special case of rational action, economic building blocks cannot be qualified as necessary either.

"Quod erat demonstrandum."

In this perspective, the time has finally come for actors and systems of actors to assume their general post-Cartesian roles within a general post-Cartesian theater on a general post-Cartesian stage in front of a general post-Cartesian audience. The ongoing plays on the classical Cartesian theater should be recognized as special variants only, which prove their usefulness in restricted and comparatively small domains. With this conclusion as well as with the short list of theoretical principles, an important bridge has been constructed which should lead directly from the multi-level architectures (Hollingsworth's chapter 2) to the domains of institutional analyses (part 2) and to the social systems of production (part 3). And this bridge which for obvious reasons may be called the "bridge of multiple paths of embeddedness" has to be crossed by practically anyone in order to gain new and deeper insights on the economic behavior of actors or on the performance of economic systems.

NOTES

1 The present chapter is the end product of a very profound and complex transformation process. Originally, it was drafted under the heading of "Visual Socio-economics" and contained a large number of tables and diagrams. Due to the criticisms by J. Rogers Hollingsworth and under his "nurturing leadership," the chapter shifted more and more into a systematic foundation of the concept of socio-economic embeddedness. Thanks go also to Jerry Hage and to an anonymous referee who were confronted with earlier versions of the chapter.

2 Socio-economics can be characterized as the science of embeddedness, namely of the embeddedness of economic elements in social ones.

3 See, for example, Bunge (1999), Dretske (1988), Holland (1995, 1998), Kauffman (2000), Rescher (1994, 1998), Schank and Abelson (1977), or Schank, et al. (1994).

4 The notions of actors and actor systems used throughout this chapter are to be understood in the same ways in which they have been introduced by J. Rogers Hollingsworth in his first two chapters in this book. Thus, actors can be distributed across different spatial levels, and actor systems are present at different spatial levels as well. A careful distinction should be observed between levels of actors or actor systems on the one hand and levels of analysis on the other hand. An investigation at a specific level can be undertaken which includes actors or actor systems at different levels.

5 Quite obviously, a multi-variate regression model can be separated in many different ways and the partitioning offered in the text is only one of the most obvious ones. But the basic argument rests on the mere separability of behavioral schemes into several building blocks.

6 Other variants of a single goal to be maximized include profits in the case of firms, votes in the case of political parties, and the like.

7 The neoclassical behavioral scheme knows many additional building blocks like prices, quantities of goods, demand-curves, supply-curves, etc. Compared with the four building blocks, these additional components are of secondary importance. One could leave these additional building blocks out and would still be able to produce a genuine behavioral scheme of the neoclassical variety. Nevertheless, prices, demand-functions,

supply functions and the like, since they form part and parcel of the neoclassical paradigm, qualify as economic building blocks.

8 See for example Becker (1975, 1981).

9 See, above all, Amitai Etzioni's early synthesis in Etzioni (1988) and Etzioni (1993) or Etzioni (1998a, 1998b).

10 See Etzioni's chapter in this book "Towards a Socio-Economic Paradigm" where the complex interplay between economic goals and social norms or moral obligations occupies a central position.

11 The focus of the entire chapter lies on economic action, rather narrowly conceived. Thus, economic action should be restricted to routines which fulfill the Weber condition of scarce resources, a limited number of possible actions and need satisfaction and the Luhmann focus on money as medium of exchange simultaneously. Consequently, actions like buying, selling, investing, or saving belong to the core of economic action in which both restrictions are clearly met.

12 The focus of the subsequent examples will be within the core-domains of economic action only, processes like buying, investing, selling, trading, exchanging, etc. If the overall structure of the embeddedness of economic components within a wider circle of non-economic elements can be maintained and justified within the core domains of economic action, it follows by necessity that this embeddedness structure can be upheld in less economically structured arenas as well like the decision to marry, to have a child, to retire, to vote, etc.

13 The discussion on the status of economic building blocks has been whether they are necessary and sufficient for the explanation of economic action. Almost nobody has contested their necessary status, however. Thus, the claim within the present article must be considered as unusually radical.

14 One can identify entire research programs which are exclusively concentrated on one particular side of the embeddedness structure. For example, on the side of contextual embeddedness, one finds the behavioristic paradigm which has practically marginalized and eliminated the internal organization and architecture of actors.

15 See Etzioni's chapter 3 in this book.

16 Other complex behavioral schemes run under the headings of "multiple selves" or of the "alchemy of the mind" (Jon Elster, 1999) or of a "society of mind" (Marvin Minsky, 1990), to name just a few. In these, a design for behavioral schemes has been specified where economic building blocks become embedded in a wider and broader class of non-economic components.

17 On trust as significant component of economic action and interaction, see Fukuyama (1991, 2000) or Putnam (2000).

18 On the "path-dependency" of "past dependencies," see, e.g., the learning algorithms in Holland (1989, 1995, 1999).

19 Situated action has become a highly important issue within contemporary cognitive sciences. For an interesting survey, see, e.g., Sternberg and Wagner (1994) or Sternberg (1999).

20 Of course, the considerations on contexts for economic actions are not restricted to the level of individuals or households only. The behavior of a regional, national, multinational, or global actor, too, can be described as contextual or situated. For a large transnational enterprise as global player, its behavior or action sequences occur on local,

regional, national, multi-national, and global levels where contextual factors play a significant role at each of these levels.

21 For example, the context of a global actor like a large transnational enterprise consists of a multiplicity of local, regional, national, multi-national, and global contexts. At any single point in time, a trans-national enterprise acts across the different levels simultaneously. It may have a business meeting with other global players, a lobbying effort with representatives of a multi-national agency, a conference with national state officials, the negotiation of a contract with a regional supplier, and a discussion on environmental hazards within a local community. Nevertheless, each of these different contexts can be characterized by an internal design, by social characteristics, by the socio-technical infrastructure, or by a wider socio-economic environment.

22 To be more precise, institutions have been included in the neoclassical paradigm under the heading of new institutionalism. Following largely Rutherford (1994), the new institutionalism has tried, however, to give institutions a derivative character only, emerging as a by-product of the neoclassical core. (See also Schotter, 1981.)

23 Rules, norms, regulation, laws, etc., can be analyzed with respect to their changes over time. Here, the main focus lies, to borrow a term from Tom R. Burns, on the "rule systems" themselves and on their evolution in time. Moreover, economic actors or systems of actors can be studied with respect to the role and function, rules, norms, laws, regulations, etc., at play in "shaping" the behaviors at the actor or at the systems levels. Finally, an important perspective for institutional analysis lies in those types of investigations which stress the "encoding processes" of rules, norms, laws, etc. Put differently, this perspective analyzes the processes of the construction of norms, laws, regulations, rules, etc., and is, thus, predominantly policy-oriented. Each one of the three examples above exhibits one particular type of vertical embeddedness in general and of institutional analysis in particular. Thus, formally the three main groups of analyses on vertical embeddedness can be summarized as investigations on the changes in the institutional bases themselves, "bottom-up" changes between institutional bases and actors/actor systems and "top-down" changes between actors/actor systems and the institutional bases.

24 On situation theory, see mainly Barwise (1983, 1989) and Devlin (1993) or (1999).

25 On this framework, see especially DiMaggio and Powell (1983).

26 This specific structure of socio-economic behavioral schemes can be transferred from the sphere of economic actors to the domains of economic systems as well.

27 As a highly interesting summary and overview, see, e.g., Fox (1985).

28 On the formal background of master-equations, see especially Weidlich and Haag (1988).

29 On genetic algorithms, see John Holland, et al. (1989) and Goldberg (1988) or Rawlins (1991).

30 For an early application of genetic algorithms in the field of pipeline regulation, see Goldberg (1988).

31 As potentially relevant literature, see, e.g., Cleermans (1993), Holland, et al. (1989) or (1995), Kaelbling (1993), Marchetti (1981), or Petsche (1995).

32 For descriptive accounts which cover the rich spectrum of potentially relevant non-economic building blocks, see, for the social domains, Lesser (2000); for cognitive

areas, Norretranders (1998); for institutions, Hollingsworth and Boyer (1997) or Smelser and Swedberg (1994); for contexts, van Maanen (1988).

33 On the classical action types, see Weber (1982). For stimulating re-formulations and adaptations, see Elster (1999), (2001a), or (2000b).

34 Here, the locus classicus is Bourdieu (1982), (1985), or (1991).

35 On structuration theory, see Giddens (1984), (1989), or (1991).

36 On rich behavioral-explanation sketches of the non-economic variety from different disciplinary perspectives, see, e.g., Deacon (1997), Geertz (1983, 2000), or Hauser (1997).

37 On master-equations, see Haken (1981), Weidlich and Haag (1983, 1989), Haag (1989), or Müller and Haag (1994); on prospect theory see the impressive collection in Kahnemann and Tversky (2000); on other modeling approaches of the cognitive variety, see, among others, Engstrom and Middleton (1998), Haken (1991), Hofstadter (1982, 1985, 1995, 1997), or Newell (1990).

38 On multiple agents, see, aside from Gilbert and Troitzsch (1999), also Gilbert and Conte (1995) or Woolridge, et al. (1996).

39 For a more elaborate account on these special domains, see Müller (1996) using an interesting reference frame of different epistemic cultures in the scientific arena, developed by Karin Knorr-Cetina (1999).

40 On this point, see Weber (1982).

41 In sharp contrast to the Weberian distinctions, the socio-economic behavioral scheme assumes that human action in its reference form is to be conceptualized as a mixture or a compound of all four domains of the Weberian rationality-sequence and not as strictly dominated by one of these four groups respectively.

Part II

On Institutions

J. Rogers Hollingsworth, Karl H. Müller

Many of the essays in this volume assume that institutions are rules, norms, habits, conventions, and values, and that these are among the major determinants of the social world. These assumptions are explicitly articulated in the following chapters by J. Rogers Hollingsworth and by Tom Burns and Marcus Carson. In these two essays, they develop a theory about rules systems. For them, social rule systems are collectively shared, and they structure and regulate most forms of social behavior. Geoffrey Hodgson, not only in the essay which follows, but in much of his other work, has demonstrated that rules and norms tend to structure social interaction by specifying who may participate in relationships, how participants should conduct themselves, and what the goals of participants are. In short, they influence who does what, when, where, and how. As a result, rule systems permit patterns of social action and interactions among actors to be predictable. Without consensus on rules and norms, there would be difficulty in establishing order, stability, and continuity in social life.

Rules and norms are learned in many ways, but many are part of social traditions to which individuals are socialized as children. As a result, most rules and norms are never questioned. It is through such a pattern of learning that one acquires an understanding of one's rights, responsibilities, and obligations. And it is through rules, norms, habits, and conventions that one learns how to participate in specific situations, to understand which behaviors are frowned upon by society, and to be aware of which kinds of behavior are rewarded.

Modern societies are highly differentiated into a variety of important sub-systems, each with its own rules and norms. These subsystems include the business system, the system of education and science, the financial system, and the industrial relations system. The various institutional arrangements (e.g., markets, associations, networks) of a society also have their logics and rules for the coordination of various actors. Despite the differentiated nature of modern societies, there are meta-rules which are collectively shared throughout the society. It is the collective sharing of meta-rules which permits linkage of the various sub-systems together. But in the final analysis, the degree of coherence among the various sub-systems in each society must be determined empirically. The different sub-systems may be either loosely or tightly coupled. Through meta-rules and higher order meta-systems, societies attempt to deal with their societal contradictions and to bring about some degree of integration in the entire social system.

Rules and norms are intricately related with a society's institutional arrangements (i.e., markets, the state, associations, network) for coordinating relationships among social actors. Thus, if the rules and norms of a society are such that people have a very low degree of trust beyond the family and if they will cooperate only under a set of highly formal rules and regulations, then the state must become highly involved in establishing regulations for the governance of the society. "Widespread distrust in a society . . . imposes a kind of tax on all forms of economic activity, a tax that high-trust societies do not have to pay" (Fukuyama, 1995: 27–28). Without an understanding of a society's rules and norms, it will be very difficult to comprehend each of its institutional arrangements. While Burns and Carson have a very rich theoretical statement about role systems in the essay which follows, the next task that we should confront is to comprehend the relationship between the society's rules and norms and each of the institutional arrangements of a society.

All contemporary capitalist societies consist of a variety of social actors who continually engage in diverse interactions with each other. As Claus Offe suggests in chapter 10, relationships among actors are coordinated by different institutional arrangements (e.g., markets, states, networks, associations). The institutional arrangements which are the dominant forms for coordination in a society are very much influenced by the norms, rules, conventions, habits, and values which are prevalent in a society. In other words, in each society some institutional arrangements are more dominant than others. But in no society does any single institutional arrangement coordinate relationships among actors. There are always configurations of institutional arrangements, even though one institutional arrangement may be more important than others. Thus, in Switzer-land and Austria, associations are far more important in coordinating actors than is the case in the British, American, and Canadian societies. But in Switzerland and Austria, associations alone do not coordinate economic actors, as the state and the market are also very important coordinating mechanisms. In these societies, all three institutional arrangements make up a configuration in order to coordinate economic actors.

Historically, the state has permitted associations in some societies to engage in cartel-type behavior, while elsewhere, cartels are forbidden, and associations, instead of fixing prices and determining the quality of output of certain products, serve the function of lobbying and providing information to customers about the quality of products. And prices are determined more by markets rather than by associations. In short, the way that associations, the state, markets, and networks configure to coordinate social relations varies from society to society.

The meta-norms and rules of a society structure the constellations or configurations of institutional arrangements, and in all societies, there is a logic with which these configurations behave. One of the chief tasks of institutional analysis is to comprehend this logic. The configurative logics of institutional arrangements shape relationships within and among institutional sectors, such as the business system, the system of research, the system of education, etc.

The configuration of institutional arrangements in a society is not necessarily the most efficient means of coordinating economic activity nor should it be viewed as part of some universal pattern of development. In chapter 9, Frans van Waarden demonstrates in his arguments about path dependency that the potential for a society to change its configuration of institutional arrangements is always limited or constrained by the dominant norms, rules, habits, conventions, and values. And these configurations evolve with a logic which is somewhat societally specific. Thus, the dominant rules and norms of a society influence the configurations of institutional arrangements, and both of these institutional components influence the structure and behavior of institutional sectors of a society.

All of this becomes very apparent when one engages in comparative institutional analysis of total societies. For example, many scholars (Orru, Biggart, and Hamilton, 1991; Gerlach, 1992) point out that East Asian societies are coordinated by configurations in which networks are the dominant institutional arrangement, but the logic with which networks coordinate relationships varies from society to society. These different logics have enormous implications for how each society organizes its business system and education system, its industrial relations system, its financial markets, and the state. Thus, Japan has had a configuration of institutional arrangements which has evolved according to a communitarian logic, Korea according to a patrimonial logic, and Taiwan according to patrilineal logic. And within each society, there is a kind of isomorphism in the forms of coordination of actors in different societal sectors, as the forms of coordination of each institutional sector (the business system, industrial relations system, financial markets, etc.) have evolved according to a common logic.

But in Anglo-American societies, there is a vastly different form of logic which has influenced the development of institutional arrangements. There, the institutional arrangements have evolved from a set of rules and norms by which individuals have been very much engaged in the pursuit of individual self-interest, with much less concern with the communitarian-type norms and rules so prevalent in East Asian societies. As a result of the American-type logic, the market has become far more dominant in the configuration of institutional arrangements than has been the case in any East Asian societies. Rules and norms in Anglo-American societies emphasize individual rights and obligations. Whereas East Asian societies have configurations of institutional arrangements which facilitate close relationships among social actors, in Anglo-American societies, the configurative logics influence tendencies toward individualism and arm's length transactions. Thus, in the business systems of Anglo-American societies, buyers tend to favor suppliers who provide goods at the lowest price, whereas in East Asian societies, buyers prefer suppliers with whom they have long-established relationships (Gerlach, 1992).

Offe in chapter 10 employs a strategy for explaining institutional arrangements very different from most state and Marxist theorists. Most state and Marxist theorists attempt to explain the role and structure of the state in terms of the functions it performs for the economy. In short, the economy shapes the role of the state, which is to sustain a well-functioning capitalist economy. Most neoclassical market theorists assume that the economy is made up of large numbers of rationally calculating individuals who are engaged in the pursuit of individual self-interests, and that the aggregation of individuals through spontaneous and voluntaristic action can construct their world (Williamson, 1985). This mixing of full rationalist with market competition is expected to produce whatever institutions are necessary to coordinate a complex capitalist economy.

In the essays which follow, the authors suggest in varying degrees that the coordinating mechanisms of modern societies have configurative coordinating structures, each containing the state. However, the role and structure, not only of the state but also of the entire configuration of coordinating mechanisms, vary across societies. Each configurative structure should be seen as a larger effort to legitimate a system of rules, norms, habits, conventions, and values which have evolved in a society's history. In no society has the configurative institutional arrangement been determined exclusively or primarily by the economy. The strength of the state relative to the other institutional arrangements (associations, markets, networks, etc.) has varied considerably. As Hollingsworth suggests, it is the configurative institutional arrangements of each society which are very important in influencing the structure and behavior of societal sectors, the organizational structures across sectors within each society, and the overall performance of the society.

6

On Institutional Embeddedness

J. Rogers Hollingsworth

There are innumerable signs that we are living in an age of great institutional change: the demise of the Soviet empire; the processes of European political and economic integration; the rapid transformation of parts of the global economy; the disintegration of the family structure; the weakening of voluntary associations and the decline in political participation in a number of advanced capitalist societies; the weakening of welfare states. European law is superseding national law and is even changing complete national legal systems. The list could go on and on. Even though scholars discuss institutional change at length, their ability to measure the rate of institutional change is very limited. And far more crucial than the limited ability of scholars to measure institutional change is their very limited understanding of how to build new institutions or to promote institutional change. One of the reasons for these shortcomings is that the social sciences are deficient in a theory of institutions. The building of new institutions and redressing the decline of some of the most important institutions of our societies are among the most important problems of our time. If we are to advance in the development of a theory of institutions, we need to work collaboratively across the social sciences, and we need to define the parameters of institutional analysis.

This essay focuses on the role of institutional analysis in the research agenda of socio-economics. Institutional analysis has attained high relevance in virtually all the social sciences. For example, political scientists, anthropologists, sociologists, economists, and historians are very much engaged in institutional analysis. Thus, the subsequent discussion should be of general importance well beyond the field of socio-economics.

DIFFERENT APPROACHES TO INSTITUTIONS

We need to be very much aware of the obstacles confronting us as we attempt to advance an agenda of institutional analysis. There is at present no consensus in the social sciences as to what is meant by institutions, or by institutional analysis. These terms are very widely used, but they are used with different conceptualizations so that scholars share little common ground when they use such concepts. Until scholars have some consensus about the meaning of the concepts they use in their discourse, their potential to bring about effective advancement of knowledge is somewhat limited. To restate this point, the widespread interest in several academic disciplines in such concepts as institutions and institutional analysis may well promise more than disciplines can deliver, given the organizational and disciplinary fragmentation of contemporary universities.

There are many different approaches to the study of institutions. There are the new and the old institutionalism (Hodgson, 1998), there is historical institutionalism (Steimo, Thelen, and Longstreth, 1992; Immergut, 1998; Katznelson, 1998), and several of the social sciences have diverse approaches to the study of institutions (Hodgson, 1988; Hechter and Kanazawa, 1997). The following comments reflect some of the confusion in utilizing the concept institution. Nobel Laureate Douglass North in his book *Institutions, Institutional Change, and Economic Performance* (1990: 3) defines institutions as "rules of the game in a society." To North, institutions are constraints which shape human interaction, and the way that societies evolve through time. On the other hand, Andrew Schotter argues that institutions "are not rules of the game." Rather, institutions are the behavior that follows from rules. Briefly, he is concerned with what actors do with rules, but not with what the rules are (Schotter, 1981: 155). Many other examples might be given to illustrate the heterogeneity of approaches to institutions and institutional analysis. Even if scholars were to agree with North that rules and norms are institutions, they would not necessarily agree on what a rule is. Shimanoff, for example, has identified more than one hundred synonyms for the concept rule (Shimanoff, 1980: 57; Ostrom, 1986: 5).

Another critical issue in the institutional literature is the relationship between institutions and organizations. North (1990), following from his definition of institutions, argues that institutions and organizations are distinct entities. Which organizations come into being and how they evolve through time is influenced by a society's rules and norms, that is, by its institutions. On the other hand, a number of organizational sociologists (e.g., DiMaggio and Powell, 1991) see very little difference between institutions and organizations. For them, rules and norms are institutions, which unfold in tandem with organizational structures and processes, and changes in organizational forms internalize and reflect changes in the society's rules and norms. Using this perspective, a whole sub-discipline within sociology called the "new institutionalism" in organizational analysis has emerged. The institutionalist perspective on organizations assumes that the kinds of organizations which actors create are dictated by the cultural norms and rules in which they are embedded (DiMaggio and Powell, 1991; Zucker, 1988, 1991).

The importance of this disagreement about institutions is obvious. If institutions are so critical for understanding our socio-economic environment, it is important that we come to some systematic consensus as to what institutions are, and how they influence social actors and the organizations that they create. If we cannot do so, we risk talking past one another, and losing the opportunities for cumulative knowledge based on articulation of widely shared theoretical understanding. We need not only conceptual clarification as to what institutions are, but also greater consensus as to how to study institutions. No scientific field can advance very far if the practitioners do not share a common understanding of the key concepts used in their analysis (Ostrom, 1986: 4). But with our universities and professional associations so fragmented into academic disciplines and into various sub-specialties within disciplines, it is difficult to advance the theoretical agenda of socio-economics within the academy. Indeed, the disciplinary fragmentation of the modern university is a major barrier to the theoretical advancement not only of the field of socio-economics but also of all hybrid fields of research (Hollingsworth, 1984; Hollingsworth and Hollingsworth, 2000). Thus, the subsequent remarks should establish a common platform for various types of institutional analyses where different institutional approaches become properly combined and integrated.

FIVE TYPES OF INSTITUTIONAL ANALYSIS

At the outset, we need to recognize that when we engage in institutional investigations, we must be sensitive to multiple types of investigations. As suggested above, most scholars who engage in institutional analysis do not participate in any coordinated activity with each other, and their activity is fragmented into a variety of disciplines and sub-disciplines. To establish some coherence to the field of institutional analysis, we need a map of the field so that those working in one area can see where their research fits in relation to other areas and other practitioners on the map.[1]

Figure 6.1 presents such a map, with multiple stages at which institutional analysis occurs. Theoretically, each of these areas on the map is interrelated with each other. However, the various areas on the map are arranged in descending order of stability or permanence. Those components listed first in figure 6.1 are more permanent and durable, while those listed last change more rapidly.

Were socio-economists able to reach some consensus about where their own work fits in relation to all other practitioners in the field, we could enhance the potential for practitioners to communicate with each other. By analogy, once geneticists, crystallographers, biochemists, etc., had good understanding of how their investigations were related to each area of molecular biology, the field quickly was able to make theoretical advances (Judson, 1979).

In greater detail, each of the diagrams in figure 6.1 can be characterized by the following compositional mixtures, theoretical background assumptions, and heuristic devices.

First Type of Analysis

At the first level, there are the basic norms, rules, conventions, values, laws, regulations, and habits of a society. These are the most fundamental properties of institutions and are the most enduring and resistant to change. Rules, norms, conventions, etc., influence the nature of the other components of institutional analysis. Most human activity is organized and regulated by norms and rules and systems of rules. These concepts are extremely important for institutional analysis, as they influence the components in the next four types (depicted in figure 6.1). In most forms of socio-economic analysis, it is extremely important that we understand the social and cognitive conditions that lead to compliance or non-compliance of rules, and the conditions which lead to changes in rules.

The approach to the study of institutions employed here argues that norms, rules, habits, conventions, and values both reflect and shape the preferences of actors. Norms, rules, habits, conventions, and values influence who and what are included in different types of decision making, how information is processed and structured, what action is taken (Shepsle, 1989). It is through norms and rules that behavior is judged to be democratic, fair, or egalitarian.

Burns and Flam (1987) point out that in almost any society there are multiple rule systems. Within a family there are rules for decision making which are often quite different from rules and norms for decision making for a professor in a classroom, or for the customer in a bank. Despite the heterogeneity of rule systems, there are meta-rules and norms which encompass lesser rule systems.

Figure 6.1   A Partial Map for Institutional Analysis

1. Institutions

Actors / System of Actors
Habits, Customs, Routines, Practices

Institutional Base
Norms, Rules, Conventions, Values

2. Institutional Arrangements

Markets, Corporate Hierarchies, Networks,
Associations, Communities, States, etc.

Institutional Base
Norms, Rules, Conventions, Values

3. Institutional Sectors

Financial System, System of Education,
Business System, System of Research,
Social Systems of Production, etc.

(coordinated by Markets, Corporate Hierarchies,
Networks, Associations, Communities, States, etc.)

Institutional Base
Norms, Rules, Conventions, Values

Otherwise there would be such contradictory rule systems that the society would be paralyzed. It is because of the existence of meta-rule systems that different rule systems intersect with each other and ambiguities can be resolved. Of course, the greater the pluralism and complexity of a society, the more ambiguity there is about meta-rules and norms in a society, and of course, all ambiguities never disappear. Overall, the degree to which separate rule systems are inter-linked is an empirical problem. There are different sectors, groups, and interests pursuing their own action logic, but it is through higher-order meta-principles and rules that there can be order, consensus, and coherence in a society. It is through a set of meta-rules that class and ethnic conflicts in societies are contained (for elaboration, see Burns and Flam, 1988).

In many respects, our understanding about norms, rules, conventions, values, and habits influences our perspective on how societies are constructed and how they change. Among a group of "new institutionalists" (Posner, 1973; Schotter, 1981; Williamson, 1975, 1985) there are assumptions that at one time there was a state of nature and that there was a movement from individuals to institutions—an approach often called methodological individualism (Popper, 1961; Hodgson, 1998). And of course there are innumerable instances which methodological individualists cite to demonstrate that individuals create new rules of behavior. For example, it is possible for actors to change the rules of driving, so that instead of driving on the left side of the road, drivers adopt a new rule and drive on the right. In this essay, there is a tendency to equate social habits and institutions. As Hodgson and others (1988, 1989, 1997; Camic, 1986) remind us, habits are the results of earlier choices and are a means of avoiding endless deliberation. Because cognitive frameworks are learned through habit, individuals rely on the acquisition of such cognitive habits before reason, communication, choice, or actions are possible. (See figure 6.1.1 and note 1 at the end of this chapter.)

Whereas Schotter (1981) and other game theorists take the individual as an agent unencumbered by previous habits, Field (1984) and others have stressed that there can be no games without prior norms and rules, and thus a set of norms and rules must be presumed at the start. Those who attempt to explain institutions from individuals alone are using a bad strategy (Hodgson, 1998).

The position here—heavily influenced by Hodgson (1998, 1997, 1988)—is that individuals are embedded in a complex institutional environment and that institutions not only constrain but also shape individuals (also see Hollingsworth and Boyer, 1997). It would be a mistake, however, to get involved in an infinite regress in order to determine which came first—individuals or institutions. The main thing to keep in mind is that neither individuals nor institutions have total explanatory power. Of course, institutions are formed and changed by individuals, just as individuals are shaped and constrained by institutions. But at a macro-level, it is institutions that provide a cognitive framework whereby individuals can cope with their reality. It is in this sense that the micro- and the macro-worlds are intertwined. At the macro-level, there is stability, but at the micro-level, because individuals also have a significant level of autonomy, there is considerable diversity. As Hodgson (1988) reminds us, most institutions in a temporal sense exist prior to the individuals in any given society.

It would be a serious mistake to downplay the importance of individuals and micro-level analysis as we study institutions. In the final analysis, it is at the level of individuals that norms, rules, habits, conventions, and values exist. An individual is born into and socialized into groups and a society, and this is how one early in life acquires a sense of appropriate forms of behavior. Because of the way that individuals are socialized into a world of rules, norms, habits, conventions, and values, it is unnecessary for individuals to restructure the world anew every day (Douglas, 1987; Elster, 1989). Every action does not have to be seriously reflected upon. For this reason, institutions provide cognitive frameworks for individuals, make their environments predictable, provide the information for coping with complex problems and environments. In the words of Johnson (1992: 26) "Institutions reduce uncertainty, coordinate the use of knowledge, mediate conflicts, and provide incentive systems. By serving these functions, institutions provide the stability necessary for the reproduction of society." However, each society has different forms of habits, rules, and norms and hence different incentives and disincentive systems for learning and forgetting, for processing information. But because individuals have varying degrees of autonomy, individuals and groups can deviate from the prescribed forms of behavior in a society. And of course, these changes at the level of individuals become important in understanding processes of societal change. These views are not meant to imply that the type of institutional analysis proposed herein approximates a general theory of society. This is clearly not the case. However, it is intended to represent the first steps in a mapping exercise of the boundaries of institutional analysis and to suggest a few methodological insights for studying institutions.

In addition, it is important to make a few comments about frequent misconceptions about norms and rules. One should make an effort to see norms and rules as continuous and not as dichotomous entities. We should not think of norms and rules simply as existing or not existing, but we should recognize that they come in varying strengths. Legro (1997) has suggested that we assess the robustness of norms and rules with three criteria: their simplicity, their durability, and their concordance. Simplicity refers to how well actors understand norms and rules, how well they can be applied within a specific situation. Some norms and rules can be so complex that actors can have considerable difficulty in applying them in specific cases. Durability addresses the issue of how long norms and rules have been in effect, their level of legitimacy. While the position of this essay is that norms, rules, and values are quite durable, they clearly vary in this respect. Concordance refers to how widely applied a norm or rule is. This addresses the degree to which a rule is a meta-rule, the degree to which it incorporates a heterogeneity of other norms and rules. In sum, the clearer the norms and rules of a society, the longer they have been in existence, and the more widely applicable they are, the greater their impact on a society. Hence, the more robust the norms and rules, the greater their impact on a society, and the less their robustness, the greater their flexibility and the less their effect on shaping a society's performances.

Because norms, rules, and values are quite durable, they play an important role in shaping the history of societies, thus contributing to a great deal of path dependency. Actors are intertwined with the contemporary world in which they live, adjusting as products of their histories to their contemporary environment. The historical legacy of norms, rules, and values influences the decisions actors make. Although actors have some capacity to alter the course of their history, they are constrained by their past, and the degree to which they can move beyond their past is limited. History matters, but at critical points in history, there is punctuated equilibrium. During most periods of history, there is considerable stability in the norms, rules, and values of a society, but at certain critical moments, norms, rules, and values can quickly and dramatically be redefined.

Second Type of Analysis

The norms, rules, conventions, and values of a society lead to the next type of analysis—the institutional arrangements involved in the coordination of various social actors: In the case of a business system one finds producers and suppliers of raw materials, knowledge, etc; processors of raw materials and information; workers; customers of raw materials, finished products, information, etc.; financiers; governmental and other types of regulators. These actors regularly are engaged in contests to resolve various problems in virtually all sectors of society: How are prices to be set? What quantity of various products is to be produced? How are standards of various products, processes, etc., to be set? How is the quality of products and processes to be determined? How are various societal processes to be financed? In order to confront these problems and to address the conflicting positions of societal actors as they address these problems, societies develop various institutional arrangements for coordinating different actors. These consist of markets, various types of hierarchies and networks, associations, the state, communities, and clans (see Hollingsworth and Boyer, 1997; Campbell, Hollingsworth, and Lindberg, 1991: chapter 1). Each of these particular kinds of coordinating mechanism has many different types. For example, there are many different types of states (e.g., the regulatory state, developmental state, authoritarian state, welfare state), and of course, there is an extensive literature on each type (Kim, 1997).

Similarly, there are different types of markets, networks, different kinds of associations, etc. (Boyer, 1997; Hage and Alter 1997; Schneiberg and Hollingsworth, 1990). When we do institutional analysis, we must engage in configurative analysis, recognizing that actors are not coordinated by a single institutional arrangement. Some of the literature discusses industrial sectors as though they are coordinated or governed by a single institutional arrangement, whereas in fact each sector of an economy is coordinated by a configuration of institutional arrangements. Some configurations coordinate in certain problem areas, while other configurations of institutional arrangements coordinate other problems. The types of configuration in a society are somewhat stable and tend to persist over time within a society. It is helpful to array these various forms of coordination in a complex two-dimensional taxonomy (figure 6.2) where each position can be considered as an "ideal type." (Also, see figure 6.1.2.)

Figure 6.2 Towards a Map of Institutional Arrangements across the Dimensions of Action Motives and Power Distribution

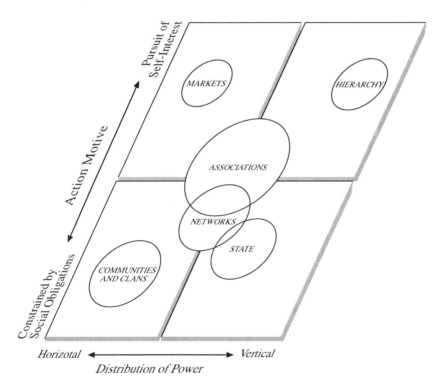

Along the vertical dimension, the economist's view of a self-interested agent is contrasted with a more sociological perspective, according to which obligation and compliance with social rules are the guiding principles shaping human

Figure 6.3 Towards a Map of Institutional Arrangements across the Dimensions of Action Motives and Coordination Structures

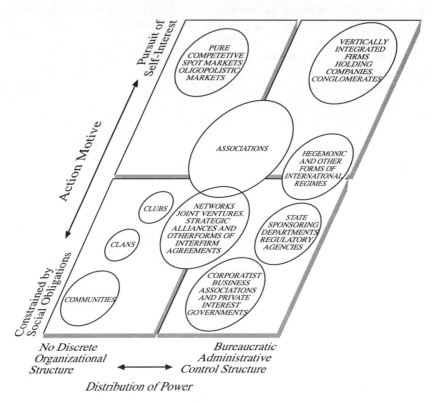

actions. Along the horizontal dimension, there is displayed a continuum of modes of coordination.

At one extreme, horizontal coordination takes place when many and relatively equal agents interact (e.g., as in a well-organized spot market).

At the other extreme, inequality in power results in a hierarchical form of coordination whereby either a private or a public hierarchy structures the interaction between principal and an agent or between a leader and a follower.

Thus, institutional arrangements can be disentangled from this combination of the two dimensions: the nature of goal setting on the one hand, and the distribution of power on the other. Markets combine "self-interest" with horizontal coordination transactions, and they reflect sensitivity to concerns about supply and demand, thus providing ex post an unintended equilibrium.

Paradoxically, the more pure and perfect the market competition, the greater the need for codified rules of the games for coordinating economic transactions.

Thus, collective associations and various forms of state intervention are required to enforce rules for transacting partners (Schneiberg and Hollingsworth, 1990; Streeck and Schmitter, 1985a, 1985b). This is an example of how the norms and rules and the institutional arrangements of a society are intertwined, and are found in a configuration of institutional arrangements. There are also networks which exhibit various mixes of self-interest and social obligation, with actors being formally independent and equal, even if some networks (the large firms and their subcontractors) partially rely upon unequal power and initiative. Networks may constitute all kinds of actors, ranging from those consisting only of firms to those that also include associations and the state (Hage and Alter, 1997).

In the right-hand cells, actors can be linked together in a high degree of integration, being joined within an organization or a firm. Hierarchy is the generic term for this institutional arrangement. Along the horizontal line, one recognizes the difference between interactions outside an organizations and those within an organization. The work of Coase (1960, 1981) and Williamson (1975, 1985) uses the role of transaction costs in explaining the emergence of corporate hierarchies which complements the perspective here.

But we should also turn to the vertical axis, which deals with action motives. Toward the upper part of figure 6.2, actors are engaged in individualistically oriented behavior, whereas toward the lower part, actors are more engaged in collective behavior and strive to cope with problems of common interest. Communities consists of institutional arrangements that are based on trust, reciprocity, or obligation, and thus are not derived from the pure selfish computation of pleasures and pains. This is an unconventional form of coordination for most neoclassical economists (however, see Arrow, 1974), but not for many anthropologists, political scientists, and sociologists (Streeck and Schmitter, 1985; Polanyi, 1946; Gambetta, 1988; Fukuyama, 1995; Sabel, 1992; Putnam, 1993). In the neoclassical paradigm, theorists argue that actors engage in those forms of exchanges that best promote their individual interests. If some structural conditions are fulfilled (absence of increasing returns to scale, the reversibility of transactions, absence of uncertainty, and complete contingent markets, with no collusion between actors), then the invisible hand theorem applies, and market-type activity functions quite well and also provides the optimum for society, therefore combining efficiency, harmony, and order. However, an excess of market activity may well lead to ruinous competition and excessive conflict. Indeed, there is variation in the extent to which ruinous competition occurs, depending on the social context within which individual transactions take place. Thus, it is important that we be sensitive to the institutional context in which transactions are embedded and that we understand the degree to which social bonds exist at both the micro- and macro-levels of analysis. Micro-bonds facilitate exchanges in a society, but at the societal level social bonds exist at the level of the collective—in the community or region, and among members of racial, religious, and ethnic groups. All other things being equal, the more powerful the social bonds among transacting partners, the more economic competition is likely to be restrained. Thus, most transactions occur not simply in an impersonal, calculative system of autonomous actors unrestrained by social ties—as implied by the neoclassical paradigm—but in the context of social ties, variation in the strength of which leads to variation in levels of trust and transaction costs (Etzioni, 1988: 211; Granovetter, 1985; Streeck and Schmitter, 1985; Hollingsworth and Boyer, 1997; Hodgson, 1988).

Another form of multilateral institutional arrangement consists of various types of associations. Unlike networks, clans, and communities, associations are more formal organizations. Whereas markets, corporate hierarchies, and obligational networks tend to coordinate economic activity among different types of actors (e.g., producers with suppliers, capital with labor, producers with customers), associations typically coordinate actors engaged in the same or similar kinds of activities. Business associations and labor unions are some of the most common forms of associations for coordinating economic activity in capitalist economies (Schneiberg and Hollingsworth, 1990; Schmitter and Streeck, 1981; Streeck, 1992).

Finally, there is the state, which is an institutional arrangement quite unlike any of the others. It is the state that sanctions and regulates the various non-state coordinating mechanisms, that is the ultimate enforcer of rules of the various mechanisms, that defines and enforces property rights, and that manipulates fiscal and monetary policy. At the same time, the state may also be an economic actor by engaging directly in production and exchange relations.

In short, the choices of institutional arrangements in figure 6.2 are constrained by the social context in which they are embedded. Depending on the nature of that embeddedness, there is variation in the collective forms of governance, Because some obligational forms of coordination tend to be configured simultaneously with those on the upper side of the typology, the forms of behavior in which actors are involved invariably influence the degree to which actors engage in markets, networks, or hierarchy.

As suggested above, each institutional arrangement is configured with other institutional arrangements, in short, a form of institutional complementarity (Amable, 2000; Hall and Soskice, 2001). Usually, one particular institutional arrangement is more dominant in a particular configuration—but because each type of institutional arrangement has its own strengths and weaknesses, there is no simple structural logic in the governance or coordination of a society. Each institutional arrangement constrains the other, but it is the inherent tension among the various institutional arrangements within a configuration that contributes to changes in the governance or coordination of a society. But it is the "logics" of each of these configurations of institutional arrangements that provide constraints and incentives for actors. And it is the way that actors perceive the incentives and constraints of these governance configurations that leads to a particular market logic, and it is the specific market logic of a society which influences its specific capacities and weaknesses. The inherent strain among the different logics in a configuration of coordination helps to provide the flexibility for a society to adapt to new circumstances.

If there were a society with pure markets or a society coordinated only by the state, there would be too much rigidity and too little diversity to cope with the vast uncertainty of the global environment. A society with very little diversity in its coordination mechanisms would have little capacity to adapt to new circumstances. Configurations with considerable diversity of institutional arrangements provide for a certain amount of incoherence in governance, but they also provide for the capacity to adapt to new circumstances. While the Soviet Union was dominated by the state as a coordinating mechanism, there were always functioning markets in the system. Moreover, the feudal society of the twelfth and thirteenth centuries consisted not only of hierarchical relationships between serfs and masters but also of urban guilds, clerical hierarchies, and markets (Johnson, 1992: 38). In sum, the robustness of institutions often depends on multiple and diverse principles and logics of action, on the inconsistency of principles and procedures, on patterned forms of disorder (Lanzara, 1998; Orren and Skowronek, 1991: 320, 329).

Third Type of Analysis

As we continue with our journey into the land of institutional analysis, the next type consists of the institutional sectors or segments of a society. An institutional sector includes all organizations in a society which supply a given service or product, along with their associated focal organizations (e.g., major suppliers, funding sources, regulators, and so forth [Scott, Meyer, et al., 1994; Campbell, Hollingsworth, and Lindberg, 1991; Hollingsworth, Schmitter, and Streeck, 1994]). While this essay does not refer to all institutional sectors, institutional sectors include, inter alia, the society's system of education, its system of research, business system, financial markets, legal system, and the state. These institutional sectors vary across societies in terms of how differentiated each sector is from every other sector and how tightly linked each sector is to the others. Indeed, the more the rules, norms, and values are widely shared throughout the society into a meta-rule system (see above), the more the different institutional sectors are highly complementary with each other. The more tightly linked the various institutions sectors are with each other, the more difficult it is for each institution to change in a fundamental way without all other institutional sectors also changing in a fundamental way. And one can determine the degree to which institutional sectors are tightly or loosely coupled only by empirical analysis. Even so, institutional sectors do undergo more change than do the two previous levels of institutional analysis: the rules, norms, values, conventions, etc., of the society and the configuration of institutional arrangements prevalent in the society. Since the third type of analysis will become the focus of the opening chapter in part 3, a more detailed discussion can be postponed to the chapter on "Social Systems of Production and Beyond." (See figure 6.1.3.)

Fourth Type of Analysis

The next type of institutional analysis, organizational structures, may be somewhat more controversial. As suggested above, Douglass North (1990) draws a sharp distinction between institutions and organizations. More recently, however, many organizational theorists (DiMaggio, 1991; Powell and DiMaggio, 1991; Kondra and Hinings, 1998) argue that institutional rules, norms, and conventions unfold in tandem with organizational structures, and this is my position. Institutional analysis involves multiple levels of society (Jepperson, 1991), and for some time, analysts have suggested that institutions and organizational forms co-evolve. But since organizations embody rules, norms, conventions, and habits, which after all are what institutions are, it must logically follow that institutions and organizations are intricately bound together. However, organizational structures change much more rapidly and are less permanent than a society's rules, norms, and conventions. Because organizational forms and institutional rules and norms co-evolve however, as organizational structures change, there will be some feedback to a society's rules and norms. (See note 1 at the end of this chapter.)

The literature which focuses on how institutions influence organizations is quite different from two other theoretical literatures which also are concerned with how organizational environments shape the behavior of organizations. There are resource dependency theorists (Pfeffer and Salancik, 1978) which emphasize the role of environmental resources in shaping organizations, while Hannan and Freeman (1977, 1984) and other population ecologists emphasize the survival of organizations, given certain kinds of organizational conditions (Orru, et al., 1991).

The institutionalist perspective, as implied above, emphasizes the normative environment in which organizations are embedded. It is a perspective which focuses on the way in which organizations, in their behavior, tend to conform to the institutional rules and norms which are dominant in the organizational environment. However, all three perspectives—the institutionalist, the population ecology, and the resource dependency—emphasize how the environment influences organizations and how organizations which are subject to the same environment tend to converge in their behavior, to have what DiMaggio and Powell have labeled organizational isomorphism (DiMaggio and Powell, 1983).

Organizations embedded in institutional environments which have common rules and norms tend to have similar structures and cultures. It is true that across different societal and industrial sectors, organizations are structured somewhat differently because they are subject to different technical environments. When one examines the structure and culture of most organizations across all sectors of a single society one sees that the variation across sectors takes place within parameters which are societally or system specific. And the specificity of these societal systems is due in large part to a set of dominant rules, norms, habits, and conventions of each society which are very much path-dependent, with long-term stability and persistence. And it is the commonality of dominant rules and norms in a society which leads to the organizational isomorphism which one finds across sectors in a society.

There is now a rapidly emerging literature which demonstrates that within each society there are fiscal, political, judicial, and other regulatory norms which limit and shape the culture and structure of organizational behavior. And it is the normative institutional environment of organizations that limits the options of what organizations do in a particular society and which influences the patterns of ownership, relations with suppliers, and customers. In short, it is the normative environment of organizations which defines within a particular society what is socially acceptable behavior for organizations (Hamilton and Biggart, 1988; Hollingsworth and Hollingsworth, 1998; Meyer and Rowan, 1977; Zucker, 1987, 1988; Orru, Biggart, and Hamilton, 1991).

Thus far, most of the analyses on isomorphic pressures operating on organizations have been cross-sectional in nature. However, the entire concept of isomorphism implies that there are strong environmental pressures exerted on organizations, and in order to observe this phenomenon it is important that we have longitudinal studies which assess how changes in an organization's institutional environment influences changes in the organization. Moreover, the expectation here is that when one analyzes the patterns of organizational change over time, the isomorphism will be holistic—that is within a particular society there will be a tendency for the entire internal structure of particular types of organizations to be similar, due in large part because of the pressures to conform to the changes in the external norms, rules and values. A close reading of Chandler (1962, 1990), Aoki (1988), and Slack and Hinings (1994) finds that variation in the national institutional environment of organizations—both across countries and over time within specific countries—has influenced conformity in the internal structure of organizations within a specific industry of a particular country.

The logic of the perspective herein suggests that within every society, there is variation in the structure and culture of business firms, universities, and other complex organizations (Kondra and Hinings, 1998). However, this variation takes place within parameters which are system specific. For example, every German firm and every German university is different from every other German university and firm, but there are a set of cultural and structural characteristics which distinguish German firms and universities from those in America.

In all societies, each organization has its own distinctive organizational rules, norms, and conventions which are subordinate to the meta-norms and rules of the larger society in which they are embedded. However, the strength of the institutional environment within which organizations are embedded varies from society to society. In those societies in which the institutional rules are most developed and in which the institutional pressures to conform are the greatest, there is less variation in the structure and culture of business forms and various kinds of research organizations. In such societies, the connectedness between research organizations and their institutional environments is sufficiently strong for organizations to have low autonomy to pursue independent strategies and goals; in these societies there is a great deal of organizational isomorphism. Conversely, the weaker the institutional environment in which research organizations are embedded, the greater the variation in the structure and culture of business firms and research organizations. Moreover, where the institutional environments are more weakly developed, organizations have greater autonomy and flexibility to respond to the development of new knowledge and to be highly innovative. Hence, it is in those societies where the institutional environments are most developed and most rigid that there is less organizational autonomy and flexibility and fewer radical innovations in basic and applied science as well as in totally new products have been made (Hollingsworth, Hollingsworth, and Hage, 2002, forthcoming).

Fifth Type of Analysis

We come next to the outputs and performance of the various institutional and organizational components of a society. It is at this very detailed focus of analysis that institutional components seem to be more pragmatic and flexible. For example, within the legal sector, there are specific statutes and court rulings; within the state sector, there are specific policies. Within the business sector, there are new products, new technologies, and market strategies. It is at this final type of analysis where institutions are most open and susceptible to change and cross-national mimicry is easiest and most common. (See note 1 at the end of this chapter.)

Moreover, it is through the outputs of the society's organizations that we can access how well the societal institutions are performing. For example, it is here that we can evaluate how egalitarian the society is in the distribution of its resources, how egalitarian it is in terms of levels of health, education, etc. We can assess how innovative it is. But just as it is complicated to measure how egalitarian a society is, similarly it is difficult to assess how innovative it is. For example, societies vary in the degree to which they make instrumental and radical breakthroughs in basic and applied science; in the frequency with which they develop totally new products and new kinds of organizations; in the degree to which they engage in incremental and process innovations in existing products and organizations; in the degree to which they develop new and different forms of marketing and commercializing products both domestically and globally. And of course, societies vary in their rates of economic growth, in their rates of economic productivity, in their quality of life (e.g., rates of crime, life expectancy, etc.). All of these performance criteria feed back and influence each of the levels of institutional analysis discussed above—rules, norms, values, etc; institutional arrangements, institutional sectors; the structure and form of organizations. Moreover, each type of performance measure may influence other performance criteria. For example, if a society has very low rates of growth, it may not be very innovative in some of the types of innovative activities mentioned above. Good or poor performances of certain kinds influence other performance indicators (Hollingsworth, Hage, and Hanneman, 1990).

Not only are different institutional arrangements associated with different social systems of production, but also different institutional arrangements and different social systems of production result in different types of economic performance (Hollingsworth, 1997). Hence, as long as countries vary in the type of coordinating mechanisms and social systems of production that are dominant in their economies, there are serious constraints on the degree to which they can converge in their economic performance. Different social systems of production tend to maximize in more or less explicit manner different performance criteria, usually mixing considerations about static and dynamic efficiency, profit, security, social peace, and economic and/or political power. In short, in contrast to the implications of the neoclassical economic theory, in real-world economies there are no universal standards all economically rational actors attempt to maximize. Economic history provides numerous examples of how a variety of principles of rationality are implemented in different societies.

Whether or not a social system of production can sustain its particular performance standards depends not only on its intrinsic economic rationality, but also on where it fits into a larger system. If a particular social system of production is immune from the competition of an alternative system, survival can be long lasting. But if different social systems of production, with diverging criteria of good economic performance, meet in the world arena, the arbitrariness of nationally imposed constructed performance standards may be superseded by alternative performance criteria as a result of international competitiveness. Even if different social systems of production are competing in the international arena, it is not always possible to determine which is more competitively effective at any moment in time. Hegemonic nation-states can shape, *within the short run*, the rules of trade that favor their industrial sectors and firms. But the history of hegemonic powers suggest that in the longer run, social systems of production, sustained largely by military and political power, eventually give way to more dynamic and competitive social systems of production. In our own day, as nation-states are increasingly integrated into a world economy, economic competition of production loses its international competitive advantage, its share of world output decreases, even if it is a hegemonic power. Such a country will slowly experience de-industrialization and/or will

attempt to restructure its institutional arrangements and to readjust its performance preferences. But such a restructuring generally calls for a major redistribution of power within a society. Largely for this reason, societies have historically had limited capacity to construct a social system of production in the
image of their major competitors. Each country's social system of production is
a configuration of a host of norms, rules, and values as well as of institutional
arrangements. Each system is constantly changing and is open to influence from
other systems. And indeed many technologies and practices diffuse from one
society to another, but the direction of change is constrained by the existing
social system of production. Thus the same technology may exist in numerous
countries, but how it is employed and how it influences societal outcomes and
performances varies from one institutional configuration or society to another.

PERSPECTIVES ON INSTITUTIONAL CHANGE

A fundamental problem which remains unresolved in institutional analysis
involves the nature of institutional change. And yet this is the next logical
problem which we need to address in institutional analysis. There is much
confusion and miscommunication in the social sciences about institutional
change, in large part because we do not know how to measure the rate of
change. Of course we know that there are both external and internal focuses for
change, and we have had a good bit of scholarship on this subject. What is not
clearly understood is that institutions and institutional arrangements within
societies are historically rooted—that there is a great deal of path dependency to
the way that institutions evolve. This is very critical to the problem of how
much freedom do we have to create new institutions afresh, to what extent do
institutions diffuse from one society to another? This is a fundamental question
for analysts of socio-economics. We need to understand how various sectors are
linked together and how each sector is in turn shaped by a society's rules and
norms. The more intricately linked each sector is with each other and with a
society's rules and norms, the less choice actors have to devise new institutions
and institutional arrangements.

There are a variety of reasons why there is confusion in studying institutional
change. One problem results from the fact that the scholarly community does
not know how to measure the rate of change. But there are even more fundamental problems. A key issue is the degree to which actors have the freedom to
build new institutions arrangements, and if they do, to what extent may the new
arrangements and organizational patterns depart from past practices? Among
some institutional economists (Williamson, 1985), there is a basic assumption
that national actors have a self-interest in building efficient institutions in order
to promote their strategic goals. Moreover, there is the assumption that a mixing
of full rationality with market competition tends to produce all of the optimal

institutions that are needed in order to coordinate a complex capitalist economy (Hollingsworth and Boyer, 1997: chapter 14). However, the argument developed here is much more complex.

Social institutions are historically rooted, and there is a great deal of path dependency in the way that various institutional components evolve. The shape of institutional configurations at any moment in time limits the type of options for change. In short, there is a great deal of institutional inertia. As a result, radical change in the institutional components of a society is uncommon (Lanzara, 1998).

Even so, as we take into consideration the constraints which existing institutions exert on actors, we also need to be mindful of the idea that existing institutional arrangements, institutional sectors, and organizational properties can also limit the degree to which norms and rules can change. Most scholars (North, 1990; Ostrom, 1986, 1990) have emphasized the role of norms, rules, ideologies, and values in limiting the ability of actors to develop new institutional arrangements which radically depart from existing ones. Thus as Friedland and Alford (1991: 244) argue, actors develop new institutional arrangements by extending existing practices, habits, and conventions to new types of problems.

The work of Campbell (1997) advances our understanding of how existing institutions enable actors to construct radically new institutions. Campbell acknowledges the existing literature by recognizing that most institutions and institutional arrangements embody a degree of rigidity from which it is different for actors to depart. Moreover, the differential power relations among actors make it extremely difficult for less powerful actors to change the existing power structure of a society. Most change in the institutional components of a society evolves through a process of constrained selection which reflects to a considerable degree the existing arrangements, and power relations. This becomes the interpretive frame for social actors, with institutionalized scripts and rituals which tend to be taken for granted and appear to be quite ordinary and natural. And it is this institutionalized scripting of the social world which is an extremely important source of social stability and inertia.

Campbell has developed a very fruitful explanation of change in terms of the various institutional components outlined in this essay. He points out the obvious distinction between incremental and radical institutional change. Moreover, he argues that radical institutional change occurs when social actors with widely differing norms, cultural scripts, and rituals for action engage in intense interaction with each other. The more diverse the interactions, the greater the potential for institutional change. Campbell argues that as the changes in the composition of interaction among social actors occur, changes in the interpretation of problems and interests will follow. If there are only minor changes in the extent to which diverse actors interact, there will be only modest institutional change. But the more fundamental the changes in the interaction of diverse social actors, the greater the change in the way that actors interpret their world. And the greater the change in the way that actors interpret their world, the more likely that radical changes in the various institutional components outlined above will follow. In other words, diverse decision making tends to create a wider range of interpretive frameworks of the social world than is likely to be the case if social actors operate in isolation.

This perspective of diverse interactions among social actors facilitates our ability to move beyond the traditional view that existing institutions simply constrain the range of institutional alterations which actors face. This view has tended to suggest that actors engage in institutional change by extending existing institutional principles, habits, and conventions. But by specifying the conditions which facilitate fundamental institutional change, we believe that we can develop a much richer perspective for institutional analysis. Significantly, Campbell's perspective about the conditions under which fundamental or radical change in institutional components occurs is consistent with my own research about the conditions under which major discoveries or fundamental new knowledge occurs: the more scholars with diverse backgrounds interact with intensity and frequency, the greater the likelihood that they will develop new and alternative ways of thinking.

CONCLUSION

In closing, several already developed themes will be reiterated. Most importantly, institutional analysis is at the heart of socio-economics. And in order to advance socio-economics theory, institutional analysis should be high on our research agenda. But the study of institutional components is a complex subject requiring multiple levels of analysis, multiple sectors within societies, and the study of the various components of institutional analysis in different societies. The lessons from the biological scenes over the last forty years are very instructive: once practitioners from various biological disciplines began to collaborate in studying biological phenomena by using the same concepts at the molecular level, theoretical advance was very rapid (Judson, 1979; Olby, 1979). A similar phenomenon took place in the development of bio-chemistry, bio-physics, and other hybrid fields (Kohler, 1982, 1994). Similarly, if social scientists in various disciplines would work collectively on the study of social institutions, there would very likely be an acceleration in the theoretical literature on institutions.

This is not a plea that everyone engaged in institutional analysis should do the same kind of research. Indeed, just as biologists working at the molecular level work on many separate kinds of problems, similarly social scientists engaged in institutional analysis would also work on many separate problems, but there would be a collective enterprise. Some would concentrate their attention on the study of rules, norms, habits, conventions, and values, while others would study how these are associated with configurations of various institutional arrangements—various types of markets, hierarchies, networks, associations, clans, states, etc. (see Hollingsworth and Boyer, 1997). And others would be specialists on specific institutional sectors (e.g., education, business systems, financial markets, and a society's system of scientific research). But what would be distinctive is how each of these sectors is linked together and how each institutional sector was linked to a society's norms, rules, values, etc. and its configuration of institutional arrangements. Similarly, other institutional analysts might focus on the study of organizations, but a major concern would be with how the institutional environment of organizations (e.g., norms, rules, values; configurations of institutional arrangements; institutional sectors) influenced the structure, culture, and outcomes of organizations. And finally, others would study how all of the aforementioned aspects of institutional analysis influenced a society's overall performance.

The examples from my study of hybrid fields of knowledge and research organizations suggest that once we have a common set of concepts, we can have genuine theoretical advance if researchers can bring their diverse expertise to bear on a common set of problems. There is considerable evidence that institutional analysis offers an enormous potential for advancing socio-economics.

NOTE

1 The five components in this note are arranged in descending order of permanence and stability. That is, norms, conventions, etc., are more enduring and persistent than each of the other components within other types of institutional analysis. Each type of analysis is highly inter-related with every other type. Moreover, changes in one component of institutional analysis are highly likely to have some effect in bringing about changes in each of the other components. Below one finds essential references which must be considered as highly relevant for the particular type of institutional analysis.

1. Institutions = Norms, Rules, Conventions, Values and Habits, Practices (see North, 1990; Burns and Flam, 1987).

2. Institutional arrangements = Markets, States, Corporate Hierarchies, Networks, Associations, Communities, etc. (Hollingsworth and Lindberg, 1985; Campbell, Hollingsworth, and Lindberg, 1991; Hollingsworth, Schmitter, and Streeck, 1994; Hollingsworth and Boyer, 1997).

3. Institutional Sectors = Financial System, System of Education, Business System, System of Research, Social Systems of Production (Hollingsworth, 1997; Hollingsworth and Hollingsworth, 2000).

4. Organizations (Powell and DiMaggio, 1991).

5. Outputs and performance = Statutes; Administrative decisions; the Nature, Quantity and the Quality of Industrial Products (Hollingsworth, 1991, 1997); Sectoral and Societal Performance (Hollingsworth and Streeck, 1994; Hollingsworth, Hage, and Hanneman, 1990; Hollingsworth and Hanneman, 1982).

7

Actors, Paradigms, and Institutional Dynamics: The Theory of Social Rule Systems Applied to Radical Reforms

Tom R. Burns, Marcus Carson

THE UNIVERSALITY OF SOCIAL RULE SYSTEMS AND RULE PROCESSES

Most human social activity—in all of its extraordinary variety—is organized and regulated by socially produced and reproduced rules and systems of rules.[1] Such rules are not transcendental abstractions. They are embodied in groups and collectivities of people—in their language, customs and codes of conduct, norms, and laws and in the social institutions of the modern world, including family, community, market, business enterprises, and government agencies. The making, interpretation, and implementation of social rules are universal in human society,[2] as are their reformulation and transformation. Human agents (individuals, groups, organizations, communities, and other collectivities) produce, carry, and reform these systems of social rules, but this frequently takes place in ways they neither intend nor expect.

There is often a vigorous situational "politics" to establishing, maintaining, and changing social rules and complexes of rules. Actors encounter resistance from others when they deviate from or seek to modify established rules. This sets the stage for the exercise of power either to enforce rules or to resist them, or to introduce new ones. Actors may disagree about, and struggle over, the definition or interpretation of the situation, the priority of the rule system(s) that apply, or the interpretation and adaptation of rules applied in the situation. Questions of power are central in our approach, since politics is typically associated with rule processes—especially those organizing and regulating major economic and political institutions. This includes not only the power to change or maintain social rules and institutional arrangements, but also the power relationships, and social control opportunities engendered by such arrangements. Many of the major struggles in human history revolve around the formation and reformation of core economic, administrative, and political institutions of society; the particular rule regimes defining social relationships, roles, rights and authority, obligations and duties; and the "rules of the game" in these and related domains. The world changes, making rule system implementation problematic (even in the case of systems that previously were highly effective and robust). Consequently, there are pressures on actors to adjust, adapt, reformulate, and reform their organizing principles and rules. Also, rules never specify completely or regulate actions fully (even in the most elaborate rituals and dramaturgical settings). The implementation of rules—and the maintenance of some order—always calls for cumulative experience, adjustment, adaptation, etc. In such ways, normative and institutional innovation is generated. There is a continual interplay—a dialectic, if you will—between the regulated and the unregulated (Lotman, 1975). Social situations—in continual flux and flow—persistently challenge human efforts to regulate and to maintain order. By means of rule systems and through the reform of established systems, social actors try to impose order on a changing, unstable, and sometimes chaotic world.

While social rule systems undergird much of the order of social life, not all regularities or patterns of social activity are explainable—or understandable—solely in terms of social rules. Situational conditions may block the implementation of particular rules and rule systems in social activities or make it costly to do so. By shaping action opportunities and interaction possibilities, ecological and physical factors limit the range of potential rules that can be implemented and institutionalized in practice. Because concrete material conditions constrain actors from implementing established rules in most situations, the actors are forced to adapt them. They may in some instances even be compelled—or strongly motivated—to radically transform or replace them in order to increase effectiveness, to achieve major gains, or avoid substantial losses. Thus, at the same time that social rule systems strongly influence actions and interactions, they are formed and reformed by the actors involved. Human agency is manifest in this dialectical process, with particular actors having their specific competencies and endowments, their situational analyses, interpretations, and strategic responses to immediate pushes and pulls to which they are subject.

The implementation or application of rules and rule systems is often problematic and requires special cognitive and practical skills—a complex process in its own right (see Burns and Gomolinska [2000a, 2000b] on rule-following, rule application, and the realization of rules in practice). Actors' cognitive and normative modes of analysis and judgment through which they apply or implement rules are organized through a shared operative institutional paradigm. The latter includes not only knowledge of the rule system but also interpretative rules and learned capacities for semantic and pragmatic judgments relating to the application of the system. The operative paradigm mediates between an abstract and often ideal(ized) rule system, on the one hand, and concrete situations in which actors implement or realize a rule system and its practices, on the other. In a word, they situate or contextualize abstract rules in relevant action situations.

Social rule system theory formulates and applies an approach to the description and analysis of institutions such as bureaucracy, markets, political systems, and science—major orders in modern societies. This entails more than a study of social structure, or a contribution to neo-institutionalism. It is a theory that analyzes the links between social structure in the form of particular institutional arrangements including role relationships, on the one hand, and social action and social interaction, on the other. The theory shows, for example, in what ways markets and bureaucracies are organized and regulated by social rules at the same time that actors, both inside and outside these institutions, maintain or change the organizing principles and rules through their actions and interactions.[3] This chapter focuses particularly on processes of radical rule change and institutional dynamics where human agency plays a key role. An important feature of such change is the mechanisms—and consequences—of institutional reform and transformation.

SOCIAL RULES AND THE PATTERNING OF ACTION

Social rule systems play a key role on all levels of human interaction. They provide more than potential constraints on action possibilities. They also generate opportunities for social actors to behave in ways that would otherwise be impossible, for instance, to coordinate with others, to mobilize and to gain systematic access to strategic resources, to command and allocate substantial human and physical resources, and to solve complex social problems by organizing collective actions. In guiding and regulating interaction, social rules give behavior recognizable, characteristic patterns, and make such patterns understandable and meaningful for those who share in the rule knowledge.

On the macro-level of culture and institutional arrangements, we speak of rule system complexes: language, cultural codes and forms, institutional arrangements, shared paradigms, norms, and "rules of the game."[4] On the actor level, we refer to particular norms, strategies, roles, action paradigms, and social grammars (for example, procedures of order, turntaking, and voting in committees and democratic bodies).[5] Social grammars of action are associated with culturally defined roles and institutional domains, indicating particular ways of thinking about and acting. In that sense, the grammars are both social and conventional. For instance, in the case of gift giving or reciprocity in defined social relationships, actors display a competence in knowing when a gift should be given or not, how much it should be worth, or, if one should fail to give it or if it lies under the appropriate value, what excuses, defenses, and justifications might be acceptable. Someone ignorant of these rules, e.g., a child or someone from a totally different culture, would obviously make mistakes (for which they would probably be excused by others). Similarly, in the case of "making a promise," rule knowledge indicates under what circumstances a promise may or may not legitimately be broken—or at least the sort of breach of a promise that might be considered acceptable (Cavell, 1979: 294). In guiding and regulating interaction, the rules give behavior recognizable, characteristic patterns[6]— making the patterns understandable and meaningful for those sharing in the rule knowledge. Shared rules are the major basis for knowledgeable actors to derive, or to generate, similar situational expectations. They also provide a frame of reference and categories, enabling participants to communicate readily about and to analyze social activities and events. In such ways, uncertainty is reduced and predictability is increased. This is so even in complex situations with multiple actors playing different roles and engaging in a variety of interaction patterns. As Harre and Secord (1972: 12) point out, "It is the self-monitoring following of rules and plans that we believe to be the social scientific analogue of the working of generative causal mechanisms in the processes which produce the non-random patterns studied by natural scientists."

Social rule systems play an important role in cognitive processes, in part by enabling actors to organize and to frame perceptions in a given institutional setting or domain. On the basis of a more or less common rule system, questions such as the following can be inter-subjectively answered: what is going on in this situation; what kind of activity is this; who is who in the situation, and what specific roles are they playing; what is being done; why is this being done? The participating actors—as well as knowledgeable observers—can understand the situation in intersubjective ways. In a certain sense, they can simulate and predict what will happen in the interactions on the basis of the applied rules. Hence, our notion of rule-based paradigms that are interpretative schemes but also the concrete basis for actors to plan and judge actions and interactions.[7]

Social rules are also important in normative and moral communications about social action and interaction. Participants refer to the rules in giving accounts, in justifying or criticizing what is being done (or not done), in arguing for what should or should not be done, and also in their social attribution of who should or should not be blamed for performance failures, or credited with success. Actors also exploit rules when they give accounts in order to try to justify certain actions or failures to act, as part of a strategy to gain legitimacy, or to convince others that particular actions are "right and proper" in the context.

So-called formal rules are found in sacred books, legal codes, handbooks of rules and regulations, or in the design of organizations or technologies that an elite or dominant group seeks to impose in a particular social setting. For instance, a formal organization such as a bureaucracy consists of, among other features, a well-defined hierarchical authority structure, explicit goals and policies, and clear-cut specialization of function or division of labor. Informal rules appear less "legislated" and more "spontaneous" than formal rules. They are generated and reproduced in ongoing interactions. The extent to which the formal and informal rule systems diverge or contradict one another varies. Numerous organizational studies have revealed that official, formal rules are not always those that operate in practice. In some cases the informal unwritten rules not only contradict formal rules but take precedence over them under some conditions. Informal rules emerge for a variety of reasons. In part, formal rules fail to completely specify action (that is, provide complete directions) or to cover all relevant (or emergent) situations. The situations (in which rules are applied or implemented) are particularistic, even idiosyncratic, whereas formal rules of behavior are more or less general. In some situations (especially emergent or new situations), actors may be uncertain or disagree about which rules apply or about the ways in which to apply them. They engage in situational analyses and rule modification, or even rule innovation out of which emerge informal rules (which may be formalized later).

However strongly actions are patterned by rules, social life is sufficiently complex that some imagination and interpretation are required in applying rules to a specific action and interaction context. Imagination generates variability in action from actor to actor, and even for a given actor over time. Rules are also interpreted in their application. Even highly formalized, systematic rules such as laws and written rules of bureaucracy are never complete in their specification. They have to be interpreted and applied using situational information and knowledge. Adaptations and improvisations are common, even in the most formally organized institutions. In this sense, rules are generative, and their interpretation and implementation more or less context-dependent. Interpretation varies across a population sharing a rule system, and also across time. In addition, rules will sometimes be learned or implemented with error, providing in some cases an incorrect model for others. Both of these factors result in variability. Moreover, if an action at deviance with cultural rules or standard interpretations is perceived by other actors as advantageous, it may be copied. Its ability to spread, providing a new cultural variant, depends on three factors: (1) its perceived desirability; (2) the ability of those with interests in the content of the rule system to sanction the use of the new rule (and to overcome the opposition of others); (3) the difficulty in acquiring, retaining, and implementing a rule at variance with core key social rules of the cultural system (Burns and Dietz, 1992a).

ADHERENCE TO AND COMPLIANCE WITH SOCIAL RULES

Contemporary social science research points up that social rule systems such as cultural formations, institutional arrangements, and norms are ubiquitous and regulative of much social action and interaction. However, actors adhere to and implement rules and rule systems to varying degrees. Compliance with, or refusal to comply with, particular rules are complicated cognitive and normative processes. Typically, there are diverse reasons for rule compliance. Several of the most important factors are:

(1) Interest factors and instrumentalism (stressed by public choice and Marxist perspectives on self-interested behavior). Actors may advocate rules to gain benefits or to avoid losses. For instance, interest groups introduce particular rules to exclude others from an institutionalized sphere or domain, whether a market, professional community, or political system, thereby attaining a monopoly or exclusive sphere for themselves and other "insiders." Such exclusionary rules may be enforced either by the authority of the state and/or by private authority (in the modern world private authority is often backed up by the state).

(2) Identity and status. Adherence to rules—and commitment to their realization—may be connected to an actor's identity, role, or status, and the desire to represent self as identified by or committed to particular rules. Elite actors are especially likely to be committed to a particular rule regime—not only because of vested material interests but because their identity, status, and meaning as significant social agents are closely associated with the rule regime, which defines their material and/or spiritual worth. It follows from the above that a major motivation in maintaining (or changing rules)—e.g., roles or distributive rules—is to maintain or change their social status.

(3) Authoritative legitimacy. Many rules are accepted and adhered to because persons or groups with social authority have defined or determined them, possibly by associating them with sacred principles or identifying their causal or symbolic relationship to actors' interests and status. In the contemporary world, we find the widespread institutionalization of abstract meta-rules of compliance that orient people to accepting particular definitions of reality and rule systems propagated by socially defined and often certified authorities, e.g., scientists and

other experts. The authority may be scientific, religious, or political (for instance in the latter case, the fact that a democratic agency has determined the rules according to right and proper procedures). Certain rules may even be associated with God, the sacred, and, in general, those beings or things that actors stand in awe of, have great respect for, and may associate with or share in their charisma by adhering to or following their rules.

(4) Normative cognitive order. Actors may follow rules—and try to ensure that others follow them—because the rules fit into a cognitive frame for organizing their perceptions and making sense of what is going on. Within any given institutional domain, particular rules or systems of rules make sense. For example, in a market context, certain norms of exchange have emerged, found support, and been institutionalized. They facilitate exchange, in part by reducing risks and transaction costs. In a certain sense, there is something reasonable about them (Boudon, 1995). In many functioning relationships and institutions, the participating agents seek trust and a sense of cooperativeness and order. Stealing, lying, cheating, murder, etc., violate basic principles of social order, of social solidarity and trust, and, therefore, are to a greater or lesser extent unacceptable. They do not make sense in terms of the type of social relationship and development actors want or hope to develop. People react negatively—even in cases where they are not directly affected (that is, there are no direct apparent self-interests), because the order is disturbed, potentially destabilized, and eroded.

(5) Social sanctions. Laws and formal organizational rules and regulations are typically backed up by specific social sanctions and designated agents assigned the responsibility and authority to enforce the rules. There are a variety of social controls and sanctions in any social group or organization which are intended to induce or motivate actors to adhere to or follow rules, ranging from coercion to more symbolic forms of social approval or disapproval, persuasion, and activation of commitments (in effect, "promises" that have already been made). Social sanctioning (for example, by a moral community, or by an elite or their agents) may take the form of various types of social disapproval and symbolic sanctions as well as material and physical sanctions. Group or community norms are typically enforced through diffuse networks. Group power rests in part on the individual's dependence on the group, and its ability to enable him or her to realize certain values or goals through the group (including the value of sociability). In order to gain entrance or to remain in the group, one must comply with key group rules and role definitions. Exclusion from the group, if there are no alternative groups, becomes a powerful sanction.

(6) Inherent sanctions. Many rules, when adhered to in specific action settings, result in gains or payoffs that are inherent in following those rules, such as going with (or against) automobile traffic. In many cases, the reasons for compliance are consequential. As Boudon (1996: 20) points out: in automobile traffic, we adhere to or accept as proper traffic rules, those relating to stopping, turning, etc., because without them, we recognize that the situation would be

chaotic, dangerous, even catastrophic. Most technical rules, for example relating to operating machines or using tools, entail inherent sanctions. Following them is necessary (or considered necessary) for the proper functioning or performance of the technology, or achieving a certain desirable outcome or solution. There-fore, many technical rules are followed habitually. Disregard of or casualness in following the rules leads to failure, and even damage to the technology or to the actors involved. Because technical rules often have this compelling aspect to them, they can be used to gain acceptance or legitimacy and to resolve social conflicts, at the same time that they can advantage some actors and disadvantage others.

(7) Veil of ignorance. Actors may not know the consequences of rule com-pliance and follow rules because they are given, taken for granted, or believed generally to be right and proper. The benefits of adhering to some rule systems can, however, mask hidden costs. For example, adherence to stereotypical gender roles may produce an ease and certainty about what one "ought" to do, and elicit positive response from others, but it may also produce psychic conflicts and limit individual or collective development. Ignorance is one aspect of the cognitive frame actors utilize, or may derive from the type of complex situation in which they find themselves. Often data about the consequences of implementing particular rule systems are not immediately available (or they concern states of the world long in the future), and both internalized beliefs and authorities play a decisive role in addressing such states of ignorance.

(8) Habits, routines, and scripts. Much rule-following behavior is unreflec-tive and routine. Many social rules are unverbalized, tacit, that is, part of a collective subconscious of strategies, roles, and scripts learned early in life or career, and reinforced in repeated social situations, for instance, sex roles or even many professional roles.[8] Of particular importance is the fact that rule systems learned in early socialization are associated with very basic values and meanings—even personal and collective identity—motivating at a deep emo-tional level commitment to the rules and a profound personal satisfaction in enacting them. Conformity is then a matter of habitual, unreflected, and taken-for-granted ways of doing things.

As indicated above, some social rules are enforced, others not: indeed, rules can be distinguished on the basis of the degree to which, and the circumstances under which, they are socially enforced or enforceable. Of course, regardless of the degree of enforceability, they may be complied with because of a desire for order, internal sanctions, or realizing one's role and self-identity. Many rules that actors rigorously adhere to are not socially enforceable, but nevertheless actors utilize them in organizing social activities and in shaping social order. Harre and Secord (1972: 17) emphasize the freedom of choice in relation to rules and roles.

> The mechanistic model is strongly deterministic; the role-rule model is not. Rules
> are not laws, they can be ignored or broken, if we admit that human beings are

self-governing agents rather than objects controlled by external forces, aware of themselves only as helpless spectators of the flow of physical causality.

In sum, actors conform to rule systems to varying degrees, depending on their identity or status, their knowledge of the rules, the meanings they attribute to them, the sanctions a group or organization imposes for noncompliance, the structure of situational incentives, and the degree competing or contradictory rules are activated in the situation, among other factors.

INSTITUTIONS AND COMPLEX INSTITUTIONAL ARRANGEMENTS

An institution is a complex of relationships, roles, and norms which constitute and regulate recurring interaction processes among participants in socially defined settings or domains. Any institution organizing people in such relationships may be conceptualized as an authoritative complex of rules or a rule regime (Burns, et al., 1985; Burns and Flam, 1987). Institutions are exemplified by, for instance, family, a business organization or government agency, markets, democratic associations, and religious communities. Each structures and regulates social interactions in particular ways; there is a certain interaction logic to a given institution. Each institution as a rule regime provides a systematic, meaningful basis for actors to orient to one another and to organize and regulate their interactions, to frame, interpret, and analyze their performances, and to produce commentaries and discourses, criticisms. and justifications. Such a regime consists of a cluster of social relationships, roles, norms "rules of the game," etc. The system specifies to a greater or lesser extent who may or should participate, who is excluded, who may or should do what, when, where, and how, and in relation to whom. It organizes specified actor categories or roles vis-à-vis one another and defines their rights and obligations—including rules of command and obedience—and their access to and control over human and material resources. More precisely, the following listing of institutional characteristics can be provided.

(1) An institution defines and constitutes a particular social order, namely positions and relationships, in part defining the actors (individuals and collectives) that are the legitimate or appropriate participants (who must, may, or might participate) in the domain, their rights and obligations vis-à-vis one another, and their access to and control over resources. In short, it consists of a system of authority and power.

(2) It organizes, coordinates, and regulates social interaction in a particular domain or domains, defining contexts—specific settings and times—for constituting the institutional domain or sphere.

(3) It provides a normative basis for appropriate behavior including the roles of the participants in that setting—their interactions and institutionalized games—taking place in the institutional domain.

(4) The rule complex provides a cognitive basis for knowledgeable participants to interpret, understand, and make sense of what goes on in the institutional domain.

(5) It also provides core values, norms, and beliefs that are referred to in normative discourses, the giving and asking of accounts, the criticism and exoneration of actions and outcomes in the institutional domain.

Finally, (6) an institution defines a complex of potential normative equilibria which function as "focal points" or "coordinators" (Schelling, 1963; Burns and Gomolinska, 2001).

Most modern institutions such as business enterprises, government agencies, democratic associations, religious congregations, scientific communities, or markets are organized and regulated in relatively separate autonomous spheres or domains, each distinguishable from others on the basis of distinctive rule complexes and each of which contributes to making up a specific moral order operating in terms of its own rationality or social logic. The actors engaged in an institutional domain are oriented to the rule system(s) that has (have) legitimacy in the context and utilize it (them) in coordinating, regulating, and talking about their social transactions.

Many modern social organizations consist of multi-institutional complexes. These combine, for instance, different types of institutionalized relationships such as market, administration, collegial, and democratic association as well as various types of informal networks. When different institutional types are linked or integrated into multi-institutional complexes, the resultant structure necessarily entails gaps and zones of incongruence and tension at the interfaces of the different organizing modes and social relationships (Machado and Burns, 1998). For instance, a modern university consists of scientific and scholarly communities, administration, democratic bodies with elected leaders, and internal as well as external market relationships. Such diverse organizing modes are common in most complex organizations or inter-institutional complexes. Rule system theory identifies several of the institutional strategies and arrangements including rituals, non-task-oriented discourses, and mediating or buffer roles that actors develop and institutionalize in dealing with contradiction and potential conflicts in complex, heterogeneous institutional arrangements (Machado and Burns, 1998). Moreover, it suggests that social order—the shaping of congruent, meaningful experiences and interactions—in complex organizations, as in most social life, builds not only on rational considerations but on non-rational foundations such as rituals and non-instrumental discourses. These contribute to maintaining social order and providing a stable context, which is essential for "rational" decision making and action.

PARADIGMS AND INSTITUTIONAL ARRANGEMENTS

The actors involved in a given institution use their institutional knowledge of relationships, roles, norms, and procedures to guide and organize their actions and interactions. But they also use it to understand and interpret what is going on, to plan and simulate scenarios, and to refer to in making commentaries and in giving and asking for accounts. Rule system theory stresses rule-based cognitive processes such as framing, contextualizing, and classifying objects, persons, and actions in a relevant or meaningful way (Burns and Engdahl, 1998a, 1998b; Burns and Gomolinska, 2000a, 2001; Carson, 1999, 2000a; Nylander, 2000). It also considers the production of appropriate or meaningful accounts, discourses, and commentaries in the context of the given institution.

Institutional rule knowledge is combined with other types of knowledge as actors engage in judgment, planning, interpretation, innovation, and application of rules. Such organization of rule knowledge and its applications—in perceptions, judgments, and actions—is accomplished through a shared cognitive-normative frame which we refer to as an institutional paradigm. It provides people a basis on which to organize and to define and try to solve concrete problems of performance and production in a given institutional domain (others using paradigm in this sense are Carson, 2000a, 2000b; Dosi, 1984; Dryzek, 1996; Gitahy, 2000; Perez, 1985).[9] Our conception builds upon institutional concepts such as rules and procedures as well as social relationships such as those of authority; it concerns the organization and regulation of concrete activities and the solution of concrete problems of action as much as the modeling and explanation of events. In acting and interacting within an institutional arrangement, social agents operate with one or more institutional paradigms as well as supportive discourses.

An operative institutional paradigm—associated with a particular institution—is a cognitive-normative framework which institutional participants use to contextualize and situate a rule system in concrete settings, as they define, make interpretations, carry out situational analyses, and make judgments concerning the application or implementation of the rule regime, or parts of it. At the core of such a paradigm is the rule regime itself—that is, the key organizing principles, values, norms, relationships, and roles that give form and identity to the institution—used in constituting and regulating interactions in appropriate settings. The rules and principles in the core are idealized in a certain sense.[10] Also found in such a paradigm—but more peripherally and discretionary—are the rules of interpretation, rules defining practical situational conditions to take into account, "rules of thumb," and other rules for making adjustments or adaptations of core rules and principles in some settings.

In sum, paradigms are actors' operative cognitive models, used in their concrete judgments and interactions to contextualize institutional rules, to conduct situational analyses, and to apply rules in their actions and interactions in the institutional domain. These operative models are constructed on the basis of core institutional rules and principles and incorporate complexes of beliefs, classification schemes, normative ideas, and rules of thumb which are used in conceptualizing and judging key institutional situations and processes, relevant problems, and possible solutions for dealing with key problems.

Figure 7.1   Core and Periphery of Operative Institutional Paradigms

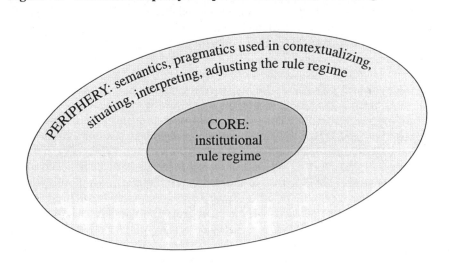

Single rules or rule systems are adjusted and compromised in concrete, practical interaction situations, taking into account situational or local conditions. Also, integrated into the operative paradigm—in its periphery—are rules of pragmatic interpretation and analysis, local styles and other cultural elements including values, norms, special social relationships that are not right and proper or legitimate parts of the institutional regime. The core and periphery components of an operative institutional paradigm are indicated in figure 7.1.

Clearly, (an idealized) system of rules is part and parcel of the paradigm and is institutionalized in particular arrangements and practices.[11] Although obviously interlocked, institutions and paradigms are affected differently in change processes, particularly those driven by tangible institutional problems. If, on the one hand, actors have a great investment in protecting the concrete institutional arrangements themselves, for reasons of power, security, predictability, and so on, rules are tightened, enforcement mechanisms are deployed, even strengthened (as in Michels's Iron Law of Oligarchy [1962]). The emphasis is on protecting ideas and principles that are already materialized, and sometimes this is done at great cost. If, on the other hand, actors have—or would like to make—a much greater investment in solving a problem(s) that the institutional arrangement and its operating paradigm have proven unable to manage, the actions taken are quite different. Rules are consciously broken in spite of possible or likely sanctions, supporters are rallied around possibilities rather than certainties, and short-term, concrete interests may be set aside in favor of long-term possibilities. There is a substantial shift in risk-taking orientations.

Operative Institutional Paradigm and Its Gaps and Anomalies

An institutional paradigm contains, among other things, a generally coherent complex of ideas, beliefs, assumptions, systems of classification, organizing principles, norms and procedures, and practical rules of thumb. It provides the cognitive basis upon which actors conceptualize, make decisions, and act together within an institutional domain. Within a given paradigm, actors mediate between abstract institutional principles and rules, on the one hand, and concrete interaction settings in which the rule system is to be implemented or realized in practice, on the other hand. Such mediation takes form in a variety of activities.

(1) In implementing or following rules, actors engage in processes of judgment, and make use of situational and interpretative knowledge for contextualizing and interpreting rules, ultimately applying them in order to organize and regulate their interactions.

(2) Actors use the institutional paradigm to interpret and understand what is going on (and also to define what should or should not be going on). It is the basis upon which actors generate concrete, contextualized expectations, predictions, and simulations.

(3) Actors concretely judge actions in the situation on the basis of appropriate rules, and thus can judge whether or not rule violation or deviance has taken place.

(4) An institutional paradigm is used in identifying, defining, and classifying institutional problems (and "non-problems"), potential solutions (including the use of appropriate and effective technologies and techniques), and source(s) of authority in the institutional arrangement. These judgments play a key role in the giving and asking of accounts and in justifying or legitimizing actions (see below).

Each paradigm is grounded in a particular set of fundamental assumptions and beliefs that a group of actors shares about reality.[12] It forms the frame for organizing their perceptions, judgments, and action that determines which phenomena are included in the picture—and which are excluded (Berger and Luckmann, 1969; Kuhn, 1970; Lakoff and Johnson, 1980). It is also the basis for operationally assigning values to certain actions and conditions, and encouraging and pursuing certain activities (or discouraging or even prohibiting others). A paradigm, as a collectively produced and maintained entity, is usually changed with reluctance—collective identities and interests are often closely associated with it, making difficult changes that are judged to alter its core elements that give it and the concrete institutional practices their identity. A paradigm whose core principles, values, and normative practices are deeply embodied in concrete institutional and identity-giving practices will tend to be durable and resilient.

Much of the day-to-day work of actors in a given institutional arrangement has the effect of cementing and normalizing the operative paradigm in a sense similar to that which Kuhn (1970) characterized as "normal science." Problems appear manageable, there is a high degree of consensus, and there is no sense of crisis or bold challenge. A paradigm necessarily focuses attention on certain phenomena while obscuring others—it is used to select and also restructure data so that they fit with its basic assumptions, categories, and rules.[13] Because of the paradigm's selectivity, its biased rules of interpretation, and its bounded character, the actors utilizing it experience difficulties understanding and explaining, or knowing how to deal in practical ways with some types of situation or problem. Some of these problems arise in connection with, or as a byproduct of, actions guided by the paradigm itself. That is, meaningful action—viewed from the perspective of the paradigm—generates anomalies and failures, which some participants define as problems (Spector and Kitsuse, 1987). These problems are not only cognitive but practical. Problems fail to be recognized or adequately addressed. Goals fail to be achieved. The stage is set for entrepreneurial actors to suggest new approaches and solutions, although these need not be radical.

In the context of a complex institution and a dynamic environment, some entrepreneurial actors creatively press limits and challenge what have been normal practices. They initiate and foster processes of change and give them direction. Certain developments—gaps and anomalies—inevitably emerge that can neither be adequately understood nor dealt with within the framework provided by the paradigm. These developments may be initially explained away or simply ignored. Or attempts may be made to understand and to deal with them through ad hoc interpretations and adaptations. However, if their effects are sufficiently powerful, or if they attract a sufficiently influential constituency of actors, the anomalies may motivate either major reformulation of the existing paradigm—or its replacement by a competing paradigm. The process of paradigm shift may entail both political struggle and confrontation (Hall, 1992) or may entail a more gradual and negotiated change with marginal conflicts and piecemeal adjustments (Coleman, et al., 1997).[14] Paradigm shift or replacement is not a purely cognitive development. It is associated with reorientation in actors' choices and actions, in their definitions of and practical attempts to deal with problems, and is expressed over time in concrete changes in the institutional arrangements and everyday practices.

One operative institutional paradigm can be distinguished from another paradigm in that it entails a distinctly different, and often incommensurable, way of framing, conceptualizing, judging, and acting in relation to particular classes of "problems" and "issues." This becomes of particular interest when actors guided by alternative paradigms compete with one another or each tries to impose her respective paradigm in a given institutional domain. Two competing institutional paradigms—each with its reality-defining features and discourses—may concern, for instance, "bureaucratic hierarchy" versus "democratic procedure," or "market problem-solving" versus "redistributive or welfare problem-solving" (see later).[15]

Institutional Paradigms and Their Discourses in an Institutional Context

An operative institutional paradigm is communicated and articulated through discourses—both descriptive narratives and conceptual metaphors—and through social action and interaction. These discourses and actions define social problems and potential solution complexes, and suggest the assignment of authority and responsibility in a given or appropriate area of activity. Through their characterizations of goals and purposes, and accounts of institutional performance—successes as well as failures—actors express or reveal their common paradigm. It is the means by which they perceive and judge the world, and organize, understand, and regulate their activities in the institutional domain.

Particular institutional discourses, serving as a means of describing, interpreting, and dealing with reality, are inspired and organized—directed and purposeful—on the basis of the institutional paradigm. The discourses indicate, among other things, parameters of acceptable problems, leaders, and performance. For instance, they may concern whether the current performance or status of the institution represents improvement or deterioration over earlier performance or status. In general, an institutional paradigm encompasses a range of institutional practices and strategies for addressing issues considered to be problems and for establishing authority for how to address various types of problems.

Key Components of Discourse

Paradigms are expressed and articulated, in part, through discourses concerning institutional "problems" or "threats" and "crises," the expressed distribution of institutional "authority and responsibility," the distribution of "expert authority," and "appropriate solutions" to deal with defined problems. The discourses refer to written rules and laws, and deeper, underlying principles that define the location and other particulars of rule-making authority, and set(s) of institutional strategies and practices for dealing with specific types of problems and issues (concerning public policy areas, see Sutton, 1998; Carson, 2000a, Carson, 2000b). The approach outlined here analyzes the ways in which discourses, on the one hand, express and articulate a paradigm and, on the other hand, frame and define reality (see, for example, Spector and Kitsuse, 1987; Hardy and Phillips, 1999; Kemeny, 1999). Discourses can be analyzed in terms of the categories or complexes of definitions they contain (Carson, 1999, 2000a, 2000b; Sutton, 1998).

(1) Problem/issue complexes—definition and characterization of key issues/problems, including characterizations of who is affected and how, and the broad categorizations of an issue or problem as social, moral, economic, political, etc. Here we find causal narratives—or narratives and statements that contain either implicit or explicit assumptions about the sources or causes of public issues and problems as well as narratives of threat which indicate or describe who is affected and the likely consequences if it is not "solved."

(2) Distribution of expert authority—the location and distribution of legitimate sources considered to be knowledgeable and authoritative on the issue or issues. It also defines who has the legitimacy to define a particular problem into—or out of—existence or to redefine an issue or problem into another institutional domain.

(3) Distribution of problem solving authority and responsibility—the location and distribution of appropriate problem-solving responsibility and authority, that is, the authority which has the formal or informal responsibility for addressing and/or resolving the issues or problems. Who is the legitimate authority (or authorities) for addressing and resolving the problem(s). This includes both institutional authority and legitimacy for making policy, and the responsibility for taking specific corrective action. This is related to expertise but, equally important, is grounded in the social roles and norms for determining who should be empowered to pass judgment, adopt new problem-solving strategies, or initiate necessary action on behalf of other members of the institution.

(4) Solution complexes—the form and range of acceptable solutions to institutional problems. Solution complexes include the particular way(s) in which the resolution of an issue or problem should be constructed, including the use of appropriate, available institutional practices, technologies, and strategies. Problems are often deliberately defined in ways that permit an issue to land in particular parts of an institutional apparatus (Nylander, 2000). This, in turn, dictates the range of both possible and likely responses (Sutton, 1998).

One challenge to discourse analysis is distinguishing between the "talk" that has weight and that which does not. One method is to make this distinction by tracing discourses that have been (1) adopted by key actors, and manifested in their discourses and actions, and (2) reflected at the institutional level in public statements and accounts, operating principles and rules, and/or organizational structure. Patterns of change are apparent whenever these discourses deviate in principle and content from previous ones. The processes by which paradigms shift and transformation of institutional arrangements take place through interaction processes are examined in the following sections. The major principle in the analyses is that the formulation and diffusion of significant new paradigms accompany and underlie many, if not most, radical reforms and structural revolutions. They provide new points of departure for conceptualizing, organizing, and normalizing social orders.[16]

DYNAMICS

Institutional change entails changes in the rules and/or enforcement activities so that different patterns of action and interaction are encouraged and generated (Burns, et al., 1985; Burns and Flam, 1987; Levi, 1990). Such changes may be initiated by various social agents. For instance, an elite "legislates" an institutional change, or a social movement brings about change through coming to direct power or effectively pressuring and negotiating with a power elite. Changes may also be brought about through more dispersed processes, e.g., where an actor discovers a new technical or performance strategy and others copy the strategy, and, in this way, the rule innovation diffuses through social networks of communication and exchange.

In general, there are several mechanisms that explain rule formation and change. (a) A well-known and common motivator underlying initiatives to establish new policies, laws, or institutional arrangements is self-interest, that is, the pursuit of opportunities to make gains (economists refer to "rent-seeking") or to avoid losses through changing rules. (b) Actors mobilize and struggle to realize what they consider an institutional ideal, for instance, a principle of distributive justice or common good that can be more effectively or more reliably realized through reforming institutional arrangements. (c) Key actors or groups in an institution encounter normative failure or gaps in applying a rule system in an appropriate domain, and try to overcome the failure or gap. Such a development may arise because of the emergence and influence of new social values. For instance, the rise of more radical egalitarianism or the spread of the normative idea of citizen autonomy draws attention to particular legal and normative limitations or gaps and leads to demands for new legislation and institutional arrangements, for example to advance gender equality. New technological developments often expose the limitations of existing laws and institutional arrangements. In the area of contemporary information technologies, existing laws concerning intellectual property rights have proven inadequate and have led to a number of reform efforts. Another example concerns Internet developments that have led to demands for increased regulation, because of the ready availability on the World Wide Web of pornography, extremist political, and racist pages, among other problems. Or new medical technologies—organ transplantation, life support technologies, and the new genetics—call for new normative principles, legislation, and institutional arrangements (Machado, 1998; Machado and Burns, 2000a, 2000b). In these and similar cases, rule formation and development must be seen as a form of normatively guided problem-solving.

Power, knowledge, interest, and values are key ingredients in institutional transformation. The power of elites to mobilize resources including wealth, legislative authority, and legal or coercive powers to maintain or change institutional orders is, of course, critical. But emerging groups and movements may also manage to mobilize sufficient power resources with which to challenge established elites, and to force or negotiate institutional change. The interaction between the establishment and challenging groups or movements is a major factor in institutional dynamics (Andersen and Burns, 1992; Flam, 1994). Such power mobilizations and conflicts are fueled by actors' material interests as well as ideal interests reflected in the particular paradigm to establish and maintain "right and proper" institutional arrangements.

In times of social change, the circumstances and actions of individuals and groups may come to deviate substantially from prescriptions and proscriptions of an institutionalized rule system. Since core rules are likely to be more deeply held, this generates a great deal of intra- and inter-personal conflict. Most men and women in Western societies have been raised (until rather recently) with a view of, for instance, the family as an institution in which the man provides economic support while the woman nurtures children and manages the household. Yet people attempting to follow these rules often find them neither practical nor satisfying. The "breakdown" of the family as an institution is an indication that the rules of the institution, as typically transmitted, internalized, and codified, no longer "fit," or are compatible with, reality and necessity. Thus, individuals actively seek to modify and reform the rules, creating new institutional arrangements or redefining old ones. Over time, a new paradigm of "family" has emerged. This process is conflictual and often painful.

Institutionalized changes may be brought about by the direct action of social agents or by the "selective forces" of social as well as physical environments. In the following discussion, we focus on the human problem-solving and creative capacities. We examine which agents or entrepreneurs initiate rule reform or, more radically, a paradigm shift, and why? Typically, the agents must have some basis of power or influence to bring about a paradigm shift or even changes in key rules, particularly the core rules through which a paradigm shift materializes. The particular basis of such power and the pattern of transformation may vary, as we discuss below.

Institutional entrepreneurs bring about changes in rules or, more radically, paradigm shift for a number of reasons. The following are not mutually exclusive). (a) For instance, the agents of change adopt a new paradigm because they believe it to be a better basis to solve problems—more effective, more powerful—than the existing paradigm. (b) The new paradigm may be seen as providing greater status or more legitimacy, because it represents a more advanced or "modern" form of institutional arrangement as opposed to "traditional" or non-modern forms. (c) The actors who introduce a new paradigm strongly identify with it—and may derive a new identity and status from it—as in the case of many "reform" and other social movements.

Actors who introduce and develop a new paradigm may not have intended to do so initially, but drift into it. For instance, an institutional elite or a decentralized agent adopts a new technology or technique which it considers to entail relatively minor changes in institutional procedures and rules. As additional problems emerge or are identified—which cannot be effectively analyzed and dealt with within the framework of the established paradigm—more rule changes and new approaches are considered for adoption. But failures and anomalies may continue to occur and to accumulate, and the elite—or some key members in it—develop a growing awareness of performance failings and a critical judgment of the old paradigm. Receptivity to alternative paradigms—or, at least, to the abstract notion of a possible alternative—increases.

A paradigm shift implies a change in all or part of the core of a paradigm, in particular, key organizing principles, normative ideas, and expectations regarding social relationships. For instance, in the shift from a communist society to a more liberal society in a number of Eastern European countries, emphasis was put on introducing market principles as well as values of civil rights and democratic multi-party systems. Of course, the concrete realization of such a shift required learning the practicalities of making such institutions operate properly. In other words, a certain development of the "semantics" and "pragmatics" of the new regimes also had to take place. In addition, shifts in discourse took place in connection with the transformation of several key components. (1) There was a shift in values and in defining the major problems facing the economy and society as a whole. Stress was placed on the problem of "liberating production" and "increasing productivity and wealth" rather than on "equality of distribution" or "rational central control and planning." Threats to a well-functioning economy and society were no longer "opposition to socialism" and "bourgeois economic behavior," but "state controls" and "monopoly powers" (in the economy as well as they polity). (2) The solutions were "privatization" and "political pluralism" in the form of parties and competitive politics. The role of the state would become more regulative rather than controlling-in-detail political and economic activities. In the case of the economy, for instance—rather than the state deciding the quantities and distribution of goods and services as well as prices and wages—independent, decentralized enterprises were to assume responsibility and authority to make plans and to determine quantities and qualities of goods and services as well as prices. Thus, solutions to economic problems were not expected solely or largely from the state, but from enterprises and market mechanisms. State organized "solutions" were to concern only a few, selected areas such as monetary policy, competition policy, and research and development policy. The policy measures to be taken tended to operate indirectly (for instance, monetary policy) rather than directly and in detail (price and wage controls, or detailed regulation of imports and exports). (3) Expertise was not embodied in the political leadership but in professional experts such as economists, lawyers, and business leaders. Three major patterns of institutional innovation and change may be identified.

Elite Adoption or Development of a New Paradigm and Institutional Arrangement

One common mode of institutional change takes place when authoritative or powerful agents acting within an institution or institutional arrangement reform it. This shift may take place through the elite or elite networks learning about and adopting a new institutional paradigm with its complex of beliefs, norms and values, organizing principles, and situational semantics and pragmatics. This implies, of course, new institutional conceptions and arrangements. Part of such a learning process may be connected with the elite facing new types of problems, e.g., connected with initiating a major project such as introducing radical new technologies or techniques (with unanticipated and unintended consequences), or dealing with new participants with different competencies or commitments than those recruited earlier. The emergence of such problems sets the stage for further problem-solving and institutional innovation. In some cases, the problems or problem situations appear intractable within the established paradigm and its institutional arrangements. On the basis of critical discussion and subsequent social learning, the stage is set for a paradigm shift—that is, changes occurring on the level of principles, values, and general norms—which results in innovation and transformation of institutional arrangements.

One such example can be seen in the recent shift in the EU's guiding principles for food policy from prioritizing market principles and goals to those of public health and consumer protection (Carson, 2000a). Numerous "technical" problems emerged during the deregulation associated with the establishment of the internal market in food and agricultural products. These necessitated the development of a number of new regulations at the European level, even under the guidance of a generally "free" market paradigm that emphasized the removal of regulatory obstacles to trade. However, the number of technical problems emerging continued to expand, until significant food-related crises developed (the best-known among these is "mad cow disease," or BSE). As a result of these crises, the European Commission adopted a new paradigm—new by virtue of a reordering of guiding principles to place public health and consumer protection not only above free-market deregulatory principles, but even establishing it as the means of protecting the progress made to date in establishing the internal market in food. These new priorities and the socially focused values of which they are a part have steadily been institutionalized in the subsequent regulatory actions with regard to food, the clearest example of which was the commission's response to discovery of dioxin contamination of Belgian poultry with an immediate ban on exports—quite different from the early treatment of the BSE case (in which the commission sided initially with the British government). Strong movement is now taking place toward the institutionalization of the reordered principles in the form of a reorganization of the commission. Primary responsibility and authority for dealing with food policy has been moved from the directorates dealing with agriculture and markets to a new directorate, Health and Consumer Protection. The proposed European Food Authority represents a further institutional expression of the new paradigm and its principles and values. Food policy in Europe is no longer seen as only, or even primarily, a commodity or market issue.

Physical Replacement of One Elite by Another with a Different Paradigm for Institutional Arrangements

An agent or agents with a new or different paradigm come into a dominant position—replacing an earlier elite—and introduce and institutionalize their own paradigm. These actors closely identify with the new paradigm as a basis for constructing and operating an institutional order and defining people's roles and status. This may occur through force (coup d'état, violent revolution), through democratic process (elections), or through demographic transition (e.g., generational shift). In other words, a new group or coalition with a new paradigm or model of social organization appears on the scene and assumes a position of power, enabling it to bring about a substantial shift in the institutional paradigm and arrangements. The shift in power and authority favoring actors—a new elite or coalition of elites—with a different paradigm may be preceded by a breakdown in consensus among established power elites about the appropriate paradigm or about reform of the existing paradigm. Some groups may refuse to obey established authority or to adhere to the established rule regime and its organizing principles and norms. Such shifts are apparent in the case of social revolutions such as those that took place in Eastern Europe in 1989, bringing to power through negotiated settlements and elections groups advancing liberal market and political paradigms (Saxonberg, 2000).

Diffusion and Adoption of a New Institutional Paradigm and Rule Systems

A new paradigm may be established through a process of diffusion in a community or social network; that is, there is a decentralized situation with multiple agents who enjoy control over their own situations and make independent decisions. In other words, learning and reorientation take place not at the level of an institutional elite, but on a decentralized or local level. Yet, this process results on an aggregate level in a definitive transformation of a prevailing paradigm and its particular institutional arrangements. The shifts need not be connected only with practical problems such as introducing new technologies and techniques, as part of "modernization initiatives." For instance, democratic concepts and norms have tended to spread from the political arena into other institutions such as the family, business enterprise, and health care system, implying that people have the right to know, to express themselves, and to engage in deliberations on matters that concern them and influence their conditions of life. In general, new ideas diffuse through social networks, in some cases in connection with economic and political crisis (see later discussion of the transformation of communist countries). One recent example concerns the spread to health services across Western and even Central Europe of market-oriented concepts along with new management and accounting techniques. This took place without solid evidence of their effectiveness, or knowledge about some of the more serious unintended negative consequences. Many health care units—and national policy makers—adopted such strategies in the context of economic pressures to reduce health care costs (and welfare costs generally) because management consultants and other experts advocated the step. Also, the fact that the same step was being taken in nation after nation, and system after system, apparently reassured many that such an approach must be on the right track.

Cultural change, associated with an eventual paradigm shift, may occur in the most subtle and incremental ways. Thus, an institutional order may be eroded as a result of participating actors introducing and applying in an ad hoc way alien or inappropriate rules to activities in the domain. For example, market concepts and rules such as profit-seeking strategies might be applied to what were previously "inappropriate" domains such as the family, community, or health care system, and result in the weakening or breakdown of these institutions. By breakdown we mean the inability to maintain or reproduce the institutional core; this might entail the loss of organizing principles or rules that define it or the disappearance of its most essential patterns of activity and social logic (provided, for instance, by particular principles of solidarity and justice).

Innovators and entrepreneurs—individuals and collective—initiate and carry through projects and play strategic roles in the shaping and reshaping of paradigms and particular institutional arrangements and practices: whether economic, political, technological, or scientific projects (Baumgartner and Burns, 1984; Andersen and Burns, 1992; Woodward, et al., 1994). Such agential driving forces are not restricted to business, government, or political elites initiating "from above." In a wide variety of social processes, individual and collective agents make history but not according to conditions of their choosing.

INSTITUTIONALIZATION OF PARADIGM SHIFTS AND INSTITUTIONAL INNOVATIONS: COMMITMENT, SOCIAL CONTROLS, AND SELF-REPLICATION

The maintenance and reproduction of an institutional paradigm and its concrete arrangements depend on sustaining the commitment of key actors and their knowledge of the paradigm and the situations in which it is to be implemented. In some cases, a large proportion of those involved must be committed and knowledgeable if successful reproduction of an institutional paradigm and its concrete arrangements is to take place. Reproduction also depends on the power and resource base which enable those committed to effectively execute and/or to enforce it. At the same time, the social and physical environments in which institutionalized activities are carried out operate selectively so that in a given time and place, institutional arrangements tend either to persist and be reproduced, or decline and disappear (Burns and Dietz, 1992a, 1992b; Dietz, et al., 1990).

In other words, actors' relative power resources, knowledge, and commitment play a key role in the maintenance and reproduction of a paradigm and its institutional order. Many paradigm changes and institutional innovations may be imagined or even initiated, but fail to be realized and reproduced. Consolidation and maintenance depend on there being a group of actors committed to the paradigm shift, whatever the basis of this commitment, who can mobilize resources and enforce or persuade adherence to the rules. In order to strengthen an institution and protect it from attack, one delivers concrete benefits (including security and predictability) to supporters and withdraws benefits and delivers concrete sanctions to those who oppose it. To strengthen a paradigm, one seeks to institutionalize it, but while it is the challenger, it must inspire supporters to forgo benefits and face possible hardships in pursuit of a greater principle—or greater promise down the road.

The development of cognitive capabilities as a sort of conceptual infrastructure is equally as important as material resources and the capacity to sanction. The paradigm contains, on the one hand, knowledge about particular institutional organizing principles, relations, and norms to be implemented and maintained and, on the other, situational and technical knowledge enabling them to realize or implement the organizing principles and rules in relevant settings.

The processes of paradigm maintenance—or social reproduction as sociologists refer to it—may be organized by the ruling elite who allocate resources and direct and enforce maintenance. Typically, institutional reproduction takes place through both elite direction as well as the active engagement of non-elite members. Thus, reproduction may also be organized with a broad spectrum of participants engaged in processes of knowledge transmission, socialization, sanctioning, and pressures to demonstrate institutional loyalty. In cases where elites and other participants (or more generally central and peripheral groups) stand in opposition to one another, this generates not only tensions, but also uncertainty about the effective reproduction of an institutional order, opening up the possibility of future transformations.

In transformations brought about in connection with elite learning and reorientation, the elite manages the process of transformation themselves. In a deliberate way, they can determine its speed, composition, and scope. They typically will make use of their powers to try to determine the scope and speed of introduction of the new arrangements (although they often fail, as we suggest later). With elite replacement, the new elite struggles with the old elite and competes with allies that participate in the transformation. There is often distrust of the old order and its apparatus of social control and self-replication. As a result, the new leadership is likely to try to establish quickly a variety of projects setting up entirely new institutional arrangements and mechanisms to deliver on promises; they also institute systems of control, socialization, and recruitment of loyalists into governance structures. Irrespective of such ambitions, they are often forced—by constitutional constraints, societal norms, or resource limitations—to rely on many established components of the old order.

In both elite reorientation and elite replacement, the initiation of major reforms and developments result in manifold unintended consequences as well as new problems and predicaments. Further reforms, not anticipated initially, must be undertaken. Many of these affect, directly or indirectly, the apparatus for maintenance and self-replication of the institutional order. That is, if the initial reform is to succeed, the elite may be compelled to introduce further reforms of institutional arrangements that earlier operated selectively and more or less predictably in maintaining and self-replicating the previous order (through the strategic mechanisms of institutionalized selection, socialization, conditions of incumbency and career, and capacity to inspire legitimacy and respect). As a result of such reforms—albeit selective ones—unanticipated consequences are generated. New power bases emerge, and in connection with these, group initiatives and coalition formation take place challenging the governing elite. In this way, reforms undertaken by the ruling elite may erode or destabilize unintentionally (and typically, unexpectedly) key components of the apparatus for social control and self-replication. This type of development is suggested by the Gorbachev reforms, since he neither intended nor anticipated the developments that would destroy the Soviet regime.

In general, an institutional reform will be historically vulnerable when one or more of the conditions for rule enforcement, rule transmission, and self-reproduction are not satisfied (cf. Stinchcombe, 1968: 112). Even initially successful institutionalization of a reform may be undermined by the complex processes suggested above. There are numerous historical examples of what appeared initially to be successful radical institutional reforms, or revolutions—with great visions of new, even utopian orders, collapsing and being transformed into a quite different order—typically not the one preceding the revolution. Another major type of factor affecting the fate of revolutions concerns powerful outside forces. For a radical reform to be successful, it is essential that outside forces cannot or do not operate to undermine or to block the continuation or spread of the new order. This is particularly problematic when a radical reform creates a particular "alien," threatening order—materially as well as symbolically. The revolutionary orders of an expansive imperial Japan, Nazi Germany, and Revolutionary France—in their aggressiveness and wars against others—were initially very successful. But they all were confronted eventually with external forces that brought them down. Failed attempts at establishing and maintaining new orders fill the pages of history. Failure may take place quickly, or it may be drawn out for a considerable period of time. This is part of the evolutionary processes of history (Burns and Dietz, 1992a, 1992b, 1997).

APPLICATIONS: RADICAL REFORM AND REVOLUTIONARY TRANSFORMATION OF INSTITUTIONAL ORDERS

Social rule system theory has been applied especially to the analysis of markets (Burns and Flam, 1987; Burns, 1990, 1995) administration (Burns and Flam, 1987; Machado, 1998; Woodward, et al., 1994), and politics (Andersen and Burns, 1992, 1996; Burns and Flam, 1987; Burns 1999; Fowler, 1995) as well as the tensions and dynamics of their interfaces (Machado, 1998; Machado and Burns, 1998). Among other things, analysis has been directed at the politics of rule processes, in particular, initiatives—and opposition to attempts—to reform or transform particular rule systems.

The systematic, collective reflection on—and discourse about—many rules and institutional arrangements in modern society gives expression to societal values relating to conceptions of effectiveness as well as of distributive justice and morality. Critical reflection sets the stage for reform efforts and social struggle. This is not only an apparent part of modern social life, but also one of the most important forces bringing about the frequent reformation of paradigms and institutional arrangements. Actors mobilize and negotiate, setting in motion concrete cultural and institutional mechanisms of change.[17] There is a strategic aspect—and politics—to maintaining or changing the rules of constitutions, laws, administrative regulations, and "rules of the game."

Here we focus briefly on radical reforms and revolutions. These are transformations of institutional orders entailing a fundamental, comprehensive, multi-dimensional alteration of an institutional paradigm with its particular structural arrangements and practices (Sztompka, 1993: 305).[18] Revolutions highlight not only some of the major processes whereby human agents shape and establish a new institutional order, displacing an old order, but also the variety of roles agents play in these processes. However the transformation of an institutional order is brought about—whether through violence, normative persuasion, negotiation, or elections, or some combination of these—it entails the interaction of social agents and the intended and unintended consequences of their actions. They generate social variety in the form of innovations in conceptions and beliefs, values, technologies and institutional arrangements. There emerge new paradigms including new principles and rules for organizing economic, political, or cultural activities. For example, "political revolution" means not only changes in particular institutional arrangements of government and politics, but new normative concepts and values as well as new symbols and discourses—in short, the establishment of a new paradigm of political order.

Violence—as well as speed of change—is often included in definitions of revolutionary change. Many if not most major structural developments are associated with social conflict—for instance, the conflict between those initiating a transformation in trying to establish a new institutional order, and those opposing the initiative and trying to maintain the old order. Different actors are committed or opposed in differing degrees to a particular transformation, its speed, its means of realization, or its scope. But in many instances, conflicts associated with revolutionary change are not violent, or the level of violence is highly circumscribed. Indeed, the history of much human structural development, including "political revolutions," is marked by the absence of major violence. Even transformations in systems of government, whether for better or worse, have taken place with a minimum or low degree of violence, as in the case of the recent division of Czechoslovakia, the secession of Norway from Sweden in 1905, or the 1989 uprising in Eastern and Central Europe that led to the collapse of communism, for example the "Velvet Revolution" in Czechoslovakia. Sztompka (1993: 305) notes that these entailed popular revolts before which well-armed governments collapsed: "The threat was not one of force but of passive resistance and mass strikes, which would bring a modern society to a standstill."

The following are among the key features often distinguished in the literature on revolutions (Sztompka, 1993): the degree that violence or force plays a role as opposed to other means of social influence and control; the particular roles of different social agents, especially the level of popular participation; the rapidity of transformation; the scope of the transformation; the extent to which a transformation is deliberative or designed as compared to one that results from the uncoordinated and spontaneous actions of many agents. These features need not be included in the definition of revolution as radical social transformation— rather, they distinguish between different transformative processes and outcomes in ways that call for analysis and explanation.

This approach to revolutionary transformation conceptualizes structural stability and change as a function of agential as well as structural factors. Structural factors may be of a purely social character—particular cultural forms and institutional arrangements—or of a physical or material character—for instance, natural resource distributions—or combinations of these. Agential forces may operate in deliberate ways, or spontaneously; they may be global or largely local; the agents may be relatively few or many, similar in type or substantially very different. The theory enables us to identify agents and structural mechanisms that undermine or block the maintenance and reproduction of the old institutional order or set the stage for the establishment and evolution of entirely new orders. An established order—a type of structural equilibrium—fails or is rejected, and a new institutional order—a new structural equilibrium—is established and reproduced (possibly, only temporarily) through the institutionalization of a new paradigm with its identifying organizing principles and system of rules.

Utilizing the distinctions introduced above, we shall focus on agential-driven processes of transformation; for a treatment of social structural and environmental selective mechanisms underlying social transformation, see Burns and Dietz (1992a, 1992b, 1997). Transformations associated with either elite reorientation (I) or replacement (II) typically entail decisive events and actions; that is, they are "legislative" in character. They involve the design, development, and implementation of a new order through deliberative choice. Such an agent is either a ruling elite or a new power group which replaces a former ruling elite.[19] The first two types of revolutionary change are characterized by identifiable, more or less organized agents, whether with few or many participants. The transformations, even if drawn out over considerable periods of time, have a decisive character. Through particular collective actions, a new institutional order is, in a certain sense, legislated. The third type (III) entails the accumulative effect of a multitude of "local" or decentralized actions that add up to a major social transformation. The agents involved are autonomous but typically interconnected, for instance in communication and exchange networks. New paradigms and types of relationship, institutional arrangement, and power bases emerge through ongoing, diffused activities and developments. Of course, such "organic processes" may be combined with "legislative" type processes. Stinchcombe (1968: 119) noted that workers, spontaneously forming labor unions and struggling to gain the right to form such unions and to bargain, created new forms of organized power and eventually contributed to the institutionalization (sanctioned by the state) of labor-management negotiation and conflict-resolution and increased egalitarianism in the society. Most historical revolutions consist of varying mixtures of all three transformative processes.

Elite Paradigm Adoption

A ruling elite is converted to a new paradigm of institutional order, and uses its position of power to bring about transformation of the established order. This may come about through effective persuasion or "missionary efforts" of outsiders, or it may come about gradually as the elite is confronted with types of problem for which they feel compelled—after failure in earlier, decisive attempts to apply established solutions—to seek radically new solutions. In such instances, there already exists a more or less established institutional order, with authority and power relationships, within which the transformative initiatives are initiated and implemented.

Of particular interest here are processes that entail learning, creativity, and entrepreneurship whereby an elite or elite network change their perspective on the institutional order, and adopt or develop a paradigm with new beliefs, value orientations, and organizing principles, which it tries to realize or implement (Baumgartner and Burns, 1984; Woodward, et al., 1994). These changes are accompanied by, and give expression to, new discourses. That is, discursive transformations accompany a paradigm shift and institutional transformation (Carson, 2000a, 2000b). Typically, there is a critique of the old institutional order—for its failings, its anomalies, its low status or legitimacy—and discourses on the advantages of the new. These judgments may be based on the apparent success of other communities or societies which utilize the new paradigm in constructing and operating their institutional arrangements, whether in government, armed forces, or economic areas. In general, whether there is a "push" to overcome a crisis or a "pull" to make gains through innovative efforts, the stage is set for the adoption of a new paradigm and institutional reform and innovation.

(1) A new problem situations appear to the elite as intractable within the established arrangements, or the elite believes that major problems can be handled within the new institutional order more effectively than within existing arrangements.

(2) The new problems may derive from earlier innovations in connection with the introduction of new institutional arrangements or new technologies, which result in types of problems that are believed solvable only by forging ahead with and elaborating the new arrangements.

(3) Elite actors may be faced with problems or issues, social conflicts or potential conflicts, major institutional constraints, or performance "failings" or "gaps" that are seen as hindering or blocking successful competition with rivals.

(4) The elite takes restructuring initiatives in order to mobilize support or to gain internal or external status and legitimation.

(5) A paradigm shift among elite actors—that is, changes occurring on the level of ideas, values, norms, and organizing principles—need not be directly connected to practical problems such as dealing with internal or external competition or opposition, or trying to introduce and develop new technologies and techniques. New values may be entertained by the elite as a result of a moral or religious conversion, or a gradual acquisition and commitment to new values and ways of seeing the world, as in the spread of modernization concepts.

The elite exploits its position of domination to mobilize human and material resources and to promote a new paradigm and impose its embodiment in concrete institutional arrangements and practices. A historically important class of transformations of this type occurs when a leader, group, or party uses the power of the state to drive modernization, entailing revolutions of several types: industrialization; commercialization and rationalization of markets; the development and use of new types of knowledge including technological and scientific; educational transformation; and changes in organizational, administrative, political, and legal arrangements; professionalization of public administration and the armed forces, among other things (Kamali, 1998). The paradigm(s) of modernization has been imposed selectively—for instance, typically limiting democracy. This has been a recurrent pattern of social transformation since the industrial revolution: Among others, the Meiji revolution in Japan (1868), Haile Selassie's transformation of Ethiopia (1930–74), Pahlavis Shah's (1925–79) restructuring of Iran, and Gorbachev's initiatives launching glasnost (opening) and perestroika (restructuring). For example, those who engineered the Meiji revolution in Japan were motivated largely by the desire to meet effectively military and political threats from Western powers. Or, the motive may be to overcome economic and technological failings (with military and strategic implications) as in the case of the reform efforts of Gorbachev in the eighties in the face of Soviet economic and technical stagnation. He and his allies believed that some degree of reform and restructuring were necessary in order to assure the viability of the Soviet Union as an economic, technological, and military power. Using the authority of the party and the government, Gorbachev and his allies not only initiated a paradigm shift in the former Soviet Union but at least permitted major initiatives for restructuring in other communist countries of Eastern Europe and the Baltic states.

In sum, transformations characterized by reorientation of a ruling elite entail processes of learning, conversion, and entrepreneurship. Using their power and authority to initiate and institutionalize substantial transformations, the elite is in a position to introduce and act on the basis of a new paradigm. Power and authority are highly concentrated, rather than diffused or divided among different societal agents. Under the direction of the elite adhering to a new paradigm, a new institutional order is launched and unfolds. A major structural feature of such transformations is the more or less intact domination by a ruling elite, at least initially (see later discussion on unintended developments, including erosion of elite power as an unintended consequence of such innovations).

Elite Replacement

In some radical transformations, a distinct group from inside or outside society with a substantially different paradigm takes power.[20] Such shifts in power may be brought about by military or democratic means.[21] The group uses its newly acquired power to implement its paradigm of institutional order. Such a power shift translates into a paradigm shift and the transformation of institutional arrangements and practices (as opposed to mere replacement by a group or corporate actor keeping in place the same paradigm and its social order). This type of transformation is apparent in the social revolutions that have taken place in Eastern Europe since 1989–90 where opposition movement(s) came to power and replaced to a greater or lesser extent a planned economy and a monopolistic political structure with market and liberal political paradigms. But the shift may also take place more gradually and surreptitiously. Typically, a power shift may be preceded by a breakdown in consensus among power elites about the problems of the institutional order and the appropriate ways of dealing with them. At the same time, peripheral or outside groups refuse loyalty or obedience to an established paradigm or its authority, and mobilize sufficient powers of their own to countervail the efforts of the governing elite to enforce the old institutional order. These struggles may be relatively peaceful or they may be violent; they may be rather focused—simply dealing initially with governmental and legal spheres—or broad in scope, as was the case of many of the communist "revolutions," commencing with the Bolshevik revolution. As in all of the communist revolutions, such revolution entails the introduction of party monopoly and domination of government ("dictatorship of proletariat"), nationalization of most means of production, establishment of a planning and control apparatus over the production and distribution of goods and services, control of the movements of people and resources, provision of universal education and health care, rapid deployment of women in the labor force, etc.

Challenges to institutionalized authority entail agents criticizing, deviating, and innovating—in general, refusing to accept the established institutional order and practices. These are moments of acts of heroism, charisma, and collective effervescence (Tiryakian, 1995: 273). An individual or group is able to put into play and to articulate the strong emotions, the aspirations, the pent-up feelings of the larger collectivity. This creates the sense of a moment of decisive break with the past and the opening toward a substantially different (although not fully knowable) future. Defining characteristics of revolutions with elite replacement are power struggles, the mobilization and organization of opposing forces, the development of strategies, and the interactions between, for instance, state agencies and opposition groups or movements (Flam, 1993).

In sum, the pattern in a revolution with elite replacement is one of more or less open struggle for, and ultimately a shift in domination relationships. A group, organization, or movement with a new paradigm of institutional order takes political power. Such shifts may take place through the replacement of an elite by a relatively few persons or groups leading a coup d'état;[22] or they may take place with great popular participation, as in the classical popular revolutions.[23] The struggle over power may be short, as in coup d'états, or drawn out as in guerrilla warfare (eventually turning into conventional war as in, for example, the Chinese and Cuban revolutions). There are typically even drawn out conflicts and struggles among those who succeed in taking power—the struggles are intense and extended in part because of the very erosion and destabilization of the old order. The outcome or subsequent development of revolutionary transformation is not a given or predictable. There is more than a simple unfolding or elaboration of a particular paradigm. The concrete struggles of revolutionary processes drive innovation and transformative efforts further—especially in the case of an elite shift that is accompanied by competition for revolutionary leadership. Thus, there is not only struggle between opposition movement(s) and the established order but also struggle among the different factions of a revolutionary movement. The factions differ in their perspectives, aims, and strategies—that is, there is variation in their paradigms or in the interpretations of a more or less common paradigm—and they modify and develop these in the course of the struggle. Indeed, the initiating agents often start out with rather different conceptions of a new social order, and modify and elaborate these over time. Typically, the eventual paradigm that emerges as triumphant is likely to have been modified substantially during the course of struggle and the revolutionary process, as in the conceptualizing of the Islamic Republic of Iran (Kamali, 1998). In general, elite replacement processes—particularly in broad-based revolutionary movements—tend to be highly competitive. Competitive mechanisms typically drive innovation and the generation of variety. Historically, this is a major evolutionary mechanism (Burns and Dietz, 1992a).

Organic Transformation

Organic types of transformation entail multiple actors initiating decentralized or local change, without coordination or obvious direction, although the actors are typically engaged in communicative and other types of networks. On the aggregate level, these initiatives add up to substantial transformation. The participating actors in the purest case have no intention to bring about such a global transformation. The process of transformation is diffused in time and space. It is difficult, if not impossible, to define a moment of change or transition. There are spatial and temporal continuities, but from a larger perspective, transformation is accomplished through the "spontaneous," uncoordinated actions of many social agents. Although revolution is not directed or determined on a global or macro-level, macro-institutional arrangements and polices are likely to affect the course of the transformation, and a certain directedness may emerge from such a "spontaneous order." Arguably, much of the early industrial revolution was of this type, creating and developing new types of socio-technical systems.[24] These included new institutional arrangements combined with machines and machine processes to make use of coal, iron ore, and other raw materials on a scale and with a rapidity never before achieved (or imaginable). Industrialization also entailed a technical revolution in the conception and use of mechanization, of steam and the steam engine, of electricity and of the internal combustion engine, and eventually of the atomic reactor and of air and space-craft. But strategic in all these engineering developments was the diffusion and establishment of organizational and institutional forms to exploit and develop the new and varying possibilities.

In sum, organic transformations of social orders entail the emergence and diffusion of a new paradigm to multiple decentralized agents, resulting in changes in technologies, relationships, roles, and norms. Such transformations occur without any single agent or group of agents planning or negotiating the overall pattern. The rate of change and the scope of any given change are variables of interest in the systematic study of revolutions as are the social conflicts and struggles around these changes, and the specific forms such struggles take in different phases of societal transformation.

CONCLUSION

Competition, in which particular actors struggle more or less openly for power, is one of the major mechanisms driving social change in an organic mode—but not, of course, according to a program, plan, or design. Weber (1951) stressed the importance of such "competitive processes" in social change, under conditions where there is no simple power structure or domination. Thus, Europe as a system of interconnected states in competition with one another operated to drive the transformative process of rationalization. There was no unified empire, as, for example, in China.[25] Weber (1951: 61) argued, "Just as competition for markets compelled the rationalization of private enterprise, so competition for political power compelled the rationalization of state economy and economic policy in the Occident and in the China of the Warring States. In the private economy, cartellization weakens rational calculation which is the soul of capitalism; among states, power monopoly prostrates rational management in administration, finance and economic policy."[26] In plain terms, a lack of competition tends to inhibit or restrain transformative processes. However, this is not the case under the conditions of transformations based on elite reorientation, where a leader or elite undergoes learning and conversion and initiates significant restructuring, whatever the reason for which it does so.

Competitive processes may be constrained in varying degrees. Some social orders have elaborate institutionalized systems for regulating competition and resolving conflicts. Others have few such arrangements; or the arrangement collapses under the pressures of crisis or revolutionary conditions, when key actors no longer adhere to or accept the arrangements. The degree of violence will depend on whether there are established, institutional arrangements within which to negotiate the proposals for change—and whether these arrangements remain intact under conditions of rapid social transformation. Struggle carried out within established institutional arrangements makes peaceful or negotiated power shifts more probable (Burns and Flam, 1987: 94–98; Tumin, 1982). The transition to more modern forms of government and the establishment of democracy and the rule of law in Europe have taken place in many different ways and taken different forms: gradual, largely peaceful transformations in some of the smaller countries such as those of Scandinavia; violent transformations that appeared to lead to a more or less new stable order as in France, Germany, Portugal, Russia, and Spain, among others. These processes take decades or longer—and still continue as in the case of major transformations in China and Russia in this century.

Given the complexity of the societies and the transformation which we have considered, multiple transformations can be expected to take place simultaneously, and one transformation leads to another. For instance, modernization entails such multiple transformations, as pointed out earlier. These have been typically distributed over social space and time, and they are neither particularly coherent nor orderly. The Chinese, Russian, and Iranian revolutions were not isolated events but part of much larger modernization transformations that still continue. Russia (1905, 1917, 1990), China (1911, 1949), and Iran (1909, 1979) have each had two or more socio-political revolutions of this century. After each socio-political revolution, a type of partial or quasi-equilibrium was established—that is, a social order with its configuration of social agents, key organizing principles, power and authority relationships, and mechanisms of governance, social control, and reproduction. These structures each had certain properties and development tendencies. There were also lingering problems and anomalies. In all of these countries, industrialization, urbanization, and educational and scientific transformations have entailed types of revolutions in their own right, although not as visible or as dramatic as their socio-political revolutions. Further transformations and uncertainties continue.[27] Claude Fohlen (1973: 8), referring to the industrial revolution in France, stresses rightfully, "We must recognize that the process once launched knows no limits and that the revolution is rather a series of revolutions." Furthermore, if, in these processes, there are few institutionalized means to deal with the sense of disorientation, loss, and injustice experienced in some groups, then the likelihood of major social confrontations and struggle, socio-political crisis, and institutional failure are increased greatly.

History offers not only rich variety but also patterns of great complexity. A key feature of institutional innovation and revolutionary processes are, in many instances, the positive feedback loops that amplify the initial changes that first may have appeared to be minor (Burns, et al., 1985). An initial step—even a cautious one—may lead to intensification and radicalization of the process. The process may be initiated by actors with moderate or limited aims within a particular paradigm. The actors do not expect, and even fail to anticipate, that the introduction of a particular concept, technology, or change in an institutional arrangement would have the radical consequences that ensue. Even limited, piecemeal reforms of laws and administration, may add up over the longer term to the formation of a radically new order—a revolution (Sztompka, 1993: 305). A sequence or cascade of such changes can result in a major transformation, as in the case of the transition from monarchy to democracy in many of the smaller nations of Europe such as the Scandinavian countries. If one traces such developments over a sufficiently long time frame, a revolution can be discerned in the form of significant, identity-changing transformations from, for example, strong monarchy to a weak monarch and eventually to democracy or constitutional democracy, or from rural, agricultural societies to industrialized, urban societies.

Notwithstanding the importance of agents in social change, structural factors remain key factors in the theory, as pointed out earlier. These factors include not only the institutional arrangements but also material conditions external to a social system. Elsewhere Burns and Dietz (1992a, 1992b, 1997) have examined transformations where the availability of natural resources and transformations of the biological and physical environments are critical factors, although human agents and their cultural and institutional frames with which they operate still play an important role. Most historical processes entail the interplay between agential and structural factors. Typically, agency and structure interact and combine, recombine, and are transformed in new ways (Tiryakian, 1995: 270). Tiryakian (1995) is correct in pointing out that specific individuals play key roles in the face of structural failings and anomalies—Gorbachev with his dramatic initiatives that brought about important structural changes, or Rabin and Arafat in the negotiations between Israel and the PLO, or Mandela and DeKlerk in South Africa in 1992–93. They all addressed critical problem complexes that could not continue indefinitely. The complex of serious problems constitutes a political agenda. Sooner or later, if not these agents, others would have taken some initiative. Of course, the particular ways the initiatives were eventually taken, the configuration of actors involved, and the immediate set of conditions operating imply different processes, possibly radically different scenarios. These are the historical contingencies—the sources of surprise—that Tiryakian (1995) rightfully stresses.

NOTES

1 We are grateful to Craig Calhoun, Shmuel N. Eisenstadt, Mats Franzen, Rogers Hollingsworth, Mark Jacobs, Masoud Kamali, Nora Machado, Bryan Pfaffenberger, Steve Saxonberg, and Nina Witoszek for their comments and suggestions on parts of earlier versions of this chapter.

2 Among researchers who have developed and applied rule concepts in the social sciences are Burns and Flam (1987), Cicourel (1974), Giddens (1984), Goffman (1974), Harre (1979), Harre and Secord (1972), Lindblom (1977), and Twining and Miers (1982).

3 Rule system theory was developed within a complex of interrelated theories—actor

system-dynamics (Burns, et al., 1985; Burns, et al., 2000). The latter encompasses a theory of socio-cultural evolution (Burns and Dietz, 1992a, 1992b, Burns, et al., 2000; Dietz, et al., 1990), a sociological theory of games and interaction (in which the classical theory of games is a special case (Burns, 1990; Burns and Gomolinska, 2000, 2001)), and a theory of institutions and institutional dynamics, namely rule system theory (Burns and Flam, 1987). The latter provides analytic leverage on several levels: (1) As a meta-theory: it indicates a way of conceptualizing and analyzing norms, roles, social relationships, and institutions. (2) As a basis of classification: it distinguishes types of rules and rule governed situations. For instance, inclusion and exclusion rules, time and space rules, or rules defining types of appropriate situations, participants, technologies and resources, and activities. (3) As a basis to orient the social scientist to particular empirical phenomena, among others: (a) the complexity of, and contradictions in, rule systems such as norms, roles, and institutional arrangements; (b) the fact that rules not only organize and regulate social action and interaction but play a role in cognitive processes in enabling actors to understand and make sense of what is going on, a basis to simulate or predict social interaction and development; they are also used in the asking and giving of accounts and the formulation of normative arguments and discourses; (c) the clash or contradiction between actors adhering or committed to different paradigms and rule systems which they try to apply in a given interaction situation or domain; (4) As a basis to explain rule formation and change.

4 Lotman (1975) and Posner (1989) offer valuable semiotic perspectives with important (not yet analyzed on our part) parallels.

5 There are not only role grammars but semantics and pragmatics. See later discussion on processes of meaning, interpretation, and adaptation associated with rule application and implementation.

6 To varying degrees actors collectively produce and reproduce patterns of appropriate or acceptable possibilities. This can be conceptualized and mathematically developed as an ideal point or collection of "approximations." Thus, a community of actors sharing a rule complex recognize a wide variety of varying performances of a given rule as a family of resemblances, or "the same thing" (Burns, et al., 1994). Both in this sense—and in the sense that social rules are never learned identically and undergo different rates of adaptation and change over time—our concept of rule, and of culture generally, is distributive (Hannerz, 1990).

7 The cultural complex of rule systems contributes to making social life more or less orderly and predictable and solves problems of "existential uncertainty" within the group or community bearing and adhering to the culture (Burns and Dietz, 1992a). As suggested earlier, however, there is always a tension and a dynamic between the regulated and the unregulated, order and disorder (Andersen and Burns, 1992; Machado, 1998; Woodward, et al., 1994).

8 Human beings acquire and learn cultural rules and roles—in part through being taught, in part through observing and learning the patterns generated by others (that is, both through verbal and nonverbal communication).

9 This is a usage which differs substantially from Kuhn's (1970) notion of "scientific paradigm" which refers to a theoretical model or framework for representing and explaining empirical phenomena, the theoretical and methodological rules to be followed, the instruments to be used, the problems to be investigated, and the standards

by which research is to be judged. There are, of course, a number of parallels with our conceptualization of an institutional paradigm, a matter that we shall take up in a later publication.

10 The paradigm is a "rough" or "fuzzy" rule complex. Levels of knowledge of it vary among participants. Also, it is "distributed knowledge" with variants among different individuals and groups.

11 In practice, most actors do not (or cannot) think about institutional arrangements and practices and the ways in which they work as distinct from the ideas that guide them, nor do they distinguish clearly between practices and deeper guiding principles. But as we have emphasized, there are always gaps and incongruities between the ideal and the institutionalized rules, and these are often quite separate from the gaps between the things the institution promises and what it is actually able to deliver.

12 A shared paradigm must be simplified for purposes of communication. At the same time it has definitional power, that is, the power to define, interpret, and prescribe action for dealing with, reality.

13 In this respect, it relates to the notion of "master frame" used in the social movements literature (Nylander, 2000), or that of "meta-narrative," within which individual issues or policy questions can be contextualized and "framed" (Gottweis, 1998: 30–33).

14 But note the emphasis here on discontinuity, in which one paradigm replaces another. The notion of crisis and qualitative transition in perspective—that is, the incommensurability of paradigms—was a major idea introduced by Kuhn in his conception of scientific "revolutions."

15 Such inconsistencies can be conceptualized as a source of cultural/institutional dissonance, a sociological version of the cognitive dissonance experienced by individuals and described by Leon Festinger's theory (Festinger, 1957; Machado, 1998; Machado and Burns, 1998).

16 In this sense, the introduction and spread of Christianity and Islam—and, undoubtedly, the other Axial Transformations (Eisenstadt, 1982)—entailed socio-cultural revolutions.

17. However, the theory can be readily applied to more non-discursive, unreflected, and informal rules of everyday life (see Burns and Flam, 1987: chapters 3 and 11 on the interplay between formal and informal rules).

18 We cannot review here the vast sociological work on revolution (Arjomand, 1988, 1995; Eisenstadt, 1978; Skocpol, 1979, 1994; Taylor, 1988; Tilly, 1993, 1978; among others). Suffice it to say that in these as well as other works, there is a variety of different conceptions and definitions of revolution.

19 Such a ruling or governing elite consists of a group of actors (it may be an organization such as the Communist Party in the former Soviet Union and its satellites; the group may or may not be dominated by an autocrat or supreme figure), The group holds or takes key positions in the institutions of governance (typically including, of course, the means of coercion). It might recruit new members from non-elite populations—or conversely have a policy proscribing such recruitment (see Shils, 1963; Eisenstadt, 1978; Czudnowski, 1983).

20 A recent example of an outside group taking power and establishing new

institutional arrangements by "constitutional" means is the case of the integration of West and East Germany. West Germany negotiated basically with the former Soviet Union, and East Germany was compelled to accept in large part the West German paradigm and institutional order, its elites, etc.

21 Electoral and other formal democratic processes are also also channels of elite replacement. A revolutionary group or party may come to power through electoral means, as Hitler did in 1933, by leading the largest party in the German Reichstag. Once legally in power, Hitler and his associates were systematic and ruthless in exploiting legal and semi-legal possibilities to transform the more or less democratic state into a totalitarian state. Ataturk and Peron, in addition to their military actions, both utilized electoral processes to establish and legitimize their revolutionary regimes. Many more or less peaceful transformations have been been initiated through democratic transfer of state power: The Swedish Social Democrats (1932), the Norwegian Labor Party (1929), among others, brought about significant social, economic, and political restructuring.

22 A group of military or one with close military allies takes state power through military action, in large part without mass mobilization or movement. For example, Communist regimes were introduced into Eastern European countries with the backing of the Red Army at the end of World War II. There are many other examples of such forms of transformation: Ataturk in Turkey (1922), Peron in Argentina (1944), and Nasser in Egypt (1952). Or the disillusioned officers who in April 1974, ended the Portuguese dictatorship and its colonial wars and set in motion the dissolution of the empire and the democratization of Portugal.

23 The major revolutions of this century—but also the English (1648), American (1783), and French revolutions (1789)—engaged large masses of people acting in revolutionary movements. The most dramatic cases involved peasant and worker revolts led by organized groups or parties (for instance, the Russian and Chinese revolutions) and urban revolutions (such as the Iranian Islamic revolution led by a coalition, from which the radical clergy emerged triumphant).

24 Gitahy (2000), Perez (1985), among others, have investigated and analyzed the paradigm shift from Taylorism/Fordism to new forms (flexible specialization) of organizing and regulating industrial mass production.

25 According to Weber, during the periods of warring states, the very stratum of state prebendaries who blocked administrative rationalization in the empire became its most powerful promoters.

26 Weber (1951) suggests that in the Orient, it took military or religious revolutions to bring about transformations: to shatter the firm structure of prebendary interests, thus creating completely new power distributions and in turn new economic conditions. Attempts at internal innovation through reforms were wrecked time and time again by the opposition of officialdom. Rationalization concerned not only administration but taxation and budgeting as well as military and diplomatic areas.

27 Like Iran under the Pahlavis Shahs (1925–1979), the established secular states of Algeria, Egypt, and Turkey initiated their authoritarian modernization some time ago. Major contradictions and incoherencies emerged. Western-type modernization came into conflict with many aspects of Islamic culture and sets the stage for counter-movements, as it has in Algeria, Egypt, and Turkey today (Kamali, 2001).

8

Institutional Blindness in Modern Economics

Geoffrey M. Hodgson

By mainstream economics we refer to the type of economics that dominates the modern core journals of the subject.[1] It includes a variety of doctrines and the critic must be careful to distinguish them. But there are particular themes and assumptions that pervade modern mainstream economics. Among these is the notion of a universal "science of choice." The argument here is that, as a result of its pursuit of such universal theories, mainstream economics becomes largely incapable of dealing with cultural or historical particularities. As a result— despite the rise of the "new institutional economics"—mainstream economic theory, in a sense, remains predominantly *institution-blind*. Little attention is given to establishing theories that apply to particular, historically specific, economic mechanisms or institutions.

This is a sweeping condemnation and would seem to ignore the large mainstream literature on institutions. It is not that modern mainstream economics is unaware of institutions or is still keen to avoid them. There has been a huge explosion in the literature of attempts to relate economics to institutional phenomena, including the firm, the state, the family, and other important economic and social institutions. It is now widely accepted that "institutions matter" for economic order and development.[2] There has been much important empirical work on institutions in economics, sociology and political science. All these positive achievements should be recognized and commended.

The blindness may be partial, but the impairment is nevertheless serious and disabling. What is meant by this allegation of blindness is that, despite their intentions, many mainstream economists lack the conceptual apparatus to discern anything but the haziest institutional outlines. The argument here is that mainstream economists, with relatively few exceptions—and despite a wide-spread modern interest in institutions—have not got adequate visual tools to distinguish between different types of institution, nor to appraise properly what is going on within them.[3]

As noted in preceding chapters, we cannot discern nor understand any phenomenon with data alone. Well-chosen concepts and precise theoretical instruments are required. However, in its pursuit of theoretical precision, mainstream economics deploys concepts that are too blunt and universal. They are too sweeping and undiscriminating. Without a theory that is both adequate and conceptually sensitive we remain blind. Such a theory has to be grounded on a well-developed and appropriate methodology.

BUMPING BLIND INTO MARKETS

Despite its limitations, mainstream economics is sometimes forced to engage with institutional realities. At least to maintain some credibility as the science of economic phenomena, economics has to discuss such institutions as markets and firms. Indeed, some consideration of the market is unavoidable, because a legitimate and enduring aim of economic theory is to show how markets allocate resources and how prices are formed. Furthermore, the ideological predisposition of many economists towards markets makes such considerations inevitable.

Given this, it is rather strange that definitions of the market in the textbooks are infrequent and often imprecise. The institutional relations and properties of markets are rarely explored in these texts. For example, Hugh Gravelle and Ray Rees (1992: 3) wrote with some vagueness: "a market exists whenever two or more individuals are prepared to enter into an exchange transaction, regardless of time or place." There is no mention here of the institutional structure of markets themselves, or of the price mechanism, or of the establishment and enforcement of property rights. Throughout economics, the institutional structure of markets is largely unexplored. As Nobel Laureate Douglass North (1977: 710) has remarked:

> It is a peculiar fact that the literature on economics and economic history contains
> so little discussion of the central institution that underlies neoclassical econom-

ics—the market. . . . I am not aware of any existing systematic analysis of the preconditions for price-making markets.

Typically, the market assumes a de-institutionalized form, as if it was the
primeval and universal ether of all human interactions. It is believed that when
people gather together in the name of self-interest, then a market somehow
always emerges in their midst. Mysteriously, the market springs up simply as a
result of these spontaneous interactions, not as a result of a protracted process of
multiple institution-building, nor of the full development of a historically
specific commercial culture.

Related key concepts such as "exchange" and "transaction" are also rarely
discussed in the mainstream literature. These problems are not confined to
economics. Other social sciences fail to come to grips with the institutional and
structural realities of the modern world. We have already noted the generalities
of "exchange theory" in sociology (Blau, 1964; Homans, 1961). The concept of
"exchange" therein is so broad that it covers all sorts of social interaction,
without being confined to exchanges of property.

In sociology such general theorizing has reached its apogee in the work of
James Coleman (1990). Following in the tradition of Homans and Blau, Coleman (1990: 37) saw exchange as simply a "pairwise exchange of resources"
without the necessity of a reciprocal exchange of property rights. Accordingly,
in modern social science, even concepts such as "exchange" and "transaction"
cannot be taken for granted. Yet they are used habitually and without explanatory ado, as if their meaning is always crystal clear.

In common business parlance, an exchange means something more than the
reciprocation of a polite greeting, a wave, or a smile. It is even more than a
reciprocal transfer of resources. As John Commons (1924) rightly insisted,
exchange proper involves the contractual interchange of property rights, along
with the transferred goods and services. Unless a transfer of property rights is
involved, it is not properly described as an exchange. Property rights, in turn,
are backed up by custom and legal sanctions. These involve other institutions,
such as the state. Exchange has to be understood and analyzed in terms of the
key institutions that are required to sustain it.

Strangely, however, the concept of property rights is also underdeveloped in
mainstream economic theory. True, there is a sizable sub-discipline known as
"the economics of property rights" (Furubotn and Pejovich, 1974). But if we
look at this closely then it is clear that the discourse is primarily about individual incentives rather than about property. To the property rights economists, the
"structure of property rights" refers primarily to a set of incentives and disincentives for specific individual actions—an amended Benthamite calculus of
pleasure and pain—but not essentially to the institution of property itself.

Similarly, Armen Alchian (1977: 238) defined the property rights of a person
in the universal terms of "the probability that his decision about demarcated
uses of the resource will determine the use." However, this definition is about

control, not ownership, of a resource. The upshot of this definition is that if a thief manages to keep stolen goods then he acquires a substantial property right in them. But on the contrary, legal or normative considerations would suggest that they remain the rightful property of their original owner. Alchian's ahistorical definition of property removes from the picture the essential concept of rightful ownership.

Mainstream property rights economists treat property as a relation between an individual and a good, thus downplaying the fact that the institution of property also involves social relations between individuals. Crucially, social relations and structures are absent from this definition of property. The primary focus is on the individual, his goods, and his incentives. Any analysis of the construction and nature of the institutions required to sustain and legitimate property is secondary or absent.

While economists have taken such concepts as the market and exchange for granted, sociologists have tragically assumed that the study of the market can safely be left to the economists. For different reasons, sociologists too have assumed a de-institutionalized concept of the market. This is partly the result of the influence of Marxism within sociology. Marxists also tend to regard markets as uniform entities, ultimately permeated by just one specific set of pecuniary imperatives and cultural norms. Sociology has fallen prey to both Marxism and false universalism. As Viviana Zelizer (1993: 193) pointed out, sociologists have become obsessed

> with the cash nexus, with the vision of an ever-expanding market inevitably dissolving all social relations and corrupting culture and personal values.... Mesmerized by this vision of inexorable force, sociologists implicitly adopted an extremely simple conception of the process, making it resemble the sweeping away of landmarks by a giant flood. That left unaddressed the crucial question: How do real markets work? Markets were seldom studied as social and cultural arrangements. For if indeed the modern market neutralized social relations and homogenized cultural distinctions, there was nothing much left for sociologists to study. Thus the market was surrendered to economists.

However, economists have had little to say about the nature of markets, other than classifying them by their degrees of competition, related to the number of buyers and sellers they contain. Beyond this, the institutional aspects of markets are widely neglected. There is little discussion of how specific markets are structured to select and authenticate information, and of how prices are actually formed. The concept of the market is far too important to be left to the mainstream economists.

In truly biblical tones, influential economists such as Oliver Williamson (1975: 20, 1985: 143) have proclaimed that: "in the beginning there were markets." However, by giving the market a primeval identity, it is robbed of its historical, structural, and institutional character. This weakness in defining the institutional essence of the market, combined with a mission to spread his concept of "transaction cost" beyond the market alone, led Williamson to eventually blur his own vital distinction between the market and the firm. We are thus told that hierarchies in the firm are "a continuation of market relations by other means" (Williamson, 1991: 271). The result is that much of the new institutional economics, *instead of understanding markets as social institutions*, attempts to treat *institutions as if they were all markets*. But these ubiquitous "markets" are of a strange, ahistorical, and de-institutionalized kind.

The starting point of Williamson's (1985: 43) analysis is not historically specific social institutions but "contractual man." It is as if all the "economic institutions of capitalism" are found rolled up inside every single individual human psyche, rather than in the historically contingent social relations. Williamson tried to spin out the analysis from the somehow given "human nature as we know it" (1985: 3) rather than from the specific structures and institutions that constrain and constitute social actors. As Michael Magill and Martine Quinzii (1996: 11, n.) concurred, "the transaction costs arguments are derived from basic (universal) attributes of human beings." Williamson's analysis, which was claimed to apply to "capitalism" in particular, turned out to be addressed to the universal state of nature. Despite use of the word, there is no focus on the historically specific institutions of capitalism; they are blurred almost beyond recognition. For Williamson and others, "capitalism" is itself the universal state, reflecting the natural and enduring features of "human nature."

Indeed, questions are raised about the sensitivity of the new institutional economics to real institutions, particularly when it is claimed that this very same approach can also explain "the high degree of cooperation and coordination of the activities of honeybees, ants and schooling fish" (Landa, 1999: 95). If the core concepts of the new institutional economics have such a wide applicability, then one wonders about their ability to discern the general features of human nature and human institutions, let alone those human institutions with specific features. Human societies and anthills may have some things in common, but the differences are important too. Neither ants, bees, nor fish make contracts or exchange property rights. Neither do they reflect on their own society and make conscious plans to sustain or change it. Beyond the realm of human society, there are no genuine organizations or markets.

Loose thinking about key institutions such as the market pervades mainstream economics. For instance, in his work on the family, Gary Becker saw no essential distinction between the commercial world of trade and the intimacy of the family. Apart from the duration of the contract, his theory sees little differ-ence between sex with a prostitute and sexual relations between husband and wife. For Becker, they can be analyzed with the same theoretical instruments, to the neglect of their distinctive features. Rather than focusing on specific institutions and social structures, his analysis was concerned with abstract allocative choices of a de-institutionalized kind. He thus repeatedly used loose phrases such as "a market for marriages" (Becker, 1976a: 206).[4]

Similarly imprecise habits have spread to sociology. For Coleman (1990: 35–36), markets were simply "transfers of rights or resources" within "systems of relations" or a "system of exchange." His concept of the market is so general that it can be made up of "unilateral transfers." In other words, for Coleman, markets cover a wide range of phenomena including taxation and gift-giving, as well as agreed contracts between two parties. Following Becker, Coleman (1990: 22) asserted: "It is clear that marriage can be seen as taking place in a kind of market."[5] Evidently, a near-total blindness regarding different types of social institution afflicts much of modern sociology as well.

However, despite the global march of capitalism, the modern family is still not completely invaded by commercial relations, and strong cultural norms are still sensitive to this fact. Neoclassical economics either ignores the family or tries to force it into a purely contractarian analysis. Becker and Coleman do the latter, making personal relationships within the family conceptually equivalent to commercial contracts, without highlighting the distinctive features of each.

In another context, Becker (1991: 362ff.) was again sloppy in his use of market language. In some modern societies, babies may be adopted, in return for payment. Becker wrote of babies being sold, when in fact what is involved is the sale of parental rights. However, as Posner (1994: 410) rightly pointed out: "The term *baby selling,* while inevitable, is misleading. A mother who surrenders her parental rights for a fee is not selling her baby; babies are not chattels, and cannot be bought and sold. She is selling her parental rights."

This reckless and imprecise use of terms, along with a neglect of cultural and institutional realities of market economies—especially by those that claim to pursue and admire precision and rigor as well as explanatory scope—combines both tragedy and farce.

THE DANGEROUS IDEA OF THE
DE-INSTITUTIONALIZED MARKET

We see the tragic side when mainstream economic theory is applied to real-world economic problems. This was illustrated most graphically in the post-1989 economic transformation in the former Eastern bloc. Since 1989, these Eastern European economies have often been subjected to misguided economic policies, based sometimes on the Western economic textbooks. A key assumption behind these policies—of which the textbooks give no explanation—was that the market order would germinate and grow in the primordial soil of human relations, once the old state bureaucracies were swept away. As the influential Western adviser Jeffrey Sachs (1993: xxi) contended: "markets spring up as soon as central planning bureaucrats vacate the field." In fact, markets did not spring up spontaneously. The requisite rules, norms, and institutions were lacking (Kozul-Wright and Rayment, 1997; Grabher and Stark, 1997). As Nobel

Laureate Ronald Coase (1992: 718) rightly observed: "The ex-communist countries are advised to move to a market economy . . . but without the appropriate institutions, no market of any significance is possible."

Of course, to deny that markets emerge automatically does not mean that they can be instituted simply by decree. Like many institutions, markets involve elements of both spontaneous development and rule design. Both individual initiative and collective decree are ineffective unless there is an adequate cultural and institutional foundation. Lacking an adequate institutional grounding for the growth of market alternatives to state control, many of the Eastern European economies were plunged into years of recession and economic instability (Zecchini, 1997).

It is reported that Alan Greenspan, head of the Federal Reserve Bank in the United States, recognized this mistake after the event. He originally assumed that the collapse of the Soviet regimes "would automatically establish a free-market entrepreneurial system" believing that capitalism was simply "human nature." It turned out, he says, to be "not nature at all, but culture."[6] Yet mainstream economists continue to neglect the detailed study of specific cultures. Greenspan's conversion is welcome, but there is a great deal of work to be done to ensure that economics pays recognition to culturally and historically specific institutions.

Understanding the institutional nature of markets is also vital in the context of economic development. This process involves a deeply embedded cultural and moral fabric. This fabric involves the behavioral and moral norms that are necessary for the market to function. It does not necessarily emerge spontaneously, from the interactions of given individuals. Essentially, "the social structure of the society is not a malleable structure that may easily evolve or adjust to accommodate the market and the rules of the game associated with it" (Platteau, 1994: 795).

Different types of market institution are possible, involving different routines, pricing procedures, and so on. Even some mainstream economists have been obliged to notice this. General equilibrium theorists were forced to adopt particular, auxiliary assumptions concerning market procedures in order to obtain a definite outcome. Something special like the "Walrasian auctioneer" had to be assumed in order to make the model work (Arrow and Hahn, 1971). In other words, some elemental institutional structures had to be brought in to make the model function in its own terms.

As experimental economics has emerged as a major subdiscipline, it has been realized that the simulation of market phenomena necessarily involves the setting out of specific rules and procedures. Modern experimental economists, in simulating markets in the laboratory, have found that they have had also to face the unavoidable problem of setting up its specific institutional structure. Simply calling it a market is not enough to provide the experimenter with the institutionally specific structures and procedural rules. As leading experimental economist Vernon Smith (1982: 923) wrote: "it is not possible to design a laboratory resource allocation experiment without designing an institution in all its detail."[7]

Each particular market is entwined with other institutions and a particular social culture. Accordingly, there is not just one type of market but many different markets, each depending on its inherent routines, cultural norms, and institutional make-up. Differentiating markets by market structure according to textbook typology—from perfect competition through oligopoly to monopoly—is not enough. Institutions, routines, and culture have to be brought into the picture, otherwise there will not be enough information to determine outcomes. This truth is being discovered by experimental economists. Chris Starmer (1999: F13) wrote:

> The results of market experiments show that experimental markets sometimes converge to predicted outcomes, and sometimes they do not. Part of the difficulty in understanding why such differences exist between alternative market institutions derives from the fact that we have a relatively underdeveloped understanding of what determines initial decisions and the dynamics of adjustment.

Although markets have been central to the concerns of mainstream economics for two hundred years, the neglect of real market institutions means that there is still "relatively underdeveloped understanding" of the institutional parameters determining market dynamics. The reason for this is that, at least until recently, different types of market institution were rarely examined. If we were to look for the rudiments of a theory of different types of market institution, we would have to look in the very places that mainstream economists have scorned or ignored. The institutional character of markets has been emphasized by German historical economists in the nineteenth century, and by twentieth-century "old" institutional economists such as John Commons, John Hobson, and John Maurice Clark. Long ago Hobson (1902: 144) wrote: "A market, however crudely formed, is a social institution." Likewise, for Clark (1957: 53):

> the mechanism of the market, which dominates the values that purport to be economic, is not a mere mechanism for neutral recording of people's preferences, but a social institution with biases of its own.

Significantly, much of the modern analysis of market institutions has been accomplished by social scientists working outside the tradition of mainstream economics. Wayne Baker (1984) made an important study of U.S. financial markets, showing how exchanges were structured by specific networks and social relationships between actors. Mitchel Abolafia (1996) did another major study of U.S. financial markets, showing the rules and cultural norms that govern their operation. Jan Kregel (1995) examined the historical evolution of financial markets, relating this history to the different models of market arrangement that are found in neoclassical economic theory. Marie-France Garcia

(1986) showed the detailed processes of organization of a strawberry market in France, involving mechanisms of quality control, information dispersal, and pricing by auction. All the studies of real markets indicated that there are different types of market, and that the creation of a market involves a selection from a potentially infinite number of possible alternative institutional features. Furthermore, markets are often highly organized entities, imposing rules as well as benefits upon their users.

The recognition that (a) the market is an institution and (b) different, institutionally differentiated types of market may exist has important theoretical and policy implications. Institutionalists start from these very elements that are lacking in the mainstream analysis. Exchange, in the sense of Commons and other "old" institutionalists, requires, first, a common system of language—or at least mutually understood signs—so that the individuals involved can communicate. Second, an enforceable set of rules or laws must govern the contracts between individuals. Third, there must also be a system of established property rights to make property transfers meaningful and enforceable. There must be laws, and procedures to deal with disputes. In most accounts it is accepted that some of these rules and laws can emerge gradually over time, and possibly—at least in the case of language—without intention or design. The degree to which the state or other powerful organizations have been, or must be, involved in these processes is a matter of important analytical controversy, but it need not concern us in this chapter. The key point here is to notice that all these frameworks are, in an established sense of the word, *institutions*.

In general, exchange involves contractual agreement and the exchange of property rights. Not all exchanges take place in markets. Markets, where they exist, help to structure, organize, and legitimatize numerous exchange transactions. A market is an institution in which a significant number of commodities of a particular type are regularly exchanged, and in which market rules and structures pattern these exchange negotiations and transactions. They involve pricing and trading procedures that help to establish a consensus over prices, and often help by communicating information regarding products, prices, quantities, potential buyers, or possible sellers.

Markets differ substantially, especially when we consider markets in different cultures. In Japan, for example, selling prices are typically taken as fixed. Any attempt to haggle over prices is regarded as questioning the quality of the goods and insulting the integrity of the seller. On the contrary, in North Africa, extensive bargaining over prices is seen as part of a process of developing a social relationship between buyer and seller. After a long conversation, prices can be reduced by more than a half. Comparing Japan with North Africa, we can see that markets differ not simply on the question of the pricing procedure. They also differ in the very meanings attributed to these processes and in the place of market exchange in social life.

To recapitulate, the market itself is neither a natural datum nor an ubiquitous ether, but is itself a social institution, governed by sets of rules defining restrictions on some, and legitimating other, behaviors. Furthermore, the market is necessarily embedded in other social institutions, such as in some cases the state. It can emerge spontaneously, but it can also be promoted, or even in some cases created, by conscious design. Markets, in short, are organized and institutionalized exchange.[8]

A clear implication of this argument is that the familiar pro- and anti-market policy stances are both rather insensitive to the possibility of different types of market institution. In the real world, and even in a single country, we may come across many different examples of the market. We encounter informal markets for secondhand goods, fish and vegetable markets organized and regulated by the local council, and so on. The use of designated tokens to purchase babysitting services within an organized babysitting collective is also an example of a limited market. There are also markets for the sexual services of prostitutes. Such markets are clearly quite different in substance and connotation. We should thus refrain from treating them all as exactly the same.

Instead of recognizing the important role of different possible cultures and trading customs, both opponents and advocates of the market have focused exclusively on its general features. Thus, for instance, Marxists have deduced that the mere existence of private property and markets will encourage acquisitive individual behavior, with no further reference to the role of ideas and culture in helping to form the aspirations of social actors. This de-cultured viewpoint has difficulty explaining, for example, the high degree of material acquisitiveness and commodity fetishism that prevailed in the planned and allegedly "socialist" Eastern bloc before 1989, after decades of official propaganda extolling cooperation and shunning greed. This viewpoint has difficulty, furthermore, in recognizing the often limited and contrasting versions of consumerism that prevail in different capitalist societies. As strange bedfellows, both Marxists and market individualists underestimate the degree to which all market economies are unavoidably made up of densely layered social institutions.

STUMBLING BLIND OVER THE FIRM

Turning to another key institution within modern economies, what is the attitude of mainstream economists to the firm? Clearly, the reality and importance of this institution is generally recognized, even if the internal workings of the "black box" of the firm were widely ignored until the 1970s. However, as with the market, there is a scarcity of precision and an abundance of disagreement on the definition of the firm. There are a variety of views on this issue but generally they fall short of what is required.

Consider an extreme but illustrative case. Discussing "the economics of religion," Laurence Iannaccone (1991, 1998) described "churches as firms" that compete on a "religious market." True, some churches are registered as legal or corporate entities, but that misses their true essence. Churches are institutions that provide spiritual guidance. Their services are unlike those provided by an insurance company, hairdresser, or travel agent. The mistaken idea of a "religious market" ignores the fact that choice of religious belief is neither necessarily nor principally about buying and selling, nor exchanges of property rights. Crucially, churches do not charge for the services of spiritual guidance that they dispense. Services are typically provided without any legal contract or requirement of payment in return. The unqualified description of "churches as firms" ignores some vital and specific features of church organization and function. Furthermore, it robs the notion of the firm of much necessary precision and institutional specificity. If some economists can, without any qualification, describe "churches as firms" then that betrays some institutional emptiness in their concept of the firm. If "churches are firms" and essentially the same "theory of the firm" can be used to analyze them both, then this suggests some limitations of that "theory of the firm" when applied to the profit-oriented corporations of the commercial world.[9]

Some economists see little difference between the firm and the market. In their classic article, Armen Alchian and Harold Demsetz (1972) wrote: "Telling an employee to type this letter rather than to file that document is like my telling a grocer to sell me this brand of tuna rather than that brand of bread" (Alchian and Demsetz, 1972: 777). The contractual relationship between shopper and grocer was seen as virtually equivalent to the generally more enduring and complex employment relationship with the organization of the firm.

The approach of Coase was much better. He has been much more sensitive to institutional differences than most economists. But he has still tangled with the problem of historical specificity (Hodgson, 2001). In his early and famous article, Coase (1937) seemed to confine himself to a type of firm that involves employment contracts, that is the capitalist firm. By contrast, half a century later he expressed regret for this earlier emphasis and addressed a much broader conception of the firm (Coase, 1988). Nowhere did he acknowledge that this change in definition may lead to different answers to the classic questions he raised in his "nature of the firm" article. In short, Coase seemed unsure whether his theory of the firm is universal, covering all possible types of firm, or is confined to a historically specific case.

Other leading theorists have fared no better. Sanford Grossman and Oliver Hart (1986: 692) define the firm "in terms of the assets it owns." Again this made the mistake of focusing exclusively on the relationship between persons and things, to the neglect of structured relations between persons. As David Ellerman (1992: 12) rightly put it: "Being the firm . . . is a contractual role, not a property right." This contractual role is defined and supported by socioeconomic institutions. To understand and define the firm, we must look at these specific institutions.

To their credit, some "new institutional economists" have focused on structured relationships between persons. For instance, Eirik Furubotn and Rudolph Richter (1997: 272) wrote: "A *firm* is understood . . . as a network of relational contracts between individuals . . . with the purpose of efficiently organizing production." However, this definition is inadequate, because it is unable to make a distinction between a firm and a network, simply because the former is defined as an example of the latter. Yet in the real world there is such a distinction. A network is typically understood as a loosely structured but enduring cluster of *several* contractors or firms, linked together by ongoing relational and legal contracts, and perhaps also by agreed rules between them. A network is not a single firm. The firm itself is recognized in law as a "legal person," capable of making legal contracts and exchanging its products with others. By these criteria, the firm is a historically specific entity.

As well as confusing the (vaguely defined) "market" with the (vaguely defined) "firm," another common error is to confuse the term "organization" with "firm." This habit is so widespread in economics and business studies that the two terms are often taken to mean the same thing. Yet a firm is a very particular type of organization that produces, owns, and sells goods and services. Not all organizations do this. Furthermore, not all organizations have the status of a singular "legal person" that is always accorded to the firm. Accordingly, if the terms "organization" and "firm" are conflated then the temptation is to miss out on the key legal and contractual aspects of the firm. Regrettably, the modern economic theory of the firm is pervaded with a quasi-Maoist disregard of the value and force of formal legal relations of contract and ownership.[10]

Overall, in the literature on the theory of the firm, the desire to create a universal theory of the nature and behavior of the firm gets in the way of the discussion of historical specificities. What is insufficiently prominent is the notion of the firm as a historically specific formation. If we abandon the aim to create a universal and ahistorical concept of the firm, then we can examine its nature by looking at the specific institutional realities.

In the modern business world, the firm is treated as an organization with a defined legal status. It is treated in law and society as a singular "legal person." Although we transact through individuals within the firm, we understand that these individuals are acting in the name of the firm, and that the firm as a whole is taking upon itself any contractual responsibilities into which we may enter. These responsibilities may outlive the individuals involved. This commonplace idea of the firm as a "legal person" is in line with its etymology from *firmus,* or (legal) signature. The idea of the firm as a "legal person" is widely known and understood, except by mainstream economists, who refuse to acknowledge historically specific legal realities in their quest for a universal theory.

In this sense of a "legal person," firms have existed for hundreds or even thousands of years. Originally, one person or a partnership owned the firm. The status of "legal person" emerged in law as the firm evolved beyond its previously frequent ownership by a single individual or small group.[11] The idea of a "legal person" is now established in modern statutes of corporate law. Hence it is important not to confuse the firm with a network of multiple legal persons, who may have separate ownership of their own products. A network involves multiple "legal persons." By contrast, a firm is one "legal person" capable of owning resources and making contracts as a singular corporate body, despite the fact that it is an organization composed of several people.

The firm is an organization that manages the resources in its possession, essentially by administrative control rather than by internal contract. Accordingly, one of the key features of a firm is that it is an organized enclave, apart from the market. Failing to recognize this, many observers are unable to draw clear and well-established boundaries around the firm. There is widespread confusion over this issue. This confusion allows economists to ignore the reality of non-market organization in the private sector and bring everything there under the conceptual umbrella of market analysis. Corporate control and authority is treated purely as a matter of free contract. They can thus ignore the reality of control and authority within the private capitalist corporation but remain critical of public sector bureaucracy and state planning. Such misconceptions are aided by the lack of clear and adequate definitions of "firm" or "market" in social science.

Like many, Steven Cheung (1983: 11) has some difficulty in surveying the boundaries of the firm. He raised this example:

> A landlord who wants to build a high-rise finds a building contractor. This con-
> tractor subcontracts with a hardwood floor contractor on an agreed price per
> square foot—a piece count. The subcontractor, who imports the wood materials
> and adds finishing work to the wood on a piece-rate basis, in turn finds a sub-
> subcontractor, provides him wood, and offers him a price per square foot laid. Fi-
> nally, the sub-subcontractor hires workers and again pays them per square foot
> laid.

Such a complex integration of contracts and subcontracts is very common. But, contrary to Cheung, it offers no great taxonomic difficulty. Cheung's problem was that he seemed to think that, on the one hand, piece-rate payments imply the existence of "a 'market'" (p. 10). This explains his repeated—but irrelevant— stress on payments per square foot in the above (p. 11) quotation. However, Cheung gave no reason why piece-rate payments imply the existence of "a 'market.'" On the other hand, he (p. 17) argued that "economists may well argue that because they are all vertically integrated by contracts, with transfer pricing, only one firm exists." However, contrary to Cheung, being "vertically integrated by contracts" is not the same as vertical integration *within* a firm. Blind to this important distinction, Cheung suggested that the hardwood floor example is something with the characteristics of both "a 'market'" and "one firm." The myth of the firm-market hybrid was born. In truth, the hardwood floor example involves (market or relational) exchange, between not one but four "legal persons": the landlord, the contractor, the subcontractor, and the sub-subcontracted firm with its employees. By the legal criterion, four firms were clearly present, not one. Cheung argued that the definition of the firm is arbitrary. He wrote: "according to one's view a "firm" may be as small as a relationship between two input owners or, if the chain of contracts is allowed to spread, as big as the whole economy" (p. 17). He then jumped to the conclusion: "Thus it is futile to press the issue of what is or is not a firm" (p. 18). Cheung's argument is essentially that different definitions of X are possible, therefore it is futile to define X. But this is a non sequitur. The problem here is in the eye of the beholder. The taxonomic problem diminishes greatly once we define the firm as a legal and non-market entity.

A more genuine query emerges: why do so many economists evade the obvious, everyday, legally grounded, definition of the firm? There are two likely and related reasons. One is the tendency to associate the so-called "economic" attributes of a social arrangement with specific subjective perceptions of the agents involved, rather than with the character of the social structures or institutions. The other is the related desire to make economics general and ahistorical, rather than to associate it with historically specific institutions.

Some writers repel attempts to define the firm as an identifiable legal and non-market entity. It is suggested, for instance, that the boundaries between the firm and the market are being eroded in modern capitalism. It is claimed that this development undermines the idea of the firm as a non-market entity. Nevertheless, we would still have the problem of defining and identifying the past historical phenomenon of the firm. Even the extinction of a species does not exempt us from the task of taxonomy. The truth, however, is that the firm is not extinct. It is true that there is a huge variety of possible forms of industrial organization. Open markets, relational contracts, cartels, networks, joint ventures, strategic alliances, and business groups are examples. But these are all different types of relationship *between firms*, sometimes with the addition of another legal entity set up by the firms involved. These relationships between firms are of constitutional, coordinative, and behavioral significance for the industry as a whole but they do not necessarily alter the (legal) boundary between the individual firms and the world outside.

A muddled reality is no excuse for muddled definitions. Likewise, a mutable reality is no justification for elastic ideas. Accordingly, even if the boundaries between the firm and the market are breaking down in reality, the conceptual distinction between these two terms is still necessary to make sense of such a statement. In order to describe or understand such a tangled reality we need clear concepts and careful definitions to guide us. Without them we are conceptually blind. Clear and unmuddled concepts are necessary to penetrate a muddled world.[12]

THE MYTH OF THE INTERNAL MARKET

For lack of adequate definitions and concepts, the real boundary around the firm in the real world is often missed, sometimes when writers look inside the firm, and sometimes when they look outside, at relations between firms.

Contrary to much talk in the literature, true markets rarely, if ever, exist within firms. It is true that many modern firms have separate functional divisions, each with accounting procedures and their own profit targets. A key test is whether or not these divisions have separate legal status, and are recognized as "legal persons." If so, these divisions themselves constitute firms, even if they are largely owned by, and subordinate to, another company. There are examples of this, with the modern conglomerate subdividing itself into legally separate units. That means that we must have two words, not one: "firm" and "conglomerate." We can happily use both words, but it is important not to confuse the two, as they refer to different things. Yet in the literature the distinction is rarely made. Of course, the formal legal status of any organization tells us far from the whole story. Furthermore, legal formalities can sometimes have a fictional status, masking a different reality. For example, a conglomerate of different firms may in practice act as a single firm, because control of the conglomerate is concentrated in the hands of a single group. In this case, additional criteria come into play. However, a case is made elsewhere in favor of the legal criterion being the primary one in circumstances where the rule of law prevails (Hodgson, 1998a, 1999b). In general, legal relations are not mere formalities, but are backed with the powers and sanctions of the legal system of the state. Accordingly, if legal criteria are regarded as less important, then the onus is on the researcher is to identify the powers and forces that are sufficient to counter the sanctions and powers of state authority.

There are often internal negotiations and transfers of resources between divisions of the modern firm. But are there "internal markets" within firms? Many firms use price indicators for internal accounting, and products may be "exchanged" by one internal department with another. It may be concluded that this is evidence of an "internal market." But typically these exchanges do not involve the exchange of legal property rights. The objects of "exchange" remain the property of the firm. These "exchanges" are not legally enforceable contracts of trade. They are internal measures of organizational procedure and accounting. They are accounting transfers, rather than genuine commodity exchanges. Even if a subdivision of the firm is delegated the power to enter into contracts with outside bodies, then the firm as a whole is legally the party to the contract. The subdivision is merely exercising delegated powers: it acts "in the name" of the corporation, and the corporation as a whole is legally responsible for its liabilities under the agreed contract. Because the firm is a singular legal entity, trading and contract *within* a firm are highly limited.

There is a widespread supposition that "internal labor markets" exist inside the firm. Employment contracts may be renegotiated, for example. However, these would be cases of the renegotiation of contracts for *inputs* of goods or services *into* the firm. Even the pioneers of the idea, Peter Doeringer and Michael Piore (1971: 1–2) admitted that "internal labor markets" are not governed primarily by the price mechanism but by "a set of administrative rules and procedures." David Marsden (1986: 162) went further: "internal labor markets offer quite different transaction arrangements, and there is some doubt as to whether they fulfill the role of markets." What Doeringer and Piore pointed to was a competitive fluidity of labor within the organization. They did not show that a true market existed within the firm.

Would a competition between employees for an advertised post within the firm be an "internal labor market"? Not strictly, because this would not constitute regularized and organized exchange but a series of one-off competitions for advertised internal posts. These would be periodic instances of contract reallocation, rather than a true labor market. The regular, repeated, and institutionalized exchange that characterizes true markets would be lacking.

As another example, the discussion of the modern multi-divisional form suggests that each division within a firm competes in the firm's "internal capital market" for the budget allocated by the firm's head office (Williamson, 1975). To be sure, some substantial competition and rivalry is involved, but it is not competition on a market. It is completely different from the true capital market where shares in individual firms are bought and sold. The division of the firm has no independently owned share capital to use as a lever to obtain loans from outside agencies. This internal competition is more a power struggle between different parts of the corporate bureaucracy. This mistaken idea of an "internal capital market" obscures rather than explains the true corporate reality.

Much of the loose talk about "internal markets" within firms derives from a sloppy use of the term "market" which, unfortunately, pervades mainstream economics today. In terms of genuine, regular, and organized exchanges of goods or services, "markets" are rarely, if ever, found *within* the firm. This pervasive confusion over the nature of markets and exchange allows free-market and other economists to ignore the reality of non-market organization in capitalist firms and to understand everything in "market" terms.

CONFLATING THE FIRM AND THE MARKET

Strikingly, however, a similar but inverted defect is found among some non-mainstream economists. The same lack of a clear and adequate definition of the market and of the firm, allows others, often from a very different ideological perspective, to ignore legal and contracting realities and to focus exclusively on questions of control. As an example, the very idea of "market hierarchies"

(Pitelis, 1991) encapsulates this confusion. As in mainstream economics, "market" and "organization" become conflated. Here, however, instead of seeing everything through market lenses, the power relations within organizations become eyeglasses to view the system as a whole. From this particular perspective, the universal conceptual focus becomes one of coordination and control. The crucial error here is that legal and historical specificities—particularly concerning markets and contracts—are downplayed. As a result, instead of the "new institutionalist" mistake of treating institutions as if they were all markets, the inverted error becomes one of treating all markets as if they were non-market organizations, and all contracts as is they were all simply matters of administrative control.[13]

Also conflating the firm and the market, Ken-ichi Imai and Hiroyuki Itami (1984) discussed the supposed "interpenetration of organization and market" in Japan. However, they defined both market and organization without any reference to property rights or contracts, referring instead to factors such as the durability of the relationship and the use or otherwise of price as a major information signal. By this flawed methodology it is not difficult to find elements of so-called "organization" in the highly structured and regulated "markets" of Japan, and to find elements of an alleged "market" inside many firms. These conclusions follow, however, from the inadequate definitions of "market" and "organization" in the first place. In contrast, superior definitions of these terms would lead to the conclusion that markets—in Japan and elsewhere—are often organized to a greater or lesser degree, but that any market is a quite different type of organization from the property-owning and contracting legal entity of the firm.

As another real-world illustration, consider the case of a large corporation that has a number of smaller subcontractors and suppliers—such as Benetton, or Marks and Spencer. If we mistakenly defined a firm in terms of a broad notion of control, then the large corporation, plus all the subcontracted suppliers, would together be regarded as a single firm. However, this would simply—and confusingly—shift the definition of "the firm" from one type of phenomenon to another. Clearly, we require two terms. One—the firm—would describe a productive organization constituted as singular legal entity. The other—such as a "supplier network"—would describe the entire clustered complex of subordinate subcontractors that are dependent on the contracts of a dominant organization. It is simply confusing to shift the word "firm" from the former to the latter.

A firm, a conglomerate, and a "supplier network" are different things. A firm is a single "legal person." A conglomerate is a set of firms, wholly or partly owned by a holding firm and acting as a single entity. A supplier network is a set of firms, each of which may be dependent on the contracts of a single firm, without necessarily being wholly or partly owned by the dominant firm. Once we establish legal and historical specificities, then we can be much more careful in our definitions.

In three classic articles, George Richardson (1972), Victor Goldberg (1980), and Ronald Dore (1983) argued that the relationship between a large corporation and its subordinate contractors is often more durable and intensive than a typical market relationship. This valid and important observation does not change the above argument. It is no excuse for fudging the distinction between a firm and a market. Indeed, it points not to two but to three types of institutional relationship: the firm, the market, and relational exchange. An enduring relationship between a dominant firm and a subordinate subcontractor is not an open-market relationship, but it is still one of commodity exchange, involving the legal transfer of property rights. It remains a relationship of commodity exchange between two distinct firms. It is not evidence of commodity exchange, nor evidence of a "market" within a single, encompassing firm. Firms, markets, and relational exchange are different things.

MORE ON THE MYTH OF THE FIRM-MARKET HYBRID

In modern economies, there are many cases of complex forms of interaction between productive agencies (Cheung, 1983; Ménard, 1996). However, on inspection most of these allegedly "hybrid" cases turn out to be interlocking relations or networks between multiple and distinct legal firms, rather than a single, encompassing, organization or firm.

Part of the problem here is a failure to recognize that markets are but one special case of commodity exchange (Hodgson, 1988). As North (1977: 710) has rightly observed: "most exchanges do not take place in markets." As a result, instead of just firms and markets, there are three possibilities: the firm, market exchange, and non-market exchange. If we adhere to the false dichotomy between firms and markets then truly we have some difficulty in classifying the kind of non-market contractual relations between firms, identified by Richardson, Goldberg, and Dore. The real-world ensemble of such interactive relations is neither a firm nor a market so—according to the logic of this false dichotomy—it must assume the "strange" form of a "hybrid" or a "quasi-market." The first error here lies in the adoption of a false dichotomy, ignoring the third (Richardsonian) possibility of non-market contractual exchange.

The second error is to have an inadequately precise definition of the firm, even to the extent that the difference between terms such as "firm," "organization," and "industry" may potentially dissolve. A wide notion of an "organization" is adopted, which is then confused and conflated with the firm or corporation.

Williamson's discussion of hybrids is similarly defective. Williamson (1999: 1091) saw "hybrids" as "long term contractual relations into which security features have been crafted." Admittedly, Williamson was attempting to describe a very important set of phenomena within modern capitalism. Much modern contracting is of this "long-term" type. However, such "contractual relations" are not themselves firms, nor within firms. Furthermore, the long-term, relational, and "security" features of the contractual relations mean that they are not markets either. Market relations are generally more impersonal and are typically short term. But Williamson too is a victim of the false dichotomy. He assumed that if long-term contractual relations are neither firms nor markets, then they must be "hybrids" of the market and the firm. One must ask, however: what agencies make the (long-term) contracts? In fact, these "contractual relations" are all between, not within, firms. If we accept and understand the third (Richardsonian) possibility, of non-market contracts of a "relational" type, then the whole picture is one of relational contracts between firms. There is now no "hybrid" to be seen. By adopting the obfuscatory concept of a firm-market hybrid, Williamson muddles his former claim that the firm is essentially different from the market.

To his credit, Claude Ménard (1995) defined terms such as "market" and "organization" more precisely than most others. In particular, he defined the market as an institution. His notion of organization, however, is extremely broad. On this basis, he rightly pointed to the possibility that markets themselves involve elements of organization and regulation. He thus argued: "In all of these situations, the market activities are significantly permeated with organizational factors" (p. 176). So far so good. He then went of the rails. He tried to demonstrate that "organizations can be internally structured as quasi-markets." His arguments for this included the consideration of franchising "when very strict standards are imposed on independent participants." He noted that

> Classification [into markets or organizations] becomes particularly difficult when firms are interconnected by a dense web of transactions, with strong commitments to each other and complementaries of their assets, but without formal agreements and, moreover, with property rights on these firms clearly maintained as distinct. (p. 176)

On this basis he argued for "a *continuum* between markets and hierarchies." Along this imagined continuum were hybrids, described as follows:

> Hybrid forms are characterized by specific combinations of markets incentives and modalities of coordination involving some form of hierarchical relationship. (p. 175)

The problem began when Ménard conflated the notions of "organization," "firm," and "hierarchy." Indeed, he never provided an adequate definition of the latter two terms, and he seemed to use the terms "firm" and "organization" interchangeably. Consider his example of strictly monitored and regulated franchising. With a broad definition of "organization," this could be described as an "organized" relationship, but between *two or more* firms or "legal persons." Although the relationship has an "organized" character it does not mean that it is a single firm. Once we realize that every firm is a special kind of organization but not all organizations are firms, then Ménard's argument collapses. The case when "firms are interconnected by a dense web of transactions, with strong commitments to each other" is a case of relational contracting between multiple firms. Again, the "organized" character of the relationship does not imply that they everything is organized within a single firm. The fact that "property rights on these firms [are] clearly maintained as distinct" does not create any taxonomic difficulty. It simply underlines the fact that multiple firms may exist within a single organizational network. Essentially, Ménard's primary error was to confuse the broadly defined organization with the firm. His secondary error was to overlook the fact that relational contracting involves the exchange of commodities between *different* firms but *not* on an open market. It is thus a third option, after a market and a firm.

Recognition of the general absence of markets and commodity exchange inside all firms is important for several reasons. It dispenses with sloppy and confused terms such as "internal market," "continuum," and "hybrid." It also helps to show the relevance of the boundaries of the firm and the vital interface between non-market and market modes of coordination. Any analysis of the formation and role of these boundaries has vital implications for corporate and public policy. To blur these boundaries is both to confuse the analysis and to make the policy issues less vital.

Although many of the purported "hybrid" cases disappear when we examine them closely, there is one important case where the boundaries are often difficult to draw. This concerns the classic distinction between an employment contract and a contract for services. A firm may change the status of its workers from employed to self-employed, hiring them to do the same work much as before. The key legal and substantive difference here is that, under an employment contract, the employer has the right to control and interfere with the manner and process of work. There is no such right over a self-employed worker: there is simply the right to obtain the contracted good or service at the agreed quantity and quality.

In practice, however, it is widely recognized that the line between employment and self-employment is difficult to draw. The outcome is important for conceptual as well as policy reasons. The determination of the employment status of the worker will affect the boundaries of the firm itself: self-employed workers may contract with the firm but they are not part of the firm. Although the line is difficult to draw, the distinction is still real. Difficulties of demarcation between types do not imply that differences of type are non-existent.

It is argued here that the firm exists as a distinct legal entity: it is technically a "legal person." It owns its products and sells or hires them to others. It enters into contracts with its workforce and its customers. Accordingly, its external relations are dominated by commodity exchanges or markets. Internally, however, the firm is not ruled primarily by prices, markets, or commodity exchange. It is essentially a sphere of administration, organization, and managerial direction. Unless we understand that institutional reality we do not understand the firm.

CONCLUSION

Markets and exchange cannot govern all relations, even in a capitalist society. However, neoclassical economics fails to distinguish adequately between commercial and non-commercial relations and thus it side-steps the problem. Blind to the nature and boundaries of real markets, all relations are treated as if they were market transactions. At the same time there is an inadequate depiction of markets themselves. Yet the distinction between market and non-market relations is both indelible and central to the reality of the modern world. The precise boundaries of the demarcation profoundly affect the nature of the specific variety of the system.

The conflation of the firm with the market has affected the work of authors such as Williamson who have originally made a sharper distinction between the two. Partly as a result, his concept of "transaction cost" becomes broadened not only to cover the costs of trading in markets but also the costs of organizing and managing the firm. Having blurred the boundaries between the two, the notion of transaction cost is broadened beyond the sphere of exchange. It becomes a universal, catchall phrase, seemingly explaining everything but in substance very little. To restore meaning to this conceptual chaos, a much clearer distinction between the firm on the one hand, and exchange and markets on the other, is required. Accordingly, following Harold Demsetz (1988), it would be useful to use "transaction costs" to apply to exchange and "organizational costs" to refer to the cost of managing and organizing the firm.[14]

Other problems arise when mainstream economics addresses different economic systems. Generally there is inadequate sensitivity to different cultures and institutional frameworks, involving different structures and combinations, of market and non-market institutions. Accordingly, there is an inadequate understanding of different types of capitalism, say in Britain, Germany, Japan, and the United States (Hodgson, 1999a). Especially when this conceptual blindness is combined with a free-market ideology, then an adequate policy analysis is disabled. It is sometimes simply assumed that if an economy is a successful economy then it must be a market economy, and if it is suffering recession or slow growth, then the "obvious" remedy is to extend and deregulate the market. There is little discussion of the way in which the market can be helpful in some contexts but harmful in others. The possibility that pro-market policies can be destructive as well as beneficial often escapes notice.[15]

Typically, mainstream economics starts from the individual, and tries to spin out the analysis of economic institutions from given, ahistorical agents. A remarkably candid admission of the flaw in this approach was by the econometrician Trygve Haavelmo in his 1989 lecture on receipt of the Nobel prize. He argued that

> existing economic theories are not good enough. . . We start by studying the be-
> havior of the individual under various conditions of choice. . . . We then try to
> construct a model of the economic society in its totality by a so-called process of
> aggregation. I now think this is actually beginning at the wrong end. . . . Starting
> with some existing society, we could conceive of it as a structure of rules and
> regulations within which the members of society have to operate. Their responses
> to these rules as individuals obeying them, produce economic results that would
> characterize the society. (Haavelmo, 1997: 15)

Haavelmo rightly suggested that historically specific institutions should be brought into the analysis at the beginning. Institutions are not simply human nature writ large. A few years earlier, another Nobel Laureate had made similar points and drew attention to the malaise at the core of modern economics. Robert Solow (1985: 330) complained:

> My impression is that the best and brightest in the profession proceed as if eco-
> nomics is the physics of society. There is a single universally valid model of the
> world. It only needs to be applied. You could drop a modern economist from a
> time machine . . . at any time, in any place, along with his or her personal com-
> puter; he or she could set up in business without even bothering to ask what time
> or place.

Solow (1985: 328) also regretted that "economic theory learns nothing from economic history, and economic history is as much corrupted as enriched by economic theory." However, the goal that economics has set itself of becoming the universal physics of society is luring the subject into a formalist morass. For Solow, "the attempt to construct economics as an axiomatically based hard science is doomed to fail." From this standpoint, Solow implicitly recognized the problem of historical specificity:

> all narrowly economic activity is embedded in a web of social institutions, cus-
> toms, beliefs, and attitudes. . . . If economists set themselves the task of modeling
> particular contingent social circumstances, with some sensitivity to context, it
> seems to me that they would provide exactly the interpretative help the economic
> historian needs. That kind of model is directly applicable in organizing a histori-
> cal narrative, the more so to the extent that the economist is conscious of the fact
> that different social contexts may call for different background assumptions and
> therefore for different models. . . . If the proper choice of a model depends on the

institutional context—and it should—then economic history performs the nice function of widening the range of observation available to the theorist. . . . One will have to recognize that the validity of an economic model may depend on the social context. (Solow, 1985: 328–331)

Close to the end of the twentieth century, both Solow and Haavelmo pointed to a line of conceptual and theoretical enquiry that would revive a central project of the nineteenth-century German historical school. This project involves making economics much more sensitive to specific historical, geographical, and cultural circumstances.

If we go down this road then a preliminary but important task is to provide social science with the precise concepts that are required to differentiate different types of institution and economic system. This is not a task of bland description, because the generation of adequate concepts requires a secure and prior methodological foundation. If taxonomies fail to relate to underlying structural differences then they are without value. Accordingly, conceptual clarification along these lines leads in a theoretical direction, towards the understanding and explanation of underlying causal mechanisms. This is a pressing task to which all interdisciplinary and open-minded social scientists can contribute. In this way, economics can regain its vision.[16]

NOTES

1 This chapter makes extensive use of material from Hodgson (1999b, 2001).

2 It is particularly significant that the importance of institutions is now recognized by the World Bank. See, for example, Burki and Perry (1998).

3 The affliction is not universal and uniform. For instance, the works of Aoki (1990), Chandler (1977), Greif (1998), Hirschman (1986), North (1977, 1990), and others are much better than the norm, exhibiting a deeper awareness of historical change and structural differences in socio-economic systems.

4 Efforts to explain this phrase away as a mere "metaphor" make matters no better. Becker and Posner (1993: 423) explain that the term "marriage market" means little more than that the matching of partners is "systematic and structured rather than the result of random shots from Cupid's bow." This inadequate explanation gives little recognition either of the institutional character of markets, or of the fact that marriages per se are never themselves bought or sold.

5 Coleman (1990: 22) goes on to state that marriage involves the "barter," by each partner, of "one commodity—himself or herself." Yet in no legal marriage contract does one person purchase another. Outside of slavery, people are not chattels. Many writers have described marriage using the metaphor of slavery; but Coleman is proposing a structurally impossible kind of slavery where each is equally the owned slave of the other.

6 Quoted by William Pfaff in the *Boston Globe*, 30 August 1999.

7 See Holt (1995) and Kagel (1995) for discussions of the evidence from experimental economics of the varying impacts of different market structures or mechanisms.

8 While this is a broad definition of a market, it does not rule out the need for internal subdivision, to delineate different types of market institution. On the contrary, it is essential to make such distinctions, in order to acknowledge many different types of mechanism and outcome. The markets of two thousand years ago were very different from (say) the electronic financial markets of today. For discussions of the shared and contrasting features of different markets see Polanyi, et al. (1957) and Callon (1998).

9 Leathers and Raines (1992) have disputed a claim by Iannaccone (1991) and others that Adam Smith treated churches simply as competitive firms.

10 For a good discussion of the role of legal relations in an institutional context see Bromley (1989).

11 For an interesting historical study of the evolution of the firm see Greif (1996).

12 In an excellent discussion of different types of business system, Whitley (1999) made a useful distinction between ownership and non-ownership coordination between firms. Ownership coordination depends on the exercise of ownership and other contracted rights, such as through strategic alliances. Non-ownership coordination depends on more informal relationships. Note that this important distinction is sustained only by recognizing—rather than ignoring—the importance of formal ownership, although it is far from the whole story.

13 See Cowling and Sugden (1993), Pitelis (1991), and the critical discussion in Hodgson (1999b).

14 Notably, Coase (1937) did not use the term "transaction cost." Instead, he used phrases such as "contract costs," "marketing costs," and "cost of using the price mechanism." For Coase, these costs were found principally outside the firm, and the firm exists to virtually abolish—rather than simply minimize—such costs. In contrast, Williamson accepts in principle that such "transaction costs" can apply extensively to firms as well as markets.

15 There is substantial evidence to support the view that the economic crises in East Asia in the 1990s were partly the result of unrestrained free-market, deregulatory policies. See the journal symposium in Chang, et al. (1998).

16 See, once again, the material in Hodgson (2001).

9

Market Institutions as Communicating Vessels: Changes between Economic Coordination Principles as a Consequence of Deregulation Policies

Frans van Waarden

INTRODUCTION AND SUMMARY

From Sweden to New Zealand, and from Pennsylvania to Mongolia, governments have been deregulating their economies, or at least are attempting to do so. Everywhere, the free unfolding of market forces through deregulation and privatization has become a key issue of socio-economic policy. The United States under Reagan and Britain under Thatcher took the lead in attempting to reduce state intervention and regulation of the economy. Their policies were continued under their successors, and their example was—in particular after the demise of the "real existing socialism" in Eastern Europe—also followed by many other countries including countries with formerly heavily organized and regulated economies, such as Sweden, New Zealand, and the Netherlands.

Illustrative for this broad policy trend can be the Dutch deregulation program. Its symbol and manifesto is the project "Market Forces, Deregulation and Legislative Quality" (MDW) of the Ministries of Economic Affairs and of Justice. However, in addition a wide variety of policy and legislative initiatives are aimed at reducing economic regulation and extending the scope for market forces and competition. The new measures include a major revision of the Economic Competition Act (from an abuse to a prohibition regime), a weakening of business licensing legislation, the relaxation of employment protection, the promotion of competition in the pensions market and the increased application of market forces in the insurance sector, the revision of legislation on shops' closing hours, the privatization of the sickness benefits system, the introduction of market forces into the implementation of the Disability Insurance Act, the debate on mandatory collective bargaining agreements and their statutory extension, the tendering out of bus services and telecommunication concessions, the encouragement of competition on the railways, in telecommunication, and in the supply of energy, the deregulation of the taxi market, the abolition of fixed tariffs for real estate agents and notaries, the elimination of the professional monopoly enjoyed by lawyers, competition in health care, relaxation of driving hours in road haulage, the discontinuance of proportional allocation of cargoes in inland navigation, the revision of the Food Quality Act, allowance of private television, and even the termination of the statutory minimum size of the beer glass.

"Fewer rules, more market," seems to be the maxim of such deregulation policies. The somewhat trivial assumption seems to be that deregulation will automatically result into more market competition. And that is a good thing. This chapter questions the self-evidence of such assumptions. It is built up from the following theses:

- Markets need institutions, and one of the most important functions of such institutions is to reduce risk and uncertainty. Such uncertainty reduction is needed for economic transactions, and hence for prosperity and growth, e.g., to reduce uncertainties about and increase the trust of transaction partners in the generalized means of exchange—money—institutions such as central banks have been created.
- Various coordination and allocation mechanisms can perform this function: markets themselves (i.e., commercial service–providing firms), communities, associations, firm hierarchies, the state, and courts. Most economies have all of these coordination mechanisms, but they do so in different combinations, and with some mechanisms being more dominant than others.
- Through a process of evolution, of competition and selection, certain institutions over time have survived because they tended to be more effective and efficient in reducing risk and uncertainty. In many cases it

turned out that a monopoly was needed, and that was most legitimate in the hands of the state. Hence, over time the state has assumed responsibilities for the currency, for standardization, product quality control, etc. This view contradicts the well-known economic theory of regulation (Stigler, 1971; Posner, 1972) which argues that public regulation will be less effective and efficient, because it is considered to be the unintended outcome of uncoordinated rent seeking behavior by various special interest groups.

- Deregulation is a policy trying to turn back this historical trend. Its intent is to reduce the relative importance of social and economic regulation, i.e., of statute law, created by the state. Its proponents could argue that even if the third thesis above is right, the historical circumstances, which selected out state coordination as the more effective mechanism for reducing uncertainty, may have changed; and that institutions have a tendency to become sclerotic. Hence a regular "cleaning of the stable" is necessary.

- Against this I will argue that deregulation does not reduce the need for risk and uncertainty reduction. It will merely lead to changes in the "mix" of coordination mechanisms in an economy. And these changes may be different from what has been intended.

  - Often fewer statute rules do not result in more market. Instead, deregulation may lead to an increased importance of firm hierarchies, of associations, or of case law. Associations may fill the void created by the state with self-regulation; firm hierarchies may introduce their internal rules; transaction partners may want to write more "complete contracts" and have to organize monitoring and enforcement; more commercial conflicts will come for the courts; and case law—which may be just as, or even more, detailed—will replace statute law. Countries that have deregulated tend to experience an increase in liability litigation.

  - Where stiffer competition law limits the regulatory possibilities of associations (cartels!) firms could replace "associations" (horizontal and voluntary forms of cooperation) with "firm hierarchies" (vertical and involuntary cooperation). While anti-cartel legislation prevents an association of shopkeepers to coordinate prices, such is quite acceptable for a large supermarket chain or even for a franchise. Such chains and franchises introduce much and detailed "internal regulation," regarding product assortment, handling, etc.

  - Furthermore, more market competition may require more rather than less regulation. Studies indicate that sectors that have been "deregulated" and privatized, such as telecoms or the railroads in Britain, need sector regulators that provide even more detailed regulations than the former state monopolies had.

Therefore, the unintended effect of deregulation policies—and/or of policies trying to enhance market competition—could very well be more rather than less rules; only rules in different forms—e.g., case law by the courts rather than social and economic statutory regulation; or rules emanating from other actors or representing different coordination mechanisms, such as internal rules of large firm hierarchies, or self-regulation by associations. In this sense one could perceive the various coordination mechanisms as *communicating vessels*: less of the one may lead to more of another—only not, as intended, more market.

- Such a shift between coordination mechanisms is usually not neutral. It is quite likely that other institutions that gain in importance as a consequence of deregulation are less effective and less efficient. Coordination of economic action by firm hierarchies or by courts and case law introduces new and higher costs, and can be less effective in reducing risk and uncertainty. Such will be demonstrated with reference to the higher transaction costs in the United States due to the tendency of juridification, in the absence of general civil law: more detailed contracts, more monitoring activity, more litigation, higher costs of lawyering, of compensatory and punitive damages in liability cases; and less legal certainty. Where one tries to reduce the "bureaucracy," one may end up with a more costly and less efficient "lawyerocracy."

- The conclusion relevant for policy makers is "look before you leap." It can do no harm to think twice about possible unintended consequences of deregulation. Attempts to turn the long term historical trend of increasing importance of public regulation should be aware of the costs and benefits of the various economic coordination mechanisms, and of the possible driving forces behind this historical trend. What is needed is a comprehensive approach, being aware of, and balancing the pros and cons, of the various economic coordination mechanisms. A "hydraulics of communication vessels" is needed, in a double sense of the word: as knowledge about the relations between the institutional vessels; and as praxis, as a master plan—"Wasserwirtschaft"—of such vessels, based on such knowledge.

And a bit closer link between policy making and social science can do no harm. As the American economic-sociologist and historian Rogers Hollingsworth and the French economist Robert Boyer note in their study on the relations between social institutions and economic performance: "We are witnessing a major paradox. Governments are relying more and more upon markets in order to solve the many difficult issues which they are confronting, at the very moment when theorists are discovering that the efficiency of markets is restricted to a very small set of products" (Hollingsworth and Boyer, 1997: 1).

MARKETS AND THEIR NEED FOR INSTITUTIONS

Are Markets Natural Social Orders?

Many proponents of market competition seem to consider markets to be natural and spontaneous social orders. And these supposedly can flourish and develop best in the absence of any intervention. The assumption is that there can never be too much freedom on markets. "Many economists correlate freedom only with negative rights—the absence of governmental interference" (Scully, 1992: 11). Maximum freedom, openness, and competition provide the most optimal allocation of goods and production factors and those in turn the greatest prosperity possible. The self-regulatory capacity of parties on markets is often overrated and there is not enough awareness of the potentially disruptive effect of conflict and competition. For this there is no room in the standard economic models. And neither is there for the possible benefits of ordering and moderation.

Whereas many economists assume natural order, by contrast, political theorists and lawyers often start from an opposing assumption. According to them, the "natural" societal condition is one of chaos, destruction, insecurity, and an unlimited and all-destructive battle of all against all. The political philosopher Hobbes described in 1651 the "natural conditions of humanity" with the famous and timeless words:

> Againe, men have no pleasure, (but on the contrary a great deale of griefe) in keeping company, where there is no power able to over-awe them all . . . So that in the nature of man, we find three principall causes of quarell. First, Competition; Secondly, Diffidence; Thirdly, Glory. The first maketh man invade for Gain; the second, for Safety; and the third, for Reputation. . . . Hereby it is manifest, that during the time men live without a common Power to keep them all in awe, they are in that condition which is called Warre; and such warre, as is of every men, against every man. (Hobbes, 1968, orig. 1651: 185)

Conflict, violence, and deception are also the "natural" condition on unregulated markets. They are of all times and places. Just a few out of an endless list of examples. The "robber barons" (Josephson, 1934), the railroad magnates, mine owners and steel barons of the late nineteenth century in the United States did not refrain from having their competitors eliminated by professional gunman or from fighting trade unions and their leaders literally with fire and sword. The Dutch nineteenth-century capitalists went less far, as they were already constrained by regulations, but they too did hire once in a while a fighting squad to threaten strikers. At the moment, capitalism probably shows its most unrestrained face in Eastern Europe, where the institutions that formerly regulated economic exchange have lost their legitimacy and new ones have yet to be developed. Whereas Eastern Europeans were told for a long time that capitalism was a crime, now they believe that crime is capitalism. The *Volkskrant* reported on the Wild West methods of taxi drivers in Prague:

> The exorbitant growth of the number of taxi's (there is no legal limit) has led to all out war for the best of the approximately five-hundred taxi-stands. In the tourist center, the law of the jungle reigns. Places at the Wenceslas square are defended with all available means. Competitors find their tires slashed or are molested. One driver was kicked to death in broad daylight on the Wenceslas square when he summoned a colleague who pushed a lady out of his car because she wanted only a very short drive. (*De Volkskrant,* 3-12-1994)

The examples should make clear that markets cannot exist without rules and organizations, without a legal framework.

It might be countered that it is now generally accepted among economists that there are many types of market failures that reduce the effectiveness and efficiency of market allocation. Much of modern-day microeconomics deals extensively with such market failures as information asymmetries, moral hazard problems, externalities, or the underproduction of collective goods. It is accepted that regulation may be necessary to correct for such market failures. But that there are "market failures" even before there are markets, that markets may need rules to exist at all is often overlooked. This might be because throughout history markets have become more and more regulated, so that the problem of order on markets is no longer perceived (and reflected upon) as a problem. It has become taken for granted, in particular in the deregulation debate.

Insofar as there are economists who do realize that markets are no spontaneous orders, these are yet mainly located in the margins of the discipline, such as economic history (North and Thomas, 1973; North, 1990), institutional economics (Hodgson, 1988, 1993a, 1993b; Williamson, 1975, 1985; Eggertson, 1990) and economic sociology (Granovetter, 1985; Granovetter and Swedberg, 1992; Smelser and Swedberg, 1994; Etzioni and Lawrence, 1991; see for an overview Steiner, 1995).

As a consequence, fundamental categories, such as market, competition, or optimal allocation, which have long been taken for granted by many mainstream economists, are again being problematized. "Social theory is experiencing something of a revival within economics. . . . Economists are again addressing such issues as the relationship between agency and structure, between economy and the rest of society, and between inquirer and the object of inquiry. There is renewed interest in elaborating basic categories such as causation, competition, culture, discrimination, evolution, money, need, order, organization, power, probability, process, rationality, technology, time, truth, uncertainty and value, etc.," so said editor Tony Lawson at the presentation of a new contribution to his series "Economics as Social Theory" (Maki, 1993: frontispiece).

Functions of Institutions: The Generation of Incentives

Of course economists are right in emphasizing that economic actors need incentives in order to engage in transactions, to buy, sell, invest, or look for work. The basic incentive is of course the human need for food, shelter, protection, and derived from that, for money, power, and wealth. And they are right in arguing that markets and competition enhance this incentive. The fear of losing out in the competitive struggle stimulates economic actors to take initiatives, to engage in more transactions, and to do so in a quicker, more decisive, effective, and efficient manner. It stimulates business to invest and innovate, and to look for new markets. It stimulates workers to invest in their skills and to search the labor market for better opportunities to acquire income and influence. That makes for more efficient allocation, i.e., that scarce resources find their way to those that put them to the best use.

Furthermore, of course freedom is important for allowing and instigating economic actors to engage in transactions, investment, and innovation: freedom to think, to experiment, to associate, to discover, to try out new and daring, uncommon and not obvious combinations, to travel through unknown lands, to delve into mysterious spaces. Freedom also to exchange information, to travel, to choose one's profession, and to follow one's interests. Such freedoms enhance creativity. This is of course all very true.

However, this argument tends to overlook the obvious fact that freedom can exist only in an ordered context, where basic needs are safeguarded. And that incentives need to be amplified—by organizing and protecting competition.

North and Thomas (1973), North (1990), and Scully (1992) have pointed out that property rights have to be secured in order for economic transactions to occur. The incentive of serving self-interest works only when one has some minimal security that what is being exchanged can also be disposed over, at the exclusion of others. Similar securities are needed for the enforcement of contracts. Pay is only an incentive for a worker when he can have the relative security that what has been promised will actually be paid.

The "whip of competition" is neither a naturally occurring phenomenon. It has to be organized. First of all, there must be a minimum number of firms competing. But left to itself many markets tend to monopolization. Mergers and takeovers take place in order to realize economies of scale, to save on transaction costs, or merely to accumulate economic power. Sunk costs and technological expertise give the incumbents such a large advantage that newcomers experience great difficulties entering stabilized markets. One merely has to reflect on the history of the American oil, chemical, automobile, and aircraft industries, the railroads and air traffic (Chandler, 1962, 1977) to realize this. Antitrust policy is needed to secure a minimum number of competitors. By law monopolies of Standard Oil in the United States and IG Farben in Germany had to be broken up.

Competition requires furthermore that customers are able to monitor prices and qualities of offers of producers. The market must have some minimal transparency. That does not come by itself. Producers often have an interest in creating intransparency. Or they produce so many price/quality combinations in their search for market niches that customers lose overview. The examples are there for the asking: airline fares, automobile models, and most recently computers and mobile telecom services. Although the differences are marginal, the diversity of products, tariffs, and services is so great that hardly any consumer can get a complete and comparative overview. Incomplete and asymmetric information can frustrate the working of markets. Institutions are needed to correct for these "market failures," e.g., some authority who creates uniform units for prices and possibly also for quality. In this way in the past many standards have been created for products, services, and production factors, varying from the decimal system of weights and measures, to standards for advertising mortgage interest rates, to diplomas standardizing skills.

Many markets have their own specific standards that organize them. Agricultural auction marts organize the coming together of supply and demand. The rules determine who can (and sometimes also who have to) sell on this market. Usually that right is limited to members of the cooperative, but they are forbidden to sell outside of the auction hall. Thus supply and demand come together only on that specific place at a specific time. The rules also determine who can buy, and how the price is determined. Other nice examples of socially constructed markets are Wall Street and the London City. Only registered traders that satisfy a number of conditions can trade on these markets, and they have to do so according to quite detailed prescriptions, including bans on insider trading. These rules all serve to make trading transparent and to give everyone equal and honest chances. Hence, institutions are needed to organize the incentive of competition.

Reduction of Risk and Uncertainty

Incentives and fear of competition are usually not enough to get economic actors to engage in transactions and to invest. They must also believe that this is a meaningful activity, that there is some minimum chance for success. The chance of success should not be too small. If economic actors do not see many possibilities to realize their interests, they are not likely to take action and to engage in transactions. And less economic activity implies less prosperity and growth.

The unemployed may be stimulated to look for work by lowering their benefits; however, they should also believe in the possibility of really finding work. If five years of applying for jobs have not rendered any results, they will not be very active anymore. Competition or tax incentives may entice entrepreneurs to invest. However, if they see no useful technology available or new market niches, they may refrain from investing. In particular, there should be some reason to believe that the relevant circumstances on their markets will not have changed too drastically in a number of years, when their investments should finally start generating profits.

Nobody gets motivated by the prospect of performing Sisyphus labor. Whoever does so is certainly not a rational acting *Homo economicus*. An economic actor should see some minimal possibilities. It is as with gambling. One gambles, because the chance of winning big can be a strong incentive. However, it is particularly thrilling and addicting if one indeed wins occasionally, if only a little bit, because that increases the belief that one day one might win big. If one never wins even a little bit, gaming soon becomes pretty boring. That is known in Las Vegas. One wins regularly, and casinos advertise with payout ratios of 97 or 98 percent. That makes it so addictive that the casinos can get rich from the difference of 2 percent.

Belief in the possibility and sensibility of investment and innovation depends in particular on the nature and degree of *uncertainties and risks*. (The difference between both being that uncertainty cannot be predicted, whereas risk can be to some extent. This implies that probabilities can be calculated—and hence insured. See Knight [1921], on this still the classic statement.) The greater the risks and uncertainties, the more economic choices become a gamble. And the greater the gamble, the greater the chance that no action will be taken at all, that transactions will not take place. Reduction of risk and uncertainty brings stability and predictability, and makes economic transactions more likely and hence also prosperity and growth (North, 1990: 3ff.).

In the "natural" economic disorder the uncertainty and risk are much too great. In a situation where everybody is everybody's competitor—read enemy—no transactions take place and no growth can be generated. In the words of Hobbes:

> In such condition, there is no place for Industry; because the fruit thereof is uncertain: and consequently no Culture of the Earth; no Navigation, nor use of the commodities that may be imported by Sea; no commodions Building; no Instruments of moving, and removing such things as require much force; no Knowledge of the face of the Earth; no account of Time; no Arts; no Letters; no Society; and which is worst of all, continuall feare." (Hobbes, 1968, orig. 1651: 186)

There are many sources of risk and uncertainty. A major and elementary one regards property rights. Safeguarding those through regulation is not only necessary in order to provide economic actors with incentives, but also to allow for transactions to occur in the very first place. A potential buyer will want to be sure that the seller is the real owner of the good to be sold. How uncertainty over property rights can bring an economy to a standstill became clear at the unification of East and West Germany, when it was unclear for a while who was the rightful owner of real estate: the original owner who had fled to the West and who had been disowned by a regime which had now lost legitimacy and legality; or the person whom the GDR-regime had assigned the property and who now lived in it. As long as this remained uncertain, no one wanted to buy real estate and that prevented investment in business as well.

Uncertainty exists also as to the transaction process itself. How should a price be determined? Is the price demanded the price that the seller expects? Or does he start higher in the expectation of coming out at a lower price? Is bargaining expected? Various cultures have developed different unwritten rules for this. At a Turkish bazaar both parties expect lengthy bargaining. In a West European supermarket such is considered highly unusual. But with trade in real estate bargaining is again accepted practice in Western societies.

Differences in Place and Time as Source of Uncertainty

The uncertainty increases, the moment transactions go beyond simple exchange. What to do if I want to sell something, but the one who needs my good does not have anything I want? While a third person has something I need, but he is not interested in what I have to offer. Such transactions—whereby my transaction partners are different individuals and whereby transactions are often separated over time and space—require an abstract generalized means of exchange, such as shells, gold, coins, or checks. The agreement that these represent a specific value is such an institution that makes these transactions possible. But the partners need some certainty regarding the value of the gold or check—and regarding the durability of this value. Someone who wants to sell something today against "money" will want the certainty that he will get the next day about the same counter-values in goods for that money. If not, he will not be inclined to sell for this "money" and transactions may not take place. Like uncertainty about property rights, galloping inflation can also halt transactions and dislodge an economy completely.

Future-transactions involve risk by definition. Today an agreement is reached, but only in the future will delivery take place: of the house or the ship that has yet to be built, of the holiday for which one has only the necessary free days in six months' time, of the raw materials and machines that will have to be delivered "just in time" in exactly forty days from now. Such a contract creates extra risks. The supplier is unsure whether the customer will really accept the product upon delivery and hence presses for prepayment or at least a down payment, also because he has to make costs in the meantime. That creates risks and uncertainty for the buyer. Will the holiday trip meet the expectations? Will the hotel be really as close to the beach as promised? What if the travel agency goes bankrupt before the trip starts? Will the service be delivered or will I get my money back? Such risks and uncertainties can be translated into transaction costs: the costs that have to be made to reduce risks and uncertainty to an acceptable level.

More in general is to factor in time as a major source of risk and uncertainty (Traxler and Unger, 1994). This holds in particular for entrepreneurs who have to invest enormous sums in research and development, or in complex and large-scale manufacturing technology, which takes years to build and which will generate profits only in some years from now. Much can be different by then. Consumer preferences may have changed, new alternative products may have appeared, unforeseeable technical innovations may make the investments obsolescent, political regimes may be different. The uncertainty over time implies that the rationality behind short-term investment decisions is often another one than that behind long-term decisions. Thus institutions help reduce risk and uncertainty that can have a major impact on such rationalities.

Distrust and Fraud as Sources of Uncertainty

An important and specific source of uncertainty concerns the behavior of the transaction partner. Can he be trusted? Won't he deceive me? Will he live up to his promises? Or should I expect him to be an opportunist? In case of a futures contract: will he deliver the expected goods in time and of the expected quality and on the conditions agreed? Even in a direct exchange this is far from being certain. Do I really get forty liters of gasoline in my tank when the meter indicates so? Can the meter be trusted or has it been manipulated? Anybody who has traveled in Mexico with a car will know that that is not self-evident. Is the meat hormone free, the eggs without salmonella, and do they really come from free-roaming chickens? How much room do the latter actually have? What if we do not agree on a transaction? How will conflicts be settled? Is there any chance of me getting an honest process or will the law of the jungle reign?

Differences of opinion are not imaginary. Partners will not be inclined to trust each other a priori. On the contrary. Each one knows that the other is after his own interest. Competition, which on the one hand provides positive incentives, can on the other hand increase distrust. It can become also an incentive for fraud and violence. Distrust is the "natural" state on any unregulated market. Actors need a minimal trust in the honesty of others, trust that these others will abide by the rules of the game, trust in the quality of the goods that they will not be poisonous or spoil quickly, trust also that the value of the money they trade their goods for will still have the same value tomorrow, trust in the correctness of information, and so on.

Conclusion: A Balance between Incentives and Uncertainty Reduction

Economic actors need incentives in order to be stimulated to take initiatives, but they must also be able to believe in the sense of such initiatives. Incentives bring flexibility, movement. They stimulate actors to look for new profit possibilities. Uncertainty reduction brings stability and predictability. It allows people to make rational decisions, including the making of long-term investments. Therefore, institutions are needed, rule systems that reduce distrust and transaction costs. Without them, transactions become less likely.

In that sense, institutions are the "dikes" of an economy. Dikes are physical constructs that create physical space and reduce risk and uncertainties within it due to flooding; they make life within the polder possible, and make it sensible for economic actors to invest in farms and factories in the polder. Similarly, institutions are social constructs that create social spaces and markets, and reduce risk and uncertainties in them; they make life in markets possible, and make it sensible for transaction partners to invest in manufacturing and trading.

Uncertainty must be reduced, but not so much that the incentives disappear or that moral hazard problems arise. The demands from the need for incentives and for uncertainty reduction can be contradictory. Incentives depend on some degree of insecurity, the insecurity provided by competition. Therefore, institutions have to strike a balance between the need for incentives and flexibility on the one hand, and the need for security and stability on the other. There has to be some fear, but also some security. Economic actors should feel pressured to invest, but also feel able to do so, that this makes sense. And exactly where the balance between these contradictory needs lies depends on the cultural importance of both needs for incentives and for uncertainty reduction, which tends to differ between societies.

INSTITUTIONAL ALTERNATIVES FOR UNCERTAINTY REDUCTION IN TRANSACTIONS

Individual Strategies

Transaction partners can of course first try to solve their problems of uncertainty and lack of information themselves. They can conduct their own checks. They can gather information from the neighbors of the transaction partner to find out whether the latter really owns the house he wants to sell, or whether he is often drunk. One can hire lifeguards and threaten with fighting squads, not an uncommon method in criminal circles to reduce the uncertainty of transactions. Less drastic is to demand securities from the trading partner, like a bank guarantee or a bank deposit. Loans are given against collaterals or after inquiries have been made with the employer. Landlords demand a deposit from renters. And customers could take a scale to the supermarket to check on the real weight of the chocolate in the box. And do you see yourself already filling eight times a five-liter jerrycan with gasoline, in order to be sure that you tanked forty liters? Or take a microscope along to the butcher to check the meat for salmonella?

It seems farfetched, but in the past, when institutions that provided for such control were still lacking, this was not uncommon behavior. This occurred because the chance of opportunistic behavior of the other is so great on markets. On medieval markets, gold and silver pieces were weighed very carefully, because others had often tried to file a little bit off.

An interesting example is provided by the early Dutch cotton trade. There was a time, around the middle of the eighteenth century, when traveling salesmen put out yarn to house-sitting weavers in order to weave it into fabrics. Yarns and fabrics formally remained the property of the salesmen. The weavers tried, by weaving a little less tight, to keep some yarn for themselves. The salesman was of course aware of this and hence carefully weighed yarn before and fabric after. The weavers counteracted by making the cloth a little damp, in order to make it heavier. That forced the salesman not only to weigh the fabric, but also to estimate its degree of humidity. That required time, energy, and skill and led easily to conflicts between weaver and salesman. Records of many of them can be found in the archives.

A second individual strategy to reduce uncertainty is to conclude contracts. By making clear agreements before and fixing them formally, so that they can be verified later on, one can also try to reduce risk and uncertainty. However, that too requires information: ex ante about what exactly to fix and how, and ex post about whether the contract partner has lived up to his commitments. The observation of contracts has to be monitored, and if necessary enforced. Therefore one has to dispose over sanctions. If the partner is dependent on resources that are at one's disposal—future orders or supplies, work, knowledge—and that partner has little or no alternative suppliers, then an efficient sanction is the threat of withholding such resources in the future. In the absence of a long-lasting and non-anonymous relation—required for such sanctions—one may have to seek recourse to the threat of violence. In criminal circles, where one cannot so easy call upon the strong arm of the state, this is not an uncommon means for contract enforcement.

Fighting squads cost money, the measuring of gasoline takes time, and salmonella are difficult for the layman to recognize. Individual strategies to counter distrust and reduce uncertainty cost time and money. They are literally "transaction costs," which tend to be high, because the individual cannot profit from economies of scale. Therefore, they can seriously frustrate transactions.

Institutions

Societies have over time developed institutions which serve to reduce such transaction costs and which aid in reducing risk and uncertainty, thus facilitating transactions and increasing prosperity. Building upon typologies made earlier by Williamson (1975), Ouchi (1980), Streeck and Schmitter (1985), and Hollingsworth (1997), the following allocation and coordination principles, which can perform these functions, can be distinguished:

1. The market, that is, commercial firms making a business out of the reduction of risk and uncertainty
2. Communities or clans, i.e., informal groups based on primary relations such as the family, and whereby "trust" is an important lubricant
3. Associations, a more formal and goal-oriented form of social cooperation, as compared with communities
4. Firm organizations, which internalize transactions (or private hierarchies)
5. The courts, which coordinate through case law. This is the state in a more passive role: it reacts to conflicts brought to it by market parties
6. The state, or a public hierarchy, which coordinates through statute law, both basic civil/commercial private law and social and economic public law. This is the state in a more active, initiative-taking role.

Common to all of these coordination mechanisms is that they are forms of organized cooperation. They differ, however, on a number of dimensions. First of all is that of informal-formal. Formalization of group relations by the creation of a formal organization enlarges the binding character of the group and with that its capacity to create uncertainty-reducing regulations. Second, groups can be structured internally either horizontally or vertically. In a horizontal structure the members are more or less equal, but in a vertical one there is a hierarchy of super- and subordinates. A vertically structured group has an internal central authority, which improves decisiveness and hence its capacity for regulation. Third, formal organizations can be either private or public. Being public means that this organization has access to the state, i.e., can be supported by the monopoly of the state on the legitimate exercise of force. With that, the degree of bindingness increases further. Because courts act only upon initiatives from civil society (conflicts that are being brought before them), they can be considered a mixed public-private institution. Statute law, created on its own initiative by the state, can be considered a more pure public institution. Combinations of these three dimensions produce the various institutions that can coordinate markets. Except for the market itself these are captured in table 9.1. As one comes further down the rows, the coordination principles have a greater capacity for creating and maintaining more specific rules and regulations that are to reduce risk and uncertainty. It is an ordinal rank order of weaker to stronger developed principles. On these now a bit more.

Table 9.1   Comparison of Economic Coordination Principles

Coordination Principle	Nature of Relations	Nature of Relations	Legal Status
1 The Market, Commercial Services	None or contractual	private	private
2 The Community or Clan	Informal	horizontal	private
3 The Association	Formal	horizontal	private
4 The Firm Organization	Formal	vertical	private
5 The Court	Formal	vertical	semi-public
6 The State	Formal	vertical	public

Commercial Services on Markets

Can the market itself provide solutions for the problems of risk and uncertainty? To a certain extent it can. The history of the market economy, capitalism, and industrialization is one of institutional innovations that have helped to reduce extremely high risks and uncertainties to more manageable proportions in order that higher risks can as yet be taken and sizable amounts of capital can be made available for such enterprises.

That started in medieval markets. In order to satisfy the need for quantity and quality controls, new trades developed, such as those of gold and silver weighers. Future transactions were put in writing in order to increase the clarity of the agreement and to allow for ex post control. At a time when few people were able to read and write, this need led to the development of the profession of official writer, out of which the function of the notary public later developed.

With the general differentiation of the economy since the end of the nine-teenth century the business of uncertainty reduction has also been further differentiated. Enterprising businessmen saw market niches. Others have followed and are still following. Uncertainty reduction has become big business. As fewer people are involved in the primary and secondary sectors of the economy, an increasing share of output and employment is produced by economic sectors that specialize in the reduction of risk and uncertainty, that is, in controlling others on behalf of still others. Much of what is called "commercial services" is concerned with this activity. It has become one of the fastest growing sectors of the economy. As with other products and services, division of labor and specialization have also led to higher productivity and cost reduction in the business of risk and uncertainty reduction. In due time, reduction of risk and uncertainty has become a major service sector. Businessmen have specialized in the collection of information (detectives, credit registration bureaus, consultancy firms, marketing agencies), in the evaluation of actors (credit rating organizations), the distribution of information (advertising, more neutral: consumer organizations), the certification of the truthfulness of information on behalf of transaction partners (accountants, auditors, notary publics), the drafting of contracts (lawyers and notary publics), their monitoring and enforcement (assault groups, debt collection agencies, process servers, bailiffs), the covering of calculable risks (insurance companies, options trade), the investigation of the suitability of job candidates (professional recruiting agencies, head hunters, psychological testing bureaus), private trade marks and private certification agencies that reduce the risk among consumers regarding the stability and nature of product quality, etc.

The market can also contribute to uncertainty reduction. Important in this respect are the stock and option exchanges. But the labor markets and parties on it (temporary work agencies) also contribute. The stock market allowed for the easy marketability of ownership shares. "Marketability of assets and the existence of efficient markets for the sale of these assets meant that owners were not undertaking commitments equal in during to the life of long-lived capital assets. On the contrary, they could realize their financial gains or cut their financial losses whenever doing so appeared to be expedient. In this way a capitalist proprietor's long-term risk was converted into an investor's short-term risk" (Rosenberg, 1994: 97).

However, commercial solutions do have their problems. For many forms of uncertainty reduction they are less appropriate. Commercial businesses are also prone to the seductions of opportunistic and corrupt behavior. They are often paid by only one of the transaction partners and "whose bread one eats, those word one speaks." Product information supplied by advertising agencies for their producers tends to be incomplete and biased. It still entails uncertainty for others, be it at a different level. Who controls the controllers, the accountants, risk analysts, and insurers? Could their professional associations do it? And who controls those?

Furthermore, private institutions usually cannot do without the backing of an external authority. One can try to build up a trademark image. However, as long as this is not protected and competitors are free to market products, also of lesser quality, under the same brand name, the image cannot serve its purpose. That is, free riders can destroy the reputation of an image or brand of a group of producers. Bad products drive out good products from the market, and bad entrepreneurs good entrepreneurs. Brand names need protection. Lawyers cannot do much without a system of law and without public agencies and functionaries, such as public prosecutors, judges, policemen, bailiffs, and prison guards, who enforce that law.

A third problem of market solutions is that where uncertainty reduction requires generally valid and accepted norms and standards, the competition which is typical for market solutions is likely to create problems. Commercial organizations compete among others by trying to impose their own technical standard on the market. That may produce a plurality of standards, i.e., confusion. However, the customer is interested in one universal standard, rather than the best one. One can still live with less efficient standards. The United States still has weights and measures with which it is difficult to calculate. However, lack of universal standards seriously hinders trade and production, as it reduces complementarity and interchangeability of products, as was the case in the early days when every city and region had its own weights and measures. Efficiency requires an organization with a monopoly position on setting technical standards.

Finally, commercial solutions still imply large transaction costs, and these costs now have to be paid to commercial organizations. Compared to individual firm strategies for uncertainty reduction, "outsourcing" to specialized organizations offers economies of scale. But other forms of uncertainty reduction, by institutions to be discussed below, can provide further savings. Furthermore, such alternatives are often more effective, with the result that many commercial uncertainty-reducing institutions have been replaced sooner or later by other institutions. More on those now.

Community and Trust

A "cheaper" means to save on transaction costs is "trust" between the partners. An efficient economy runs—like society in general—largely on trust.

Trust is not self-evident. It cannot be based in a belief in the "natural" goodness of man. Certainly not in capitalism, where competition tempts if not forces transaction partners to cheat each other if possible. Those who do not join in cheating may find that they lose out in the competitive struggle in an unregulated economy.

There can be three bases for trust between transaction partners: (a) somewhat durable mutual dependencies, (b) cultural norms, and (c) institutions.

Transaction partners who are mutually dependent on each other for some length of time, such as a shipbuilder and its supplier or a textile manufacturer and his workers, can develop trust in these longer lasting relations. Game theoretical experiments have shown that cooperation and trust can be rational strategies between players who know that they will also remain dependent upon each other in the future ("iterative games"). Furthermore, parties in a durable relation can develop gradually mutual expectations, which can, in the context of their dependence, be regularly affirmed and hence fortified. In time, such expectations will develop into unwritten rules. The history of capitalism also shows, however, that sooner or later the temptation or pressure of competition can get so great that such mutual expectations are broken and trust disappears. Loss of foreign markets to competitors can force employers to reduce wages and to lay off workers with whom they have had a mutual commitment of decades. That might make it very difficult to win back that trust, as the Dutch textile entrepreneurs learned. In the 1930s they halved the wages and fired thousands of long-term employees. After World War II they again needed workers, but many did not trust the manufacturers anymore. Such is likely to happen on large markets where transaction partners are relatively anonymous for each other— that is, the ideal market in economic theory.

Trust is not something that can be easily created. It is there or it is not (and if it is, one better be careful about it). Trust is more likely to be found in a "community" with a certain identity. One strategy to reduce uncertainty is to conclude transactions preferentially with people that one trusts because one shares a common group identity with them, or because there is for other reasons a durable mutual dependency relation. That could be members of the same (extended) family, religion, ethnic group, or minority. The chance that they will commit deceit is smaller than with anonymous transaction partners in a market.

Trust is enhanced by the diffuse and multiplex character of relations in such groups. The members are in different roles related to each other, as family, as neighbors in the same village, as churchgoers to the same church, as carers in sickness, as members of the same hobby club—and as partners in economic transactions. The polymorphic character of these relations offer ever so many channels for social control and social interdependence. Misbehavior in economic transactions can be punished, one extreme form being excommunication.

Transactions remain limited to within a certain homogeneous social group. The social structure of that group is the institution that reduces uncertainty and transaction costs. Subsequently Ouchi (1980), Piore and Sabel (1984), Sabel (1992), Porter (1990), and Fukuyama (1995) have pointed to the importance of clan and culture for economic transactions. The classic examples are the industrial districts of mid-Italy, textiles in Prato and ceramic tiles around Sassuolo. But examples can also be found elsewhere in time and place: the communist silver smiths in Oneida in New York State, or the Jewish confection industry in New York City.

It will be clear that dependence on this institution limits the scale of transactions. One is therefore tempted to think that this institution only works for more primitive, less differentiated societies, and that they would be outdated in the present time of globalization. Nothing is further from the truth, as the competitive advantage of the social community structure of the Italian districts shows. Multinational network organizations like Benetton owe their existence to them. Geographically dispersed communities can serve as channels for internationalization. Such was a competitive advantage of the Jews in former days. Family and religious ties in the diaspora were channels for trust relations, even to third persons. In a time when there was hardly any international banking, Jews could give off bills of exchange on family members in distant cities.

A group identity is also a source of social norms, of what is acceptable and not, also in economic transactions. Jews won't trade on the Sabbath, Catholics were originally not allowed to charge interest, and Calvinists were expected to be thrifty and not to indulge in luxuries. That too increases the predictability of the intentions and choices of transaction partners. Many cultures and religions have norms that condemn deceit. This has as effect—if not intention—to mitigate mutual distrust among the members of the group.

As norms differ, so do mutual trust and distrust between groups. Cultures differ also as to those whom one trusts, family members, strangers, organizations, the state. According to Fukuyama (1995) Chinese and Italians have in common that they trust their family, but distrust "strangers," that is, those in the society at large. He calls these "low trust" societies. Germans, Japanese, and Americans by contrast have relatively more trust in people and agencies outside of their family relations, including associations and the state. He calls them "high trust" societies.

Cultures—also on submarkets—develop unwritten rules that prescribe how transactions are to take place, how one should negotiate, how one can appeal, and how conflicts between transaction partners should be settled. In short, such rules structure mutual expectations between transaction partners. On a Turkish bazaar both parties expect that the buyer will bargain. In a department store in a Western society this is unusual and is not expected. But even in Western societies one should bargain in the markets for real estate and secondhand cars. Is it possible to return goods that do not satisfy and get one's money back? In the United States that is no problem, but in the Netherlands that is uncommon. Here the rule "buying is buying" reigns informally.

Often, however, cultural norms and values do not suffice. Agencies are needed to back up such norms, to formulate and interpret them clearly, and to monitor and enforce them. Norms without supporting agencies are rarely long lasting—certainly in capitalism! The pressure of unrestrained competition can get so fierce that even originally good willing and obedient members of the group feel forced to forget about the norms. Therefore, institutions are needed to keep capitalist competition in check, institutions that regulate and enforce what are legitimate and illegitimate fighting methods. Murder, thievery, and manifest fraud are certainly not such methods—not only because they are immoral, but also dysfunctional: the risk of competition can get so great that incentives no longer work and no one is willing to engage in transactions. There are various types of agencies that can generate and back up such rules.

Associations

A first one is self-organization and self-regulation by the sector concerned. They may form a kind of "private" government in the form of an association, which enacts and tries to enforce "laws," in the form of internal rules. There have been many forms of them.

Early forms of horizontal cooperation have been social clubs, with predominantly businessmen as members, such as the Free Masons, local elite societies, and presently service clubs such as Rotary, Lions, or Kiwanis. They too have played a role in uncertainty reduction. They were places where the local elite, including potential business partners, could meet informally, exchange information and opinions, and check mutual expectations. It still is a golden rule to building contractors to be member of several local clubs. They have to "network," establish relations with local dignitaries and politicians who may have jobs to tender out, and check if not try to influence expectations of possible clients. Furthermore, such clubs are locations where local social elite identities and social ties get established. In that sense business clubs are a combination of the two allocation principles "community" and "association."

More important, however, are the specialized interest associations of economic actors: trade associations, trade unions, and consumer organizations. Unlike clubs they have businesslike goals, such as political interest representation, providing services to members, creation of sectoral collective goods, and self-regulation, including cartellization. There are many of them, and many types. In various ways they help to reduce uncertainty. Some examples may be helpful.

The Dutch Association of Insurance Companies has created a code, which prescribes to members how they have to list returns and risks of life insurances in order that potential clients can better compare offers. This is a typical attempt to increase market transparency. The increased competition has led to a diversity of calculation methods which has complicated comparison. Dutch associations of contractors and travel agencies have created guarantee funds, which give clients the certainty that the future trip or house bought from a member in the fund will really be provided, even if the firm goes bankrupt. Cartels mitigate competition, and thus reduce the pressure on market parties to behave opportunistically. Dutch dairy associations have created a system of quality control, which secures the trust of consumers, both domestic and foreign, in the quality of Dutch dairy products. The association of electricity companies has created minimal safety standards for electrical products, which provide consumers with the certainty of buying safe products and which prevent higher transaction caused by connecting products of different standards, and so on.

Associations of consumers and workers also help reduce uncertainty. The Dutch consumer organization compares products on price and quality, and has negotiated contracts with the bankers association which regulates liability in electronic payments. This reduces uncertainty for customers over whether the amount of cash received from an ATM machine will actually be the same as the amount deducted from their account. Uncertainty over this did initially lead to hesitation in the Netherlands among consumers to use such machines. Trade unions conclude collective wage agreements and help reduce distrust among workers that all employers want to exploit them. Sometimes such associational regulation has been sanctioned and supported by the state, as with the statutory extension of collective wage agreements and of the dairy quality control system.

Private Hierarchies

In the absence of community and trust—as in an internationalizing and consequently more anonymous market—and with too high costs of commercial uncertainty reduction, entrepreneurs can also limit uncertainty through mergers and takeovers with transaction partners. Competitors can be conquered—as in horizontal integration—or customers/suppliers—as in vertical integration. Transactions that were to take place before in a market can henceforth take place in a bureaucratic organization, which thus increases in importance as an allocation and coordination mechanism. Actors actually enter into transactions with themselves, and this allows them to reduce uncertainty about intentions and possible opportunistic behavior of others. Greater size also means more market power, and allows economic actors to influence or even steer developments in markets, which reduce uncertainties for long-term investments. Even uncertainties about the value of money can be reduced, by the creation of one's own value-units for internal exchange. Competing technical standards, which produce uncertainty, can be co-opted and adopted, or abolished, or pushed out of the market by the greater market power of the larger firm. Philips might not have lost out with its video 2000 standard, if it had been able to take over its Japanese competitors, which produced VHS. The example shows how high the transaction costs of losing out in battle over technical standards can be.

This is all, of course, common knowledge since the work of Williamson (1975), who, following Coase (1937), tried to find an answer to the problem mainstream economics could not solve: "why are there organizations if markets are such efficient coordination mechanisms?" His answer was that market failures like information asymmetries create possibilities for fraud and deception, that strategies to reduce such asymmetries involve costs—transaction costs—and that organizations can help reduce such uncertainties and costs. Therefore organizations can be more efficient. Lazonick (1991) goes further and states that "what mainstream economists view as 'market failures' I view as 'organizational successes.' . . . By their unquestioning acceptance of the ideology that views the perfection of market coordination as an economic ideal, the new theorists of 'imperfect markets' have become intellectual captives of the myth of the market economy" (1991: 8).

The State I: The Courts and Case Law

Many economic transactions sooner or later give rise to conflicts over the quality of the products supplied, over the payment of product or labor, over the observation of contracts. Such conflicts often have come, after outbursts of violence and social unrest, sooner or later to some arbitrator for settlement. Already early on, the state has—given its responsibility for social order— provided such arbitrators: the judiciary financed and employed by, but relatively independent from, the other state powers. For the implementation and enforcement of its decisions the judiciary is supported by the legitimate monopoly of the state over the exercise of force. As judges orient themselves in their decisions to earlier decisions by other judges, these have acquired power of precedence. The accumulated decisions have produced de facto regulation: case law, which regulates economic transactions and which has substantially contributed to the reduction of uncertainty. Already in this manner the state has become involved in the regulation of economic transactions. Even governments that are otherwise wary of intervention in the economy and advocate a liberal "nightwatch" state have in this way, willy-nilly, become market regulators and are becoming more so every day.

The State II: The Legislative and Executive Powers, with Statute Law

Is the uncertainty-reducing role of the state via the courts still a passive one? It reacts to conflicts which are brought to it from civil society. Sooner or later the state has also come to intervene and mediate more actively in economic transactions. This has happened through the production of abstract civil law and social and economic public law. In part such statutes were a codification of earlier formed case law; in part it was also new law. To some extent such has happened at the instigation of market parties. Thus much of social and economic regulation in the Netherlands has been created at the initiative of trade associations and trade unions.

Various motives got the state to do so. First of all was its interest in and responsibility for the maintenance of social order. Legal protection of workers could reduce their risks and uncertainties in the labor market and were to contribute to a reduction of social conflict. Threats of strikes and revolutions can be considered as back-ups of attempts at private regulation of transactions of the labor market. Not coincidentally, much social regulation came about in periods of great social unrest, like the revolutionary year 1919 and the crisis of the 1930s. Protection of consumers was to prevent conflicts between consumers and suppliers. In both cases the state again was addressed in its primary responsibility of maintainer of law and order and conflict settler.

Another motive of the state for intervention was its interest in economic growth and prosperity. Reduction of uncertainty in transactions could promote growth-inducing transactions, and thus eventually also the tax income of the state itself. Such early economic intervention was an important legitimation of the state. In fact, the process of state formation can be considered as a history of uncertainty-reducing interventions on behalf of the market. The formation of states and capitalist markets has been a parallel and inter-linked process. One might even maintain that uncertainty reduction is the central "business" (and legitimation) of the state.

There were various reasons for a special role of the state. First was its monopoly on the legitimate exercise of force, and then the inter-linking of its monopoly on taxation and on the enactment of binding regulation for everyone. Many forms of uncertainty reduction require such a monopoly. Either there was a need for a generally valid institution and a single general and uniform standard or such a monopoly was necessary to prevent and discourage free ridership. Many forms of state regulation are typically collective goods.

A second reason for state involvement was that, of all actors, it could most legitimately claim to represent a "general interest." And that was important for the legitimation of uncertainty-reducing regulations. Potential transaction partners need a minimal trust that the rules of the game are relatively neutral, that they do not advantage certain parties over others. Furthermore, only a more or less neutral party can provide legitimation to private uncertainty reducers, such as certification agencies of insurers. History has shown that there is a need for neutral certification of the certifiers, and neutral control of the controllers.

Third, centralization of the exercise of force to back up contractual obligations had the advantages of economies of scale—as compared with private bodyguards or even armies.

Just to mention some examples: Sooner or later the state monopolized the provision of a generalized medium of exchange such as money in order to guarantee its value. It "stamped" specified amounts of gold and silver—certifying their value. The use of money still reflects a trust in the state and its central bank—notwithstanding the saying on the rim of a well-known coin that it is "in God we trust." Product quantity control also became the domain of the state. The weighing of goods in transaction in medieval cities eventually became a state monopoly: the institution of the city municipal weighing house was introduced. Later the weights and measures gauging office (IJkwezen) evolved out of this. Now private individuals do the weighing again, but with instruments calibrated by state agencies. Similarly, product quality is controlled by public authorities. The Leyden fabric controllers ("lakenkeurders") of the sixteenth century have evolved into a variety of control agencies: the Food Inspectorate, the Meat Control, the Drug Inspectorate. And they control detailed norms, fixed in public law, varying from the "Meat Inspection Law" to the "Baby Food Ordinance."

A major function of civil law is to back up private property and contracts. In return, law sets conditions of contracts. State law also establishes the rights and responsibilities of the limited liability company, the insurance company, or the stock market, institutional innovations that developed in society but needed sanctioning by the state in order to effectively reduce uncertainty for the investors.

In general many privately created institutions function thanks to state supervision. People are prepared to pay for decades of insurance premiums to private companies because state supervision of the sector provides some minimal guarantees against loss of entitlements due to bankruptcy of the insurance companies. Passive public oversight on disciplinary law of the professions and of self-regulation by the stock exchange increases their trustworthiness. State and semi-state agencies implement such regulations. Examples are the courts, also publicly appointed notary publics or the registry offices for land and ships, who fix property rights. Formal ownership of firms is registered by the Chambers of Commerce. Intellectual property is protected by patent law and brand law, an important precondition for entrepreneurs to invest in research and development and to built up brand images.

A large part of law, both civil and economic public law, serves to discourage corrupt and opportunistic behavior and to mediate in conflicts over transactions. The security that there are fixed procedures for conflict mediation which minimize the chance of arbitrariness and make outcomes somewhat predictable reduces the frequency with which mediation is called upon, and that in turn lowers transaction costs and facilitates transactions. It helps also in reducing conflict in labor relations.

The most important and most general function of the state regarding the reduction of uncertainty is to provide for a stable and predictable legal, political, and social environment for firms, thus allowing them to calculate risks better, in the knowledge that the basic parameters in the environment will not change erratically. The provision of stability and predictability is of course a major function of the rule of law. This reduces the likelihood of arbitrary interventions by the state. Constitutional law limits the authority of the state and provides for procedural rules regarding rule-changing, which guarantee that such rule-changing will take time, be cautious and prudent, and allow for public debate and the hearing of the subjects concerned. But not only constitutional law has a function here; social and economic public law have a role as well. Labor law reduces strike incidence, and market ordering regulations and social security reduce the chance of erratic and fierce demand fluctuations.

Combinations of Coordination Mechanisms

Combinations of the various coordination principles have in turn created specific institutions that reduce uncertainty. A nice example thereof—and of central importance in the history of capitalism—is the invention of the limited liability company. This was produced by the principles market, hierarchy, and state, in combination. It is an organization, active in markets—in particular the capital market—and sanctioned if not created by the state.

The limited liability company allowed entrepreneurs to reduce their personal risk by "sharing" it with others. As a result, the group as a whole could take larger risks. Furthermore, the company limited liability of the partners by separating private and corporate property. The corporation became a separate legal entity that could own property and enter into transactions and assume commitments and debts. Its property was separated from that of its shareholders. That reduced the risk of bankruptcy for the latter. Claims on the company could no longer be directed against the personal property of the participants. Given this significant reduction of the personal risk of the entrepreneur, he dared to engage, through his company, in more risky investments than he would be likely to do when he would still be liable with all his personal assets. Of course this did imply greater risk for the transaction partner. He was less certain that commitments made in future contracts would be observed, that deliveries would be paid. To reduce such risks, formal rules were introduced regarding the procedures to be followed in case of bankruptcy and the rights of creditors. Furthermore, the larger capital reserves of the shared liability company provided transaction partners with added securities.

An institution that bears resemblance to the stockholding company is the insurance company. Where stockholders shared risks among themselves, the insurance company allowed basically the same on a larger scale: the sharing of risk between all those taking insurance. The insurance company is a go-between that, on the basis of mathematical knowledge, did the work of calculating the probability of risks. It could reduce risk through scientific calculation. It could then risk the taking of risk of others. And it is no accident that both developed simultaneously. It was in the Netherlands, where the emergence of "parten-rederijen" and "compagnieschappen" was linked to large and risky investments in radical innovations, that there was the construction and maintenance of windmills, the huge engines of proto-industrialization, and the organization of ship convoys to the Indies.

In the seventeenth and eighteenth centuries, the oldest industrial region of the Netherlands, and one of the oldest in the world, emerged along the Zaan River to the northwest of Amsterdam. For those days, enormous capital goods—driven by wind power—sawed wood, pressed oil seeds, ground grain, and beat ingredients for paper manufacture. More than six hundred windmills adorned around 1725 the flat and wet Zaan region (Boorsma, 1950). The growth of this windmill park was made possible by risk distribution. The construction and exploitation of a mill was quite a risky enterprise. In the flat country, very costly tall wooden constructions were quite vulnerable to storm, lightning, and fire. On average once every forty years a mill burned down. Hence, the mill owners entered into agreements to distribute the risk. Rather than one person owning one mill, each of thirty owners owned one-thirtieth share in thirty mills. The owners cooperated in so-called "partenrederijen," corporate bodies that formally owned the mills (Van Braam, s.a.). Furthermore, they also cooperated in mutual insurance contracts, through which the owners collectively insured their property against fire. Such contracts were also early forms of associational self-regulation. The contracts provided for associations that imposed a number of preventive measures on the members, such as the presence of buckets and rope to fight fires, and the associations actively organized the supervision of these rules (Walig, 1912).

Earlier on, similar forms of risk distribution had been developed in trade, in particular the trade to the Indies. The Dutch East-India Company (VOC) and West India Company (WIC) were also limited liability corporations, whose shares were in the hands of municipal chambers. In the latter, leading merchants and their families participated. For each individual trip to the Indies separate "compagnieschappen" were created within these chambers. A successful return of a ship full of spices could reap extraordinary profits. That was the incentive to invest. However, the risk on these long and dangerous journeys was high. Only one in two ships returned. To reduce this risk, such ships were financed collectively. These were major factors facilitating investment in risky undertakings, and hence were major instruments for industrialization. All these techniques made it possible "to convert a long-term risk involving large amounts of capital into a short-term risk that was limited to small amounts of capital" (Rosenberg, 1994: 97).

Effectiveness and Efficiency of Coordination Principles

Which of these coordination principles are now to be preferred, and under what conditions? Which ones are the most effective and efficient ones? Which have the greatest legitimacy? Present-day deregulators and privatizers seem to assume a priori explicitly or implicitly that "market solutions" will be more effective and cheaper. That remains to be seen. How could "organization" ever have been able to maintain the competition with the "market" as a coordination mechanism—and under certain conditions even have won it—if it would be less efficient?

History has shown that many market solutions to the problem of uncertainty in transactions have their deficiencies. New forms of order through the principles of association, hierarchy, courts, and state have developed and have eventually been selected by history as the more effective and efficient ones. Market solutions often require support of public regulation. It is not without reason that gold- and silverweighers in medieval markets were replaced by state-certified coins and later central banks, or that private quality seals were substituted by public hallmarks. The latter were simply "better:" more effective to enforce, less free rider problems, less ambivalent and contradictory interpretations, greater clarity and more uniform and equal application, economies of scale, etc.

Many non-state solutions to the problem of risk and uncertainty have eventually needed state support in order to be effective. We realize better that associations find themselves confronted with what Olson called "the logic of collective action," the threat of free riders (Olson, 1965). In practice associations were very much aware of this and they have often lobbied the state for support. That has frequently come, e.g., in the form of statutory compulsory membership (as for the Austrian, German, and Swiss Chambers and the Dutch statutory trade associations), statutory extension of private contracts of and between associations (cartels, collective wage contracts, covenants in several continental European countries), or the statutory monopoly on the provision of specific services (e.g., export licenses, collection of statistical data).

The coordination principles of "community" and "trust" can often exist only thanks to the presence of supporting institutions created by the state, especially in the larger and more anonymous societies in which we live. Examples are quality standards and inspections, supervision of insurance and banking, or regulation that mitigates competition and bans some more aggressive forms of association. These trends reduce the compulsion economic actors may feel to behave strictly as self-serving and opportunistic partners, seizing every means to advantage themselves in complete disregard of the interests of others.

INSTITUTIONS AS COMMUNICATING VESSELS

Risk and uncertainty in economic transactions can be reduced by different coordination and allocation principles. This makes these principles functional alternatives for each other. They are likely to be a kind of communicating vessels. Less of the one leads to more of the other. And that has implications for deregulation policies. Less statutory regulation does not necessarily mean that the outcome will be less overall regulation. It may increase the demand for coordination by other principles. Transaction partners will continue to need reduction of risk and uncertainty. And that need may not necessarily be filled by the "market," by commercial services. It could also lead to more associations, more hierarchies, or a greater role for the courts and case law. And it is questionable whether those alternatives for statutory regulation are to be preferred and whether they will be just as effective and efficient.

As suggested above, public regulation has often turned out to be necessary in order for other uncertainty-reducing institutions to function well. Deregulation may therefore also have the consequence of undercutting such supports. Mutual trust between economic actors and trust in each other's products may wane when statutory product regulation gets abolished; associations may find it more difficult to ensure the observation of their self-regulation by their members if they lose statutory supports. It is questionable whether such costs compensate for the advantages of simpler and lesser regulation. A more flexible monetary policy can undercut public trust in a currency and lead to a drastic drop of its value on exchange markets. More flexible meat inspection can lead to sudden loss of public trust in meat. The BSE scandal might have been prevented if British agricultural standards would from early on have banned turning herbivores into carnivores, by serving them ground-up congeners. The scandal well illustrates how high the costs of ineffective risk and uncertainty-reducing institutions can be. Similarly, people may be less likely to have a building firm do some renovation if the chance to be cheated increases because of deregulation.

Deregulation may lead to an increase in the importance of other coordination principles; some deregulation measures can also undercut the effectiveness and efficiency of other principles. In the first case it is a matter of *fewer* rules and *more* other coordination principles; in the second, *fewer* rules and *fewer* other principles as well. But in both cases there may be a loss of effectiveness and efficiency in the reduction of risk and uncertainty on markets. Below I will discuss first some cases of "fewer rules, more others," and then some "fewer rules, also fewer others."

Fewer Rules, More Community?

Fewer rules, more mutual trust and community: that may look like an ideal situation. The latter are not only usually "cheap" coordination principles, but for many people coordination by informal community processes has positive connotations.

It is, however, questionable whether there will be many deregulation initiatives which could lead to an informal community taking over the role of formal regulation. Coordination through informal communities usually requires face-to-face contacts, typical for a local community (but, of course, also a locally centralized market such as the London stock exchange or the Antwerp diamond market). Such principles are not really an alternative for most markets in modern society, which tend to be large scale, separated in time and space, even international, and anonymous. Historically, the trend has also been the other way around. Markets and transactions on the basis of spontaneous trust and informal communities usually did not survive. Sooner or later such informal agreements were formalized to self-regulation by associations, created by such communities.

One area where communities could again become more influential is in the case of the deregulation of establishment licensing, which existed in many continental European countries. Proof of skills was needed in order to be able to open certain businesses. In the Netherlands these rules have been deregulated because they were considered unjustified barriers to market entry (and it is considered in Austria and Germany). A more specific motive was to make it easier for ethnic minorities to establish a business. It is quite likely now that out of newly found ethnic businesses new business communities emerge, and that these may try to regulate their markets with more informal regulations. Such happened in the thirties in the Netherlands with Italians who created terrazzo businesses (and now completely monopolize it), and after the war with Chinese restaurants, Italian ice cream shops, and Turkish sewing ateliers in Amsterdam. These communities often formed their own informal establishment standards— regarding skills, implicit knowledge, social/ethnic relations, capital, reputation and reliability. Such informal standards may become quite effective market entry barriers and their power of social exclusion may be much greater than that of formal statutory standards, which at least do not explicitly discriminate.

Whether such a development is desirable remains to be seen. Are informal market entry barriers not worse? The legal system created by the Enlightenment and French Revolution that treats everyone formally equal was inspired by the desire to abolish group privileges and informal social inequalities.

Fewer Rules, More Association?

Deregulation may also be countered by business with a strengthening of self-regulation by associations. It even seems to be the explicit goal of some de-regulation measures. If licensing for butcher shops will be abolished it may not take long before consumers may see a sign on the door "recognized by the Royal Association of Butchers." There is no establishment regulation for brothels, as they are still formally illegal in the Netherlands; however, many brothels have a sign on their door, "Recognized by the Association of Safe Sex Relax Houses" (which means that they have to live by the rules of the association: regular health inspections for prostitutes, obligatory use of condoms, etc.). If the government gives consumers fewer guarantees about the quality of the entrepreneurs and their services, businessmen will try to do so themselves.

It is unclear whether self-regulation is always to be preferred over state regulation. Self-regulation certainly has advantages: broader legitimation among the businesses concerned; closer adjustment to practice, hence more practical and technically better, sometimes also more flexible, regulation; etc. But there are disadvantages, too. It may be less effective, as self-regulation may be undercut by moonlighting and dabbling outsiders, which may destroy the image of a sector. One rotten apple may spoil the whole basket since, with information asymmetries, the bad firms drive the good ones from the market. This is especially true when self-regulation is not allowed to have cartel-like elements, due to strict competition law, because such cartel-like elements (e.g., exclusive trading agreements) can provide supporting sanctions to self-regulation.

A second disadvantage of self-regulation is that there is a greater chance that it serves particular interests, which may undermine credibility among consumers. Product scandals tend to suddenly reduce public trust in such arrangements and invariably lead to calls—sometimes from unlikely sides—for more state intervention. In 1997, when the Dutch stock exchange was haunted by some sensational insider-trading scandals, the liberal leader, Bolkestein, who otherwise pleaded for deregulation, demanded that self-regulation by the stock exchange should be replaced by stricter government control. That demand had already been voiced in the United States, where stock market scandals had been the order of the day and where investors defend their interests more assertively. Thanks to pressure from the United States, even the Germans have had to replace their reasonably effective self-regulation of financial markets by public regulation (Lütz, 1997).

Fewer Rules (Less Association), More Hierarchy?

Abolishment of statutory establishment licensing can be replaced not only by a private recognition regulation of a trade association, but also by attempts of a larger individual firm to establish a trade mark reputation for itself and its products. As this succeeds, the firm will enlarge its market share, buy up competitors, and get larger. Conversely: as the firm is larger, its name recognition will increase, and as long as the firm succeeds to link positive associations of reliability, trustworthiness, efficiency, and quality to that name, this form of "quality certification" becomes more effective. In this way many firms have grown to organizational giants: Shell, Philips, Mercedes, McDonald's, Nike, Benetton. Nothing wrong with that. Even excellent, from the perspective of uncertainty reduction.

One should realize, however, that deregulation policies may have such consequences for the relative importance of different coordination principles. A retreat of public quality regulation increases the importance of trademark reputations and that tends to enhance concentration in the economy. In short, "hierarchy" increases in importance as a coordination principle.

Other deregulation measures can enhance such a trend. The Netherlands recently has changed its regulation of competition from an abuse to a prohibition system. Whereas the past price agreements between cement manufacturers, pickle producers, and collective purchasing associations of independent retailers were allowed, now that is no longer the case. Will that produce more "market?" Or will sectors be stimulated to transform horizontal forms of cooperation in trade associations and cartels into vertical ones? Franchises and collective purchasing associations are no longer allowed to set prices for their members; a large supermarket chain can do so, however, without restrictions for its shops. Small building firms cannot collude before tendering; a large contractor can, however, freely exchange information among its subsidiaries, i.e. strict cartel legislation forces small firms into each other's arms. A plurality of smaller firms that cooperate in an association will be replaced by a more limited number of larger firms. Market agreements are then replaced by internal firm regulations, and those are of no concern to the cartel authority. Its business is inter-firm regulations, not intra-firm ones. A similar process took place earlier in the United States. The relatively strict anti-cartel tradition of English common law stimulated firms to form large trusts, until the United States introduced anti-trust laws. Such merger controls are, however, a far cry in many European countries.

There are still more deregulation measures that are likely to contribute to a concentration movement: relaxation of shop opening hours legislation; the abolishment of zoning laws that limit the building of large stores at the periphery of cities (introduced earlier on to protect the inner cities); the deregulation of the liberal professions of lawyers, accountants, and notary publics, such as the ban on advertising and on contingency fees, etc.

Until recently, cartels, establishment licensing, shop closing hours, and zoning laws have protected the small retailers and made for diversity. Thus there is as yet a diversity of publishers and bookstores. In every little town one still finds a bookshop. They are protected by the statutory book price cartel, which fixes the retail price of books for two years and allows the bookstores a markup of 40 percent. This enables them to keep a relatively large stock of books, and not just huge piles of only bestsellers, as is the typical picture in many American bookstores. Abolishment of this cartel will enable supermarkets to cream off the market with bestsellers, a deathblow to many smaller bookstores. They will go bankrupt or be taken over by a large bookseller. Or the association of bookstores might transform itself into a business firm, a direct change of horizontal voluntary coordination into vertical compulsory. This has happened in the Dutch dairy industry, where cooperative associations of over two hundred independent small dairies were transformed into one very large dairy manufacturer, with the associational staff becoming the company staff. Liberalization of markets will enhance competition and eventually lead to further concentration. The liberalization of the American airline industry has after a short period in which the number of airlines increased led to a merger and concentration movement, in which the consumer has fewer and fewer independent companies to choose among. A similar trend is likely to occur in the telecom sector, now a proliferation of firms. However, soon there will be a shakeout and concentration.

Curiously enough, competition stimulates—because it increases risk and uncertainty—economic actors to try to reduce such competition, by cooperation, or by "conquest." Feudal lords fought in earlier times a battle in which eventually one of them, the monarch, gradually acquired a monopoly on using violence. They did so by means of war, raids, occupations, negotiations, and marriage. Now business firms do the same. They use similar means: price wars, raids on the stock exchange, and mergers. Liberalization both facilitates and stimulates this process. Will each economic sector sooner or later get its own Leviathan? With the merger of Boeing and McDonnell-Douglas the airline industry is not very far removed from that anymore. As the public state withdraws, do we get a private "business state" instead?

What is more in the interest of consumers and citizens? It is not easy to evaluate the coordination principle "hierarchy." Large firms no doubt have many advantages: economies of scale resulting in lower prices and high-quality standards, reduction of uncertainty and transaction costs in internal economic traffic, trademark reputations that provide certainty to consumers and facilitate transactions, a stronger competitive position of such large firms in internationalizing markets, enough capital to invest in a knowledge infrastructure, allowing for innovation and adaptation to changing circumstances, etc. Only large firms can invest the huge sums needed for developing high-speed train systems or UMTS networks. And up to a limit, concentration does not necessarily have to reduce alertness, flexibility, and innovation. The cola wars illustrate that oligopolistic markets can still be very competitive.

However, there are also disadvantages to concentration. Uncontrolled concentration of power is everywhere in society a threat to freedom, and in this the economy is not excepted. In politics concentration of power has led citizens over time to create many checks and balances on such power: the rule of law, periodic democratic elections, judicial review, administrative law, an ombudsman, etc. Such checks and balances on the concentration of economic power clearly lag behind. Furthermore, concentration can and does reduce diversity and create more uniformity. Symbolic may be the average shopping street in many European cities: everywhere the same shields of the same chains and franchises. Concentration is not yet so far progressed as in Canada, where 80 percent of all restaurants are franchises, but the trend is in that direction. Finally, there are indications that large-scale production can inhibit flexibility and innovation. Among others, Saxenian (1994) showed in her comparative study of the computer industry of the American West Coast (Silicon Valley) and East Coast (Route 128 around Boston) that small-scale firms in flexible networks on the West Coast were much more flexible, dynamic, and innovative, and performed better, than the industry on the East Coast, which was organized in older, larger, and more closed hierarchies such as IBM and Wang.

Whether one puts the emphasis on the advantages or disadvantages of hierarchy, it serves to stress that the enhancement of hierarchies is contradictory to the intentions of many deregulation programs. Their intent is to increase economic dynamism: more new market entrants, greater mobility in and out of markets, more room for small-scale initiatives. While this may be the short-term effect, in the long run concentration will be stimulated. Furthermore, it may be that liberalization of market regulations will only have a limited effect. Markets are also limited by other factors, which are positive for the economy and the consumer: accumulated internalized implicit and codified knowledge in the established firms, accumulated capital goods stock, and trademark reputations. Deregulation of banking and insurance will not lead to the creation of thousands of new local banks and insurance providers, which come and go as nine-day wonders. And it is questionable whether such is desirable.

Fewer Rules, More Courts, and Case Law?

Fewer rules do not mean fewer social situations that require regulation. Public regulation reduces uncertainty and contributes to the predictability in economic transactions. Codified civil law fixes property rights and the rights of contract partners. It provides for standard contractual rules, whether for a marriage, a will, or a business contract. Social and economic public regulation also fixes basic rights and duties of societal actors. That saves on transaction costs. What is already regulated in law does not have to be specified by partners in contracts. Labor law protects the interests of workers, so that it is less risky for them to engage in a labor relation with an employer. They are less dependent on their own power, and hence will be less likely to strike, which in turn reduces uncertainty for employers. Similarly, consumer protection legislation corrects for information asymmetries and enhances the development of trust in products and their suppliers.

Less codified and statute law does not mean that there is less to be regulated, but that others actors and other institutions will have to do so. And if no one else, transaction partners may have to do so themselves. Where there is less certainty about mutual expectations and less legal protection of the interests of the parties concerned, they will have to try to provide such certainty themselves and specify their mutual expectations, rights, and obligations. This requires detailed contracts, and active monitoring of these. Where mutual expectations are less clear and stable, the chance of conflict is also greater. Parties will bring such conflicts to court, where judges are forced to take decisions, which set precedents and become case law. Contracts and case law are hence an alternative for statute and codified law.

Comparison with a legal system where statute law and codified law is relatively less important, such as that of the United States, can be illuminating. Dutch firms that go to the United States to found a subsidiary are often shocked by the amount of contracts, the degree of detail, and other paperwork involved in establishing a business. It can take over two years before all the legal formalities are taken care of. In the absence of standardized business law, each individual contract has to specify in detail all the possible future states of the world—the more so as the general reliance on case law and litigation forces transaction partners to try to conclude as "complete" contracts as possible. I had a personal experience with this difference in legal systems. A family will drawn up in the Netherlands took only two pages; Dutch civil law regulated most issues. When my parents moved to the United States, a new will had to be drawn up. To specify the same issues, the document became forty-five pages long, trying to specify any imaginable but unlikely future situation, such as the chance that someone might claim to be an illegitimate grandchild.

Where workers or consumers have less protection from collective law or collective welfare state provisions, they seek recourse to tort law and engage in lawsuits. A case in point is the incidence of asbestos-based tort cases. Although the incidence of asbestos-related diseases among Dutch workers was five to ten times as high as in the United States in the seventies and eighties (Kagan and Axelrad, 1996: 5), Dutchmen rarely took to the courts. By 1991 fewer than ten cases had been filed (Vinke and Wilthagen, 1992), although Dutch law authorizes tort claims against employers. By contrast, an estimated two hundred thousand asbestos tort cases had been filed in the United States. The explanation is that victims had other roads open to them in the Netherlands. For about one century, compensation for damage caused by work accidents and diseases has predominantly been based on social security. Financial consequences of the risks of labor were collectivized.

> In Great Britain, where asbestos victims' medical costs and lost earnings are taken care of by the National Health Service and government-provided disability pensions, the rate of asbestos-related tort suits has been far lower than in the US, tort recoveries are about half as large, and British asbestos firms have not been driven into bankruptcy. (Kagan and Axelrad, 1996)

A similar contrast is found in job protection. In the Netherlands, workers are protected against sudden dismissal. Employers have to ask the State Labor Exchange Offices for formal permission to lay off groups of workers. The director of the office decides. Only rarely is permission refused. The procedure is informal and flexible. Laid-off workers are compensated by their former employer or by the collective unemployment insurance. This makes them much less prone to appeal decisions of employers in court. Not so in the United States, where no such statutory job protection exists. Workers can be dismissed starting the next day. As a result, many workers sue their employer in court, claiming to be discriminated against or sexually abused. A director of Ikea in Los Angeles, who had been Ikea director in Austria, told me once that he spent as much on liability insurance in the United States as he did formerly on social security in Austria. That is, "fringe benefits" for workers cost about the same. In Austria any laid-off worker had the right to an unemployment benefit. In the United States it was a gamble for the dismissed worker. He could win big and get sizable damages paid; or he could go out empty-handed.

American research shows that where new collective regulations or provisions are created, tort litigation tends to decrease. Kagan (1984) noted that in the period 1950–84 the number of cases involving transaction partners trying to collect debts in American state supreme courts and trial courts declined sharply, despite the large increase in the volume of loans and delinquent debts, and despite the sharp increase in overall litigation. The explanation: there were new alternatives. In the past,

> the farmer who could not pay off his crop mortgage was threatened simultaneously with the loss of his home and livelihood. The shopkeeper or small manufacturer who could not pay his debts faced similar ruin. For them it made sense to fight for survival in the courts if any plausible legal argument could be made. (Kagan, 1984: 365)

Now farmers, businessmen, and workers have more alternatives and can most easily find other jobs, "and their debts are backed by relatively reliable sources of income and various forms of social insurance" (ibid.).

The inclination of the Dutch to go to court has until recently been in comparison extremely low. Indicative was the low lawyer density in the Netherlands. In 1988 there were thirty-five lawyers per one hundred thousand inhabitants, almost ten times fewer than in the United States, with a density of 312 lawyers. Other European countries score higher: Germany 190, Britain 134, Italy 81 (Lipset, 1996: 50; Blankenburg, 1994; Blankenburg and Bruinsma, 1994). The explanation is the presence of much legislation which is quite clear about what parties can expect from each other, the presence of collective social security provisions, of collective sectoral institutions that compensate the aggrieved, and of alternative arbitration institutes.

This is changing, however. Litigation is increasing. Health and safety at work issues may stand as examples. Injured workers more often file liability claims against their employers, for having been exposed to unsafe working environments or for being laid off. An important factor is the advance in scientific knowledge about the relation between work environment (e.g., hazardous substances) and illness, making for better, more convincing, evidence in court. Furthermore, some legal changes are fostering the decollectivization of the compensation for the risks of labor. Since 1967 an individual employee can make a tort-based claim against the employer; previously this possibility was excluded by law for almost seventy years. Furthermore, the duty of proof in tort law, placed on the employee, has become less severe. Also, the demands entailed by the duty of care grew with regard to employers. Employers are becoming increasingly responsible and liable for the risks of labor, and their responsibility and liability are based on a non-fault jurisprudence. There has been a cutback in social security-based benefits since the 1970s. The measures taken are increasingly forcing both employers and employees to insure themselves by means of private insurance. As a consequence, tort law and private insurance companies are growing in importance with respect to compensating workers as victims of occupational accidents and diseases.

Indicative for the juridification trend is the lawyer density. It has doubled between 1988 and 1998 from thirty-five to seventy lawyers per one hundred thousand inhabitants. A new specialty, that of tort lawyer, is developing, and— in line with Dutch corporatist traditions—already an association of such lawyers has been founded. The first compensatory damages of more than one million guilders (five hundred thousand dollars) have been awarded.

This trend is likely to be enhanced by deregulation measures. More protective legislation and collective provisions may then, according to the research of Kagan, lead to less (lengthy) contracts and less litigation; the opposite is probably also true. Retreat of the legislature will increase litigation. Deregulation does not reduce the amount of conflict in society. On the contrary, it is likely to increase it. And such conflicts have to be managed.

Workers, no longer protected by statutory dismissal regulations or with less unemployment insurance are more likely to take to the courts. Ex ante, new workers may try to safeguard their interests in individual employment contracts, if they have the bargaining power (scarce skills) to do so. Deregulation of establishment licensing could lead to bunglers entering the market, and a consequent increase of fraud, deception, and adulteration. Victims have an incentive to sue their suppliers in court, at least if these have not yet been bankrupt. Indicative is the case of Dutch victims of fraudulent marriage counseling bureaus and time-sharing sellers (sectors that were never regulated). They have formed an association to represent their interests in court. The initiator was a lawyer, who smelled business (*De Volkskrant*, 12–11–97). Liberalization of the legal profession, easier access to the bar, contingency fees, allowance of advertising—all measures planned in the Netherlands—are likely to stimulate such entrepreneurship among lawyers. Research of Steven Vogel (1996) into deregulation and privatization of the British telecom and financial sectors has, at least for Britain, indicated a relation between deregulation and a more adversarial policy style of regulatory agencies and to increasing litigation.

How to evaluate such a trend? There are no doubt positive aspects to the fact that people have easier access to their rights in court. It fits well with the individualization trend in society. For business it means more uncertainty and higher transaction costs, because litigation and case law tend to be less effective and efficient in reducing risk and uncertainty, as the American example demonstrates. How *effective* are both systems in the reduction of uncertainty? It should be noted at the outset that neither legislation nor litigation can provide for complete stability and predictability. Ideally—in the interest of stability—statute law would have to be highly detailed, specifying all the possible future states. But that is of course not possible. Lawyers, the legal designers, have a bounded rationality and imperfect foresight. Therefore, such rules need later interpretation by the courts, through litigation. That is not only necessary but also desirable to keep legislation flexible and capable of adjusting to changing circumstances and changes in the sense of justice of society. Regulatory systems have to strike a balance between predictability at the cost of rigidity on the one hand, and flexibility at the cost of uncertainty and arbitrariness on the other hand.

However, in the United States the emphasis is on the side of flexibility and unpredictability. In the literature and the media there are many complaints about the unpredictability of judicial decisions. Medical malpractice is a case in point. Law often looks like a lottery. In a review of cases against anesthesiologists, in 46 percent of the cases the claimant received appropriate care, according to an expert panel; 42 percent of these 46 percent who received appropriate care nevertheless received compensation. "At the same time, many of these malpractice studies demonstrate, many malpractice victims, and some legal claimants, who did receive inadequate care—according to expert review panels—received no or relatively little compensation" (Kagan, 1996: note 88).

Such unpredictability creates uncertainty. Huber (1989) compared verdicts by juries in cases of allegedly dangerous products. "Most juries, in accordance with the evidence, found the product not responsible for the plaintiff's injuries. However, in each sequence of trials concerning a particular product, one or two juries, hearing the same evidence as those which found no liability, decided otherwise and awarded the plaintiff massive compensatory and punitive damages. The modal jury award was $0, but the 'average' was in the millions of dollars. For the manufacturer in question, the result was inescapable legal uncertainty, which has a large impact on settlement strategy." Even when a defendant may be in the right, according to all legal advice, there is still an inclination to invest in out of court settlements: "The notable point is that defendant firms are uncertain whether theirs will be in the minority of cases in which firms are hit with enormous judgments. To foreclose this risk of catastrophic loss, they are likely to settle out of court more often than they would if there were less uncertainty" (Kagan, 1996: note 82).

Even lots of expensive legal advice does not safeguard a company. A veritable legion of well-paid and experienced attorneys and investment advisers was not able to prevent Texaco from being fined eight and one-half billion dollars in actual and punitive damages in the infamous Pennzoil-Texaco dispute over Getty Oil, one of the most expensive liability cases ever. In reaction, firms are going to avoid risky transactions and risky customers. Doctors refuse to do certain operations, and accounting firms refuse to audit risky clients. (Berton and Lublin, 1992; Berton, 1995). And firms may become more careful with innovation. When specific transactions are avoided, markets may shrink.

More litigation and more activist lawyers may be a good thing for their individual customers; it remains to be seen whether that will also be the case for society at large. It can lead to greater fluctuations in case law and make court decisions less consistent and predictable. That means case law is less effective as a collective good that reduces uncertainty. Law becomes then merely a private good, good for the individual client. Activist litigation is not only rather ineffective in reducing uncertainty in economic transactions; it is also not very efficient. The costs of legal advice and litigation can get very high with ongoing juridification of society and economy. Contract regulations and case law are by their nature less general, less abstract, and more specific to certain transactions. They emanate from a variety of actors: transaction partners, regulatory agencies, courts. There are more of them, and they are more complex. The rules that are produced are less transparent and predictable. In the face of such uncertainty, business needs batteries of lawyers that assist it in drawing up contracts. "American business executives engaged in negotiating sales franchises, seeking approval for real estate projects, acquiring other companies, issuing stock, and launching new products are surrounded by larger phalanxes of expensive attorneys than their counterparts in, for example, Europe or Japan—where the legal risks corporations face are less problematic" (Kagan, 1996: 12).

Given the adversarial nature of legal proceedings, lawyers provide work for each other. The defendant does not have a voluntary need for advice, but is forced by the plaintiff to get it. Thus the system can acquire a self-propelled momentum of ever more juridification, adversarial legalism, lawyers, and lawyer fees. Once this trend has been set in motion, it is difficult to stop. It is like an arms race, in which the parties in the race, the attorneys on both sides, have an incentive in escalating the adversarial relations, to lengthen cases, to devise new rules and exceptions to the rules that can be challenged again. It is not only a self-reproducing system, but an endogenous growth system.

The high costs of lawyering can be read from the earlier presented comparative data on lawyer density. The costs of legal services by the 780,000 lawyers that existed around 1990 in the United States have been estimated at one hundred billion dollars a year, or 2.4 percent of the American GDP. With that, the U.S. legal industry was, measured in terms of value added, larger than the U.S. steel industry or the domestic automobile industry (Sander, 1992). In the larger Western European nations, lawyering costs amounted to 0.5 to 0.6 percent of GDP. In the Netherlands it was negligible (Lipset, 1996).

"American litigation, with its wasteful, lawyer-dominated pretrial discovery and its cumbersome jury trials, is far less efficient than Continental European or British methods." In motor vehicle accident lawsuits in the United States, payments to lawyers account for more than 40 percent of total liability insurance payouts. In Japan and the Netherlands, a variety of alternative dispute resolution and legal mechanisms produce compensation for motor vehicle accident victims at dramatically lower transaction costs.

Claims agents who deal with cargo damage disputes arising from trans-Atlantic shipments say that lawyers' bills are far higher if a legal dispute is processed in New York rather than in Rotterdam, even though the relevant substantive law in the two countries is essentially identical. (Kagan, 1996: 10)

Proponents of a regulatory system based on tort law often argue that the threat of high liability claims provides an economic incentive to business to refrain from harming transaction partners and thus increasing trust in economic transactions. This would be much more effective than "command and control" regulation. American scholars are not so convinced. Kagan and Axelrad (1996: 17) summarize the evidence: "Many thoughtful scholars have come to the conclusion that the vaunted deterrent effect of the uniquely fierce American tort law regime is in fact minimally or only erratically effective. Steven Sugarman points out that the liability system's deterrent threat is severely muted by: (1) liability insurance, which means that tortfeasors do not bear the full cost of the harms they do; (2) the uncertainty and delayed effects of tort liability, which cause potential tortfeasors to discount the threat, regarding tort suits more like random lightning bolts than a source of systematic guidance about what precautions to take; and (3) the all-but-inevitable persistence of human incompetence, inattentiveness, and calculated corner-cutting that lead truck drivers, emergency-room doctors, and the crew of the Exxon Valdez to make mistakes, no matter how large the potential liability. . . . Case studies of the motor vehicle and small aircraft manufacturing industries, in a book edited by Peter Huber and Robert Litan, did not support the presumed safety-enhancing effect of American product liability litigation."

The American may pay less taxes for a bureaucracy that sets and enforces codified and statute law. However, he pays at least as much on costs of lawyers and liability insurance. If the average European transaction partner is confronted with a "bureaucracy," the American has to do with a "lawyerocracy." Both are functional alternatives for each other. But a comparison shows that a lawyerocracy is less effective and efficient in reducing risk and uncertainty.

Fewer Rules, Less Community, and Less Trust?

Instead of fewer rules leading to more community and trust, the reverse may be more likely. Liberalization of markets tends to undercut trust and informal cooperation.

Scandals have often been the direct occasion for state regulation of markets and products. The Dutch history of social and economic regulation has been one of scandals. In the 1910s dairy scandals led to statutory standards for agricultural products. In the 1920s, bankrupting insurance companies led to a call for stiff regulation of the insurance business. In 1963 the Thalidomide scandal led in many countries to state regulation of the admission of drugs to the market. In the 1970s food regulation was further tightened after twelve elderly citizens died from eating unhygienic shrimp, and recently the country has had scandals over insider trading on the stock market, explosions of fireworks factories, the BSE scandal, and poor services by the partly privatized railroads.

Liberalization of markets leads sooner or later to such scandals and suddenly and drastically reduces trust of consumers. Free markets do not produce that trust themselves. On the contrary. Markets and competition invite self-servingness, opportunism, and fraud. And the freer the market, the fiercer the competition, the greater such pressures and temptations. A pig farmer still quickly smuggles a load of pigs away from his contaminated farm, the butcher processes not-so-fresh meat in the strongly seasoned sausage, and the stock trader abuses insider knowledge. It happens wherever consumers, clients, or competitors are for lack of knowledge unable to control economic power. Fighting fraud is hence not so much necessary for moral as for functional reasons. It has to repair trust and promote transactions.

Fewer Rules (Freer Markets), Eventually More Rules?

Deregulation may in the short run lead to freer markets; in the long term it often leads again to a stiffening of standards. "Freer markets, more rules," notes Steven Vogel in the book under this title (1996). He compares the deregulation of the telecom and financial services sectors in Britain and Japan. As these sectors preeminently experience the consequences of technological change and globalization, it is here where deregulation should be most effective. Still, that was not the case. Vogel speaks of a deregulation revolution that wasn't. Deregulation and privatization first led to freer markets. But soon regulation of these markets increases again. Parties conclude contracts, which become more and more detailed; these give occasion to court cases, and to very detailed case law. Liberalized sectors get their own sector regulator. Either that happens as part of the deregulation measures, because the state realizes that it has to compensate for its loss of influence with the privatization of former state monopolies; or it happens somewhat later, as the conflicts between competitors and customer/suppliers increase and a need emerges for a regulator that sets rules of the game. That regulator may tender concessions out, and conclude very detailed contracts with those that won the public tender. The contracts in Britain between the railroad regulator and the railroad companies are thousands of pages thick. The more detailed the contracts, the greater the chances for conflict, and for development of case law. Thus deregulation leads eventually to more conflict and re-regulation of the sector.

CONCLUSION

Economics is a science of "trade-offs." It investigates how economic actors make reasoned and balanced ("rational") choices from among a number of alternatives. The science tries to increase the rationality of such decisions by studying costs and benefits of the various options. In many cases the choice is one between "two evils," whereby a bit more of the one (less inflation) goes at the cost of another (less growth). Policy makers also have to make such choices. Their policies will be more rational, the more alternatives are considered, and the more possible unforeseen consequences of such alternatives are thought through.

This essay has had the goal to think through some possible consequences of deregulation and privatization policies. It has argued that such policies may have unintended and unforeseen consequences: not "more market," as intended, but more and more detailed contracts, more social and legal conflict and litigation, more case law, more and larger firm hierarchies, more self-regulation by associations. When risk and uncertainty are reduced less by statutory regulation, transaction partners will turn to alternative institutions that may do so for them. In that sense, the various risk and uncertainty-reducing institutions are functional alternatives, even communicating vessels. This chapter has also argued that it remains to be seen whether such alternatives are to be preferred over statutory regulation. They may turn out to be less effective, involve higher transaction costs, or create more uncontrolled concentrations of economic power. For these very reasons such institutions have in the past been replaced by state regulation.

That does not mean of course that whatever institution has proven to be superior at one particular point in time and in one particular country will be so for all times and places. Institutions have a tendency to persist and can become sclerotic and bureaucratic, contradicting their ideal goal through their real functioning. Some "cleaning of the institutional stable" may be appropriate at regular times.

Furthermore, as conditions change, so does the appropriateness of specific market ordering institutions. New markets, new products, and new generations may require new solutions to the problems of risk and uncertainty. The internationalization of markets can make solutions by national states less effective. Standardization and certification have to become international, and in the absence of a supra-national state with enough authority, "associations" such as the WTO or international courts can be a second-best option. In addition, changes can take place in the trust of transaction partners in the state or in associations, and with that in the legitimacy and effectiveness of such institutions to regulate transactions.

Finally, it is likely that the need for risk and uncertainty reduction—the willingness of people to engage in risky activities—differs among cultures and countries, and as cultures develop, and over time as well. This would be a topic of a separate essay. There are many indicators that Americans are less risk averse than Dutchmen. Consequently, the Dutch have created many more institutions to reduce risk and uncertainty—varying from dikes to welfare state programs to strict food quality regulations—and have given associations and the state a larger role in these. This can be seen as reflecting a greater priority in society and politics to risk and uncertainty reduction.

10

Civil Society and Social Order: Demarcating and Combining Market, State, and Community

Claus Offe

Whenever we speak of social change, it helps to specify in which of its two major meanings we wish to employ the concept. For the social sciences have always analyzed social change in two perspectives. First, social (or "historical") change is conceived of as a set of blind and impersonal forces, structural trends and contradictions to which human agents are exposed as objects, if not as passive victims to whom change "happens." Social change of this sort consists of trends (ranging from global warming to shifting consumer tastes) which have neither been initiated by someone nor can they be stopped by anybody. Second, social change is seen as something that results from deliberate and intentional efforts of rational human agents to cope, individually or collectively, with needs and problems that they encounter in social, economic, and political life. Social change in this second sense is deliberately "accomplished" and executed by agents. This activist and purposive version of the concept emphasizes subjectivity, cooperation, and the rational pursuit of interests and values—the "making" of history rather than the exposure to anonymous historical fates and forces.

A synthesis of these seemingly incompatible modes of understanding social change is classically suggested by Karl Marx in his *The Eighteenth Brumaire* and later writings on the political economy of capitalism: the fateful forces of historical change[1] to which agents fall victim are themselves triggered and set in motion by human agency and its aggregate and unanticipated side effects—the critical implication being that the deficiencies of human agency and of the standards of rationality it follows are the causes both of those fateful forces themselves and of the agents' failure to cope with them in sustainable ways and with desirable results. The theory that ties fateful results to such institutionally necessitated blindness and other deficiencies of agency is a theory of crisis. As is well known, Marx and some Marxists believed that the institutions that make for the misdirection of agency can themselves be altered through a very special kind of agency—an agency conceptualized in terms of "revolution" and "class struggle." But much of the evidence accumulated in the twentieth century suggests that revolutionary sorts of second-order agency (or agency acting upon the institutional framework of agency) suffer from the same kind of blindness and deficiency that is being held against first-order agency and its deficiencies.

Nevertheless, the same problematic of how agents fail and how agency can be reconfigured is still central to many of today's social theorists, be they guided by "institutionalist" (Hall and Taylor, 1996) or game-theoretic and rational choice paradigms (cf. the telling title of a collection edited by Barry and Russel Hardin, 1982). In these traditions of social and political research, two key questions are being pursued, one positive and one normative. The positive question is this: how are particular configurations of agents (e.g., those which we find in markets, in firms, in international relations) related to particular outcomes of their agency? From this, the normative consideration follows: which changes in the configuration of agents would result in outcomes that are superior to the ones observed, in terms of evaluative criteria such as peace, sustainability, or social justice?

These are the terms of reference of our contemporary debates on the institutional design of state—society relations. In my present discussion of these relations, I proceed as follows. First, I shall reiterate a few dominant trajectories of social change that all of us, almost irrespective of what part of the world we come from, are critically exposed to. Second, I want to switch from the passive to the active mode in order to discuss the agents (namely citizens), as well as their modes of action (namely civility) that might cope with and turn into tolerable or even desirable outcomes the forces of change which we must confront. Finally, and building upon the discussion of civility, I'll specify six fallacies that must be avoided in order for citizens within civil society to arrive at an adequately competent configuration of agency.

CURRENT TRAJECTORIES OF
TRANSITION AND CHANGE

Democratization

Let me start by reiterating that the overwhelming change that has taken place in the past twenty-five years on a global scale and that is still going on has occurred on the level of the political order, or the polity, of many societies. Authoritarian regimes of various sorts—military dictatorships, state socialist regimes, theocratic regimes—have crumbled to an unprecedented extent and given way to (at least nominal) liberal constitutional democracies. These are roughly defined by equal political participation rights of all citizens, the guarantee of human, civic, and political rights, and the accountability of governing elites. The global phenomenon of mass transition to democracy was pulled by intentions inspired by the ideals associated with the democratic regime form, as well as pushed by causal mechanism. Let us briefly consider each of these factors.

What were the reasons that have led so many people, elites and masses alike, to advocate and adopt some version of the democratic regime form? What is democracy deemed to be "good for," or capable of accomplishing? Four cumulative answers come to mind. First, there is the "liberal" achievement of rights and liberties being guaranteed and the drawing of a clear demarcating line between what can be contingent upon the outcome of the political process and the conflicts of interest entering into it, and what can not, or only under particular circumstances, be the object of such conflict because it is constitutionally entrenched. It is worth noting that in a democracy most of the conditions that are of great interest to citizens (e.g., who can voice which opinions or own which resources) are not normally a potential object of the collective decision making of even vast majorities because they are constitutionally entrenched. As a consequence of both rights and procedures being thus guaranteed as well as supposedly implemented through the day-to-day operation of the judicial system, democracies make for a nonviolent, limited, and civilized character of political conflict and incremental change.

This civilizing potential of the democratic regime form is probably its overwhelming attraction for those who had emerged from the horrors and terrors of defunct predecessor regimes. A second reason for the normative attractiveness of the democratic regime form is its "international" accomplishment, normally expressed in the "democratic peace" hypothesis, dating back to Kant's famous formulation of 1795. It posits that democracies will not wage war against other democracies.[2] Third, the "social progress" accomplishment. As democracies rest upon majority rule, and as majorities are typically made up of those who do not share in economic privilege and social power, and as democratic state power, constitutionally entrenched rigidities notwithstanding, is in fact able to affect the size and distribution of economic resources (e.g., through policies of growth, taxation, and social security) in more than marginal ways, democracies will normally work to serve the interests of the less privileged segments of the population, thereby promoting "positive" or "social" rights and, more generally, growth, prosperity, and social justice.

Finally, the "republican" accomplishment of transforming "subjects" into "citizens," i.e., agents committed to and capable of employing their cognitive and moral resources in deliberative and intelligent ways so as to solve political problems, according to a logic of collective learning, and eventually striving to serve the "public good."

But democratization is not just pulled by those reasons and the hopes attached to them. Its introduction was also pushed by causes. The internal decomposition of authoritarian regime forms and their failure to sustain the functions of a state in confrontation with domestic and international challenges made democracy the regime form chosen "by default." Democracies come typically into being as a compromise entrenching the second most-preferred option of all those who are too weak to impose their respective (non-liberal-democratic) most preferred option. As neither military leaders nor party elites could successfully claim sovereignty, "the people" remained the only conceivable bearer of sovereignty. This choice has been enforced by two types of external agents. Liberal democracy was often installed through pressures and encouragements coming from other liberal democratic nations and their supranational organizations. Moreover, it has often been the preference of investors (whose investment is urgently needed by new democracies for the sake of their economic development and recovery) to operate under regime forms which meet the minimum requirements of rule of law, security of contract, and accountability of political elites.

Taken together, the combined outcomes of the push and pull factors underlying the mass transition to democracy that we have experienced over the past three decades are today often being commented upon with a sense of disenchantment. While the new wave of democratization has virtually everywhere confirmed the democratic peace hypothesis, it has not consistently redeemed the hopes for a reliable protection of equal human, civil and political rights, elite accountability, economic progress, social justice, or civic virtue practiced by the citizenry. In particular, there is no evidence that prosperity and social justice (in any of its various meanings) are promoted by democracy as a matter of course.[3] As the number of democracies increases, their quality seems to decrease (Beetham, 1994; Diamond, 1996), giving rise to well-founded complaints of new democracies having degenerated into mere "electoralist" or "delegative" democracies (O'Donnell, 1995), if not outright defective democracies with "reserved domains" (Linz and Stepan, 1996) controlled as a privilege by non-accountable elites. In sum, we can say that the democratic regime form is an indispensable prerequisite, but evidently no automatic assurance, of the qualities that have been associated with it by the protagonists of the transition to democracy.

"Globalization"

One explanation for this mixed and often somewhat disappointing experience of democratic transitions has to do with the weakening of the nation state and its governing capacities. This is the theme of global interdependence (or, at least, macro-regional interdependence, as in the European Union). The condition of intensified transnational connectedness shapes the fates of societies. It brings forces to bear upon social and economic life which are largely outside the control of even the most determined national political elites. As borders are permeable and perforated, the range of what can be collectively and effectively accomplished by domestic political forces shrinks,[4] because of the damaging repercussions from the outside international arena that any "wrong move" is anticipated to provoke. Borders, it seems, have lost not only their limiting, but also their protective and hence enabling, capacity. The media through which the governing capacity of nation states is partly disabled due to interdependency and the ensuing loss of autarchy and self-sufficiency can be summarized through the formula, perhaps to be taken half-seriously, of "six M's": money, mathematics, music, migration, military force and meteorology (or climate):

- money, as the medium of commerce and investment: between 1955 and 1989, the world GDP index has grown from 100 to 350, while the world export index increased to almost 1,100;
- mathematics: universalization of cognitive culture and technologies based upon it, all using Arabic numbers, incidentally the only truly universally understood medium of written communication;
- music/movies, as well as architecture: non-verbal means of expression and communication; cross-national standardization of patterns of life as informed by these aesthetic forms and their ethical content;
- migration: as many states cannot protect or provide minimal living conditions and liberties to all of their people, many other states receive (and have no practical and legitimate means to avoid receiving) growing numbers of aliens, refugees, migrant workers, denizens, etc., within their resident population;
- military resources: probably a minority of states enjoy military autarchy, as they have either joined supranational military alliances (such as NATO), depend upon the defense provided by other states, or are constrained in their domestic and international policies by the presence of military threat from other states; moreover the uncoupling of "stateness" and "military capacity" becomes manifest in the fact that the capacity to

make war is increasingly acquired by non-state actors (such as separatist armies, ethnic movements, terrorist groups, or armed gangs deployed by warlords);

- meteorology: the supply and quality of air and water, both within relatively narrow tolerable ranges of temperature as well as its seasonal and regional fluctuation and long-term change, are known to be basic parameters of human life and economic activity; the availability of these resources is also known to depend upon the stability of an immensely complex system of interaction which can be upset, entirely regardless of state borders and on a global scale, by the externalities of production and consumption.[5]

The classical response to the threat of loss of governing capacity is supranational integration and the formation of transnational regimes; EU, ASEAN, NAFTA, MERCOSUR, as well as various transnational military alliances and regimes of international regulation are cases in point. Equally important, however, seems to be the opposite response to the perceived weakness of the capacity of states to control their fates: the retreat to smaller, subnational units. Only seemingly paradoxically, globalization involves incentives for "lifeboat behavior" and subnational separation of the (relatively) rich, who quite rationally, from their point of view, strive to defend, exploit, and insulate their local or regional competitive advantages, rather than sharing the proceeds with the wider (and supposedly more vulnerable) state units to which they belong, preferably through secession and separate state building,[6] or at least through far-reaching forms of federalist fiscal autonomy.

The "multi-media" process of globalization, together with the dual transnational and subnational responses to it, amount to two kinds of predominantly bad news concerning distributive justice. One is the bad news pertaining to the advanced countries: their labor market performance and social security is seen to be undermined by the mobility of capital to the low-wage countries of the South, with widening gaps of social inequality within the advanced countries being one of the consequences. This factor of mobility is currently dramatically enhanced by new technologies of transportation and communication. There is also the reciprocal bad news for the poorer and economically less developed countries: the Western standards and style of living which they try to achieve and imitate constitute a "positional" good which cannot be universalized (for resource and ecological reasons). As obvious as it is that not everybody can earn twice the median income, it is evident that Western ways of living, of consumption and transportation, cannot be universalized for reasons of resource limitations and ecological sustainability. But as there is no model of housing, transportation, and consumption at hand that would pose a viable alternative to Western styles, distributional inequalities will widen, as some in the non-Western world will manage to imitate Western role models successfully, while most will fall. The combined result of both of these bad news is this: as the number of owners of luxury cars and air-conditioned apartments grows in what was the Third World, so does the number of people who search for food in the garbage containers in what was the First World.

Post-Modernization

After having hinted at some of the trajectories that drive the transition of polities, namely democratization, and those of economies, namely globalization, let me briefly refer to post-modernization as the driving force of cultural change.

Three generalizations can be offered, pertaining alike to the aesthetic, cognitive and moral-political ingredients of culture. First, there are powerful trends towards the transnational homogenization of culture. At least as far as the male and the urban segments of global society are concerned, movies, music, everyday dress, food, and life styles are in the process of losing much of their distinctiveness and evident rootedness in national and regional cultural traditions, as much as English is in the process of becoming the global idiom. But, second, powerful counter-tendencies are also to be observed, leading to the rediscovery and revival of local aesthetic and religious traditions which are adopted as symbolic means of resistance to the uniformity of global culture and which give rise to a post-modern cultural politics of identity, difference, and tribalism. Third, the moral and political impulse provided by ideas of liberation, social justice, and international peace seems to have lost much of its appeal and potential for political mobilization. This applies, in particular, to any notion of progress that would involve, as once did liberal modernization theory, revolutionary Marxism, or the missionary zeal of Christianity, a universalistic notion of desirable ends towards which history should move and can actually be moved by properly constituted agents and their strategies of change. If anything, this notion of progress, to the extent to which it survived at all the disorganizing forces of cultural post-modernism, is now being reformulated: progress is now conceived of as the continuous avoidance of a collective relapse into barbarism and catastrophic forms of de-civilization.

INNOVATING AND DESIGNING THE RELATIONS BETWEEN STATE, SOCIETY, AND COMMUNITIES

If these are the internally highly contradictory and ambiguous historical forces in which political agency is embedded and with which it must deal, the problem lies in determining what kinds of institutions are best suited to cope with them. Our problem is most definitely not Lenin's problem, as captured in his famous question of "What is to be done?" Instead, our problem can be formulated as the logically prior question of "who," i.e., what configuration of agents, might at all be capable of doing whatever "is to be done." Questions of institutional reform are conventionally framed in terms of which spheres of life should be governed by political authorities, contractual market exchange, or self-governing and responsible communities and associations (Streeck and Schmitter, 1985). Concerning this ever-contested division of domains, social scientists, the basis of their professional expertise, have little privileged insights to offer. At best, they can elaborate, on the basis of empirical observation and the analysis of causal mechanisms, as well as feasibility and consistency assessments, some critical arguments which can inform judgment on these matters. What to avoid is more obvious than what actually to do. Old design options are obsolete, regardless of whether we already know this or are in the process of slowly coming to understand it. Old design options are monistic, relying on the state, the market, or the community as the ultimate guarantors of social order and cohesion.

More promising solutions are essentially "impure": none of the three principles of social order is to be relied upon exclusively, but none of them is to be denied some role within a composite and complex "mix" of institutional arrangements. These three partial components of social order stand in a precarious relation to each other: on the one hand, they rely on each other, as each of the components depends upon the functioning of the two others. On the other hand, their relationship is antagonistic, as the predominance of any one of them risks to undermine the viability of the two others (Streeck and Schmitter, 1985c: 119f.). Let us examine the three components in turn. The state, the market, and the community represent ideal-typical modes in which people live and act together, the mode of coordination of individuals and their action.[7] Each of them, as it were, activates and relies upon one of the three collectively relevant capacities by which human beings can shape the social world: reason, interest, and passion.

The state can be thought of, as the seventeenth-century political theorists in fact did, as a creature of human reason, both in terms of its coming into being through a rational contract and in view of its day-to-day "formal rational" operation through bureaucratic rule (Weber). Reason is the capacity of individuals to find out and recognize what is good for all; in this sense, Hegel could even equate the state with reason.

The market is, of course, driven by the interest of human agents in the purposive acquisition of individual goods without any or much of a consideration of, or control over, what the pursuit of acquisitive purposes will do to others or to our future selves, be it in the positive sense (as the wealth of nations being promoted through an "invisible hand") or in the negative sense (with crises, injustices, social conflict, or environmental damages as an aggregate outcome that, as market logic implies, nobody can foresee and nobody is accountable for).

Finally, there is the notion that social order presupposes or, at any rate benefits from, the rights and duties that are attached to the members of concrete communities of persons. The cement that integrates the members of such communities is human passion (such as love, honor, pride, or a sense of loyalty and faithful attachment). From these communities, be they families, religious groups, or those defined by shared ethnic traditions, we derive our identity, our sense of belonging, and the commitment to an ethical model that informs our life plans.

Each of these three types of human capacities, generating corresponding patterns of social order, specializes in maximizing one distinctive value. This value is equality of legal status, comprising duties and rights, in the case of states; freedom of choice in the case of markets; and identity and its preservation (through commitment, solidarity, and loyalty) in the case of communities. While justice is an important consideration within all three of these patterns of social order, the operational meaning of justice differs significantly (Miller, 1979). In the case of the modern state, the mark of justice is the extent to which the rights, most often equal rights of all citizens under a constitution and the rule of law principle, are guaranteed and enforced by state agencies. Market justice, in contrast, emphasizes the entitlement of partners in market transactions to obtain what was agreed upon between them in contracts they voluntarily entered into, i.e., desert on the basis of contractual agreements. Finally, justice within communities is a standard defined according to the criteria of recognized need. The members of communities are called upon, in the name of some community-specific justice, to come to the assistance of needy members even if they have in no way "earned" the claim to such assistance through contributions made by them or through legal entitlements assigned to them by state authorities, with the group deciding, according to its standards and traditions, who is in legitimate need of what.

What this brief exercise in sociological basics is intended to help us understand is the truth of two related propositions. First, providing for social order and stability through institutions cannot rely on one of these patterns—state, market, community—alone. Any "monistic" institutional design tends to ignore (on the theoretical plane) and destroy (in its practical implications) the contributions that the other two components of the social order have to make. Second, it cannot even rely on a combination of any two (that is, excluding the respective third) of these patterns, be it a market—state, state—community, or community—market synthesis. We need all three foundations of social order, and in a mix that prevents them from undercutting each other.[8] The problem of designing appropriate institutions can thus be formulated as that of keeping an appropriate distance from the extremes of "pure" solutions while at the same time avoiding "too little" use of any one of them. This demarcating of the components of social order, of correcting, maintaining, and fine-tuning the mix within the bounds of a complex balance, is what, I submit, "civil society" is about.

The "pure" doctrines are easily recognized. First, social democratic statism (although that is the doctrine least often advocated as a "pure" public philosophy these days) emphasizes the activist use of strong governing capacities as the key to social order and social justice. It is opposed by market liberalism, or rather libertarianism, as a doctrine that proposes to rely on social coordination to be effected through price signals and little else, thus advocating privatization, deregulation, and the demolition of status rights, particularly the status rights of labor. Finally, there are religious as well as non-religious communitarian and social conservative public philosophies which emphasize the shared meaning, mission, and identity of family, religious, and national communities as the ultimate foundation of social cohesion. These are the three competing types of public philosophies that stand out at the end of the twentieth century. Needless to observe, systems of political parties in many countries reflect this configuration of public philosophies, divided as they are into socialist/social democratic parties, market liberal parties, and parties envisaging social order in terms of religious or ethnic identities.

The problem of designing and defending state-society relations, however, is not that of opting simplemindedly for one of the three, but of engaging in, or, at the very least, tolerating a process of the ongoing design, readjustment, and fine-tuning of a rich and adequate mix in which all three building blocks of social order have a mutually limiting and variable role. The capacity to invent, implement, and tolerate such ideologically and quintessentially impure patchworks of social order is the mark of civility or "civilness," i.e., the ability and willingness of citizens to utilize open and peaceful deliberation as well as the institutional methods of carrying out social and political conflict. Civilness and the political resources afforded by liberal democracy enable us to address the dilemmas posed by the fact that we live beyond the age that could (if only seemingly) be mastered by the clean and simple pronouncements of some "correct line," "ruling doctrine," "one best way," or, for that matter, "Washington consensus." Civilness, in other words, can be conceived of as the Archimedean point outside the force of gravity of any of the three paradigms of social order from which their relative scope can be evaluated and reconfigured. Civilness is the virtue encouraged by those cooperative and deliberative practices which are the common core of the various notions and models of civil society currently proposed.

To insist upon any "correct line" is to silence democratic voice by claiming superior and privileged insight. Such silencing has been, for instance, the epistemological principle of Thatcherism, with its key slogan "There is no alternative!" rightly ridiculed as the TINA rule. If, however, institution building according to some "correct line" can no longer be performed by philosophers and ideologues, it follows *a contrario* that the key role of designing and preserving social order must, in an age that has outgrown the schemes of ideologists, reside with the citizens and their civic associations themselves. In an essentially "mixed" institutional world, we need informed public judgment and deliberative civic engagement instead of authoritative expert knowledge as to what to do and what not to do. Needless to emphasize, such judgment will always come as the result of often vehement conflicts of interest, ideology, and identity which the democratic regime form allows to emerge and to be carried out in civilized ways. It appears that today both socialist statist egalitarians and social conservative communitarians have come to recognize and heed the need for self-limitation in applying their respective inherited guiding principles of social order; yet most market liberals are lagging behind in the reflexive art of relativizing their own creed. Many of them have still to overcome their often almost "revolutionary" and single-minded belief in the salutary potential of an ever more unscrupulous unleashing of market forces.

The only correct answer to a question such as "What is the optimal size of government?" is: we don't know! Or rather: the answer is not one that can be given in the form of a compelling economic or philosophical argument, but only in the course and as the outcome of well-informed democratic deliberation carried out within and between collective actors, both formal and informal, within civil society. To be sure, demonstrating by scholarly methods inconsistencies and unfeasibilities will help the public to make more enlightened choices. But the answer remains ultimately a matter of "voice," not of "proof," or of some objective measure of "rationality." The relationship and demarcation line between market, state, and community is itself a matter of politics (Stretton and Orchard, 1994). As a consequence, almost any answer to the question of the proper role and desirable relative size of macro-social organizing principles of the political economy will be controversial and essentially contested.

SIX FALLACIES

If we pursue further the idea of an ongoing "civic mix" of the various ingredients of social order as opposed to an elite-sponsored imposition of any single one of those ingredients, we arrive at a list of six pathological approaches to the building of social and political institutions, or six fallacies. Three of them result from the single-minded reliance upon any one of our three building blocks, and the other three from the premise that any of the three can entirely be left out of the architecture of social order. I hasten to add that these various fallacies will probably differ as to the seriousness of their impact and the frequency with which they occur under the regime of the current Zeitgeist. In spite of these differences in seriousness and probability, let me briefly review each of the six fallacies in turn.

The Fallacy of Excessive Statism

It might seem that after the breakdown of the type of state socialism that reigned in the Soviet empire, as well as after the collapse of much of the intellectual hegemony of Keynesianism in the eighties, the orthodoxy of excessive statism has become an entirely unlikely affliction. The breakdown of state socialism has rendered obsolete a model of statist authoritarian protection and productivist dirigisme, leaving behind in many of the post-socialist societies the craving for a "market economy without an adjective." (This is the prescription of the former Czech Prime Minister Vaclav Klaus, who proposed to eschew the specification of the market economy as "social.")

However, it seems all-important to keep in mind the difference between a big state (as measured in terms of the size of the budget or the number of state employees) and a strong state, i.e., a state whose governance has a significant impact upon the level and distribution of life chances within civil society (World Bank, 1997). It may well happen that a state is oversized and undereffective at the same time, and that the goods it generates are in fact not public goods, but categorical (or "club") goods enjoyed by what has been called the "state bourgeoisie," which may come in a military as well as a civilian version. However, "big" states usually also pretend to be "strong" states. Instead of serving civil society in any tangible sense, they exercise oligarchic control over actors within civil society. There is an ongoing debate within advanced societies as to which spheres of life and collective provision should be adopted or maintained by the state authorities, and which should be left to, or transferred to, markets or communities.

A healthy antidote to the pathology of a reliance upon the "strong" (or rather "big") state is to scrutinize whether the practice of governance does actually live up to the statist version of the ideal of justice, namely the legally guaranteed equality of opportunities.[9] Does a marginal increase in state capacity demonstrably enhance the equal enjoyment by citizens of the provision of such basics as access to the courts, legal protection, the provision of health services, education, housing, and transportation? Or would, conceivably, a marginal decrease in the size of the state apparatus and its responsibilities serve this goal better? If so, we might even get "more for less." The burden of proof in answering such questions must reside with those who advocate more state spending and public sector employment.

Liberal critics of big government must be granted the point that excessive statism often inculcates dispositions of dependency, inactivity, rent-seeking, red tape, clientelism, authoritarianism, fiscal irresponsibility, avoidance of accountability, lack of initiative, and hostility to innovation, if not outright corruption (and often so on either side of the administration-client divide). In order to stem these temptations that are built into large-scale public authorities and state responsibilities, a highly developed ethos and commitment, as well as professional competence, of the public sector personnel must be presumed, often counterfactually. All these considerations tend to be unduly dismissed by the (evidently rapidly shrinking numbers of) those who still believe that more public expenditures and public sector employment is needed for, and will result in, the better production and more equitable distribution of public goods.

The Fallacy of "Too Little" Governing Capacity

But we should pay equal attention to the pathologies that become manifest when the state is made to "wither away" under the onslaught of libertarian political forces or under the impact of severe fiscal crises. As we all know, the state, at the very minimum, is called upon to protect the life, property, and liberty of citizens, with the implication for modern society that the majority of (adult) citizens who operate on the supply side of labor markets will neither have their "property" (i.e., their labor power) nor their liberty protected in the absence of state-organized schooling, vocational training, housing, individual and collective labor law, and social security. For in the absence of these services and status rights that we associate with the modern welfare state, the labor market turns into what Polanyi (quoting Blake) has called a "satanic mill." Similarly, markets for financial assets, goods, and services cannot come into being nor, once in being, continue to exist without the continuous generation and adjustment of the norms of civil law, as well as the state-organized and guaranteed enforcement of these norms through the court system within the constraints of the rule of law, to say nothing about "targeted" industrial policies aimed at the growth of particular sectors of industry. Much the same applies to the protection of "life" that states must supply through military defense, and also the provision of basic health services, and the protection of citizens from "civil" violence committed against them by other citizens (and, a fortiori, state agents themselves). In order to perform all these functions that are essential to a state, states must also be capable of extracting the resources necessary for the performance of these functions through a regime of taxation (Holmes and Sunstein, 1999) that is, and is seen to be, both fair and effective. Both in the developed world and in Latin America, state reform aiming at the restoration of crumbling state capacity is today seen as the top item on the agenda of domestic politics (Kaufman, 1997). Such deficiencies in the performance of states are being diagnosed today with respect to all aspects just mentioned: social protection, civil law, law and order, and the power to extract revenues. If anything, we seem to be threatened more by the pathology of severe state deficiencies than by the pathology of state hypertrophy, although market liberals routinely emphasize the latter. Or, perhaps more accurately, we suffer from the combined malaise of the oversized and underperforming state.

The Fallacy of Excessive Reliance on Market Mechanisms

Markets, i.e., the competitive allocation of both the factors and the results of production mediated through the price signals, are very peculiar institutional arrangements. Allegedly, markets respond to individual desires, as expressed through effective demand. But it is well documented that even highly favorable individual market outcomes do not contribute much to the satisfaction of people's desires (Lane, 1991; Oswald, 1997; Frank, 1997). For, except for the very lowest income categories, life satisfaction and self-reported happiness are but very weakly correlated with increases in market income and the subsequent effective demand such income allows to be made for goods and services. The higher the incomes are, the less they are sought for the satisfaction of needs other than the—entirely market-induced and negative—"need" to avoid a relative loss of income. Few would disagree that non-tradable pleasures play a role for overall life satisfaction, including, arguably, the pleasure derived from the perception of living in a just society. Also, the market is said to reward efficiency, provided, that is, that competitive advantages come as a premium for better production methods or better products only, rather than as a premium for better methods of tax evasion, of deceiving consumers, or of dumping parts of the production costs upon the state budget or the general public. But efficiency is valued almost exclusively in an environment where efficiency laggards are punished, i.e., within markets. This is one of the reasons why the market has been compared to a "prison" in which we are coerced to perform activities that are unrelated to our needs, while being prevented from performing those which respond to them (Lindblom, 1982). Outside of markets, there is no self-evident and absolute value attached to greater efficiency. After all, non-market societies have sustained themselves for centuries without any noticeable increase in efficiency. Markets place a premium upon outcomes that are measured by markets as superior in terms of efficiency. It is worth keeping in mind the circular logic of markets. If we do so, we will be less impressed by the conventional argument that market arrangements are preferable over other arrangements because they yield greater efficiency. For that argument is virtually as powerful as the argument that cherry trees are preferable over all other trees because they bear cherries.

Furthermore, markets are supposed to "clear." But the very conditions that make the very special market for labor tolerable as a social arrangement (cf. the "satanic mill" argument in Polanyi, 1944), namely workers' status rights and the protective regulation of employment (summarily referred to as "decommodification"), hinder the clearing of the labor market and exclude growing numbers of potential workers from the possibility of becoming actual workers, particularly after the level of efficiency of production has been driven up through labor saving technical change. This market-inflicted exclusion from the (labor) market, however, is in itself one of the strongest known causes of decline in life satisfaction and self-reported happiness.

Moreover, markets are known to be self-destructive in still another sense. Once markets are left to themselves, rational actors will conspire, in the interest of increasing their profits, to escape the competitive threat coming from other market participants by forming cartels or monopolies, thus subverting the ideal of "freedom of choice" in whose name markets are often defended. In other words, once competitive markets are in place, it can by no means be assumed that they stay competitive in the absence of some non-market agents enforcing competitiveness. In addition, markets are known to be deaf and blind: deaf as to the present negative externalities they cause, e.g., of an environmental sort, as well as blind to the long term consequences of market transactions for those involved in them.

Finally, not only do markets lack a self-reproductive mechanism, as they constantly tend to subvert themselves into arrangements of monopolistic power, but they also lack a self-restraining mechanism. Because they have no way of distinguishing between "marketable" and "non-marketable" items, they tend to flood the universe of social life and marketize everything—unless, that is, the distinction is being imposed upon them, again, from the outside—through a legal ban on marketability (e.g., to some extent, of addictive drugs or prostitution) or/and through the standards of good taste and proper behavior established and enforced by the ethics of communities. It is somewhat ironic to see that the advocates of markets, committed as they are to competition and the freedom of choice afforded by competition, tend to shy away from appreciating the legitimacy of a second-order competition between the market and other methods of generating and distributing valued items.

To illustrate, it can be said that in the European Middle Ages, the scope of marketable items was much wider than it actually is within modern market economies. Such a seemingly nonsensical proposition does in fact make good sense if we remember that in the Middle Ages among the goods traded were, as ordinary objects of commercial exchange, items such as the salvation of one's soul, military force, the right to marriage, and other goods that we have come to consider as "non-tradables." Arguably, we are actually on our way back into the Middle Ages, as increasingly fewer items appear to be solidly immune from being "for sale." Examples might include doctoral titles, physical attractiveness, public attention, court decisions, and even political careers (to be acquired, respectively, through purchasing the services of some academic institutions, beauty surgeons, media time, expensive lawyers, or campaign staff). As markets are structurally intolerant of non-market methods of generating and allocating valued items, they can cause what has been called a "low-level trap." Countries (such as the United States) where private commercial forms of provision are widely considered the standard response to conditions of social need—and where any expansion of state and federal budgets is viewed with habitual alarm—are at the same time those where complementary welfare state provisions, to the very limited extent they exist, are most easily demolished—the somewhat paradoxical generalization being that the smaller the welfare state is, the more precarious and vulnerable its residual arrangements, and the more easily any attempt at its expansion will be frustrated.[10]

Given all these features of the market and its mechanisms, it can hardly be invoked as a self-evidently superior contribution to social order. To the contrary, the market has rightly been considered, from Marx to Schumpeter and beyond, as an "anarchic," "subversive," "revolutionizing," and disorganizing pattern of social arrangements. At best, the market's contribution to the creation of social order is strictly contingent upon its being firmly embedded in constraints, restrictions, regulations, limitations, status rights, and informal social norms imposed upon it from the outside, by either the state or the community.

The Fallacy of an Excessive Limitation of Market Forces

Yet still, and as is the case with many poisonous substances, markets are indispensable as powerful medicines, if administered in reasonable doses. Such is also the case with appropriately constrained and regulated markets. A doctrinaire ban of market mechanisms from all spheres of social life would deprive us of the salutary functions that markets can perform. Although such a ban is rarely proposed today, it is still useful to remember for a moment what markets are in fact good for. Four points come to mind. First, market exchange, if properly supervised and policed, is usually peaceful and nonviolent, as eighteenth-century political economists were well aware when they praised the virtues of *doux commerce* (Hirschman, 1977). While this "pacifist" defense of markets, as applied to the history of the twentieth century with its experience of the conquest and defense of markets through imperialist powers, may well be called into question, it maintains much of its validity at the micro-level. People who relate to each other as actual or potential partners in market exchange normally have little reason to go at each other's throats. To the contrary, they may even develop some sense of "sympathy" for each other, as Adam Smith was the first to suggest. This is so because market outcomes, i.e., the terms of trade of inputs and outputs (e.g., income earned per hour worked) cannot plausibly be attributed to the (hostile) intentions of any actor, but are due to some anonymous causation for which "I" have no one to blame but "myself." Markets are learning environments that favor self-attribution of both favorable and unfavorable outcomes and, as a result, a cognitive frame of responsibility.

A further formative impact of the "hidden curriculum" of markets is that it favors learning. It has been claimed that markets, through their continuous imposition of negative and positive sanctions upon participants in market transaction, make people more intelligent than they would be outside of market contexts. But that proposition must be qualified in that it applies only if the positive and negative rewards come in the form of relatively moderate increments or losses. In contrast, if rewards change in quantum jumps, people stop learning and begin either to mistake the market for a lottery[11] (in the case of big gains that cannot be accounted for in terms of the recipient's prudent behavior) or to respond fatalistically or in panic in the case of "big" losses, the disastrous proportions of which exceed the individual's capacity for intelligent adjustment.[12] Finally, the market has a powerful liberating potential, as it allows the holder of marketable assets to escape the control of either communities or state bureaucracies.[13] To the extent that markets can be demonstrated to actually redeem its potential for inculcating the spirit of peaceful and civilized interaction, of responsibility, of intelligent adjustment, and of liberation from the grip of authoritarian and paternalistic powers, they can certainly not be dismissed as essential building blocks of the institutional structure of social life.

The Fallacy of Excessive Communitarianism

A powerful representation of current realities is multiculturalism. This doctrine of political post-modernism tends to code people not in terms of citizenship, but in terms of "identity." It emphasizes a "politics of difference," a difference that is not always conceived of as being bridged or reconciled by common national, civic, or class interests. It responds to the mass phenomenon, both present and historical, of voluntary as well as involuntary transnational migration. In the North Atlantic West, the politics of difference and identity is a philosophical response to the widespread disenchantment with the premises of liberal individualism and its socialist concomitant of universalism. In order to become aware of yourself, you must discover, recognize, and cultivate the distinctive "roots" that tie you to your family of origin and, beyond that, to ethnic, linguistic, religious communities and their life-forms. Feminism provides another cognitive map that emphasizes gender identities, and the "politics of the body" (age, food, health status, sexual orientation) is further invoked in the construction of difference based on physical characteristics, practices, and preferences (see especially Heller, 1996).

Following the model of group rights conceded to Black Americans in consideration of the lasting discrimination against their citizen status and life chances, identity politics has become a widely copied strategy of self-declared "groups" to gain access to cultural and other privileges. Similarly, in post-communist countries, we see a dramatic rise of the politics of ethnic, religious, and linguistic identity politics and ethnic nationalism which, however, is not limited in its potential for violent separatism to the post-communist world; Northern Ireland and the Basque country, and not just Chechnya and Bosnia, illustrate the potential of identity politics for terror and horror. In East and West alike, doctrines of ethnic nationalism have rarely failed to unfold hostile and repressive inclinations that interfere with "dissenting" citizens' and "strangers'" civil and political rights. Even in its more benign forms (such as Quebec), the communitarian politics of identity and difference tend to be exclusive, anti-egalitarian, and notoriously difficult to reconcile with civic principles of neutrality and "color-blind" toleration. Even if it is not openly exclusive, the emphasis upon ascriptive groups and group solidarities violates egalitarian standards due to the simple fact that not everybody does actually belong to, or at any rate identify with, a group thus defined. Even those who share in ascriptive characteristics that supposedly make up a "group" may wish to "opt out" of its solidarity networks because of the often authoritarian or paternalist patterns such quasi-tribal groups tend to develop.

The tensions that exist between identity politics and principles of egalitarian citizenship can be explained by the particular difficulties encountered by the attempt at civilized resolution of identity conflicts when compared to the resolution of class conflict (Offe, 1998). Identity, or the passionate identification with some community, is almost by definition inalienable and non-negotiable. While class conflict is carried out between collective actors who depend upon each other (even if asymmetrically so) and for that reason take some, at least implicit, interest in the well-being of their opponents, the protagonists of identity conflicts at least in their most radical version, tend to portray outsiders as people whose very absence from "our" community or national territory is the condition of the fulfillment of "our" aspirations for "purity"—an aspiration that all too often has led to the practice and justification of ethnic cleansing.

The Fallacy of Neglecting Communities and Identities

But, again, this is just one side of the debate. On the other side it is claimed, with some plausibility, that communities and identities that we are "born into" are the most potent generators of our moral commitments and capacities. Communities such as families, religious associations, and ethnic nations provide individuals with a sense of meaning and mission, as well as with all the feelings of pride, trust, love, guilt, honor, commitment, etc., that can perhaps only be acquired in communities, which thus play a uniquely important role in the reproduction of cultural traditions and ethical values. Only communities can generate, or so the communitarian argument goes, "strong" individuals who are prepared to be held accountable for their acts and thoughts, as opposed to spineless opportunists. And it is not only the unique contribution that communities presumably can make to solving problems of social order and social integration that then deserve recognition and protection through state policies. They are deserving also because communities, almost like a cultural genetic pool of society, cannot be manufactured or artificially reproduced. The need to protect communitarian cultures applies specifically, or so it is argued, if they are seen to be exposed to a threat of extinction originating with market or political forces of modernization.

At any rate, much of the evidence demonstrates that "ascriptive" collectivities based on religious, gender, age, regional, ethnic, and other identities that people are "born with" have provided the moral energies which have driven public-regarding innovation and social and political advances. The same can be said of less ascriptive, but still relatively permanent identities that are based upon people's belonging to local communities or professional categories (Tendler, 1997). The new social movements of the sixties and seventies are cases in point (Marwell and Oliver, 1993). In many places, movements of students, women, and ethnic or racial minorities, as well as local communities have been the pioneer promoters of civil rights and a sharpened moral and political awareness of issues of liberation, toleration, social justice, and ecological or environmental concerns. Granting and guaranteeing the necessary space for the social and political action of these communities and promoting their associative practices (rather than displacing them through paternalist and/or repressive state action) would therefore appear to be a necessary pre-condition for the further collectively beneficial use of these communal forces and modes of action.

CONCLUSION

The three antinomies of social and political order I have discussed are not to be resolved by grandiose schemes that either philosophers or political ideologists might supply. What we are left with is a repertoire of partly contradictory, partly complementary arguments and observations that can be brought to bear upon the critique and reconstruction of existing institutional arrangements. For there is no such thing as uniquely "rational" institutions or state-society relations. On the contrary, these antinomies and ideological rivalries must (and, I believe, can) be resolved through practices of civility and deliberation which unfold "in between" the poles of our conceptual triangle of "pure," if largely obsolete, solutions.

The three forces, or options for institution building, that I have discussed here in a rather schematic fashion, tend to undercut each other (Streeck and Schmitter, 1985: 119f.). They also depend upon each other. As none of them is dispensable, the need for self-limitation of the proponents of each of them becomes evident. Emerging institutional forms of public-regarding agency do in fact emphasize, if only in negative ways, necessary limitations. For instance, we speak of "non-governmental" organizations or the "non-profit" sector. With equally good reasons, we might call for "non-sectarian," i.e., non-exclusive or non-discriminatory kinds of communities. These three negations combined are, or so it seems, a very good approximation to the idea of civic associability and the social capital that enables people to engage in associative practices.

The civic use of social capital and the associative practices in which it manifests itself may be deemed to be an overly idyllic and harmonistic way out of the dilemma of social order. For advocates of such practices often seem to ignore or belittle the realities of social power and powerlessness. Categories of social actors may take a rational interest in the spreading of hegemonic discourses which favor community-centered, statist, or market-based versions of social order. Social scientists do not have a good understanding as to which strategies, conditions, and perceptions drive such hegemonic discourses which actually succeed in privileging one model of social order at the expense of its effectively discredited alternatives. And neither do we understand the sometimes abrupt changes that give rise to new hegemonic discourses, such as the free-market orthodoxy, and the sudden disestablishment of previously institutionalized models of social order. All we can perhaps say is that the semantic class struggles which lead to the spread and consolidation of hegemonic cognitive frames and moral intuitions are subject, as to their outcomes, to the formation of judgment and the autonomous confrontation of experience and evaluative standards to which civic associations can give rise. In this sense, social capital is not neutral with respect to power, but the very essence of the capacity of civil society to challenge and limit its reach.

It is a truism that such a culture of civility does not automatically emerge with the demise of authoritarian regimes and the transition to—or even consolidation of—the democratic regime form. The ongoing fine-tuning and critical, flexible, as well as imaginative recombination of the three disparate components of the institutional order is driven by the "social capital" (see especially Putnam, 1993) available within civil society, widely referred to in contemporary social science as the source of energy that "makes democracy work." By the term "social capital" we refer to a syndrome of cognitive and moral dispositions of citizens that lead them to extend trust to anonymous fellow citizens (as well as the political authorities that, after all, one's fellow citizens have endowed with political power), to practice the "art of association" (Tocqueville, 1961), and to be attentive to public (as opposed to their own narrowly circumscribed group-specific) affairs and problems. Fair and transparent institutions of government, the prosperity that carefully regulated markets can generate, and the life of communities restrained by the principle of toleration can and must all contribute to (and in turn benefit from) the formation and accumulation of social capital within civil society, the associational forces of which are better capable of defining and constantly refining the "appropriate mix" of institutional patterns than any self-declared "experts" or intellectual protagonists of some "pure" doctrine of social order.

NOTES

1 Rather than the clearly desirable ones brought about by Smith's "invisible hand!"

2 We might note, however, that in a world of international regimes and security alliances, democracy is a sufficient, but not a necessary, condition for the prevention of international war. The Gulf War had demonstrated that even dictators can be stopped from attacking and occupying neighbors.

3 It used to be argued by the "structuralist" school of democratic theorists that an advanced economy is a determinant or prerequisite of democracy, and that in turn

democracy will enhance the potential for growth and prosperity. Neither side of this feedback model is supported by much of the current evidence.

4 As some have argued, to the point of making democracy pointless. Cf. Guéhenno (1993).

5 It is worth noting in passing that one item, a seventh M, is missing from this list. The moral ideas and principles governing particular national communities have largely proved to be resistant to "globalizing" processes of diffusion and convergence.

6 At any rate, from the mineral-rich Congo province of Katanga in the early sixties to the rise of Catalan demands for independence in the eighties to the independence of the Baltic states, as well as of Croatia and Slovenia in the post-Soviet early nineties, it was consistently the richest regional sub-units of established states that have had strong motives to defect from the encompassing unit.

7 Cf. Etzioni (1961) for a similar conceptualization of modes of coordination through social norms, coercive power, and material incentives. Also, Schuppert (1997).

8 The standard cases of such undercutting and mutual displacement are, on the one hand, the "dependent state" whose regulatory and governing capacity is reduced by national and international monetary markets and investors' decisions and, on the other, the "over-regulated" economy. Cf. also the notion of a "depletion of the moral heritage" by political and economic modernization in Hirsch (1976).

9 For instance, it can be easily demonstrated that the system of tertiary education in Germany, an almost entirely statist system, serves the professional upper middle class and their offspring much better than it does any other stratum in German society. In contrast, private university systems might easily be regulated in ways that give greater weight to considerations of social equality.

10 Arguably, there is also the reverse paradox of a "high-level trap," with "big" welfare states (such as the Netherlands) defying downward revisions and behaving stubbornly path-dependent.

11 This is a view of how markets operate that is widely encountered in post-socialist economies with their sudden and conspicuous emergence of the nouveaux riches.

12 This is nicely illustrated by a story that was being told in the context of the economic transition in Poland. Suppose the price of coal doubles during a cold winter. In response, people will economize on heating and work harder (which in itself keeps them warm) in order to earn the necessary additional income to buy coal. Now suppose the price of coal increases by the factor of five. What will be the response? People give up and stay in bed.

13 It is this experience of escaping the control of power holders that young entrants to the labor market enjoy when for the first time earning their own money, and thus escaping the control of parents, or that clients of newly privatized telephone companies enjoy when given the chance to put together their own service package, rather than being forced to pay for what the former state monopoly would offer as the single standard package. It must be noted, however, that the experience of such enthusiastic feelings of liberation may be more of a transition phenomenon. Nevertheless, the desire of both states and communities to extend authoritarian or paternalistic control over individuals can only be checked by keeping the exit option of markets permanently open.

Part III

On Social Systems of Production—
and Beyond

J. Rogers Hollingsworth, Karl H. Müller

There has been considerable confusion in public discourse about the meaning of the concepts "the market" and "capitalism." Many discussants have tended to equate the market with capitalism. However, the two concepts are by no means synonymous. The market is a mechanism for coordinating specific types of relationships in transactions among economic actors (Boyer, 1997; Williamson, 1975, 1985). And as Polanyi (1944) and others (Hollingsworth and Boyer, 1997) have emphasized, the market, if left untamed and unconstrained by other coordinating mechanisms, is destructive of trust and other traditional values, on which its very existence is dependent.

On the other hand, capitalism is a much more complex and encompassing subject. It involves the entire institutional environment in which economic transactions of a society occur. Indeed, J. Rogers Hollingsworth in the following essay suggests that we need to think of capitalism as being synonymous with a society's social system of production. Of course, some scholars recognize that the market and capitalism are not identical phenomena, but they then equate capitalism only with the way that economic transactions occur within a particular society (see the discussion of the literature on business systems in Whitley, 1992a, 1992b). However, the essays in this volume are distinctive in the way that they demonstrate that capitalism consists of a configuration of economic, political, social, and cultural organizations which are intricately linked with each other. In order to understand the behavior of any particular system of capitalism, one must comprehend the interaction of the constituent parts of the entire system.

A social system of production consists of a society's norms, rules, habits, conventions, and values, which in turn influence the institutional arrangements (e.g., markets, the state, association, networks) which are dominant in a society. These in turn influence the structure and interaction of a society's business system with its institutional environment, which consists of the society's financial markets, its industrial relations system, its educational and training system, and the state. The state plays multiple roles in any social system of production. It both influences the rules of the system and is the ultimate enforcer of rules. Moreover, it can also be an owner of the means of production. Thus, because the state is unlike all other parts of the social system of production, it is treated repeatedly in this volume. These are themes which emerge in the essays in part 3, all of which complement some of the recent literature on varieties of capitalism (Crouch and Streeck, 1997; Hall and Soskice, 2001).

There has been an extensive literature about business systems (Whitley, 1992a, 1992b), but business systems are only a part of the larger domain of social systems of production. At the same time, the concept of a business system is much broader than that of the firm. The business system involves the relationships between firms and their suppliers, their customers, their competitors, their owners and other sources of capital, and their employees. And across societies, there are many ways that these relationships get defined.

In some countries—for example, the United States—there has been a long history of firms integrating vertically, that is, suppliers and processors are integrated within a firm. In other countries, these relationships may be defined by competitive pricing, by long-term relationships, and by other strategies. In Japan, suppliers and processors exist in industrial groups which have been defined from the subcontracting relationships between large firms and their suppliers. These relationships are strengthened by neutral stockholding and interlocking directorships. The extensive cross-company pattern of stock ownership among firms in many industrial sectors is an important reason why Japanese firms can forsake short-term profit maximization in favor of a strategy of long-term goals. Moreover, the pattern of inter-corporate stockholding encourages many long-term business relationships in Japan, which in turn reinforce ties of interdependence, exchange relations, and reciprocal trust among firms (Aoki, 1988; Whitley, 1992a; Gerlach, 1992).

In the literature on social systems of production, a standard problem is whether societies have a single social system of production. Hollingsworth in the following essay suggests that although there is heterogeneity in terms of how firms within a single country define their relationships with their suppliers, customers, competitors, employees, and financiers, there does tend to be a dominant pattern in most societies by which these processes are defined. As a result, the relationships between firms and their institutional environment are more complex in the United States than in most countries—due in part to the fact that the United States is not only a very large country in terms of space and population, but it also has considerable ethnic heterogeneity. In three of the following essays, Peter Hall, Steven Casper, and Sigurt Vitols focus on certain aspects of the contemporary German social system of production. In chapter 12, Peter Hall calls our attention to the important point that even though there are powerful forces of globalization very much at work in the world, the way these play out within societies is quite varied. It is the distinctiveness of social systems of production of societies which is responsible for this variation.

In chapter 13, Steven Casper emphasizes how the long established institutional structures of a society influence the kind of incentives and constraints which shape the development of particular industries—in this case, biotechnology in Germany. His essay makes important contributions to the literature of institutional theory, national systems of innovation, and varieties of capitalism.

Sigurt Vitols in chapter 14 emphasizes the important role of financial markets in shaping the distinctiveness of social systems of production. The way the financial markets are shaped in each society is extremely important in shaping its entire social system of production. In all capitalist societies, capitalists are motivated to earn a profit, but how profit is pursued is socially shaped. In some countries, profits are sought in the short term, while in others capitalists have a long-term perspective. And one of the major features influencing whether capitalists have a long- or short-term perspective is how the financial markets are organized in the society. Indeed, not only does the structure of the financial markets influence the time perspective of capitalists, but the time perspective also influences the relationships between labor and management. For example, in the United States, large firms—in comparison with those in other societies—have tended to expand on the basis of retained earnings or to raise capital from the bond or equity markets, but less frequently to use bank loans. As a result, over time American corporate managers have become dependent on the whims and strategies of stockholders and bond owners. Once financial markets became highly institutionalized, securities became increasingly liquid, as the owners of such securities have tended to sell their assets when they have believed their investments were not properly managed. Since management embedded in such a system has tended to be evaluated very much by current price and earnings of the stocks and bonds of their companies, it has had high incentives to maximize short-term considerations at the expense of long-term strategy. This kind of emphasis on a short-term time horizon has historically limited the development of long-term, stable relations between American employers and employees—a prerequisite for a highly skilled and broadly trained work force. Instead, the short-term maximization of profits has meant that firms in such a social system of production have been quick to lay off workers during economic downturns, and thus to remain heavily dependent on a lowly and narrowly skilled workforce.

But in contrast to the Anglo-American economies, the securities industries in Japan and Germany have been less well-developed, with the result that banks have long been much more important in supplying capital to firms than the equity and bond markets. How this has been done in Japan and Germany has varied, but the interesting thing is that where firms are dependent on bank loans rather than on the kind of equity markets found in the Anglo-American environment, the consequences have had some similarities despite their many differences. All of these factors also shape the behavior and performance of different market segments—as the Casper essay demonstrates. In short because the banking system and the bio-technology sector are part of the same social system of production, their behavior feed backs onto each other.

Chapter 15 by Raymond Russell and Robert Hanneman is a fascinating analysis of worker cooperatives. As suggested above, a critical issue which firms face is their relationship with their owners (e.g., sources of capital) and their employees. Their chapter is rich with suggestions of how the institutional environment of firms (e.g., the social system of production) influences the relationship between firms and their owners as well as their employees. Unfortunately, the social sciences thus far have a paucity of studies which explain why workers become owners of firms and how the institutional environment in which workers and employers are embedded influences their particular relationships. We believe that the kind of institutional analysis proposed in this book will advance an understanding of this important problem.

The concept social system of production suggests that societies have distinctive norms, habits, conventions, and values which are historically path-dependent. For this reason, it is a concept which suggests that there is still great variation rather than convergence in the social makeup of societies. It is in this context that Marie-Laure Djelic in chapter 16 has written "Exporting the American Model—Historical Roots of Globalization." Hers is perhaps the most sophisticated analysis yet to appear which discusses the interaction of the processes of societal convergence, divergence, and globalization. As a result of her essay, it will be necessary for scholars to reassess their views of how processes of globalization are restructuring relations among national societies.

In chapter 17 Jerald Hage and J. Rogers Hollingsworth pick up on a theme of variation in the institutional makeup of societies and argue that this leads to considerable difference in the way that market segments (i.e., industrial sectors) perform across societies. Because of the distinctiveness of the social system of production of each society, there is considerable variation in the industrial sectors in which societies perform well. This chapter also ties these themes to different types of innovativeness.

11

Social Systems of Production and Beyond

J. Rogers Hollingsworth

The third part of this volume focuses primarily on societal macro-research. In this introductory essay, an important socio-economic concept will be discussed at some length, one which is labeled "social system of production" (Hollingsworth, 1997; Hollingsworth and Boyer, 1997). In the subsequent parts of this overview, the concept of social systems of production will be presented as a heuristically fruitful perspective especially for the purpose of comparative socio-economic macro-investigations.

In the latter part of the essay, the concept of "social systems of production" will be generalized and applied to a variety of different societal macro-domains. Centered around the products and services of a "caring state," different social systems of health, education, law, or security, broadly conceived, will be introduced. These societal configurations exhibit a high degree of variation across space and time and show an astonishing amount of substitution and "path-dependencies." In doing so, a highly relevant conceptual instrument for the study of the contemporary macro-world will gradually emerge.

ON SOCIAL SYSTEMS OF PRODUCTION

The starting point for the subsequent exposition lies quite obviously in the definition of a "social systems of production." In general, a social system of production is the way that the following socio-economic ensembles or industrial structures of a country or a region are integrated into a macro-social configuration:

1. the industrial relations system
2. the system of training of workers and managers
3. the internal structure of corporate firms
4. the structured relationships among firms in the same industry
5. the structured relationships between firms with their suppliers and customers
6. the financial markets of a society
7. the structure of the state and its policies
8. the conceptions of fairness and justice held by capital and labor
9. a society's idiosyncratic customs and traditions as well as norms, moral principles, rules, laws, and recipes for action

Figure 11.1 presents an overview of the main components in the definition of a social system of production. All these institutions, organizations, and social values tend to cohere, although they vary in the degree to which they are tightly coupled with each other into a full-fledged system. While each of these components has some autonomy and may have some goals that are contradictory to the goals of other institutions, an institutional logic in each society leads institutions to coalesce into a complex social configuration (Hollingsworth, 1991a; 1991b). This occurs because the institutions are embedded in a culture in which their logics are symbolically grounded, organizationally structured, technically and materially constrained, and politically defended. The institutional configuration usually exhibits some degree of adaptability to new challenges, but continues to evolve within an existing style. But under new circumstances or unprecedented disturbances, these institutional configurations are exposed to sharp historical limits as to what they may or may not do (Schumpeter, 1983; David, 1988; Arthur, 1988a, 1988b; Håkansson and Lundgren, 1997). Why do all of these different institutions coalesce into a complex social configuration, which is labeled here as a social system of production? The literature suggests two contrasting interpretations. Part of the answer—indeed a controversial one—is that these institutions are functionally determined by the requirements of the practice of capitalism in each time and place (Habermas, 1975). Another explanation emphasizes the genesis of the actual configuration, via a trial and error process, according to which the survival of firms, regions, or countries is the outcome of

Figure 11.1 Social Systems of Production

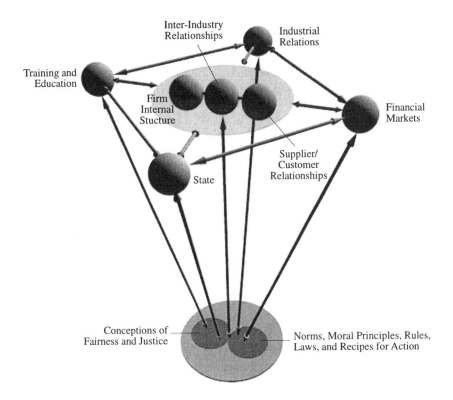

complex evolutionary mechanisms (Maynard-Smith, 1982; Nelson and Winter, 1982).

However, the problem is even more complex. Markets and other mechanisms for coordinating relationships among economic actors place constraints on the means and ends of economic activity to be achieved in any society. The other coordinating mechanisms include different kinds of hierarchies and various types of networks and associations (e.g., trade unions, employers, and business artisan associations; [Hollingsworth and Lindberg, 1985; Campbell, Hollingsworth, and Lindberg, 1991]). These various coordinating mechanisms provide actors with vocabularies and logics for pursuing their goals, for defining what is valued, and for shaping the norms and rules by which they abide. In short, in contrast to the logic of the neo-classical paradigm, the argument here is that economic coordinating mechanisms place severe constraints on the definition of needs, preferences, and choices of economic actors. Whereas the neoclassical paradigm assumes that individuals and firms are sovereign, this chapter is based on the assumption that firms are influenced by the hold that institutions have on individual decision making (Campbell, Hollingsworth, and Lindberg, 1991; Etzioni, 1988; Streeck and Schmitter, 1985a; Hollingsworth, Schmitter, and Streeck, 1994; Hollingsworth and Boyer, 1997; Magnusson and Ottosson, 1997; North, 1990).

Moreover, firms utilize and organize available technologies in quite distinct ways and follow along different technology trajectories. The same equipment is frequently operated quite differently in the same sectors in different countries, even when firms are competing in the same market segment (Hollingsworth, Schmitter, and Streeck, 1994; Maurice, Sorge, and Warner, 1980; Sorge, 1989; Sorge and Streeck, 1988). Variations in production and process technologies are influenced, partly, by variations in the social environments in which they are embedded. In other words, firms are embedded into complex environments, which, among other things, place constraints on their behavior. Thus, a social system of production is of major importance in understanding the behavior and performance of an economy. How the state and other coordinating mechanisms (e.g., markets, networks, private hierarchies, associations) coalesce and are related to particular social systems of production are important determinants of economic performance.

During the past sixty or seventy years there have been several broad types of social systems of production in the histories of Western Europe, North America, and Japan. One system, labeled in the literature as a Fordist or a mass standardized social system of production, tended to produce highly standardized goods on a large scale with highly specialized equipment, operated by semi-skilled workers. In contrast to Fordist production systems, there have been various types of flexible social systems of production, each tending to produce a wide array of products in response to different consumer demands, supported by a skilled workforce with the capability of shifting from job to another within a firm.

Because both standardized and flexible social systems of production are ideal types, it is important to emphasize that, for analytical purposes, each is subject to the usual strengths and weaknesses of ideal types. They are not meant to be descriptive statements about specific firms, industrial sectors, or individual firms at specific periods of time. Rather, they are heuristic devices to sensitize us to possible inter-relationships that might exist among a broad set of variables or social categories. Neither type ever existed in a pure form in space or time. Even where a standardized mass social system of production was the dominant paradigm, there were always firms, or even entire industries, that were organized on opposite principles. The two organizing principles were complementary one with another: Mass standardized production tended to respond to the stable component of demand, while batch or medium-size production systems tended to cope with the variable part of the same demand. So the co-existing forms of production broadly shared the same short-run flexibility and long-run performance. It is not uncommon for different components of varying social systems of production to exist simultaneously in a particular country (Herrigel, 1995). For example, standardized social systems of production have always required customized machines or some form of flexible production. And flexible social systems of production have required standardized equipment and therefore some standardized production processes. In other words, the customization of products has long been based on the standardized production of component parts and equipment. A number of scholars (Hirst and Zeitlin, 1989; Pollert, 1988; Sabel, 1991) have made the important point that firms frequently engage in hybrid forms of production, producing both long and short runs or particular products, sometimes engaging in both flexible and standardized production, but that these hybrid-type firms are usually embedded in a dominant type of social system of production.

Of course, flexible systems of production predate Fordist systems of production. Sabel and Zeitlin (1985), as well as others (Hounshell, 1984; Zeitlin, 1992), have demonstrated that flexible social systems of production existed in a number of nineteenth-century industrial districts of Europe and Great Britain, from Lyon to Sheffield, as well as in parts of the United States. Though flexible systems of production both pre- and post-date Fordist, mass standardized systems of production, we must recognize that in recent years flexible social systems of production have become further differentiated into various sub-types. In the literature, one is labeled the flexible specialization system of production (FSP) and another is labeled the diversified quality mass system of production (DQMP) (Aoki, 1988; Boyer and Coriat, 1986; Hirst and Zeitlin, 1989; Streeck, 1991). Originally, these models emerged from an analysis of local structural conditions. They were mainly concerned with coordination among actors and were less concerned with technology or innovation. For example, industrial districts with flexible systems of production existed long before the development of recent information technologies (Sabel and Zeitlin, 1985). On the other hand, the adoption of new, micro-electronic production technology has increased the number of areas of the world that have social systems of flexible production (e.g., either flexible specialization or diversified quality mass production). Therefore, the existing institutions are filtering the emergence and diffusion of new technologies, and conversely, over the long run, some radical technological innovations seem to call for epochal changes in institutions. The success of those changes and the ultimate outcome of these changes is quite uncertain.

In any case, the high flexibility of micro-electronic equipment and the speed with which it can be shifted to a variety of products have permitted previous mass producers to engage in customized quality production and producers with only small batches of specific items to shift to larger batches of production. Thus, there has been a restructuring of two different trajectories of production. Craft producers have been able to extend their production volume without sacrificing their high-quality standards and customization, and many mass producers have had the capacity to upgrade their product design and quality and thus to reduce the pressures of price competition and shrinking mass markets (Sorge and Streeck, 1988).

There was no single and unique pattern of industrialization. Forms of flexible specialization existed in the United States during the nineteenth century— for example in the textile industry (Scranton, 1984). As dominant forms of production, however, they were defeated by standardized mass production, at least in the United States but not everywhere else, especially in Germany and Italy (Herrigel, 1995; Piore and Sabel, 1984; Sabel and Zeitlin, 1985). This was because the social environments in which production was embedded varied greatly from society to society.

In our own day, there are both similarities and differences between the social system of flexible specialization (FSP) and social system of diversified quality mass production (DQMP). Rather than viewing these two perspectives as competing or conflictual, it is best to see them as complementary (Elam, 1992; Sorge, 1989; Sorge and Streeck, 1988). In contrast with social systems of standardized mass production, both FSP and DQMP require workforces with broad levels of skills, i.e., employees who have "learned to learn" about new technologies and who can work closely and cooperatively with other employees and management. Moreover, these systems tend to require that firms develop long-term stable relations with their suppliers and customers.

Social systems of mass production have performed best when firms serve large and stable product markets, and have products and process technologies that are relatively stable or have a low level of technological innovation (Chandler, 1962, 1977, 1990). However, technological complexity and the speed of technical change are not to be confused. For example, the car industry used to implement rather simple components but nevertheless exhibited complex coordination problems (Tolliday and Zeitlin, 1991). Markets, corporate hierarchies, and inegalitarian and short-lived networks are the dominant forms of coordination in social systems of mass production. On the other hand, social systems of flexible specialization and diversified quality mass production tend to function more effectively when firms are responding to small market niches with product markets that are unstable and volatile (the Italian garment industry) or whose product and process technologies change rapidly (micro-electronics, bio-technologies) and are quite complex (aircraft industry, luxury cars). For firms to perform well under these circumstances, they require different forms of coordination from those that are most effective for social systems of mass standardized production.

Markets and hierarchies as coordinating mechanisms can work effectively in mass standardized systems of production even if the transacting actors are embedded in an impoverished institutional environment—one in which such collective forms of coordination as associations and promotional networks are poorly developed (Hollingsworth, 1991a, 1991b). But social systems of flexible specialization and diversified quality mass production work best when transacting actors are embedded in an institutional environment in which collective forms of coordination are highly developed. Broadly speaking, both of these social systems of production are basically incompatible with neo-liberal regimes of unregulated economies (Pyke and Sengenberger, 1992; Streeck, 1991). Nevertheless, the relative success of the Japanese transplants in the United States and the United Kingdom does challenge the view that these alternatives to typical Fordism cannot be implemented in countries with weakly developed collective forms of coordination (Florida and Kenney, 1991; Kenney and Florida, 1988, 1993; Oliver and Wilkinson, 1988). The long-term success of flexible specialization and diversified quality mass social systems of production requires a high degree of trust and cooperation among economic actors—between workers and managers within firms and between firms on the one hand and their suppliers and customers on the other (Boyer and Orlean, 1991; Hollingsworth, 1991a, 1991b). This can be organized in some localities with a strong tradition of providing the collective goods of trust and cooperation (examples are the German cooperative partnership between labor and management and the Italian industrial districts). Firms operating in isolation from such collective goods may provide local examples of flexible production or diversified quality mass production, at least in the short run (e.g., Japanese transplants in the United States and the United Kingdom). But in the long run, successful firms that are involved in flexible social systems of production must engage in cooperative behavior with suppliers, competitors, and employees far in excess of what is needed for markets and hierarchies to function effectively and in excess of what single firms can develop for themselves (Streeck, 1991; Hollingsworth and Streeck, 1994). But in order to understand why these different types of production exist, it is important to understand the different social environments in which they are embedded and the different historical traditions from which they have evolved.

Convergence or Divergence among Social Systems of Production

Discussions about convergence and divergence are still very much alive in the social science community. For example, some of the industrial organizational literature argues that firms competing in the same product markets tend to become similar in their structure and behavior, else they disappear. In other words, the convergence thesis assumes that there is one best solution for organizing labor, raw materials, and capital in order to manufacture and distribute goods. Producers, processors, and distributors must at least emulate if not surpass their most efficient competitors in order to survive. Every time a group of innovators discovers a new, but highly efficient method of increasing output, their competitors are likely to follow. Thus competition and survival involve discovering and implementing the best techniques and strategies (Chandler, 1962, 1977, 1990).

However, the argument for such a convergence is far from convincing (Whitley and Kristensen, 1996). The key to understanding the degree to which the economic performance of countries will converge is influenced very much by the extent to which they have similar social systems or production. Because the social systems of production of modern societies are complex configurations of numerous institutional sectors, however, it is problematic that they can diffuse across countries, except over an extraordinarily long period of time. In fact, given the strong complementarity and syncretic flavor of any national system of innovation (Nelson, 1993), it would be surprising to observe an easy catching up by followers: the structural advantage taken by a leading country or industry initially prevents an easy imitation. Followers, while trying to imitate, usually encounter unexpected problems, which trigger a series of induced adaptations or even innovations that may finally deliver a different model, building on their own national specificities. When France and Germany tried to follow the first British industrial revolution, both countries moved toward quite different new models (Gerschenkron, 1962). Similarly, after World War II, many Japanese manufacturers wanted to follow American mass production practices, but got, quite unintentionally, diversified quality mass production (Ohno, 1989).

But firms in lagging economies do attempt to mimic some of the management styles and work practices of their more successful competitors. We observed this in both the United Kingdom and the United States during the eighties, where there emerged the concept of "the Internationalization of Japanese Business" (Trevor, 1987). However, this phenomenon was grossly exaggerated. Many who contended that there was an emerging Japanization of the world economy had not confronted the problem of what is distinctively Japanese. True, some Japanese practices were exported elsewhere. But much of our scholarship on Japanese firms in foreign settings demonstrates that they pragmatically adapt to foreign conditions rather than duplicate Japanese practices. As Levine and Ohtsu (1991) observe, Japanese companies in foreign settings generally find that they must contend with the foreign culture as well as the laws and rules of alien governments, foreign unions, and employers, all of which are at great variance with Japanese institutions. Of course, one may point to the joint venture which developed between Toyota and General Motors in Fremont, California, as well as the cases of Honda and Nissan in the United States, as examples in which a number of Japanese management practices appear to have diffused to the American setting. But close examination of even these more extreme cases demonstrates a hybridization of Japanese and American practices. Nevertheless, this kind of hybridization did result in much more flexible patterns of production than were previously observed in the American automobile industry.

This, of course, raises the larger issue of joint ventures and strategic alliances taking place in advanced capitalist societies. In an era when the rate of technological change was relatively low and there were homogeneous demands for a particular product, production processes in an industry were relatively standardized, production runs were quite long, and vertical integration was an appropriate strategy for firms that faced high uncertainties and small numbers in their interdependent relationships with other firms. However, when technology changes very rapidly and the costs of technology are very expensive, firms are less inclined to engage in vertical integration, and joint ventures and strategic alliances become more frequent, particularly among firms in different societies. Of course, the motives for this form of coordination are varied: the search for economies of scale, the need for market access, the sharing of risks, the need to have access to technology, and the need to pool know-how if no one firm has the capability to achieve its goals. Such projects have occurred in a variety of sectors, but especially in the pharmaceutical, computer, aerospace, nuclear energy, electronics, and automobile industries. Is the increasing frequency of this form of coordination leading to the convergence of national economies?

Undoubtedly, the increased frequency of joint ventures and strategic alliances does lead to some convergence in certain management styles and work practices among cooperating partners. However, the diffusion of these practices does not bring about convergence in social systems of production. Before World War II, foreign firms attempted to borrow certain principles of scientific management that had become widespread in the United States, but in general the American practices were greatly modified when implemented. Moreover, in making these modifications, foreign actors did so within the developmental trajectory of their own social systems of production. Similarly in our own day, selected principles of Japanese management styles and work practices did diffuse to other countries, but they were selectively integrated into local institutional arrangements.

The institutional configurations that coordinate or govern the behavior of actors in the various institutional sectors of one society cannot easily be transferred from one society to another, for they are embedded into a social system of production that is societally distinct. Societies do borrow selected principles of foreign management styles and work practices, but their effectiveness is generally limited. Economic performance is shaped by the entire social system of production in which actors are embedded and not simply by specific principles of particular management styles and work practices. Moreover, a society's social system of production tends to limit the kind of goods that it can produce and with which it can compete successfully in international markets.

True, some scholars (Kenney and Florida, 1993; Oliver and Wilkinson, 1988) have assumed that the diffusion of particular forms of management styles and work practices across societies could lead to system convergence. Referring to the Japanese production system, Kenney and Florida argue that it consists of organizational practices whose fundamental genetic code can be successfully inserted into another society and can then begin to successfully reproduce in the new environment (1993: 8). Their argument is in the intellectual tradition of

Antonio Gramsci (1971) who contended decades ago that the American system of mass production would most certainly diffuse to Europe over time.

However, the argument of this essay is that even though British, French, and American firms may adopt certain aspects of Japanese management styles (e.g., just-in-time production complexes, self-managing teams, quality circles, the use of statistical process controls etc., or some variant of the German vocational system) one should not conclude that their economies will be transformed. A nation's financial markets, educational system, industrial relations system, and other socio-political factors influence sectoral and national economic performance. In order to understand how and why a society's economy performs, it is necessary to understand its entire social system of production. If a society is to improve the performance of its economy, it cannot adapt only some of the management and work practices of its foreign competitors. It must alter its entire social system of production.

In any social system, there are pressures to have consistency in the norms, rules, and values across institutional sectors, though in any complex society, social systems are obviously imperfectly integrated. Indeed, the degree to which the institutional norms and rules making up a social system of production are loosely or tightly coupled is a variable of considerable importance.

In sum, the emergence of social systems of production is a long-term, evolutionary process with each part interacting with its environment and resulting in a configurative whole—but with no previous design by either a single actor or a collectivist of actors.

CHARACTERISTIC FEATURES OF
SOCIAL SYSTEMS OF PRODUCTION

Having introduced the notion of "social systems of production" at some length, we can now lay out their essential and principal features in a more systemic manner which, in addition, summarizes the preceding discussions. These main features can be clustered in three different groups.

Compositional and Structural Complexity

One of the basic characteristics of social systems of production lies in their compositional complexity. Social systems of production consist of a large number of different actors, ranging from small-scale enterprises to transnational corporations and from the governing bodies of small town halls to multinational or global agencies. Structural complexity is linked to the organizational complexity (variety of institutional arrangements) and to hierarchical complexity (number of levels). Moreover, each social system of production has a diversified, hierarchical, and partially conflicting set of institutional arrangements in terms of norms, rules, regulations, values, laws, and the like which adds up to the compositional as well as to the structural complexity of these macro-societal ensembles.

High Variations across Space and Time

One of the most prominent features of social systems of production lies in the high degree of variations across space and time. Not only are different coordinating mechanisms associated with different social systems of production, but also different coordinating mechanisms and different social systems of production result in different types of economic performance. As long as countries vary in the type of coordinating mechanisms and social systems of production that are dominant in their economies, there are serious constraints on the degree to which they can converge in their economic performance. Different social systems of production tend to maximize in a more or less explicit manner different performance criteria, usually mixed considerations about static and dynamic efficiency, profit, security, social peace, and economic and/or political power. In short, in contrast to the implications of neo-classical economic theory, in real-world economies there are no universal standards that all economically rational actors attempt to maximize. Economic history provides numerous examples of how a variety of principles of rationality are implemented in different societies.

Another feature, directly related to the high degree of variation across space and time, lies in the astonishing amount of substitution within social systems of production. Thus, major functions within a social system of production like training and education or conflict resolution can be fulfilled with different actors and actor groups. Thus, the dual vocational training system, highly characteristic for countries like Germany or Austria, can be substituted by a variety of other arrangements, ranging from internal training programs to specially designed "youth employment programs."

A third generic trait of social systems of production which follows immediately from the first two characteristics lies in the limited transferability of "comparative advantages" from one social system of production to another. In general, the institutions and actors making up a social system of production are interdependent, and changes in one institutional domain generally result in changes in other institutional arenas. Each institutional sphere is dependent on the others for various types of resources, so there is interdependence among the differing institutional spheres. Moreover, each society has its norms, moral principles, rules and laws, recipes for action, as well as its own idiosyncratic customs, traditions, and principles of justice (Burns and Flam, 1987) which generally lead to two transfer errors. The first and most frequent error lies in transfers from one context into a different one where the necessary mechanisms required for a successful adaptation are not available. The second transfer error occurs in all those instances where unsuccessful experiments in other contexts are not considered as suitable objects of transfers, although the available context would generate a positive outcome. Both "transfer errors" point to a severely restricted transfer potential and to the serious limitations on "benchmarking" and on the usefulness of "best practice standards."

Complex Dynamics

In line with the two features just presented, the third set of patterns follows almost logically. Social systems of production are characterized by a complex, non-linear dynamics which can be identified in various ways.

The first dynamic pattern of social systems of production lies in their general "path dependencies." National trajectories of social systems of production which have existed for long periods of time are very difficult, if not outright impossible, to reverse and to change substantially. One recent comparative study (Hollingsworth, Schmitter, and Streeck, 1994) has demonstrated that, across countries, clusters of industries develop along particular trajectories, each having its distinct microeconomic dynamics within which markets, corporate hierarchies, networks, associations, and governments operate. Because skills, management techniques, and modes of governance are embedded in distinctive social systems of production, they do not easily diffuse from one society to another.

As a result, variation across countries in social systems of production remains substantial, even if there is convergence at the global level in how selected industries (e.g., chemical, oil, large-scale aircraft) are coordinated. This variation remains substantial for there have been great differences in the path dependencies of countries. For more than a century, the German economy had an emerging diversified quality system of production (Herrigel, 1995), whereas since the fifties, the Japanese have hybridized mass production along with diversified quality production. In both countries, specific institutional arrangements allowed for the distinctiveness of their particular social system of production. In contrast, the United States has been very much constrained by its earlier Fordist mass production system and its "short-termism" under the influence of its distinctive financial markets, weak unions and business associations, and specific norms, rules, and recipes for action. Despite the emphasis on the logic of institutional continuity and of "path-dependencies" this is not an argument that systems change along some predetermined path. There are critical turning points in the history of social systems of production, but the choices are limited by the exiting institutional terrain. Being path-dependent, a social system of production continues along a particular logic until or unless a fundamental societal crisis intervenes (Milgrom, Qian, and Roberts, 1991; Krugman,

1991; Durlauf, 1991; Hollingsworth, 1991a, 1991b; Pred, 1966; David, 1988; Hodgson, 1998).

At this point it is important to confront the question of how social systems of production evolved. And this question gets to the heart of the problem of building complex institutions. Certainly, social systems of production did not emerge from some process of social engineering. Moreover, the various component parts of each social system of production were not designed to be part of a social system of production. Indeed the component parts of each social system of production emerged as unintended by-products of goals which various actors had in mind at earlier moments in time. It is usually the case that actors at time *t* do think seriously about the long-term consequences of their actions. However, Wolfgang Streeck convincingly argues that the design of institutional sectors which were created for one purpose generally had quite unintended consequences over time (Streeck, 1997a, 1997b; Wright, 1998). In describing the configuration which made up the German social system of production of the seventies and eighties, Streeck points out that it was the unintended by-product of multiple points in history. Some elements were pre-Wilhelmian, others were introduced by the Allied powers after 1945, and others emerged during the years of the German Federal Republic.

There are inherent obstacles to convergence among social systems of production, for where a system is at any one point in time is influenced by its initial state. Systems having quite different initial states are unlikely to converge with one another's institutional practices. Existing institutional arrangements block certain institutional innovations and facilitate others (Roland, 1990). Thus, the institutions making up a social system of production provide continuity, though institutional arrangements are always changing, but with a particular logic. While Williamson (1975, 1985) suggests that actors tend to choose the institutions which are most efficient, North (1990) is much closer to the mark in his argument that most societal institutions exist as a result of custom and habit and are therefore inefficient. At any moment in time, the world often appears to its actors as very complex and uncertain. For this reason, actors often engage in contradictory forms of behavior—pursuing different strategies as hedges against what is viewed as a very uncertain world. And their hedging and contradictory forms of behavior may lead to somewhat different societal directions, but ones constrained by the institutional fabric within which the actors are embedded.

Recapitulating, it is difficult to overlook the co-evolutionary "deep structure" found in complex, dynamic systems. Analysis of embedded macro-societal formations is one of the most promising intersections where socio-economics meets with evolutionary theorizing, co-evolutionary frameworks, and non-linear systems theory.

MORE EMBEDDED SOCIAL SYSTEMS

At this point, we confront the question of whether other societal systems can be identified which exhibit a similar composition, and dynamic features like the ones which have been summarized for social systems of production. Even a brief glance at the long-term development of national systems of health, national systems of education, or national systems of innovation makes it clear that other societal configurations can be constructed which, like the social system of production, exhibit the same basic structure and the same group of essential characteristics.

All the different components of social systems of production also exist for these other societal configurations as well. The main reason for this similarity lies in the similar degrees of compositional and organizational complexity across different embedded societal formations. Thus, dynamic features like "path-dependencies" or the absence of a "global attractor" to which all different national systems might converge should be considered as the only constant and unchangeable elements which this current age of rapid changes, uncertainties, and complexities is able to offer.

12

Globalization and Economic Adjustment in Germany

Peter A. Hall

As Schumpeter (1950) observed half a century ago, modern capitalist economies are not static entities but are marked by dynamic processes that pose continuous challenges to those who manage or govern them. From this perspective, we can discern four periods in the years since 1945, each of which generated a distinctive set of economic challenges for the developed democracies.

For a decade after World War II, the energies of Western Europe were concentrated on economic reconstruction. That required the accumulation and allocation of capital with which to rebuild industry and the development of institutions for economic coordination within and across nations (cf. Shonfield, 1969; Eichengreen, 1997). For another twenty-five years, rapid economic growth meant that the principal challenges facing the European nations were to stabilize the business cycle and allocate the fruits of growth fairly among profits, wages, and social benefits (Boltho, 1982; Marglin and Schor, 1990). The seventies generated a new set of challenges, as rising commodity prices and the exhaustion of Fordist models of production brought lower rates of growth as well as higher levels of inflation and unemployment (Piore and Sabel, 1984; Boyer, 1990). Inflation loomed as the main problem facing the industrialized democracies, and they responded with a variety of experiments with incomes policies and ultimately stricter monetary policies and efforts to mount fixed exchange-rate regimes (Salant, 1977; Hirsch and Goldthorpe, 1978; Berger 1982).

Since 1980, the general complexion of the economic challenges facing the industrialized nations has again changed. Three developments have set the stage. The first is a technological revolution, centering around information technology and biological science that has created whole new industries and changed production and distribution in many other established industries (Ziegler, 1997; Lane, 1995). Closely allied to this is a managerial revolution, initially associated with the diffusion techniques for quality control, team production, and supply-chain relations pioneered in Japan but now extending to innovative forms of standard-setting, subcontracting, and technology transfer utilized around the world (Womack, et al., 1990; Streeck, 1987). Reinforcing these twin revolutions is the substantial growth in international trade and finance of recent years, facilitated by the liberalization of trading regimes, financial deregulation, falling transportation and communication costs, and the collapse of communism (cf. Milner and Keohane, 1995; Berger and Dore, 1995).

Together, these recent developments have put substantial pressure on the firms and governments of the developed economies to adjust. Business enterprises have come under pressure to alter their modes of operating in order to cope with more intense international competition. As a result, they have put pressure on their suppliers and workforce to find new and more "flexible" ways of doing things. Governments have been asked to alter their regulatory structures in order to accommodate new forms of production, distribution, and innovation. In some nations, higher levels of unemployment, especially among the less skilled, associated with these shifts in resources have placed new demands on many of the social benefits schemes and institutions that traditionally secure social order (cf. Wood, 1994; OECD, 1994; Rodrik, 1997).

In such a context, many firms, trade unions, and governments seem beleaguered by international forces. They face a new set of adjustment problems defined by demands to alter corporate strategy, industrial relations, and public policy so as to secure prosperity in a rapidly changing environment. The purpose of this chapter is to examine these adjustment problems and the capacity of the German political economy, in particular, to cope with them.[1] The German case is an especially important and interesting one, not only because it is the leading European economy but because it is a "coordinated market economy" quite different in operation from the "liberal market economies" of the United States and Britain where markets provide the principal means of adjustment. As such, Germany is representative of many of the northern European economies, where powerful trade unions and employers associations exist alongside markets, limiting their operation in some cases and supplementing them in others. Here, adjustment must often be negotiated among the social partners or stakeholders in firms; and many question whether economies such as these can prosper in the face of contemporary economic challenges (cf. Streeck, 1997). An examination of the German case will tell us much about the viability of European models of capitalism in an era of globalization.

I begin by outlining the basic problems that the forces associated with "globalization" pose to the German political economy. Then, I provide a basic framework for understanding the central differences among political economies, based on joint work with David Soskice (Hall and Soskice, 2001). From this, I derive a theory of comparative institutional advantage and ela-borate the alternative perspective on globalization it implies. Equipped with this view, I assess the adjustment capacities of the German political economy in both economic and political terms and conclude with some overarching observations about the future of organized models of capitalism in Europe.

THE GLOBALIZATION PROBLEM

The economic challenges of the contemporary era are frequently described as a problem of "globalization." I use the term here to refer to rapid growth in the amount of goods and capital flowing across national borders in the wake of falling trade barriers, lower communication costs, financial deregulation, and shifts in political regimes. From it, two problems of central importance to Germany and many other economies have followed. First, globalization raises the prospect that many firms will take advantage of greater economic openness to shift some or all of their production to foreign nations. Second, this prospect puts pressure on national governments to alter their regulatory frameworks in order to keep these firms at home and attract others from abroad.

For several reasons, these problems are especially intense in Germany. The collapse of communism in Eastern Europe dismantled what had once been substantial trade barriers. German firms now sit close to large, low-cost labor markets that can provide attractive alternative sites for production. Thanks to powerful trade unions and high levels of productivity, German labor costs are now among the highest in the world, intensifying fears that the price of goods produced in Germany may be undercut by foreign competitors. The monetary policies that followed German unification and the effort to create a European Monetary Union also generated high levels of unemployment that have called into question Germany's framework for social and economic regulation (cf. Carlin and Soskice, 1997). In this context, it is inevitable that German firms will move some parts of their production abroad, while others face more intense competition from foreign firms. In the long run, however, the growth of foreign economies, especially in East Central Europe, will provide new markets for

German goods. This is the sort of adjustment process that has long been associated with the opening of borders. The central questions are: how much production should we expect to see shift abroad and how much do German institutions have to change in order to remain competitive? To these questions, the perspective on globalization commonly found in the literature gives a frightening answer. There are several components to this view. First, it sees firms as essentially similar across nations, at least in terms of basic structure and strategy. Second, it associates firm competitiveness almost exclusively with labor costs. From this, it follows that many firms will find it tempting to move their production offshore if they can find cheaper labor there.

Many expect the result to be a familiar political dynamic. In the face of threats from firms to exit the national economy, governments will come under increasing pressure from business to alter their regulatory frameworks so as to lower domestic labor costs, reduce rates of taxation, and expand internal markets via deregulation. What resistance there is to such steps will come from trade unions attempting to protect the wages of their members and social democratic parties seeking to preserve social programs. On these premises, the effects that each nation suffers in the face of globalization will be determined largely by the amount of political resistance that labor and the left can mount to such proposals for change. If their resistance is low, the economy will adjust and prosper but at the cost of radical deregulation. If it is high, regulatory regimes will not change dramatically, but it may be difficult for the economy to flourish. In essence, this perspective defines an inescapable frontier in which nations face a sharp tradeoff between deregulation and unemployment.

Most predict that, when faced with such choices, governments will choose deregulation. Business is said to gain power as the economy opens because capital is more mobile than labor, and governments may not be able to resist its pressure (Kurzer, 1993). As a result, the conventional model predicts substantial convergence in economic institutions and public policy across nations (Ohmae, 1991; Reich, 1994; cf. Berger and Dore, 1995). It contains a "convergence hypothesis" analogous in force, but less sanguine in social implications, to the one generated forty years ago by theories of industrial society (Kerr, 1973; Graubard, 1964).

To date, those who have challenged this model of globalization have done so by arguing that the internationalization of trade and finance is not as extensive as the model suggests or that national governments are not subject to its pressures but active collaborators in the changes to international regimes that then seem to generate these pressures (cf. Wade, 1996; Boyer, 1996; Cohen, 1996). There is some validity to both arguments. However, there are even stronger grounds for rejecting the conventional view of globalization, to which I now turn. I lay the groundwork for that argument by outlining a new approach to comparative capitalism and the implications for comparative economic advantage that follow from it.

COORDINATED AND LIBERAL MARKET ECONOMIES

If we are to understand the adjustment problems that an economy faces and its capacity for coping with them, we must begin from an accurate representation of how that economy operates. For this purpose, it will not do to posit an ideal type based entirely on neoclassical images of a market economy because the shapes of many economies diverge in substantial and systematic ways from such an image. Instead, we need a fine-grained appreciation for the multiple "varieties of capitalism" to be found in the developed world.

Accordingly, I draw on the formulations of Hall and Soskice (2001; Soskice, 1991, 1998) built on the work of many other scholars (Katzenstein, 1985; Scharpf, 1991; Hall, 1986; Zysman, 1983; Goldthorpe, 1984). This approach to "varieties of capitalism" sees firms as the central actors in the economy, responsible for the key decisions that will ultimately determine the shape and quality of economic adjustment. The principal challenges that firms face are said, in turn, to be relational. In order to accomplish its core tasks associated with the recruitment, compensation, and training of labor, securing access to finance and technology, and managing relations with suppliers, clients, and employees, a firm must develop effective relations with other actors. On the quality of these relations depend the core competencies of the firm (cf. Milgrom and Roberts, 1992; Aoki, 1990). But these relations can be construed as coordination problems. How well a firm performs each task will depend on the effectiveness with which it coordinates with other actors.

From this, it follows that we can distinguish among economies according to the extent to which their firms rely on "market" versus "non-market" mechanisms to coordinate their endeavors. In some nations, firms rely primarily on standard market mechanisms to coordinate their relations with other actors. In others, firms make more extensive use of non-market arrangements where coordination takes the form of a strategic interaction that is supported by a set of institutions supplying the flows of information, monitoring, sanctioning, and deliberative capacities necessary to effective coordination. Several kinds of institutions can provide such capacities, including employer associations, trade unions, networks of cross-shareholders, and quasi-public organizations. Thus, economies can be arrayed along a spectrum according to the extent to which firms there depend on "market" versus "non-market" modes of coordination.

I will term the type of economy found at one end of this spectrum a "liberal" market economy, and we find good examples of it in Britain, the United States, Canada, Australia, Ireland, and New Zealand. At the other end of the spectrum sit "coordinated" or "organized" market economies, where firms rely more heavily on non-market modes of coordination to accomplish their tasks. Although there are some fine-grained differences in the modes of coordination their firms employ, we can think of Germany, Japan, the Netherlands, Sweden, Austria, Norway, and many of the other economies of northern Europe as coordinated market economies. What are the principal differences between these two types of economy?[2]

The defining feature of a liberal market economy is the degree to which its firms rely on the price signals arising from competitive markets and formal contractual relations to resolve such coordination problems. Here, firms typically secure finance via arm's-length relations in which equity markets play a large role and bank lending turns heavily on cash flow or collateral. The access of most firms to finance depends heavily on their short-term profitability. Labor is recruited from relatively unconstrained labor markets where trade unions are often weak. Wage determination lies primarily at the firm or plant level and management retains substantial prerogatives over firing. Access to production inputs and technology is generally secured by competitive bidding among suppliers, licensing or hiring technical personnel from fluid labor markets. Vocational training is the responsibility of the worker or individual firm and emphasizes general skills.

By contrast, a coordinated market economy is defined by the extensive degree to which it relies on institutions other than market mechanisms to resolve the coordination problems facing firms, including relatively encompassing trade unions, works councils, employers associations, cross-shareholding, and other linkages between firms. These institutions allow firms to engage in high levels of "non-market coordination" with each other and their employees that have the character of strategic interactions, by providing facilities that allow the actors to exchange information in a context of credibility, to monitor others' behavior more closely than market relations allow, to sanction deviation from agreed courses of action, and to deliberate about changes to such arrangements. Thus, corporate finance is usually provided on terms that are more sensitive to a firm's long-term strategy than its short-term profitability by banks or other firms with extensive capacities for network monitoring of firm behavior. Equity markets featuring high levels of cross-shareholding inhibit hostile takeovers and facilitate the exchange of inside information among firms. Labor is recruited on markets that are dominated by powerful trade unions or employer associations often accompanied by institutions that limit managerial prerogatives over layoffs and work reorganization. Firms typically secure access to inputs and technology via long-term collaborative arrangements whose viability depends on collective capacities for standard setting and the enforcement of implicit contracts. Vocational training is often accomplished through collaborative schemes that encourage the development of industry-specific skills.

Although this is a schematic account identifying two ideal types, it allows us to identify some of the distinctive strengths and weaknesses that each type of economy has for coping with the adjustment problems of the contemporary era.

The principal strengths of liberal market economies flow from the capacities they vest in corporate managers to redeploy resources quickly both within the firm and across sectors. Labor can be recruited, laid off, or redirected with relative ease. Well-developed equity markets push capital quickly from spheres offering low returns to those promising higher ones. As a result, these econo-mies tend to be propitious sites for radical innovation of the sort that involve very new technologies or entirely new product lines and high-risk investments (Soskice, 1994a). Firms in such economies also tend to be effective at control-ling labor costs.

The central weaknesses of liberal market economies derive from the low levels of support they provide for the long-term relationships associated with incomplete contracting among firms or between firms and their employees (cf. Milgrom and Roberts, 1992). This is notable because the absence of such arrangements in some spheres inhibits their development in others. For instance, the salience of short-term profitability to finance limits the capacity of firms to offer long-term employment contracts, which may reduce the willingness of employees to share their private knowledge or to acquire firm- or industry-specific skills. Accordingly, companies in liberal market economies often find it difficult to raise some kinds of skill levels, to sustain new projects through a downturn in demand or to develop the kind of long-term relations with custom-ers and suppliers that facilitate incremental innovation in products and produc-tion processes.

The strengths and liabilities of coordinated market economies are virtually the mirror image of those in liberal market economies. Such economies draw their strengths from institutional infrastructures that support long-term relation-ships alongside market relations. Thus, firms enjoy superior capacities for vocational training and competitive advantages in sectors that demand highly skilled labor (Finegold and Soskice, 1988). The availability of long-term finance allows firms to develop "implicit contracts" with employees that encourage them to share knowledge with management (cf. Aoki, 1990). Thus, quality control is easier and close relations with suppliers facilitate continuous innova-tion. Organized producer groups provide mechanisms for aligning wage growth with productivity growth in the economy as a whole (cf. Golden, 1993; Soskice, 1990).

The weaknesses of coordinated market economies flow largely from the slow speed with which they redeploy resources. Financial systems that rely heavily on network reputations and discourage hostile takeovers can be slow to shift funds from areas of low return to those offering higher ones. Where layoffs are more difficult, it is harder for firms to cut costs and riskier for them to invest in new sectors or technologies where failure might leave them holding labor they cannot shed. Although long-term relationships inside and among firms offer gains from reorganization that might not otherwise be possible, realizing those gains may be a slow process demanding the renegotiation of skill categories, task assignments, and resource allocation with multiple actors.

COMPARATIVE INSTITUTIONAL ADVANTAGE

One of the most important features of this approach to comparative capitalism is the theory of comparative institutional advantage that it generates. At the heart of international trade theory is the doctrine of comparative economic advantage. It suggests that particular nations or groups of nations enjoy advantages in the production of certain kinds of commodities, whether agricultural or industrial, by virtue of endowments specific to those nations. Where this is true, expanding trade will not impoverish a country by sending all of its production abroad, but enhance its prosperity, because each nation will be able to specialize in the goods for which its endowments are most suited, thereby producing them more efficiently so that they can be exchanged for even more goods from other nations.

In its initial versions, the theory was applied to agricultural commodities where one could readily see that both Portugal and Britain would prosper by trading if one specialized in wine and the other in grain. Here, the emphasis was on the physical endowments of a nation that make some kinds of agricultural production more feasible others. In later versions, the theory emphasized the relative abundance of labor and capital across nations, suggesting that nations with abundant labor could specialize in labor-intensive industries, while those with more capital pursued capital-intensive endeavors (Stolper and Samuelson, 1941). With some modifications to allow for differences between skilled and unskilled labor, relative factor mobility, and the like, theories based on relative factor endowments have dominated analyses of comparative economic advantage.

In recent years, however, a number of analysts have begun to suggest that relative factor endowments may not be the only sources of national economic advantage (Zysman, 1994; Nelson, 1993). One indicator pointing in this direction has been the discovery that the total productivity gains of a nation cannot be explained fully by reference to the amounts of capital and labor that it utilizes. Like firms, many nations seem to experience increases in productivity beyond those that could be expected to derive from additions to their base of capital or labor. Based on this observation, a set of "endogenous growth theories" have been devised to explain how other features of the character or organization of an economy may allow it to secure higher levels of productivity or growth than one would predict on the basis of factor inputs alone (cf. Romer, 1986, 1994; Grossman and Helpman, 1994). These theories open the door to arguments suggesting that the organization of the economy may affect what firms there can do. But we need to know more about precisely which features of that organization matter most. To date, these theories have emphasized gains secured through economies of scope or scale, network externalities, and appropriate property-rights regimes.

The approach to comparative capitalism outlined here directs our attention in another direction, toward the modes of coordination that firms employ. It may well be that the efficiency with which a firm can accomplish certain tasks (or produce particular kinds of products) may depend on its capacities to coordinate with the relevant actors; and these capacities, in turn, should depend on the level of institutional support available for that kind of coordination in the political economy as a whole. In short, firms that enjoy the coordinating capacities provided by a coordinated market economy may be able to produce some kinds of goods more efficiently, while those in liberal market economies produce other kinds of goods more efficiently. If so, we can say that the organization of the economy generates comparative institutional advantages.

Much remains to be done to develop this line of analysis. But Soskice (1994a) has already developed a powerful argument linking the organization of the economy to the kind of innovation likely to be accomplished most effectively there. Liberal market economies (LMEs) tend to provide propitious settings for radical innovation, understood in terms of the capacity of firms to develop very different product lines, to move into radically new endeavors, or to make and exploit dramatic advances in science or technology. By contrast, coordinated market economies (CMEs) tend to be more effective at incremental innovation, namely at making gradual but steady improvements to products and production processes, and at securing high levels of quality control. We can see why this might be the case.

In liberal market economies, the financial markets generally provide substantial amounts of venture capital for entrepreneurs seeking to establish new companies built around radically new technologies or product lines. Fluid labor markets also encourage such innovation because they allow companies to recruit employees with new kinds of technical expertise and readily release them if the new endeavor does not prove fruitful. As Lehrer (1997b) shows, the corporate hierarchies of liberal market economies that concentrate power in top management make it easier for firms to undertake radical reorganizations in response to shifting market conditions. Systems of standard-setting that turn heavily on market races to patent new technologies encourage investment in radical innovation.

However, firms in liberal market economies face some disadvantages in the sphere of innovation. Because their institutions provide little support for coordinating training at the industry level, they can have difficulty securing labor with high levels of industry-specific skills and may find it costly to improve the skill levels of the workforce.

Low job tenures and high rates of turnover make it more difficult for many firms to secure the high levels of loyalty from the workforce required to maintain high levels of quality control, to sustain collaborative work arrangements, or to operate strategies that turn on employee-led process innovation.

It is here that firms in coordinated market economies enjoy distinctive advantages. These economies are marked by institutional settings that support long-term employment contracts and guarantees that employees will not be exploited by management of the sort embodied in works councils. As a result, firms find it easier to secure the incremental process or product innovation that draws on the knowledge of the workforce. The presence of institutions for coordinating vocational training makes it easier for these nations to upgrade industry-specific skills to cope with technological advance and to diffuse such skills widely across an industry. Industry-based systems of standard setting of the sort found in Germany also help to diffuse new technology across sectors (Casper, 2001).

Conversely, the institutional settings of coordinated market economies tend to militate against radical innovation. Since employment tenures tend to be long, firms find it riskier to hire in new personnel in order to secure access to technology. Instead, they rely more heavily on collaborative endeavor with other firms for technology transfer, an approach that encourages incremental innovation but offers fewer incentives for radical innovation. Because the discretion of top management is limited by more influential supervisory boards and/or works councils, it can be difficult to mobilize consent for radical changes in corporate strategy in these economies (Lehrer, 1997b). Collaborative standard setting, usually at the industry level, encourages firms to make incremental improvements to their products and production processes but discourages efforts at radical innovation.

It should be apparent that the portrait drawn here is a stylized one. There are some significant differences among nations that can be described as coordinated or liberal market economies; and some firms will find ways of pursuing corporate strategies in any one of them that the overall institutional structure does not encourage (cf. Soskice, 1994b). In some cases, regional or sectoral institutions offer support for strategies that cannot be found in the political economy as a whole, and there are firms that remain profitable even without exploiting their nation's comparative advantages.

However, the overall point remains an important one. Systematic institutional differences across nations in the support provided for different kinds of coordination tend to confer on the firms of each nation some distinctive advantages for pursuing certain kinds of activities, notably in the sphere of innovation, relative to those of other nations. There are good grounds for thinking that each nation enjoys some "comparative institutional advantages."

AN ALTERNATIVE PERSPECTIVE ON GLOBALIZATION

This approach to comparative capitalism calls into question each of the key tenets underpinning conventional views of globalization. First, it suggests that we should not assume that firm strategy is largely similar across nations. Differences in the levels of institutional support provided for particular kinds of coordination tend to generate systematic differences in firm strategies across nations. Firms in coordinated market economies will favor strategies that take advantage of the extensive support provided there for non-market coordination, while firms in liberal market economies will rely more heavily on market-oriented strategies.

There is support for this contention in the literature. Soskice (1994a) has found systematic differences in the approach that firms take toward innovation across nations. Knetter (1989) finds that German firms behave quite differently from British firms when faced with a similar challenge. Faced with an appreciation of the exchange rate, German firms tend to lower their prices in foreign markets, sacrificing profitability to preserve market share, while British firms move to higher prices in order to maintain their current profits. This is precisely what we would expect. German firms need to maintain market share because they cannot lay labor off readily but their access to "patient capital" allows them accept lower rates of profit for a period. By contrast, British firms need to maintain their profits to retain access to capital, given the structure of capital markets in LMEs, and it is easier for them to shed labor in order to do so, given the fluid labor markets there. In short, systematic differences in corporate strategy across LMEs and CMEs mean that we should not expect the firms of all nations to respond similarly to the challenge of globalization.

Second, this approach to comparative capitalism suggests that firms will not always seek lower-cost labor abroad, even when they can find it more readily there. Provided it comes with commensurate levels of skill and productivity, lower-cost labor is always attractive to firms. But I have argued that many firms also benefit from the specific forms of inter-firm coordination available in their home country. Many will be reluctant to give up the institutional support available for such coordination there simply to reduce their wage costs. The importance of institutional support to the modes firms develop to resolve their coordination problems renders many less mobile than theories that do not adopt this relational perspective to the firm acknowledge.

Indeed, one of the implications of this analysis is that firms in liberal market economies—whose institutional arrangements privilege corporate strategies oriented toward cost-competitiveness, standardized production, and low-cost labor—may be more inclined to move their activities abroad when lower-cost labor becomes available there. By contrast, firms in coordinated market economies tend to adopt strategies that are more dependent on forms of coordination for which it is difficult to find institutional support in countries where cheap labor can be secured, and they may be less inclined to move.

Third, this approach suggests that the dynamics driving the movement of firms in the face of greater economic openness may be at some variance with the postulates of conventional theory. Instead, of roaming the world for cheap labor, companies may decide to locate some of their activities abroad in order to benefit from the comparative advantages that the institutional frameworks of specific nations offer. That may entail locating research and development facilities in liberal market economies where radical innovation is easier to pursue, but it may also entail movement toward coordinated market economies to secure access to skilled labor, quality control, and process innovation.

We can already see many examples of this "institutional arbitrage." Deutsche Bank acquires facilities in London and Chicago to access the radical innovation in financial services available in those settings, and Mazda locates design functions in California to benefit from the advantages its institutional setting provides, but General Motors locates a new engine plant in Dusseldorf, rather than Britain or Spain, to secure the skills and quality control that German institutions offer. In sum, we should expect higher levels of economic openness to increase the rate at which firms move activities abroad, but we need to shift our expectations about the direction of this movement. We should see movement not only toward low-wage and low-regulation environments but toward high-wage and highly regulated economies as well.

Finally, the view presented here calls into question the presumption that business will always press governments toward greater deregulation when faced with the pressures of globalization. We can expect this response in liberal market economies, where many firms coordinate their activities through market mechanisms whose effectiveness can be sharpened by selective deregulation. But there is likely to be substantial resistance to deregulation in coordinated market economies from those segments of the business community that benefit from the regulatory structures underpinning complex forms of non-market coordination. Firms that rely on various forms of non-market coordination to generate their competitive advantages will want to preserve the institutions that support such coordination.

There is good evidence for this in the case of Germany. Wood (2001) shows that German employers mounted significant resistance to the efforts of the newly elected Kohl government to weaken the trade unions by altering the legal basis for strike payments, to reform works councils, and to introduce fixed-term employment contracts. Many firms were reluctant to disrupt the balance of power that had ensured relatively peaceful and stable labor relations, and long-term employment relations had become a component of corporate strategy (see also Thelen, 2000).

In short, the presence of comparative institutional advantages renders the pressures for institutional convergence stemming from globalization less powerful than many think. Firms will certainly shift some of their activities abroad, but that movement is likely to be multi-directional and less extensive than conventional views imply. Thus, the pressures to deregulate that governments face may be lower, especially in coordinated market economies where parts of the business community will join with labor in support of the regulatory arrangements that form important components of their competitive advantage.

THE INSTITUTIONAL SETTING FOR ADJUSTMENT IN GERMANY

This analysis provides a new perspective on the adjustment challenges facing Germany. It suggests that the issue facing the nation is not "how to deregulate" but "how to preserve Germany's institutional comparative advantage." The problem is not "how to prevent German firms from moving abroad" but "how to secure the continuing competitiveness of German firms in more open markets." Even redefined, however, these are significant challenges that will demand some adjustment in firm strategies, trade union positions, and public policy. They will require action in both the economic and political arenas and that will be conditioned by the nature of German institutions in both arenas. What kinds of capacities for adjustment are built into the character of German institutions? I take up this issue from a broad, comparative perspective.

In comparison to other countries, two overarching features of Germany's institutions for economic and political decision making stand out. First, Germany's institutional setting is one in which multiple interests generally have entrenched power over decision making. More groups are in a position to veto key decisions than is the case in many other nations. Second, the German setting contains a substantial number of institutions designed to facilitate collective deliberation among these groups. Although those institutional features often accompany each other, they do not always do so.

This broad institutional pattern is visible in both the political and economic arenas. In the political arena, Germany's system of government divides power between the federal government and the Länder, and between the Bundestag and a Bundesrat that are often controlled by opposing political parties. Within the Bundestag itself, the power to govern is usually shared among a coalition of parties. In short, Germany has a political system that is marked by power sharing among the representatives of many diverse interests. Agreement from most of those interests must be secured if action is to be taken. Katzenstein (1987) is quite right to say that Germany has a "semi-sovereign state."

In the economic arena, power inside firms is not as concentrated as it is in liberal market economies. Although top management enjoys considerable power, it must secure consent for many moves from works councils, where the trade unions are strongly, if informally, represented and from supervisory boards that give providers of finance and other stakeholders a significant voice in corporate strategy (cf. Lehrer, 1997a; Thelen, 1991; Turner, 1991). Many of the most important decisions about vocational training, standard setting, and technology transfer cannot be taken unilaterally by a firm but must be agreed among groups of firms and workers (cf. Finegold and Soskice, 1988; Casper, 1997; Hancke and Casper, 1996).

Consequently, the style of decision making adopted in both the economic and political systems of Germany is normally one that attaches great importance to consultation among all the affected interests and to securing consensus on the course of action to be taken (Richardson and Jordan, 1978). A large number of institutional arrangements, both formal and informal, have been devised for conducting such consultation and securing the relevant consensus.

These characteristics are not unique to Germany. A number of other nations with political and economic systems often described as consociational or corporatist have similar institutions (cf. Katzenstein, 1985; Lijphart, 1975). However, they form a striking contrast to the institutions of some other nations, such as Britain, where decision making in both the economy and polity takes place in much more hierarchical contexts, ones that concentrate power in the hands of a few actors. British managers, for instance, generally have much more discretionary authority over the direction of the firm than their German counterparts. And the Westminster system of cabinet government concentrates power in the hands of the prime minister and his colleagues.

In general terms, these institutional features seem to confer three distinctive advantages on decision making in Germany.

First, they provide decision makers in both the economic and political arenas with what might be termed "strategic capacity."[3] By this, I mean that such institutions encourage the actors to agree on a diagnosis of the overall problems they confront and to formulate a conscious and collective strategy for tackling those problems. Germany is replete with institutions designed to diagnose problems as they emerge, ranging from influential economic institutes, whose pronouncements receive considerable publicity, to trade associations, ever watchful for problems developing in their sectors.

Second, German institutions provide formidable mechanisms for what might be termed the "mobilization of consent."[4] I am referring to the resources that German institutions bring to bear on the problem of securing agreement among a wide range of groups on the course of action that should be taken. This entails compromise but, once it has been secured, the outcome is often more stable than those found in other nations facing similar problems.

This is not to say that the system is non-conflictual. It is common to see open conflict break out among political parties or between employers and trade unions. But this is a normal feature of this kind of negotiated economy. In such settings, the organizations representing specific interests must assure their rank-and-file that they are acting aggressively on their behalf. And, from time to time, they need to test the resolve and strength of the other side. Strikes, lockouts, and other kinds of conflict can be important means of doing so. But that conflict tends to strengthen the overall system of bargaining. It rarely results in its breakdown precisely because national institutions entrench the power of the relevant actors to such a degree that none can afford to ignore the others for long (see also Streeck, 1995). This is a system in which periodic conflict ultimately reinforces the capacity of the actors to secure agreement.

Finally, German institutions are also effective at extracting information relevant to resolving a problem from those affected by it, extending a substantial distance down the hierarchies found in firms and other large organizations. This "capacity to mobilize information" is of great value to German firms seeking to improve their production processes, but can also be a valuable asset for other kinds of decision making, as when the federal government and the Länder must coordinate their endeavors (cf. Herrigel, 1996; Sabel, 1994; cf. Berg, 1997; Scharpf, 1995).

In short, German institutions embody considerable strengths for problem solving. Against these, however, we must set the limitations that flow from such institutional arrangements. Of these, several seem most important.

In an institutional setting such as this, it can be difficult to implement measures that impose significant costs on specific groups, unless those costs are relatively evenly distributed across all those represented in decision making. From the perspective of distributive justice, this may be an advantage. From the perspective of efficient adjustment, it can be a disadvantage. Under the Thatcher governments of the eighties, for instance, Britain was able to improve the efficiency of its economy relatively quickly by imposing the costs associated with those efficiency gains on specific groups, including those employed in marginal firms and less productive occupations. Entire sectors were virtually eliminated and many people were left without jobs, while others gained substantially from resource reallocation. In both Britain and the United States, the industrial reorganization of recent decades has been accompanied by a substantial widening in income differentials, as those with market power have prospered and those without it have been left far behind. In Germany, it is much more difficult to pursue an adjustment path that rewards "winners" so substantially, while imposing such high costs on those in less advantageous positions.

Similarly, it can be difficult in such settings to secure adjustment rapidly. Where power over decision making is concentrated and markets can be used to reallocate resources, adjustment can often be accomplished relatively quickly. Fluid markets discourage investment in specific assets that cannot readily be diverted to other uses and encourage investments in general skills and other types of assets with the result that assets of many types tend to be more mobile in such settings. Corporate hierarchies that concentrate power at the top make it easier for firms to divest themselves of less profitable subsidiaries and to reorganize those that remain. For all of these reasons, liberal market economies can shift resources into new endeavors and into new sectors relatively rapidly.

But coordinated market economies cannot do so. It takes time to win consensus from a variegated and powerful set of stakeholders. The relevant negotiations are often slow and painful. The institutions that support non-market coordination in such economies also encourage investments in specific assets, where investments by individuals in industry- or firm-specific skills or investments by firms in activities that are tied to active collaboration with other firms. As a consequence, assets are less mobile and it can be costly for firms to move them from one endeavor to another. Moreover, where firms rely more heavily on collaboration and less heavily on market mechanisms to coordinate their endeavors, whether with employees or other firms, changes must be negotiated and negotiation can be a protracted process. The reallocation of resource is likely to take more time in a nation such as Germany both because of the nature of the assets that must be shifted and because of the extensiveness of the negotiations required to accomplish such shifts. We can expect an adjustment process that is slower than it would be elsewhere.

The German institutional setting tends to privilege the interests of those groups represented in the principal forums for negotiating adjustment at the cost of those not well represented there. This is a natural concomitant of systems for adjustment that rely on negotiation. The German system of industrial relations, for instance, serves skilled workers relatively well because they are strongly represented on works councils, but it is biased against the interests of unskilled workers and others not in the labor force who are rarely represented there. In general, the German system tends to privilege the interests of producers relative to those of consumers simply because the former are well represented in the many forums to which the government has delegated some responsibility for industrial decision making. We can see this if we compare (1) telecommunications reform in Germany and the United States, where the executive branch of government played a greater role and gave greater weight to consumer interests, and (2) consumer regulation in Germany and France, where the government took a more active stance on behalf of consumers while decisions in Germany were left to forums in which consumer groups found themselves outnumbered or outgunned by the producer groups with whom they were to negotiate (Trumbull, 1999). In Germany, economic adjustment is largely a matter for negotiation but it is industrial trade unions and employers who are most strongly represented in the forums charged with much of the negotiating (see also Manow and Seils, 2000).

THE GERMAN ADJUSTMENT PATH

In short, the German political economy contains formidable capacities for adjustment, but these make some kinds of adjustment more feasible than others, thereby making some adjustment paths more likely than others. Although any analysis at this stage must be tentative, we can identify some of the directions that adjustment is likely to take in Germany. To do so, I focus on five of the most important adjustment challenges currently facing all the developed democracies.

The first of these challenges entails maintaining competitive unit labor costs in the face of increasing foreign competition. In Germany, where average hourly labor costs are among the highest in the world, at $32 versus $18 dollars in the United States, the problem is especially acute. In other times and places, this kind of problem has often been addressed by currency depreciation or large-scale layoffs among firms. But neither of these solutions is feasible in Germany, where the European Central Bank now controls monetary policy, and monetary union means that Europe can devalue only against the rest of the world; Germany's principal trading partners now share its currency. Social regulations and powerful trade unions also discourage large-scale layoffs. Instead, we can expect most German firms to concentrate their efforts to remain competitive in securing improvements in productivity of the sort based on the reorganization of production (see also Streeck, 1987).

In the past, German firms have been highly successful at such endeavors. In the face of rapid technological change, however, the relatively rigid skill categories of a collaborative vocational training system pose special problems. They can limit the ability of firms to secure workers with new skills, to deploy them in tasks that cut across skill categories, or to shift workers from one task to another. As a result, adjustment will require some reform of the skill categories underlying the vocational training system (cf. Herrigel, 1996). However, the institutional machinery for doing so is in place and progress is being made, even though it takes time to negotiate such changes.

The second challenge facing the industrialized nations is to secure footholds in the new sectors that are emerging as future centers of growth, especially in spheres of new technology. The latter include micro-processing, telecommunications, and bio-engineering. As I have noted, German firms are not normally well placed to move into sectors where they have no experience. Radical innovation is more likely in the United States or Britain. Thus, Germany may continue to be under represented in some sectors of the "new economy" such as semiconductors and some parts of information technology.

However, German firms have long had firm footholds in telecommunications and pharmaceuticals, from which they can exploit many new technological developments, if they can secure access to them. Precisely for this reason, we should expect to see these firms expand research and development facilities in the United States and Britain from which they can import innovations back into their home production processes. Moreover, by virtue of the kinds of coordination available to them, German firms have historically been good at diffusing new technology into their existing product lines and production processes. Thus, we can expect German industry to take advantage of new technology even if it is developed elsewhere. Adjustment is likely to take the form of improvements to existing product lines of the sort that Mercedes and Volkswagen have undertaken with their entry into markets for mini-automobiles and family vans.

The third challenge facing nations such as Germany is to adjust their managerial strategies in order to take full advantage of the just-in-time inventory systems, new forms of quality control, closer client-supplier relations, and other techniques emblematic of the recent managerial revolution. Here, German firms have significant advantages over their competitors in liberal market economies. Many of these techniques demand the development of close and collaborative relations with the workforce and other firms of the sort that German companies have long cultivated and for which the institutions that have long supported non-market coordination there can be very useful. German firms have long had substantial capacities for customized production, quality control, and technology transfer along supply chains of the sort that these new managerial techniques emphasize.

Turning to the macro-level, the fourth problem that Germany faces, in common with many other European nations, is how to cope with levels of unemployment that have crept into double-digits. Although the structure of the labor market may contribute to these figures, it should be remembered that Germany has long been able to secure low levels of unemployment. Much of the recent increase can be traced to the effects of unification and the contractionary macro-economic policies associated with efforts to create Economic and Monetary Union in Europe (cf. Carlin and Soskice, 1997; Soskice, 1999). However, jobs lost are not easily recovered, and unemployment remains a significant problem for Germany.

Here, too, adjustment is likely to take a distinctive path. We can expect widespread resistance to calls for Germany to approach the problem by deregulating labor markets. Instead, the problem will be tackled through intensive negotiations at the firm, sectoral, and peak levels between employers, the government, and trade unions. The emphasis, as I have noted, will be on distributing the costs of adjustment fairly and evenly among those negotiating the relevant measures. This institutional approach tends to privilege schemes for work-sharing and early retirement over those designed to lower wage costs or to increase the flexibility of hiring and firing. Accordingly, we should expect to see work-sharing schemes that provide the labor force with shorter working hours in return for providing employers with greater flexibility in how they use labor. Schemes of the sort pioneered by Volkswagen are likely to be adopted in sites where they are feasible.[5]

The more difficult challenge is how to secure employment growth in the service sector, now the most dynamic sector in all the developed economies (Iversen and Wren, 1995). Since 1981, employment in the German service sector has grown by 1.2 percent a year on average, while it has fallen in industry by 3 percent a year. Germany should not find it difficult to increase employment in high-end services, such as education, health care, and business services, but its high wage costs limit employment in personal services, restaurants, and retailing where wages are normally lower and the rates of productivity increase modest. Some loosening of regulations on shop hours, part-time employment, and small business could help here, as would efforts to subsidize the social charges on low-wage labor (Scharpf and Schmidt, 2000). What remains to be seen, however, is whether the social partners in Germany will agree to such measures, since the trade unions are both powerful and reluctant to countenance that rise of a low-wage sector that might widen income differentials and ultimately push down wages in the industrial sectors where their membership is concentrated.

Finally, like many of its neighbors, Germany faces the problem of controlling the social costs of an extensive welfare state. Generous health care and pension provisions, rising rates of life expectancy, and falling birthrates combine to raise the specter that a shrinking workforce may be asked to devote a much larger share of its income to support for the retired. Germany's record of coping with such problems is not altogether auspicious. A series of attempts to reduce the costs of early retirement schemes produced few real economies, and successive governments have found it difficult to secure agreement on changes to pensions schemes from the political parties and social partners (Mares, 2000). It is clear that it takes longer to resolve such distributive issues in Germany than in some nations and there are risks that the results will be inefficient (Scharpf, 1995).

Nevertheless, most of the distributive issues associated with reunification, which entailed massive transfers from west to east, were resolved with relatively little open conflict; and the Schröder government has secured agreement on reductions in pensions and significant economies have been found in the health care system. Like many European nations, Germany is likely to allow the expansion of various kinds of private pension arrangements that will reduce some of the fiscal pressures on the state.

In sum, the recent efforts made in Germany to adjust to challenges within specific problem areas correspond to the adjustment paths we would expect from an inspection of German institutions. Much attention has been paid to developing a full diagnosis of the problem. Major initiatives have been preceded by extensive negotiations among the political parties and producer groups. Movement has been relatively slow and reform incremental, but significant progress has been made on the major problems facing the nation.

THE CHALLENGE TO GERMAN INSTITUTIONS

There are two dimensions to the challenge that globalization and other contemporary economic developments pose to the developed democracies. On the one hand, they call for some adjustment within the context of existing institutions of the sort I have just discussed. On the other, these developments also put pressure on those institutions themselves. Thus, the second-order question is: can the principal institutions regulating the German political economy survive the challenges that globalization poses to them? Although some reforms are inevitable, can nations such as Germany make them without going so far towards deregulation that they dissolve into liberal market economies, thereby erasing the alternative economic model they have developed?

There are some grounds for skepticism on this point implicit in the analytical framework developed here.[6] Perhaps the most important turn on the *institutional complementarities* that can be found among the multiple sub-spheres of the economy. Two institutions are complementary when the presence of one raises the returns available from the other; and such complementarities are often found within liberal or coordinated market economies (Milgrom and Roberts, 1992, 1995). Financial institutions that provide capital on terms independent of short-term profitability make labor-market institutions associated with long job tenures more feasible, for instance, and the latter render corporate strategies and structures based on implicit contracts with employees more productive (cf. Aoki, 1990; Hall and Soskice, 2001). Since coordinated market economies often have tight institutional linkages of this sort, the important implication is that deregulatory reforms to institutions even in one restricted sphere of the economy may put significant pressure on institutions in other spheres that can snowball into wider deregulation across the economy.

The prospects for this kind of dynamic in Europe stem primarily from initiatives to deregulate financial markets (Streeck, 1997). Powerful trade unions and differences of opinion among the member nations of the European Union (EU) have limited deregulatory initiatives in the spheres of social policy and labor markets. But the EU has actively encouraged deregulation of financial markets and many of the large European banks have been receptive as they seek market share in increasingly global capital markets. More firms have turned to these markets for finance where it is often provided on Anglo-American terms that stress financial transparency, short-term profitability, and the corporate strategies associated with "shareholder value" (Ziegler, 2000; Vogel, 1999).

Financial deregulation not only threatens the dense network-monitoring systems associated with house-bank relationships, cross-shareholding, and close inter-firm collaboration. Through institutional complementarities, it could result in widespread changes to labor-market practices. Without access to patient capital, many firms would have difficulty maintaining long-term employment contracts, and more liberal layoff strategies could precipitate changes in industrial relations systems, affecting works councils and wage coordination. Financial-market deregulation could be the wedge that drives large-scale deregulation in coordinated market economies.

Although this dynamic is a lively possibility, to see it as inevitable would be premature. To date, German firms have used well-publicized efforts to increase "shareholder value" mainly to improve their control over subsidiaries without radically altering their overall style of corporate governance. Although the large German banks are internationalizing, regional financial institutions continue to maintain close relationships to firms and the dense networks that link firms through employers associations and chambers of commerce remain largely intact. The tax reforms of the Schröder government will make it easier for the banks and insurance companies to divest themselves of cross-shareholdings, but we have yet to see how extensively those cross-shareholdings, which protect German firms against hostile takeovers and allow them to remain responsive to stakeholders, will erode.

The other challenge to institutional stability in the coordinated market economies is more sociological. Effective non-market coordination depends on more than the presence of appropriate institutions. Since there may be multiple equilibria on which the actors can coordinate even in the presence of one set of institutions, effective coordination also depends on shared understandings among the actors, the reputations they cultivate with each other, their capacities to work out ongoing problems, and the level of consensus among them about appropriate goals. In sum, achieving effective economic performance in such settings also requires an appropriate social underpinning (Streeck, 1992, 1997).

However, high levels of unemployment, rapid technological change, globalization, and the movement toward a post-industrial economy threaten the social understandings that underpin coordinated market economies by placing new issues on the agenda and disrupting long-standing compromises among social actors. Greater international interdependence intensifies cleavages between the traded and sheltered sectors of the economy (Frieden, 1991; Pontusson and Swenson, 1995). Efforts to expand the low-wage service sector can unsettle hard-won compromises about wage equality and social benefits. High levels of unemployment can deepen insider-outsider conflicts and call into question the good faith of those who bargained peaceably under full employment.

Indeed, there may be processes of *political hysterisis* whereby rising levels of unemployment intensify conflict among the relevant producer groups to such an extent that it becomes more difficult for them to negotiate those adjustments that would bring unemployment down. Rothstein (1999) argues that some of Sweden's recent problems stem from precisely such a breakdown in trust among the key social partners. High levels of unemployment also destabilize collaborative systems of vocational training as firms facing low levels of demand decline to train and as those seeking apprenticeships find there are no positions for them; and they can make it difficult to maintain the effectiveness of coordinated wage bargaining as skilled workers with substantial organizational power protect their wages at the expense of unemployed outsiders (cf. Culpepper, 2001). In short, coordinated market economies may not operate as effectively when unemployment is high, and frustration with the difficulties of negotiating adjustment when settled understandings have been disrupted may fuel initiatives for deregulation. Such problems put heavy political demands on nations.

In Germany, however, there are grounds for cautious optimism. Its actors do not operate on a tabula rasa. They have long experience of resolving such problems in the past and deliberative institutions available for doing so. Moreover, the key producer groups operate from bases of entrenched organizational power substantial enough to remind their counterparts that reaching agreement is likely to be less costly than trying to impose a unilateral settlement. The capacity of the "social partners" in these political economics to find negotiated adjustment paths is ultimately founded on a finely tuned balance of power among them that remains robust even when consensus founders.[7]

Moreover, the experience of the Netherlands and Denmark indicates that selective deregulation can be implemented without unraveling the coordination processes that underpin such economies (Visser and Hemerijck, 1997). There may be many ways to improve their functioning without impairing their capacities for non-market coordination. As Levy (2000) points out, Germany also has a social policy regime that facilitates incremental reform. Although the shift to a European Central Bank disrupted the German industrial relations system, wage settlements there have remained moderate. Bargaining continues to be coordinated even though some firms, especially in the east, are demanding greater flexibility than sectoral settlements normally countenance (Thelen, 2000).

CONCLUSION

There is no doubt that international economic developments in the contemporary era pose profound challenges to coordinated market economies of the sort that Germany has developed. These economies performed well during the industrial era of the second half of the twentieth century, delivering superior economic performance and high levels of social well-being. However, they are now being called upon to respond to technological and managerial revolutions, higher levels of international integration, and movement towards a post-industrial economy. These developments demand adjustment at both the micro- and macro-levels of the economy. On the success with which this adjustment can be accomplished hangs the fate of the alternative economic model that nations with coordinated market economies have evolved. Here, I consider that problem in the context of the German case.

I have identified the principal challenges facing the German political economy, located the character of that economy within the analysis of varieties of capitalism recently developed by Soskice and others, outlined the principal institutional features of the German polity and economy pertinent to the character of adjustment there, and assessed the kind of adjustment path we are likely to see in Germany in the light of this analysis. My premise is that a nation's adjustment path is likely to be conditioned both by the nature of the challenges it faces and by the institutions it has in place for coping with such challenges.

The conclusions that follow from this analysis are mixed. On the one hand, the adjustment process in a coordinated market economy, such as that of Germany, is likely to be more protracted than it might be in nations that can depend on market mechanisms to accomplish much of that adjustment. This is a negotiated economy in which consent must be mobilized for the reallocation of resources that adjustment entails. On the other hand, Germany has robust institutions for undertaking these negotiations, some of which operate at the sectoral and even sub-sectoral levels while coping with problems at the national or regional levels, and a long track record of successful negotiation. There are good reasons to believe that the nation will ultimately adjust well to the challenges it faces.

The character of German institutions, however, is likely to push adjustment in specific directions that may well be quite different from those that would obtain in a liberal market economy. We can expect outcomes that privilege the interests of producer groups that are already well organized and represented in the nation's bargaining systems. As a consequence, Germany may be slower than some other nations to bring outsiders into the labor force, more reluctant than many to reduce social benefits substantially, and more likely to seek new forms of "internal flexibility" than to rely on the "external flexibility" that more liberal hiring and firing policies provide (Streeck, 1987). Like all adjustment paths, this is one with distinctive distributive implications, which in this case give some priority to maintaining job security, real wage levels, and relatively low levels of income inequality. We will see in the coming years whether these predictions are borne out. However, the overarching point of this chapter is to draw attention to the analysis of adjustment paths and to provide some indication of how we might understand them. I have suggested that the adjustment paths of a nation will be affected by three sets of factors: (1) the nature of the economic challenges it faces, (2) the existing organization of its political economy as reflected in its position among varieties of capitalism, and (3) the character of the political and economic institutions that it has in place for managing adjustment. This is a framework we can use to analyze other cases with a view both to explaining their adjustment paths and to improving our understanding of economic adjustment more generally.

NOTES

1 This chapter draws heavily on joint work with David Soskice to whom I owe many insights (Hall and Soskice, 2001) and on my 1997 article, "The Political Economy of Adjustment in Germany," pp. 293–317 in Frieder Naschold, David Soskice, Bob Hancké and Ulrich Jürgens, eds., *Ökonomische Leistungsfähigkeit und Institutionelle Innovation* (Berlin: Sigma).

2 For a more extensive account of this theory and of the differences among these economies, see Hall and Soskice, 2001.

3 I owe this term to conversations with David Soskice.

4 I owe this term to Samuel Beer.

5 In return for job guarantees to 1999 and more generous provision for early retirement, the workers at Volkswagen have agreed to a Saturday shift. In the chemical industry and automobile industries, the trade unions have shown themselves willing to concede wage increases for guarantees of employment; and firms in all sectors are making extensive use of early retirement schemes (cf. Mares, 1997).

6 The discussion in this section draws on my 2001 article, "Organized Market Economies and Unemployment in Europe: Is It Finally Time to Accept Liberal Orthodoxy?" in Nancy Bermeo, ed., *Context and Consequence: The Effects of Unemployment in the New Europe* (New York: Cambridge University Press).

7 Of course, socioeconomic developments can alter this balance of power in significant ways by shifting the interests of the actors and thus the opportunity costs of alternative courses of action, but even those disadvantaged by such shifts often retain residual bases of organizational power (cf. Swenson, 1999).

13

National Institutional Frameworks and High-Technology Innovation in Germany: The Case of Biotechnology

Steven Casper

Since the early eighties, the U.S. political economy has evolved to support commercial innovation in biotechnology, software, and a variety of other industries relying on radical innovation, often with close links with basic science. U.S. national institutional frameworks have fostered a dramatic expansion of innovative activities within the economy. Institutional frameworks have been reconfigured to foster high-risk venture capital financing of dynamic start-up companies, new links between university scientists and companies, and the reorganization of large company decision-making and incentive schemes. In Germany firms and policy makers are anxiously experimenting with their own institutional frameworks to foster organizational structures supporting radical science-based innovation in their own countries.

Can German national institutional frameworks be reconfigured to allow radical innovation in science-based industries? This chapter is part of a larger project examining the transfer of science-based commercial technologies in

277

pharmaceutical-based biosciences developed initially in the United States to the United Kingdom and Germany. The broader goal is to examine the degree to which national institutional frameworks can be reconfigured to better support commercial innovation in radically innovative high-technology industries. National institutional frameworks provide incentives and impose constraints that influence the ability of firms to create a variety of organizational structures and human resource competencies needed to innovate. In the biotechnology case important national institutional frameworks include the financial system, the education and training system, laws and other institutions influencing the development of careers and decision making within large companies, and the system governing relations between companies.

Germany presents an especially intriguing case. In Germany there is currently a large push by the government to promote the development of a biotechnology sector comparable to that in the United States. The official goal of the German government is to be the European leader in biotechnology by the turn of the century. To promote this goal, the federal and Länder governments have jointly spent well over a billion deutsche marks in support of "Gene centers" that include new basic research facilities, "incubator labs" for start-up companies, and the inclusion of matching funds up to a 50 percent basis for virtually all private venture or bank-based capital for biotechnology activities. This catalyst has created a small biotech boom in Germany, particularly within the Munich area. From scarcely a handful of companies at the beginning of the nineties, there are now several hundred biotech start-up firms in Germany.

The technological regime underpinning biotechnology necessitates the creation of company organizational structures that are difficult to sustain within Germany's business-coordinated market economy. Long-term career structures within most German firms, combined with the willingness of German courts to uphold anti-poaching clauses within labor contracts, limits the active labor market of scientists and financial experts needed to form start-up companies. Similarly, the lack of a strong NASDAQ-style market by which start-ups can go public limits the availability of high-risk venture capital. This makes it difficult for German start-up companies to create high-powered incentives for employees. Furthermore, the lack of an exit option limits the emergence of a refinancing mechanism for start-up capital based on funds generated through initial public offerings (IPOs). This also may prevent venture capitalists from engaging in "portfolio" strategies when investing in start-up companies.

The recent success of German biotechnology promotion programs presents an important puzzle for research. The short-term success of German industrial policies to support biotechnology indicates that, at the local level, the company organizational structures, financial links, and networks with universities needed for radical innovation can exist in Germany. This chapter focuses primarily on only one part of the puzzle: the creation of viable institutional structures to stimulate and nurture high-technology start-up firms in biotechnology. It thus ignores equally important problems associated with the creation of biotechnology competencies in large firms as well as the creation of links between universities and other public research institutes and the private sector.

The chapter is organized into two general sections, followed by a conclusion. The first section examines the generally static situation during the eighties. During the eighties commercial biotechnology research was largely moribund in Germany. I first briefly describing the newfound importance during the eighties of biotechnology methodologies to pharmaceutical research strategies through examining the comparative performance of U.S. and U.K. firms (which had access to new biotechnology start-up firms) to German firms (which generally did not). I then examine more carefully the technological regime underpinning biotechnology and how German national institutional frameworks broadly disadvantage the creation of financial, company organizational, and career-structure competencies that have been developed by U.S. biotech firms to successfully innovate. Examining the largely static institutional frameworks during the eighties allows a more careful appraisal of institutional reforms and governmental promotional policies that have been created during the nineties.

The second section attempts to create a framework for examining the more fluid situation during the nineties. It first examines general industry dynamics during this period, which are generally favorable to new entry in biotechnology. I then examine three scenarios for institutional reform in Germany: convergence, specialization, and accommodation. There is little evidence supporting the view that German national institutional frameworks are converging to a U.S./U.K. liberal market economy model. There is strong evidence supporting the view that German national institutional frameworks promote a specialization in a wide variety of high-value niche markets in process technologies while U.S. and U.K. frameworks better conduce towards radically innovative product market strategies. However, there is also evidence supporting the view that some forms of high-technology start-up activity can be "accommodated" within Germany's generally unfavorable institutional environment. Incremental reforms in German financial laws supported by the bulk of German industry, combined with a number of sectoral industrial policies, have created opportunities for firms to create alternative governance structures needed to accommodate some forms of biotech start-up activity.

THE SITUATION DURING THE EIGHTIES

Market and Technological Dynamics in Pharmaceuticals and the Performance of German Firms

During the eighties there were substantial performance differences across the German as opposed to the U.S. or U.K. pharmaceutical industries. Table 13.1 includes a number of aggregate market characteristics for the five largest pharmaceutical producing nations. Using several summary measures, we can construct a picture of a given nation's competitive position at the beginning of the nineties. The number of products in the Top 50 is included to account for the fact that although some new chemical compounds (NCEs) introduced are genuinely original, others may be marginal improvements only, which could then make the NCE figures somewhat misleading. Market share in the United States is included as a crude measure of competitiveness, because the U.S. market is the most open and competitive market in the world.

Table 13.1 International Comparison of Market Characteristics

	U.S.	Japan	Germany	France	U.K.
Market Size ($ bn)					
1987	39.3	30.2	11.8	10.2	8.2
1993	70.8	51.1	19.5	17.1	14.9
R&D Intensity (%)					
1983	10.6	6.7	8.4	7.1	11.7
1992	14.3	9.8	9.2	8.7	16.3
New Chemical Entities					
(NCEs)					
1971-80	154	74	91	98	29
1981-90	142	129	67	37	28
No. of Products					
in Top 50					
1985	23	5	5	1	9
1990	27	2	5	0	12
Patent Trends					
1980-84	49.8	13.3	10.4	5.1	7.5
1990-94	54.6	14.7	7.8	4.7	5.3
Firm's Market Share					
in the U.S.					
1991	70.2	0.3	4.6	1.2	14.6

Source: Casper and Matraves, 1997.

A comparison with the United Kingdom is a good gauge for the strength of the German pharmaceutical industry during the eighties. Taking R&D intensity into account, the German and U.K. pharmaceutical industries spend roughly equivalent absolute sums on R&D. However, the U.K. industry substantially outperformed Germany. Its leading firm, Glaxo, for example, rose from 17th in the world in terms of sales in 1983, to 1st in the world in 1995. There has also been a relative increase in R&D expenditure in the U.K., and furthermore, its companies are extremely good at developing NCEs that are commercially successful. During the 1981–90 period, only 28 new drugs were developed, but a relatively high percentage of these turned into blockbusters. Germany, on the other hand, has a much weaker position. It developed far more drugs (67 NCEs between 1981 and 1990), spends approximately the same amount on R&D, but has a very low number of blockbusters to account for this (only 5 in 1990). As a final measure of international competitiveness. Germany's share of the U.S. market is only 4.6 percent, compared to 14.6 percent for the U.K.

Beginning in the late seventies, competitive industry dynamics became more complex. This was due to radical changes in the nature of the innovation process and the introduction of new marketing and distribution techniques. Though both are important (see Casper and Matraves, 1997), this project focuses primarily on changes in the technological process and their impact on company organizational competencies and alliances.

How has the development of biotechnology impacted the performance of large pharmaceutical firms? Biotechnology has displaced traditional "chemical" capabilities. The traditional methodology, prevalent in the fifties and sixties when knowledge about the properties of the compounds that could be used to synthesize new drugs was still lacking, screened thousands of chemical compounds for efficacy against a given disease (Schwartzman, 1976). In the seventies, basic biomedical knowledge increased. The traditional methodology has been replaced by "rational drug design," i.e., the development of more precise models of how particular diseases function, and the design of molecules designed to target particular cells or cause particular biological interactions within the body (see Werth, 1995; Powell, 1996: 204). In addition, genetic engineering techniques have allowed biotechnology companies to manipulate the structure and functioning of so-called "large molecule" proteins that cannot be synthesized through traditional chemical processes.

When a fundamentally new research methodology is created, it is often the case that organizational rigidity and inertia hinder incumbents' ability to take advantage of new opportunities. Following the logic of technological life cycles, radical innovations in biotechnology have created incentives for hundreds of new firms to enter the market, paralleling periods of rapid market entry following similar periods of rapid technological change in semiconductors, software, and other high-technology industries. As research is one of the highly specialized and hence value-added processes, the fact that most biotechnological research is taking place within small start-ups rather than large firms is an important change (see Powell, 1996). However, although the discovery process is changing, the specialized assets needed for development and commercialization are not, and these assets continue to be owned by the largest firms (see Teece, 1986). Only about 10 percent of the total R&D costs of a new patented drug are in discovery; the vast majority of costs are found in development, clinical trials, and the regulatory approval process. Tiny biotechnology start-up firms rarely evolve into large pharmaceutical firms. Rather, due to the high cost and long time-horizons in therapeutics research (see below), most biotechnology companies sell or license their patents to pharmaceutical firms for continuing financing long before their discoveries reach the market. Further development and commercialization is then taken over by large pharmaceutical firms.

The challenge created by biotechnology for large firms is primarily one of rivalry with other integrated pharmaceutical companies. Having access to new competencies in drug design, disease modeling, and screening created by biotechnology is widely viewed as critical for competitive success (McKlevey, 1997). In the world of rational drug design, research in complex disease areas usually takes place along a number of distinct research trajectories. For example, Penan (1996) identifies over fifteen distinct research programs to fight Alzheimer's disease, each of which was supported by a different constellation of university departments, large pharmaceutical firms, and in some cases, biotechnology firms. In addition, the therapies for some of the more complicated diseases, such as AIDS and most likely Alzheimer's disease, often consist of "cocktails" of two or more compounds developed through separate research programs. Developing alliances with biotech firms helps pharmaceutical firms diversify the lines of research within which the large firm can take part.

Developing licensing arrangements and research collaborations with biotechnology firms helps diversify the pharmaceutical firm's "bets" across a number of research programs. Each therapeutic area becomes a platform from which the firm can monitor the field, purchase promising compounds from third parties, or develop collaborative research projects with universities or research firms, or starting in-house research projects. Nurturing third-party research firms can also help to diversify commercial risks. Developing drugs is an inherently risky business: it is estimated that one compound from an initial 5,000 will be successful (PhRMA, 1997). If in-house research in one therapeutic area is unsuccessful, purchasing compounds developed by third parties can help to fill gaps in the development pipeline.

It follows from this discussion that the pharmaceutical firms with easy access to biotech start-up firms, via strategic alliances, research networks, mergers, and so forth should have an important competitive advantage in responding to these changed technological conditions over firms that do not. The superior performance of the U.K. and U.S. industries compared to Germany follows directly from this second conclusion. The United States and, to an increasing extent, the United Kingdom, have national systems of innovation conducive to the support of high-risk start-up firms in emerging technologies. Large clusters of biotechnology start-up firms were created in the United States and (to a substantial, but lesser extent) United Kingdom. To obtain long-term financing and access to development and to marketing expertise, and to forge research networks, large numbers of these start-up firms quickly formed alliances with local pharmaceutical companies. Through these networks large pharmaceutical companies could monitor technology developments, license or co-develop compounds, and begin to develop internal competencies through mergers, equity holdings, or the recruitment of scientists working within biotech firms.

These performance differences may be linked to the inability of firms in Germany to plug into emerging networks of commercial biotech research that were blooming in the United Kingdom and especially the United States but largely moribund in Germany. During the nineties the situation has changed. To close the technology gap, German pharmaceutical firms have created a massive network of international research networks, primarily with U.S. biotechnology firms and public research universities and hospitals (Sharpe and Patel, 1996). At the same time, German national and regional government offices have undertaken a number of substantial technology promotion programs in the area of biotechnology. This raises the possibility of institutional reforms that could lead to a national system of innovation more conducive to the creation and nurturing of high-tech start-up firms. However, during the eighties German pharmaceutical firms relied primarily on domestic R&D while a variety of national institutional frameworks that are important in nurturing clusters of start-up firms were stable. This allows a relatively clear analysis of the German situation in the eighties, which can then be used later to understand scenarios for reform during the nineties.

NATIONAL INSTITUTIONAL FRAMEWORKS AND COMPETENCY BUILDING

How do national institutional frameworks impede the creation of the human capital skills and organizational relationships needed for small firms to innovate in biotechnology? National institutional frameworks influence the governance costs of embarking on particular product market strategies. My argument differs from the "embeddedness" approach often found in sociological studies (see Hollingsworth and Boyer, 1997; Granovetter, 1985). In its simplest form, this position holds that company organizational structures are shaped directly by the orientation of national institutional frameworks. Rather, I assume that company management, faced with international competition, can survey the spectrum of possible organizational arrangements prevalent within their industry, and attempt to shape a coherent strategy. National institutional frameworks play a strong role through influencing the relative cost of building the organizational competencies needed to pursue each strategy.

To create successful product market strategies, the management of companies must create and sustain relationships with a number of different groups: workers, technicians and scientists, owners and banks, and other companies. Economists, game theorists, and political scientists have in recent years combined rational choice theory, strategic bargaining models, and organizational analysis to form a broad body of theoretical and empirical analysis exploring each of these relationships (see Milgrom and Roberts, 1992, and Miller, 1992, for overviews). This literature, the economics of organization, has developed a unified methodology showing that most substantive management problems are not just technical challenges but also pose strategic conflicts of interest between participants (so-called "relational problems").

The economics of organization approach has, along these lines, developed a competency-based view to understanding technology and innovation. The technologies needed to innovate rarely consist of specialized machines or codifiable knowledge that can be transferred to any organization regardless of institutional environment, and simply be "turned on" (Winter, 1987). Rather, most technologies are dispersed across highly skilled experts embedded within complex organizational structures. Innovative capacity usually consists of tacit knowledge spread over networks of managers, scientists, and skilled workers within a complex organizational environment (which often spreads across several discrete firms or, in science-based industries, firms and public research institutes).

The complex of legal and private rules that are created to manage organizational relationships are commonly called "governance structures" (Williamson, 1985).   Because its goal is the development of a universal approach to understanding industrial organization, economics of organization scholars often implicitly assumes that companies create their own, private governance structures to solve their contracting dilemmas. This ignores the fact that there are systematic differences in the governance structures developed within Germany and the United States. These variations will be linked to differences in national institutional frameworks governing company relationships in these countries. I first present thumbnail sketches of the institutional differences, and then examine more specifically how particular aspects of these institutions influence the creation of viable company organizational competencies needed for radical innovation (see Soskice, 1994).

The United States is characterized by a liberal market economy. Business organization depends primarily on market transactions and the use of a flexible, enabling private legal system to facilitate a variety of complex contracting situations. Because courts refuse to adjudicate incomplete contracts (see Schwarz, 1992), market participants need to specify control rights in contract to as full an extent as possible or, when this is not possible, to use extremely high-powered performance incentives to align interests within and across organizations. Rather paradoxically, this system of legal and corporate governance advantages the creation of governance structures suitable for two very dissimilar product market strategies. On one hand, it promotes a variety of price-based mass production industries dependent on complete, often asymmetrical and opportunistic contracts between large firms/top managers and dedicated suppliers/unskilled workers, respectively. On the other hand, and of more interest in this project, the U.S. system of legal and corporate governance also advantages the creation of complex, incentive based governance structures needed to support radical innovation in "bubbling" technologies (see Casper, 1998, for a fuller exposition of this argument).

Germany is characterized by a "coordinated market economy" (Soskice, 1994) underpinned by a regulatory private law system. German business is organized in nature, primarily due to the embeddedness of large firms within networks of powerful trade and industry associations, as well as a similar, often legally mandated, organization of labor and other interest organizations within para-public institutions (Katzenstein, 1987, 1989). Businesses engage these associations to solve a variety of incomplete contracting dilemmas and create important non-market collective goods. For example, German employers associations maintain tacit norms and a monitoring capacity to prevent employee poaching and in doing so lower the risks to large German companies of training highly skilled workers within nationally specified curriculums. To discourage individual companies from exiting the collective business system, German public policy uses private law to regulate a wide variety of inter-firm and labor contracts as well as create neo-corporatist bargaining environments through the delegation of issue-area specific bargaining rights to unions and other stakeholders within firms. German courts use standardized business agreements produced through neo-corporatist arrangements as the basis to apply regulatory corporate laws throughout the broader economy (again, see Casper, 1998, for a fuller exposition).

German national institutional frameworks advantage what Streeck labels "diversified quality production" (DQP) product market strategies that lead to specialization in a wide number of high-quality niche markets such as industrial machinery, specialty chemicals, high-end automobiles, and so forth (Streeck, 1992). The German system also creates strong prohibitions against opportunistic (largely low price competitive) product market strategies that depend on the delegation of important risks to weaker market participants. As already noted, German industry has suffered in high-technology industries such as biotechnology. I argue that this weakness in high-technology industry is a direct consequence of laws and other institutions constructed by German business and public policy makers. Through creating institutional frameworks to advantage a series of company organizational competencies for DQP-style industries and— to discourage free-riding on the collective goods necessary to make this system viable for companies competing on world markets—punish opportunistic strategies, German firms and public policy makers simultaneously create institutions that dramatically raise the governance cost of creating the competencies needed to innovate in high-technology industries. To explore this argument in more detail, I now compare how U.S. and German institutional frameworks influence the creation of three of the most important competencies for innovative start-up firms: high-powered incentive structures for employees, high-risk financing, and the creation of viable career structures for employees of firms that run a high risk of failure.

High-Risk Financing

Requirement: Biotechnology start-ups need access to a continuous stream of high-risk finance. Three industry characteristics combine to make biotechnology one of the riskiest segments in high-technology industry. First, the failure rate is very high. The vast majority of biotechnology firms do not succeed in bringing a product to market. In addition to cases when the firm simply is not able to successfully innovate, even successful innovators can quickly see their intellectual property eroded by technological advances by other firms who are quicker to market. To give an indication of the failure problem, while there are hundreds of biotechnology start-ups active in therapeutics research, as of 1997 only 40 drugs designed through biotechnology research techniques had reached the market (BIO, 1998). Second, the "burn rate" is very high in biotechnology. Basic research costs for specialist equipment, high salaries for scientists and researchers, and supplies (cell cultures, tissue samples, etc.) are high. Therapeutic companies face additional costs for testing and trials; even early stage animal and human clinical trials can run into the tens of millions of dollars. The total R&D cost to bring a new drug to market is between 200 and 325 million dollars (PhRMA, 1997). High burn rates are compounded by a third problem, the long time-horizons before most biotech products reach the market. This is particularly the case for therapeutic companies, which must bear a minimum clinical trial and regulatory approval period of five to seven years before their discoveries are approved and reach the market.

Solution: In the United States most biotechnology firms are initially funded by venture capitalists (see Florida and Kenney, 1988). There are important institutional reasons why the venture capital market is so large. First, very substantial private legal competencies exist and, due to the "enabling" nature of ownership and contract law, can be used to create sophisticated legal structures used to support risky new ventures. These include the high-powered performance incentives for managers and scientists discussed above. Second, and probably most important, in the United States the ownership of firms is primarily financial in structure, and rooted in large capital markets (e.g., NASDAQ, NYSE). A liquid market for corporate control is critical for venture capitalists, as it creates a viable *exit option* via initial public offerings and mergers or acquisitions by other pharmaceutical companies. Without this exit option, it is difficult for venture capitalists to diversify risks across several investments or create a viable refinancing mechanism. Typically, a venture capitalist will invest in a number of companies, expecting one or two to become successful in a few years, one or two to survive, and several others to fail.

Successful start-ups will be given supplementary "mezzanine" financing and eventually taken public through an IPO or sold to a larger pharmaceutical company, usually creating a very high return for the venture capitalists. These profits may be used to offset the losses on other companies and thus make a portfolio strategy more viable. The exit option created by large capital markets allows venture capitalists to shorten the time-horizon for investments (usually to three to five years). Finally, by taking a firm public within a few years, venture capitalists create a viable refinancing mechanism. They can use the profits from IPOs to seed new ventures as well as provide secondary funding for other start-ups (for example, to take promising candidate compounds into clinical testing).

Problem: In Germany the ownership of most firms is only partially financial in nature. It is also based on non-financial rights of employees and other "stakeholders." In connection with the historical development of German financial markets, German company law creates incentives for most investment to be debt-based (see Vitols et al., 1997). Shareholdings of German public firms have traditionally been concentrated and dispersed through stable cross-shareholding arrangements between the large German commercial banks and other large firms. The low-risk nature of bank loans entails that most German firms have traditionally financed R&D and other speculative investments with retained earnings. Germany has never developed a "hostile" market for corporate control. Until very recently, share offerings have not served as a primary source of funding for German firms, large or small.

The lack of developed capital markets willing to invest in speculative IPOs for technology firms creates important barriers for prospective venture capitalists. If share offerings cannot be supported, then the "exit option" for venture capitalists becomes limited. This has two important consequences. First without an established IPO market, possible refinancing mechanisms are decreased. The profits from IPOs are the primary continuing source of seed money for venture capital. Without this, venture capitalists must return to original investors to obtain new funds. Lacking a relatively short-term prospect of a high return, it seems unlikely that investors can be relied on to continually finance high burn-rate biotech start-ups. Second, without the short-term returns created by IPOs, it becomes difficult for venture capitalists to diversify risks through a portfolio strategy. The venture capitalist must assume that it is making a long-term investment in each firm that becomes successful, making it difficult to quickly offset loses on unsuccessful firms.

- Hypothesis: Legal restraints combined with the bank-based financial system limits the creation of market structures needed to support high-risk venture capital. High-risk start-ups in biotechnology are thus difficult to fund in Germany.

Low Career Risk from Failure

Problem: For the reasons already discussed, most biotech start-ups eventually fail. In addition, because research trajectories within biotechnology can be very volatile, firms need to build new competencies as well as shed assets in unsuccessful areas quickly. As a result, the career risk from failure must be low. This entails the development of an active labor market for scientists, technicians, and managerial experts within biotechnology. If one firm fails or decided to shed competencies in one area, employees must be able to obtain similar employment without severe loss of salary or status. Top executives at start-up firms typically come from large pharmaceutical companies or public university research laboratories. These often senior scientists/managers would hesitate in making the move to a start-up if the career risk of doing so were large. Furthermore, as Powell (1996) and others have discussed, biotechnology is a network-based industry. Innovation is dependent on the flow of knowledge between university labs, start-up research firms, and large pharma. While joint research projects, strategic alliances, and so forth facilitate this exchange of knowledge, these network externalities are also supported by the rapid movement of scientists and technicians across firms. Thus, if the labor market did not support extensive lateral career mobility across firms, these network externalities would be difficult to sustain.

Solution: In the United States there is an extremely active labor market. Particularly in California (but generally throughout the United States), courts have refused to enforce "competition clauses" written into labor contracts. While firms can ask employees to sign non-disclosure agreements covering specific technologies, scientists and managers are generally free to move from firm to firm as they see fit. This has facilitated extensive poaching and the organization of career paths within firms based on the probability of frequent employee turnover. As a result, the risk of failure is very small (see Saxenian, 1993, for a general discussion of career-paths in Silicon Valley).

Problem: In Germany the organization of labor and company law combined with the organizational strategies of most large companies severely constrains the development of U.S.-style active labor markets. Both sides of the "hire and fire" equation are muted. German courts routinely uphold competition clauses written into employment contracts, with the result that scientists/managers often cannot leave one firm to perform a similar job at a competitor for up to one to three years after leaving the original firm. Similarly, German company law grants important representative rights over personnel and working-time policy (training, overtime, work organization) to legally mandated councils of works and middle management, as well as seats on the supervisory boards of public companies to employee representatives, unions, and other "stakeholders." In return for cooperative labor and employee relations and acceptance of very low-powered performance incentives within the firm, German companies have traditionally offered lifetime employment to any employee that survives an initial six months to two-year probationary periods. While large German firms can sell entire subsidiaries or send some lower-productivity older employees into early retirement, individual employees or groups of employees cannot be fired within German firms as part of the "normal" course of business.

Though there is often some lateral movement across firms very early in a person's career, the vast majority of German employees build careers within one firm. Partly as a consequence, the structure of decision-making, remuneration, and career-paths within German firms differ fundamentally from common practice within the United States or United Kingdom (see full discussion in Vitols et al., 1997). Because employment is usually long-term, German firms must refrain from alienating particular constituencies. As a result, most decision-making is consensual. Career paths tend to be well-specified, incremental, and based on rank hierarchies. Salary is primarily determined by seniority and educational status, rather than short-term performance. Higher levels of salary and responsibility are only obtained as a result of long careers within the firm. This structure of large company organization has been found ideal for a number of "DQP" industries dependent on long-term investment strategies in relatively stable technologies and the diffusion of deep skills throughout the firm (see Streeck, 1992, and Vitols et al., 1997). In particular, it encourages the creation of tacit organizational knowledge throughout the firm that enhances flexibility. However, this system creates fundamental obstacles to the creation of high-risk technology start-up firms. The risk of "jumping ship" from an established large company (or—though there is less research in this area—a prestigious university professorship) to a start-up firm is extremely high. This risk includes not just the possible legal consequences (if competition clauses are enforced), but the risk of finding oneself on the outside of an extremely rigid labor market at mid-career. Because large German firms encourage the creation of firm-specific tacit knowledge, mid-career managers cannot easily find similar positions inside other large firms. Because status tends to be firm specific, the cost of leaving one organization must be higher in Germany than in more permeable U.S. firms. In order to compensate for the career risk of joining a risky start-up, it would seem that the start-up would have to offer very high levels of status and/or salary in order to successfully recruit higher-level management or scientists.

- Hypothesis: German start-up biotech companies have a difficult time recruiting mid-career and especially senior-level management and science staff, due to the career risk of leaving positions in large companies.

High-Powered Performance Incentives

Problem: Successful research in high-technology firms requires the recruitment of scientists with very specialized knowledge. The decentralization of knowledge creates agency problems within the firm. It is difficult for non-scientist managers and, in many cases, even fellow scientists to determine whether or not specialist workers within the firm are efficiently working towards firm goals (see generally Miller, 1992). Scientists often have strong incentives to work on projects with substantial *private* returns but inferior *collective* returns for the company. In addition to pure agency problems, the existence of "high-powered" incentive structures is commonly associated with the willingness of employees within high-technology firms to "sign-on" to extremely challenging work assignments requiring long hours and an extraordinary commitment to the firm.

Ethnographic accounts of U.S. biotechnology firms contain numerous examples of agency dilemmas. One example comes from Werth's book *The Billion Dollar Molecule* (1993). A goal of many biotech firms is to uncover the chemical structure of large proteins involved in disease processes. Werth examines problems encountered by the biotech start-up Vertex in its quest to uncover the structure of an important protein thought to be involved in the immune system. The firm invested in two approaches, traditional X-ray crystallography and a newer approach based on MRI scanning. The firm hired a specialist for each area, both of which began working independently to discover the protein structure. Each scientist had a tremendous incentive to discover the protein by himself, in order to gain sole credit for an important discovery in the subsequent journal publication. As a result, the two scientists refused for months to share their partial results, which could have been combined to uncover the complete structure at an earlier stage of research. Finally, company management forced the scientists to work jointly, but the delay eventually forced the firm to share publication priority with rivals outside the firm.

Solution: In the United States, agency problems are perhaps the major reason why most biotechnology firms are small (rarely more than 10 to 50 people, including administrative staff) or, in the case of larger companies investing in biotechnology, organized into semi-autonomous decentralized labs. Small numbers facilitates mutual monitoring. However, the vast majority of U.S. start-up technology firms have complemented small numbers with very strong financial incentives. Most companies do this with share options, coupled with the announced intention of owners and venture capitalist to take the firm public within a few years (usually three to five). In the cases of successful firms that have gone public, share options can be worth tens of thousands of dollars to junior staff to millions to senior scientists and owner/managers. The prospect of large financial rewards helps align the private incentives of scientists with those of companies and is a prime reason why U.S. high-tech firms have become associated with extremely long workweeks and general dedication to projects.

Problem: In Germany, financial incentives cannot easily be used to resolve agency problems within firms. This area underwent extensive change during the late nineties, but during the eighties the organization of German financial markets and property rights law made share-based financial systems difficult to implement. In order to limit share-price speculation, German financial laws have until very recently prohibited listed companies from buying back shares already on the market.

Doing so eliminates pure share options as a possible strategy. Privately held start-up companies could instead grant shares to employees. However, particularly during the eighties and early nineties, nothing comparable to the NASDAQ or other small-firm technology market existed in Germany. Stock market capitalization was, even for large companies, small, and there was no established IPO market for high-tech firms. At most, employers holding shares could hope that another firm would acquire the company. Table 13.2 summarizes this discussion.

- Hypothesis: The lack of "high-powered" incentives within German start-up firms exacerbates agency problems while making it difficult for mangers to convince employees to "sign-on" to complex projects (i.e., through long workweeks, intense work environments, and so forth).

The Situation during the Nineties and Possibilities for Institutional Reform

During the nineties the creation of high-tech industry became a major preoccupation with German political and business leaders. In Germany there is currently a large push by the government to promote the development of a biotechnology sector comparable to that in the United States. The federal and Länder governments have created a framework to support over a dozen local "BioRegio" technology promotion infrastructures. While the total amount of money spent on the BioRegio program is difficult to assess due to the program's decentralization, over a billion DM has been spent in support of the Munich Gene Center alone, and Berlin, Cologne, Stuttgart, and the Heidelberg region each have significant programs of smaller size. Public spending has been aimed primarily in two areas: infrastructure and subsidies. Infrastructure includes the creation of technology parks and "incubator labs," often tied closely to existing or newly created basic research facilities tied to local universities or Max Planck Institutes. Subsidies are usually provided as seed-capital for start-up firms. Programs vary, but in general money is provided only if applicants are able to concurrently secure private venture capital.

This catalyst has created a biotech boom in Germany. From scarcely a handful of companies at the beginning of the nineties, as of mid-1998 there were over 400 firms in Germany (Ernst and Young, 1998c). Given these substantial institutional hurdles to the creation of viable organizational, financial, and career-structures for biotechnology, why has German technology policy targeted biotechnology as a major "industry of the future"?

Before returning to the core theme of creating a viable institutional environment for start-up firms, it is first important to examine whether, from an industry-dynamics perspective, large-scale entry into the biotechnology industry is still possible during the nineties.

IS IT FEASIBLE FOR GERMAN FIRMS TO COMPETE IN BIOTECHNOLOGY?

From the perspective of industry dynamics alone, barriers to entry into most segments of the biotechnology sector remain low. This conclusion derives from three major features of the biotechnology sector:

The Markets for Biotechnology Are Booming

In recent years the spectrum of molecular biology–based advanced drug design and gene-engineering techniques has emerged as the dominant science paradigm in the pharmaceutical and life-science industries more generally. As a result, biotechnology-based drugs should obtain an increasingly larger share of the world pharmaceutical market. Revenues for the biotechnology industry were over $13 billion in 1997 (of which $9 billion went to the U.S. industry), and while the number of drugs actually approved remains small, over 290 drugs are in clinical testing phases in the United States (BIO, 1998:5).

As a response to this boom, biotechnology during the nineties took off in Europe. The European industry is now approaching in size that of the United States. As of 1997 there were 1,287 biotechnology companies in the United States and 1,027 in the European Union (though overall employment was much higher in the United States due to relative maturity of the U.S. industry) (BIO, 1998: 5; Ernst and Young, 1998b: 3). High-risk venture capital for biotechnology has shifted to Europe. Ernst and Young estimates that in 1998 European biotech firms raised about 380 million euros, compared to the 843 million euros in the United States (Ernst and Young 1998a: 49; Ernst and Young 1998b: 19; Ernst and Young, 2000). While there has been a moderate biotech boom in Germany, biotechnology start-up firms have particularly thrived in the United Kingdom, a country that has developed an institutional environment for high technology that mimics crucial aspects of that in the

Table 13.2   Company Organizational Requirements and Institutional Frameworks for Therapeutics

Company Organizational Requirement		"Solution" in the United States	"Problem" in Germany
High-powered performance incentives	Risky research requires recruitment of scientists with very specialized knowledge. High-powered incentives needed to reduce monitoring problems and to align interests with management.	Extensive use of share options or outright share dispersal coupled with possibility of IPO or buy-out is used to align private preferences with firms.	Stock options illegal until March 1998; lack of IPO market limits the "strength" of other share schemes.
Competency destruction risks	Low technological cumulativeness creates frequent failures and often forces firms to reorganize R&D competencies through hiring and firing. Innovation might require knowledge transfer created by networks of scientists moving between start-ups, university labs, and pharma firms.	Extremely active labor market creates "asset recycling" mechanisms within technology clusters. This facilitates extensive poaching and the organization of career paths within firms based on probability of frequent employee turnover.	Long-term career paths at large German firms inhibit the creation of an active labor market for mid-career scientists and managers. "Asset recycling" difficult.
High-risk financing	Most biotech start-ups in therapeutics require very high risk financing due to long-term nature of discovery and development process plus risk of losing innovation races.	Large venture capital market. IPOs and large market for M&As allow venture capitalists to diversify risks across several investments and also create a short to medium term refinancing market.	Bank-centered financial system. Small IPO market limits private-sector refinancing mechanisms. Venture capitalists do not have viable "exit strategy," meaning most investments are long term.

United States. In both 1995 and 1996 well over half of all European biotech venture capital has been invested in the United Kingdom (Ernst and Young 1998b: 41), and the United Kingdom continues to support the most biotech start-ups in the European Union (Ernst and Young, 1998b: 3).

Of particular importance to German firms is the emergence in recent years of a large market for "platform technologies." While intellectual property and general know-how remain extremely specialized across therapeutic areas, there are an increasing number of generic biotechnology competencies applicable across large segments of the field. Examples include firms that apply information technology and advanced testing methods to small-molecule drug design (combinatorial chemistry), firms specializing in gene sequencing and the construction of specialized libraries from the human genome, and firms that specialize in the creation of equipment and research methods used in genetic engineering. Lead times are much shorter for most platform technology firms, since sales are usually on a contract basis and immediate. As we will see below, targeting platform technologies is an especially viable option for German firms, since the relative financial and technological stability of these firms may "fit" better with normal German financial and labor market institutions.

Existence of Advanced Lead Users

In industries where technologies are changing very quickly, the success of particular companies often depends on the development of dynamic relationships with the users of the end-technology. For example, Borrus and Zysman (1997) argue that U.S. networking firms have dominated data-driven communication markets in part because large American corporations demanded a wealth of new IT technologies much earlier than their European or Japanese counterparts. A similar logic exists in pharmaceuticals. The large pharmaceutical companies are the primary the market for biotech start-ups; it is the existing large pharmaceutical companies that eventually purchase or license, or market, most of the drugs or other products created at biotech companies. Pharmaceutical companies have access to vast small-molecule libraries, testing facilities, manufacturing process expertise, and, of particular importance, know-how in guiding candidate drugs through clinical testing and regulatory approval. Pharmaceutical companies have massively invested in joint-research projects with biotech start-ups—creating the network-based learning possibilities that are often crucial to success in quickly changing technologies.

In Germany advanced lead users exist, in the form of the pre-existing large integrated chemical/pharmaceutical companies (Hoechst, Bayer, BASF, Schering). While German computer and telecommunication firms languished in part because German business was very late to switch to advanced IT networks, German pharmaceutical companies have in recent years recognized that biotechnology (broadly defined) has become a defining methodology in life-science industries. Hoechst and Bayer are shedding industrial chemical subsidiaries to focus primarily on "life-science" competencies. Hoechst has gone the farthest down this route, announcing that biotechnology has become the core unifying science methodology throughout the company. While German pharmaceutical companies have invested large amounts of resources in the U.S. and U.K. biotechnology industries, they have a natural interest in nurturing German biotechnology. This is in part because local research networks are easier to maintain (e.g., fewer cultural barriers, plus the local firms should have an advantage in accessing the German market). Moreover, by nurturing German biotechnology firms, human resource and organizational expertise will be developed that can (through buy-outs or alliances) then be transferred to the existing pharmaceutical companies as they develop their own in-house biotechnology competencies.

Technological and Intellectual Property Structures Favor Entry

Ease of market entry is a chief reason why thousands of biotechnology start-ups have emerged worldwide over the last 25 years. For an industry some 25 years old, the lack of concentration within biotechnology is amazing. Firm size remains relatively small: some 39,000 people are employed in the European Union industry, while the average employment within the EU's top ten biotech firms, in terms of market capitalization, stands at only 390 (Ernst and Young, 1998b: 12–13). Notwithstanding the recent appearance of platform technologies, intellectual property in pharmaceuticals is very fragmented across literally hundreds of separate research trajectories. Though patents for individual drugs (and artificially created gene sequences) are strong, in very few disease areas do "blocking" patents exist. For example, in the study of Alzheimer's disease mentioned earlier, Penan showed that there were 15 ongoing separate research clusters for this one disease. Intellectual property across these separate research clusters apparently has not overlapped in such a way as to "block" ongoing research within competing research clusters. To give another indication of the ease of entry, according to a recent industry analysis, some 90 percent of patented drugs have direct competitors, and there exist three or more direct competitors for 15 of the 20 top selling drugs (Powell, 1996: 204).

The situation in pharmaceuticals differs hugely with semiconductors and computers, another industry in which intellectual property plays a defining role. Grindley and Teece (1997) have argued that intellectual property in semiconductors can block new entry. Patents in this area tend to be very broad, in that patents for new circuit designs cannot be easily "reengineered" and thus circumvented. Furthermore, there tend to be a number of key technologies in each area that tend to be held by several firms. These firms must sign cross licenses for each other's intellectual property in order to innovate. This creates a severe handicap on small start-ups that lack tradable patents.

Possibilities for Institutional Reform

German national institutional frameworks are likely to develop along one of three trajectories. A first scenario is *convergence*. According to this view, given the pressures of globalization and the inability to reconfigure existing German institutional arrangements to support radical innovation, Germany must be transformed into a liberal market economy, allowing German companies to adopt forms of organization advantaged by liberal market economies. Resistance to these changes, driven by a robustness of the current institutional equilibrium, could result in a second scenario, *specialization*. This is the arrangement widely seen to exist in the eighties and early nineties (see, e.g., Hollingsworth, 1997). Differences in national institutional structures advantage a different constellation of organizational structures and associated product market strategies. In this scenario, globalization, rather than a cause of convergence, could actually strengthen national differences, as large multinational companies create international product chains locating activities in the political economy best advantaging the required company organizational characteristics. A final advantageous solution for Germany is an *accommodation* of the present institutional frameworks to support at least minimal forms of radical science-based innovation, without undermining the country's unique ability to support other medium-tech high value–added industries. Organizational patterns might differ substantially from those in the United States, but nevertheless allow successful radical innovation strategies to ensue.

Although some interesting changes are taking place, there is little evidence that the convergence scenario is coming to pass. The case against the convergence scenario is best presented through data comparing the relative specialization of the United States and Germany during the nineties in a broad array of industries. Recent EPO patent data suggest that, as of 1993/94, extreme differences continue to exist in U.S. and German industry specialization (see Casper, Lehrer, and Soskice, 1999). These data reveal that Germany excels relative to the United States in construction, engineering, weapons, transport, agricultural machinery, machine tools, motors, environmental technologies—all of which are process-oriented industries that broadly fit into the "diversified quality production" classification. U.S. industry, on the other hand, excels relative to Germany in an array of high-tech industries that include biotechnology, organic chemistry, semiconductors, telecommunications, materials, and optics. Even more revealing is a comparison of 1983/84 data with that from 1993/94. This data reveals that the United States *increased* its relative specialization in each of the high-tech industries just mentioned between

1983/84 and 1993/94, while the Germans similarly increased its relative specialization in the DQP industries.

Based on these industry specialization statistics, the convergence scenario appears weakly supported. Furthermore, while changes to German national institutional changes are ongoing, these changes are incremental in nature and still aim primarily to advantage DQP rather than high-technology company organizational strategies.

Among the most important institutional reform is a new law that permits companies to introduce share-option schemes. As knowledge continues to become more decentralized across most sectors in the economy, a general interest within the German business community in developing sharper incentive structures has emerged. This led to a debate over the role of share options in large German firms. The advantage of share options is that they can be introduced on a collective basis across the firm, without disturbing normal consensus-based decision-making patterns. After circulating within the German parliament for over two years, a legislative bill allowing companies to buy and sell their own shares (the prerequisite for share-option schemes) was approved in March 1998.

Otherwise, there are no other signs that the broadly "social" constitution of German large firms will be replaced by a more U.S./U.K. style financial system of ownership. There has been very little debate on dismantling other aspects of German company organization, such as the two-tier board system or the installation of powerful employee counsels for labor and middle management. Similarly, competition clauses are still upheld by courts while German company and labor law continues to continues to promote the stakeholder model, which strongly encourages firms to adopt the lifetime employment model and its consequent impact on company decision making, career-trajectories, and remuneration. As a result, active labor markets for mid-career managers and scientists continue to be underdeveloped.

Incremental changes are also occurring within the financial system. Often in combination with the introduction of share-option performance incentives, many large German firms have embraced dispersed equity offerings as a common instrument to raise investment capital. Public interest has been catalyzed by the highly publicized Deutsche Telekom share offering in 1996, the emergence of numerous low-cost stock brokerages in Germany (especially on the Internet), and exuberance created by the soaring level of the blue-chip DAX index, which has more than doubled in the last two years. In 1997 a new exchange tailored for smaller, higher risk companies was created, the Neue Markt. As of mid-2000 over 250 firms have taken listings on the Neue Markt, including several German biotechnology firms.

What do these changes entail for prospective German high-tech start-up companies? Most promising, German start-up firms will soon be able to offer high-powered incentive structures in the form of share options. In addition, the Neue Markt, if it continues to develop, presents the opportunity of a legitimate market for small-firm IPOs in Germany. If a legitimate market for German high-tech IPOs is sustained, this will also go a long way towards creating an "exit option" for venture capitalists. As already noted, this is critical if a viable refinancing mechanism is to develop in Germany and also allows venture capitalists to more easily diversify risks.

While these changes are important, it is important to ask which *type* of firms are likely to be funded through these new markets. As of mid-1998, extremely high market valuations for not just "blue chip" established large firms but also most of the higher risk Neue Markt suggests that German investors are willing to accept risks on a level with those commonly found in the United States or United Kingdom. Such a conclusion, however, ignores several important facts about the structure of German equity markets and the effect of German company law on company strategy.

The major source of finance in Germany continues to be debt and, for established firms, retained earnings. German equity market capitalization in November 1996 was only 27 percent of GDP, compared to 122 percent in the United States and 152 percent in the United Kingdom (of the major OECD countries, only Austria comes in lower, at 14 percent) (Deutsche Bundesbank, 1996: 28). Furthermore, despite increased interest in the stock market, actual equity ownership is extremely narrow: while some 47 percent of U.S. citizens directly own stocks or equity-based mutual funds, only about 5 percent of Germans directly hold equities. Though international investors (e.g., U.S./U.K. pension funds) are an important new source of finance, as a source of finance German equity markets remain much thinner than in the United States or United Kingdom.

It is also questionable whether the current, highly speculative company valuations can be maintained in Germany. As the current expansion of the DAX into a market with widely traded and dispersed shares is only a few years old, the market has no track record of performance through the normal business cycle. Furthermore, it is likely that new and especially international holders of German equities hold the mistaken assumption that German firms are operating within a similar institutional environment as U.S. or U.K. companies. While important changes are taking place, it would be erroneous to conclude that Germany is marching towards the U.S./U.K. national institutional infrastructure. As already highlighted, virtually no changes have occurred in German company or labor law. German firms are encouraged to make long-term bets on market and technological trajectories, to train deeply within the firm, and make use of these resources when making decisions. German management cannot quickly cut assets or embark on the "hire and fire" trajectories often seen in the United States (and increasingly, the United Kingdom). In part because they are controlled by coalitions of company representatives and concentrated shareholders (e.g., banks), German supervisory boards have systematically refused to offer top management the extremely high performance-related pay packages coupled with extreme managerial control that is typical in U.S./U.K. public firms.

While German firms have successfully competed in the variety of "DQP" product market segments noted above, these established, largely process-innovation based markets usually do not create the growth opportunities presented in the high-tech product innovation based markets that U.S. and U.K. firms tend to dominate. In contrast to the Anglo-Saxon "high-risk, high-return" model of company strategy, the strategies advantaged in Germany are best seen through a "low-risk, low-return" lens. While German organizational structures usually prevent firms from making huge mistakes, this means that these firms are usually much slower to react and fully commit to major changes in technology or market organization. Biotechnology is a good case in point. As discussed above, the big-three German chemical/pharma companies were very slow in reacting to the changed scientific and market conditions in pharmaceuticals during the eighties.

In general, there is little evidence that German national institutional frameworks have converged to a liberal market economy model. They do not facilitate the use of similar governance structures to support high-technology start-up firms that have been created in the United States and Germany. More open to debate is whether German managers, scientists, and investors can embrace piecemeal reforms in company law as well as a slight deepening in German equity markets to make the accommodation scenario viable.

The "Accommodation" Strategy

This strategy, while recognizing that important national institutional frameworks in Germany are oriented primarily to advantage other company strategies, attempts to use a variety of alternative private sector or governmental devices to create governance structures supporting at least minimal forms of the desired company organizational structures. For this to happen, however, German companies would need to create new governance structures for biotechnology that do not merely mimic those already developed in the United States. Because the accommodation strategy relies on the creative design or reconstruction of new governance structures, it is difficult to specify with precision what this strategy might entail. However, focusing again on biotechnology start-ups, there are at least four components of an accommodation strategy that firms and interested governmental actors might usefully keep in mind.

Specialize in Lower-Risk Niche Markets

Table 13.3 summarizes the four principal market segments in bio-medical-related biotechnology. Important differences exist in risk profile across these segments. Given the difficulties that exist in sustaining high-risk strategies within the German institutional environment, it follows that German firms should gravitate into market niches that avoid the high-risk "races" to develop highly specific intellectual property in particular disease areas and long-lead

Table 13.3 Bio-Medical-Related Market Segments

Category	Definition	Examples	R&D costs	Time to Market	Competency Destruction	Risk Profile
Thera- peutics	Develop products to improve the treatment of disease	Apply a variety of molecular biology methodologies to discover/design drugs	High (due to uncertainty of research results and high costs of preclinical and clinical testing)	Long (usu- ally 7–10 years, due to length of testing and regulatory approval process)	High (volatility of research trajectories, high failure rate due to racing activity)	High
Diag- nostics	Develop tools to help identify diseases	Develop anti-bodies for use in diagnostic procedures; Some use of genetic technologies (e.g., PCR) to test for hereditary or acquired genetic diseases	Medium to high (research risk can be high; testing and regulatory costs exist, but are lower than in therapeutics)	Medium (regulatory approval and testing require- ments are less restrictive)	Medium- High	Medium to High
Platform Technolo- gies	Create enabling technolo- gies with broad appli- cation	Genetic sequencing or engineering services; the creation of consumables for use in molecular biology lab procedures; combinatorial chemistry and other automation technol- ogies; genomics	Low to medium (technolo- gies can be very uncertain, but usually few regulatory approval or testing re- quirements)	Short (direct sales to other life- science companies/ labs)	Low to Medium (technologi- cal cumula- tiveness higher and racing activity less intense)	Varies, but generally Low to Medium
Contract Research/ Manufac- turing	Perform customized biochemi- cal-related services for other companies	The manufacturing of customized biochemical products; specialized services like equipment servicing or quality control certification	Low	Short (direct sales to other life- science companies/ labs)	Low	Low

Source: Categories and definitions paraphrased from Ernst and Young, 1998, European Life Sciences Report, pp. 5–6.

times that characterize the therapeutics area. In fact, this is the preferred strategy of most German biotech start-ups. In a recent survey of Europe's biotech firms, Ernst and Young found that while close to 40 percent of European biotech firms are developing high-risk therapeutic products, less than 20 percent of German firms are in this field. Conversely, about 30 percent of German firms are developing platform technologies, compared to less than 20 percent for the European industry as a whole (Ernst and Young, 1998c: 19). When German biotech firms were asked to list the areas of their research activities, therapeutics came in fifth, ranked well below contract research and manufacturing, platform technologies, diagnostics, and "other services" (Ernst and Young, 1998c: 17).

The process-oriented innovation strategies of platform technology strategies entail the creation of organizational structures that resonate well with the "competency preserving" orientation of German institutions (Casper, 2000). The leading German biotechnology firms, such as Qiagen, a world leader in the creation of high-value-added consumable kits for DNA purification, and Lion Bioscience, a bioinfomatics firm, come from the platform technology segment. These firms are not "typical" German organizations, in that they use high-powered incentive structures and often rely upon the intense work-environments that characterize American or British high-tech firms. However, because the platform technologies are generic, scientific competencies are generally much more stable than in therapeutic firms while much shorter lead times reduce failure rates. This lowers both the need for long-term high-risk finance and the career risk of working within such a firm.

Create New Governance Structures

Firms can create supplementary governance structures to compensate for underlying institutional weakness. Organizational patterns might differ substantially from those in liberal market economies, but nevertheless allow successful radical innovation strategies to ensue. For this to happen, however, German companies would need to create new governance structures for biotechnology that do not merely mimic those created in the U.S. or U.K. Such hybrid organizational forms might emulate characteristics of the U.S. model (smaller network forms of organization with high-powered performance incentives), but with more stability in structure of labor markets or finance.

One example of this strategy has originated within large pharmaceutical firms. Hoechst and BASF have both initiated in-house incubator labs designed to allow employees to organize start-up firms. Ownership will be divided between the host-firm and the managers and scientists that organize the new venture. Successful firms are expected to be placed on German or international equity markets through IPOs. While these incubator firms will have preferential access to materials, scientific equipment, and other assets, the hope is that high-powered incentive structures and autonomy will help recreate the highly creative atmospheres found in "true" start-ups. Schemes of this sort should provide an effective solution to the career-structure problem: if a large company incubator firm fails, the managers and scientists presumably can return to normal positions within the firm.

A second new organizational form has originated out of many of the regional "BioRegio" programs in connection with universities and other public research labs. In contrast to the wide engagement of U.S. academics in the biotechnology industry, during the eighties and early nineties German academic researchers in the biosciences were usually portrayed as aloof from commercial developments in their research fields. During the late nineties this situation dramatically changed: perhaps the most common source of most biotech start-ups are established public research labs in the biosciences. German research labs differ from those in the United States and the United Kingdom in one key regard: while U.S./U.K. universities have jealously guarded intellectual property developed by their employees, German universities generally cede full control over intellectual property to the professor/student inventors.

This intellectual property has become a prime source of collateral used to secure venture capital start-up financing for biotech start-ups. Many German universities and public research institutes have worked with regional "BioRegio" technology agencies to develop "gene centers" affiliated with established institutions. These often include "incubator labs" located in technology parks in close proximity to public bioscience labs. Many of Germany's biotech start-up firms are actually tiny offices designed to manage commercial spin-offs that emerge out of basic research conducted within public bio-medical labs. If a discovery merits further development (i.e., early stage trials) that cannot be paid through normal basic research grants, scientists connected to the basic research lab can take full-time employment at the company. However, this governance form again provides employment protection for senior scientists. If the spin-off company becomes extremely successful and obtains long-term financing (through, for example, the licensing of a discovery to a large pharmaceutical firm), senior scientists may leave their public research posts to work in the private sector. Otherwise, senior scientists can safely retain their public professor/research post while retaining a large financial stake in the associated spin-off firm.

Embrace Globalization to Develop Competencies That Cannot Be Easily Developed within Germany

While large German pharmaceutical firms during the late eighties attempted to bridge their internal technology gaps through investing in U.S. biotech, the opposite can also be true. One option is to tap into international equity markets through taking listings on foreign exchanges. For example, Qiagen used its success to tap into U.S. financial markets through being listed on NASDAQ.

A second option is to recruit foreign scientists and managers to work in German start-ups. Personnel recruited from the United States or United Kingdom, for example, can easily move back into their more flexible home labor markets. Recruiting foreign specialists is a core strategy of firms working in connection with the Munich Gene Center, the most successful of the German biotech clusters. According to the director of the Munich Gene Center, most start-up firms affiliated with the Munich Gene Center have recruited American or British nationals with expertise in international finance to fill key chief financial officer positions (Interview, December 1998). Similarly, having created a world-class infrastructure to support molecular biotechnology, the University of Munich has been able to use a large fellowship program to attract a number of top-rate scientists from foreign countries, many of whom spend part of their time within local start-up firms.

Make Selective Use of Governmental Policy to Fill Gaps in Private-Sector Incentive Structures

German industrial policy has circumvented the critical problem of finding seed-money for most of the current crop of biotech start-up firms. Most of the German subsidy programs demand that each applicant find a private investor (usually a venture capital firm or large pharmaceutical firm). Governmental subsidies then supplement the seed money provided by venture capitalist. The vast majority of German biotech start-ups grounded since 1995 have depended on governmental matching grants (Casper, 2000). Through essentially halving the cost of capital, governmental subsidies have created incentives for foreign and domestic venture capital firms to invest in German biotech. According to German biotech experts, the subsidies provided by the BioRegio and various Länder programs have essentially solved the capital formation problem in Germany (see Adelberger, 2000).

Governmental subsidy programs are short term in nature, since they do nothing to assure a viable long-term source of capital for German start-up firms; neither are these programs geared to provide the "mezzanine" financing needed to sustain the high burn-rates commonly found in biotechnology. In the long term, German firms should work to develop governance structures that do not rely on direct governmental intervention. Only then will institutional frameworks exist that can create and reproduce viable governance structures for high-tech firms over the long-term. Both the U.S. and U.K. biotech industries rely primarily on favorable national institutional frameworks in the finance and company organizational areas discussed throughout this chapter. In the long-term, the best German governmental policy for biotechnology will most likely consist of large financing for basic research in molecular biology and medicine.

Though the BMBF now spends some DM 1 billion on Max Planck Institutes and university labs involved in bio-medical research, this pales in comparison with the some $14 billion spent by the U.S. National Institutes of Health.

CONCLUSION: RECONFIGURING NATIONAL INSTITUTIONS TO PROMOTE INNOVATION

Why has the creation of viable institutions to support biotech start-ups in Germany been so difficult? A general conclusion emerging from this case study is that national institutional frameworks are *complementary* in nature. Complementarities are present when "doing more of one activity increases (or at least does not decrease) the marginal profitability of each other activity in the group" (Milgrom and Roberts, 1992: 108; see also Hall and Soskice, 2001). While in Germany the institutional complementarities between finance, career development and skill-formation, and company organization advantage a variety of "DQP" product market strategies, we have seen how, especially during the eighties these same institutions create severe problems for German firms attempting to create high-technology start-up firms.

When institutional frameworks are highly interdependent in this sense, dramatic institutional reforms that run counter to the broad logic of industry coordination in an economy become difficult. While some German high-tech firms currently demand the opening of labor markets and the deregulation of wage bargaining, most German firms resist this because it could radically lower the value of vocational and career training while increasing wage costs for highly skilled workers and managers. Reforms to support high technology are possible only when they gain the support of German industry more widely. The important reform of German financial law that allows high-tech start-ups to distribute share options was viable because most German large companies are interested in using share options to strengthen group performance incentives.

Given these constraints, the short-term success of German promotional policies for biotechnology is quite remarkable. We have seen that the governance structures used to organize start-ups generally follow the "accommodation" strategy. Firms have made use of generous infrastructure provision and financial subsidies provided by the numerous German "BioRegio" programs to reduce much of the financial risk imposed by biotechnology. Career risks have been reduced through importing foreign financial and scientific specialists to fill many of the higher-risk positions, while creating new employment relationships that have allowed senior German mangers and scientists to maintain positions public research labs or larger firms while working within start-up firms. Finally, German firms have by and large avoided the higher-risk, longer time-horizon therapeutic area by specializing in the lower-risk product segments in platform technologies and related service areas.

However, the problem of creating viable institutions to promote firms with radical innovation competencies is by no means resolved in Germany. German technology policy has been aimed primarily to fill gaps in the institutional frameworks that influence new firm creation. Now that large numbers of start-up firms exist, new problems associated with nurturing these firms in viable commercial enterprises are inevitable.

For example, the German industry must develop viable refinancing mechanisms to satisfy the constant hunger of biotech start-ups for fresh investment capital. In their recent survey of German biotechnology, the consulting firm Ernst and Young see the lack of capital investment in new product development equipment as a key weakness of the German industry (Ernst and Young, 1998c: 8). German venture capital is currently abundant, but due to the availability of large subsidies for start-up firms, might be flowing primarily in this direction rather than as "mezzanine" financing for established firms. This would force firms to invest their initial seed capital much more conservatively than their competitors with fairly secure access to secondary financing, accounting for lower capital investment in Germany.

Similarly, it is unclear if the German biotechnology industry has developed institutions that can effectively deal with firm failures. Will unsuccessful firms be allowed to fail and, if so, can the resources within these firms be efficiently recombined into new ventures or absorbed by other companies? What will happen to the scientists and mangers of failed start-ups? Will they be quickly absorbed into other start-ups along the U.S./U.K. labor market model, or will they retreat back into their prior public research or large firm careers? Overall, creating viable governance structure to support high-technology start-up firms in Germany will remain a difficult challenge for the foreseeable future.

14

The Financial System of Industrial Finance and the Social System of Production

Sigurt Vitols

INTRODUCTION

In the past decade a considerable amount of research has been done on the differences between national economic organization and performance. This interest has been driven by the perception that economies have reacted differently to the twin oil shocks of the seventies, the dismantling of the Bretton Woods system, and the deep worldwide recession of the early eighties. While earlier research focused mainly on industrial relations and labor markets, recognition of the importance of differences in the financial system is growing.[1]

In the United States, interest in other national financial systems is driven by the perception that the investment time horizons on financial markets are too short to foster internationally competitive manufacturing (Jacobs, 1991; Porter, 1992). The German universal bank system in particular has attracted great attention because of its great stability and the ability of its large banks to provide industrial companies with abundant "patient capital." While less well understood, the Japanese financial system with its bank-centered industrial groups has also been seen as sharing virtuous features of the German system.[2]

One major body of literature which addresses the differences between national financial systems and which is having a major impact on policy debates is the new institutional economics (NIE). The NIE approach focuses on the problem of moral hazard arising from incomplete contracting, which is especially severe in the case of long-term asset-specific investments. Contracting mechanisms vary in their capacity to deal with information and incentive problems and the associated conflicts of interest between classes of investors as well as between investors and management. NIE suggests that the U.S. regulatory system places too many constraints on financial institutions, preventing them from engaging in efficient financial contracting; banks in particular are constrained from making large equity investments in companies and playing an active role in corporate governance. This approach thus recommends financial deregulation to enable U.S. banks to engage in the kinds of financial contracting that German and Japanese banks routinely use in supplying patient capital.

This chapter argues for an alternative approach to the problem of long-term investment by focusing on the systemic requirements for the provision of patient capital. Financial institutions are organizations which are exposed to a variety of risks; in addition to credit risk (which NIE focuses on), financial institutions must also manage liquidity and interest rate risks, which are especially high in long-term investment. Thus the capacity of the financial system to provide patient capital is dependent on the presence of patient owners of financial institutions, stable savings behavior on the part of households, stable competitive relations within the financial sector, and stable demand for patient capital from companies. In contrast with the microanalytic focus of NIE, this alternative approach focuses on the embeddedness of financial institutions within the broader social system of production; norms and values, state policies, the industrial relations system, and inter-firm coordination all have an impact on the financial environment.

The utility of this broader approach is illustrated in an analysis of the U.S., German, Japanese, and British cases. When examining the first three countries, NIE suggests that Japan is an "intermediate" case sharing some but not all of the restrictions on banking activity that exist in the United States; data on the degree of shareholding and long-term lending to corporate firms by banks seem to support this ordering. When extending the analysis to all four countries, however, the British case constitutes a paradox; U.K. banks are unrestricted in the type of contracting they may engage in, yet their shareholding and lending patterns are more similar to the U.S. case than the German case.

The alternative approach developed here resolves the "British anomaly" by showing that the British social system of production, including the features which are crucial for supporting long-term relational investment, is more similar to the United States than to Germany and Japan. In the absence of change in other aspects of the social system of production, deregulation of the U.S.

banking system will thus not have the intended effects of creating a U.S. variant of the bank-centered industrial groups typical of Germany and Japan; in the worst case scenario, deregulation will actually decrease the capacity of U.S. banks to provide patient capital by increasing instability in the financial system.

MARKET-BASED VERSUS RELATIONAL FINANCIAL SYSTEMS AND FINANCIAL PERFORMANCE

Financial systems can be classified according to the relative importance of financial assets which are marketable versus those that are relationship-specific. In the first case ownership rights of the asset can be easily transferred; in the second case the asset expires with the termination of the relationship. In industrial finance, equity investments in privately-held companies and long-term loans are the most important forms of relational investment; bonds and stocks tradable on securities exchanges and negotiable commercial paper are the main form of market-based assets. In general, relational investing is associated with patient capital since investors are constrained to following "voice" strategies in supporting company restructuring if the company experiences financial distress; marketable assets in contrast allow investors to follow "exit" strategies by selling the securities of companies they loose confidence in.[3]

Banks play a central role in relational financial systems. Banks have a greater organizational capacity than the other major types of financial institutions (pension funds, insurance companies, and mutual funds) to perform the credit evaluation and monitoring needed for relational investments. Relational investing is particularly important for small and medium-sized enterprises (SMEs), since they are generally too small to have access to finance through securities exchanges. Banks also play a special role in monitoring the financial condition of publicly traded companies and in restructuring companies in the event of financial distress. Thus, the relative importance of banks has implications for the capacity of the financial system to provide patient capital (Fama, 1980; Santomero, 1984; Gertler, 1988).[4]

A comparison of the world's four most important financial systems show major differences in financial structure; the United Kingdom and United States can be classified as market-based financial systems while Germany and Japan can be classified as relational along a number of important indicators (see table 14.1). In the United Kingdom and United States, banks account for less than half of all financial sector assets; in Germany and Japan in contrast they account for about four-fifths of all such assets.[5] Banks are also less important repositories of household savings in the United Kingdom and United States, accounting for only about one-quarter of household financial assets in these countries; in Germany and Japan they account for over one-half of household financial assets.

Table 14.1 Bank Shares of Financial Assets and Liabilities, 1989

	U.K.	U.S.	Germany	Japan
Bank Share of Financial Sector Assets	45%	45%	83%	79%
Bank Share of Household Financial Assets	25%	25%	61%	51%
Bank Share of Corporate Equities	4%	<1%	10%	21%

Sources: U.K. National Accounts (1993), Statistical Abstract of the U.S. (1991), Statistisches Jahrbuch (1991), Japan Statistical Yearbook (1991), OECD Non-Financial Enterprises Financial Statements (1990), Tatewaki (1991: 100).

Finally, banks in the market-based systems are less able to provide patient capital to industry than in the relational systems. Banks in the United Kingdom and United States rarely provide loans with maturities of more than four years to industrial and commercial companies, and those loans with maturities of greater than one year are generally made with floating rates of interest. U.K. banks hold a small amount of corporate equities; U.S. banks own virtually none.[6] German banks in contrast directly own 10 percent of outstanding corporate stock and vote on another 30 percent held in trust with them, i.e., German banks control about 40 percent of corporate stock. Furthermore, about half of German bank loans to industry have maturities of four years or more, the bulk of these long-term loans carrying fixed interest rates. Japan represents an intermediate case; Japanese banks hold 21 percent of outstanding corporate shares and the long-term credit banks are able to provide long-term loans at fixed interest rates.

While resolving the debate on the contribution of financial systems to economic performance is beyond the scope of this chapter, it is nevertheless instructive to note a strong correlation between the type of financial system and a number of indicators of economic and financial performance, including investment and growth, financial stability and efficiency, and support of SMEs. These indicators consistently classify the market-based systems on the low end of the performance scale and the relational systems on the higher end of the scale (see table 14.2).

One broad measure of economic performance is the growth rate in GDP per capita. Growth rates between 1980 and 1992 have been higher in the relational systems (3.3% in Japan and 1.9%) than in the United States and United Kingdom (1.4% and 1.8%). One of the most important factors supporting national economic growth is capital investment, here measured by the rate of net fixed capital formation (the net addition to the nation's capital stock) as a share of gross domestic product; according to this measure, net investment in this same period has been significantly higher in the relational systems (16.2% in Japan and 8.2% in Germany) than in the market-based systems (5.7% in the U.K. and 5.5% in the U.S.).

Table 14.2 Economic and Financial Performance Indicators, 1980–92

		U.K.	U.S.	Germany	Japan
Growth in GDP per Capita	Annual Average	1.8%	1.4%	1.9%	3.3%
Rate of Net Fixed Capital Formation/ GDP	Annual Average	5.7%	5.5%	8.2%	16.2%
Long-Term Interest Rates	Annual Average	11.1%	9.8%	7.8%	6.5%
	Variance	3.23	3.07	1.28	2.65
Net Interest Margin	Annual Average	3.2%	3.4%	2.2%	1.2%

Source: OECD Historical Statistics and National Accounts, 1960–1992.

A second important set of performance indicators relates to financial system stability and efficiency. Stability in interest rates affects the risks that financial institutions face in providing patient capital as well as the willingness of non-financial companies to make long-term investments (Dixit and Pindyck, 1994). Nominal interest rates between 1980 and 1992 have been significantly lower and more stable in the relational countries than in the market-based countries.[7]

Banks in the relational systems are also been more efficient than banks in the market-based systems, as measured by the spread between the interest that banks pay on their deposits and the interest they charge on their loans. Ceteris paribus, a lower spread means that the cost of capital to non-financial companies is lower since banks can make loans at lower interest rates. Average net interest spread as a percentage of total assets between 1980 and 1992 was significantly lower in the relational systems (1.3% in Japan and 2.2% in Germany) than in the market-based systems (3.4% in the U.S. and 3.2% in the U.K.).

Finally, it is important to note that the four countries have significantly different industrial structures. In terms of the relative share of manufacturing employment, SMEs are much more important in the relational systems than in the market-based systems. Firms with up to five hundred employees in the late eighties accounted for 35 percent of employment in the United States, 40 percent of employment in the United Kingdom, and 58 percent of manufacturing employment in Germany. Firms with up to three hundred employees alone accounted for 72 percent of total manufacturing employment in Japan (Acs and Audretsch, 1993; Sengenberger, 1991). In the past decade smaller firms have received much attention because of their potential contribution to flexible production (Piore and Sabel, 1984; Sengenberger, 1991). Relational finance is especially important to SMEs because smaller firms lack access to securities markets (Vitols, 1994).

THE NEW INSTITUTIONAL ECONOMICS APPROACH TO INDUSTRIAL FINANCE

One major body of literature which addresses the problem of variations in financial structure is the new institutional economics (NIE). While NIE has a number of important variants, the common core of NIE is a critique of the neo-classical theory of the firm as a profit-maximizing production function.[8] In contrast with neoclassical financial economics which treats financial structure as essentially independent of real investment, employment, and production decisions, NIE seeks to integrate the analysis of financial structure with a more general theory of the firm.[9]

NIE stresses the difficulties in writing complete contracts, which specify each party's obligations and payoffs in every conceivable future state of nature. Many contracts are incomplete due to the prohibitive costs of writing and enforcing contracts. Contracts may also be incomplete due to the problem of asymmetric information, i.e., the problem that one party may have in verifying the effort of another party.

The problem of moral hazard arises from the incompleteness of contracts and the possibility of opportunism, i.e., of one actor maximizing his or her utility to the detriment of others. Moral hazard is especially severe in the case of long-term and asset-specific contracts. The longer the time horizon of the contract, the more likely it is that unforeseen contingencies will arise. Contracts involving asset-specific investments are prone to moral hazard since the party making the investment suffers more from the premature termination of the relationship and is thus vulnerable to demands for ex post facto renegotiation of contracts.

The provision of external finance regulated by financial contracts represents one type of contracting. The most common types of financial contracting are debt and equity. Debt contracts typically specify a fixed repayment schedule and give creditors priority claims to the firm's assets in the case of bankruptcy. Providers of equity have nominal control rights over the firm, receive the increment of income after expenses and interest payments, and in the case of bankruptcy have claim to the firm's residual assets once other interests are paid off.

Complete financial contracting would mitigate conflicts of interest between the different parties by specifying each party's obligations and claims in each possible state of nature. However, difficulties in financial contracting arise from asymmetric information and conflicts of interest between different categories of investors and between investors and management in different economic states. Management may prefer "private consumption" in the form of company perks and empire building at the expense of investors.

Furthermore, if the company experiences financial distress and the value of equity approaches zero, stockholders will have little to loose and will undertake risky investments in the hope that a gamble will pay off. They may also attempt to liquidate firm assets and receive the payoff in the form of dividends. Creditors in contrast will have an interest in conservative investment policies which preserve the value of the assets of the firm and the repayment of debt.

Both of these types of conflict of interest may prevent socially efficient investments from being made. It may be possible however to construct mechanisms which mitigate these conflicts and permit the investment to go ahead. For example, conflicts between investor groups may be mitigated by allowing investors to hold both debt and equity. Information flows to investors may be improved by creating a board of directors and including investors on this board. Empirical research on Germany appears to confirm the view that these types of mechanisms improve large company performance and access to external capital (Cable, 1985; Audretsch and Elston, 1994).

The U.S. financial regulatory system severely constrains these types of contracting arrangements. Commercial banks are prohibited from making substantial equity investments and effectively constrained from nominating representatives to company boards; this prohibits a mitigation of the creditor—shareholder conflict and an improvement in the flow of information from management to the bank. Geographical restrictions on bank branching have constrained the growth of banks, and even the largest U.S. banks lack the financial capacity needed to make substantial equity investments in large industrial companies (Roe, 1990).[10]

The NIE approach suggests that a deregulation of the U.S. banking system is desirable in order to improve the efficiency of financial contracting; "strict regulation has prevented banks from effectively exercising control in non-financial corporations, affecting their willingness to extend credit" (Berglöf, 1990: 108). Given the freedom to, investors will naturally develop the kinds of financial contracting needed in order to support patient capital (Porter, 1992).

This view superficially appears to work when examining the U.S., German, and Japanese cases. As indicated in the previous section, German banks have the greatest capacity to provide patient capital; they also have fewer restrictions than Japanese or U.S. banks on the equity investments in non-financial companies they may make or on the nomination of members of the supervisory boards of these companies. Japan appears to be an intermediate case in terms of constraints on financial contracting and the capacity to supply patient capital. The U.S. occupying forces imposed a version of the Glass-Steagall Act on Japan after World War II which limits the equity investments Japanese banks may make; however, there are fewer constraints on active participation in corporate governance than is the case for U.S. banks. While Japanese banks typically do not nominate members to the supervisory boards of the companies they hold a stake in, they do review the investment plans of these companies and play an active role in restructuring them in case of financial distress (Hoshi et al., 1990; Prowse, 1990; Tsusui, 1988).

The NIE approach, however, runs into difficulties when trying to explain the British case. Britain lacks the formal relational contracting restrictions that the United States has in acquiring equity stakes, nominating directors, and playing an active role in corporate governance. However, the British clearing banks have exploited this opportunity only to a limited extent and generally limit their investments in companies to shorter-term credits. British insurance companies, which hold about ten times as much stock as banks do, play a much greater role in corporate governance (Scott and Griff, 1985; Berglöf, 1990).

A second major problem for NIE lies in dealing with the problem of finance for SMEs. In none of the four countries examined do banks typically hold shares in or nominate directors of the SMEs they lend to. Nevertheless, national differences in industrial finance may in fact be larger among SMEs than in the case of large joint-stock companies. The most important form of bank finance for small British companies is a short-term overdraft facility on their checking accounts. In Germany in contrast dependence on long-term bank credits increases with decreasing firm size (Deutsche Bundesbank, 1992).

These two anomalies suggest that factors other than the financial contracting mechanisms identified by the NIE must be sought in order to explain cross-national differences in industrial finance.

A Social System of Production Approach to Financial Systems

In contrast to microanalytic focus of NIE, the alternative approach developed here views financial institutions as organizations embedded in a social system of production. The capacity of financial institutions to perform specific functions is influenced by the risks that these institutions face. The extent of these risks as well as the ability of financial institutions to manage these risks is influenced by the characteristics of other elements of the social system of production. These other elements include the general norms and values of a society, the state and its policies, industrial relations, and inter-firm relations.

The core thesis of the social systems of production approach is that these different elements are interdependent; one must understand the inter-relations between these elements in order to understand the performance of the system as a whole. Change in any one of these elements will have an impact on the performance of the whole system, thus the success of attempts to import a feature of another system will be dependent upon the interaction of this new feature with other system elements (Hollingsworth, 1994).[11]

The function of financial institutions is to create, administer, and exchange financial assets and liabilities. The performance of these functions involves a number of risks. The main risks that financial institutions face in providing patient capital to industry are credit risk, which is the risk that payments will not be made according to an agreed schedule; interest rate risk, which is the risk that the interest rate margin a financial institution receives will be squeezed by an increase in the cost of funds or a decrease in the income from loans made; and liquidity risk, which is the risk that funds will be withdrawn without adequate reserve coverage. These risks generally increase with the duration of an invest-ment.[12]

Four characteristics of financial systems influence their capacity and will-ingness to manage the risks involved in providing patient capital to industry (see table 14.3): 1) the ownership structure of financial institutions, 2) the sectoral organization of the financial system, 3) the characteristics of sources of funding for financial institutions, and 4) the characteristics of the demand for funds from financial institutions. These characteristics are significantly determined by other elements of the social system of production.

Table 14.3 Factors Promoting Patient Capital

Characteristic of Financial System	Factors Promoting Patient Capital
Ownership Structure	Public and Cooperative Alternatives to Private For-Profit Institutions
Sectoral Organization	Regulatory Coherence Continuity in Structure of Competition High Degree of Intra-Sectoral Cooperation
Characteristics of Sources of Funds	Stability in Cost of Funds Stability in Household Savings Behavior Capture of Long-Term Savings by Banks
Characteristics of Demand for Funds	Stability in the Demand for Funds Greater Relative Weight of SMEs Low Business Failure Rate

Ownership of Financial Institutions

The nature of ownership will influence the behavior of the financial organi
zation, including the universe of investments considered by the organization, the
targets for financial return, the overall attitude towards risk, and the priority
placed on long-term investment. The primary purpose of cooperative banks is to
service their members, thus the spectrum of investments considered will be
limited to lending to the membership or safe investments for surplus funds;
speculative investments will not be considered. Profitability is only a secondary
objective and losses may be taken during a downturn in order to continue
lending to the members. Similarly, the primary purpose of most state-owned
financial institutions is to "fill in the gaps" in the private sector provision of
credit; many of these institutes are dedicated to SME lending and/or the provision of long-term credit. State-owned financial institutions also generally
operate under a soft budget constraint; losses will be tolerated in a business
downturn in order to maintain the supply of credit to the customer group.

Privately owned banks in contrast are less reliable providers of patient capital. These banks are less willing to incur losses in order to stick with specific
customers. The larger private banks in particular rapidly shift their investment
policies in response to shifting opportunities and risks. Service to specific types
of customers is typically subordinated to goals such as growth and profitability.
Thus in general the greater the relative importance of public and cooperatively
owned financial institutions, the greater the capacity of the financial system to
provide patient capital.

The extent of state ownership and of state support for cooperative banks is
influenced by the general norms and values of the society towards state intervention in the economy. The structure of the state such as the strength of
regional and local government and of departments of industry will also influence the state's capacity to play a direct role in the financial system. Finally, the
extent of interfirm coordination influences the capacity of firms to cooperatively
own banks or to influence the lending policies of state-owned banks (e.g.,
through inclusion of business association representatives on bank boards).

Sectoral Organization

A second factor influencing the capacity of financial institutions to provide
patient capital is the nature of organization of the financial sector. A high degree
of regulatory coherence is important for the provision of patient capital, since
shifting regulations and standards force financial institutions to change their
investment policies. The presence of competing or partially overlapping regulatory regimes also discourages patient capital, since financial institutions will
be encouraged to shift regimes or to force down standards in their regime

through regulatory arbitrage; these types of changes are also likely to lead to changes in investment policies and possibly in the types of companies invested in.

Continuity in the structure of competition within the financial system is also important for the capacity to provide patient capital. Much instability is caused by the aggressive attempts of new entrants to gain market share, forcing financial institutions to subordinate long-term policies to the short-term struggle for market share. Regulatory coherence contributes to stability in competition by allowing for the orderly introduction financial innovations.

Finally, a high level of cooperation between financial institutions also encourages the provision of patient capital. Cooperation reduces liquidity risk through the pooling of surplus funds and the riskiness of individual loans through loan participations. Cooperation may also allow for a lengthening in the maturity of lending activity, since cooperating institutions will be better able to achieve the minimum size needed to have access to long-term funds from capital markets.

Sectoral organization is influenced by the state's structure; fragmentation of the state is often reflected in fragmentation of the regulatory apparatus. State policies also determine the degree of segmentation of the financial system into (noncompeting) groups of specialized financial institutions and influence the barriers of entry into and exit out of these segments. Finally, the degree of intra-sectoral cooperation is constrained by general societal norms and values; strong norms against collusion will discourage a high degree of cooperation.

Characteristics of Sources of Funds

The characteristics of sources of funds have a major influence on the capacity of financial institutions to provide patient capital. The greater the volatility of funds provided to financial institutions, the greater the liquidity risk faced by these institutions. The greater the volatility in interest rates and thus in the cost of funds provided, the greater the interest rate risk faced by financial institutions. Greater stability in these variables in contrast will help support patient capital.

State regulation of interest rates or coordination between financial institutions encourages the provision of patient capital by stabilizing the cost of funds. Greater stability of household income and savings behavior will promote the capacity of the financial system to provide patient capital, since the household sector is the largest net saver in industrialized economies. Finally, due to the importance of banks in relational investing, the greater the share of long-term household savings flowing to banks, the greater will be the capacity of the system to provide patient capital.

Stability in the cost of funds is influenced by the general societal norms and values of a society towards state regulation of interest rates or towards business coordination. Industrial relations influence the stability of savings behavior through the regulation of pension and insurance schemes; industrial relations also influence the stability of household income and savings by constraining the extent to which the labor force can be reduced during downturns. Finally, state policies influence the form and characteristics of long-term household savings such as pension funds, life insurance policies, and state savings schemes, as well as bank access to these long-term savings.

Characteristics of Demand for Funds

The fourth factor determining the capacity of financial institutions to provide patient capital is the characteristics of the demand for funds from industrial companies. Stability in the demand for funds will reduce the exposure of financial institutions to interest rate risk, since demand for credit will be steady through high as well as low interest rate phases. Stability in demand will also reduce the exposure of financial institutions to liquidity risk, since companies are unlikely to suddenly draw down uncommitted lines of credit. Volatility in the demand for funds on the other hand will discourage financial institutions from developing long-term sources of funds. The greater the relative weight of SMEs, the greater will be the incentives of financial institutions to develop long-term sources of capital. In general these companies have a greater demand for external long-term capital than large companies, since investment patterns are "lumpy" due to sporadic large investments; large companies in contrast are able to smooth out investment through spacing out individual capital projects and financing these through internal funds or shorter-term external capital. Finally, a low business failure rate will reduce the credit risks associated with providing patient capital.

State fiscal and macro-economic policies influence the volatility in the general level of demand and thus in the investment levels and demand for credit from companies. Industrial relations influence the level of investment and the demand for credit by determining the wage level and the ease of laying off workers during downturns. Finally, state policies influence the industrial structure and the company failure rate, for example in influencing the barriers of entry for new companies and the costs of bankruptcy.

FINANCIAL SYSTEMS IN FOUR SOCIAL SYSTEMS OF PRODUCTION

In this section the social systems of production approach is applied in the analysis of financial systems in the United States, United Kingdom, Germany, and Japan. Special attention is paid to the banking sector due to its importance for the provision of patient capital. While each financial system has important national peculiarities, this analysis emphasizes the broad similarities between Japan and Germany on the one hand and the United States and United Kingdom on the other. Thus the British financial system, though lacking the formal restrictions on financial contracting of interest to NIE, actually has a more unstable financial environment and is less able to provide patient capital than the United States.

Ownership of Financial Organizations

Germany and Japan are distinguished by the relative importance of alternatives to the privately owned, for-profit financial institution, particularly in the banking sector (see table 14.4). These financial institutions are either state-owned or have a cooperative structure. They are legally charged with serving specific types of customers; in many cases their mandate specifies provision of long-term capital to these customers. Their governance structures also help ensure that these goals are fulfilled through the inclusion of representatives of their customers. In the United Kingdom and United States the relative importance of alternatives to private for-profit banks is much smaller.

Table 14.4 Relative Share of Different Bank Ownership Forms

	U.K.	U.S.	Germany	Japan
Publicly Owned Banks	< 1%	< 1%	48%	24%
Cooperatively Owned Banks	24%	10%	16%	23%
Privately Owned Banks	75%	90%	36%	53%

Sources: Central Statistical Office Financial Trends, Federal Reserve Board Flow of Funds Accounts, Deutsche Bundesbank Monatsberichte, Tatewaki (1991: 100).

The importance of state ownership of banks is especially great in Germany. The public savings banks constitute the largest segment of the banking sector; most cities, many rural counties, and regional governments established savings banks in the nineteenth century to take care of their own financial business, to encourage savings among the working classes, and to finance local and regional infrastructure. These savings banks have expanded their lending activity to local and regional companies and have become the most important source of long-term credit for SMEs (Deeg, 1991). Germany also has a number of public and quasi-public special banks for long-term lending. These banks accept long-term deposits and issue long-term bonds, which enable them to provide long-term finance for SMEs, housing, agriculture, and other purposes (Vitols, 1994). Publicly owned banks alone account for half of all German banking assets.

Germany also has an important cooperative banking sector. The cooperative banking movement was started in the mid-1800s by artisans and small farmers who needed capital in order to modernize. Small business owners are the most important members of the cooperative banks and play an active role in their governance (Kluge, 1991). Cooperative banks account for 16% of total banking assets. Together, the publicly owned and cooperative banking sectors account for almost two-thirds of all banking assets in Germany (64%). This importance is surprising given the amount of attention that is paid to the three big joint-stock banks (Deutsche Bank, Dresdener Bank, and Commerzbank), who actually only account for 8 percent of total German bank assets.

In Japan state-owned and cooperative banks also are an important alternative to private for-profit banks and account for almost half of all banking sector assets (47%). Government-owned institutes include the Post Office Bank and the Trust Fund Bureau and account for a quarter of all banking sector assets; both of these use their deposits to fund public projects and to buy the bonds of the long-term credit banks. The long-term credit banks are also under government influence. Cooperative banks are also very important, accounting for almost another quarter of the banking sector's assets. Cooperative banking groups specialize in servicing specific sectors such as artisans, farmers, and fisheries (Tatewaki, 1991).

The relative importance of alternative ownership forms in the United States is much smaller. Concerns about adequate provision of financial services to communities traditionally have been addressed by protecting small privately owned community banks. These banks are assumed to be responsive to the needs of the community since their owners and directors are generally part of that community and because the prospects of the bank are clearly tied to the economic health of the community. The aggressive expansionary strategies of the large "money center" banks prompted most state legislatures at the beginning of the past century to protect their community banks by placing restrictions on branching activity, in the most extreme cases only allowing banks to have one office (unit banking) (White, 1983). Throughout the postwar period these restrictions have been increasingly circumvented through the use of bank holding companies and in the eighties many states partially or completely lifted branching regulations. As a result the private banking sector is increasingly dominated by large banks.

Only a handful of U.S. banks are publicly owned and account for less than one percent of total banking assets (Wyatt, 1988). More significant are the credit unions and the mutual savings banks, accounting for 10 percent of U.S. banking assets. Deposits also function as ownership shares, and the credit unions in particular make an effort to include their depositor/members in governance. However, these institutions are constrained in the extent to which they may lend to small businesses.

In the United Kingdom, the commitment to alternative ownership forms is also weak and has weakened further during the eighties. Since the beginning of this century, the banking sector has been dominated by a handful of London-based commercial ("clearing") banks. After the privatization of the Trustee Savings Bank, the only major public bank is the National Girobank, run by the Post Office.[13] The primary form of cooperative ownership is the building society; however, the building societies were only recently allowed to lend to small businesses (Mullineux, 1987).

The diverging ownership structures of financial institutions are influenced by the different general norms and values in the four countries. Anglo-American individualism has taken a much more critical view of government intervention in the economy and the barriers to gaining popular support for public institutions has been greater in the United Kingdom and United States than in Germany and Japan. Similarly, business organization in the Anglo-American countries has been weaker and less able to mobilize state support for the cooperative provision of services.

Sectoral Organization

The second major factor influencing the capacity of the financial system to provide patient capital is the stability of relations between financial institutions. A high degree of regulatory coherence encourages stability by constraining regulatory arbitrage and providing continuity in the standards financial institutions must adhere to. This in turn contributes to continuity in the structure of competition, which is important since instability can be caused by the attempt of new entrants to gain market share. Finally, a high degree of intra-sectoral cooperation contributes to stability by allowing for the collective management of liquidity and interest rate risk associated with long-term investment.

The greatest degree of regulatory incoherence among the four countries examined here exists in the United States. For most types of financial activities a dual regulatory structure exists, with regulatory agencies and standards at both the state and federal level. In addition, regulation is typically fragmented along functional lines. The typical U.S. bank is subject to three or four different regulators with partially overlapping responsibilities (Reinicke, 1994). At the federal level these include the Federal Reserve Board, the Comptroller of

Currency, and the Federal Deposit Insurance Corporation. Each state also has its own set of regulatory authorities.

This incoherence allows for regulatory arbitrage and instability in the competitive structure of the U.S. financial system. Banks can choose to be members of the Federal Reserve System as a national bank or as a state bank, or they may opt out of the Federal Reserve System as a state bank but remain part of the Federal Deposit Insurance scheme. Substantial differences exist between these regulatory regimes, and banks shift regimes or try to press down standards in their regime. Regulatory incoherence also allows for the emergence of new types of financial institutions and services in unregulated or lightly regulated settings. One of the most important new competitors to the banks for funds is mutual funds, which first appeared in the mid-seventies. These funds, which were not subject to interest rate regulation or insurance fund charges, were able to offer higher interest rates than banks and caused a large flow of funds out of the banking system during the high interest rate environment of the late seventies and early eighties (Greider, 1987). Finally, the level of cooperation between financial institutions is relatively low in the United States. In the banking sector, cooperation typically takes the form of bilateral "correspondent bank" relationships between a smaller community bank and a larger regional bank for check-clearing services, liquidity management, and loan participations. Concentration in the U.S. banking system in the eighties has often taken the form of regional banks buying up the smaller community banks they have a banking relationship with.

The degree of formal regulatory coherence is higher in the United Kingdom; supervisory responsibility for commercial banks rests squarely with the Bank of England and for building societies with the Building Societies Commission. Nevertheless, since the early seventies the regulatory authorities have been wrestling with the problem of different degrees of regulation among similar categories of financial institutions. Under the old system of informal regulation, a bank could gain more "recognition" from the Bank of England as it progressed up the ladder of regulatory standards. This system was set up under the assumption that greater recognition was enough of an incentive to adhere to stricter standards. In the second half of the sixties, however, this assumption broke down as the largest "clearing banks" themselves set up subsidiaries in the less-regulated categories in order to participate in more speculative lending activity such as real estate. Much of this lending was done through "liability management," i.e., loans were made and then the funds to cover them were sought by offering higher interest rates (Grady and Weale, 1986). Steps have been taken to increase regulatory coherence by imposing common standards on all banks. However, the contribution of these steps to stability has been undermined by the lifting of deposit interest rate regulations and lending restrictions on building societies in the mid-eighties. Building societies have aggressively moved into consumer and small business lending and contributed to the inflationary "credit boom" of the second half of the eighties (Mullineux, 1987). The degree of cooperation between financial institutions is also low in the United Kingdom. Banking is dominated by a few large banks and most risk management takes place within the individual banks themselves. The main institutionalized form of cooperation is the Committee of London Clearing Banks, which provides check clearance services. Liquidity management is done by the banks through a small number of discount houses on the London money market.

The German financial system in contrast has had a high degree of regulatory coherence throughout the postwar period. The ultimate supervisory responsibility for each category of financial institution is clearly defined and rests with one regulatory agency. For the banking sector, the Federal Banking Supervisory Office has clear oversight over all banks. Common standards are defined for all types of banks in the central piece of legislation regulating the banking sector (*Kreditwesengesetz*) and in the regulations of the supervisory office. The high degree of regulatory coherence has allowed for an orderly introduction of new financial services; such new services are authorized after a process of consultation of the banking associations with the federal supervisory office. The fact that the three main banking groups (private, public and cooperative) all offer the same broad array of financial services and introduce new services at roughly the same time has also helped stabilize the structure of competition within the financial system. The pattern of foreign entry has also contributed to stability, since new foreign competitors have entered the German financial markets through the purchase of existing institutions rather than the establishment of new subsidiaries. Finally, the German financial system is characterized by a high degree of cooperation between financial institutions. In the banking system, inter-bank deposits account for about one-quarter of total bank liabilities. Much of these inter-bank liabilities exist between members of the public savings bank or cooperative banking associations as part of their liquidity and interest rate risk management strategies. However, there is substantial cooperation between bank groups as well, for example in loan participations (Deeg, 1991).

The Japanese financial system also has a high degree of regulatory coherence, though not quite as high as in Germany. Regulatory responsibility for the banking system is lodged in the Bank of Japan and in the Bank Bureau of the Ministry of Finance. The Japanese financial system is highly segmented by type of financial product and customer group, clearly defining the competitive structure of each of these segments. Financial service innovations have been introduced in an orderly fashion after a period of consultation between the banking associations, the Bank of Japan, and the Ministry of Finance (Hall, 1993). Moreover, the Japanese financial system is characterized by a relatively high degree of cooperation. Banks and insurance companies in the same *keiretsu* have a division of labor, with the latter providing longer-term finance to industrial companies. Each of the cooperative banking groups has a national bank assisting the local banks in the management of lending risk. Finally, the Bank of Japan itself is a substantial lender to other Japanese banks (Tatewaki, 1991).

Financial system organization is influenced by the structure of the state and the nature of state policies in the four countries. In the United States, fragmentation of public power between the state and federal level is reflected in the regulatory incoherence of the dual banking system. In the United Kingdom, an emphasis on informal state regulation through personal supervision and moral suasion allowed for the emergence of a largely unsupervised "secondary" financial system in the sixties. In Germany and Japan, in contrast, a greater emphasis on formal national regulation allows for the development of clear common standards for entire classes of financial institutions. The importance of interfirm coordination also affects the organization of the financial system and its capacity to provide patient capital. In Japan and especially in Germany, associations help stabilize competition and support long-term lending through joint risk management.

Characteristics of Sources of Funds

The third factor influencing the capacity of financial institutions to provide patient capital is the degree of stability in funding sources. The interest rate risk involved in long-term investment will be low if the cost of funds is stable over time. Similarly, the liquidity risk involved in long-term investment will be low if there is a steady supply of new funds to financial institutions. Financial institutions in systems where there is much volatility in these characteristics such as the United States and United Kingdom will be exposed to much greater risk in the provision of patient capital than in countries with less volatility, such as Japan and Germany (see table 14.5).

Japan has the greatest stability in the cost of funds. This is largely attributable to the strict regulation of interest rates on deposits for most of the postwar period. In 1987, 80 percent of deposits at Japanese banks were interest-rate regulated (Federation of Bankers Associations of Japan, 1993). Regulation of interest rates also helps stabilize the quantity of funds supplied in Japan, since financial institutions are constrained in their ability to increase their share of funds at the expense of other institutes by bidding up interest rates.[14]

German financial institutions also enjoy a high degree of stability in the characteristics of their funding sources. While formal regulation of interest rates on deposits was ended in 1967, German banks run an informal interest rate cartel.[15] The ability of German banks to increase the maturity structure of their deposits also contributes to stability; almost half of bank liabilities have maturities of four years or more. Finally a very high degree of stability in household savings behavior results in a steady flow of new funds to financial institutions.

In the United States in contrast there is a high degree of volatility in the characteristics of sources of funds. Bank deposits are overwhelmingly short term in nature and the cost of these deposits is highly responsive to short-term interest rate fluctuations. Since the lifting of regulations on deposit interest rates with the Depository Institutions Deregulation and Monetary Control Act of 1980, competition between different groups of financial institutions such as commercial banks, S&Ls, and money market funds for household savings has become fierce. Large commercial banks pursuing aggressive expansionary strategies through liability management techniques have also contributed to a high degree of volatility by bidding up interest rates to attract funds (Greider, 1987). The household rate of savings has declined during the eighties and U.S. banks have increasingly depended on volatile international markets for funding; the banking system actually experienced a net outflow of funds in 1990 and 1992.

Table 14.5 Characteristics of Sources of and Demand for Funds, 1980–92

		U.K.	U.S.	Germany	Japan
Cost of Bank Funds as a % of Assets	Annual Average	8.1%	6.1%	5.3%	4.7%
	Variance	1.69	1.94	0.85	0.73
Increase in Quantity of Bank Deposits	Annual Average	16.3%	5.6%	6.6%	8.8%
	Variance	68.08	17.5	2.35	8.46
Net Borrowing of Non-financial Corporations as % of GDP	Annual Average	0.74%	1.2%	3.59%	6.11%
	Variance	3.65	2.46	4.11	5.05
Business Failure Rate per 10,000 firms		120 (est)	92	57	90 (est)

Sources: OECD National Accounts 1960–1992, OECD Bank Income Statistics, Central Statistical Office Annual Abstract of Statistics, Statistical Abstract of the U.S., Statistisches Bundesamt, Japan Statistical Yearbook.

Financial institutions in the United Kingdom have experienced the greatest degree of volatility in their funding sources. As in the United States, bank deposits are overwhelmingly short term and the cost of these deposits is highly responsive to money market interest rate fluctuations; less than 5 percent of British sterling deposits have maturities of one year or more (Grady and Weale, 1986: 23). Since the late sixties the more lightly regulated subsidiaries of the large clearing banks have followed aggressive liability management techniques. The deregulation of building societies in the mid-eighties and their subsequent aggressive bid for deposits also contribute to this instability. In 1991 the British banking system also experienced a net outflow of sterling deposits.

The greater stability in the characteristics of savings in Germany and Japan can be attributed to a number of elements of the social system of production. Cooperation between firms is sanctioned by the general norms and values of these two societies; these norms are reflected in law, which in both countries distinguishes between "good" and "bad" cartels. The strong emphasis on individualism and competition in the Anglo-American countries contributes to a more critical view of inter-firm cooperation and stronger antitrust policies. The industrial relations systems in Japan and Germany also enhance the financial system's capacity to provide patient capital by contributing to stability in household income and savings behavior. Large Japanese companies are committed to lifetime employment and go to great lengths to keep their workers despite business slowdowns. German companies face numerous legal constraints and costs in laying off workers; in addition, the government offers subsidies for short-time working arrangements. U.S. and British companies in contrast face few effective constraints on rapid workforce reduction and household income is more severely affected during downturns.[16]

Characteristics of the Demand for Funds

A fourth factor influencing the financial system's capacity to provide patient capital is the characteristics of the demand for funds from non-financial companies. Volatility in the demand for credit from companies reduces the incentives of financial institutions to develop patient sources of funds. The greater the relative weight of SMEs, especially of high-wage high-investment SMEs, the greater will be the demand for patient capital. Finally, a high business failure rate discourages financial institutions from providing patient capital due to the high credit risks involved in long-term lending.

The demand for new funds by non-financial companies in Japan and Germany is steadier than in the United States and United Kingdom. (see table 14.5).[17] In addition, non-financial companies in Germany and Japan are consistent and substantial net borrowers. U.K. and U.S. companies in contrast have accumulated substantial financial assets of their own and become net lenders competing with financial institutions when financial conditions become favorable. The U.S. non-financial corporate sector was a net lender in three years (1980 to 1983) of the twelve years between 1980 and 1992; the British non-financial corporate sector was a net lender in six of these years (1981 to 1986).

As indicated earlier in section one, the relative importance of SMEs is greater in Germany and Japan than in the United States and United Kingdom.

Furthermore, the demand for patient capital from the average German or Japanese SME is greater than from comparable SMEs in the United States and United Kingdom due to the greater incentives for long-term investment; supplier SMEs in Germany and Japan typically enjoy more stable relations with their larger customers, and single sourcing is widely used in Japan. Many German SMEs are also producers of sophisticated capital goods and they invest heavily in R&D, worker skills, and new technology. Finally, German SMEs are constrained to pay high wages and benefits and thus have an incentive to follow high-investment strategies (Vitols, 1994).

There are also substantial differences in the business failure rate between the countries. Germany has the lowest business failure rate and thus the lowest degree of credit risk associated with long-term investing. Japan and the United States have roughly similar business failure rates. The United Kingdom has by far the highest business failure rate.

A number of aspects of the social system of production affect stability in the demand for patient capital. The high degree of inter-firm cooperation in many German and Japanese industries between supplier and customer firms increases the incentives for asset-specific investment and thus the demand for patient capital. Industrial relations systems in large Japanese companies and in German industry as a whole, which encourage stability in employment and high investment strategies, also increase the demand for patient capital. Finally, state policies regarding the ease of new business formation influence the credit risk involved in long-term lending; the bankruptcy rate is lowest in Germany, and is partially attributable to the exclusion of marginal firms through high barriers to the establishment of new firms.

CONCLUSION

One of the basic lessons of the social systems of production approach is the difficulty of successfully transferring aspects of one country's institutional structure to other countries. Elements of the social system of production are complexly interwoven and the performance of the system as a whole is dependent upon these links. Thus the transference of one element of this system to another country without its supporting links is unlikely to bring about the change in performance desired. While the ceteris paribus nature of reasoning in the NIE approach allows it to develop powerful microeconomic models, the limits of usefulness of this approach become apparent when applied to cross-national differences. National systems differ along a whole set of variables, thus the "other things being equal" assumption typically does not hold. Furthermore, institutional changes designed to alter one element will typically feed back and change other elements.

The policy recommendations of the new institutional economics with regard to the financial system are an excellent illustration of this point. One aspect of the financial system, the financial contracting links between financial institutions and non-financial companies, is examined and a correlation with economic performance is noted. Models generating results consistent with the performance variable are developed and, in the case of the United States, deregulation is advocated in order to allow financial actors greater freedom in financial contracting. However, the social systems of production approach shows that the system as a whole must be examined in order to anticipate the changes induced by introducing changes in the regulation of financial contracting. In the worst-case scenario, deregulation may actually decrease stability for the system as a whole and thus defeat the intention of the original policy initiative.

Attempts to increase the supply of patient capital in the United States must therefore look beyond the relationship between financial institutions and non-financial companies. Policy initiatives must take into account the dependence of patient capital on factors such as stability in industrial relations and the employment relation, the coherence of financial regulation, the stability of relations between financial institutions, and the nature of ownership of these financial institutions. Given the differences between countries in these arrangements, solutions for the problem of patient capital and for other problems in the United States and other countries must be tailored to the existing social system of production.

NOTES

1 Earlier work stressing convergence includes Kerr, et al. (1960) and Schonfield (1965). An important early statement of the differences in national financial systems is Zysman (1983).

2 Interest is also being driven by the crisis in the regulation of the savings and loan and commercial banking sector. The German universal banking system, which allows financial institutions to diversify risk across different product markets, has also been seen as an attractive alternative to the fragmented U.S. system.

3 For an analysis of exit versus voice strategies see Hirschman (1970). For an analysis of the negative consequences of exit strategies for company investment see Porter (1992) and Jacobs (1991).

4 This distinction between market-based and relational financial systems differs somewhat from the traditional distinction between bank-based and market-based systems stemming from Gerschenkron (1962). This alternative distinction recognizes that, under certain circumstances, other financial organizations may also be important relational investors; Japanese insurance companies for example are important lenders to industry.

5 Unless otherwise noted, all figures in this section will refer to 1989. The broad definition of bank is used here to include all institutes authorized to take deposits and

make loans.

6 Equity held for long-term investment is the most patient form of capital; however, equity held for speculative purposes is impatient. Loans with long maturities are more patient than loans with shorter maturities. Finally, loans made with floating rates of interest are less patient than loans with fixed rates of interest, since uncertainty in the finance costs of investment due to fluctuations in general interest rates are borne by the company, not by the bank.

7 This article focuses on nominal financial indicators, since financial contracts are generally denominated in nominal rather than in real terms.

8 Williamson (1988) distinguishes between transaction cost economics and the property rights approach. Berglöf (1990) further breaks down the latter into traditional property rights theory, agency theory, and the new property rights approach.

9 For many decades financial economics had been based on the Modigliani-Miller theorem, which stated that the choice of different financial instruments was inconsequential for real decisions within the firm (Modigliani and Miller, 1958). Financial structure could thus be studied separately from other aspects of the firm. Explanations for variations in capital structure were thus sought primarily in differences in taxation or the costs of bankruptcy.

10 In the late eighties, only one U.S. bank, Citibank, was among the world's largest forty banks. Japan accounted for twenty-three of these banks, Germany for five, France for four, the United Knigdom for three, Switzerland for two, and Italy and Hong Kong each for one (American Banker, 1989).

11 This core thesis is also shared by the national models of capitalism approach (Soskice, 1992) and the regulation school (Boyer, 1990).

12 Financial institutions are also concerned with *inflation risk*, which is the risk that the real value of long-term assets may be wiped out by inflation; and for those institutions involved in international investment, *exchange rate risk*, which is the risk that an asset is denominated in a currency that will decrease in value.

13 The Trustee Savings Banks (TSBs) could be considered a stunted version of the German public savings banks. The TSBs originated in the nineteenth century as pure savings repositories, and only in the seventies did they develop into full-fledged banks. In 1973 a government commission recommended that the TSBs be developed into a "third force" alongside the clearing banks and building societies; in that year a central TSB was established to act as a banker to the regional TSBs and in 1976 the TSBs were permitted to lend. The TSBs were high on the Thatcher government's privatization list and were publicly floated in 1986.

14 Recently, however, Japan has deregulated its deposit interest rates; the impact of deregulation on the cost of funds will be dependent upon the success of banks in coordinating in the determination of interest rate policies and in capturing long-term fixed-rate deposits.

15 German regulatory authorities have often sanctioned or even encouraged the development of cartels in order to foster stability and control the problem of excess competition among financial institutions as well as in other sectors. In response to the

banking crisis of 1931, the German state authorized an interest rate cartel among banks. In response to the financial chaos in the reconstruction period, a committee of banks was also formally authorized to organize the timing and volume of securities issues; this committee controlled access to these markets until the late eighties.

16 Increases in household income are roughly twice as volatile in the United States and United Kingdom as they are in Germany and Japan (own calculations from OECD data).

17 The variance in the demand for funds is roughly equal to the average level of net borrowing in the first two countries; in the United States and especially in the United Kingdom, the variance is considerably higher than the average demand for new funds.

15

The Role of Institutional Processes in the Formation of Worker Cooperatives in Israel, 1924–1990

Raymond Russell, Robert Hanneman

Social scientists in many disciplines are increasingly inclined to view the decision to form a new business as not simply a rational response to economic opportunity by individual entrepreneurs, but as a consequence of a wide range of sociological processes. "New institutionalists" like DiMaggio and Powell (1983, 1991), for example, have argued that choices about organizational structure are shaped not only by "competitive" processes, but also by a number of "institutional" processes that are political, cognitive, or normative. Population ecologists like Delacroix and Carroll (1983) and Carroll and Hannan (1989) see the formation of new firms as not just a result of isolated choices by individual actors, but as also being determined by the influences of one entrepreneur on another, and of the aggregate of all past decisions on each subsequent choice. In recent work, Carroll and Hannan (1989) also now view these decisions as being governed not only by "competitive" processes, but by processes of "legitimation" as well. These points may be particularly applicable to the formation of cooperative organizations. The motivation to form a cooperative is often attributed to the values of founders who reject conventional capitalist structures for normative reasons (Rothschild-Whitt, 1979; DiMaggio and Powell, 1983). Where such explicitly anti-capitalist values are absent, the formation of a cooperative is at the very least a rejection of individual rationality in favor of some form of collective self-help (e.g., Russell, 1984). Because cooperatives are innovative organizations whose economic viability has often been questioned (e.g., Weber, 1978: 137–138; Williamson, 1975: chapter 3, 1985: chapters 9 and 10; Jensen and Meckling, 1979), their formation is also likely to be highly subject to the "cognitive" processes of legitimation featured by DiMaggio and Powell (1983) and by Carroll and Hannan (1989), in which the success of pioneering organizations plays an important role in demonstrating the feasibility of a new organizational form, and in which failures of such innovative organizations can have equally important discouraging or "delegitimating" effects.

The present study explores the role of such processes in the formation of worker cooperatives in Israel from 1924 through 1990. These "worker cooperatives" are not the cooperative agricultural settlements of Israel's countryside, the "kibbutzim" and "moshavim." They are instead a lesser-known population of production, service, and transportation cooperatives located in Israel's cities and towns. Although they are less famous than their rural counterparts, these urban worker cooperatives have also been quite prolific (see figure 15.1 and table 15.1).

Figure 15.1   Worker Cooperatives in Israel 1924–1992

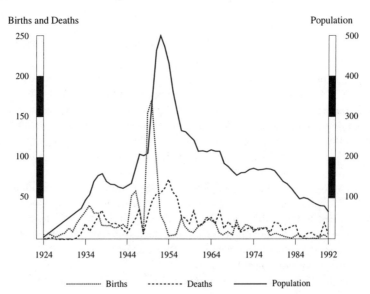

Table 15.1 Births, Deaths, and Density by Sector and Industry

Industry	Initial Year	Initial Density	Total Births	Mean Birth Rate	Total Deaths	Mean Death Rate	Density in 1990	Mean Density
Transport	*(1926)*	1	*169*	*15.2*	*160*	*7.5*	*10*	*22.6*
Passenger Transport	(1929)	2	36	8.8	34	5.3	4	7.2
Motor Freight	(1926)	1	50	10.4	45	6.0	6	9.9
Other Transport*	(1930)	3	78	16.6	81	15.3	0	9.5
Services	*(1926)*	2	*277*	*13.1*	*255*	*8.2*	*24*	*39.3*
Food	(1935)	1	38	14.4	36	8.4	3	5.7
Restaurants/Hotels	(1929)	1	30	10.4	28	7.1	3	5.4
Cultural Activities	(1927)	1	44	12.6	41	7.8	4	6.8
Other Services	(1926)	2	173	12.7	161	8.3	14	23.5
Production	*(1924)*	*3*	*731*	*14.7*	*695*	*8.7*	*39*	*93.3*
Baking	(1933)	3	94	9.8	93	7.2	4	23.3
Woodworking	(1926)	1	71	14.3	64	7.4	8	10.3
Printing/Paper	(1925)	2	48	8.7	41	5.2	9	9.3
Electrical/Metal	(1924)	2	82	12.4	77	8.1	7	12.2
Building	(1924)	1	127	17.6	122	10.7	6	12.3
Cement/Sand/Drill	(1932)	1	31	13.4	30	7.2	2	4.0
Textiles	(1929)	1	72	14.4	72	10.4	1	7.3
Food Processing	(1937)	4	54	12.4	56	10.7	2	7.2
Leather/Shoes*	(1926)	1	33	14.5	34	13.0	0	5.0
Other Production*	(1927)	1	105	26.6	106	21.4	0	12.3
Sector Unknown	*(1924)*	*1*	*30*	*14.7*	*30*	*10.1*	*1*	*3.1*
Total	*(1924)*	*4*	*1210*	*14.7*	*1140*		*74*	*156.3*

* Statistics are calculated from the first year in which organizations existed in the industry and sector, i.e., from the first year in which density was non-zero. Each subsequent birth was treated as a 100% increase when density was zero. Initial densities are for the beginning of the year shown. Total number of births and deaths are to year-end, 1990. Average annual births and deaths are a percentage of population density at year start. Mean density is the average of annual density adjusted for initial year. All means are estimated through the end of 1990, with the following exceptions (*): Other Transport (1930–69); Leather/Shoes (1926-77); and Other Production (1927–77).

The population of these cooperatives is much smaller now than it has been at any time since the 1920s, but it continues to employ about 1.5 percent of Israel's non-agricultural labor force, making this in relative terms one of the largest populations of worker cooperatives in the Western world (Ben-Ner, 1988: 8). Most of this employment is accounted for by two large bus cooperatives, Egged and Dan, which together provide almost all of the regularly scheduled bus transportation in contemporary Israel.

This chapter explores the role played by institutional processes in the initial growth and later decline of this population. After a brief discussion of data and measures, we examine the effects of demographic variables derived from population ecological theories of density dependence and population dynamics. This analysis explores the extent to which the effects of ecological variables like population density and the number of recent formations and dissolutions within a population depend on inferences that potential organizational founders draw from them regarding the appropriateness and feasibility of an innovative organizational form. A later section turns to the role played by the changing historical, social, and political environment of Israel in accounting for the waxing and waning of worker cooperative births.

Putting together these two sources, and eliminating duplications, we were able to obtain at least partial records on a total of 1,356 worker cooperatives. The principal requirement for the analyses that follow was to obtain data on the year of formation and the year of dissolution, where applicable, of each coop- erative in this population. One or both of these two pieces of information was missing for a total of 142 cases, which were therefore deleted from our sample. We do not consider the loss of these cases to be a serious omission, because they constitute only about a tenth of all recorded births. Moreover, since these cases with incomplete information appear for the most part to be unusually short-lived cooperatives, we suspect that our data underestimate by no more than 5 percent the number of Israeli worker cooperatives that were alive at any given time.

Of the two sources we used to identify our total sample of 1,214 usable cases, it was the Registrar's records that proved to be more complete, as the Cooperative Center did not begin to maintain a systematic roster of all its member cooperatives until the mid-forties. Even after that time, its records omitted information about unaffiliated cooperatives. We were able to find slightly less than half of our cases (582) on both lists. For 508 cases we have information from the Registrar alone, and 124 cases are known to us only from information supplied by the Cooperative Center. It was somewhat surprising to find so many cases that are unknown to the Registrar. Some of these appear to be extremely short-lived cases that went out of business before they could complete the process of being registered. A report by the Registrar published in 1938 noted that many worker cooperatives were going through a trial phase of one or two years before formally registering; while technically against the law, this practice was being tolerated by the mandatory officials (Registrar of Cooperative Societies, 1938: 106, 108). The absence of other cooperatives from the Registrar's records is less easy to explain, but they appear to be valid cases, as this group includes several living cases such as Egged. Since Egged was created as a merger of several existing cooperatives, it seems likely that its official registration is in one of these extinct names.

For the 582 cooperatives for which we had two sets of records, we compared the two dates of formation and two dates of dissolution, and when they differed, we always took the earlier date. Like Don (1968), who used similar data, we were concerned that the Registrar or the Cooperative Center might have incurred delays in receiving or recording information about cooperative births and deaths. In general we found that the two sets of estimates were reasonably close. Where the two sets of estimates differed by more than two years, we attempted to resolve the discrepancy by consulting the complete listings of the Cooperative Center membership that were available to us for a total of six years (1931, 1949, 1960, 1975, 1988, and 1989).

COMPETITION, LEGITIMATION, AND THE POPULATION ECOLOGY OF COOPERATIVE BIRTHS

Density Dependence

According to the theory of density dependence (Hannan and Freeman, 1987; Caroll and Hannan, 1989) the number of new formations in any population of organizations in any time period is a positive but curvilinear function of the "density" or size of the population at the beginning of that period. The effect of density is curvilinear because population increases have different consequences for "competition" and "legitimation," depending on whether density is low or high. When density is low, even small additions to the population can have a strong legitimating effect, demonstrating the viability of a new form of business, and offering concrete examples to imitate. Competitive pressures, on the other hand, remain low at this point. When density is high, on the other hand, further additions to the population no longer carry a significant legitimating effect, as the virtues of the given organizational form are already widely known. At these high population levels, however, further increments to the population do cause competitive pressures to become increasingly problematic, and these pressures have the effect of discouraging additional births.

This theory of density dependence has now been successfully tested on a number of diverse populations (Hannan and Freeman, 1987; Carroll and Hannan, 1989; Singh and Lumsden, 1990). Before testing it in this population, however, it is first necessary to ask whether the assumptions of the theory are in fact applicable here. The set of all worker cooperatives in a single country may not qualify as a "population" in the conventional sense of the term. Its members are heterogeneous with respect to industry, or economic "niche," and in most cases they constitute only a small fraction of the firms in any single industrial branch. Is it reasonable to expect the formation of cooperatives in one industry to stimulate the formation of cooperatives in another? Can one validly speak about competitive pressures among firms that together account for only a small portion of the total output of any given industrial field?

These questions add special significance to the testing to hypotheses within individual industries and sectors that will be presented later in this section. But for the present, we will note only that we do believe that the answer to both of these questions is yes. It is our impression that in a country as small as Israel, if not elsewhere, the various members of the worker cooperative movement do constitute a single population, in at least some senses of this term. They keep a close watch on one another, and stimulate each other's development. And they do compete for many of the same resources, even when they operate in different fields. For example, they have competed in the past for the financial resources and technical assistance that have occasionally been made available to worker cooperatives by such sources as the Jewish Agency, the Israeli government, and the Cooperative Center. Perhaps above all, they compete for the limited supply of workers who wish to help found cooperative organizations, about which we will have more to say below. The results of our effort to test the predictions of the theory of density dependence with data on the full population of Israeli worker cooperatives are shown in the first column of table 15.2. As predicted by the theory, the linear form of density has a statistically significant positive effect on cooperative births. The squared form of density appears here to have a negative or discouraging effect on births, as predicted by the theory, but in this case the effect falls short of statistical significance.

Population Dynamics

An alternative view of organizational formations is the "population dynamics" theory of Delacroix and Carroll (1983) and Carroll and Huo (1986). This model looks at the effects on organizational founding rates not of population size or density, but of the two component processes that make it up: organizational births and organizational deaths. In the simplest version, also known as "rate dependence," the number of new organizational births in any given time period is posited to be a positive but curvilinear function of the number of births in the previous period. Unlike the theory of density dependence, the population dynamics theory gives no consideration to the consequences of population changes for processes of legitimation; it confines its attention to their implications for processes of competition alone. Thus small increases in the number of births are seen as stimulating additional births, because they act as "signals" of a hospitable competitive environment. As in the theory of density dependence, however, large numbers of births are seen as discouraging additional births, because they cause competitive pressures to set in.

The neglect of legitimation processes is not serious in this case, because taking them into account has no other consequence than to uncover additional reasons for making the same prediction. As in the theory of density dependence, small numbers of births can be expected to increase legitimation by demonstrating the viability of a new form or organization, and offering a set of examples to imitate. As births proliferate, on the other hand, additional births would yield increasingly diminishing returns, as the potential demonstration effect attributable to each new population member would gradually be exhausted. This reduction in the positive mimetic effect of births at higher values would produce a negative coefficient for the square of births along with a positive coefficient for the linear form of births, as the theory predicts on the basis of reasoning about competitive processes alone. For both of these sets of

Table 15.2 Negative Binomial Regression Models on ln (Birth Counts), 1924–1990[a]

	I		II		III		IV		V	
	b	S.E.	b.	S.E.	b.	S.E.	b.	S.E.	b.	S.E.
Intercept	1.119*	(.638)	1.592**	(.236)	1.661**	(.301)	1.652**	(.241)	0.894**	(.230)
Density	0.014**	(.007)							0.011**	(.002)
Density Squared[b]	-0.018	(.015)							-0.016**	(.005)
Recent Births			0.075**	(.024)	0.076**	(.024)	0.076**	(.024)	0.058**	(.009)
Recent Births Squared[b]			-0.348	(.227)	-0.350	(.227)	-0.347	(.226)	-0.253	(.069)
Recent Deaths					-0.007	(.042	-0.004	(.008)	-0.024	(.005)
Recent Deaths Squared[b]					0.039	(.717)				
Dispersion	1.599**	(.366)	0.993**	(.186)	0.985*	(.189)	0.985*	(.189)	0.343**	(.059)
Log Likelihood	-249.66		-239.61		-239.46		-239.46		-244.93	
Baseline Log Likelihood	-257.30									

* p < .10   ** p < .05.

a Estimates of parameters are calculated by maximum likelihood under the assumptions of a negative binomial process generating log(births), using LIMDEP. The model is equivalent to exponential Poisson regression with the exception that overdispersion is modeled parametrically. Overdispersion is often interpreted as serial correlation within observations, or positive contagion.

b In thousands.

reasons, we join the population dynamics theorists in expecting the number of new formations of Israeli worker cooperatives in any given year to be a positive but curvilinear function of the number of new formations in the previous year. This prediction is tested in the second column of table 15.2. The results shown there are once again supportive. As expected, the linear form of recent births of worker cooperatives has a significantly positive effect on births in the current year. As in the case of density, the squared term once again appears to have the predicted negative effect, but this effect falls short of statistical significance.

The population dynamics theory views the "rate dependence" of current births on recent births as a "baseline" against which the effects of all additional influences on organizational formations are to be measured and judged. Within the population dynamics theory, the next most important of these additional influences is the frequency of recent "dissolutions" or organizational "deaths." As in the case of the effect of recent births on current births, the number of current births within a population is posited to be a positive but curvilinear function of the number of recent deaths. The reasoning for this is once again based solely on a consideration of the consequences for competition of organizational deaths. According to Delacroix and Carroll (1983), a small number of recent deaths creates competitive opportunities, in the form of former customers of defunct firms whose demands are no longer being met, and idle factories and equipment that a later entrant to the field might readily put to use. Large numbers of recent deaths, on the other hand, signal that something has gone wrong with an environment as a whole.

This prediction from population ecology has received less consistent empirical confirmation than have the theories of density dependence and rate dependence. While the findings of a number of studies have been confirmatory (Singh and Lumsden, 1990), those of others have been unsupportive, including the findings of Carroll and Huo (1986). In a study of foundings of state bar associations, Halliday, Powell, and Granfors (1987) predicted and found a linear negative effect of prior failures on current foundings, arguing that even small numbers of failures can signal environmental adversity. Similar linear negative effects of prior failures on current foundings have been reported by Barnett and Amburgey (1990), by Olzak and West (1991), and by Budros (1992).

This frequent incidence of disconfirmatory results becomes more understandable when the consequences of recent failures for legitimation are taken into account. While the consequences of recent deaths for competition have been conceived by various authors to be either positive or negative and possibly dependent on their levels, their consequences for legitimation are unambiguously and uniformly negative. From the point of view of legitimation, recent deaths should decrease rather than increase the current rate of births, because they would discourage potential organizational founders, and cast doubt on the viability of an organizational form. And there is no reason to expect this negative effect of recent deaths on the perceived legitimacy of any form of organization to be reduced at higher values, as deaths that reach epidemic proportions might have a de-legitimating effect that is still greater than that caused by small accumulations of individual dissolutions.

We consider a negative and linear effect for recent deaths on current births to be especially likely in the present case, because this is a population in which the negative effects of dissolutions on legitimation can be expected to outweigh whatever favorable consequences they may have for processes of competition. Cooperatives in general seem particularly vulnerable to concerns about their legitimacy, given the long history of skepticism about their viability as an economic form. The population dynamics theorists' arguments about competition, on the other hand, seem less relevant to the present case. Given the heterogeneity of this population with respect to industry, it is hard to see how the death of a cooperative in one industry could stimulate the formation of new cooperatives in another. Even within a single industry, the death of a cooperative might indeed free up resources, but the availability of alternative ownership models within the same industry makes it highly likely that it will be a noncooperative organization that makes use of the idle equipment and satisfies the unmet demand.

Population dynamics models that test these two alternative formulations of the effects of recent deaths are shown in the third and fourth columns of table 15.2. The third column tests for the positive and curvilinear effect of recent deaths as posited by Delacroix and Carroll (1983). The prediction is not confirmed, as neither the linear nor the squared form of recent deaths has a significant effect, and the signs of both coefficients are in directions opposite to that predicted by the theory. The fourth column tests for a linear negative effect of recent deaths as reported by Halliday, Powell, and Granfors (1987), Budros (1992), and other researchers, and as predicted for this population on the basis of the arguments invoked above. In this case the expectation is supported, although the negative linear effect of recent deaths shown here does not quite attain statistical significance. In the final column of table 15.2, the terms of this last population dynamics model are brought together with the terms of the density dependence model to produce a more comprehensive model of the population ecology of the formation of new organizations in this population. When introduced simultaneously, all five terms retain the signs that were predicted and observed in the previous analyses, but in this case all also attain statistical significance.

Competition and Legitimation within Industries and Sectors

In tables 15.3 and 15.4, we retest the final and more comprehensive model from table 15.2 within a number of specific sectors and industries. Table 15.3 tests the effects within each sector or industry of the density, recent births, and recent deaths in the entire population of worker cooperatives in Israel. Table

15.4 tests the effects of the density, recent births, and recent deaths recorded in that specific sector or industry. Our expectation was that the population parameters from the full population and from the specific industries or sectors would in all cases be similar in their effects, with one exception. For the reasons discussed above, we expected the effects of recent deaths in the full population on current births in specific sectors and industries to be negative in all cases. Within specific industries, however, we saw a greater chance that the negative effect of recent deaths on legitimation might be countered by the positive effect of reduction in competition that was posited by Delacroix and Carroll (1983). That is, there is a much greater chance in these instances that deaths within a given industry might indeed be freeing up resources that lead to the creation of new firms within the same field. For this reason, we expected recent deaths within specific industries to show a pattern of weaker or more mixed effects, while the effects of recent deaths in the entire population are more uniformly negative.

A comparison of the effects of recent deaths in table 15.3 with those in table 15.4 shows that this expectation is largely met. The effects of recent deaths in the entire population are estimated to be negative in every test, and are statistically significant in most. The effects of the industry- or sector-specific count of recent deaths on current births are statistically significant in only four out of seventeen industries, not much more than one would expect if the relationship between these variables was governed by chance alone. The signs of the effects estimated for recent deaths within industries are also quite erratic, as they are negative in ten cases, and positive in seven. This supports our expectation that recent deaths within specific industries have few systematic effects on organizational births in those industries, while recent deaths in the full population have a consistent pattern of negative effects that are in keeping with the arguments and evidence that were introduced above.

The effects estimated for the other variables included in these models are also generally consistent with the predictions and findings presented earlier. Of parameters taken from the full population, the effects of the linear and squared forms of density and recent births are in the predicted direction in almost every test, and attain statistical significance in most. This highly consistent pattern of findings further validates the arguments invoked earlier in support of our treatment of the Israeli worker cooperatives as a single population, despite their heterogeneity with respect to industry.

The effects attributed to the industry- and sector-specific forms of density and recent births in table 15.4 are also generally as predicted, although less frequently significant. We suspect that the lower incidence of statistically significant results on this table may be more attributable to statistical considerations than to theoretical ones. Counts of recent births and density within specific industries are generally confined within a small range. The lower variances in these variables leads to a loss of statistical power. And when counts of births are

Table 15.3. Negative Binomial Regression Models of ln (Birth Counts) on Cooperative Movement Levels of Independent Variables, by Sector and Industry[a]

	Density	Density Squared[b]	Recent Births	Recent Births Squared[b]	Recent Deaths	Dispersion	Log Likelihood[c]
Transport (1926–90)	-.001 (.006)	-.006 (.015)	.103** (.023)	-.459** (.141)	-.046** (.021)	.944** (.393)	-115.39 (-131.75)
Passenger (1929–90)	-.007 (.009)	.029 (.018)	.140** (.048)	-1.505** (.625)	-.083** (.035)	.746 (.878)	-53.26 (-62.91)
Freight (1926–90)	.020** (.007)	-.034** (.017)	.050** (.021)	-.177 (.130)	-.040* (.021)	.410 (.407)	-64.01 (-77.31)
Other Transport (1930–69)	.024 (.025)	-.172 (.114)	.058 (.055)	.034 (.889)	-.043 (.045)	.334 (.328)	-45.91 (-67.61)
Services (1926–90)	.020** (.003)	-.028** (.006)	.022* (.012)	-.075 (.077)	-.030** (.009)	.257** (.092)	-150.39 (-165.31)
Food (1935–90)	.003 (.018)	.004 (.004)	.084 (.052)	-.452 (.349)	-.038 (.045)	2.197** (1.270)	-55.59 (-60.29)
Restaurants/Hotels(1929–90)	.009 (.009)	-.016 (.013)	.049** (.016)	-.199** (.090)	-.018 (.026)	0.000	-49.26 (-59.81)
Cultural Activities (1927–90)	.016** (.008)	-.026 (.017)	.021 (.022)	-.082 (.147)	-.016 (.020)	.393 (.438)	-67.78 (-72.96)
Other Services (1926–90)	.027** (.005)	-.044** (.011)	.019 (.016)	-.021 (.093)	-.023* (.013)	.388* (.197)	-113.45 (-134.38)
Production (1924–90)	.015** (.004)	-.021* (.011)	.055** (.020)	-.235 (.202)	-.023** (.009)	.792** (.217)	-195.43 (-221.79)
Baking (1933–90)	.040** (.006)	-.041** (.009)	.026** (.010)	-.109** (.054)	-.094** (.018)	0.000	-85.52 (-173.55)
Woodworking (1924–90)	.015* (.008)	-.018 (.021)	.038 (.031)	-.156 (.350)	-.016 (.018)	1.084* (.611)	-80.40 (-90.05)
Printing/Paper (1925–90)	.022* (.007)	-.040** (.012)	.033** (.013)	-.137* (.078)	-.008 (.017)	0.000	-64.85 (-82.58)
Electrical/Metal (1924–90)	.017** (.005)	-.016 (.013)	.042* (.025)	-.187 (.162)	-.063** (.023)	.642 (.408)	-86.63 (-100.18)
Building (1924–90)	.015** (.004)	-.018 (.013)	.069** (.015)	-.304 (.195)	-.059** (.012)	.295** (.111)	-100.92 (-117.61)
Cement/Sand/Drill (1932–90)	.040** (.011)	-.045* (.015)	.032* (.018)	-.118 (.101)	-.093** (.034)	0.000	-40.40 (-73.39)
Textiles (1929–90)	.034** (.006)	-.034** (.009)	.025** (.011)	-.110* (.063)	-.099** (.020)	0.000	-87.48 (-92.95)
Food Processing (1937–90)	.040** (.008)	-.063** (.013)	.034* (.020)	-.065 (.103)	-.079** (.013)	.028 (.211)	-78.89 (-97.99)
Leather/Shoes (1926–77)	.020 (.015)	-.032 (.032)	.017 (.036)	-.007 (.221)	-.013 (.022)	.730 (.947)	-48.89 (-55.65)
Other Production (1927–77)	.024** (.010)	-.035 (.026)	.025 (.026)	-.050 (.264)	-.039** (.014)	.488* (.295)	-78.72 (-94.92)

*p < .10
** p < .05

a Estimates of parameters are calculated by maximum likelihood under the assumptions of a negative binomial process generating log(births), using LIMDEP. The model is equivalent to exponential Poisson regression with the exception that overdispersion is modeled parametrically. Overdispersion is often interpreted as serial correlation within observations, or positive contagion.

b In thousands.

c The first figure shown is the log-likelihood for the model. In parentheses, the log-likelihood for the intercept-only model is given.

Table 15.4. Negative Binomial Regression Models of ln (Birth Counts) on Sector and Industry-Specific Levels of Independent Variables, by Sector and Industry[a]

	Density	Density Squared[b]	Recent Births	Recent Births Squared[b]	Recent Deaths	Dispersion	Log Likelihood[c]
Transport (1926–90)	.054 (.037)	-.574 (.751)	.441** (.117)	-18.673* (9.747)	-.088 (.060)	.727** (.288)	-114.02 (-131.75)
Passenger (1929–90)	.410 (.427)	-20.480 (25.742)	1.213** (.625)	-162.534 (120.253)	.174 (.283)	1.323 (1.022)	-56.75 (-62.91)
Freight (1926–90)	.178 (.215)	-7.937 (11.481)	.159 (.526)	49.494 (177.017)	-.521 (.352)	.998 (.556)	-71.36 (-77.31)
Other Transport (1930–69)	.201** (.057)	-3.880** (1.505)	.294** (.101)	-17.225** (7.006)	-.180** (.055)	0.000	-68.48 (-117.87)
Services (1926–90)	.032 (.030)	-.187 (.267)	.156 (.091)	-3.039 (4.735)	-.034 (.060)	.810** (.253)	-154.18 (-165.31)
Food (1935–90)	.399 (.525)	-.019 (.036)	1.645 (1.242)	-379.062 (334.992)	.169 (.695)	2.799** (1.722)	-57.56 (-60.29)
Restaurants/Hotels (1929–90)	.410 (.405)	-32.022 (34.423)	.691 (1.469)	-1.618** (.737)	-.498 (.365)	.267 (.650)	-54.16 (-58.08)
Cultural Activities (1927–90)	-.174 (.306)	18.471 (20.348)	-.442 (.509)	49.530 (171.296)	-.400 (.312)	.383 (.496)	-68.26 (-72.96)
Other Services (1926–90)	.104** (.050)	-1.781** (.906)	.144 (.145)	.122 (10.379)	.013 (.106)	.745** (.295)	-112.30 (-134.38)
Production (1924–90)	.020** (.008)	-.049 (.031)	.093** (.035)	-.559* (.304)	-.032 (.020)	.990** (.262)	-200.83 (-221.79)
Baking (1933–90)	.014 (.096)	-.336 (1.402)	.462 (.463)	-14.606 (48.843)	-.047 (.236)	1.742** (.630)	-82.15 (-90.78)
Woodworking (1926–90)	.040 (.147)	-1.074 (6.814)	.189 (.438)	2.592 (78.513)	.047 (.213)	1.765** (.723)	-85.69 (-90.05)
Printing/Paper (1925–90)	.359 (.309)	-22.421 (19.002)	.777 (.584)	-84.533 (204.152)	.184 (.256)	.457 (.443)	-71.41 (-77.57)
Electrical/Metal (1924–90)	.048 (.119)	-2.040 (4.336)	.417 (.446)	-15.304 (81.094)	.121 (.318)	1.311** (.465)	-94.21 (-100.18)
Building (1924–90)	.117 (.112)	-1.671 (2.271)	.443** (.200)	-14.687 (18.216)	-.290** (.138)	1.269 (.485)	-101.77 (-117.61)
Cement/Sand/Drill(1932–90)	.219 (.412)	-13.390 (24.057)	.259 (1.172)	27.595 (185.500)	-.058 (.446)	2.280 (1.654)	-47.09 (-70.39)
Textiles (1929–90)	.486** (.119)	-5.847 (4.535)	-.335 (.509)	11.406 (100.476)	-.819** (.310)	1.141** (.599)	-70.39 (82.95)
Food Processing (1937–90)	.304** (.064)	-6.515** (1.601)	.462** (.092)	-8.733 (7.223)	-.152 (.148)	0.000	-62.79 (-109.37)
Leather/Shoes (1926–77)	.428 (.372)	-27.593 (23.946)	1.283 (.926)	-145.247 (189.283)	.285 (.558)	.986 (.933)	-43.70 (-55.65)
Other Production (1927–77)	.122** (.045)	-2.257 (1.166)	.582* (.196)	-14.983 (9.790)	-.403** (.180)	.355 (.250)	-78.26 (-94.92)

* p < .10
** p < .05
a Estimates of parameters are calculated by maximum likelihood under the assumptions of a negative binomial process generating log(births), using LIMDEP. The model is equivalent to exponential Poisson regression with the exception that overdispersion is modeled parametrically. Overdispersion is often interpreted as serial correlation within observations, or positive contagion.
b In thousands.
c The first figure shown is the log-likelihood for the model. In parentheses, the log-likelihood for the intercept-only model is given.

limited to relatively low numbers, they may not grow high enough to allow the initially positive linear effects of this variable to tip in a negative direction at higher values. We believe that this is why the squared form of recent births appears to have positive effects on current births in some of these industries.

These differences in statistical power between the estimates in tables 15.3 and table 15.4 may also have played some role in producing the generally weaker and more mixed pattern of effects for recent deaths in table 15.4 than in table 15.3. In this regard it may be relevant to note that in the four instances in table 15.4 in which estimates of the effects of recent deaths attain statistical significance, this variable has the same negative effect as that reported in table 15.2 and table 15.3. This in turn would suggest that even within industries, where they seemed most likely to be applicable, arguments about the consequences of recent dissolutions for competition have little relevance, or are at least outweighed by the delegitimating institutional consequence of recent deaths. But the estimates of the effects of recent deaths in table 15.4 continue to stand out by virtue of being so widely mixed in sign. We also continue to suspect that the capacity of recent deaths within a given industry to liberate resources may have played a role in producing this unique pattern of results.

THE EFFECTS OF THE SOCIAL AND POLITICAL ENVIRONMENT ON THE FORMATION OF COOPERATIVES

While the population ecology of organizations emphasizes the influence on individual organizations of the experiences of other similar organizations, it also directs attention at influences of the environment in which a population is embedded. In table 15.5, we test the effects of a number of characteristics of the Israeli social and political environment on the formation of worker cooperatives in Israel over the period of this study.

Of the factors within Israeli society that seemed most likely to influence the number of new worker cooperatives that were created in each year, we gave pride of place to the number of new immigrants that had arrived in the country in the previous year. Several considerations prompted us to attach special significance to this factor. The formation of worker cooperatives has long been viewed in Israel as a particularly appropriate way to create jobs for new immigrants, both by many of the immigrants themselves, and by the political and philanthropic organizations that sought to help them find employment. In the pre-state period, both the values and the interests of many immigrants and of the organizations that assisted them led to a preference for forms of organization that would be collectively rather than individually owned (Russell, 1995). By the time of independence in 1948, if not before, newly arriving immigrants showed distinctly less socialist or Zionist fervor; but by this time the past pattern had already been well institutionalized, and Israel's new socialist government continued to treat the formation of worker cooperatives as a favored technique for the absorption of new immigrants.

To test the effects of immigration on the formation of worker cooperatives in this study, we obtained data on the annual number of new immigrants entering Israel between 1948 and 1990 from the Statistical Abstract of Israel 1991. Information about the years from 1924 to 1947 was obtained from Janowsky (1959). In the analyses that follow, we examine the effect on the number of cooperatives formed in a given year of the number of immigrants who arrived in the previous year. We conceive the effect of immigration as a lagged effect on the grounds that new immigrants must spend a certain amount of time learning a new language and establishing contacts before they can proceed to the establishment of a new firm.

The effect of the number of immigrants in the immediately previous year on the number of worker cooperatives formed in the current year is shown in the first column of table 15.5. The effect is significantly positive as predicted. This finding is also consistent with those reported by previous studies that dealt only with the post-state period (Don, 1968; Russell and Hanneman, 1992). In analyses not shown here, we also found that the unlagged form of immigration appears to have effects on the formation of worker cooperatives that are similar to but slightly weaker than the effects obtained with this one-year lag. We also observed that immigration in a given year continues to raise the annual count of new cooperatives for several years after it occurs.

The second and third columns of table 15.5 attempt to measure the effects of another major set of influences, in this case the entire set of changes that have taken place in Israeli society between 1924 and the present. Israel is a far different society today than it was in the twenties, thirties and forties. In the early years, the Jewish community in Palestine was led and typified by its Zionist pioneers, the people who tamed the wilderness and created the kibbutz. This was a period in which Israel's entire cooperative movement enjoyed exceptionally high legitimacy and prestige. Members of bus cooperatives like Egged, who maintained contact with isolated settlements in times of trouble at great personal risk, shared in the same high esteem in which the kibbutzniks were held. In recent decades, on the other hand, the public standing of Israel's cooperative institutions has almost steadily declined. The cooperative bus companies are now regularly accused of price gouging. The moshavim have lurched from chronic crises to almost total collapse, and the kibbutz itself has been mired for more than a decade in economic losses, soul-searching, and self-doubt (Rosner, 1993). Israeli society as a whole, in the meantime, now strikes many observers as being a much more individualistic and materialistic society than it was in the days of its pioneers (Eisenstadt, 1985; Chafets, 1986).

Thus Israeli society in general seems to be a less conducive environment for the formation of worker cooperatives today than it was in the past. For this reason, we introduce a term for "Year" in the second and third columns of table

15.5. The second column indicates that as predicted, the passage of time has indeed had a significantly negative impact on the formation of worker cooperatives in Israeli society. The third column shows that this effect of "Year" is independent of the effects of changing patterns of immigration, as each of these variables retains a statistically significant effect when both are included in the same model.

Table 15.5 Effects of Social and Political Environment on ln (Birth Counts), 1924–1990[a]

	I		II		III		IV		V		VI	
	b	S.E,	b.	S.E.	b.	S.E.	b.	S.E.	b.	S.E.	b.	S.E.
Density	0.04	(.003)	.031**	(.003)	.028**	(.003)	.029**	(.004)	.025**	(.004)	.026**	(.004)
Density Squared[b]	-.009*	(.005)	-.041**	(.006)	-.038**	(.005)	-.038**	(.005)	-.034**	(.006)	-.032**	(.006)
Recent Births	.063**	(.008)	.002	(.012)	.002	(.010)	-.007	(.012)	.004	(.010)	-.008	(.012)
Recent Births Squared[b]	-.330**	(.044)	.025	(.128)	-.007	(.006)	.025	(.061)	-.017	(.058)	.028	(.059)
Recent Deaths	-.007	(.007)	-.047**	(.007)	-.039**	(.009)	-.041**	(.010)	-.036**	(.008)	-.038**	(.009)
Lag Immigration	.011**	(.002)			.007**	(.004)	.010**	(.004)	.007**	(.003)	.011**	(.004)
Year			-.066**	(.007)	-.066**	(.007)	-.055**	(.013)	-.056**	(.010)	-.039**	(.016)
Statehood							-.586	(.603)			-.871	(.594)
Likud									-.856*	(.481)	-1.037**	(.487)
Dispersion	.287**	(.047)	.224**	(.085)	.191**	(.074)	.184**	(.091)	.183**	(.070)	.173*	(.093)
Log Likelihood	-242.21		-200.57		-197.07		-196.51		195.54		-194.33	

* p < .10   ** p < .05
a See note a to table 15.2.
b In thousands.

These two columns of table 15.5 also indicate that when this control for the effect of "Year" is introduced, the coefficients for the linear and squared forms of recent births are greatly reduced in size, and lose their statistical significance. This suggests that in the face of this long-term trend of declining societal legitimacy, recent births lack the capacity to be a sufficiently potent legitimating force on their own. The effects of density, density squared, and recent deaths, on the other hand, appear to be sharpened by the inclusion of this control for the effects of changing years, and are strongly significant throughout the remaining analyses in table 15.5.

In the final three columns of table 15.5, we test the extent to which the effects of the past six and a half decades of Israeli history can be attributed to two discrete historical events: the attainment of independence in 1948, and the ascent of the Likud bloc to power in 1977. Our expectation regarding independence is that it would have a negative impact on the formation of cooperatives in Israel in the long run, despite the fact that annual birth counts soared to their highest levels ever in the first two or three years after statehood was attained. The spike in cooperative formations in 1949–51, we suspect, was more an effect of immigration than of statehood itself. We expect the impact of statehood itself on cooperative births to be negative, because it deprived the Israeli cooperative movement of much of its rationale. In the period before statehood, the Israeli cooperative movement in its many forms served the Zionists as their main weapons in the struggle for independence. After statehood was achieved, this struggle had been won; and for Israelis who still wished to serve their country, the principal threats were now external, and the path to public service led into the army or the government, not the cooperative movement.

We also expected to find that the Likud victory in 1977 would prove to have been another major blow to the Israeli cooperative movement. This prediction was based in part on the fact that the ascent of Likud meant a withdrawal of patronage, as cooperative institutions like the kibbutz and the Cooperative Center would no longer receive from the Likud government the preferential treatment they had enjoyed in the past from their socialist allies in the government. More broadly, the Likud victory has been seen as a sea change in Israeli society as well as in Israeli politics (Shalev, 1990). The defeat of the socialist leaders who had dominated Israeli society since the twenties did much to help transform Israel into the pro-capitalist, individualistic, and materialistic society that it appears to be today (Eisenstadt, 1985; Chafets, 1986).

These expectations are tested in the final three columns of table 15.5. The estimates suggest that statehood may indeed have had a slight depressing effect on the formation of worker cooperatives in Israel, but that this effect falls short of statistical significance. The effect of the Likud victory is more strongly negative, and is clearly significant. Interestingly, however, neither statehood, nor the Likud victory, nor the two in combination can fully account for the negative influence of "Year." This variable continues to exert a negative and statistically significant effect on the formation of worker cooperatives in Israel, even after the effects of these two distinct historical events have been taken into account. We interpret the residual negative influence of this variable as capturing the cumulative effects of numerous smaller and unmeasured changes in Israeli society that have helped to make it a less conducive environment for the formation of worker cooperatives over time.

CONCLUSION

We have had much to say about legitimacy, values, and other "institutional" influences in this paper, without introducing any direct evidence about any of these things. We have not measured any attitudes, have not actually observed any norms in operation, and never caught any organizations in the act of imitating one another.

We regret the absence of more direct measures of institutional processes in this study, but believe that the indirect manner in which we have explored these phenomena can readily be justified. First of all we would note that in confining ourselves to this inferential approach, we are in excellent company. Some of the best and most persuasive demonstrations of the importance of the normative and mimetic processes that are the subject of this study have relied on many of the same indirect approaches to measurement that we have used here (e.g., Tolbert and Zucker, 1983; Fligstein, 1985; Singh, Tucker, and House, 1986; Carroll and Hannan, 1989). Insofar as one can validly study these processes inferentially, we have found plenty of additional evidence for them here. In light of the impressive accumulation of evidence that documents their effects, we believe that the burden of proof is now increasingly shifting onto those social scientists who continue to leave no room for normative or mimetic processes in their models. It is they who should now be called upon to defend their positions, or to begin to revise their theories.

A theory that strikes us as being particularly ripe for such revision is the population dynamics theory of Delacroix and Carroll (1983). Population ecology has already seen a demonstration of the value of incorporating processes of both competition and legitimation into one theory in the form of the density dependence theory of Carroll and Hannan (1989). While density dependence has at least temporarily eclipsed population dynamics in the work of population ecologists, the life and range of population dynamics theory could also be extended, if it could simply be broadened to bring the effects of births and deaths for legitimation as well as for competition into its scope.

Consider first the implications of processes of legitimation for the relationship between recent foundings in an organizational population and current foundings. A positive relationship between recent foundings and current foundings might have been predicted on institutional grounds alone; in the vocabulary of DiMaggio and Powell (1983), for example, it would be an instance of "mimetic isomorphism." The reasoning about "competition" invoked by population dynamics theory thus deserves unambiguous credit only for the additional stipulation that this effect is curvilinear. That both sets of processes contribute to such compatible predictions may help to explain why this set of predictions of population dynamics theory is so empirically robust (Singh and Lumsden, 1990). The implications of recent deaths for competition and legitimation, on the other hand, may work at cross-purposes, making their effects on current foundings in general a weaker and less universal set of effects. The net effects of these contradictory processes might add up differently, depending on whether the consequences of recent deaths for competition or legitimation are more salient in any particular case. Thus recent organizational failures may indeed stimulate new formations in an industry like wine production, in which recent deaths do relatively little to undermine the legitimacy of an organizational form, but clearly do free up resources like grape fields that readily contribute to the formation of new firms (Delacroix and Solt, 1988). The deaths of worker cooperatives in Israel, in contrast, served as signals that an innovative form of organization was in trouble, and on that other hand probably left few usable resources behind.

These considerations may also help to explain an apparent discrepancy between our findings and those of Staber (1989). Staber examined the effects of recent failures on current foundings in three populations of cooperatives in Atlantic Canada: consumer cooperatives, marketing cooperatives, and worker cooperatives. Among consumer cooperatives and marketing cooperatives, recent failures had the same linear negative effect on current foundings as we have found here, and has been reported by Halliday, Powell, and Granfors (1987), and by Budros (1992) and others. Among worker cooperatives, however, Staber found the positive curvilinear effect of recent failures on current foundings predicted by Delacroix and Carroll (1983). A partial explanation of the difference between his findings and ours on this point may lie in the fact that the worker cooperatives in his sample were much longer lived than those in ours. His Canadian worker cooperatives had a median life expectancy of nearly eighteen years, while those in Israel lived only about four years. The inference is justifiable, therefore, that the deaths of worker cooperatives in Atlantic Canada were much more likely than in Israel to leave meaningful resources behind, and were less likely to cast doubt on the viability of an organizational form.

The main point of these examples is to argue that by explicitly taking into account the implications of organizational births and deaths for processes of legitimation as well as for competition, population dynamics can acquire the flexibility to cover all of these situations. Without such amendments, its scope is inherently limited to the narrow universe of organizational populations to which institutional processes do not apply. With these additions, on the other hand, it joins the theory of density dependence in illustrating how an "institutionally informed" population ecology of organizations can "extend the reach" of ecological analysis (Fombrun, 1988). Thus the ecological analyses in the first half of this paper have a theme that is in fact very similar to those of the second half, which were much more explicitly devoted to the effects of social and political contexts. Both of these discussions have emphasized the fundamental point that economic choices are not made in a social vacuum. We hope that this paper has helped to identify some of the many ways in which this is true.

NOTE

Research for this chapter was carried out with the help of a grant from the United States–Israel Educational Foundation. We thank Amnon Bar-On of Israel's Cooperative Center and Uri Seligman, Israel's Registrar of Cooperatives, for making available to us the data on which this article is based. We have received valuable assistance in this research from Asaf Darr, Orna Al-Yagon, Neal Hickman, Vered Mirmovich, and Patricia Hanneman. We have also benefited from the comments and suggestions of Howard Aldrich, Art Budros, Glenn Carroll, Michael Conte, Jacques Delacroix, Yehuda Don, Michael Hannan, Arie Shirom, Udo Staber, and Avi Weiss.

16

Exporting the American Model—Historical Roots of Globalization

Marie-Laure Djelic

The world, we are told, is getting smaller, increasingly seamless and it all has to do with "globalization" (Ohmae, 1994; Held, et al., 1999; Giddens, 1999; Friedman, 1999). The movement seems to lead inexorably to the worldwide convergence of economic, technological, and institutional conditions, fostering in the process a homogenization of organizational recipes and national systems of economic organization (Scott and Meyer, 1994; Kanter, 1997). Furthermore, if we believe the popular business press, the Internet revolution is significantly accelerating the pace at which this transformation is taking place.

There is evidence, though, that the Panglossian discourse characteristic of much writing on economic globalization is often little more than that—unduly optimistic discourse. Whole regions or continents are still entirely excluded from the global world economy (Sachs, 2000). In those countries that are part of it, the divide is in fact increasing between institutions, organizations, and social groups that welcome and benefit from a global economy and those that dread, resent, and resist it. Furthermore, there are clear signs that important differences persist to this day between national systems of economic organization, including within the small circle of countries that participate in the global economic game. In spite of global pressures, national recipes for organizing the economy are apparently quite resilient (Hollingsworth and Boyer, 1997; Whitley, 1999; European Business Forum, 2000a, 2000b).

There has been little overlap between the prophets of a global world economy and those who point to the long-term persistence of "national variants" of capitalism (Albert, 1993). The tendency has been to either account for convergence beyond national boundaries or document significant and resilient differences across countries. While those two approaches differ on many grounds, their common weakness is that each provides only a partial picture of our economic world and its evolution after 1945. In contrast, this chapter starts from the observation that both trends characterize at the very same time the post-World War II period. A key puzzle is the fact that differences between national systems of economic organization have persisted while similarities were undeniably increasing. The challenge is to propose an account that can make sense of the co-existence of these two apparently contradictory trends and of their lasting interplay throughout the second part of the twentieth century. This requires, on the one hand, a deconstruction of globalization—in terms of both historical origins and mechanisms. It also calls for a systematic focus at the point of articulation between "global pressures" and national legacies.

After briefly reviewing the existing literature and its shortcomings, we define "national systems of economic organization" and operationalize our dependent variable, documenting the co-existence, after 1945, of the double trend identified above. Building on detailed historical studies of three countries—France, Germany, and Italy—and on their systematic comparison (Djelic, 1998), we then put forward the following story. The current episode of globalization finds its historical roots in the attempted process of Americanization that marked the years following the end of World War II. Starting in those years, the American system of economic organization—which had itself emerged earlier in peculiar and unique conditions—was constructed as a universal model for the Western world. The large-scale and systematic attempt to transfer this one and single model accounts in the end for the increasing similarities that can be documented across national systems of economic organization in the second half of the twentieth century. A key driving force behind the attempt at cross-national transfer was, at least throughout the early period, a multi-national network of "modernizers" working with or around the Marshall Plan administration. The attempted transfer did not take place in a vacuum, though, and it turned out as a consequence to be more or less successful in each country. To a significant extent, differences in the degree to which national peculiarities have persisted reflect the strength of incumbent rules and institutional legacies in a particular country, the effectiveness of channels of transfer, and the level of resistance nationally.

BEYOND GLOBAL CONVERGENCE AND NATIONAL PATHS—THEORIZING THE INTERPLAY

The literature on national systems of economic organization is by now rich and varied. There have been two major preoccupations, each often in practice exclusive of the other. The first has been with convergence and increasing similarities across national borders, particularly throughout the twentieth century. The other has been with the unique character and long-term resilience of national models.

Pointing to economic and technological drivers, evolutionary arguments emphasize convergence (Chandler, 1962, 1977, 1990; Williamson, 1975, 1985). The logic of change, in those arguments, is neutral and universal. It has to do with the "laws of the market," with "technological progress" or with "transaction costs." The defining claim of evolutionary arguments is that under those unavoidable pressures, national systems of economic organization are bound to evolve quite significantly. They move ultimately towards a common—most efficient—set of institutional and organizational arrangements.

Another research tradition also focuses on convergence, explaining it, though, from quite a different perspective. For neo-institutionalists in the "phenomenological tradition" (Djelic, 1999) structural convergence is driven by increasingly homogeneous institutional environments the world over (Scott, Meyer, et al., 1994). Human life is structured by sets of cultural rules and norms. The latter have had a tendency, particularly throughout the second part of the twentieth century, to become more and more similar across national boundaries—rationalization describing the overall evolution. In this research tradition, national economies and their constituent parts are defined as emergent social constructions embedded in larger institutional environments understood as sets of cultural rules and norms. Homogenization of institutional environments across national boundaries logically drives worldwide isomorphism in structural arrangements and behavioral scripts, including—but not only—in the economic and business realm.

While there are important differences between evolutionary arguments and "phenomenological" neo-institutionalism, some of the conclusions are shared. In both cases, systems of economic organization evolve in response to inescapable demands stemming from the environment—whether understood in its economic and technological dimension or as a set of cultural rules. Transformations at the national level are understood to take place along a predetermined trend or continuum, implying parallel convergence towards a unique—and in the case of evolutionary arguments, superior—set of structural arrangements. Both evolutionary arguments and "phenomenological" neo-institutionalism tend to see differences across countries as temporary. They tend to explain away remaining national specificities by the particular stage of evolution of a given country or by unduly strong obstacles on the evolutionary path. Ultimately, those are likely to fade. Altogether, evolutionary arguments and "phenomenological" neo-institutionalism can help us account for increasing similarities between national systems of economic organization. However, their common determinist and quasi-functionalist nature means that they have a tendency to remain blind to timing, historical embeddedness, actors and resistance. They do not allow us to understand the long-term resilience of differences and the stubborn multiplicity of national systems of economic organization.

In striking contrast to the preoccupation with convergence and isomorphism, research on national variants of capitalism highlights resilient differences. The double objective in that research tradition has been to account for the peculiarities of any given national system of economic organization and to explain the long-term persistence of structural differences across national boundaries. A common argument emerges where systems of economic organization are described as embedded in unique institutional environments, historically structured, at least in their modern form, at the national level. Overall, and as a consequence, we propose to label that tradition "historical neo-institutionalism" (Djelic, 1999). There are two slightly different understandings, though, of the nature of institutional environments that coexist under this broad label. One is cultural (Dobbin, 1994; D'Iribarne, 1989). The other is more structural (Fligstein, 1990; Campbell, Hollingsworth, and Lindberg, 1991; Hollingsworth and Boyer, 1997; Whitley, 1999).

The proponents of a cultural understanding point to national cultures as socially constructed belief and rule systems embodied in a set of basic practices. Historically, the argument goes, different sets of beliefs have been stabilized and institutionalized at the level of each nation, creating the context for different logics of action and multiple "rationalities." Ultimately, national systems of economic organization are shaped by those stable and long-standing rules (Dobbin, 1994; D'Iribarne, 1989). The structural perspective underscores on the other hand the importance of states and political institutions as key elements of the constraining institutional framework (Evans, Rueschmeyer, and Skocpol, 1985; Fligstein, 1990; Campbell, et al., 1991; Hollingsworth and Boyer, 1997; Whitley, 1999). Early patterns of state building and political choices at key turning points become structural constraints that channel individual action and significantly limit the possibility for change. Those structural institutional legacies create path dependencies at the national level, which national systems of economic organization tend to reflect.

Beyond differences between the cultural and structural perspectives, all arguments in the "historical neo-institutionalist" tradition tend to share a common weakness. By restricting the embedding environment to its national dimension, they forget or disregard cross-national isomorphic pressures, which as a matter of fact are working their way in the real world despite or around local peculiarities. Tracing differences across national borders to country specific constraints, those accounts fail to consider the geopolitical environment as a potential source and engine of change and transformation.

In the end it seems that there is room for theoretical cross-breeding. If we are going to account for the paradoxical interplay between increasing worldwide isomorphism and national path dependencies—and not merely for one trend or the other—then we need a framework that allows us to focus on both trends at the same time. We will show below how a combination of phenomenological neo-institutionalism with historical neo-institutionalism of the structural kind make it possible to go quite a way in that direction.

NATIONAL SYSTEMS OF ECONOMIC ORGANIZATION—
DEFINITIONS AND METHODS

A system of economic organization is defined here as a particular constellation of rules and structures that shapes economic activity. Historically, and in the age of the nation-state, these constellations have tended to be defined by national states (Weiss, 1988; Dobbin, 1994; Whitley, 1999). Since those national states have been characterized by varying levels of autonomy and infrastructural power (Mann, 1986), there is bound to be, in some cases, a degree of decoupling between the dominant national system of economic organization and the particular functioning of any given region or industry. The discussion that follows will tend to neglect decoupling and internal variation, remaining for the sake of simplicity at the national aggregate or ideal type level. Our question can thus be reformulated in the following way. How can we explain that quite distinct national ideal types have persisted throughout the second part of the twentieth century in spite of increasing similarities between national systems of economic organization?

Although exact definitions differ slightly, the concept of "national system of economic organization" proposed here is compatible with Chandler's "forms of capitalism," Whitley's "business systems," and Piore and Sabel's "industrial divides" (Chandler, 1990; Whitley, 1999; Piore and Sabel, 1984). We picture a national system of economic organization as having six constitutive dimensions. As illustrated in figure 16.1, the productive entity dimension represents the central one into which the other five feed. This chapter focuses on the productive entity dimension reducing in a somewhat schematic, but nevertheless expedient way, national systems of economic organization to their centrally constitutive dimension. The productive entity dimension covers both the nature of firms and the nature of their interactions. As shown in table 16.1, the nature of firms is operationalized through size, ownership, and internal (or organizational) structure. The dominant structure and logic of markets is used as a proxy for firm interaction.

Figure 16.1 National Systems of Economic Organization—Six Constitutive Dimensions

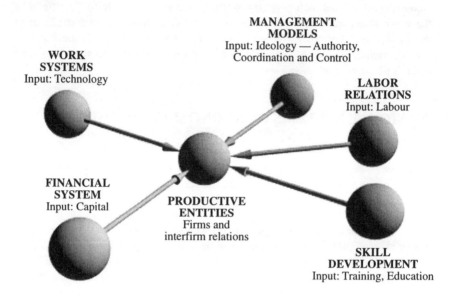

Table 16.1 Productive Entity—Operationalization

	Nature of Firm		Firm Interaction
Size	Ownership structure	Organizational structure	Logic of markets

The productive entity dimension varies in some or all four elements from country to country. Regular patterns can be identified throughout history, though, pointing to a typology of systems of economic organization or forms of capitalism. In this typology, presented in table 16.2, family and organized capitalisms are two variants of the same type, dominant in Western Europe until World War II. Corporate capitalism, on the other hand, is a radically different type, emerging in the United States at the turn of the twentieth century. In the post-World War II period, the transformation—when it took place—of national systems of economic organization was generally towards the structural model originally pioneered by the United States and labeled here corporate capitalism. This is documented below for productive entities, by looking at evolution on all four elements—size, ownership, organizational structure, and logic of markets—in three Western European countries, France, West Germany, and Italy. The choice of countries was oriented by methodological requirements. Considering the nature of the research question, comparative historical analysis appeared to be the most appropriate methodological framework (Skocpol, 1979; Djelic, 1998).

Combining detailed case studies with systematic comparison, it could handle at the same time both regularities across cases and national specificities. The choice of cases, though, is key for this methodological framework to work. Comparison becomes a real tool of analysis if selected cases allow for both the "method of agreement"—positive comparison—and the "method of difference"—negative comparison (Mill, 1843; Skocpol, 1979; Djelic, 1998). France and Germany were selected here as positive cases, where outcomes proved sufficiently similar and systems of economic organization have tended to evolve towards the American model, although in a somewhat different context. Italy was included as a negative case, where the national system of industrial production appeared comparatively much less affected by isomorphic trends.

Table 16.2 National Systems of Economic Organization—A Typology

	Laissez Faire Capitalism	*Family Capitalism*	*Organized Capitalism*	*Corporate Capitalism*
Size	Small firms	Small / medium-sized firms	Small / medium-sized firms	Large firms
Ownership Structures	Personal ownership	Personal ownership or partnership	Partnership or mixed forms*	Joint stock, dispersed public ownership
Organizational Structures	Not mentioned "black box"	Not formalized or rationalized	Not formalized or functional	Functional or multidivisional
Logic of markets	Free markets	Loosely organized markets	Formally organized markets	Antitrust— "hierarchies" and oligopolies

* By "mixed forms," we understand here those legal structures which are essentially crossbreeds of "partnerships" and "joint stock companies," such as for example the German GmbH, the French SARL or "Société en commandité." Those forms are located somewhere in between personal and public ownership.

Size

In a number of Western European countries, the number and role of large firms increased quite significantly during the two decades that followed the end of the war (Cassis, 1997). As shown in figure 16.2, the twenty years following the end of World War II have been characterized in West Germany or in France by rapid and radical changes in the size structure of productive entities.

Figure 16.2   Distribution of Industrial Labor Force by Size of Establishments

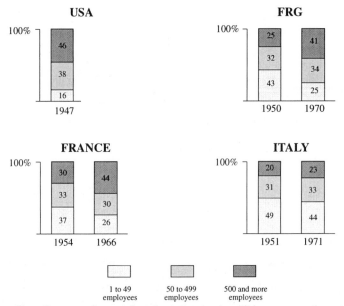

Note: Those figures are for manufacturing industry only; utilities, energy and construction are not included.
Sources: Bureau of the Census (1951, 1971), Statistisches Bundesamt (1954, 1974), INSEE (1956, 1974), Istituto Centrale di Statistica (1955, 1976).

Over those twenty years, West German and French firms became increasingly similar to their American counterparts at least as far as size and physical boundaries were concerned. The relative stability of Italian productive entities with respect to their size, also documented in figure 16.2, appears in contrast all the more striking. Small units retained in that country a predominant role throughout the period.

Ownership Structures

Together with variation in the size of productive entities and in the physical boundaries of firms came an evolution of their legal identities and of ownership structures. From 1950 to 1970, ownership structures characterized by a dispersion of ownership and limited liability—defining elements of the corporate structure—became increasingly popular in France and in West Germany as figure 16.3 underscores. In both countries, the widespread adoption of corporate ownership structures came with a sharp decrease in the total number of sole proprietorships. In the meantime, in Italy, the number of firms adopting corporate structures also increased but to a less significant extent while the overall number of sole proprietorships remained relatively stable.[1] There were, on the other hand, national specificities with respect to the types of corporate ownership structures adopted in each country. In France and in Italy, the preference went to joint-stock companies. In West Germany, limited liability companies and limited partnerships were clearly favored over the public joint-stock corporation.[2]

Figure 16.3 Joint-Stock Companies, Limited Liability Companies, and Limited Partnerships. Percent of Total Industrial Firms

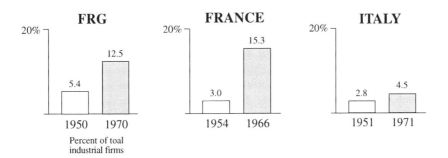

Note: Those figures are for manufacturing industries only; utilities, energy and construction are not included.
Sources: INSEE (1956, 1974), Statistisches Bundesamt (1953, 1973), Istituto Centrale di Statistica (1955, 1976).

Organizational Structures

The postwar period also witnessed the adoption of new modes of internal organization in Western European firms. The multi-divisional firm, in particular, pioneered in the 1920s by a couple of American corporations, spread at a quick pace among large French and West German firms, starting in the 1950s. The multi-divisional structure, or M-form, was characterized by decentralization and a rational reorganization of the firm's activities along product lines. A general office was in charge of coordination and long-range planning (Drucker, 1946; Chandler, 1962; Sloan, 1963). Figure 16.4 below shows that the multi-divisional structure was unknown in Europe in 1950.

Twenty years later, around 40 percent of the largest French- and German-owned manufacturing concerns had adopted the M-form. Large Italian firms,

Figure 16.4 Multidivisional Structure in Large Manufacturing Firms

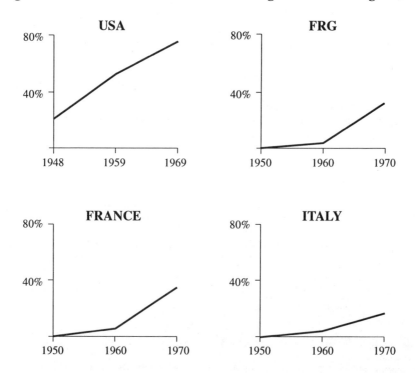

Sources: Fligstein (1990: 336), USA = 100 largest companies. Dyas and Thanheiser (1976: 29), FRG = 78 largest German-owned companies; France = 79 French-owned companies; Italy = 61 Italian-owned companies.

on the other hand, were clearly more reluctant and by 1970 a mere 25 percent of the largest Italian firms had settled for the M-form. Still, over half of this same sample had already chosen diversification as a strategy by 1950. The slow adoption of the M-form in Italy thus cannot be accounted for, as traditional arguments would have it, only by a failure to diversify.[3]

Logic of Markets

While the nature of inter-firm relations did also undergo changes in the postwar period, particularly in France and in West Germany, measuring precisely such an evolution is more difficult. The size of West German and French industrial legal entities increased significantly over the period, which can be taken as a fairly good indication that "hierarchies" were in the process of being created on a large scale in those two countries. Those new large firms, or "hierarchies," often the product of mergers and acquisitions, internalized a number of formerly inter-unit relationships thus redefining in the process the market logic in some sectors of the economy. This was not so much the case in Italy, naturally, where small or medium-sized family-owned firms remained predominant.[4]

While industrial concentration was increasing both in France and in West Germany, legislative bodies were in the meantime crafting and adopting acts outlawing cartels and most forms of loose agreements. Organized markets thus became illegal in most industrial sectors. Due in part to American pressure, the American anti-trust tradition was being transferred and "translated" in France, West Germany, and the emerging European economic space (Djelic, 1998; Djelic and Bensedrine, 2001). While exact figures on cartels and loose agreements are not available for the period, the new legislation undeniably deterred informal organization of markets. It also stimulated the redefinition of many French and West German industrial sectors into competitive oligopolies, following the model pioneered by American industry (Dyas and Thanheiser, 1976; Berghahn, 1986; Djelic, 1998).

FRANCE, GERMANY, AND ITALY—LEARNING FROM HISTORY AND COMPARISON

Until the end of World War II, French, German, and Italian capitalisms all ranged somewhere between family and organized types (Chandler, 1990; Cassis, 1997; Djelic, 1998). Altogether, they were much more similar to each other than to the corporate and managerial model that was then being institutionalized in the United States. On the whole, structural features proved quite stable during that period in Europe and if there was at all an evolution, it was undeniably towards increasingly organized markets and structured forms of interfirm cooperation (Djelic, Koza, and Lewin, 1999). During those years, Europeans tended to observe with disbelief and concern rather than enthusiasm the corporate and managerial revolution that was transforming the economy and the society in the United States (Duhamel, 1930; Siegfried, 1927; Djelic, 1998).

The figures presented above show two things, however. First, that this apparently started to change after 1945. From that point on, the evidence is there of an evolution in Western Europe of national systems of economic organization. And the common direction of that evolution was clearly towards the corporate and managerial model pioneered by the United States. Second, the figures also show that the extent of the transformation and its impact were clearly not the same in all Western European countries. The challenge is thus two-pronged. We need to understand what happened in the post-World War II period to bring about the disruption of a long-standing relative equilibrium. We also need to understand what explains national differences. We rely for that on historical case studies, a summary of which is presented below.[5]

France

Formally, France was one of the winners of World War II and as such was granted a seat on the United Nations Security Council. In reality, France emerged from the war a weak, divided, and humiliated nation. The men who came to power in 1945 had been the leaders of the French *Résistance*. This partly underground, partly exiled movement had fought not only the Germans but also the official French regime, the Vichy government of Marshall Petain. The sense of national crisis was particularly acute in this group. The dominant analysis was that both the military defeat and political shame of the war period could be traced to prewar political, social, but also economic arrangements (Michel and Mirkine-Guetzevitch, 1954). Members of the resistance coalition argued that the French economy had not been equal, before the war, to the historical prestige of the nation and had not served its ambitions. They claimed that it had been characterized by backwardness and *Malthusianism*—a systematic and organized policy of limiting productive capacities in order to keep the balance in favor of producers. Both backwardness and *Malthusianism* were themselves seen as the consequences of rigid structures and of a conservative attitude on the part of business communities. Despite ideological differences, members of the resistance coalition agreed on one thing. There was a need for a radical break away from this past (Michel and Mirkine-Guetzevitch, 1954; de Gaulle, 1964; Monnet, 1976; Bloch-Lainé and Bouvier, 1986).

A clean slate entailed a radical questioning of prewar economic structures and their "modernization"—if only as a means to regaining "Great Power" status (de Gaulle, 1964). There was disagreement, though, on what "economic modernization" should mean. In a world that emerged as bi-polar, there were two models of "Great Power"—the Soviet and the American. Since the French coalition brought together communists, socialists, and more conservative

Gaullists, debates were heated. French hesitation only lasted, though, until the geopolitical showdown of 1947. Truman's Cold War speech in March and General Marshall's generous June plan both significantly contributed to bringing about a watertight division of the world. In that context, France chose its side and communist ministers were expelled from the government. By the end of 1947, France had been thrust into and solidly anchored within the Western camp. Its economic and geopolitical dependence on the United States had increased significantly and it had lost most of its bargaining power. All these conditions combined, in the end, to make the American economy and system of economic organization the only available and acceptable model for the modernization of French structures.

It would take a small group of men to turn availability and likelihood into process. In France, a "modernizing" network took over or created in those early postwar years key institutions at the border between state and economy and at the point of articulation of Franco-American relationships. For the most part those men originated from the public sphere if they were not civil servants. Planning and preparing the large-scale transformation of national economic, industrial, and even social structures, French modernizers looked towards the United States for models they could borrow. They worked in close synergy with a small group of Americans, soon spinning a dense cross-national web. The group of progressive American businessmen, civil servants, and economists with whom they collaborated had been closely involved in the American war effort. Losing some leverage on the national scene after the end of the war, this group turned to foreign affairs and took over in particular the Marshall plan machinery—the Economic Cooperation Administration (ECA). Members of this cross-national network had compatible objectives and they shared a common ideology, a mixture of Keynesianism, productivism, and fordism. They also came to be institutionally contiguous, in particular through the French planning council and the ECA mission in Paris, thus increasing the likelihood of collaboration. Jean Monnet was the cornerstone of this Franco-American network. While American support proved significant and instrumental, French initiative was ultimately the main driver. The French modernizing group spontaneously took upon itself the task of transferring the American structural model to the national economic scene. Working from key positions of institutional power, this small group elaborated and operated, on its own initiative, a set of mechanisms that were to bring about radical transformations within the French economy. The infrastructural power of the French state after World War II made it possible for this small group to have a significant impact over the national economy (Cohen, 1969; Kuisel, 1981). French modernizers had the necessary means and tools to implement their ambitious project—from nationalized industries, a central but flexible planning system, a centralized system of credit, and relays in all key decision-making centers. In the end, though, theirs was not an easy task and they sometimes encountered significant resistance. In some cases, they had to turn to their American friends, who helped them by playing "bad cop." The French planning council more than once pushed its own projects for France—generally highly compatible with American objectives—by asking the ECA to threaten to block or delay the release of Marshall funds (Djelic, 1998).

At the same time that the French modernizing network was a key transmission belt for American models in that period, it was also an intervening variable. It played a part as such in the reinterpretation and translation of the foreign model, while privileging some dimensions over others. Thus, together with transfer came editing and diffraction. French modernizers reinterpreted the American corporation as the state-owned "national champion." In the "American model," they picked and chose mergers, large size, and mass-production techniques. Highly distrustful of French business communities, they rejected—for the time being—private or public ownership, favoring instead the control of a new breed of civil servants (Kuisel, 1981; Kesler, 1985). Other elements of the original model were also paid scant attention, at least in relative terms—smooth industrial relations for example or strict anti-trust legislation.

While involved in reshaping national structures, the French team also turned out to be a driving force in the process of construction of a West European economic space. Defining new rules of competition and market regulation at the European level, this economic space was to have an impact ultimately, through trickle down types of processes, on national systems of economic organization. Once again, the models were American and the vision was that of a peaceful and united, mass-producing, and mass-consuming European continent—the "United States" of Europe (Djelic, 2000). In the medium to long term, the European economic space was expected to work through an in-depth redefinition of the rules of the economic game, bringing the latter much closer in line with the rules dominant in the American economic space. Rather than constraining economic actors into certain types of behaviors or hoping that they could be brought to mimic them, the rationale was that to be long lasting, changes should become deeply embedded. This could take time, naturally, and the impact was not likely to be felt in the short term. It would take new generations that would come to be socialized under those new rules of the game. In the process, those generations would come to appropriate them as their own rather than seeing them as foreign. This implied not only structural change but also a radical shift in mentalities, values, and economic and industrial ideologies, which would only foster and ground further the structural changes already in progress. The logic behind the European project was thus quite similar to that which led to the emergence and development of management and business education in European countries (Engwall and Zamagni, 1998) or to the spread to the region, in time, of American anti-trust principles (Djelic and Bensedrine, 2001). Unsurprisingly, there was a common base to the groups and individuals involved in those different projects and the early group of American and French modernizers proved particularly crucial.

Conditions in France were thus quite favorable to a large-scale, cross-national structural transfer. A deep sense of national crisis, the clear dependence in time on the American superpower, and the existence of a small but institutionally powerful cross-national network, the members of which worked in close synergy, all combined to make such transfer a reality. This never was, though, a laboratory experiment. The challenger set of structural features was being imported into a pre-existing economic and institutional landscape. It threatened in the process an incumbent system of economic organization and ran, unsurprisingly, into vested interests and a fair amount of resistance. As it turned out, the main source of resistance lay within civil society and more particularly within labor and business communities.

Business leaders, for one, had trouble accepting the radical questioning of their traditional ways of organizing and doing business—radical questioning that was explicit in the modernization project. They could not reconcile themselves with the transfer of a foreign model they generally considered unfit for European conditions and disruptive of their interests. In the period that immediately followed the end of the war, those business communities were particularly weak in France, lacking in resources and for a while even in the right to organize (Ehrmann, 1957). This prevented reaction on their part at least for a few years. By the early fifties, though, they had regained the right to organize and were rapidly reasserting their power and influence. The Conseil National du Patronat Français was getting ready to fight. Among the resources that played a role were naturally the financial contributions of members. The control business groups exercised, directly or indirectly, over a number of press outlets was also an important tool for them, allowing them to orchestrate large-scale propaganda campaigns. The political route, finally, was also important and business communities in France nurtured their relationships with politicians and deputies, in particular through donations for campaign funds. Making use of these various resources, the French business communities launched a war against the large-scale transfer of what they denounced as an "American model." The issues of size and ownership structure were at the heart of business resistance in France. In the end, though, French business communities achieved little and they were not able to prevent the structural transfer engineered by the cross-national network from taking place. A weak point for them was that they were targeting in their lobbying efforts deputies and politicians who, in the France of that time, had comparatively much less power and leverage than technocrats and civil servants, at least when it came to economic affairs. The pattern of resistance, though, turned out to have an impact on the transfer process itself. It undeniably contributed to the deep distrust of private capitalism characteristic of French technocrats in that period. In the end, it thus certainly had an impact on their editing of the American corporation into the French state-owned national champion.

Business communities were another powerful source of resistance in France. The communist CGT was by far the most powerful trade union (Dreyfus, 1995). Its significant reach at the grassroots level together with its rigid centralization explained that it could rapidly mobilize a large share of the French working class. The strength of communist influence over the French labor movement meant that resistance and opposition to the modernizing project—generally symbolized by the close links between the French plan and the Marshall plan— took, within the working class, a political and geopolitical dimension. Starting in the summer of 1947, Soviet directives were calling for an all-out war on the part of Western European labor against what Moscow denounced as an American imperialist scheme and a declaration of war to the communist world. The French communist trade union as a consequence launched violent social movements bordering on insurrection and monitored, together with the French Communist Party, fierce propaganda campaigns. The strategy of the modernizing network with respect to such an obviously political opposition was to bypass communist groups and actors. Since the cooperation of labor still appeared necessary to the modernization project, the American element of the cross-national network worked together with the CIA and American labor federations to identify, co-opt, and sponsor interlocutors in the French labor movement. The split of the CGT in April 1948 and the creation of the French CGT-FO, a more reformist trade union, owed a lot in fact to this American intervention (Carew, 1987).

West Germany

On May 8, 1945, Germany surrendered unconditionally. In a matter of days, the end of the war brought along the collapse of the national order. The power vacuum that followed was unparalleled in its extent but did not last. Soon after surrender, the four victorious Allied powers, the U.S., the U.K., the U.S.S.R., and France were exercising complete political and military control, each in its own zone of occupation. An Allied Control Council, made up of the four Allied commanders-in-chief acting jointly, was created to allow for coordinated policy making. It rapidly became clear, though, that this was a poor forum for collective decision making. Even before the Cold War split, the Soviets were doing what they wanted while the Western zones of Germany increasingly fell under American control. By the spring of 1948, Western powers had merged their three zones, which were to become the Federal Republic of Germany. For some time already, the United States had shouldered most of the financial burden for all three zones and their power had increased to the point where they had "the right of final decision in financial and economic matters" (Clay, 1950: 178). In an obvious way, West German territories were thus in a highly dependent relationship to the United States. This would still be the case after the creation of the Federal Republic of Germany in 1949. Although direct American presence and power seemed to fade somewhat, West German dependence was perpetuated through the launching of the Marshall plan and following the onset of the Cold War. From occupying power, the United States turned into a generous and regular provider of economic and financial but also technical assistance. In a divided world, where the threat from the East seemed real, the western superpower also appeared to be the only potential protector of a weak and highly exposed West Germany.

In the early years that followed the end of the war, debates raged within the American military government in Germany, within the Washington administration, and between both, as to what the American policy in Germany should be (Clay, 1950; Martin, 1950; Djelic, 1998). Altogether, though, there was widespread agreement within American ranks that prewar German political and economic institutions had in one way or another been tainted by the Nazi era. When the dust had settled, the American objective was to bring about a radical transformation of German economic and industrial structures. This was only reinforced by the onset of the Cold War, which turned western territories of Germany into a front bulwark against communism. The United States set out, as a consequence, to transform the Federal Republic of Germany into a wealthy and prosperous country. The West German economy was to become the engine of reconstruction in Western Europe and an outpost of American-type capitalism. For that, a large-scale transfer of the American system of economic organization was in order.

Americans were convinced that a West German economy, revamped along the lines of the "free competitive economy, which has been so successful in the US" was a prerequisite to political stability, peace and democracy in West Germany but also in Europe. They were also convinced that the "German people could be taught to understand and want such an economy" (OMGUS, Bd 18). By 1948, American officials in Germany meant by "free competitive economy" the American form of corporate capitalism rather than the "free market" of classical economists. The model they were intent on transferring was an economy dominated by large-scale, mass-producing firms, competing on oligopolistic markets and policed by anti-trust legislation in the American tradition. From the perspective of OMGUS members, it seemed that two features of this model of reference were particularly important for the projected restructuring of the West German economy and industry. They pointed, first of all, to the large size of American production units and firms, allowing rationalization, economies of scale and scope, and mass production. They also pointed out the regulation of anti-competitive behavior through anti-trust legislation, identifying such regulation as a necessary step towards a redefinition of the West German economy and industry.

Key to the project of large-scale transfer was the decartelization and deconcentration program. This program had initially been designed as a punitive one. Its object was to "destroy Germany's economic potential to wage war" and to break up German firms and cartels that had been the economic backbone of Nazi Germany. After much debate and internal infighting, this program was reinvented. By 1948, it had become the basis of anti-trust legislation in the American tradition—nothing more, nothing less. The team in charge of the program was not striving for "the ideal of perfect competition with hundred of firms competing in the production of each product." Rather, following the model set by American industry, it was advocating "an oligolistic structure policed by the vigorous enforcement of antitrust or anticartel laws." The claim was that large corporations competing in oligopolistic markets were the surest way to combine, in West Germany, "technical efficiency" and "economies of scale" with competition (OMGUS, Bd 18). Americans used the powers granted to them through the revamped decartelization and deconcentration program to foster the structural redefinition, along those lines, of firms and interfirm relations in many industries (Berghahn, 1986; Djelic, 1998). As OMGUS members acknowledged, they could do at the time "anything they wanted, within some limits, to the German economy" (OMGUS, Bd 42).

While aware of their power and using it to further their project for Germany, Americans also understood that reforms would not last if they were merely being imposed on the Germans. After all, the period of acute German geopolitical dependence was bound to end at some point. What would be left then of the radical American project? The solution to that problem, OMGUS soon realized, was to co-opt as early as possible a group of German decision makers that were sympathetic enough to the American project. As it turned out, they managed to identify such a group, around the then marginal German economist, Ludwig Erhard. The Freiburg school, as this group was known, had been before the war and still was small, powerless, and a clear outsider in the German landscape. The "social market economy" they envisioned had been defined in radical opposition to the tightly cartelized prewar and Nazi German economy. It centered around the "principle of freedom and liberalism" (Peacock and Willgerodt, 1989). While Erhard's colleagues meant by that the "free market" of classical economists, Erhard himself pleaded for a reconciliation of competition with efficiency and productivity. He thus advocated large-scale productive entities competing freely in oligopolistic markets as the most direct route to a mass-producing and mass-consuming society which he clearly championed (Erhard, 1958). This program was music to American ears and the close fit between this program and the American project for West Germany explains that OMGUS did a lot to bring this group in the center of German political life.

Ludwig Erhard once called himself an "American invention" (Berghahn, 1984; Nicholls, 1984). In political terms, this is indeed true. From virtual outcasts, intellectually and institutionally, in their own country, Ludwig Erhard and members of the Freiburg school were thrust in positions of power by American authorities (Wallich, 1955; Nicholls, 1984; Peacock and Willgerodt, 1989). In 1946, the American military government appointed Ludwig Erhard Minister of Economic Affairs in his home state of Bavaria. After the merging of the British and American zones of occupation in 1947, a number of new German institutions were created. In particular a German economic council was granted some responsibility over bizonal economic issues. The chairman, who was to act as a Minister of Economic Affairs with limited powers, was to be elected by his peers. This election had been planned by the occupying powers as a political process, a first step towards democracy and it was to reflect the balance of power between German parties. Johannes Semler, a member of the Bavarian Christian Democratic Party (CSU) was elected in July 1947 and became the first chairman of the German economic council. His public speeches, highly critical of American military government, and some of his actions as chairman soon attracted a lot of attention. In January 1948, members of the American military government decided unilaterally to dismiss him. In a move that was not quite democratic this time, they imposed Ludwig Erhard in his place (Peterson, 1977). This was the beginning, for Ludwig Erhard, of a long career, first as Minister of Economic Affairs until 1963 and, from 1963 to 1966, as Chancellor of the Federal Republic of Germany.

In the process, this meant the institutionalization of a cross-national network. Both the German and American elements of this network were to work, throughout the years, in close synergy and in the same direction. The Ministry of Economic Affairs around Ludwig Erhrard—and later on the West German government—appropriated most of the structural reforms that had initially been launched by American occupation authorities. Those reforms were thus lastingly embedded in the West German context, gaining legitimacy in time albeit painfully, together with their German proponents. Throughout his career, Ludwig Erhard consistently received the full support of the American administration—the American Military Government in Germany or OMGUS and later the American High Commission / ECA Mission in Germany, but also the Washington administration.

With hindsight, it seems unlikely in fact that Ludwig Erhard and his team could have done without such support. Their program and the American project for West Germany were radical and the system of economic organization both were advocating was a clear challenge to German structural and ideological traditions. Civil society once again reacted to what was then perceived as large-scale attempt at grafting on the national soil a foreign economic logic. And reactions proved sometimes in the German case to be of an extreme violence, particularly within the national business community.

German business leaders fought fiercely on the issue of cartels and competition. Both the German and American elements in the cross-national network had declared a war on cartels, which they saw as essentially collusion schemes set up to control competition, preserve stability, and ensure high profits. Those systematic attacks against cartels and organized capitalism infuriated most German business leaders from the very beginning. In the early postwar period, though, reactions could at best be muted. In those times of "denazification" when all form of official representation was prohibited, resistance was by necessity limited and unorganized. By the early months of 1950, when the Allied prohibition on the formation of trade associations was finally allowed to lapse, a federation of business associations—the Bundesverband der Deutschen Industrie (BDI)—was created in West Germany. Most members of the BDI had belonged, before and during the war, to the former German federation, the

Reichsverband der Deutschen Industrie (RDI). A number had been involved in the corporatist institutions of Nazi Germany. Altogether, the BDI was therefore quite conservative and attached to prewar patterns of economic organization. In defense of cartels and collective agreements, West German business leaders initially used fairly traditional arguments, carried through from the prewar period. Free competition, they claimed, led to dangerous price wars, the consequence of which in turn was generally a series of failures, particularly among smaller and medium-sized concerns. They presented, on the other hand, cartels and collective agreements as essentially sound mechanisms to "avoid ruinous competition and to prevent the waste of material and labor capacities" (OMGUS, Bd 42).

When they realized that such arguments did not carry, West German business leaders turned to much more aggressive and violent strategies and rhetorics. Feeling increasingly secure and powerful after the creation of the BDI, they launched a systematic and violent propaganda campaign against competition and its champions in the West German political and administrative elite. Ludwig Erhard and the West German Ministry of Economic Affairs were clearly the main targets of these attacks. Throughout the fifties, the West German business community repeatedly accused the Ministry of Economic Affairs of being the instrument of American occupation authorities and of implementing an American policy that had originally been designed to weaken the German economy. Members of the BDI found it "hard to understand why the Federal Minister of Economic Affairs wished to lead and force industry into economic freedom against its own will" (Erhard, 1963: chapter 16). There were two main fronts to the war of the BDI—nationally, the passing of a German anti-cartel act and in Europe, negotiations around the Schuman plan.

One of the first commitments of Erhard upon his nomination as chairman of the German Economic Council was to sponsor a German anti-cartel law that was to replace the Allied act of 1947. The confrontation with the German business community lasted for close to ten years and the German parliament only voted such a law in July 1957. Throughout those years the fight was violent. The BDI used the media it controlled, such as the economic weekly *Der Volkswirt*, to orchestrate harsh attacks. It also turned to more direct means of pressure, through its political contacts within the Christian Democratic Party. Members of the BDI threatened to reduce their campaign contributions to the CDU for the 1953 elections if the bill was not modified (Braunthal, 1965). Bypassing Ludwig Erhard, they also tried to appeal directly to Konrad Adenauer, German chancellor and leader of the CDU. In the end, Ludwig Erhard and his collaborators held fast mostly thanks to American support and to the scarecrow of a tougher U.S.-imposed legislation. The West German act prohibited cartels in principle, following in that the American Sherman Act (Djelic and Bensedrine, 2001). The violent resistance of the German business communities had left its marks, though, and the exceptions that were included in the act were the result of compromise.

While confrontation was still in full swing on the national scene, the West German business community became involved in a parallel fight on the European level. The emerging coal and steel community (ECSC) was a source of significant concern for West German industries, particularly with respect to the cartel issue. Although the confrontation was taking place in a different context, the pattern was fairly similar. On one side, a few European—and even more precisely French—technocrats and civil servants were working with members of the American administration to institutionalize a competitive logic in the emerging European market for coal and steel. On the other side, national representatives of heavy industries were apparently intent on fighting this project. There was no institutional framework, however, that could formally bring together all Western European coal and steel industries. Common objectives and interests, furthermore, were often offset by national rivalries. As a consequence, opposition to the coal and steel community remained structured nationally. The strategy of Jean Monnet and his team had been to exclude entirely from ECSC negotiations all national representatives of European heavy industries. However, they could not prevent—except in the French case—the weaving of informal links between industry members and members of national delegations. Private interests and corporatist claims were thus bound to influence negotiation proceedings, even if only partially and indirectly. This was illustrated when, under strong pressure from heavy industries' representatives, the West German delegation denounced the anti-cartel provisions of the ECSC treaty. Negotiations were consequently stalled for several months and if it had not been, once again, for American intervention, they may never have started again. Indeed the American administration and John McCloy in particular, then American High Commissioner in Germany, were instrumental in dragging the German delegation back to the negotiation table and in bringing Germans finally to accept and ratify the anti-cartel provisions of the ECSC treaty.

Those provisions are much more than they seem. Articles 60 and 61 in the ECSC treaty were directly transferred in 1957 to the Treaty of Rome—that founded the European Economic Community—where they became articles 85 and 86. In the words of Jean Monnet, those articles "represented a fundamental innovation in Europe." Robert Bowie had drafted those two articles, building unmistakably on American anti-trust tradition. A Harvard Law School anti-trust specialist, Bowie was also General Counsel to the American High Commissioner in Germany and as such closely involved in the drafting of the national German legislation. For Jean Monnet, the "essential antitrust [*sic*] legislation reigning over the common market today ha(d) its origins in those few sentences for which (he did) not regret to have fought during four months" (Monnet, 1976: 413). And indeed, articles 60 and 61 of the ECSC treaty laid the foundations of anti-trust legislation for the common European market with a significant impact, over time, on national systems of economic organization as well as on transnational patterns of collaboration and competition.

Italy

Like many other countries in Europe at the time, Italy was after World War II in a state of utter destitution. The country had been highly dependent on the United States for emergency relief and other resources ever since September 1943 when the fascist government had surrendered. At the same time, though, that the United States were playing such a key role on the Italian scene, the strength of the Communist Party was the source of bargaining power for that country at least between 1945 and 1947 (Hughes, 1965; Romano, 1977; Miller, 1986). The year of 1947 marked a turning point, though, as it did in France. Italians could not postpone taking sides in the Cold War anymore. During a trip to the United States, early in 1947, the Italian Premier Alcide de Gasperi tried to secure renewed American economic assistance. He was told in no uncertain terms that financial and economic aid would be much more forthcoming if communist ministers left the Italian government.

Clear advice of that sort combined with rumors that Washington was preparing a large-scale aid package for Europe to speed up action on the Italian national scene. In May 1947, Alcide de Gasperi set up a new government without communist or left-wing socialist ministers. When Marshall dollars started to flow in, by 1948, Italy was well and truly anchored to the West and most of its bargaining power in the relationship with the United States had been lost. The American system of economic organization was therefore, and from that point on, available as a model for Italy as much as it was for France. Contacts between Italy and the United States became increasingly numerous throughout the Marshall plan period, multiplying the opportunities for the Italian population to become familiar with American economic structures. Those structural arrangements characterized a Great Power that also happened to be, for Italy, the main provider and the sole protector. Conditions thus seemed to have been fulfilled for the American system of economic organization to become a model, both familiar and superior, for Italian reconstruction.

It was soon obvious, however, that the American model was much less likely to be considered in Italy than it was in France. The first reason for that was that the Italian power elite lacked, after the war, the sense of crisis and urgency that defined its French counterpart. The group controlling political and institutional positions of power in Italy did not define itself in radical opposition to the former regime and system, nor did it declare a state of national emergency and crisis that would call for radical structural transformations. In Italy, the rejection of fascism had taken place during the war and had been, as a consequence, relatively short-lived. After the surrender of the fascist government in 1943, a number of Italians had shared in the Allied war effort. When the war came to an end in 1945, Italy was in a relatively ambiguous situation. That special status, neither winner nor loser, clearly had to be preserved in order to prevent issues such as military occupation or reparations to surface. Italians were better off forgetting their fascist past than loudly rejecting it (Miller, 1986).

A second reason explains that the American model never became in Italy the type of reference that it was in France or West Germany. In Italy, the cross-national network broke down. Members of the ECA failed to identify and co-opt, on the Italian national scene, actors with whom they could collaborate to bring about a radical transformation of economic and industrial structures. After March 1947, the main objective of the United States in Italy was to weaken the communist movement (Hughes, 1965; De Cecco, 1972; Miller, 1986). In that context, the American administration came to support the Christian Democratic Party as the only alternative it could identify in Italy to communism or fascism. This party was heir to the prewar Popolari, the people's party. By the end of the war, the people's party brought together all those Italians wary of extremism and fearful, in particular, of communism. It thus emerged as a patchwork of many different political trends, united essentially around a preference for the West in the geopolitical confrontation that was dividing the world. Middle classes were dominant in the electorate of the Christian Democratic Party, with a prominent group of craftsmen, shopkeepers, and small business entrepreneurs.

In the end, the Christian Democratic Party and the governments it sponsored in Italy proved somewhat disappointing to the American administration and in particular to the sponsors in that administration of a "European neo-capitalism" (Hogan, 1985). The Christian Democratic elite and the American group involved in Italian affairs turned out to have little in common, with regard to both ideology and objectives. There was clearly no equivalent, within the Italian public sphere, to the generation of French modernizing technocrats or to the group in Germany around Ludwig Erhard. This left Americans from the ECA with no valid interlocutor within the Italian government—nobody that talked the same language, nobody to rely on. From 1948, the ECA country mission in Italy was headed by James Zellerbach, former chairman of the board of the Crown Zellerbach Corporation. He had a project for Italy that was similar to ECA projects for the rest of Western Europe. The transformation of Italy towards a mass-producing, mass-consuming society would, according to him, quell political conflicts and rule out the possibility of communist takeover. This transformation, however, would require the creation of large firms in most industrial sectors and necessitate a significant increase in productivity levels (Miller, 1986; Harper, 1986). The ECA mission in Italy was ready to elaborate and to help implement programs that would increase production capacities and bring about the modernization and restructuring of Italian industry. Members of the ECA mission in Italy, in fact, pointed to what was being done in France. Marshall aid should be used to invest in a few key industries that would have, in turn, a multiplier effect on the rest of the economy. But Keynesian productivists in the ECA did not find any collaborators sympathetic to their project on the Italian political and technocratic scene. Members of the ECA mission in Rome and those men in positions of institutional power in Italy seemed separated by an abyss. Communication, most of the time, was impossible and both groups worked at counter purposes.

Retrospectively, things could have turned differently. There was, after all, a tradition of modernizing technocrats in Italy dating back to the period of national unification. Even after 1945, the tradition was perpetuated but Italian modernizers were to be found mostly among those businessmen and managers running the few large Italian firms, not in the public, technocratic, or political sphere. Amongst those few large Italian firms, the state holdings inherited from the fascist years—the ENI or IRI—could have been used as powerful tools in a state-led strategy of economic modernization. Enrico Mattei at the head of ENI (the energy holding) or Oscar Sinigaglia, who was leading IRI's Finsider (steel arm of IRI) were sympathetic to Keynesian and productivist values. As a matter of fact, they often developed and nurtured direct contacts with the ECA mission in Rome and with American business leaders. Although they were quite powerful, their impact on the Italian economy as a whole was altogether quite limited. The gap was significant between them and the mass of Italian business owners, running small and medium-sized family firms tied together through dense, often local, networks mixing collaboration and competition.

In the Italian case, Americans had thus failed in their strategy of co-optation. The lack of a national sense of crisis combined with the breakdown of the cross-national network to make it highly unlikely that a large-scale transfer of structural arrangements would be considered let alone undertaken. Postwar Italian power holders did not engage in a radical questioning of prewar economic and social arrangements. Nor did they advocate a radical transformation of industry structure and the transfer, to their country, of the American system of economic organization. American modernizers, present in Italy through the Marshall plan administration, nevertheless attempted to institutionalize in that country the same types of transfer mechanisms that were proving quite effective in France and in West Germany. For the most part, those attempts failed. The absence of Italian interlocutors and institutional relays frustrated and curtailed the efforts of American modernizers in that country. In the longer term, the creation of a Western European economic community, of which Italy was an early member, would end up having an impact on the Italian economy. As documented earlier, though, the scale and scope of transformations that were to affect the Italian system of economic organization in the twenty years after the end of the war could clearly not compare with what was taking place at the same time in France or in West Germany.

TOWARDS A DECONSTRUCTION OF GLOBALIZATION

Building on the historical case studies briefly summarized above and on their systematic comparison, we propose a new perspective on the contemporary episode of globalization. In contrast to the literature on national variants of capitalism, we believe that there are indeed pressures pushing for structural isomorphism and the homogenization of national systems of economic organization. But those pressures, we argue, are far from being neutral and a-historical. While the literature on globalization tends to emphasize economic and technological determinism or even a neutral but inescapable rationalization of the world, we have asked here about origins, defining moments and enabling contexts. We argue that the transformation of economic institutions over the second half of the twentieth century, in Western Europe but also in the rest of the world, cannot be understood without taking into account the peculiar nature of geopolitical relationships in the early postwar years. At that point, pressures for change had a lot to do with the clear imbalance of power between the United States as a dominant superpower and a more or less dependent set of countries. Unmistakably, the historical roots of our contemporary episode of globalization lay in the early attempt, following World War II, at large-scale "Americanization" of economic institutions. In the end, however, convergence following the "American model" was partial at best. The transfer of that model came together with its local reinterpretation, editing and thus with hybridization. This filtering process and the enduring nature of pre-existing national legacies explain that local peculiarities persist to this day, allowing us to set apart national variants of capitalism.

The attempt at large-scale "Americanization" of the post-World War II period took place, we have shown, in the context of a significant redefinition of the geopolitical environment. When the United States took on the leadership of the Western world, parallels were quickly drawn between, on the one hand, American geopolitical and economic power and, on the other, the peculiar and unique system of industrial production then dominant in that country. In the context of national crisis and radical questioning that characterized a number of Western European countries, the American system of industrial production unsurprisingly became a model to be transferred and adopted.

At the same time, the large-scale structural transfer was made possible and fostered by the emergence of a small cross-national network controlling key resources and positions of power. The transfer process was institutionalized through the systematic setting-up and operation of various cross-national transfer mechanisms, whether of mimetic, coercive or normative types. Such a transfer was naturally bound to disrupt preexisting economic and social arrangements. It did encounter obstacles and sometimes even triggered organized resistance and opposition within national units. As a direct consequence, the transfer was not equally successful in all Western European countries. The original model was adapted, "translated," edited, leading quite often to hybrid forms of structural arrangements. This largely differences accounts for the persistence, in the long term, of significant not only across Western European national industries but also between European and American industries.

History tells us, therefore, that globalization is a process—not a state of things. It is historical and political—and not universal and neutral. It is about the cross-national transfer of dominant models rather than about the spontaneous and parallel emergence in many different countries of similar solutions. This historic and political cross-national transfer process we see as having three main moments. As underscored in figure 16.5, cross-national transfer will not take place in the absence of enabling conditions. It can be characterized by multiple combinations of mechanisms and it is bound to run into obstacles, although the nature and strength of these obstacles will vary.

Figure 16.5   Three Moments in the Cross-National Transfer Process

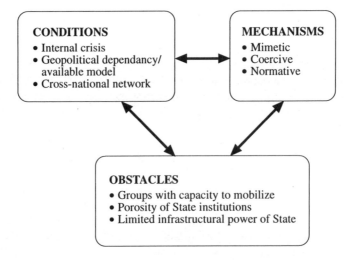

Conditions

In order for a large-scale, cross-national transfer process to be possible, to be contemplated and eventually to be launched, it appears that a number of conditions should be met simultaneously. First of all, a traumatic disruption should bring, at the national level, an acute sense of crisis and a questioning of the legitimacy of pre-existing institutional and structural arrangements. Then, a redefinition of the geopolitical environment and, in particular, the emergence of relationships of asymmetrical dependence should turn a foreign system of economic organization into an available model, in other words both familiar and perceived to be superior. Finally, a cross-national network of actors, sharing similar and compatible if not common objectives should bridge the gap between both countries. These "modernizing" individuals may be only a small minority within their respective national environments. They should nevertheless hold and control key positions of power both within cross-national institutional channels and in those national institutions located at the articulation of state and economy in the receiving country, which are bound to play an essential role in the transfer process. This set of three conditions, it is proposed here, will significantly increase the likelihood that a large-scale, cross-national transfer process be considered and eventually launched in a given situation.

Mechanisms

The concrete implementation, however, of such a large-scale, cross-national transfer process will also require that a number of transfer mechanisms be not only elaborated but also operated. The comparative and historical study has made it possible to identify three main types of transfer mechanisms. Using DiMaggio and Powell's (1983) terminology, these mechanisms are labeled respectively "coercive," "mimetic," and "normative." Varying degrees of geopolitical dependence account for differences in the mix of transfer mechanisms. The nature of this mix, on the other hand, is bound to have an impact on the transfer process, for example on its speed and on the extent of the "translation" or adaptation of the original model. It may also to some extent determine national reactions, and in particular the degree of local resistance and the violence of opposition movements. Table 16.3 proposes a summary description

Table 16.3 Dominant Mechanisms and Different Paths of Transfer

	COERCIVE	*MIMETIC*	*NORMATIVE*
CONDITIONS	Asymmetrical Dependence	Dependence or asymmetrical dependence	Dependence or interdependence
AGENTS	Model country	Local	Foreign or local
PROCESS	Imposing	Imitating	Embedding
SPEED	Rapid	Medium	Slow
IMPACT	Short-lived and fragile	Stable and long lasting	Fairly permanent
RESULT	Similar to model	Partial adaptation	Partial adaptation
REACTIONS	Rejection, opposition	Resistance or support	Indifference to support

of the different paths a cross-national transfer process could take depending on the type of transfer mechanism predominant in each case.

Obstacles

The concrete operating of those various transfer mechanisms is naturally not likely to run smoothly. Obstacles could emerge from the existence of powerful and organized groups with a significant capacity to mobilize and intent on resisting the transfer process. The porosity of state institutions could apparently increase further the ability of those groups to impose their own views and thus to successfully resist the transfer process, while limiting at the same time the autonomy of political or administrative actors. Furthermore, notwithstanding the degree of resistance and the impact of opposition groups, a large-scale cross-national transfer process may be considerably slowed down, if not brought to a halt, because of the limited infrastructural power (Mann, 1986) of political institutions and state actors, and in particular because of their limited leverage over the national economy and industry.

Cross-national processes of transfer or diffusion thus cannot be uncoupled from a concomitant process of diffraction, partial reinterpretation, "translation," editing, or hybridization of the original model to be transferred. The combination of those two indissociable processes seems to require the theoretical crossbreeding of two variants of neo-institutionalism. On the one hand, the tradition of "phenomenological" neo-institutionalism (Meyer and Rowan, 1977; Scott and Meyer, 1994) can be used to account for diffusion. On the other hand, the associated processes of reinterpretation or editing will be better explained using the variant of neo-institutionalism that was labeled earlier "historical" (Fligstein, 1990; Hollingsworth and Boyer, 1997; Whitley, 1999). The cross-fertilization between those two traditions has undeniable implications for the thriving but multi-faceted "neo-institutional" school in economic sociology and point to potentially quite fruitful research directions.

NOTES

1 1,249 Italian firms (with more than 50 employees) were sole proprietorships in 1951 (1,781 in 1971). In France, the numbers were 1,408 in 1954 and 901 in 1966.

2 INSEE (1956, 1974), Istituto Centrale di Statistica (1955, 1976), Statistisches Bundesamt (1953, 1973).

3 Chandler (1962). Neither could Italian reluctance to the M-form be explained by peculiarities of the environment. Indeed, most foreign-owned subsidiaries in Italy (thirty-three out of thirty-nine) had adopted the form by 1970.

4 Both in France and in West Germany, the total number of industrial units was stable over the period at around six hundred thousand. Some very small firms (less than ten

employees) disappeared, but they were replaced, for the most part, by small or medium-sized entities (between ten and five hundred employees). Statistisches Bundesamt (1953, 1954, 1973, 1974), INSEE (1956, 1974), Istituto Centrale di Statistica (1955, 1976).

5 For the full versions of these national case studies, see Djelic (1996, 1998).

17

Institutional Pathways, Networks, and the Differentiation of National Economies

Jerald Hage, J. Rogers Hollingsworth

Countries have long had various forms of cooperation among organizations (e.g., cartels, cooperatives, and cottage industries)[1] but in the past several decades there has been an increasing presence of varied forms of interorganizational cooperation (Alter and Hage, 1993; Doz and Hamel, 1998; Dussauge and Garrette, 1999; Gomes-Casseres, 1996; Hagedoorn, 1993; Harbison and Pekar, 1998; Johanson, 1994; Jungmittag, Reger, and Reiss, 2000; Mockler, 1999). Some examples of these trends include the proliferation of joint ventures for either product development, production or marketing (Hladik, 1988; Jungmittag, Reger, and Reiss, 2000), research consortia (Aldrich and Sasaki, 1995), and complex alliances involving rivals (Gomes-Casseres, 1996). In some sectors, increases in inter-organizational cooperation have been spectacular. Perhaps the most dramatic examples are in biotechnology and pharmaceutical industries where a variety of different inter-organizational relationships have been established, with most of the increase occurring after 1992 (Jungmittag, Reger, and Reiss, 2000; Powell, 1998). Harbison and Pekar (1998: 25–30) report that in just the two years of 1995–97, approximately twenty thousand international joint ventures of one kind or another were formed. The number in the United States has been growing by 25 percent per annum since 1987. While about one-half of these joint ventures are concentrated in what might be called the high-tech industries such as telecommunications, computer hardware and software, biotechnology, and medical services (Hagedoorn, 1993), one increasingly finds them in all sectors of the economy.[2] One form of joint ventures consists of consortia. Prior to 1985, the United States had relatively few research consortia, but since then more than three hundred have been created, including the highly successful SEMATEC (Aldrich and Sasaki, 1995; Browning, Beyer, and Shetler, 1995).

The direction of this evolution towards more and more inter-organizational relationships and thus (Hage and Alter, 1997) greater cooperation may be described by three distinctive characteristics: First, the fastest growth has occurred *across* economic sectors rather than being concentrated within the same sector as are cartels, cooperatives, and cottage industries. In other words, there is increasing hybridization across industries (Alter and Hage, 1993). Second, these changes involve the coordination of many activities, particularly research and development and/or the manufacturing of complex products such as airplanes and cars (Killing, 1988). This, of course, is part of the process of the hybridization of industries. A modern airplane must have a sophisticated computer system, communications, radar, air conditioning, engines, exotic alloys in both the engine and skin, etc. Indeed, the complexity of many products is so great that firms in a large number of industries must cooperate in producing the final product. These processes are quite different from many of the more traditional forms of industrial cooperation when cartels or cooperatives emerged in order to solve problems distinctive to firms in the same industry (Hollingsworth, 1991a, 1991b; Kanter, 1994).

Third, joint ventures and inter-organizational networks tend to involve particularistic relationships among specific firms for a set of products (Gomes-Casseres, 1996; Johanson, 1994; Mockler, 1999). Thus, Microsoft, Intel, IBM, and countless other firms now are engaged in a rapidly expanding number of joint ventures and strategic alliances to address particular research and production problems (Gerlach, 1992; Gomes-Casseres, 1996; Jarillo, 1993; Alter and Hage, 1993). Again, this is quite different from the more general relationships found in cartels, cooperatives, and the typical cottage industries which involved most producers in a particular sector and/or locality when there were efforts to regulate or coordinate problems common to all firms in a particular industry (Hollingsworth, 1991a, 1991b). The relationships become particularistic as different companies in the same industry join together to produce distinctive products (Mockler, 1999).

These movements toward new forms of *cooperation* are a consequence of two major *competitive* forces operating across the world. The first is the rapid growth in industrial research and its consequences for making product/process innovation a criterion for commercial success (Hage, 1999; National Science Foundation, 1996, 1998). The second is the large reduction in tariffs and the resulting increase in the variety and number of competitors even in what are labeled the high-tech industries (Gilpin, 2000). These two competitive forces are further augmented by two other major societal changes: (1) consumers have become more affluent and have higher levels of education, meaning more diversity of tastes and thus smaller market niches for products, and (2) technologies have become more complex with more rapid rates of technological change. As a result, product lives in an increasing number of sectors have become very short. And as firms are embedded in an increasingly more global environment with consumers tastes changing rapidly, with products becoming more complex, with technologies changing constantly, and with more products having short lives, firms must have the capacity to adapt rapidly to their changing environment in order to survive. To adapt to these competitive forces, states (Casper, 1999; Cohen, 1992; Matthews, 1997) and firms have found it necessary to develop more complex institutional arrangements for research, development, production, and distribution (Hage and Powers, 1992; Hollingsworth, 1991a, 1991b), including a variety of different kinds of linkages among firms (Hage and Alter, 1997; Hage and Hollingsworth, 2000; Harbison and Pekar, 1998; Jungmittag, Reger, and Reiss, 2000; Nooteboom, 2000; Powell, 1998). However, it would be wrong to assume, as many who advance the thesis of globalization do, that these forces are creating convergence in the way in which firms and sectors are structured. Indeed, not all firms in all industrial sectors are creating joint ventures and inter-organizational networks at the same rate and in the same way. Indeed, our argument is to the contrary. We argue that national economies, in both the developed and developing world, are moving towards greater divergence than existed in the industrial age, roughly the period from 1875 to 1975 (Hollingsworth and Streeck, 1994). One reason for this divergence is the *differential development* of joint ventures and networks influenced by the national institutional context and cultural norms in which firms are embedded, a complex institutional environment which influences the choice of businesses relationships in a particular society. These institutional environments also influence the comparative advantages of firms and industries in specific countries (Porter, 1990). Because societies vary in their pattern of institutional arrangements, there is also societal variation in the speed with which particular industrial sectors are evolving towards inter-organizational cooperation (see table 17.1). In other words, the pace of the movement is influenced in large part by the nature of the institutional context that filters or mediates these general forces.

The argument that institutions influence the processes of economic change and the choice of organizational form is not new (Polanyi, 1957; North, 1990; Hollingsworth, 2000; Williamson 1985). What is distinctive in our argument is that inter-organizational networks are becoming more prevalent, especially ones involving the coordination of complex activities, such as research and production with particularistic relationships across industrial sectors (Hage and Alter, 1997; Hage and Hollingsworth, 2000; Hladik, 1988; Inkpen and Dinur, 1998; Mockler, 1999; Powell, 1998). Furthermore, we are also suggesting that competition in the marketplace is increasingly dominated by a new set of factors, not only particular kinds of consumer tastes for high quality products but also those involving the importance of innovation, and rapid adaptiveness to the increasingly global environment of firms (Hage, 1987). Indeed, our network argument is quite different from that of Williamson (1985) who emphasizes the importance of vertical integration in order to achieve efficiency. Rather than accentuate the role of such economic institutions as contracts or property rights as influencing business relationships, we stress the importance of a variety of non-economic institutional arrangements as well as cultural norms that influence the evolution towards networks and their performance (Whitley, 1992a, 1992b).

Table 17.1 Forces Shaping Joint Ventures and Networks

Global Forces of Change	Societal Mediating Forces	Outcomes
1. Growth in knowledge which creates need for: a. Flexibility and adaptiveness b. New skills c. Speed of response d. Structure of financial markets e. Industrial relations system f. System of scientific research	1. Social system of production a. Rules and norms b. State structure and policies c. System of training labor and management	Extensiveness and form of joint ventures and networks across industrial sectors both within and across countries.
2. Growth in competitiveness across countries caused by reduction in tariffs and reduction in transportation costs	2. Societal values	

While our emphasis is more on the consequences of non-economic institutional patterns which influence the type of networks which emerge, our arguments are still relevant to recent developments in economics as well as the social sciences more generally: Joint ventures and inter-organizational networks facilitate innovation, as well as rapid responses to competitive moves in the marketplace, both of which relate to current work on adaptive costs and benefits (Hage and Jing, 1993), time to market (Schoenberger, 1994; Stalk and Hout, 1990), and adaptive efficiency (North, 1990). Economic growth increasingly depends on the capacity of a nation to develop new products and technologies (Landes, 1998). Thus, our analysis is applicable to the new endogenous theories of economic growth, which address the problem of how institutional arrangements lead to innovation and thus to continued economic development (Romer, 1986, 1990).

THE GENERAL FRAMEWORK: FORCES OF COMPETITION

To address these questions, we need an understanding of why particular forms of networks exist in particular sectors or geographical regions in some countries but not others. We must distinguish between such general forces as knowledge growth and global competition that have attracted the most attention, and the specific forces, institutional context, and cultural norms, that influence the speed and form that influence the evolution of these networks (see table 17.1).

The Growth in Knowledge

More and more industrial sectors are becoming research intensive as both public and private research expenditures increase in absolute terms (National Science Foundation, 1996, 1998). As well, the total expenditure for R & D has grown significantly in most advanced industrial societies. Between 1981 and 1998, total expenditures on non-military research in constant U.S. dollars (1992) increased by 66 percent in the United States and nearly doubled in Japan. In Germany, France, and Italy there was nearly a 50 percent increase during the same time period. Only the United Kingdom remained relatively stagnant (National Science Foundation 1998: appendix 4). In the case of the United States, most of the increase reflected spending by business firms. Nor is this expansion in industrial research limited to only the developed world. As more and more states and firms become concerned about their competitive position in the world economy, they are adopting policies to facilitate industrial innovation (Casper, 1999; Cohen, 1992; Matthews, 1997). Knowledge—as reflected in the rapid rise in the number of university-trained people—has changed the nature of market demands in the following ways. The expansion of education has meant that more educated consumers with complex cognitive structures demand products that are not only high in quality but safe for both the environment and the user (Hage and Powers, 1992). Beyond this, consumers increasingly demand that products be technologically advanced, be of high quality, and have aesthetic characteristics. The most visible sign of the sophistication of new products is that many are being married to the computer chip, and this in turn has meant that the labor force must be flexibly and broadly trained. Equally important is the growth of services, with customers wanting to be treated with tender loving care. Indeed, the distinction between products and services is collapsing as increasingly firms provide after-sales service, and more and more service organizations supply products. These service requirements push organizations into networks with other firms that have more experience in handling customers. Such consumer demands have created a very complex set of product design requirements for manufacturers, requiring technical expertise that the organization frequently does not have. This is especially the circumstance when organizations attempt to market, advertise, and distribute their products in countries where they have not previously been involved, again the impact of global competition (Hergert and Morris, 1988; Kogut and Singh, 1988; Mowery and Nelson, 1999).

The expansion of university graduates has also generated more demand for individualized life styles. Throughout the world, consumers are increasing their demands of individualized goods, at the same time that the world is becoming more differentiated in its particular tastes and combinations of tastes. Indeed, a number of products/services have become quite highly differentiated according to price/quality. High fashion, ready to wear, and discount clothes within the apparel industry is one example and one where even the same product (e.g., the blue jean) varies within each price gradient. Overall, these trends have meant that one firm does designing, another product development, another production, and yet another marketing and distribution, leading to a further proliferation of inter-organizational networks.

Advocates of the globalization thesis who argue the homogenization of tastes—such as Ritzer's (1993) book on McDonaldization—will note that our argument is quite different.[3] On the one hand, there are a few global products (portable phones and VCRs) and some services (American films, hamburgers, and soft drinks) that people across different regions of the world seem to want. But in contrast, most products—especially services—have to be differentiated to fit national tastes. Some of the radical increase in joint ventures represent marketing and production combinations so that these differences in demand can be accommodated.

The nature of consumer demands and how they have shifted across the last few decades is not the only impact of knowledge on organizations and their competitive situation. The growth in knowledge is also changing the task environment for manufacturing and service organizations in a variety of ways (e.g., the creation of radical new technologies such as optic fibers, computer chips, robots, gene therapies, etc., and more generally flexible manufacturing

[Piore and Sabel, 1984]). More critical in our perspective is the substantial reduction in the length of product lives as consumers shift their tastes rapidly (Schoenberger, 1994; Stalk and Hout, 1990). And as firms increase their budgets for research and development, more and more industries engage in complex technologies, particularly in advanced industrialized countries. Nor is research the only cause of short product lives. With the expansion of demands for aesthetics, more and more industries are developing a fashion/design component.

Moreover, there has been the development of joint ventures in material sciences where there are many distinct kinds of niches. In recent decades there have been an estimated eighty thousand new kinds of materials based on the combinations of existing ones. Less evident but perhaps more critical is the division of established markets into a large number of specialty niches, each with their limited customer demand. Specialty steels, chemicals, and the like are more and more common. In other words, it is not only consumer demands but increasing product availability that has allowed for the niche specialization that is occurring. In turn, increased specialization implies strong pressures towards joint ventures and networks as firms in a variety of sectors seek out competencies and expanding markets (Alter and Hage, 1993).

On the one hand, the general expansion of knowledge and the increased demand for higher-quality products in the context of global competition is encouraging the continual differentiation of markets in many industrial sectors and is requiring organizations to move away from vertical integration where it has existed and move towards small flexible units. Elsewhere (Hage and Hollingsworth, 2000) we have argued that this process is differentiating idea innovation chains in which organizations specialize in one or more of the following aspects of product/process innovation: basic research, applied research, product development, research on manufacturing processes, quality research, and marketing research. A good illustration of this process is the recently published study on the pharmaceutical industry in Germany and the United States (Jungmittag, Reger, and Reiss, 2000). The development of various kinds of inter-organizational relationships is an attempt to create connections between these different specialist organizations.

The Growth in International Competition

The impact of the expansion in knowledge and increased demand for higher quality products would be much less if competition were to remain national in scope. But there has been a reduction of tariffs on manufactured products and services (Gilpin, 2000: 21). Furthermore, within the global economy there has been the creation of large trading blocks such as the European Union and NAFTA but elsewhere as well, including the southern cone in Latin America and Southeast Asia. The corresponding lowering of transportation costs has made many markets global or at least continental in scope, thus resulting in a spiral of international competition in many economic sectors.

During the last three decades, world trade has grown much faster than the growth in the entire global economic output. However, as various critics of the globalization thesis have observed, trade was substantial prior to World War I, being almost as high in 1913 as in 1992 (Bairoch, 1996). What distinguishes the contemporary period from the early period are the following major changes: (1) many more countries are involved in the world trade of manufactured products than before; (2) many more products are now involved, most of which have been invented in the last three decades; and (3) many of these products and services—cars, commercial aircraft, and computers—are quite complex, involving a number of components which come from several nations. In other words, there is an interdependence in this trade that did not exist previously.

But those who argue for the development of a global economy are more likely to stress other aspects of interdependence than just trade. One dimension is the amount of direct foreign investment (FDI), which has been increasing at the rate of 15 percent annually, and thus much faster than the growth in world economic output (Gilpin, 2000: 22–24). In the United States alone, foreign owned assets had reached six trillion dollars in 1998, exceeding the FDI of the United States abroad by one trillion dollars (U.S. Census Bureau, 1999).

Globalization of competition has had a number of obvious implications. First, it means growth in the number of potential competitors, so that a number of markets are now literally global. Second, it means a much wider potential choice of partners with which to join forces in product development and to establish industrial standards (Gomes-Casseres, 1996). Thus, it is not surprising that a large number of joint ventures cut across national boundaries (Harbison and Pekar, 1998). And third, given the combination of differentiation of consumer tastes as indicated above, companies frequently form alliances to produce simultaneously a specific kind of car, cement, cigarette, chemical product, etc., for each country or even region within a country in order to maintain economies of scope so that efficiency and productivity can continue to grow. Thus a number of marketing and production joint ventures which emerge in order to deal with the problem of differentiated products contain some common elements. Firms often join together when the market is very small and the costs of development and production are quite high.

Another kind of production network that spans national boundaries is one in which the design is completed in one country and the production in another, which Perry (1999) calls buyer-driven commodity chains. This kind of separation across the commodity chain frequently occurs when the cost of labor is the most critical factor in production and the production is moved to the country with the lower labor costs (Korzeniewicz, 1994; Hsing, 1998; Perry, 1999: 166–168; Matthews, 1997). Obviously, every time a firm moves its production offshore, a joint venture or some form of network does not occur, but the shift of production sites from one country to another has led to an increase in the number of joint ventures, licensing agreements, partnerships, etc.

These trends parallel developments in those industries in which most of the segments of the commodity chain are high-tech, requiring high levels of education among the labor force and considerable levels of research. To appreciate why this is the case, we must observe how increases in knowledge at the societal level are impacting on both the demand for and supply of goods and services.

THE GENERAL FRAMEWORK: THE MEDIATING INFLUENCE OF INSTITUTIONAL AND CULTURAL VARIABLES

The expansion in knowledge, changes in consumer tastes, and the growth in international trade do not occur in a vacuum. Instead, they are mediated and influenced by the institutional context and cultural norms of specific societies. For example, institutional arrangements and cultural norms influence the speed with which organizations in a particular society or industry join together in either joint ventures or networks with resulting competitive advantages. Space limitations prevent an explication of all the ways in which these factors influence the evolution of organizational forms, but we suggest several themes below. One is how various institutional arrangements impact on the adoption of new technologies and product innovation, and another is how various institutions influence the ease with which different kinds of networks develop. First, however, we should provide examples of several major types of networks.

Examples of Differential Network Development

The comparative study of the global automobile industry in the late eighties indicated that the inter-organizational form of the *keiretsu* as well as other organizational and cultural factors had given the Japanese automobile industry considerable advantages in the global economy (Womack, et al., 1990). This form of inter-organizational relationship was able to develop new automobile products in a much shorter time span at lower cost as well as to produce automobiles of high quality. Meantime, in the succeeding ten years, American automobile companies began moving away from vertical integration towards a variety of inter-organizational relationships (Mockler, 1999: 20–27), and as a consequence were able to improve the speed with which they were able to develop new products as well as improve their product quality. The theoretical argument is that as both the complexity of products, and especially if these are assembled, and the quality of products increase, then inter-organizational relationships are a more effective method of coordination because they allow separate companies to specialize in specific components and develop greater quality as a consequence. The second theoretical argument is that multiple organizations in a network can respond more quickly to shifts in either technology or market tastes when they are coordinated because highly specialized companies can change more quickly, one of the original insights of Piore and Sabel (1984).

In contrast to the American automobile industry where the development of inter-organizational relationships has been slow, the American biotech industry has developed large numbers of joint ventures and contractual arrangements not only with pharmaceutical companies but with various kinds of research centers, including universities (Powell, 1998; Jungmittag, Reger, and Reiss, 2000). The latter inter-organizational relationships have allowed for quick movement of ideas from basic research into applied research and product development. It is interesting to note that the success of these biotech firms has also led to a number of foreign joint ventures for these American companies. The speed of changes in biomedical research makes an inter-organizational network of organizations specializing in various aspects of the innovation process more effective because networks absorb the necessary tacit knowledge more effectively.

In a further contrast to both the American automobile industry and the American biotech industry, the American shoe industry did not develop inter-organizational relationships, and the percentage of the American shoe market controlled by imports of shoes produced by foreign companies increased from 4 percent in 1960 to 86 percent in 1990 (Footwear Industries of America, 1992). Significantly, this kind of decline did not occur in Italy with its shoe industry, which has a complex set of inter-organizational relationships among small and highly specialized firms (Piore and Sabel, 1984; Perry, 1999) even though in 1991 it paid its workers almost fourteen dollars per hour in contrast the American shoe worker receiving only nine dollars and the Taiwanese less than four dollars per hour. The Italian inter-organizational networks have been highly adaptive to changing market tastes and have remained innovative (Perry, 1999: 93–96). These networks are located in what are called industrial districts that provide the trust for companies to become highly specialized and dependent upon each other (Lazerson, 1993; Perry, 1999; Piore and Sabel, 1984; Pyke and Sengenberger, 1992). The few American shoe firms that have done well, such as Nike and Reebok, are relatively new companies that built supply-dominated commodity chains with plants in East and Southeast Asia (Footwear Industries of American, 1992; Korzeniewicz, 1994). However, these buyer-dominated chains are quite different from the previously discussed inter-organizational networks because they are only concerned with low-price goods and they achieve adaptability with short-term contracts and quick shifts to other suppliers.

Another example of where inter-organizational networks of many small companies have proved resilient in the face of competition is the sub-contracting networks for computer components, printers, and similar equipment in Taiwan (Hsing, 1998; Matthews, 1997). These networks provide components and equipment for the major American companies such as Dell and Hewlett-Packard. Furthermore, with state help, industrial districts have been created in which complex networks have been constructed which involve both public and private organizations, including research universities. This has allowed the Taiwanese to become a world leader in customized chip making (Matthews, 1997).

One could provide many more examples of where inter-organizational arrangements of one kind or another have provided competitive advantages in both low-tech and high-tech industries, ranging from bicycle manufacturing in Taiwan (Perry, 1999: 166–167) to film making in the United States (Storper, 1997) to machine tools in Germany (Perry, 1999: 107–108) to ceramics in Japan (Perry, 1999: 101–102). However, we are faced with the problem of what are the factors that facilitate the creation of inter-organizational relationships, as well as their capacity to respond to changes in the global economy—our next topic.

The Institutional Context of the Social System of Production

Despite the presence of common global forces such as worldwide competition and the growth of knowledge, convergence in the structure of networks is not occurring in the economies of the advanced industrialized countries. Indeed, the economies of Britain, France, the United States, Germany, and Italy are much more different now than they were some twenty-five years ago, when the post-industrial phase began in earnest. Rather than convergence, there has been increased divergence in how these economies are coordinated and governed. The form and the shape of the networks, even in the same industry, are not the same. Our argument for why there has been this persisting divergence in the nature of networks is somewhat complex, involving our views of how networks fit into a theory of modern capitalism. This perspective makes several assumptions about contemporary capitalism.

First, contemporary capitalism must be comprehended in terms of changes taking place within the global economy. All advanced industrial societies are facing a number of common problems, but because of their distinctive institutional configurations, each country responds differently to common challenges. Second, the institutions which give shape to the distinctive configurations of capitalism have evolved over a long period of time and have a distinctive logic to the way they have evolved. And because of the path-dependent nature of these institutions, capitalism in any particular society is not likely to converge with or mimic in any profound way the distinctive institutional configuration of capitalism in other societies. Third, networks, along with other economic institutions, must be comprehended as part of the larger institutional environment within which they are embedded. And it is the larger institutional environment, interacting with economic institutions, which has shaped a distinctive logic to each society's brand of capitalism. We label this larger institutional environment as a society's social system of production. A social system of production is a constellation of the following (see chapter 11): the underlying values of a society which shape its norms, moral principles, rules, and recipes for action. These in turn influence such other institutional arrangements as the following: a society's system of training (e.g., type of education, skills enhancement) for labor and management; its industrial relations system; its labor markets; the structure and behavior of its financial markets; the structure and behavior of the state; and finally, the structure and behavior of its firms, including the structured relationships among firms, their suppliers, and distributors. And it is the particular configuration of these institutional factors in a particular society that shape the extent of and the form of the networks which emerge in a society. Moreover, the institutional environment in which a society's networks are embedded influences the consequences of its particular form of networks in the following ways:

- whether they lead to short- or long-term horizons in decision making
- the variability in the speed with which networks adapt to changes in the world economy

Networks in some societies have the capacity to adapt to their larger environment in such a way as to develop entirely new products but a lower capacity to make incremental changes on existing products. In other societies, the social system of production and its resulting structure of networks lead to a low capacity to develop new products but a high capacity to make incremental improvement on existing products.

It is not the case that all these inter-organizational networks can easily adapt to shifts in the nature of competition. It depends upon the social system of production in which they are embedded. For example, networks in Japan have found it difficult to move away from long-term relationships in various *keiretsu* in order to have more flexible inter-organizational arrangements similar to those in Taiwan (Perry, 1999: 202).

A society's social system of production and the structure of its networks can be understood only by being sensitive to the society's history from which they have emerged. In short, there is a high degree of path dependency in all market economies, and the direction of their change can only be comprehended by being highly cognizant of what has gone before. There is always a huge overhang of institutional inertia that exercises a powerful influence upon present and future possibilities. Thus, attempting to theorize about networks and firms requires some sensitivity to the environment from which they have emerged.

This, of course, raises larger issues about the spatial environments in which joint ventures and strategic alliances take place in advanced capitalist societies. In an era when the rate of technological change was relatively low, production processes in an industry were relatively standardized, and production runs were quite long, vertical integration was an appropriate strategy for firms which faced high uncertainties and small numbers in their interdependent relationships with other firms. However, when technology changes very rapidly and the costs of technology are very expensive, firms are less inclined to engage in vertical integration, and joint ventures and strategic alliances become more frequent, particularly among firms in different societies. Of course, the motives for this form of coordination are varied—the search for economies of scale, the need for market access, the sharing of risks, the need to have access to technology, the need to pool know-how if no one firm has the capability to achieve its goals. But is the increasing frequency of this form of coordination leading to the convergence of national economies?

Undoubtedly, the increased frequency of joint ventures and strategic alliances does lead to some convergence in certain management styles and work practices among cooperating partners. However, the diffusion of these practices does not bring about a convergence in the institutional arrangements for coordinating economic actors. Before World War II, foreign firms attempted to borrow certain principles of scientific management which had become widespread in the United States, but in general the American practices were greatly modified when implemented. Moreover, in making these modifications, foreign actors did so within the developmental trajectory of their own social system of production. Similarly in the eighties and nineties, selected principles of Japanese networks diffused to other countries, but they were selectively integrated into the local environment.

Each country's social system of production is a configuration of institutions. Each system is constantly changing and is open to influence from other systems. And indeed many technologies and practices do diffuse from one society to another, but the direction of change is constrained by the existing social system of production. Thus, the same technology may exist in numerous countries, but how it is employed varies from one institutional configuration to another.

One recent comparative study (Hollingsworth, Schmitter, and Streeck, 1994) has demonstrated that across countries, clusters of industries develop along particular trajectories, each having its distinct micro-economic dynamics within which markets, networks, corporate hierarchies, associations, and governments operate. Because skills, management techniques, and modes of governance are embedded in distinctive social systems of production, they do not easily diffuse from one nation to another. As a result, variation across countries in social systems of production remains substantial, even if there is convergence at the global level in how a few industries (e.g., chemical, oil, large-scale aircraft) are coordinated.

This variation remains substantial, for there have been great differences in the path dependencies of countries. For more than a century, the German economy has evolved toward a diversified quality social system of production (Herrigel, 1995), whereas since the fifties, the Japanese have hybridized mass production along with a diversified quality social system of production. In both countries, specific institutional arrangements have allowed for the cohesiveness of their distinctive social systems of production. In contrast, the United States has been very much constrained by its earlier fordist mass production system and its "short termism" under the influence of its distinctive financial markets, weak unions and business associations, norms, rules, and recipes for action.

Variation in Modes of Coordination

Hierarchical forms of governance are based on the assumption that in order to reduce uncertainty among actors, relationships must be coordinated within a firm. But in advanced capitalist societies, as technology and knowledge become more complex and as the product life cycle changes more rapidly, hierarchies are less effective in coordinating economic activity.

Due to high research and development costs, and rapid change in products and volatile markets, it is no longer possible, in many industries, to coordinate as many things in house as was possible during the age of mass standardization. Markets and hierarchies can work best when firms are embedded in an institutional environment impoverished by richly developed collective institutional arrangements. But for networks and joint ventures to operate with sustained effectiveness, they must be embedded in an environment which is highly developed with institutions which promote cooperation between processors and suppliers and even among their competitors. Firms must also be embedded in an environment which develops rich, broad, and flexible skills for the work force. In short, advance capitalist societies require cooperative relations and collective resources far in excess to what is needed for markets and hierarchies to function effectively, in excess of what single firms can develop for themselves, and in excess of what rational actors would perceive as important to develop, (Streeck, 1987, 1988).

As Perry (1999) observes, both industrial districts and associations have provided the trust that has made the development of networks much easier in Japan, Germany, and Italy. In contrast, in Taiwan, it has been a combination of Chinese kin networks and state coordination that has facilitated the emergence of inter-organizational networks that have been successful in a number of industries.

Highly effective and sustained sharing of information and cooperation among various actors requires all of the following: collective action on the part of competitors, rich training centers—whether within vocational schools, universities, or other institutions—and institutions willing to provide financing on a long-term basis. In other words, cooperative relations among actors function best when they are embedded in an institutional environment with rich multilateral or collective dimensions which provide these conditions, as in Japan and Germany.

The dominant social system of production in American society has been coordinated by markets and corporate hierarchies, with firms embedded in a weakly developed civil society. Of course, there has been, for some years, an emerging subordinate social system of production in American society, one in which economic coordination is taking place not within firms but within networks among cooperating actors, occasionally competing, who have developed long-term relationships with one another. This pattern is found most clearly in Silicon Valley and in Hollywood (Perry, 1999; Storper, 1997), two examples of industrial districts in the United States.

Some of the most effective American networks have involved cooperative relations among university-based firms, firms requiring a strong knowledge base for the development of their products, and the state and federal governments (National Science Foundation, 1996, 1998; Powell, 1998). Just as the American state's anti-trust activity has placed limits on the cooperative activity among firms, the key actor in promoting multi-lateral cooperative activity among producers has nevertheless been the American state. Significantly, the American state has rarely taken the lead in developing coordinating networks among manufacturing firms in more traditional industries, which historically were coordinated primarily by markets and/or hierarchies. Rather, the American state has been most active during the past half century in developing networks for manufacturing firms in relatively new industries which have addressed the military and health related needs of the society. For example, the following are some of the products and technologies derived from firms coordinated by networks which were firmly embedded in an environment involving cooperative relations with university-based scientists and engineers, the state—especially the military—and other firms, both suppliers and competitors: commercial aircraft, semiconductors, integrated circuits, computers, nuclear power, microwave telecommunications, new materials such as high-strength steel alloys, fiber-reinforced plastics, titanium, and new methods of fabricating metals such as numerical-controlled machine tools. Without networks involving multi-lateral relations with universities, various agencies and departments of the federal government, and numerous business firms, these technologies and products could not have occurred in the United States at the time they did. In the pharmaceutical and other biotech industries, networks have been extensive in linking together experts in industry, government laboratories, and land grant universities in the relatively new industries involving the fields of pharmacology, biochemistry, immunology, molecular and cell biology (Hollingsworth, 1991a, 1991b; National Science Foundation, 1998).

One important feature of such networks is that they link organizations having different knowledge bases. This kind of coordination is not possible within a single hierarchy, as no firm has had the capacity to incorporate all the knowledge and resources to develop any one of the technologies and products listed above. Nor could a single firm linked with its suppliers have developed these products. They could be developed only because firms were engaged in highly developed, cooperative, and long-term relationships involving many other organizations.

Because of the pervasiveness of a market mentality, the strong tradition of entrepreneurship, and the flexibility of the external labor market, and because venture capital markets have been quite well developed in the United States, it has been relatively easy, by world standards, for American researchers and engineers to develop their own firms with joint ventures and strategic alliances in order to commercialize new products, especially when the federal government has blessed such ventures with research and development funds and immunity from anti-trust concerns. This has been especially common in information-based industries in and around the Silicon Valley, California, as well as in the biomedical and artificial intelligence related industries throughout the United States.

With a cross-national perspective, it is apparent that network-type arrangements have performed extremely well in American society in advancing knowledge at the frontiers of science and in the development of new products derived from basic science. The Americans have been particularly successful in the development of new products which have many kinds of military and health-related applications. However, the American R & D system has been less successful in improving upon older products for commercial markets. For example, when one observes the Japanese system of research and development, one quickly becomes aware that the American system of networking facilitates creativity in developing new products, but it has had major shortcomings in improving on existing products, especially in large corporate hierarchies. Though the Japanese are much weaker in basic science, have not succeeded in developing radically new products, and are somewhat deficient in entrepreneurial leadership, they have concentrated on establishing very close communication among researchers and engineers with production and marketing personnel involved in existing product technologies. Japanese firms are also increasingly embedded in networks involving university-based scientists and engineers, but established networks are closely linked with established production facilities, whereas in the United States, manufacturing networks tend to be less involved with production personnel, or else the production activity is only at the periphery of the network (Aoki, 1988; Hollingsworth, 1991a, 1991b; Hage and Hollingsworth, 2000).

In Japan, R & D and production personnel frequently move back and forth among production sites, research laboratories, and engineering departments. Americans are socialized in their educational system to be highly individualistic, to make scientific discoveries, and to develop new products. In contrast, the Japanese are socialized to de-emphasize individualism and to cooperate within groups, to be highly attentive to detail, and to improve upon existing products. Whereas the Americans excel in entrepreneurship in the development of new products, the Japanese excel in establishing feedback types of communication within existing organizations or stable networks in improving production and redesign (Aoki, 1988: 247). In other words, the Japanese emphasis is clearly on the production phases of the industrial process, whereas the Americans have tended to be less creative in this area, but more creative in developing completely new products. And this difference in where networks focus their energies in the two countries does much to explain why the Japanese have over the long run been so successful in commercially producing and marketing products which the Americans first developed (Hollingsworth, 1997).

Similarly in Europe, especially in northern Italy and Germany, producers of more traditional products (automobiles, ceramics, textiles, furniture, machine tools, shoes) are embedded in a rich infrastructure consisting of training institutes, business associations, and local and regional governments (Schmitter and Streeck, 1981; Streeck, 1991; Piore and Sabel, 1984; Perry, 1999; Pyke and Sengenberger, 1992). And it is from this cooperative environment that diversified, high-quality production emerged in these European industries. One reason why American firms in these industries have been less competitive in recent decades, at least internationally, is because of the weakness of networks embedded in the type of institutional environment which is so richly developed in Germany and northern Italy.

Finally, there is one other aspect of American networks in high-tech industries which deserves mention. Because of the flexible external labor market in the United States, it is very difficult for American firms to keep knowledge proprietary. The moving of personnel from one organization to another undoubtedly facilitates communication, creativity, and the development of new products. But because knowledge is so easily siphoned from American firms, they are somewhat limited in their ability to focus all of their talents on the long-term development of particular products once they come into existence— whereas the rigid external labor market in Japan and Germany permits firms in these countries to focus more energy on the improvement and refinement of products. As technology in sectors of advanced capitalist societies becomes increasingly complex, changes more rapidly, and becomes more expensive, actors in these industries are increasingly finding that various types of networks are an effective form of coordinating and transacting with each other, even in rather traditional industries. But to maximize their effectiveness as governance arrangements, networks need to be embedded in a rich institutional environment involving various forms of collective behavior.

Where firms are embedded in an institutional environment rich in collective goods (e.g., employers associations, trade unions, training institutes), flexible systems of production are likely to be dominant. In such a world, the social environment plays an important role in shaping the behavior of firms, the types of products, and production strategies. And the economy is likely to be one whereby economic actors, embedded in a richly developed system of networks, are likely to engage in long-term strategies involving industrial relations and production. But in a world where there is an impoverishment of such an institutional environment, the market mentality plays a more important role in shaping the social environment, and there is a minimum development of the collective goods necessary for the type of networks essential for high-quality products and international competitiveness in the contemporary global economy, except for industries in which product lives are very short (e.g., entertainment, publishing, biotechnology, and software).

This brief comparison of networking in the Japanese, European, and American environments suggests that despite the utility of the concept of networks and despite the fact that networks are becoming more pervasive across countries, there are different types of networks, which tend to be dominant in specific sectors and in specific societies. And the form of a society's networks is shaped very much by the social system of production and culture from which it has emerged.

NOTES

1 On relevant literature on this point, see, e.g., Hollingsworth, 1991a, 1991b.

2 Classification of an industry as high tech can be done on the basis of three characteristics: (1) the amount of the sales dollar spent on research; (2) the complexity of the technology and the speed with which the technology changes; and (3) the level of training or human capital of the industry's labor force, with emphasis on technical training at all levels.

3 Given the variety of ways in which globalization has been defined, we choose to limit our definition to the variety of countries involved in exporting and importing goods and/or services within a single industrial sector. For example, if both the developed and developing countries import and export shoes, as is the case, then one can argue that this sector has been globalized. Much of the controversy over measures of trade as a definition of globalization revolve around the use of an aggregate measure rather than a sectoral one. These provide quite different perspectives on globalization, especially if one adds the requirement that a variety of countries be involved.

References

Abell, Peter. 1989. "Foundations for a Qualitative Comparative Method." *International Review of Social History*. 34: 103–109.

Abolafia, Mitchel Y. 1996. *Making Markets: Opportunism and Restraint on Wall Street.* Cambridge: Harvard University Press.

Acs, Zoltan and David Audretsch, eds. 1993. *Small Firms and Entrepreneurship: An East-West Perspective.* Cambridge: Cambridge University Press.

Adelberger, Karen E. 2000. "Semi-sovereign Leadership? The State's Role in German Biotechnology and Venture Capital Growth." *German Politics*. 9, no. 1: 103–122.

Albert, Michel. 1993. *Capitalism vs. Capitalism.* New York: Four Walls Eight Windows.

Alchian, Armen A. 1977. "Some Implications of Recognition of Property Right Transaction Costs," pp. 234–255 in Karl Brunner, ed., *Economics and Social Institutions: Insights from the Conferences on Analysis and Ideology.* Boston: Martinus Nijhoff.

Alchian, Armen A. and Harold Demsetz. 1972. "Production, Information Costs, and Economic Organization." *American Economic Review*. 62, no. 4: 777–795.

Aldrich, Howard and T. Sasaki. 1995. "R and D consortia in the United States and Japan." *Research Policy*. 24: 301–316.

Alter, Catherine and Jerald Hage. 1993. *Organizations Working Together: Coordination in Interorganizational Networks.* Beverly Hills, Calif.: Sage.

Amable, Bruno. 2000. "Institutional Complementarity and Diversity of Social Systems of Innovation and Production." *Review of International Political Economy*. 7: 645–687.

American Banker. 1989. *Top Numbers 1989.* Washington, D.C.: American Banking Association.

Amin, Ash and Nigel Thrift, eds. 1994. *Globalization, Institutions, and Regional Development in Europe.* Oxford: Oxford University Press.

Andersen, Svein S. and Tom R. Burns. 1992. *Societal Decision-making: Democratic Challenges to State Technocracy.* Aldershot, Hampshire: Dartmouth.

Aoki, Masahiko. 1988. *Information, Incentives and Bargaining in the Japanese Economy.* Cambridge: Cambridge University Press.

Aoki, Masahiko. 1990. "Towards an Economic Model of the Japanese Firm." *Journal of Economic Literature*. 26, no. 1: 1–27.

399

Archer, Margaret S. 1996. *Culture and Agency: The Place of Culture in Social Theory.* Revised Edition. Cambridge: Cambridge University Press.

Arjomand, Said Amir. 1988. *The Turban for the Crown: The Islamic Revolution in Iran.* New York: Oxford University Press.

Arjomand, Said Amir. 2002, forthcoming. "Introduction: The Concept of Revolution in Comparative History and Sociology," in *Revolution in World History.* Chicago: University of Chicago Press.

Arora, Ashish, Ralph Landau and Nathan Rosenberg, eds. 1998. *Chemicals and Long-term Economic Growth: Insights from the Chemical Industry.* New York: John Wiley & Sons, Inc.

Arrow, Kenneth J. 1974. *The Limits of Organization.* New York: Norton.

Arrow, Kenneth J. and Frank H. Hahn. 1971. *General Competitive Analysis.* Edinburgh: Oliver and Boyd.

Arthur, William Brian. 1988a. "Self-reinforcing Mechanisms in Economics," pp. 9–31 in Philip W. Anderson, Kenneth J. Arrow and David Pines, eds., *The Economy as an Evolving Complex System.* Redwood City, Calif.: Addison-Wesley.

Arthur, William Brian. 1988b. "Competing Technologies: An Overview," pp. 590–607 in Giovani Dosi, Christopher Freeman, Richard Nelson, Gerald Silverberg and Luc Soete, eds., *Technical Change and Economic Theory.* London: Pinter Publishers.

Audretsch, David and Julie Elston. 1994. "Does Firm Size Matter?: Evidence of the Impacts of Liquidity Constraints on Firm Investment Behavior." *Discussion Paper No. 1072.* London: Centre for Economic Policy Research.

Badaracco, Joseph L. 1991. *The Knowledge Link: How Firms Compete Through Strategic Alliances.* Boston: Harvard Business School Press.

Bairoch, Paul. 1996. "Globalization Myths and Realities: One Century of External Trade and Foreign Investment," p. 179 in Robert Boyer and Daniel Drache, eds., *States Against Markets: The Limits of Globalization.* London: Routledge.

Baker, Wayne E. 1984. "The Social Structure of a National Securities Market." *American Journal of Sociology.* 89, no. 4: 775–811.

Balabkins, Nicholas. 1964. *Germany Under Direct Controls.* New Brunswick, N.J: Rutgers University Press.

Barker, Roger Garlock. 1968. *Ecological Psychology: Concepts and Methods for Studying the Environment of Human Behavior.* Stanford: Stanford University Press.

Barker, Roger Garlock and Phil Schoggen. 1973. *Qualities of Community Life: Methods of Measuring Environment and Behavior Applied to an American and an English Town.* San Francisco: Jossey-Bass.

Barker, Roger Garlock and associates. 1978. *Habitats, Environments, and Human Behavior.* San Francisco: Jossey-Bass.

Barnett, William P. and Terry L. Amburgey. 1990. "Do Larger Organizations Generate Stronger Competition?," pp. 78–102 in Jitendra V. Singh, ed., *Organizational Evolution: New Directions.* Newbury Park, Calif.: Sage.

Barry, Brian. 1978. *Sociologists, Economists and Democracy.* Chicago: University of Chicago Press.

Barry, Brian and Russel Hardin. 1982. *Rational Man in Irrational Society?* London: Sage.

Barwise, Jon and John Perry. 1998. *Situations and Attitudes.* Cambridge: Cambridge University Press.

Barwise, Jon. 1988. *The Situation in Logic.* Stanford: Center for the Study of Language and Information, Lecture Notes 17.

Baumgartner, Thomas Martin and Tom R. Burns, eds. 1984. *Transitions to Alternative Energy Systems: Entrepreneurs, New Technologies and Social Change.* Boulder, Colo.: Westview.

Bechtel, William. 1986. *Integrating Scientific Disciplines.* Dordrecht: Martinus Nijhoff.

Beck, Ulrich. 1986. *Risikogellschaft: Auf dem Weg in Eine Andere Moderne.* Frankfurt: Suhrkamp.

Beck, Ulrich. 2000. *World Risk Society.* Cambridge: Polity Press.

Becker, Gary Stanley. 1975. *Human Capital: A Theoretical and Empirical Analysis, with Special Reference to Education.* Second edition. New York: National Bureau of Economic Research; distributed by Columbia University Press.

Becker, Gary Stanley. 1981. *A Treatise on the Family.* Cambridge: Harvard University Press.

Becker, Gary Stanley. 1990. *The Economic Approach to Human Action.* Chicago: University of Chicago Press.

Becker, Gary Stanley. 1991. *A Treatise on the Family.* Enlarged edition. Cambridge: Harvard University Press.

Becker, Gary Stanley. and Richard A. Posner. 1993. "Cross-Cultural Differences in Family and Sexual Life: An Economic Analysis." *Rationality and Society.* 5, no. 4: 421–431.

Becker, Josef and Franz Knipping, eds. 1986. *Power in Europe?* Berlin: Walter de Gruyter.

Beetham, David. 1994. *Defining and Measuring Democracy.* London: Sage.

Ben-Ner, Avner. 1988. "Comparative Empirical Observations on Worker-Owned and Capitalist Firms." *International Journal of Industrial Organization.* 6: 7–31.

Berg, Peter. 1997. "Fostering High Performance Work Systems in Germany and the United States." Paper presented at the EMOT conference, Berlin, January.

Berger, Peter L. and Thomas Luckmann. 1969. *The Social Construction of Reality: A Treatise in the Sociology of Knowledge.* London: The Penguin Press.

Berger, Suzanne, ed. 1982. *Interest Politics in Western Europe.* New York: Cambridge University Press.

Berger, Suzanne and Ronald Dore, eds. 1996. *National Diversity and Global Capitalism.* Ithaca: Cornell University Press.

Berghahn, Volker. 1984. "Ideas into Politics: The Case of Ludwig Erhard," pp. 178–192 in R. J. Bullen, Harmut Pogge von Strandmann and A. B. Polonsky, eds., *Ideas into Politics: Aspects of European History 1880–1950.* London: Croom Helm.

Berghahn, Volker. 1986. *The Americanization of West German Industry.* Cambridge: Cambridge University Press.

Berglöf, Erik. 1990. *Corporate Control and Capital Structure: Essays on Property Rights and Financial Contracts.* Stockholm: Institute of International Business.

Berton, Lee. 1995. "Big Accounting Firms Weed Out Risky Clients." *Wall Street Journal.* 26 June, pp. B1, B6.

Berton, Lee and Joann Lublin. 1992. "Seeking Shelter: Partnership Structure is Called into Question as Liability Risk Rises." *Wall Street Journal.* 10 June 1992.

(Biotechnology Industry Organization). 1998. *Biotechnology Editors and Reporters Guide, 1997–98.* Biotechnology Industry Organization publication, downloaded from World Wide Web and on file with author.

Black, John Stanley. 1978. "Attitudinal, Normative, and Economic Factors in Early Response to Energy-Use Field Experiment," Doctoral Dissertation, Department. of Sociology, University of Wisconsin.

Blackmer, Donald and Sidney Tarrow, eds. 1975. *Communism in Italy and in France.* Princeton: Princeton University Press.

Blankenburg, Erhard. 1994. "The Infrastructure for Avoiding Civil Litigation: Comparing Cultures of Legal Behavior in the Netherlands and West Germany." *Law and Society Review.* 28, no. 4: 789–808.

Blankenburg, Erhard, and Freek Bruinsma. 1994. *Dutch Legal Culture.* Deventer and Boston: Kluwer.

Blau, Peter. 1964. *Exchange and Power in Social Life.* New York: Wiley.

Bloch-Lainé, François and Jean Bouvier. 1986. *Profession: Fonctionnaire.* Paris: Seuil.

Boltho, Andrea, ed. 1982. *The European Economy.* Oxford: Oxford University Press.

Borrus, Michael G. and John Zysman. 1997. "Wintelism and the Changing Terms of Global Competition: Prototype of the Future?" Berkeley: BRIE working paper.

Bossuat, Gérard. 1984. "Le Poids de l'Aide Américaine sur la Politique Economique et Financière de la France en 1948." *Relations Internationales.* 37: 17–36.

Bossuat, Gérard. 1986. "L'Aide Américaine à la France après la Seconde Guerre Mondiale." *Vingtième Siècle*. 9: 17–35.

Boudon, R. 1996. "The Cognitivist Model: A Generalized 'Rational-Choice' Model." *Rationality and Society*. 8, no. 2: 123–150.

Bourdieu, Pierre. 1982. *Die feinen Unterschiede: Kritik der Gesellschaftlichen Urteilskraft*. Frankfurt: Suhrkamp.

Bourdieu, Pierre. 1985. *Sozialer Raum und "Klassen": Leçon sur la Leçon. Zwei Vorlesungen*. Frankfurt: Suhrkamp.

Bourdieu, Pierre. 1991. *Language and Symbolic Power*. Cambridge: Cambridge University Press.

Bourdieu, Pierre, et al. 1999. *The Weight of the World: Social Suffering in Contemporary Society*. Cambridge: Polity Press.

Boyer, Robert. 1996. "The Convergence Hypothesis Revisisted: Globalization But Still the Century of Nations?" pp. 29–59 in Suzanne Berger and Ronald Philip Dore, eds., *National Diversity and Global Capitalism*. Ithaca: Cornell University Press.

Boyer, Robert, 1997. "The Variety and Unequal Performance of Really Existing Markets: Farewell to Doctor Pangloss," pp. 55–93 in J. Rogers Hollingsworth and Robert Boyer, eds., *Contemporary Capitalism: The Embeddedness of Institutions*. Cambridge and New York: Cambridge University Press.

Boyer, Robert. 1990. *The Regulation School: A Critical Introduction*. New York: Columbia University Press.

Boyer, Robert and Benjamin Coriat. 1986. "Technical Flexibility and Macro Stabilization." *Ricerche Economiche*. XL: 771–835.

Boyer, Robert and Daniel Drache, eds. 1996. *States Against Markets: The Limits of Globalization*. London: Routledge.

Boyer, Robert and André Orléan. 1991. *Why Are Institutional Transitions So Difficult?* Textes Présentés à la Conférence: "L'économie des Conventions," Paris, 27–28 March. Paris: CEPREMAP.

Braunthal, Gerard. 1965. *The Federation of German Industry in Politics*. Ithaca: Cornell University Press.

Browning, Larry, Janice Beyer, and Judy Shetler. 1995. "Building Cooperation in a Competitive Industry: SEMATEC and the Semiconductor Industry." *Academy of Management Journal*. 38: 113–151.

Budros, Art. 1992. "The Making of an Industry: Organizational Births in New York's Life Insurance Industry, 1842–1904." *Social Forces*. 70: 1013–1033.

Bunge, Mario. 1999. *The Sociology—Philosophy Connection: With a Foreword by Raymond Boudon*. New Brunswick, N.J.: Transaction Publishers.

Burgess, Simon and Michael M. Knetter. 1996. "An International Comparison of Employment Adjustment to Exchange Rate Fluctuations." Working Paper 5861 of the United States National Bureau of Economic Research.

Burki, Shavid Javed and Guillermo E. Perry. 1998. *Beyond the Washington Consensus: Institutions Matter*. Washington, D.C.: World Bank.

Burns, Tom R. 1990. "Models of Social and Market Exchange: Toward a Sociological Theory of Games and Social Behavior," pp. 129–165 in C. Calhoun, M. W. Meyer and W. R. Scott, eds., *Structures of Power and Constraint: Papers in Honor of Peter M Blau*. Cambridge: Cambridge University Press.

Burns, Tom R. 1992. "Technology, Socio-technical Systems, and Technological Development: An Evolutionary Perspective," pp. 206–238 in M. Dierkes and U. Hoffman, eds., *New Technology at the Outset: Social Forces in the Shaping of Technological Innovations*. Frankfurt: Campus.

Burns, Tom R. 1995. "Market and Human Agency: Toward a Socio-economics of Market Organization, Performance, and Dynamics," pp. 15–60 in C. Mongardini, ed., *L'Individuo e il Mercato (Market and Individual): European Amalfi Prize Proceedings 1994*. Rome: Bulzoni Editore.

Burns, Tom R. 1999. "The Evolution of Parliaments and Societies in Europe: Challenges and Prospects." *The European Journal of Social Theory*. 2: 167–194.

Burns, Tom R., T. Baumgartner and P. DeVille. 1985. *Man, Decision and Society*. London: Gordon and Breach.

Burns, Tom R. and T. Dietz. 1992. "Cultural Evolution: Social Rule Systems, Selection, and Human Agency." *International Sociology*. 7: 250–283.

Burns, Tom R. and T. Dietz. 1997. "Evolutionary Sociology: Selective Environments, Human Agency, and Institutional Dynamics." Paper presented at the Conference on "Sociological Theory and the Environment," Zeist, The Netherlands, 20–23 March.

Burns, Tom R. and E. Engdahl. 1998a. "The Social Construction of Consciousness: Collective Consciousness and its Socio-Cultural Foundations." *Journal of Consciousness Studies*. 5: 67–85.

Burns, Tom R. and E. Engdahl. 1998b. "The Social Construction of Consciousness: Individual Selves, Self-Awareness, and Reflectivity." *Journal of Consciousness Studies*. 5, no. 2: 166–184.

Burns, Tom R. and Helena Flam. 1987. *The Shaping of Social Organization*. Beverly Hills, Calif.: Sage.

Burns, Tom R. and A. Gomolinska. 2000. "The Theory of Socially Embedded Games: The Mathematics of Social Relationships, Rule Complexes, and Action Modalities." *Quality and Quantity: International Journal of Methodology*. 34: 379–406.

Burns, Tom R. and A. Gomolinska. 2001. "Socio-cognitive Mechanisms of Belief Change: Applications of Generalized Game Theory to Belief Revision, Social Fabrication, and Self-fulfilling Prophesy." *Cognitive Systems Research*. 2, no. 1: 39–54.

Cable, John. 1985. "Capital Market Information and Industrial Performance: The Role of West German Banks." *Economic Journal*. 95, no. 1: 118–132.

Calhoun, Craig, Marshall W. Meyer and W. Richard Scott, eds. *Structures of Power and Constraint: Papers in Honor of Peter M. Blau*. Cambridge and New York: Cambridge University Press.

Callon, Michel. ed. 1998. *The Laws of the Markets*. Oxford: Blackwell.

Camic, Charles. 1986. "The Matter of Habit." *American Journal of Sociology*. 91: 1039–1087.

Campbell, John L. 1994. "Recent Trends in Institutional Analysis: Bringing Culture Back Into Political Economy." Unpublished paper presented at the Stanford Center for Organizations Research, Stanford University, Stanford, Calif.

Campbell, John L. 1997. "Mechanisms of Evolutionary Change in Economics Governance: Interaction, Interpretation and Bricolage," pp. 10–32 in Lars Magnusson and Jan Ottosson, eds., *Evolutionary Economics and Path Dependence*. Cheltenham, Gloucestershire, UK: Edward Elgar.

Campbell, John L., J. Rogers Hollingsworth and Leon Lindberg, eds. 1991. *The Governance of the American Economy*. Cambridge and New York: Cambridge University Press.

Campbell, John L. and Leon Lindberg. 1990. "Property Rights and the Organization of Economic Activity by the State." *American Sociological Review*. 55: 634–647.

Caporaso, James A. 1995. "Research Design, Falsification, and the Qualitative—Quantitative Divide." *American Political Science Review*. 89: 457–460.

Carew, Anthony. 1987. *Labour Under the Marshall Plan*. Detroit, Mich.: Wayne State University Press.

Carley, Kathleen, ed. 1996. "Artificial Intelligence and Computational Theorizing and Methods Within Sociology." *Sociological Methods and Research*. 25, no. 1: 138–168.

Carlin, Wendy and David Soskice. 1997. "Shocks to the System: The German Political Economy Under Stress." *National Institute Economic Review*. 159: 57–76.

Carroll, Glenn R. and Michael T Hannan. 1989. "Density Dependence in the Evolution of Populations of Newspaper Organizations." *American Sociological Review*. 54: 524–541.

Carroll, Glenn R. and Michael T. Hannan. 2000. *The Demography of Corporations and Industries*. Princeton: Princeton University Press.

Carroll, Glenn R. and Yangchung Paul Huo. 1986. "Organizational Task and Institutional Environments in Ecological Perspective: Findings from the Local Newspaper Industry." *American Journal of Sociology*. 91: 838–873.

Carson, Marcus. 1999. "Competing Discourses in the EU." Discussion paper for research project: How is EU Policy Made?" Uppsala University, Sweden.

Carson, Marcus. 2000. "From Commodity to Public Health Concern: Shifting Policy Paradigms and the Transformation of Food Policy in the European Union." Uppsala University, Sweden: D-Uppsats Graduate Thesis, Department of Sociology, 5 September.

Carson, Marcus. 2001. *From the Folkhem to the Market: Paradigm Shift to System Shift in the Swedish Welfare State*. Forskningsrapport/ Research Report Series, Uppsala Universitet. Uppsala: Institutet för Bostadsforskning.

Casper, Steven. 1998. "The Legal Framework for Corporate Governance: Explaining the Development of Contract Law in Germany and the United States." Berlin: WZB Working Paper.

Casper, Steven. 1999. "High Technology Governance and Institutional Adaptiveness: Do Technology Policies Usefully Promote Commercial Innovation Within the German Biotechnology Industry?" Wassenaar, The Netherlands: The Netherlands Institute for Advanced Studies, unpublished paper.

Casper, Steven. 2000. "Institutional Adaptiveness, Technology Policy, and the Diffusion of New Business Models: The Case of German Biotechnology" *Organization Studies*. 21, no. 5: 887–914.

Casper, Steven. 2001. "The Legal Framework for Corporate Governance: Contract Law and Company Strategies in Germany and the United States," chapter 4 in Peter A. Hall and David Soskice, eds., *Varieties of Capitalism: The Institutional Foundations of Comparative Advantage*. Oxford: Oxford University Press.

Casper, Steven, Mark Lehrer and David Soskice. 1999: "Can High-Technology Industries Prosper in Germany: Institutional Frameworks and the Evolution of the German Software and Biotechnology Industries." *Industry and Innovation*. 6: 6–23.

Casper, Steven and K. Matraves. 1997. "Corporate Governance and Firm Strategy in the Pharmaceutical Industry." Berlin: WZB Working Paper.

Cassis, Youssef. 1997. *Big Business: The European Experience in the Twentieth Century*. Oxford: Oxford University Press.

Casti, John L. 1994. *Complexification: Explaining a Paradoxical World Through The Science of Surprise*. London: Abacus.

Cavell, Stanley. 1979. *The Claim of Reason: Wittgenstein, Skepticism, Morality, and Tragedy*. New York: Oxford University Press.

Cental Bureau of Statistics. 1991. *Statistical Abstract of Israel 1991*. Jerusalem: Central Bureau of Statistics.

Chafets, Ze'ev. 1986. *Heroes and Hustlers, Hard Hats and Holy Men: Inside the New Israel*. New York: Morrow.

Chandler, Alfred D. 1962. *Strategy and Structure: Chapters in the History of the American Industrial Enterprise*. Cambridge, Mass. and London: MIT Press.

Chandler, Alfred D. 1977. *The Visible Hand: The Managerial Revolution in American Business*. Cambridge, Mass.: Belknap and Harvard University Press.

Chandler, Alfred D. 1990. *Scale and Scope*. Cambridge: Harvard University Press.

Chang, Ha-Joon, Gabriel Palma and D. Hugh Whittaker, eds. 1998. "Special Issue on the Asian Crisis." *Cambridge Journal of Economics*. 22, no. 6: 649–808.

Cheng, B. and D. M. Titterington. 1994. "Neural Networks: A Review from a Statistical Perspective." *Statistical Science*. 9: 2–54.

Chesler, Mark A., Joseph Sanders and Kebra S. Kalmuss. 1988. *Social Science in Court: Mobilizing Experts in the School Desegregation Cases*. Madison: University of Wisconsin.

Cheung, Steven N. S. 1983. "The Contractual Nature of the Firm." *Journal of Law and Economics*. 26, no. 2: 1–21.

Cicourel, A. V. 1974. *Cognitive Sociology*. New York: Free Press.

Clark, John Maurice. 1957. *Economic Institutions and Human Welfare*. New York: Alfred Knopf.

Clay, Lucius. 1950. *Decision in Germany*. New York: Doubleday.

Cleeremans, Axel. 1993. *Mechanisms of Implicit Learning: Connectionist Models of Sequence Processing.* Cambridge: MIT Press.

Coase, Ronald H. 1937. "The Nature of the Firm." *Economica.* 4: 386–405.

Coase, Ronald H. 1960. "The Problem of Social Cost." *Journal of Law and Economics.* 3: 1–44.

Coase, Ronald H. 1981. "The Coase Theorem and the Empty Core: A Comment." *Journal of Law and Economics.* 24: 183–187.

Coase, Ronald H. 1988. "The Nature of the Firm: Origin, Meaning, Influence." *Journal of Law, Economics, and Organization.* 4, no. 1: 3–47.

Coase, Ronald H. 1992. "The Institutional Structure of Production." *American Economic Review.* 82, no. 4: 713–719.

Cohen, Elie. 1992. *Le Colbertisme "High Tech": Économie des Télécom et du Grand Projet.* Paris: Hachette.

Cohen, Elie. 1996. *La Tentation Hexogonale: La Souveraineté À L'épreuve de la Mondialisation.* Paris: Seuil.

Cohen, Stephen. 1969. *Modern Capitalist Planning: The French Model.* Cambridge: Harvard University Press.

Coleman, James S. 1990. *Foundations of Social Theory.* Cambridge: Harvard University Press.

Coleman, W., G. Skogstad and M. Atkinson. 1997. "Paradigm Shifts and Policy Networks: Cumulative Change in Agriculture." *Journal of Public Policy.* 16, no. 3: 273–301.

Collier, David. 1995. "Translating Quantitative Methods for Qualitative Researchers: The Case of Selection Bias." *American Political Science Review.* 89: 461–466.

Commons, John R. 1924. *Legal Foundations of Capitalism.* New York: Macmillan. Reprinted 1968, Madison: University of Wisconsin Press; 1974, New York: Augustus Kelley; 1995, with a new introduction by Jeff E. Biddle and Warren J. Samuels, New Brunswick, N.J.: Transaction.

Coughlin, Richard M. 1991. *Morality, Rationality, and Efficiency: New Perspectives on Socio-Economics.* Armonk, N.Y.: M.E. Sharpe.

Cowling, Keith and Roger Sugden. 1993. "Control, Markets and Firms," pp. 66–76 in Christos Pitelis, ed., *Transaction Costs, Markets and Hierarchies.* Oxford: Basil Blackwell.

Crouch, Colin. 1986. "Sharing Public Space: States and Organised Interests in Western Europe," pp. 177–210 in John A. Hall, ed. *States in History.* Oxford: Oxford University Press.

Cuff, Robert D. 1973. "American Historians and the 'Organizational Factor.'" *Canadian Review of American Studies.* 4: 19–31.

Culpepper, Pepper. 2001. "Employers Associations, Public Policy and the Politics of Decentralized Cooperation," chapter 7 in Peter A. Hall and David Soskice, eds., *Varieties of Capitalism: The Institutional Foundations of Comparative Advantage.* Oxford: Oxford University Press.

Damasio, Antonio. 1999. *The Feeling of What Happens: Body and Emotion in the Making of Consciousness.* New York: Harcourt Brace.

Damm, Walter. 1958. *National and International Factors Influencing Cartel Legislation in Germany.* Doctoral Dissertation, University of Chicago.

Dankbaar, Ben. 1994. "Sectorial Governance in the Automobiles Industries of Germany, Great Britain, and France," pp. 156–182 in J. Rogers Hollingsworth, Philippe Schmitter, and Wolfgang Streeck, eds., *Governing Capitalist Economies: Performance and Control of Economic Sectors.* New York: Oxford University Press.

Danto, Arthur. 1974. *Analytische Philosophie der Geschichte.* Frankfurt: Suhrkamp.

David, Paul. 1988. "Path-dependence: Putting the Past in the Future of Economics." *IMSS Technical Report No. 533.* Stanford: Stanford University.

Deacon, Terrence W. 1997. *The Symbolic Species: The Co-evolution of Language and Brain.* New York: W.W. Norton.

De Cecco, Marcello. 1972. "Economic Policy in the Reconstruction Period, 1945–1951," pp. 156–180 in Stuart Joseph Woolf, ed., *The Rebirth of Italy, 1943–1950.* London: Longmans.

Deeg, Richard. 1991. "Banks and the State in Germany: The Critical Role of Subnational Institutions in Economic Governance." Dissertation in Political Science, Massachusetts Institute of Technology, Cambridge, Mass.

De Gaulle, Charles. 1964. *Complete War Memories of de Gaulle.* New York: Simon and Schuster.

Delacroix, Jacques and Glenn R. Carroll. 1983. "Organizational Foundings: An Ecological Study of the Newspaper Industries of Argentina and Ireland." *Administrative Science Quarterly.* 28: 274–291.

Delacroix, Jacques and Michael E. Solt. 1988. "Niche Formation and Foundings in the California Wine Industry, 1941–84," pp. 53–70 in Glenn R. Carroll, ed., *Ecological Models of Organizations.* Cambridge, Mass: Ballinger.

Demsetz, Harold. 1988. "The Theory of the Firm Revisited." *Journal of Law, Economics, and Organization.* 4, no. 1: 141–162.

Dennett, Daniel. 1995. *Darwin's Dangerous Idea: Evolution and the Meanings of Life.* New York: Simon and Schuster.

Detailhandel, Hoofdbedrijfschap. 1995. *Trendrapport Detailhandel.* Den Haag: Hoofdbedrijfschap Detailhandel.

Deutsche Bundesbank. 1992. "Longer Term Trends in the Financing Patterns of West German Enterprises." *Monthly Report of the Deutsche Bundesbank.* 44, no. 10: 25–39.

Deutsche Bundesbank. 1997. "Quarterly Report." November.

Devlin, Keith. 1993. *Infos und Infone: Die mathematische Struktur der Information.* Basel: Birkhäuser-Verlag engl. *Logic of Information.* Cambridge: Cambridge University Press. 1991.

Devlin, Keith. 1999. *InfoSense: Turning Information into Knowledge.* New York: W. H. Freeman and Company.

Diamond, Larry. "Is the Third Wave Over?" *Journal of Democracy.* 7, no. 3: 20–37.

DiMaggio, Paul J. and Walter W. Powell. 1983. "The Iron Cage Revisited: Institutional Isomorphism." *American Sociological Review.* 48: 147–160.

DiMaggio, Paul J. and Walter W. Powell. 1991. "Introduction," pp. 1–38 in Walter W. Powell and Paul J. DiMaggio, eds., *The New Institutionalism in Organizational Analysis.* Chicago: University of Chicago Press.

D'Iribarne, Philippe. 1989. *La Logique de l'Honneur.* Paris: Editions du Seuil.

Dixit, Avinash and Robert Pindyck. 1994. *Investment Under Uncertainty.* Princeton: Princeton University Press.

Djelic, Marie-Laure. 1996. *The Structural Transformation of West European Industries: The Role of the United States, 1945–1954.* Ph.D. Dissertation, Sociology Department, Harvard University.

Djelic, Marie-Laure. 1998. *Exporting the American Model: The Post-War Transformation of European Business.* Oxford: Oxford University Press.

Djelic, Marie-Laure. 1999. "From a Typology of Neo-institutional Arguments to their Cross-fertilization." ESSEC Working Paper, France.

Djelic, Marie-Laure. 2000. "The United States of Europe." *European Business Forum.* 2: 20–21.

Djelic, Marie-Laure and Jabril Bensedrine. 2001. "Globalization and its Limits: The Making of International Regulation," pp. 426–471 in Glenn Morgan, Richard Whitley and Peer Hull Kristensen, eds., *Organizing Transnationally.* Oxford: Oxford University Press.

Djelic, Marie-Laure, Mitchell Koza and Arie Lewin. 1999. "Are Networks New Forms of Organization?" Paper presented at the American Academy of Management, Chicago.

Dobbin, Frank. 1994. *Forging Industrial Policy.* New York: Cambridge University Press.

Doeringer, Peter B. and Michael J. Piore. 1971. *Internal Labor Markets and Manpower Analysis.* Lexington, Mass.: D.C. Heath.

Don, Yehuda. 1968. "Development of Production Cooperatives in Israel: A Statistical Analysis," pp. 43–72 in Yehuda Don and Yair Levi, eds., *Public and Co-operative Economy in Israel.* Liége: International Centre of Research and Information on Public and Co-operative Economy, CIRIEC.

Dore, Ronald. 1983. "Goodwill and the Spirit of Market Capitalism." *British Journal of Sociology.* 34, no. 4: 459–482.

Dorn, Walter. 1957. "The Debate Over American Occupation in Germany in 1944–1945." *Political Science Quarterly.* 72, no. 4: 481–501.

Dosi, Giovanni. 1984. *Technical Change and Industrial Transformation: The Theory and An Application to the Semiconductor Industry.* London: Macmillan Press.

Douglas, Mary. 1987. *How Institutions Think.* Syracuse, N.Y.: Syracuse University Press.

Doz, Yves L. and Gary Hamel. 1998. *Alliance Advantage: The Art of Creating Value Through Partnering.* Boston: Harvard Business School Press.

Dretske, Fred. 1988. *Explaining Behavior: Reasons in a World of Causes.* Cambridge: MIT Press.

Dreyfus, Michel. 1995. *Histoire de la CGT: Cent Ans de Syndicalisme en France.* Paris: Editions Complexe.

Drucker, Peter. 1946. *Concept of the Corporation.* New York: New American Library.

Dryzek, John S. 1996. "The Informal Logic of Institutional Design," pp. 103–125 in Robert E. Goodin, ed., *The Theory of Institutional Design.* Cambridge: Cambridge University Press.

DuBoff, Richard and Edward Herman. 1980. "Alfred Chandler's New Business History: A Review." *Politics and Society.* 10, no. 1: 87–110.

Duchêne, François. 1994. *Jean Monnet: The First Statesman of Interdependence.* New York: W.W. Norton & Company.

Duhamel, Georges. 1930. *Scenes de la Vie Future.* Paris: Mercure de France.

Durkheim, Emile. 1951. *Suicide.* New York: The Free Press.

Durlauf, Steven N. 1991. "Path Dependence in Economics: The Invisible Hand in the Grip of the Past." *American Economics Association Papers and Proceedings.* 81: 70–74.

Dussauge, Pierre and Bernard Garrette. 1999. *Cooperative Strategy: Competing Successfully Through Strategic Alliances.* Chichester, N.Y.: Wiley.

Dyas, Gareth and Heinz Thanheiser. 1976. *The Emerging European Enterprise: Strategy and Structure in French and German Industry.* Boulder, Colo.: Westview Press.

Eberly, Don E., ed. 2000. *The Essential Civil Society Reader: Classic Essays in the American Civil Society Debate.* Lanham, Md.: Rowman & Littlefield.

Edelman, Gerald M. 1987. *Neural Darwinism.* New York: Basic Books.

Edelman, Gerald M. 1990. *The Remembered Present: A Biological Theory of Consciousness.* New York: Basic Books.

Edelman, Gerald M. 1992. *Bright Air, Brilliant Fire: On the Matter of the Mind.* New York: Basic Books.

Eggertsson, Thrainn. 1990. *Economic Behavior and Institutions.* Cambridge: Cambridge University Press.

Ehrmann, Henry. 1957. *Organized Business in France.* Princeton: Princeton University Press.

Eichengreen, Barry. 1997. "Institutions and Economic Growth after World War II," pp. 38–72 in Nicholas Crafts and Gianni Toniolo, eds., *Economic Growth in Europe since 1945.* Cambridge: Cambridge University Press.

Eisenstadt, Shmuel Noah. 1978. *Revolution and the Transformation of Societies: A Comparative Study of Civilizations.* New York: Free Press.

Eisenstadt, Shmuel Noah. 1985. *The Transformation of Israeli Society: An Essay in Interpretation.* London: Weidenfeld and Nicolson.

Eisner, Mark Allen. 1991. *Antitrust and the Triumph of Economics: Institutions, Expertise and Policy Change.* Chapel Hill: University of North Carolina.

Elam, Mark. 1992. "Markets, Morals, and Powers of Innovation." Unpublished paper presented before the School for Workers, University of Wisconsin, Madison, 6 April.

Ellerman, David P. 1992. *Property and Contract in Economics: The Case for Economic Democracy.* Oxford: Basil Blackwell.

Elster, Jon. 1989. *The Cement of Society: A Study of Social Order.* Cambridge: Cambridge University Press.

Elster, Jon. 1999. *Alchemies of the Mind: Rationality and the Emotions.* Cambridge: Cambridge University Press.

Elster, Jon. 2000a. *Strong Feelings: Emotion, Addiction, and Human Behavior. The 1997 Jean Nicod Lectures.* Cambridge: MIT Press.

Elster, Jon. 2000b. *Ulysses Unbound: Studies in Rationality, Precommitment, and Constraints.* Cambridge: Cambridge University Press.

Engström, Yrjö. and David Middleton, eds. 1998. *Cognition and Communication at Work.* Cambridge: Cambridge University Press.

Engwall, Lars and Vera Zamagni, eds. 1998. *Management Education in Historical Perspective.* Manchester: Manchester University Press.

Epstein, Joshua M. and Robert Axtell. 1996. *Growing Artificial Societies: Social Science from the Bottom Up.* Washington, D.C.: Brookings Institution Press.

Erhard, Ludwig. 1958. *Prosperity Through Competition.* New York: Frederick Praeger.

Erhard, Ludwig. 1963. *The Economics of Success.* Princeton, N.J.: Van Nostrand.

Ernst and Young. 1998a. *New Directions 1998: The Twelfth Biotechnology Industry Annual Report.* Palo Alto, Calif.: Ernst and Young.

Ernst and Young. 1998b. *European Life Sciences 1998.* London: Ernst and Young.

Ernst and Young. 1998c. *Aufbruchstimmung 1998: First German Biotechnology Survey.* Munich: Ernst and Young.

Ernst and Young. 2000. *European Life Sciences 2000.* London: Ernst and Young.

Etzioni, Amitai. 1961. *A Comparative Analysis of Complex Organizations.* New York: Free Press.

Etzioni, Amitai. 1975. *A Comparative Analysis of Complex Organizations: On Power, Involvement and Their Correlates.* Revised edition. New York: Free Press.

Etzioni, Amitai. 1988. *The Moral Dimension: Toward a New Economics.* New York: Free Press.

Etzioni, Amitai. 1993. *The Spirit of Community: Rights, Responsibilities and the Communitarian Agenda.* London: Fontana Press.

Etzioni, Amitai. 1994. *Jenseits des Egoismus-Prinzips: Ein neues Bild von Wirtschaft, Politik und Gesellschaft.* Stuttgart: Schäffer-Poeschel.

Etzioni, Amitai. 1996. *The New Golden Rule: Community and Morality in a Democratic Society.* New York: Basic.

Etzioni, Amitai. 1998. "The Methodology of Socio-Economics." *The Journal of Socio-Economics.* 5: 540–549.

Etzioni, Amitai. 2001. "Social Norms: The Rubicon of Social Science." *The Monochrome Society: Essays about the Good Society.* Princeton: Princeton University Press.

Etzioni, Amitai, ed. 1998. *The Essential Communitarian Reader.* Lanham, Md.: Rowman & Littlefield.

Etzioni, Amitai and Paul R. Lawrence. 1991. *Socio-Economics: Toward A New Synthesis.* Armonk, N.Y.: M.E. Sharpe.

European Business Forum. 2000a. "Does the European Management Model Have a Future?" *At the Forum.* Issue 1 (Spring).

European Business Forum. 2000b. "Does the European Management Model Have a Future–Reactions." *At the Forum.* Issue 2 (Summer).

Evans, Peter, Dietrich Rueschmeyer and Theda Skocpol, eds. 1985. *Bringing the State Back In.* New York: Cambridge University Press.

Fama, Eugene. 1980. "Banking in the Theory of Finance." *Journal of Monetary Economics.* 6, no. 1: 39–57.

Federation of Bankers Associations of Japan. 1993. *Japanese Banks '93.* Tokyo: FBAJ.

Festinger, Leon. 1957. *A Theory of Cognitive Dissonance.* Stanford: Stanford University Press.

Field, Alexander. 1984. "Microeconomics, Norms, and Rationality." *Economic Development and Cultural Change.* 32: 683–711.

Finegold, David and David Soskice. 1988. "Britain's Failure to Train: Explanations and Some Possible Strategies." *Oxford Review of Economic Policy.* 4: 21–53.

Fischer, Ernst Peter and Carol Lipson. 1988. *Thinking About Science: Max Delbrück and the Origins of Molecular Biology.* New York: W.W. Norton & Co.

Flam, Helena, ed. 1994. *States and Anti-Nuclear Movements.* Edinburgh: Edinburgh University Press.

Fligstein, Neil. 1985. "The Spread of the Multidivisional Form Among Large Firms, 1919–1979." *American Sociological Review.* 50, no. 3: 377–391.

Fligstein, Neil. 1990. *The Transformation of Corporate Control*. Cambridge: Harvard University Press.

Florida, Richard and Martin Kenney. 1988. "Venture Capital Financial Innovation and Technological Change in the USA." *Research Policy*. 17: 119–137.

Florida, Richard and Martin Kenney. 1991. "Transplanted Organizations: The Transfer of Japanese Industrial Organization to the U.S." *American Sociological Review*. 56: 381–398.

Foerster, Heinz von. 1982. *Observing Systems*. Seaside, Calif.: Intersystems Publications.

Foerster, Heinz von. 1985. *Sicht und Einsicht: Versuche zu Einer Operativen Erkenntnistheorie*. Braunschweig: Vieweg.

Fohlen, Claude. 1973. "The Industrial Revolution in France: 1700–1914," pp. 7–75 in Carlo M. Cipolla, ed., *The Fontana Economic History of Europe: The Emergence of Industrial Societies. Part One*. Glasgow: Fontana/Collins.

Fombrun, Charles J. 1988. "Crafting an Institutionally Informed Ecology of Organizations," pp. 223–239 in Glenn R. Carroll, ed., *Ecological Models of Organizations*. Cambridge, Mass.: Ballinger.

Footwear Industries of America. 1992. *Quarterly Reports* (mimeograph).

Fowler, C. 1994. *Unnatural Selection: Technology, Politics, and Plant Evolution*. London: Gordon and Breach.

Fox, Karl A. 1985. *Social System Accounts: Linking Social and Economic Indicators through Tangible Behavior Settings*. Dordrecht: D. Reidel Publishing Company.

Frank, Robert H. 1997. "The Frame of Reference as a Public Good." *The Economic Journal*. 107: 1832–1847.

Franko, Lawrence. 1974. "The Move Towards a Multidivisional Structure in European Organizations." *Administrative Science Quarterly*. 19, no. 4: 493–506.

Frieden, Jeffry. 1991. "Invested Interests: The Politics of National Economic Policies in a World of Global Finance." *International Organization*. 45, no. 4: 425–450.

Friedland, Roger and Robert A. Alford. 1991. "Bringing Society Back In: Symbols, Practices, and Institutional Contradictions," pp. 232–263 in Walter W. Powell and Paul J. DiMaggio, eds., *The New Institutionalism in Organizational Analysis*. Chicago: University of Chicago Press.

Friedman, Thomas. 1999. *The Lexus and the Olive Tree*. New York: Anchor Books.

Fukuyama, Francis. 1995. *Trust: The Social Virtues and the Creation of Prosperity*. New York: Free Press.

Fukuyama, Francis. 2000. *The Great Disruption: Human Nature and the Reconstitution of Social Order*. London: Profile Books.

Furubotn, Eirik G. and Svetozar Pejovich, eds. 1974. *The Economics of Property Rights*. Cambridge, Mass.: Ballinger.

Furubotn, Eirik G. and Rudolph Richter. 1997. *Institutions in Economic Theory: The Contribution of the New Institutional Economics*. Ann Arbor: University of Michigan Press.

Gambetta, Diego, ed. 1988. *Trust: Making and Breaking Cooperative Relations*. New York: Basil Blackwell.

Garcia, Marie-France. 1986. "La Construction Sociale d'un Marché Parfait: Le Marché au Cadran de Fontaines-en-Sologne." *Actes de la Recherche en Sciences Sociales*. 65: 2–13.

Gardner, Lloyd. 1970. *Architects of Illusion: Men and Ideas in American Foreign Policy, 1941–1949*. Chicago: Quadrangle Books.

Geertz, Clifford. 1983. *Local Knowledge: Further Essays in Interpretative Anthropology*. New York: Basic Books.

Geertz, Clifford. 2000. *Available Light: Anthropological Reflections on Philosophical Topics*. Princeton: Princeton University Press.

Geluk, J. A. 1967. *Zuivelcoöperatie in Nederland: Ontstaan en Ontwikkeling tot Omstreeks 1930*. Den Haag: Royal Dutch Dairy Union FNZ.

Gerhards, J. and Dieter Rucht. 1992. "Mesomobilization: Organizing and Framing in Two Protest Campaigns in West Germany." *American Journal of Sociology*. 98, no. 3: 555–595.

Gerlach, Michael. 1992. *Alliance Capitalism: The Social Organization of Japanese Business*. Berkeley: University of California Press.

Gerschenkron, Alexander. 1962. *Economic Backwardness in Historical Perspective.* Cambridge: Harvard University Press.

Gibbons, Michael, Camille Limoges, Helga Nowotny, Simon Schwartzman, Peter Scott and Martin Trow. 1994. *The New Production of Knowledge: The Dynamics of Science and Research in Contemporary Societies.* London: Sage.

Giddens, Anthony. 1984. *The Constitution of Society: Outline of the Theory of Structuration.* Berkeley: University of California Press.

Giddens, Anthony. 1989. *Sociology.* Cambridge: Polity Press.

Giddens, Anthony. 1991. *Modernity and Self-Identity: Self and Society in the Late Modern Age.* Cambridge: Polity Press.

Giddens, Anthony. 1999. *Runaway World.* New York: Routledge.

Gilbert, Nigel and Rosaria Conte. 1995. *Artificial Societies: The Computer Simulation of Social Life.* London: UCL Press.

Gilbert, G. Nigel and Klaus G. Troitzsch. 1999. *Simulation for the Social Scientist.* Philadelphia, Pa.: Open University Press.

Gilpin, Robert. 2000. *The Challenge of Global Capitalism: The World Economy in the 21st Century.* Princeton: Princeton University Press.

Gilpin, Robert and Jean M. Gilpin. 2000. *The Challenge of Global Capitalism.* Princeton: Princeton University Press.

Gimbel, John. 1968. *The American Occupation of Germany.* Stanford: Stanford University Press.

Gitahy, L. 2000. *A New Paradigm of Industrial Organization: The Diffusion of Technological and Managerial Innovations in the Brazilian Industry.* Ph.D. Dissertation in Sociology, Uppsala, Sweden.

Glynn, Ian. 1999. *An Anatomy of Thought: The Origin and Machinery of the Mind.* London: Phoenix.

Goffman, E. 1974. *Frame Analysis: An Essay on the Organization of Experience.* Cambridge: Harvard University Press.

Goldberg, David Edward. 1988. *Genetic Algorithms in Search, Optimization and Machine Learning.* Reading, Mass.: Addison-Wesley.

Goldberg, Victor P. 1980. "Relational Exchange: Economics and Complex Contracts." *American Behavioral Scientist.* 23, no. 3: 337–352.

Golden, Miriam. 1993. "The Dynamics of Trade Unionism and National Economic Performance." *American Political Science Review.* 87, no. 2: 439–454.

Goldthorpe, John A., ed. 1984. *Order and Conflict in Contemporary Capitalism.* Oxford: Oxford University Press.

Gomes-Casseres, Benjamin. 1996. *The Alliance Revolution: The New Shape of Business Rivalry.* Cambridge: Harvard University Press.

Gottweis, H. 1998. *Governing Molecules: The Discursive Politics of Genetic Engineering in Europe and the United States.* Cambridge: MIT Press.

Grabher, Gernot and David Stark, eds. 1997. *Restructuring Networks in Post-Socialism: Legacies, Linkages and Localities.* Oxford: Oxford University Press.

Grady, John and Martin Weale. 1986. *British Banking, 1960–85.* New York: St. Martin's Press.

Gramsci, Antonio. 1971. "Americanism and Fordism," pp. 277–320 in Quintin Hoare and Geoffrey Nowell Smith, eds. and trans., *Selections from the Prison Notebooks.* New York: International Publishers.

Granovetter, Mark. 1985. "Economic Action and Social Structure: The Problem of Embeddedness." *American Journal of Sociology.* 91, no. 3: 481–510.

Granovetter, Mark. 1992. "Problems of Explanation in Economic Sociology," pp. 25–56 in Nitin Nohria and Robert G. Eccles, eds., *Networks and Organizations: Structure, Form, and Action.* Boston: Harvard Business School Press.

Granovetter, Mark. 1994. "Business Groups," pp. 453–475 in Neil J. Smelser and Richard Swedberg, eds., *The Handbook of Economic Sociology.* Princeton: Princeton University Press.

Granovetter, Mark and Richard Swedberg, eds. 1992. *The Sociology of Economic Life.* San Francisco: Westview Press.

Grant, Wyn. 1987. *Business and Politics in Britain.* Houndsmill and London: Macmillan.

Grant, Wyn and David Marsh. 1977. *The CBI.* London: Hodder & Stoughton.

Graubard, Stephen, ed. 1964. *A New Europe?* Boston: Beacon.

Gravelle, Hugh and Ray Rees. 1992. *Microeconomics,* 2nd edition. Harlow, U.K.: Longman.

Greider, William. 1987. *Secrets of the Temple: How the Federal Reserve Runs the Country.* New York: Touchstone.

Greif, Avner. 1996. "The Study of Organizations and Evolving Organizational Forms Through History: Reflections from the Late Medieval Family Firm." *Industrial and Corporate Change.* 5, no. 2: 473–501.

Greif, Avner. 1998. "Historical and Comparative Institutional Analysis." *American Economic Review. Papers and Proceedings.* 88, no. 2: 80–84.

Grindley, Peter and David J. Teece. 1997. "Managing Intellectual Capital: Licensing and Cross-Licensing in Semiconductors and Electronics." *California Management Review.* 39: 8–39.

Grossman, Gene and Elhanan Helpman. 1994. "Endogenous Innovation in the Theory of Growth." *Journal of Economic Perspectives.* 8, no. 1: 23–44.

Grossman, Sanford J. and Oliver D. Hart. 1986. "The Costs and Benefits of Ownership: A Theory of Vertical and Lateral Integration." *Journal of Political Economy.* 94, no. 4: 691–719.

Guéhenno, Jean-Marie. 1993. *La Fin de la Démocratie.* Paris: Flammarion.

Guillén, Mauro. 1994. *Models of Management: Work, Authority and Organization in a Comparative Perspective.* Chicago: University of Chicago Press.

Haag, Günter. 1989. *Dynamic Decision Theory: Applications to Urban and Regional Topics.* Dordrecht: Kluwer.

Haavelmo, Trygve. 1997. "Econometrics and the Welfare State (Nobel Lecture)." *American Economic Review.* 87 (supplement, December): 13–17.

Habermas, J. 1975. *Legitimation Crisis.* Boston: Beacon Press.

Hage, Jerald. 1999. "Organizational Innovation and Organizational Change." *Annual Review of Sociology.* 25: 597–622.

Hage, Jerald. 2000. "Die Innovation von Organisationen und die Organisation von Innovationen." *Österreichische Zeitschrift für Geschichtswissenschaften.* 1: 58–81.

Hage, Jerald, ed. 1987. *Futures of Organizations.* Lexington, Mass.: D.C. Heath.

Hage, Jerald and Catherine Alter. 1997. "A Typology of Interorganizational Relationships and Networks," pp. 94–126 in J. Rogers Hollingsworth and Robert Boyer, eds., *Contemporary Capitalism: The Embeddedness of Institutions.* Cambridge and New York: Cambridge University Press.

Hage, Jerald and J. Rogers Hollingsworth. 2000. "A Strategy for Analysis of Idea Innovation Networks and Institutions." *Organization Studies.* 21: 971–1004.

Hage, Jerald and Zhongren Jing. 1993. "Adaptive Costs: Another Issue in Institutional Economics." Revision of a paper presented at the annual meetings of the Society for the Advancement of Economics, March, New York.

Hage, Jerald and Charles Powers. 1992. *Post-industrial Lives.* Newbury Park, Calif.: Sage.

Hagedoorn, John. 1993. "Strategic Technology Alliances and Modes of Cooperation in High-technology Industries," pp. 116–138 in Gernot Grabher, ed., *The Embedded Firm: On the Socioeconomics of Industrial Networks.* London: Routledge.

Håkansson, Håkan and A. Lundgren. 1997. "Paths in Time and Space: Path Dependence in Industrial Networks," pp. 119–137 in Lars Magnusson and Jan Ottosson, eds., *Evolutionary Economics and Path Dependence.* Cheltenham, UK: Edward Elgar Publishing.

Haken, Hermann. 1982. *Synergetik: Eine Einführung.* Berlin: Springer-Verlag.

Haken, Hermann. 1991. *Synergetic Computers and Cognition: A Top-Down Approach to Neural Nets.* Berlin: Springer.

Hall, Maximilian. 1993. *Banking Regulation and Supervision: A Comparative Study of the UK, USA and Japan.* Aldershot: Edward Elgar.

Hall, Peter A. 1986. *Governing the Economy: The Politics of State Intervention in Britain and France.* Cambridge: Polity Press; New York: Oxford University Press.

Hall, Peter A. 1992. "The Movement from Keynesianism to Monetarism: Institutional Analysis and British Economic Policy in the 1970s," pp. 90–113 in Sven Steinmo, Kathleen Ann Thelen and Frank Longstreth, eds., *Structuring Politics: Historical Institutionalism in Comparative Analysis*. Cambridge: Cambridge University Press.

Hall, Peter A. 1999. "The Political Economy of Europe in an Era of Interdependence," pp. 135–163 in Herbert Kitschelt et al., eds., *Continuity and Change in Contemporary Capitalism*. New York: Cambridge University Press.

Hall, Peter A. and Robert Franzese. 1998. "Mixed Signals: Central Bank Independence, Coordinated Wage Bargaining and European Monetary Union." *International Organization*. Summer: 505–535.

Hall, Peter A. and David Soskice. 2001. "Introduction," in *Varieties of Capitalism: The Institutional Foundations of Comparative Advantage*. Oxford: Oxford University Press.

Hall, Peter A. and David Soskice, eds. 2001. *Varieties of Capitalism: The Institutional Foundations of Comparative Advantage*. Oxford: Oxford University Press.

Hall, Peter and Rosemary Taylor. 1996. "Political Science and the Three New Institutionalisms." *Political Studies*. XLIV: 952–973.

Halliday, Terence C., Michael J. Powell and Mark W. Granfors. 1987. "Minimalist Organizations: Vital Events in State Bar Associations, 1870–1930." *American Sociological Review*. 52: 456–471.

Hamilton, Gary G. and Nichole Woolsey Biggart. 1988. "Market, Culture, and Authority: A Comparative Analysis of Management and Organization in the Far East." *American Journal of Sociology*. 94: S52–S94.

Hancke, Bob and Steven Casper, 1996. "ISO 9000 in the French and German Car Industry." Discussion Paper of the Wissenschaftszentrum, Berlin.

Handelsblatt. 1996. "Massive Behinderung der Forschung." *Handelsblatt*. 21 March.

Hannan, Michael T. and John H. Freeman. 1977. "The Population Ecology of Organizations." *American Journal of Sociology*. 82: 929–964.

Hannan, Michael T. and John H. Freeman. 1984. "Structural Inertia and Organizational Change." *American Sociological Review*. 49: 149–164.

Hannan, Michael T. and John H. Freeman. 1987. "The Ecology of Organizational Foundings: American Labor Unions, 1836–1985." *American Journal of Sociology*. 92: 910–943.

Hannerz, Ulf. 1992. *Cultural Complexity: Studies in the Social Organization of Meaning*. New York: Columbia University Press.

Harbison, Frederick and Charles Myers. 1959. *Management in the Industrial World: An International Analysis*. New York: McGraw Hill.

Harbison, John R. and Peter P. Pekar. 1998. *Smart Alliances: A Practical Guide to Repeatable Success*. San Francisco: Jossey Bass.

Hardy, Cynthia and Nelson Phillips. 1999. "No Joking Matter: Discursive Struggle in the Canadian Refugee System." *Organization Studies*. 20, no. 1: 1–24.

Harper, John Lamberton. 1986. *America and the Reconstruction of Italy, 1945–1948*. New York: Cambridge University Press.

Harre, Romano. 1979. *Social Being: A Theory for Social Psychology*. Oxford: Blackwell.

Harre, Romano and Paul F. Secord. 1972. *The Explanation of Social Behavior*. Oxford: Blackwell.

Hauser, Marc D. 1997. *The Evolution of Communication*. Cambridge: MIT Press.

Hayward, Jack E. S. 1975. "Employers' Associations and the State in France and Britain," pp. 118–151 in Steven Joshua Warnecke and Ezra N. Suleiman, eds. *Industrial Policies in Western Europe*. New York: Praeger.

Hechter, Michael and Satoshi Kanazawa. 1997. "Sociological and Rational Choice Theory." *Annual Review of Sociology*. 23: 191–214.

Held, David, Anthony McCrew, David Goldblatt and Jonathan Perraton. 1999. *Global Transformations*. Stanford: Stanford University Press.

Heller, Agnès. 1996. *Biopolitics: The Politics of the Body, Race and Nature*. Avebury: Aldershot.

Hempel, Carl G. 1965. *Aspects of Scientific Explanation and Other Essays in the Philosophy of Science*. New York: Free Press.

Hempel, Carl G. 1966. *Philosophy of Natural Science*. Englewood Cliffs, N.J.: Prentice-Hall.

Hergert, Michael L. and D. Morris. 1988. "Trends in International Collaborative Agreements," pp. 99–109 in Farok J. Contractor and Peter Lorange, eds., *Cooperative Strategies in International Business*. Lexington, Mass.: Lexington Books.

Herrigel, Gary. 1993. "Large Firms, Small Firms and the Governance of Flexible Specialization: The Case of Baden-Wurttemberg and Socialized Risk," pp. 15–35 in Bruce Kogut, ed., *Country Competitiveness*. New York: Oxford University Press.

Herrigel, Gary. 1994. "Industry as a Form of Order: A Comparison of the Historical Development of the Machine Tool Industries in the United States and Germany," in Rogers Hollingsworth, Philippe Schmitter, and Wolfgang Streeck, eds., *Governing Capitalist Economies: Performance and Control of Economic Sectors*. Oxford: Oxford University Press.

Herrigel, Gary. 1995. *Industrial Constructions: The Sources of German Industrial Power*. New York: Cambridge University Press.

Herrigel, Gary. 1996. "Crisis in German Decentralized Production." *European Urban and Regional Studies*. 3, no. 1: 33–52.

Hickson, David, ed. 1993. *Management in Western Europe*. Berlin: Walter de Gruyter.

Hirsch, Fred. 1976. *Social Limits to Growth*. Cambridge: Harvard University Press.

Hirsch, Fred and John Goldthorpe, eds. 1978. *The Political Economy of Inflation*. London: Martin Robertson.

Hirschman, Albert O. 1970. *Exit, Voice, and Loyalty: Responses to Decline in Firms, Organizations, and States*. Cambridge: Harvard University Press.

Hirschman, Albert O. 1977. *The Passions and the Interests: Political Arguments for Capitalism Before its Triumph*. Princeton: Princeton University Press.

Hirschman, Albert O. 1984. "Against Parsimony: Three Easy Ways of Complicating Some Categories of Economic Discourse." *Bulletin: The American Academy of Arts and Sciences*. 37: 11–28.

Hirschman, Albert O. 1986. *Rival Views of Market Society and Other Essays*. New York: Viking.

Hirst, Paul and Grahame Thompson. 1996. *Globalization in Question: The International Economy and Possibilities for Governance*. Cambridge: Polity Press.

Hirst, Paul and Jonathan Zeitlin, eds. 1989. *Reversing Industrial Decline?: Industrial Structure and Policy in Britain and Her Competitors*. Oxford: Berg.

Hladik, K. 1988. "R & D and International Joint Ventures," pp. 187–204 in Farok J. Contractor and Peter Lorange, eds., *Cooperative Strategies In International Business*. Lexington, Mass.: Lexington Books.

Hobbes, Thomas. 1968, orig. 1651. *Leviathan*. Harmondsworth: Penguin.

Hobson, John A. 1902. *The Social Problem: Life and Work*. London: James Nisbet. Reprinted 1995 with an introduction by James Meadowcroft. Bristol: Thoemmes Press.

Hodgson, Geoffrey M. 1988. *Economics and Institutions: A Manifesto for a Modern Institutional Economics*. Cambridge and Philadelphia: Polity Press and University of Pennsylvania Press.

Hodgson, Geoffrey M. 1989. "Institutional Rigidities and Economic Growth." *Cambridge Journal of Economics*. 13: 79–101.

Hodgson, Geoffrey M. 1993. *Economics and Evolution: Bringing Life Back Into Economics*. Cambridge and Ann Arbor: Polity Press and University of Michigan Press.

Hodgson, Geoffrey M. 1997. "The Ubiquity of Habits and Rules." *Cambridge Journal of Economics*. 21: 663–684.

Hodgson, Geoffrey M. 1998a. "The Approach of Institutional Economics." *Journal of Economic Literature*. 36: 166–192.

Hodgson, Geoffrey M. 1998b. "The Coasean Tangle: The Nature of the Firm and the Problem of Historical Specificity," pp. 23–49 in Steven G. Medema, ed., *Coasean Economics: Law and Economics and the New Institutional Economics*. Boston: Kluwer. Revised and reprinted in Hodgson, 1999b.

Hodgson, Geoffrey M. 1999a. *Economics and Utopia: Why the Learning Economy is Not the End of History.* London and New York: Routledge.

Hodgson, Geoffrey M. 1999b. *Evolution and Institutions: On Evolutionary Economics and the Evolution of Economics.* Cheltenham: Edward Elgar.

Hodgson, Geoffrey M. 2001. *How Economics Forgot History: The Problem of Historical Specificity in Social Science.* New York: Routledge.

Hodgson, Geoffrey M. ed. 1993. *The Economics of Institutions.* Aldershot: Edward Elgar.

Hofstadter, Douglas R. 1982. *Gödel, Escher, Bach: An Eternal Golden Braid.* Fourth edition. Harmondsworth, Middlesex: Penguin.

Hofstadter, Douglas R. 1985. *Metamagical Themas: Questing for the Essence of Mind and Matter.* New York: Basic Books.

Hofstadter, Douglas R. 1997. *Le Ton beau de Marot: In Praise of the Music of Language.* New York: Basic Books.

Hofstadter, Douglas R. and Fluid Analogies Research Group. 1995. *Fluid Concepts and Creative Analogies: Computer Models of the Fundamental Mechanisms of Thought.* New York: Basic Books.

Hogan, Michael. 1985. "American Marshall Planners and the Search for a European Neo-Capitalism." *American Historical Review.* 90, no. 1: 44–72.

Holland, John H. 1986. "Escaping Brittleness: The Possibilities of General-Purpose Learning Algorithms Applied to Parallel Rule-Based Systems," pp. 593–623 in Ryszard S. Michalski, Jaime G. Carbonell and Tom M. Mitchell, eds., *Machine Learning: An Artificial Intelligence Approach, Vol. II.* Los Altos, Calif.: Morgan Kaufmann Publishers.

Holland, John H. 1995. *Hidden Order: How Adaptation Builds Complexity.* Reading, Mass.: Addison-Wesley.

Holland, John H. 1998. *Emergence: From Chaos to Order.* Reading, Mass.: Perseus Books.

Holland, John H., Keith J. Holyoak, Richard E. Nisbett and Paul R. Thagard. 1989. *Induction: Processes of Inference, Learning, and Discovery.* Cambridge: MIT Press.

Hollingsworth, J. Rogers. 1984. "The Snare of Specialization." *Bulletin of the Atomic Scientists.* 40: 34–37.

Hollingsworth, J. Rogers. 1986. *A Political Economy of Medicine: Great Britain and the United States.* Baltimore: Johns Hopkins University Press.

Hollingsworth, J. Rogers. 1991a. "Die Logik der Koordination des verabeitenden Gewerbes in Amerika." *Kolner Zeitschrift fur Soziologie und Sozial Psychologie.* 43: 18–43.

Hollingsworth, J. Rogers. 1991b. "The Logic of Coordinating American Manufacturing Sectors," pp. 35–73 in John Campbell, J. Rogers Hollingsworth and Leon Lindberg, eds., *The Governance of the American Economy.* Cambridge and New York: Cambridge University Press.

Hollingsworth, J. Rogers. 1994. "Are National Economies Converging: Perspectives from the Cases of Japan, Germany and the U.S.A." Paper presented before the Society for the Advancement of Socio-Economics, Paris, France, 15 July.

Hollingsworth, J. Rogers. 1997. "Continuities and Changes in Social Systems of Production: The Cases of Japan, Germany, and the United States," pp. 265–310 in J. Rogers Hollingsworth and Robert Boyer, eds., *Contemporary Capitalism: The Embeddedness of Institutions.* Cambridge and New York: Cambridge University Press.

Hollingsworth, J. Rogers, Jerald Hage and Robert A. Hanneman. 1990. *State Intervention in Medical Care: Consequences for Britain, France, Sweden, and the United States, 1890–1970.* Ithaca: Cornell University Press.

Hollingsworth, J. Rogers and Robert Hanneman. 1982. "Working-Class Power and the Political Economy of Western Capitalist Societies." *Comparative Social Research.* 5: 61–80.

Hollingsworth, J. Rogers, Robert Hanneman, Jerald Hage and Charles Ragin. 1996. "The Effect of Human Capital and State Intervention on the Performance of Medical Delivery Systems." *Social Forces.* 75: 999–1024.

Hollingsworth, J. Rogers and Ellen Jane Hollingsworth. 2000. "Major Discoveries and Biomedical Research Organizations: Perspectives on Interdisciplinarity, Nurturing Leadership, and Integrated Structure and Cultures," pp. 215–244 in Peter Weingart and Nico Stehr, eds., *Practising Interdisciplinarity*. Toronto: University of Toronto Press.

Hollingsworth, J. Rogers, Ellen Jane Hollingsworth and Jerald Hage. Forthcoming, 2002. *The Search for Excellence: Organizations, Institutions, and Major Discoveries in Biomedical Research*. New York: Cambridge University Press.

Hollingsworth, J. Rogers and Leon Lindberg. 1985. "The Governance of the American Economy: The Role of Markets, Clans, Hierarchies, and Associative Behavior," pp. 221–254 in Wolfgang Streeck and Philippe C. Schmitter, eds., *Private Interest Government: Beyond Market and State*. London and Beverly Hills: Sage Publications.

Hollingsworth, J. Rogers and Wolfgang Streeck. 1994. "Countries and Sectors: Performance, Convergence and Competitiveness," pp. 270–300 in J. Rogers Hollingsworth, Philippe Schmitter and Wolfgang Streeck, eds., *Governing Capitalist Economies: Performance and Control of Economic Sectors*. New York: Oxford University Press.

Hollingsworth, J. Rogers and Robert Boyer, eds. 1997. *Contemporary Capitalism: The Embeddedness of Institutions*. Cambridge and New York: Cambridge University Press.

Hollingsworth, J. Rogers, Philippe Schmitter and Wolfgang Streeck, eds. 1994. *Governing Capitalist Economies: Performance and Control of Economic Sectors*. New York: Oxford University Press.

Holmes, Stephen and Cass R. Sunstein. 1999. *The Costs of Rights: Why Liberty Depends on Taxes*. New York: Norton.

Holt, Charles A. 1995. "Industrial Organization: A Survey of Laboratory Research," in John Henry Kagel and Alvin E. Roth, eds., *The Handbook of Experimental Economics*. Princeton: Princeton University Press.

Homans, George C. 1961. *Social Behaviour: Its Elementary Form*. London: Routledge and Kegan Paul.

Hoshi, Takeo, Anil Kashyap and David Scharfstein. 1990. "The Role of Banks in Reducing the Costs of Financial Distress in Japan." *Journal of Financial Economics*. 27, no. 1: 67–88.

Hounshell, David A. 1984. *From the American System to Mass Production, 1800–1932*. Baltimore: Johns Hopkins University Press.

Hsing, You-tien. 1998. "The Work of Networks in Taiwan's Export Fashion Shoe Industry," pp. 124–140 in W. Mark Fruin, ed., *Networks, Markets, and the Pacific Rim*. New York: Oxford University Press.

Huber, Peter W. 1989. *Liability: The Legal Revolution and its Consequences*. New York: Basic Books.

Hughes, Stuart. 1965. *The United States and Italy*. Cambridge: Harvard University Press.

Huntington, S. P. 1968. *Political Order in Changing Societies*. New Haven: Yale University Press.

Huntington, S. P. 1976. "The Change to Change: Modernization, Development and Politics," pp. 25–61 in C. E. Black, ed., *Comparative Modernization*. New York: Free Press.

Iannaccone, Laurence R. 1991. "The Consequences of Religious Market Structure: Adam Smith and the Economics of Religion." *Rationality and Society*. 3: 156–177.

Iannaccone, Laurence R. 1998. "Introduction to the Economics of Religion." *Journal of Economic Literature*. 36, no. 3: 1465–1496.

Imai, Ken-ichi and Hiroyuki Itami. 1984. "Interpenetration of Organization and Market: Japan's Firm and Market in Comparison with the US." *International Journal of Industrial Organisation*. 6, no. 4: 285–310.

Immergut, Ellen M. 1992a. *Health Politics, Interests and Institutions in Western Europe*. Cambridge: Cambridge University Press.

Immergut, Ellen M. 1992b. "The Rules of the Game: The Logic of Health Policy-Making in France, Switzerland and Sweden," pp 57–89 in Kathleen Ann Thelen, Frank Longstreth and Sven Steinmo, eds. *Structuring Politics: Historical Institutionalism in Comparative Analysis*. Cambridge: Cambridge University Press.

Immergut, Ellen M. 1998. "The Theoretical Core of the New Institutionalism." *Politics and Society*. 26: 5–34.

Inkpen, Andrew C. and Adva Dinur. 1998. "Knowledge Management Processes and International Joint Ventures." *Organization Science* 9: 454–468.

INSEE. 1956. *Les Etablissements Industriels et Commerciaux en France en 1954*. Paris, France.

INSEE. 1974. *Les Entreprises et Etablissements Industriels et Commerciaux en 1966*. Paris, France.

Istituto Centrale di Statistica. 1955. *Censimento Generale dell'Industria e del Commercio, 1951*. Rome, Italy.

Istituto Centrale di Statistica. 1976. *Censimento Generale dell'Industria e del Commercio, 1971*. Rome, Italy.

Iversen, Torben. 1997. "Wage Bargaining and Macroeconomics in Organized Market Economies: One Logic or Two?" Paper presented to a workshop on Varieties of Capitalism, Wissenschaftszentrum, Berlin. June.

Iversen, Torben and Anne Wren. 1998. "Equality, Employment and Fiscal Discipline: The Trilemma of the Service Economy." *World Politics*. July: 507–546.

Jacobs, Michael. 1991. *Short-term America: The Causes and Cures of Our Business Myopia*. Boston: Harvard Business School Press.

Janowsky, Oscar I. 1959. *Foundations of Israel: Emergence of a Welfare State*. Princeton, N.J.: Van Nostrand.

Jardine, Lisa. 1999. *Ingenious Pursuits: Building the Scientific Revolution*. New York: Anchor Books.

Jarillo, J. C. 1993. *Strategic Networks: Creating the Borderless Organization*. Oxford: Butterworth-Heinemann.

Jeanneney, Jean-Noèl. 1980. "Hommes d'Affaires au Piquet: Le Difficile Intérim d'une Représentation Patronale, Septembre 1944–Janvier 1946." *Revue Historique*. January–March: 81–100.

Jensen, Michael C. and William H. Meckling. 1979. "Rights and Production Functions: An Application to Labor-managed Firms and Codetermination." *Journal of Business*. 52: 469–506.

Jepperson, Ronald L. 1991. "Institutions, Institutional Effects, and Institutionalism," pp. 143–163 in Walter W. Powell and Paul J. DiMaggio, eds., *The New Institutionalism in Organizational Analysis*. Chicago: University of Chicago Press.

Johanson, Jan and Associates. 1994. *Internationalization, Relationships and Networks*. Uppsala, Sweden: Acta Universitatis Upsaliensis.

Johnson, Bjorn. 1992. "Institutional Learning," pp. 23–44 in Bengt-Ake Lundvall, ed., *National Systems of Innovation: Towards a Theory of Innovation and Interactive Learning*. London: Pinter.

Josephson, Matthew. 1934. *The Robber Barons: The Great American Capitalists, 1861–1901*. New York and London: Harvest.

Judson, Horace F. 1979. *The Eighth Day of Creation*. New York: Simon and Schuster.

Jungmittag, Andre, Guido Reger, and Thomas Reiss, eds. 2000. *Changing Innovation in the Pharmaceutical Industry: Globalization and New Ways of Drug Development*. Berlin: Springer.

Kaelbling, Leslie P. 1993. *Learning in Embedded Systems*. Cambridge: MIT Press.

Kagan, Robert A. 1984. "The Routinization of Debt Collection: An Essay on Social Change and Conflict in the Courts." *Law and Society Review*. 18, no. 3: 323–371.

Kagan, Robert A. and Lee Axelrad. 1996. *Adversarial Legalism: Costs and Consequences*. Manuscript, Center for Law and Society, University of California.

Kagan, Robert A. and Lee Axelrad. 1997. "Adversarial Legalism: An International Perspective," pp. 146–147 in Pietro S. Nivola, ed., *Comparative Disadvantages? Social Regulations and the Global Economy*. Washington, D.C.: Brookings Institution Press.

Kagel, John Henry. 1995. "Auctions: A Survey of Experimental Research," in John Henry Kagel and Alvin E. Roth, eds., *The Handbook of Experimental Economics*. Princeton: Princeton University Press.

Kahneman, Daniel and Amos Tversky, eds. 2000. *Choices, Values and Frames*. Cambridge: Cambridge University Press.

Kamali, Masoud. 1998. *The Modern Revolutions of Iran: Clergy, Bazaris, and State in the Modernization Process*. Aldershot: Ashgate.

Kamali, Masoud. 2001. Civil Society and Islam: A Sociological Perspective." *European Journal of Social Theory*. 4, no. 2.

Kanter, Rosabeth Moss. 1994. "Collaborative Advantage: Successful Partnerships Manage the Relationship, Not Just the Deal." *Harvard Business Review*. 92: 96–108.

Kanter, Rosabeth Moss. 1997. *World Class: Thriving Locally in the Global Economy*. New York: Simon & Schuster.

Katona, George. 1971. *Aspirations and Affluence: Comparative Studies in the United States and Western Europe*. New York: McGraw-Hill.

Katona, George. 1977a. *The Powerful Consumer: Psychological Studies of the American Economy*. Westport, Conn.: Greenwood Press.

Katona, George. 1977b. *Psychological Analysis of Economic Behavior*. Westport, Conn.: Greenwood Press.

Katzenstein, Peter J. 1985. *Small States in World Markets: Industrial Policy in Europe*. Ithaca: Cornell University Press.

Katzenstein, Peter J. 1987. *Policy and Politics in West Germany: The Growth of a Semi-sovereign State*. Philadelphia: Temple University Press.

Katzenstein, Peter J. 1989. "Stability and Change in the Emerging Third Republic," pp. 307–353 in Peter J. Katzenstein, ed., *Industry and Politics in West Germany: Toward the Third Republic*. Ithaca: Cornell University Press.

Katzenstein, Peter J., ed. 1978. *Between Power and Plenty*. Madison: The University of Wisconsin Press.

Katznelson, Ira. 1998. "The Doleful Dance of Politics and Policy: Can Historical Institutionalism Make a Difference?" *American Political Science Review*. 92: 191–197.

Kaufman, Robert. 1997. "The Politics of State Reform: A Review of Theoretical Approaches" *and idem*, "The Next Challenges for Latin America." *Working Papers 98 and 108*. Madrid: Instituto Juan March.

Kauffman, Stuart. 2000. *Investigations*. Oxford: Oxford University Press.

Kay, Lily E. 1993. *The Molecular Vision of Life: Caltech, the Rockefeller Foundation and the Rise of the New Biology*. New York: Oxford University Press.

Kenney, Martin and Richard Florida. 1988. "Beyond Mass Production and the Labor Process in Japan." *Politics and Society*. 16: 121–158.

Kenney, Martin and Richard Florida. 1993. *Beyond Mass Production: The Japanese System and Its Transfer to the U.S.* New York: Oxford University Press.

Keohane, Robert and Helen Milner, eds. 1996. *Internationalization and Domestic Politics*. New York: Cambridge University Press.

Kerr, Clark, John T. Dunlop, Frederick H. Harbison and Charles A. Meyers. 1960. *Industrialism and Industrial Man: The Problems of Labor and Management in Economic Growth*. Cambridge: Harvard University Press.

Kerr, Clark, John T. Dunlop, Frederick H. Harbison and Charles A. Meyers. 1973. *Industrialism and Industrial Man*. Second Edition. Cambridge: Harvard University Press.

Kesler, Jean-François. 1985. *L'ENA, la Société, l'Etat*. Paris: Berger-Levrault.

Killing, J. Peter. 1988. "Understanding Alliances: The Role of Task and Organizational Complexity," pp. 55–67 in Farok J. Contractor and Peter Lorange, eds., *Cooperative Strategies in International Business*. Lexington, Mass.: Lexington Books.

Kim, Eun Mee. 1997. *Big Business, Strong State: Collusion and Conflict in South Korean Development, 1960–1990*. Albany: State University of New York Press.

Kim, Linsu. 1997. "The Dynamics of Samsung's Technological Learning in Semiconductors." *California Management Review*. 39: 86–101.

King, Gary, Robert O. Keohane and Sidney Verba. 1994. *Designing Social Inquiry: Scientific Inference in Qualitative Research*. Princeton: Princeton University Press.

Klein, Julie Thomson. 1996. *Crossing Boundaries: Knowledge, Disciplinarities, and Interdisciplinarities*. Charlottesville: University Press of Virginia.

Kluge, Arnd. 1991. *Geschichte der Deutschen Bankengenossenschaften*. Frankfurt: Fritz Knapp Verlag.

Knetter, Michael. 1989. "Price Discrimination by U.S. and German Exporters." *American Economic Review*. 79: 198–210.

Knorr-Cetina, Karin. 1999. *Epistemic Cultures: How the Sciences Make Knowledge*. Cambridge: Harvard University Press.

Kogut, Bruce and H. Singh. 1988. "Entering the United States by Joint Venture: Competitive Rivalry and Industrial Structure," pp. 241–251 in Farok J. Contractor and Peter Lorange, eds., *Cooperative Strategies in International Business*. Lexington, Mass.: Lexington Books.

Kogut, Bruce Mitchel and David Parkinson. 1994. "The Diffusion of American Organizing Principles to Europe," pp. 179–202 in Bruce Mitchel Kogut, ed., *Country Competitiveness: Technology and the Organizing of Work*. New York: Oxford University Press.

Kohler, Robert E. 1982. *From Medical Chemistry to Biochemistry*. Cambridge: Cambridge University Press.

Kohler, Robert E. 1994. *The Lords of the Fly*. Chicago: University of Chicago Press.

Kolko, Joyce and Gabriel Kolko. 1972. *The Limits of Power: The World and United States Foreign Policy, 1945–1954*. New York: Harper & Row.

Kondra, Alex A. and C. R. Hinings. 1998. "Organizational Diversity and Change in Institutional Theory." *Organization Studies*. 19: 743–767.

Korzeniewicz, Miguel. 1994. "Community Chains and Marketing Strategies: Nike and the Global Athletic Footwear Industry," pp. 247–266 in Gary Gereffi and Miguel Korzeniewicz, eds., *Commodity Chains and Global Capitalism*. Westport, Conn.: Praeger.

Kozul-Wright, Richard and Paul Rayment. 1997. "The Institutional Hiatus in Economics in Transition and its Policy Consequences." *Cambridge Journal of Economics*. 21, no. 5: 641–661.

Kregel, Jan A. 1995. "Neoclassical Price Theory, Institutions and the Evolution of Securities Market Organisation." *Economic Journal*. 105, no. 2: 459–470.

Krippendorf, Ekkehart, ed. 1981. *The Role of the United States in the Reconstruction of Italy and West Germany, 1943–1949*. Berlin: Materialen 16.

Krugman, Paul. 1991. "History and Industry Location: The Case of the Manufacturing Belt." *American Economic Association Papers and Proceedings*. 81: 80–83.

Kuhn, T. 1970. *The Structure of Scientific Revolutions*. Second Edition. Chicago: University of Chicago Press.

Kuisel, Richard. 1981. *Capitalism and the State in Modern France*. New York: Cambridge University Press.

Kuisel, Richard. 1993. *Seducing the French*. Berkeley: University of California Press.

Kurzer, Paulette. 1993. *Business and Banking*. Ithaca: Cornell University Press.

Lakoff, G. and M. Johnson. 1980. *Metaphors We Live By*. Chicago: University of Chicago Press.

Lakoff, Georg and Rafael E. Nunez. 2000. *Where Mathematics Comes From: How the Embodied Mind Brings Mathematics into Being*. New York: Basic Books.

Landa, Janet. 1999. "Bioeconomics of Some Nonhuman and Human Societies: New Institutional Economics Approach." *Journal of Bioeconomics*. 1, no. 1: 95–113.

Landes, David S. 1969. *The Unbound Prometheus*. New York: Cambridge University Press.

Landes, David S. 1998. *The Wealth and Poverty of Nations: Why Some Are So Rich and Some Are So Poor*. New York: W.W. Norton.

Lane, Christel. 1995. *Industry and Society in Europe*. Aldershot: Edward Elgar.

Lane, Robert E. 1991. *The Market Experience*. Cambridge: Cambridge University Press.

Lanzara, Giovan Francesco. 1998. "Self-Destructive Processes in Institution Building and Some Modest Countervailing Mechanisms." *European Journal of Political Research*. 33: 1–39.

Lave, Jean. 1988. *Cognition in Practice: Mind, Mathematics and Culture in Everyday Life*. Cambridge: Cambridge University Press.

Lawler, Edward J. 1992. "Choice Processes and Affective Attachments to Nested Groups: A Theoretical Analysis. *American Sociological Review.* 57: 327–339.

Lawler, Edward J. and Jeongkoo Yoon. 1993. "Power and the Emergence of Commitment Behavior in Negotiated Exchange." *American Sociological Review.* 58: 465–481.

Lazerson, Mark. 1993. "Factory or Putting-out? Knitting Networks in Modena," pp. 203–226 in Gernot Grabher, ed., *The Embedded Firm: On the Socioeconomics of Industrial Networks.* London: Routledge.

Lazonick, William. 1991. *Business Organization and the Myth of the Market Economy.* Cambridge and New York: Cambridge University Press.

Leathers, Charles G. and J. Patrick Raines. 1992. "Adam Smith on Competitive Religious Markets." *History of Political Economy.* 24, no. 2: 499–513.

LeDoux, Joseph. 1999. *The Emotional Brain.* London: Phoenix Press.

Legro, Jeffrey. 1997. "Which Norms Matter? Revisiting the 'Failure' of Internationalism." *International Organization.* 51: 31–63.

Lehrer, Mark. 1997a. "German Industrial Strategy in Turbulence: Corporate Governance and Managerial Hierarchies in Lufthansa." *Industry and Innovation.* 4, no. 1: 115–140.

Lehrer, Mark. 1997b. *Comparative Institutional Advantage in Corporate Governance and Managerial Hierarchies: The Case of European Airlines.* Ph.D. Thesis, Institut Européen d'Administration des Affaires (INSEAD), Fontainebleau.

Leibfried, Stephan and Paul Pierson, eds. 1995. *European Social Policy: Between Fragmentation and Integration.* Washington, D.C.: Brookings Institution Press.

Lesser, Eric L., ed. 2000. *Knowledge and Social Capital: Foundations and Applications.* Boston: Butterworth-Heinemann.

Levi, M. 1990. "A Logic of Institutional Change," pp. 402–418 in K. S. Cook and M. Levi, eds., *The Limits of Rationality.* Chicago: University of Chicago Press.

Levine, Solomon B. and Makoto Ohtsu. 1991. "Transplanting Japanese Labor Relations." *The Annals of the American Academy of Political and Social Science.* 513: 102–116.

Lévi-Strauss, C. 1963. *Structural Anthropology.* New York: Basic Books.

Lijphart, Arend. 1975. *The Politics of Accommodation.* Second Edition. Berkeley: University of California Press.

Lindblom, Charles E. 1977. *Politics and Markets.* New York: Basic Books.

Lindblom, Charles E. 1982. "The Market as Prison." *Journal of Politics.* 44: 324–336.

Linz, Juan and Alfred Stepan. 1996. *Problems of Democratic Transition and Consolidation: Southern Europe, South America, and Post-Communist Europe.* Baltimore: John Hopkins University Press.

Lipset, Seymour Martin. 1996. *American Exceptionalism: A Double-Edged Sword.* New York and London: Norton.

Locke, Richard and Wade Jacoby. 1995. *The Dilemmas of Diffusion: Social Embeddedness and the Problems of Institutional Change in East Germany.* Manuscript. Cambridge: MIT.

Locke, Richard, Thomas Kochan and Michael Piore. 1995. *Employment Relations in a Changing World Economy.* Cambridge: MIT Press.

Loewenstein, George. 1992. "The Fall and Rise of Psychological Explanations in the Economics of Intertemporal Choice," pp. 3–34 in Jon Elster and George Lowenstein, eds., *Choice over Time.* New York: Russell Sage Foundation.

Loewenstein, George. 1996. "Out of Control: Visceral Influences on Behavior." *Organizational Behavior and Human Decision Making Processes.* 65: 272–292.

Lotman, J. 1975. *Theses on the Semiotic Study of Culture.* Lisse, Netherlands: Peter de Ridder.

Luce, R. Duncan and Howard Raiffa. 1989. *Games and Decision: Introductions and Critical Survey.* New York: Dover Publications.

Lundvall, Bengt-Ake, ed. 1992. *National Systems of Innovation: Towards a Theory of Innovation and Interactive Learning.* London: Pinter.

Lütz, Susanne. 1997. "Die Rückkehr des Nationalstaates? Kapitalmarktregulierung im Zeichen der Internationalisierung von Finanzmärkten." *Politisches Vierteljahresschrift.* 38, no. 3: 475–497.

Maanen, John Van. 1988. *Tales of the Field: On Writing Ethnography*. Chicago: University of Chicago Press.

Machado, Nora. 1996. "Incongruence and Tensions in Complex Organizations: The Case of an Organ Transplantation System." *Human System Management*. 11: 23–34.

Machado, Nora. 1998. *Using the Bodies of the Dead: Legal, Ethical, and Organizational Dimensions of Organ Transplantation*. Aldershot: Dartmouth Publishing.

Machado, Nora and Tom R. Burns. 1998. "Complex Social Organization: Multiple Organizing Modes, Structural Incongruence, and Mechanisms of Integration." *Public Administration: An International Quarterly*. 76: 355–386.

Machado, Nora and Tom R. Burns. 2000a. "Discretionary Death: Cognitive and Normative Problems Resulting from Boundary Shifts Between Life and Death." Paper presented at the Third International Symposium on Coma and Death, Havana, Cuba, 22–25 February.

Machado, Nora and Tom R. Burns. 2000b. "The New Genetics: A Social Science and Humanities Research Agenda." *Canadian Journal of Sociology*. 25, no. 4.

Magill, Michael and Martine Quinzii. 1996. *Theory of Incomplete Markets*. 2 vols. Cambridge, Mass.: MIT Press.

Magnusson, Lars and Jan Ottosson. 1997. *Evolutionary Economics and Path Dependence*. Cheltenham, UK: Edward Elgar.

Maier, Charles and Günther Bischof, eds. 1991. *The Marshall Plan and Germany*. New York: Berg Publishers.

Maki, Uskali, Bo Gustafsson, and Christian Knudsen. 1993. *Rationality, Institutions, and Economic Methodology*. London and New York: Routledge.

Mann, Michael. 1986. *The Sources of Social Power, Volume I*. New York: Cambridge University Press.

Manow, Philip and Eric Seils. 2000. "Adjusting Badly: The German Welfare State, Structural Change and the Open Economy," chapter 6, pp. 144–171 in Fritz Wilhelm Scharpf and Vivien Ann Schmidt, eds., *Welfare and Work in the Open Economy: Volume I: From Vulnerability to Competitiveness*. Oxford: Oxford University Press.

March, James and Johan Olsen. 1989. *Rediscovering Institutions: The Organizational Basis of Politics*. London: Macmillan.

Marchetti, Cesare. 1981. *Society as a Learning System: Discovery, Invention, and Innovation Cycles Revisited*. Laxenburg, Austria: International Institute for Applied Systems Analysis.

Mares, Isabela. 2000. "The Evolution of Early Retirement: Explaining Policy Blockage and Policy Frustration." *Working Paper 11*. Washington, D.C.: American Institute for Contemporary German Studies.

Margalit, Avishai. 1996. *The Decent Society*. Cambridge: Harvard University Press.

Marglin, Stephen and Juliet Schor, eds. 1990. *The Golden Age of Capitalism*. Oxford: Clarendon Press.

Marsden, David. 1986. *The End of Economic Man? Custom and Competition in Labour Markets*. Brighton: Wheatsheaf Books.

Martin, James. 1950. *All Honorable Men*. Boston: Little, Brown.

Marwell, Gerald and Pamela Oliver. 1993. *The Critical Mass in Collective Action: A Micro-Social Theory*. Cambridge: Harvard University Press.

Matthews, John A. 1997. "A Silicon Valley of the East: Creating Taiwan's Semiconductor Industry." *California Management Review* 39: 26–55.

Maurice, Marc, Arndt Sorge and Michael Warner. 1980. "Societal Differences in Organizing Manufacturing Units: A Comparison of France, West Germany, and Great Britain." *Organization Studies*. 1: 59–86.

Mayer, Herbert. 1969. *German Recovery and the Marshall Plan*. Bonn: Atlantic Forum.

Maynard-Smith, John. 1982. *Evolution and the Theory of Games*. Cambridge and New York: Cambridge University Press.

McClintick, David. 2000. "The Decline and Fall of Lloyd's of London: A Legendary Institution Has Barely Escaped Bancruptcy and is Now Accused of Perpetrating the Greatest Swindle Ever." *Time Magazine*. 21 February.

McCloskey, Deirdre N. 1973. *Economic Maturity and Entrepreneurial Decline: British Iron and Steel, 1870–1913.* Cambridge: Harvard University Press.

McCloskey, Deirdre N. 1985. *The Rhetoric of Economics.* Madison: University of Wisconsin Press.

McCloskey, Deirdre N. 1990. *If You're So Smart: The Narrative of Economic Expertise.* Chicago: University of Chicago Press.

McCloskey, Deirdre N. 1998. *The Rhetoric of Economics.* Madison: University of Wisconsin Press.

McCreary, Edward. 1964. *The Americanization of Europe: The Impact of Americans and American Business on the Uncommon Market.* New York: Doubleday & Company Inc.

McKlevey, M. 1997. "Coevolution in Commercial Genetic Engineering." *Industrial and Corporate Change.* 6: 503–532.

Ménard, Claude. 1995. "Markets as Institutions Versus Organizations as Markets? Disentangling Some Fundamental Concepts." *Journal of Economic Behavior and Organization.* 28, no. 2: 161–182.

Ménard, Claude. 1996. "On Clusters, Hybrids, and Other Strange Firms: The Case of the French Poultry Industry." *Journal of Institutional and Theoretical Economics.* 152, no. 1: 154–183.

Messer-Davidow, Ellen, David R. Shumway and David Sylvan. 1993. *Knowledges: Historical and Critical Studies in Disciplinarity.* Charlottesville: University Press of Virginia.

Meyer, John and Brian Rowan. 1977. "Institutionalized Organizations: Formal Structure as Myth and Ceremony." *American Journal of Sociology.* 83, no. 2: 340–363.

Meyer, John and Brian Rowan. 1991. "Institutionalized Organizations: Formal Structure as Myth and Ceremony," reprinted pp. 41–62 in Walter W. Powell and Paul J. DiMaggio, eds., *The New Institutionalism in Organizational Analysis.* Chicago: University of Chicago Press.

Michel, Henri and Boris Mirkine-Guetzevitch, eds. 1954. *Les Idées Politiques et Sociales de la Résistance.* Paris: Presses Universitaires de France.

Michels, Robert. 1962. *Political Parties: A Sociological Study of the Oligarchical Tendencies of Modern Democracy.* New York: The Free Press.

Milgrom, Paul, Yingyi Qian and John Roberts. 1991. "Complementarities, Momentum, and the Evolution of Modern Manufacturing." *American Economics Association Papers and Proceedings.* 81: 84.

Milgrom, Paul and John Roberts. 1992. *Economics, Organization and Management.* Englewood Cliffs: Prentice Hall.

Milgrom, Paul and John Roberts. 1995. "Complementarities: Industrial Strategy, Structure and Change in Manufacturing." *Journal of Accounting and Economics.* 19: 179–208.

Mill, John Stuart. 1843. *A System of Logic, Ratiocinative and Inductive.* West Strand: John Parker.

Miller, David. 1979. *Social Justice.* Oxford: Oxford University Press.

Miller, G. 1992. *Managerial Dilemmas.* Cambridge: Cambridge University Press.

Miller, James Edward. 1986. *The United States and Italy, 1940–1950.* Chapel Hill: University of North Carolina Press.

Milward, Alan. 1984. *The Reconstruction of Western Europe: 1945–1951.* Berkeley: University of California Press.

Minsky, Marvin. 1990. *Mentopolis.* Stuttgart: Klett-Cotta.

Mitman, Gregg. 1992. *The State of Nature.* Chicago: University of Chicago Press.

Mockler, Robert J. 1999. *Multinational Strategic Alliances.* Chichester, N.Y.: Wiley.

Modigliani, Franco and Merton Miller. 1958. "The Costs of Capital, Corporation Finance, and the Theory of Intermediation." *American Economic Review.* 48, no. 2: 261–297.

Monnet, Jean. 1976. *Mémoires.* Paris: Fayard.

Mowery, David and Richard R. Nelson, eds. 1999. *The Sources of Industrial Leadership.* New York: Cambridge University Press.

Müller, Karl H. 1996. "Epistemic Cultures in the Social Sciences. The Modeling Dilemma Dissolved," pp. 29–63 in Rainer Hegselmann, Ulrich Mueller, and Klaus G. Troitzsch, eds., *Modelling and Simulation in the Social Sciences from the Philosophy of Science Point of View.* Dordrecht: Kluwer Academic Publishers.

Müller, Karl H. and Günter Haag, eds. 1994. *Komplexe Modelle in den Sozialwissenschaften*. WISDOM (Special Edition): 3/4.

Mullineux, A. W. 1987. *U.K. Banking After Deregulation*. London: Croom Helm.

Murmann, Johann Peter. 1998. *Knowledge and Competitive Advantage in the Synthetic Dye Industry, 1850–1914*. PhD dissertation, Columbia University.

National Science Foundation. 1996. *National Science and Engineering Indicators*. Washington, D.C.: Government Printing Office.

National Science Foundation. 1998. *National Science and Engineering Indicators*. Washington, D.C.: Government Printing Office.

Nelson, Richard R. 1994. "The Co-evolution of Technology, Industrial Structure, and Supporting Institution." *Industrial and Corporate Change*. 3: 417–419.

Nelson, Richard R. 1995a. "Co-evolution of Industry Structure, Technology and Supporting Institution, and the Making of Comparative Advantage." *International Journal of the Economics of Business*. 2: 171–184.

Nelson, Richard R. 1995b. "Why Should Managers Be Thinking About Technology Policy?" *Strategic Management Journal*. 16: 581–588.

Nelson, Richard R. 1996. "The Evolution of Competitive or Comparative Advantage: A Preliminary Report on a Study." *Industrial and Corporate Change*. 5: 597–618.

Nelson, Richard R., ed. 1993. *National Innovation Systems: A Comparative Analysis*. New York and Oxford: Oxford University Press.

Nelson, Richard R. and David C. Mowery. 1999. "Introduction," pp. 1–18 in David C. Mowery and Richard R. Nelson, eds., *Sources of Industrial Leadership: Studies of Seven Industries*. New York: Cambridge University Press.

Nelson, Richard R. and S. G. Winter. 1982. *An Evolutionary Theory of Economic Change*. Cambridge: Harvard University Press.

Newell, Alan. 1990. *Unified Theories of Cognition*. Harvard University Press.

Nicholls, Anthony. 1984. "The Other Germany: The Neo-Liberals," pp. 164–177 in R. J. Bullen, Harmut Pogge von Strandmann and A. B. Polonsky, eds., *Ideas into Politics: Aspects of European History 1880–1950*. London: Croom Helm.

Nooteboom, Bart. 2000. "Institutions and Forms of Co-ordination in Innovation Systems." *Organization Studies* 21: 915–939.

Nørretranders, Tor. 1998. *The User Illusion: Cutting Consciousness Down to Size*. Harmondsworth: Penguin Books.

North, Douglass Cecil. 1977. "Markets and Other Allocation Systems in History: The Challenge of Karl Polanyi." *Journal of European Economic History*. 6: 703–716.

North, Douglass Cecil. 1981. *Structure and Change in Economic History*. New York: Norton.

North, Douglass Cecil. 1990. *Institutions, Institutional Change, and Economic Performance*. Cambridge: Cambridge University Press.

North, Douglass Cecil and Paul Thomas. 1973. *The Rise of the Western World*. Cambridge: Cambridge University Press.

Nowotny, Helga, Peter Scott and Michael Gibbons. 2001. *Re-Thinking Science: Knowledge and the Public in an Age of Uncertainty*. Cambridge: Polity Press.

Nylander, J. 2000. *The Power of Framing: A New-Institutional Approach to Interest Group Participation in the European Union*. Doctoral Dissertation, Uppsala University, Sweden.

O'Donnell, Guillermo. 1995. "Delegative Democracy." *Journal of Democracy*. 5, no. 1: 55–69.

Offe, Claus. 1998. "'Homogeneity' and Constitutional Democracy: Coping With Identity Through Group Rights." *The Journal of Political Philosophy*. 6, no. 2: 113–141.

Ohmae, Kenichi. 1990. *The Borderless World*. New York: Harper Business.

Ohno, T. 1989. *L'esprit Toyota*. Paris: Masson.

Oksenberg Rorty, Amelie, ed. 1980. *Explaining Emotions*. Berkeley: University of California Press.

Olby, Robert. 1979. *The Path to the Double Helix*. Seattle: University of Washington Press.

Oliver, Nick and Barry Wilkinson. 1988. *The Japanization of British Industry*. Oxford: Basil Blackwell.

Olson, Mancur. 1965. *The Logic of Collective Action: Public Goods and the Theory of Groups.* Cambridge: Harvard University Press.

Olzack, Susan and Elizabeth West. 1991. "Ethnic Conflict and the Rise and Fall of Ethnic Newspapers." *American Sociological Review.* 56: 458–474.

OMGUS, Bd 42. *Economics Division.* Koblenz, Germany: Bundesarchiv.

OMGUS, Bd 18. *Bipartite Control Office, Economics Division and Decartelization Branch.* Koblenz, Germany: Bundesarchiv.

Organization for Economic Cooperation and Development. 1994. *The OECD Jobs Study.* Paris: OECD.

Orren, K. and S. Skowronek. 1991. "Beyond the Iconography of Order: Notes for a 'New Institutionalism,'" pp. 311–330 in L. C. Dodd and C. Jillson, eds., *The Dynamics of American Politics.* Boulder, Colo.: Westview Press.

Orru, Marcu, Nichole Woolsey Biggart and Gary G. Hamilton. 1991. "Organizational Isomorphism in East Asia," pp. 361–389 in Paul J. DiMaggio and Walter W. Powell, eds., *The New Institutionalism in Organizational Analysis.* Chicago: University of Chicago Press.

Osterman, Paul, ed. 1984. *Internal Labor Markets.* Cambridge: MIT Press.

Ostrom, Elinor. 1986. "An Agenda for the Study of Institutions." *Public Choice.* 48: 3–25.

Ostrom, Elinor. 1990. *Governing the Commons: The Evolution of Institutions for Collective Action.* Cambridge: Cambridge University Press.

Oswald, Andrew J. 1997. "Happiness and Economic Performance." *The Economic Journal.* 107: 1815–1831.

Ouchi, William G. 1980. "Markets, Bureaucracies, and Clans." *Administrative Science Quarterly.* 25: 129–141.

Palombo, Stanley R. 1999. *The Emergent Ego: Complexity and Coevolution in the Psychoanalytic Process.* Madison: International Universities Press.

Pavan, Robert. 1976. "Strategy and Structure: The Italian Experience." *Journal of Economics. and Business.* 28: 254–260.

Peacock, Alan and Hans Willgerodt, eds. 1989. *Germany's Social Market Economy: Origins and Evolution.* New York: St. Martin's Press.

Penan, H. 1996. "R&D Strategy in a Techno-economic Network: Alzheimer's Disease Therapeutic Strategies." *Research Policy.* 25: 337–358.

Perez, C. 1985. "Microelectronics, Long Waves and World Structural Change: New Perspectives for Developing Countries." *World Development.* 13, no. 3: 441–463.

Perrow, Charles. 1981. "Markets, Hierarchies and Hegemony: A Critique of Chandler and Williamson," pp. 371–386 in Andrew H. Van de Ven and William F. Joyce, eds., *Perspectives on Organization Design and Behavior.* New York: John Wiley.

Perry, Martin. 1999. *Small Firms and Network Economies.* London: Routledge.

Peterson, Edward. 1977. *The American Occupation of Germany: Retreat to Victory.* Detroit, Mich.: Wayne State University Press.

Petsche, Thomas, Stephen J. Hanson, and Jude Shavlik, eds. 1995. *Computational Learning Theory and Natural Learning Systems: Volume III: Selecting Good Models.* Cambridge: MIT Press.

Pfeffer, Jeffrey and Gerald Salancik. 1978. *The External Control of Organizations: A Resource Dependence Perspective.* New York: Harper and Row.

PhRMA. 1996 and 1997. *PhRMA Industry Profile.* Washington, D.C.: PhRMA.

Piore, Michael J. and Charles Sabel. 1984. *The Second Industrial Divide: Possibilities for Prosperity.* New York: Basic.

Pitelis, Christos. 1991. *Market and Non-Market Hierarchies: Theory of Institutional Failure.* Oxford: Basil Blackwell.

Platteau, J.-P. 1994. "Behind the Market Stage Where Real Societies Exist—Part II: The Role of Moral Norms." *Journal of Development Studies.* 30, no. 4: 753–817.

Polanyi, Karl. 1957. *The Great Transformation: The Political and Economic Origins of Our Time.* Boston: Beacon Press. (Originally published 1944.)

Polanyi, Karl, Conrad M. Arensberg and Harry W. Pearson, eds. 1957. *Trade and Market in the Early Empires.* Chicago: Henry Regnery.

Pollert, Anna, ed. 1991. *Farewell to Flexibility?* Oxford: Blackwell.

Pontusson, Jonas and Peter Swenson. 1995. "Labor Markets, Production Strategies and Wage-Bargaining Institutions." *Comparative Political Studies.* 29: 223–250.

Popper, Karl. 1961. *The Poverty of Historicism.* London: Routledge and Kegan Paul.

Porter, Michael. 1990. *The Comparative Advantage of Nations.* New York: The Free Press.

Porter, Michael. 1992. *Capital Choices.* Washington, D.C.: Council on Competitiveness.

Posner, R. 1989. "What Is Culture? Toward a Semiotic Explication of Anthropological Concepts," pp. 240–295 in W. A. Koch, ed., *The Nature of Culture.* Bochum: Studienverlag Dr. Norbert Brockmeyer.

Posner, Richard A. 1972. *Economic Analysis of Law.* Boston: Little, Brown.

Posner, Richard A. 1994. *Sex and Reason.* Cambridge: Harvard University Press.

Powell, Walter W. 1996. "Inter-organisational Collaboration in the Biotechnology Industry." *Journal of Institutional and Theoretical Economics.* 152, no. 1: 197–215.

Powell, Walter W. 1998. "Learning from Collaboration: Knowledge and Networks in the Biotechnology and Pharmaceutical Industries." *California Management Review.* 40: 228–241.

Powell, Walter W., ed. 2000. *How Institutions Change.* Chicago: University of Chicago.

Powell, Walter W. and Paul J. DiMaggio, eds. 1991. *The New Institutionalism in Organizational Analysis.* Chicago: University of Chicago Press.

Pred, Allan. 1966. *The Spatial Dynamics of U.S. Urban-Industrial Growth, 1800–1914.* Cambridge: MIT Press.

Prindl, Andreas. 1981. *Japanese Finance: A Guide to Banking in Japan.* New York: John Wiley & Sons.

Prowse, Stephen. 1990. "Institutional Investment Patterns and Corporate Financial Behavior in the United States and Japan." *Journal of Financial Economics.* 27, no. 1: 43–66.

Putnam, Robert A. 1993. *Making Democracy Work.* Princeton: Princeton University Press.

Putnam, Robert D. 2000. *Bowling Alone: The Collapse and Revival of American Community.* New York: Simon & Schuster.

Pyke, Frank and Werner Sengenberger, eds. 1992. *Industrial Districts and Local Economic Regeneration.* Geneva: International Institute for Labour Studies.

Quine, Willard Van Orman. 1969. *Ontological Relativity and Other Essays.* New York: Columbia University Press.

Raadschelders, J. C. N. 1995. *Tussen Markt en Overheid: Een Bestuursgeschiedenis van de Centrale Vereniging voor de Ambulante Handel 1919–1921–1996.* Leyden: Leyden Department of Public Administration, University of Leyden.

Ragin, Charles C. 1987. *The Comparative Methods: Moving Beyond Qualitative and Quantitative Strategies.* Berkeley: University of California Press.

Ragin, Charles C. 1994a. "Introduction to Qualitative Comparative Analysis," pp. 299–319 in Thomas Janoski and Alexander Hicks, eds., *The Comparative Political Economy of the Welfare State.* New York: Cambridge University Press.

Ragin, Charles C. 1994b. "A Qualitative Comparative Analysis of Pensions Systems," pp. 320–356 in Thomas Janoski and Alexander Hicks, eds., *The Comparative Political Economy of the Welfare State.* New York: Cambridge University Press.

Ragin, Charles C. and York W. Bradshaw. 1991. "Statistical Analysis of Employment Discrimination: A Review and Critique." *Research in Social Stratification and Mobility.* 10: 199–228.

Ratey, John R. 2001. *A User's Guide to the Brain: Perception, Attention, and the Four Theaters of the Brain.* New York: Pantheon Books.

Rawlins, Gregory J. E., ed. 1991. *Foundations of Genetic Algorithms.* San Mateo, Calif.: Morgan Kaufmann Publishers.

Rawls, John. 1971. *A Theory of Justice.* Cambridge: Harvard University Press.

Regini, Marino. 2000. "Between De-regulation and Social Pacts: The Responses of European Economies to Globalization." *Politics & Society.* 28: 4–33.

Registrar of Cooperative Societies. 1938. *Cooperative Societies in Palestine: Report of the Registrar of Cooperative Societies on Developments During the Years 1921–1937.* Jerusalem: Printing and Stationery Office.

Reich, Robert. 1994. *The Work of Nations.* New York: Knopf.

Reinicke, Wolfgang. 1994. "Consolidation of Federal Bank Regulation?" Testimony before the US Senate Committee on Banking, Housing, and Urban Affairs, 4 March.

Rescher, Nicholas. 1994. *Philosophical Standardism: An Empiricist Approach to Philosophical Methodology.* Pittsburgh: University of Pittsburgh Press.

Rescher, Nicholas. 1998. *Complexity: A Philosophical Overview.* New Brunswick, N.J.: Transaction Publishers.

Richardson, George B. 1972. "The Organisation of Industry." *Economic Journal.* 82: 883–896.

Richardson, Jeremy and W. Jordan, eds. 1978. *Policy Styles in Western Europe.* London: Macmillan.

Ritzer, George. 1993 *The McDonaldization of Society: The Changing Character of Contemporary Social Life.* Newbury Park, Calif.: Pine Forge Press.

Ritzer, George. 1998. *The McDonaldization Thesis.* London: Sage Publications.

Rodrik, Dani. 1997. *Has Globalization Gone Too Far?* Washington, D.C.: Institute for International Economics.

Roe, Mark. 1990. "Political and Legal Restraints on Ownership and Control of Public Companies." *Journal of Financial Economics.* 27, no. 1: 7–41.

Roland, Gérard. 1990. "Gorbachev and the Common European Home: The Convergence Debate Revisited." *Kyklos.* 43: 385–409.

Romano, Sergio. 1977. *Histoire de l'Italie du Risorgimento à Nos Jours.* Paris: Seuil.

Romer, Paul M. 1986. "Increasing Returns and Long-run Growth." *Journal of Political Economy.* 94: 1002–1037.

Romer, Paul M. 1990. "Are Non-convexities Important for Understanding Growth?" *American Economic Review.* 80, no. 2: 97–103.

Romer, Paul M. 1994. "The Origins of Endogenous Growth." *Journal of Economic Perspectives.* 8, no. 1: 3–22.

Rosenberg, Nathan. 1994. *Exploring the Black Box: Technology, Economics and History.* Cambridge: Cambridge University Press.

Rosner, Menachem. 1993. "Organizations Between Community and Market: The Case of the Kibbutz." *Economic and Industrial Democracy.* 14: 369–397.

Rothschild-Whitt, Joyce. 1979. "The Collectivist Organization: An Alternative to Rational-Bureaucratic Models." *American Sociological Review.* 44: 509–527.

Rothstein, Bo. 1998. "The Breakdown of Trust and the Fall of the Swedish Model." Paper presented to the Seminar on the State and Capitalism since 1800, Harvard University.

Rumelt, Richard. 1974. *Strategy, Structure and Economic Performance.* Boston: Harvard Business School Press.

Rupert, Mark. 1995. *Producing Hegemony: The Politics of Mass Production and American Global Power.* New York: Cambridge University Press.

Russell, Raymond. 1984. "The Role of Culture and Ethnicity in the Degeneration of Democratic Workplaces." *Economic and Industrial Democracy.* 5: 73–96.

Russell, Raymond. 1995. *Utopia in Zion: The Israeli Experience with Worker Cooperatives.* Albany: State University of New York Press.

Russell, Raymond and Hanneman, Robert. 1992. "Cooperatives and the Business Cycle: The Israeli Case." *Journal of Comparative Economics.* 16: 701–715.

Rutherford, Malcolm. 1994. *Institutions in Economics: The Old and the New Institutionalism.* Cambridge: Cambridge University Press.

Sabel, Charles F. 1991. "Moebius Strip Organizations and Open Labor Markets: Some Consequences of the Reintegration of Conception and Execution in a Volatile Economy," pp. 23–63 in Pierre Bourdieu and James S. Coleman, eds., *Social Theory for a Changing Society.* Boulder, Colo.: Westview Press.

Sabel, Charles F. 1992. "Studied Trust: Building New Forms of Cooperation in a Volatile Economy," pp. 215–250 in Frank Pyke and Werner Sengenberger, eds., *Industrial Districts and Local Economic Regeneration*. Geneva: International Institute for Labour Studies.

Sabel, Charles F. 1994. "Learning by Monitoring: The Institutions of Economic Development," pp. 137–165 in Neil Smelser and Richard Swedberg, eds., *Handbook of Economic Sociology*. Princeton: Princeton University Press.

Sabel, Charles and Jonathan Zeitlin. 1985. "Historical Alternatives to Mass Production: Politics, Markets, and Technology in Nineteenth Century Industrialization." *Past and Present*. 108: 133–176.

Sachs, Jeffrey D. 1993. *Poland's Jump to a Market Economy*. Cambridge: Harvard University Press.

Sachs, Jeffrey. 2000. "On Globalization—A New Map of the World." *The Economist*. June 24.

Salant, Walter. 1977. *Worldwide Inflation*. Washington, D.C.: Brookings Institution Press.

Sander, Richard. 1992. "Elevating the Debate on Lawyers and Economic Growth," *Law and Social Inquiry*. 17, no. 4: 659–666.

Santomero, Anthony. 1984. "Modeling the Banking Firm: A Survey." *Journal of Money, Credit and Banking*. 16, no. 2: 576–602.

Saxenian, AnnaLee. 1994. *Regional Advantage: Culture and Competition in Silicon Valley and Route 128*. Cambridge: Harvard University Press.

Saxonberg, S. 2000. *The Fall: A Comparative Study of the Collapse of Communism in Four Countries*. Amsterdam: Gordon and Breach Publishers.

Schank, Roger C. and Robert Abelson. 1977. *Scripts, Plans, Goals, and Understanding: An Inquiry into Human Knowledge Structures*. Hillsdale, N.J.: Lawrence Erlbaum Associates.

Schank, Roger C., Alex Kass, and Christopher K. Riesbeck. 1994. *Inside Case-Based Explanation Artificial Intelligence*. Hillsdale, N.J.: Lawrence Erlbaum Associates.

Scharpf, Fritz W. 1991. *Crisis and Choice in European Social Democracy*. Ithaca: Cornell University Press.

Scharpf, Fritz Wilhelm and Vivien A. Schmidt, eds. 2000. *Welfare and Work in the Open Economy. Vol. I: Diverse Responses to Common Challenges in Twelve Countries*. Oxford: Oxford University Press.

Scharpf, Fritz W. 1995. *Governing in Europe*. Oxford: Oxford University Press.

Scharpf, Fritz W. 1997. *Games Real Actors Play: Actor-centered Institutionalism in Policy Research*. Boulder, Colo.: Westview Press.

Schelling, T. C. 1963. *The Strategy of Conflict*. Cambridge: Harvard University Press.

Schettkat, Ronald. 1992. *The Labor Market Dynamics of Economic Restructuring*. New York: Praeger.

Schmölders, Günter. 1973. *Sozioökonomische Verhaltensforschung*. Berlin: Duncker & Humblot.

Schneiberg, Marc and J. Rogers Hollingsworth. 1990. "Can Transaction Cost Economics Explain Trade Associations?" pp. 320–460 in Masahiko Aoki, Bo Gustafsson and Oliver E. Williamson, eds., *The Firm As A Nexus of Treaties*. London and Beverly Hills: Sage Publications.

Schoenberger, Erica. 1994. "Competition, Time, and Space in Industrial Change," pp. 51–60 in Gary Gereffi and Miguel Korzeniewicz, eds., *Commodity Chains and Global Capitalism*. Westport, Conn.: Praeger.

Schonfield, A. 1965. *Modern Capitalism: The Changing Balance of Public and Private Power*. London: Oxford Press.

Schotter, Andrew. 1981. *The Economic Theory of Social Institutions*. Cambridge and New York: Cambridge University Press.

Schriftgiesser, Karl. 1967. *Business and Public Policy: The Role of the Committee for Economic Development, 1942–1967*. Englewood Cliffs, N.J.: Prentice Hall.

Schubert, Klaus. 1989. *Interessenvermittlung und staatliche Regulation*. Opladen: Westdeutscher Verlag.

Schumpeter, Joseph A. 1950. *Capitalism, Socialism and Democracy*. Third Edition. New York: Harper.

Schumpeter, Joseph A. 1983. *The Theory of Economic Development*. New Brunswick, N.J.: Transaction Books.

Schuppert, Gunnar Folke. 1997. "Assoziative Demokratie. Zum Platz des organisierten Menschen in der Demokratietheorie," pp. 114–152 in Ansgar Klein and Rainer Schmalz-Bruns, eds., *Politische Beteiligung und Bürgerengagement in Deutschland*. Baden-Baden: Nomos.

Schwartz, A. 1992. "Relational Contracts and the Courts." *Journal of Legal Studies*. 21: 780–822.

Schwartz, Thomas. 1991. *America's Germany*. Cambridge: Harvard University Press.

Schwartzman, D. 1976. *Innovation in the Pharmaceutical Industry*. Baltimore: Johns Hopkins University Press.

Scott, John and Catherine Griff. 1985. "Bank Spheres of Influence in the British Corporate Network," pp. 215–233 in Frans Stokman, Rolf Ziegler and John Scott, eds., *Networks of Corporate Power: A Comparative Analysis of Ten Countries*. Cambridge: Polity Press.

Scott, W. Richard. 1981. *Organizations: Rational, Natural, and Open Systems*. Englewood Cliffs, N.J.: Prentice-Hall.

Scott, W. Richard, John W. Meyer and Associates, eds. 1994. *Institutional Environments and Organizations: Structural Complexity and Individualism*. Thousand Oaks, Calif.: Sage.

Scranton, Philip. 1984. *Proprietary Capitalism: The Textile Manufacture at Philadelphia, 1800–1885*. Cambridge and New York: Cambridge University Press.

Scully, Gerald W. 1992. *Constitutional Environments and Economic Growth*. Princeton: Princeton University Press.

Searleman, Alan and Douglas Herrmann. 1994. *Memory from a Broader Perspective*. New York: McGraw-Hill.

Selznick, Philip. 1992. *The Moral Commonwealth: Social Theory and the Promise of Community*. Berkeley: University of California Press.

Selznick, Philip. 1996. "Institutionalism 'Old' and 'New.'" *Administrative Science Quarterly*. 31: 171–193.

Sengenberger, Werner, ed. 1991. *Industrial Districts and Local Economic Regeneration*. Geneva: International Institute for Labour Studies.

Shalev, Michael. 1990. "The Political Economy of Labor Party Dominance and Decline in Israel," pp. 83–127 in T. J. Pempel, ed., *Uncommon Democracies: The One Party Dominant Regimes*. Ithaca: Cornell University Press.

Sharp, M. and P. Patel. 1996. "Europe's Pharmaceutical Industry: An Innovation Profile," Draft Report Prepared for DG X111, European Commission.

Shils, E. A. 1963. *Political Development in New States*. Hague: Mouton.

Shimanoff, S. B. 1980. *Communication Rules: Theory and Research*. Beverly Hills, Calif.: Sage Publications.

Shonfield, Andrew. 1969. *Modern Capitalism*. New York: Oxford University Press.

Siegfried, André. 1927. *America Comes of Age*. New York: Harcourt Brace.

Singh, Jagjit. 1972. *Great Ideas of Operations Research*. New York: Dover Publications.

Singh, Jitendra and Charles J. Lumsden. 1990. "Theory and Research in Organizational Ecology." *Annual Review of Sociology*. 16: 161–195.

Singh, Jitendra, David J. Tucker and Robert J. House. 1986. "Organizational Legitimacy and the Liability of Newness." *Administrative Science Quarterly*. 31: 171–193.

Sjöstrand, Sven-Erik. 1993. *Institutional Change: Theory and Empirical Findings*. Armonk, N.Y.: M. E. Sharpe.

Skocpol, Theda. 1979. *States and Social Revolutions: A Comparative Analysis of France, Russia, and China*. Cambridge: Cambridge University Press.

Skocpol, Theda. 1994. *Social Revolutions in the Modern World*. Cambridge: Cambridge University Press.

Skocpol, Theda and Margaret Somers. 1980. "The Uses of Comparative History in Macrosocial Inquiry." *Comparative Studies in Society and History*. 22: 174–219.

Slack, Trevor and Bob Hinings. 1994. "Institutional Pressures and Isomorphic Change: An Empirical Test." *Organization Studies*. 15: 803–827.

Sloan, Alfred. 1963. *My Years with General Motors*. New York: Doubleday and Company.

Smelser, Neil J. and Richard Swedberg, eds. 1994. *The Handbook of Economic Sociology.* Princeton: Princeton University Press; New York: Russell Sage Foundation.

Smith, David, Dorothy Solinger and Steve Kopik, eds. 1999. *State and Sovereignty in the World Economy.* New York: Routledge.

Smith, Vernon L. 1982. "Microeconomic Systems as an Experimental Science." *American Economic Review.* 72, no. 5: 923–955. Reprinted in Smith, Vernon L. 1992. *Papers in Experimental Economics.* Cambridge: Cambridge University Press.

Society for the Advancement of Socio-Economics. 1999. *Madison Declaration on the Need for Socio-Economic Research and Theory.* Accessed at www.sase.org/conf99/declaration.html on 8/5/00.

Solow, Robert M. 1985. "Economic History and Economics." *American Economic Review. Papers and Proceedings.* 75, no. 2: 328–331.

Sombart, Werner. 1930. *Die drei Nationalökonomien: Geschichte und System der Lehre von der Wirtschaft.* München: Duncker und Humblot.

Sorge, Arndt. 1989. "An Essay on Technical Change: Its Dimensions and Social and Strategic Context." *Organization Studies* 10: 23–44.

Sorge, Arndt and Wolfgang Streeck. 1988. "Industrial Relations and Technical Change: The Case for an Extended Perspective," pp. 19–47 in Richard Hyman and Wolfgang Streeck, eds., *New Technology and Industrial Relations.* New York and Oxford: Basil Blackwell.

Soskice, David. 1991. "The Institutional Infrastructure for International Competitiveness: A Comparative Analysis of the UK and Germany," pp. 45–66 in Anthony Barnes Atkinson and Renato Brunetta, eds., *Economics for the New Europe.* London: Macmillan.

Soskice, David. 1994a. "Innovation Strategies of Companies: A Comparative Institutional Approach of Some Cross-country Differences," pp. 271–289 in Wolfgang Zapf and Meinolf Dierkes, eds., *Institutionenvergleich und Institutionendynamik.* Berlin: Sigma.

Soskice, David. 1994b. "Finer Varieties of Advanced Capitalism: Industry Versus Group Based Coordination in Germany and Japan." Paper presented to the Varieties of Capitalism Conference, Poitiers, September.

Soskice, David. 1999. "Divergent Production Regimes: Coordinated and Uncoordinated Market Economies in the 1980s and 1990s," pp. 101–134 in Herbert Kitschelt et al., eds., *Continuity and Change in Contemporary Capitalism.* New York: Cambridge University Press.

Sousa, Ronald de. 1991. *The Rationality of Emotion.* Cambridge: MIT Press.

Spector, M. and J. Kitsuse. 1987. *Constructing Social Problems.* New York: Aldine de Gruyter.

Staber, Udo. 1989. "Organizational Foundings in the Cooperative Sector of Atlantic Canada: An Ecological Perspective." *Organization Studies* 10: 381–403.

Stalk, George and Thomas Hout. 1990. *Competing Against Time: How Time-based Competition is Reshaping Global Markets.* New York: Free Press.

Starmer, Christopher. 1999. "Experimental Economics: Hard Science or Wasteful Tinkering?" *Economic Journal.* 109, no. 2: F5–15.

Statistisches Bundesamt. 1953. *Statistisches Jahrbuch für die Bundesrepublik Deutschlands.* Wiesbaden, Germany.

Statistisches Bundesamt. 1973. *Statistisches Jahrbuch für die Bundesrepublik Deutschlands.* Wiesbaden, Germany.

Steiner, Philippe. 1995. "Economic Sociology: A Historical Perspective." *European Journal of the History of Economic Thought.* 2, no. 1: 175–195.

Steinmo, Sven, Kathleen Ann Thelen and Frank Longstreth, eds. 1992. *Structuring Politics: Historical Institutionalism in Comparative Analysis.* New York: Cambridge University Press.

Sternberg, Robert J., ed. 1999. *The Nature of Cognition.* Cambridge: MIT Press.

Sternberg, Robert J. and Richard K. Wagner, eds. 1994. *Mind in Context: Interactionist Perspectives on Human Intelligence.* Cambridge: Cambridge University Press.

Stigler, George J. 1971. "The Theory of Economic Regulation." *Bell Journal of Economics and Management* 2: 3–21.

Stinchcombe, A. E. 1968. *Constructing Social Theories.* New York: Harcourt, Brace & World.

Stolper, Wolfgang Friedrich and Paul A. Samuelson. 1941. "Protection and Real Wages." *Review of Economic Studies.* 9: 58–73.

Storper, Michael. 1997. *The Regional World: Territorial Development in a Global Economy.* New York: Guildford Press.

Streeck, Wolfgang. 1987. "Industrial Relations and Industrial Change in the Motor Industry: An International View." *Economic and Industrial Democracy.* 8: 437–462.

Streeck, Wolfgang. 1988. "Comment on Ronald Dore, 'Rigidities in the Labor Market.'" *Government Opposition.* 23, no. 4: 413–423.

Streeck, Wolfgang. 1991a. "The Federal Republic of Germany," pp. 53–89 in John Niland and Oliver Clarke, eds., *Agenda for Change: An International Analysis of Industrial Relations in Transition.* Sydney: Allen and Unwin.

Streeck, Wolfgang. 1991b. "On the Institutional Conditions of Diversified Quality Production," pp. 21–61 in Egon Matzner and Wolfgang Streeck, eds., *Beyond Keynesianism: The Socio-Economics of Production and Full Employment.* Aldershot, Hants, England: Edward Elgar.

Streeck, Wolfgang. 1992a. *Social Institutions and Economic Performance.* Newbury Park, Calif.: Sage.

Streeck, Wolfgang. 1992b. "On the Institutional Preconditions of Diversified Quality Production," in Wolfgang Streeck, *Social Institutions and Economic Performance.* London and Newberry Park: Sage Productions.

Streeck, Wolfgang. 1994. "Pay Restraint Without Incomes Policy: Institutionalized Monetarism and Industrial Unionism in Germany," pp. 118–140 in Ronald Dore, Robert Boyer and Zoe Marn, eds., *The Return of Incomes Policy.* London: Pinter.

Streeck, Wolfgang. 1995. "From Market Making to State Building? Reflections on the Political Economy of European Social Policy," pp. 389–431 in Stephan Leibfried and Paul Pierson, eds., *European Social Policy: Between Fragmentation and Integration.* Washington, D.C.: Brookings Institution Press.

Streeck, Wolfgang. 1997a. "The Uncertainties of Management in the Management of Uncertainty." *International Journal of Political Economy.* 17, no. 3: 57–87.

Streeck, Wolfgang. 1997b. "Beneficial Constraints: On the Economic Limits of Rational Voluntarism," pp. 197–219 in J. Rogers Hollingsworth and Robert Boyer, eds., *Contemporary Capitalism: The Embeddedness of Institutions.* New York and Cambridge: Cambridge University Press.

Streeck, Wolfgang. 1997c. "German Capitalism: Does It Exist? Can It Survive?" pp. 33–54 in Colin Crouch and Wolfgang Streeck, eds., *Political Economy of Modern Capitalism: Mapping Convergence and Divergence.* Thousand Oaks, Calif.: Sage; London: Routledge.

Streeck, Wolfgang and Philippe C. Schmitter, eds. 1985a. *Private Interest Government: Beyond Market and State.* Beverly Hills, Calif., London, New Delhi: Sage.

Streeck, Wolfgang and Philippe C. Schmitter. 1985b. "Community, Market, State—and Associations? The Prospective Contribution of Interest Governance to Social Order." *European Sociological Review.* I, no. 2: 119–138.

Streeck, Wolfgang and Philippe C. Schmitter. 1985c. "Community, Market, State—And Associations? The Prospective Contribution of Interest Governance to Social Order," pp. 1–29 in Wolfgang Streeck and Philippe C. Schmitter, eds., *Private Interest Government: Beyond Market and State.* Beverly Hills, Calif.: Sage.

Stretton, Hugh and Lion Orchard. 1994. *Public Goods, Public Enterprise, Public Choice: Theoretical Foundations of the Contemporary Attack on Government.* London: St. Martin's.

Stryker, Robin. 1989. "Limits on Technocratization of the Law: The Elimination of the NLRB's Division of Economic Research." *American Sociological Review.* 54: 341–358.

Stryker, Robin. 1994. "Rules, Resources and Legitimacy Processes: Some Implications for Social Conflict, Order and Change." *American Journal of Sociology.* 99: 847–910.

Stryker, Robin. 1996. "Beyond History vs. Theory: Strategic Narrative and Sociological Explanation." *Sociological Methods and Research.* 24: 306–354.

Stryker, Robin. 2000. "Legitimacy Processes as Institutional Politics: Implications for Theory and Research in the Sociology of Organizations." *Research in the Sociology of Organizations.* 17: 179–223.

Stryker, Robin. 2001. "The Future of Socio-Economics and of the Society for the Advancement of Socio-Economics." Chapter 4, this volume.

Stryker, Robin, Martha Scarpellino and Mellisa Holtzman. 1999. "Political Culture Wars 1990s Style: The Drum Beat of Quotas in Media Framing of the Civil Rights Act of 1991." *Research in Social Stratification and Social Mobility.* 17: 33–106.

Stryker, Sheldon. 1980. *Symbolic Interaction: A Social Structural Version.* Menlo Park, Calif.: Benjamin-Cummings.

Sutton, Francis X., Harris Seymour, Carl Kaysen and James Tobin. 1956. *The American Business Creed.* Cambridge: Harvard University Press.

Sutton, C. 1998. *Swedish Alcohol Discourse: Construction of a Social Problem.* Ph.D. Dissertation in Sociology, Uppsala University. Uppsala: Acta Universitatis Upsaliensis.

Swedberg, Richard. 1990. *Economics and Sociology: Redefining the Boundaries.* Princeton: Princeton University Press.

Sweezy, Alan. 1972. "The Keynesians and Government Policy, 1933–1939." *American Economic Review.* 62: 116–121.

Sztompka, Piotr. 1991. *Society in Action: The Theory of Social Becoming.* Cambridge: Polity Press.

Sztompka, Piotr. 1993. *Sociology of Social Change.* Oxford: Basil Blackwell.

Sztompka, Piotr. 1994. "Evolving Focus on Agency," pp. 25–60 in P. Sztompka, ed., *Agency and Structure: Reorienting Social Theory.* Amsterdam: Gordon and Breach.

Sztompka, Piotr, ed. 1994. *Agency and Structure: Reorienting Social Theory.* Amsterdam: Gordon and Breach.

Tarrow, Sidney. 1995. "Bridging the Quantitative—Qualitative Divide in Political Science." *American Political Science Review.* 89: 471–474.

Tatewaki, Kazuo. 1991. *Banking and Finance in Japan: An Introduction to the Tokyo Market.* London and New York: Routledge.

Taylor, M. 1988. *Rationality and Revolution.* New York: Cambridge University Press.

Teece, David J. 1986. "Profiting From Technological Innovation: Implications for Integration, Collaboration, Licensing, and Public Policy." *Research Policy* 15: 285–305.

Teece, David J. 1993. "Perspectives on Alfred Chandler's Scale and Scope." *Journal of Economic Literature.* March: 199–225.

Tendler, Judith. 1997. *Good Government in the Tropics.* Baltimore: John Hopkins University Press.

Thelen, Kathleen. 1991. *Union of Parts.* Ithaca: Cornell University Press.

Thelen, Kathleen. 2000. "Why German Employers Cannot Bring Themselves to Abandon the German Model," pp. 138–172 in Torben Iversen, Jonas Pontusson and David Soskice, eds., *Unions, Employers and Central Banks.* New York: Cambridge University Press.

Tilly, Charles. 1978. *From Mobilization to Revolution.* Reading, Mass.: Addison-Wesley.

Tilly, Charles. 1993. *European Revolutions: 1492–1992.* Oxford: Blackwell.

Tiryakian, Edward A. 1995. "Collective Effervescence, Social Change, and Charisma: Durkheim, Weber, 1989." *International Sociology.* 10, no. 3: 269–281.

Tocqueville, Alexis, de. 1961. *Democracy in America,* 2 vol. New York: Schocken.

Tolbert, Pamela S. and Lynn G. Zucker. 1983. "Institutionalized Sources of Change in Organizational Structure: The Diffusion of Civil Service Reform, 1880–1935." *Administrative Science Quarterly.* 28: 22–39.

Tolliday, Steven and Jonathan Zeitlin, eds. 1991. *The Power to Manage: Employers and Industrial Relations in Comparative Historical Perspective.* London and New York: Routledge.

Trevor, Malcolm, ed. 1987. *The Internationalization of Japanese Business: European and Japanese Perspectives.* Boulder, Colo.: Westview Press.

Trumbull, Gunnar. 1999. *Product Market Regulation in France and Germany.* Ph.D. Dissertation, Department of Political Science, Massachusetts Institute of Technology.

Tsusui, William. 1988. *Banking Policy in Japan: American Efforts at Reform During the Occupation.* London and New York: Routledge.

Tumin, J. 1982. "The Theory of Democratic Development." *Theory and Society.* 11: 143–164.

Turner, Jonathan. 2000. *On the Origins of Human Emotions: A Sociological Inquiry into the Evolution of Human Affect.* Stanford: Stanford University Press.

Turner, Lowell. 1991. *Democracy at Work.* Ithaca: Cornell University Press.

Twining, W. and D. Miers. 1982. *How to do Things with Rules?* 2nd edition. London: Weidenfeld and Nicolson.

United States Census Bureau, Department of Commerce. 1999. *Statistical Abstract of the United States.* Washington, D.C.: U.S. Printing Office.

Van der Pijl, Kees. 1984. *The Making of an Atlantic Ruling Class.* London: Verso.

Varsori, Antonio. 1993. "Italy and European Integration from the Marshall Plan to the Pleven Plan," pp. 401–414 in *Le Plan Marshall et le Relèvement Economique de l'Europe: Colloque Tenu à Bercy les 21, 22 et 23 Mars 1991, Sous la Direction de René Girault et Maurice Lévy-Leboyer.* Paris: Comité pour l'Histoire Economique et Financière de la France, Ministère de l'Économie, des Finances et du Budget.

Veseth, Michael. 1998. *Selling Globalization: The Myth of the Global Economy.* Boulder, Colo.: Lynne Rienner.

Vinke, Harriet and Ton Wilthagen. 1992. *The Non-mobilization of Law by Asbestos Victims in the Netherlands: Social Insurance Versus Tort-based Compensation.* Amsterdam: Hugo Sinzheimer Institute.

Vitols, Sigurt, Steve Casper, David Soskice and S. Wolcock. 1997. *Corporate Governance in Large British and German Companies.* London: Anglo-German Foundation.

Vitols, Sigurt. 1994. "German Banks and the Modernization of the Small Firm Sector: Long-Term Finance in Comparative Perspective." Paper presented at the 9th International Conference of Europeanists, Chicago, 31 March–2 April.

Vitols, Sigurt. 2001. "Varieties of Corporate Governance in Germany and the UK," Chapter 3 in Peter A. Hall and David Soskice, eds., *Varieties of Capitalism: The Institutional Foundations of Comparative Advantage.* Oxford: Oxford University Press.

Vogel, Steven Kent. 1996. *Freer Markets, More Rules: Regulatory Reform in the Advanced Industrial Countries.* Ithaca: Cornell University Press.

Vogel, Steven Kent. 1999. "The Crisis of German and Japanese Capitalism: Stalled on the Road to the Liberal Market Model?" Manuscript.

Waarden, Frans van. 1984. "Techniek en Arbeid in de Twentse Katoenspinnerijen: Van de Oudheid tot Heden," pp. 113–157 in *Het Eerste Jaarboek voor de Geschiedenis van Bedrijf en Techniek JbGBT.* Utrecht: Stichting JbGDT.

Waarden, Frans van. 1995a. "Government Intervention in Industrial Relations," pp. 109–133 in J. van Hoof, R. Huiskamp, and J. van Ruysseveldt, eds. *Comparative Industrial and Employment Relations.* London: Thousand Oaks, New Delhi: Sage.

Waarden, Frans van. 1995b. "Persistence of National Policy Styles: A Study of Their Institutional Foundations," pp. 333–372 in Brigitte Unger and Frans van Waarden, eds., *Convergence or Diversity? Internationalization and Economic Policy Response.* Aldershot: Avebury.

Waarden, Frans van. 1998. "Hoe Uniek, Legitiem en Efficient is de Nederlandse Overlegeconomie in Vergelijkend Perspectief?," pp. 23–81 in Sociaal-Economische Raad, ed., *150 Jaar Grondwet: Overlegeconomie in Een Goede Constitutie.* Den Haag: Sociaal-Economische Raad.

Waarden, Frans van. 2000. *Institutions and Innovation: The Legal Environment of Innovating Firms.* Manuscript.

Wade, Robert. 1996. "Globalization and its Limits: Reports of the Death of the National Economy are Greatly Exaggerated," pp. 60–88 in Berger and Dore, eds., *National Diversity and Global Capitalism.* Ithaca: Cornell University Press.

Wall, Irwin. 1991. *The United States and the Making of Postwar France: 1945–1954.* New York: Cambridge University Press.

Wallerstein, Immanuel. 1980. *The World System II*. New York: Academic Press.
Wallich, Henry. 1955. *Mainsprings of German Revival*. New Haven: Yale University Press.
Weber, Henri. 1986. *Le Parti des Patrons:Le CNPF, 1946–1990*. Paris: Editions du Seuil.
Weber, M. 1951. *The Religion of China: Confucianism and Taoism*. Glencoe, Ill.: Free Press; New York: Macmillan.
Weber, Max. 1949. *The Methodology of the Social Sciences*. Translated and edited by Edward A. Shils and Henry A. Flinch. New York: Free Press.
Weber, Max. 1978. *Economy and Society: An Outline of Interpretive Sociology*. Edited by Guenther Roth and Claus Wittich. Berkeley: University of California Press.
Weber, Max. 1982. *Gesammelte Aufsätze zur Wissenschaftslehre*. Fifth edition. Tübingen: J. C. B. Mohr Paul Siebeck.
Weidlich, Wolfgang and Günter Haag. 1983. *Concepts and Models of a Quantitative Sociology: The Dynamics of Interacting Populations*. Berlin: Springer-Verlag.
Weidlich, Wolfgang and Günter Haag, eds. 1988. *Interregional Migration: Dynamic Theory and Comparative Analysis*. Berlin: Springer-Verlag.
Weingart, Peter and Nico Stehr, eds. 2000. *Perspectives on Interdisciplinarity*. Toronto: University of Toronto Press.
Weiss, Linda. 1984. "The Italian State and Small Business." *European Journal of Sociology*. 25: 214–241.
Weiss, Linda. 1988. *Creating Capitalism: The State and Small Business since 1945*. New York: Basil Blackwell.
Werth, Barry. 1994. *The Billion-dollar Molecule: One Company's Quest for the Perfect Drug*. New York: Touchstone, Simon & Schuster.
Westney, Eleanor. 1987. *Imitation and Innovation: The Transfer of Western Organizational Patterns to Meiji Japan*. Cambridge: Harvard University Press.
White, Eugene. 1983. *The Regulation and Reform of the American Banking System, 1900–1929*. Princeton: Princeton University Press.
Whitley, Richard. 1992a. *Business Systems in East Asia: Firms, Markets and Societies*. London: Sage.
Whitley, Richard. 1992b. *European Business Systems: Firms and Markets in their National Context*. London: Sage.
Whitley, Richard. 1999. *Divergent Capitalisms: The Social Structuring and Change of Business Systems*. Oxford and New York: Oxford University Press.
Whitley, Richard, ed. 1992. *European Business Systems: Firms and Markets in Their National Contexts*. London: Sage Publications.
Whitley, Richard and P. H. Kristensen, eds. 1996. *The Changing European Firm: Limits to Convergence*. London: Routledge.
Williamson, Oliver E. 1975. *Markets and Hierarchies: Analysis and Anti-Trust Implications: A Study in the Economics of Internal Organization*. New York: Free Press.
Williamson, Oliver E. 1985. *The Economic Institutions of Capitalism: Firms, Markets, Relational Contracting*. London: Macmillan.
Williamson, Oliver E. 1991. "Comparative Economic Organization: The Analysis of Discrete Structural Alternatives." *Administrative Science Quarterly*. 36: 269–296.
Williamson, Oliver E. 1999. "Strategy Research: Governance and Competence Perspectives." *Strategic Management Journal*. 20: 1087–1108.
Williamson, Oliver. 1985. *The Economic Institutions of Capitalism*. New York: The Free Press.
Winter, Sidney. 1987. "Knowledge and Competence as Strategic Assets," pp. 159–184 in David J. Teece, ed., *The Competitive Challenge: Strategies for Industrial Innovation and Renewal*. Cambridge, Mass.: Ballinger.
Wirtschaftswoche. 1998. "Schneller Aufstieg," 24 September 1998: 134–139.
Womack, James P., Daniel T. Jones and Daniel Roos. 1990. *The Machine that Changed the World: Based on the Massachusetts Institute of Technology 5-million Dollar 5-year Study on the Future of the Automobile*. New York: Rawson Associates.

Womack James P., Daniel T. Jones and Daniel Roos. 1991. *The Machine that Changed the World: The Story of Lean Production.* New York: HarperPerennial.

Wood, Adrian. 1994. *North–South Trade, Employment and Inequality.* Oxford: Clarendon Press.

Wood, Stewart. 2001. "From Employer Preferences to Public Policy-making in Germany and Britain," Chapter 13 in Peter A. Hall and David Soskice, eds., *Varieties of Capitalism: The Institutional Foundations of Comparative Advantage.* Oxford: Oxford University Press.

Woodward, Alison E., Jerry Ellig and Tom R. Burns. 1994. *Municipal Entrepreneurship and Energy Policy: A Five Nation Study of Politics, Innovation, and Social Change.* New York: Gordon and Breach.

Woolf, Stuart. 1972. *The Rebirth of Italy, 1943–1950.* New York: Humanities Press.

Woolridge, Michael, Jörg P. Müller, and Milind Tambe, eds. 1996. *Intelligent Agents II: Agent Theories, Architectures and Languages.* Berlin: Springer-Verlag.

World Bank. 1997. *The State in a Changing World: World Development Report 1997.* New York: Oxford University Press.

Wright, Erik Olin. 1997. *Class Counts: Comparative Studies in Class Analysis.* Cambridge and New York: Cambridge University Press.

Wright, Erik. 1998. "A Brief Comment on Wolfgang Streeck's Essay, 'Beneficial Constraints: On the Economic Limits of Rational Voluntarism.'" Unpublished paper.

Wyatt, Michael. 1988. "The Feasibility of a State-Owned Bank in Wisconsin as an Aid to State and Local Government Finance and to Economic Development." Unpublished manuscript.

Yin, Robert K. 1993. *Applications of Case Study Research.* Newbury Park and London: Sage Publications.

Yin, Robert K. 1994. *Case Study Research: Design and Methods.* Newbury Park and London: Sage Publications.

Zamagni, Vera Negri. 1986. "Betting on the Future: The Reconstruction of Italian Industry, 1946–1952," pp. 283–301 in Franz Becker and Josef Knipping, eds., *Power in Europe? Great Britain, France, Italy, and Germany in a Postwar World 1945–1950.* Berlin; New York: Walter de Gruyter.

Zecchini, Salvatore, ed. 1997. *Lessons from the Economic Transition in Central and Eastern Europe in the 1990s.* Boston: Kluwer.

Zeitlin, Jonathan. 1992. "Industrial Districts and Local Economic Regeneration: Overview and Comment," pp. 279–294 in Frank Pyke and Werner Sengenberger, eds., *Industrial Districts and Local Economic Regeneration.* Geneva: International Institute for Labour Studies.

Zelizer, Viviana A. 1993. "Making Multiple Monies," pp. 193–212 in Richard Swedberg, ed., *Explorations in Economic Sociology.* New York: Russell Sage.

Ziegler, Nicholas. 1997. *Governing Ideas: Strategies for Innovation in France and Germany.* Ithaca: Cornell University Press.

Ziegler, Nicholas. 2000. "Corporate Governance and the Politics of Property Rights in Germany." *Politics and Society.* 28: 195–221.

Zucker, Lynne G. 1987. "Institutional Theories of Organizations." *Annual Review of Sociology.* 13: 443–464.

Zucker, Lynne G. 1988. *Institutional Patterns and Organizations: Culture and Environment.* Cambridge, Mass.: Ballinger.

Zysman, John. 1983. *Governments, Markets and Growth: Financial Systems and the Politics of Industrial Change.* Ithaca: Cornell University Press.

Zysman, John. 1994. "How Institutions Create Historically Rooted Trajectories of Growth," *Industrial and Corporate Change.* 3, no. 1: 243–283.

About the Contributors

Tom R. Burns is professor of sociology, University of Uppsala in Sweden, where he is the founder of the Uppsala Theory Circle. His academic appointments have included the Clarence J. Robinson University Professorship at George Mason University, visiting professor at the Wissenschaftszentrum Berlin, fellow at the Swedish Collegium for Advanced Study in the Social Sciences, and fellow at the European University Institute. He is the author or editor of at least eleven books and numerous scholarly articles in the area of social theory and methodology (socio-economics, institutional theory and analysis, the theory of games and interaction, and evolutionary theory). In addition, his empirical research and publications are in the areas of politics, the sociology of technology and environment, and comparative analysis of institutions and organizations. Among his books are *Man, Decisions, Society* (1985), *The Shaping of Socio-economic Systems* (1986), *Creative Democracy* (1988), *Societal Decision-making: Democratic Challenges to State Technocracy* (1992), *Municipal Entrepreneurship and Energy Policy: A Five-Nation Study of Politics, Innovation, and Social Change* (1994), *Transitions to Alternative Energy Systems: Entrepreneurs, New Technologies, and Social Change* (1984), *Structuration: Economic and Social Change* (2000).

Marcus Carson is a graduate student in the Department of Sociology, Uppsala University. He has degrees in psychology (B.A., Kalamazoo College) and sociology (B.S., Södertörns University College in Sweden). Previously he was engaged in policy making in the United States, where he worked with public interest and community organizations for more than seventeen years. He is currently collaborating with Tom Burns in research on policy making and governmental process in the European Union.

435

Steven Casper is University Lecturer in the area of innovation and entrepreneurship at the Judge Institute of Management Studies, Cambridge University. Previously he was research fellow at the Wissenschaftszentrum Berlin. He has published numerous scholarly articles in the areas of institutional theory, corporate governance, national systems of innovation, and the relationship between law and technical change. His current research concentrates on the diffusion of entrepreneurial business models in Europe, focusing on the biotechnology and software industries in Germany, the United Kingdom, and Sweden. He is the current chairperson of the Network on Knowledge, Economy, and Society for the Society for the Advancement of Socio-Economics.

Marie-Laure Djelic is professor at ESSEC, France. After undergraduate studies in business and in philosophy in France, she received her Ph.D. in sociology from Harvard. For her book, *Exporting the American Model,* she received the Max Weber Prize of the Organizations, Occupations and Work section of the American Sociological Association. Her present research projects focus on the interplay among globalization, the American model of political economy, and other national business systems.

Amitai Etzioni is University Professor at George Washington University. Previously he was professor of sociology at Columbia University and during 1987–1989 he was the Thomas Henry Carroll Ford Foundation Professor at the Harvard Business School. He was the founder and the first president of the Society for the Advancement of Socio-Economics (SASE) and is a lifetime honorary fellow of SASE. He is the editor of *The Responsible Community: Rights and Responsibilities*, a communitarian quarterly. He is frequently called the "guru" of the communitarian movement. He is a former president of the American Sociological Association, and he is the author of nineteen books, including *The Limits of Privacy, The New Golden Rule: Community and Morality in a Democratic Society* (recipient of the Simon Wiesenthal Center's 1997 Tolerance Book Award), *The Spirit of Community: Rights, Responsibilities and the Communitarian Agenda,* and *The Moral Dimension: Toward a New Economics.*

David Gear is a research associate who collaborates with J. Rogers Hollingsworth and Ellen Jane Hollingsworth at the University of Wisconsin on research involving the socio-economics of innovation in science and technology. In addition, he has considerable expertise in information technology.

Greg Greenberg is a research associate at Yale University School of Medicine's Department of Psychiatry and a health sociologist at the Department of Veterans Affairs'Northeast Program Evaluation Center. He received his Ph.D. in sociology at the University of Wisconsin, Madison. His dissertation was entitled "The Ties that Grind: Institutional Investors and the Movement from Vertical to Virtual Integration in the United States Pharmaceutical Sector." His current research is on how social capital and the organizational features of health delivery systems influence continuity of care. He is also doing research on how increasing competition in the U.S. health care sector is affecting traditional providers and minority access to health care.

Jerald Hage is professor of sociology at the University of Maryland and is the author or editor of fifteen books and numerous scholarly articles. Many of his books focus on the problem of organizational theory with a special emphasis on organizational innovation. Among his books are *Social Change in Complex Organizations* (with Michael Aiken), *Theories of Organizations, Organizations, Working Together* (with Catherine Alter), and most recently *Organizational Innovation*. Several books focus on the problems of comparing institutions and examining their performances: *State Responsiveness and State Activism* (with Robert Hanneman and Ed Gargan) and *State Intervention in Medical Care* (with J. Rogers Hollingsworth and Robert Hanneman). He was recently president of the Society for the Advancement of Socio-Economics.

Peter A. Hall is Frank G. Thompson Professor of Government, Harvard College and the director of the Center for European Studies at Harvard University where he teaches courses on comparative political economy, European politics, and methods of political analysis. He holds degrees in economics and political science from the University of Toronto, Balliol College, Oxford, and Harvard University. He is the author of *Governing the Economy* (1986) as well as many articles on European political economy and policy making, and an editor of *The Political Power of Economic Ideas* (1989), *Developments in French Politics 1 and 2* (1990 and 2001) and *Varieties of Capitalism: The Institutional Foundations of Comparative Advantage* (2001).

Robert Hanneman is professor of sociology at the University of California, Riverside. He is the author of several books and numerous scholarly articles. His books include *State Responsiveness and State Activism* (with Jerald Hage and Ed Gargan) and *State Intervention in Medical* Care (with Rogers Hollingsworth and Jerald Hage). Presently, he is engaged in joint work with Raymond Russell on the dynamics of populations of organizations in Israel and Russia, as well as two studies of the U.S. dry salt industry. One study is on trade-association activity and one is on organizational population dynamics. Other work in progress includes dynamic models and simulations of formal theories in sociology.

Geoffrey Hodgson is a research professor in business studies at the University of Hertfordshire in England. He was previously at the University of Cambridge. His books include *Economics and Institutions* (1988), *Economics and Evolution* (1993), *Economics and Utopia* (1999), and *Evolution and Institutions* (1999). He has published widely in various academic journals, including the *Journal of Economic Literature*, *Economic Journal*, *Journal of Economic Behavior and Organization*, and *Cambridge Journal of Economics*.

Ellen Jane Hollingsworth, as a member of the University of Wisconsin Department of Sociology and previously, the Institute for Research on Poverty, is the author, co-author, or editor of six books and many articles on the delivery of social services in the United States and Europe. Her studies of service systems for people with severe mental illness and for people with other disadvantages have usually been framed with a socio-economics perspective. Her other work has been concerned with administration of welfare and health programs, modes for delivering social services to the needy, and administrative/legal constraints on public employees and clients. Her recent studies have centered on research institutions, organizations, and scientific laboratories, particularly in Britain.

J. Rogers Hollingsworth is professor of sociology and history and former chairperson of the Program in Comparative History at the University of Wisconsin. Awarded honorary degrees by the University of Uppsala (Sweden) and by Emory University, he is the author or editor of numerous books and articles on comparative political economy. One of his major research interests is the study of how organizational and institutional factors influence different types of innovations. His recent publications relevant to this volume include *Contemporary Capitalism: The Embeddedness of Institutions* (with Robert Boyer, 1997); *Governing Capitalist Economies* (with Philippe Schmitter and Wolfgang Streeck, 1994); *The Governance of the American Economy* (with John Campbell and Leon Lindberg, 1991); and *The Search for Excellence: Organizations, Institutions, and Major Discoveries in Biomedical Science* (with Ellen Jane Hollingsworth and Jerald Hage, forthcoming 2002). He is past president and also honorary fellow of the Society for the Advancement of Socio-Economics.

Karl H. Müller has been head of the Departments of Political Science and Sociology at the Institute for Advanced Studies (IHS) in Vienna and is currently head of WISDOM-Research, Austria's social science infrastructure center on data archiving and method-development. His main research interests range from issues in complex modeling within the social sciences, from interdisciplinary analyses of innovation processes in science, technology, and economy to the newly emerging risk-potentials for contemporary society. For his research on innovation, knowledge, societies, and risk, he has developed a special approach which operates under the title of an "epigenetic research program" (ERP). His recent publications reflect his interests in the epigenetic architectures of contemporary knowledge societies, *Market Expansion and Knowledge Integration: Double Movements within Modernity* (1999), *Socio-Economic Models and Societal Complexity: Intermediation and Design* (1998), and *Chaos 2000: The Global Time-Quake* (1999).

Claus Offe is one of Europe's most creative political scientists and sociologists. Presently, he is professor of political science, Humboldt University, Berlin. His fields of research are in the areas of social policy, democratic theory, and transformation studies. He is the author of numerous books and articles. His recent books in English include *Varieties of Transition* (1996), *Modernity and the State: East and West* (1996, with Jon Elster and Ulrich K. Preuss), and *Constitutional Design in Post-Communist Societies: Rebuilding the Ship at Sea* (1998).

Raymond Russell is professor of sociology at the University of California, Riverside. His past research has included studies of employee participation in ownership and decision making in a number of contexts, ranging from scavenger companies, taxi cooperatives, and ESOPs in the United States, to worker cooperatives in Israel, to state-owned, privatized, and new private enterprises in Russia. Articles based on this research have appeared in *Research in the Sociology of Organizations, Journal of Comparative Economics,* and *Industrial Relations.* His comprehensive account of the studies of Israeli worker cooperatives appears in *Utopia in Zion: The Israeli Experience with Worker Cooperatives* (1995).

Robin Stryker is professor of sociology and law at the University of Minnesota. Recently, she was the president of the Society for the Advancement of Socio-Economics (SASE). She has published papers extensively, in the *American Sociological Review*, the *American Journal of Sociology,* and elsewhere on institutional politics and on the use of economics in American regulatory law. Among her recent articles are "Globalizaton and the Welfare State" in the *British Journal of Sociology and Social Policy* 18: 1–49 (1998), "Legitimacy Processes as Institutional Politics" in *Research in the Sociology of Organizations* 17: 179–233 (2000), and "Political Culture Wars 1990s Style: The Drum Beat of Quotas in Media Framing of the Civil Rights Act of 1991" *in Research in Social Stratification and Mobility* 17: 33–106 (1999).

Sigurt Vitols is a senior research fellow at the Wissenschaftszentrum Berlin für Sozialforschung (WZB) His research interests center on corporate governance, financial regulation, and small business finance in advanced capitalist economies. His many publications include "Are German Banks Different?," *Small Business Economics* 10(2): 79–91 (1998); *Corporate Governance in Large British and Germany Companies: Comparative Institutional Advantage or Competing for Best Practice* (1997, with Steven Casper, David Soskice, and Stephen Woolcock); "The German Model in the 1990s" (co-edited with Steven Casper); Special Issue of *Industry and Innovation*, June 1997; "German Industrial Policy: An Overview," *Industry and Innovation* 4(1): 15–36 (1997); "Financial Systems and Industrial Policy in Germany and Great Britain: The Limits of Convergence," pp. 221–55 in D. Forsyth and T. Notermans, eds., *Regime Changes: Macroeconomic Policy and Financial Regulation in Europe from the 1930s to the 1990s* (1997).

Frans van Waarden is professor of policy and organization at Utrecht University in the Netherlands. He has taught at the universities of Leyden, Konstanz, and Leipzig and has been visiting scholar at the Center for European Studies of Stanford University and the European University Institute in Florence. He has published on labor relations, co-determination, history of technology, textile industry, industrial policy, collective action, business associations, corporatism, and state-industry relations. His books include *Fabriekslevens* (1987); *Het geheim van Twente* (1987); *Organisatiemacht van belangenverenigngen* (1989); *Organizing Business for War: Industrial Policy and Corporatism during the Second World War* (1991); *Cultures of Unemployment* (1993); *Convergence or Diversity? Internationalization and Economic Policy Response* (1995); *Ruimte rond regels: Stijlen van regulering en beleidsuitvoering vergeleken* (1999) (on national administrative regulatory styles and discretionary authority of civil servants), and *Deregulating Imperfect Markets: On the Role of Institutions on Markets* (1999).

Index

441